Perhaps no other people in the world say 'Welcome' so frequently – and mean it every time. Egypt's ancient civilisation still awes, but today's Egyptians are pretty amazing, too.

(left) Camels at the Pyramids of Giza (p125)
(below) Loom weaver, Aswan (p253)

psychedelic vibrancy below – rewarding to explore on a multiday outing to one of the globe's great wreck dives or on an afternoon's snorkelling jaunt along a coral wall.

Desert Beauty

Whether you're watching the sun rise from the lofty heights of Mt Sinai (Gebel Musa) or the shimmering horizon from the comfort of a hot spring in Siwa Oasis, Egypt's desert landscapes are endlessly fascinating – good thing, because they make up 95% of the country. In a land where time is measured by dynasties, and distance by the setting sun, there are plenty of opportunities to relax into the infinite expanse of sand and sea.

Human Kindness

Egypt is the most traveller-friendly country in the Middle East. This means you'll enjoy cheap buses, decent budget places to sleep, English spoken to some degree everywhere and even good cold beers. It also means that if you ever get into a jam, an Egyptian will likely be there to help you out. Then again, an Egyptian will also be there to sell you some papyrus or perfume – an undeniable reality of travel here. But the souvenir sales are a minor irritant when compared with the chance to connect with some of the world's most generous people.

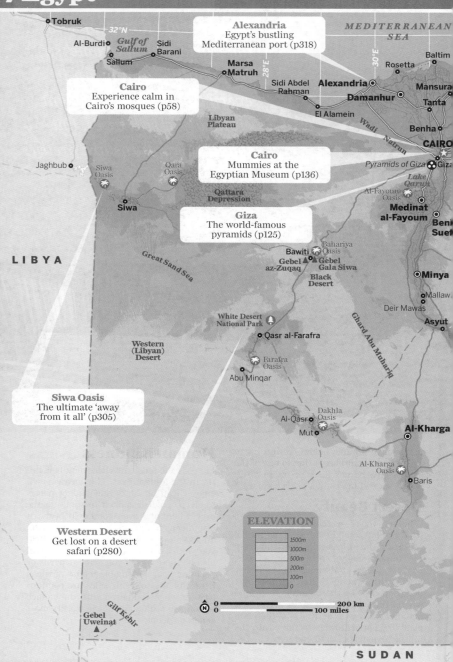

› Egypt

Alexandria
Egypt's bustling
Mediterranean port (p318)

Cairo
Experience calm in
Cairo's mosques (p58)

Cairo
Mummies at the
Egyptian Museum (p136)

Giza
The world-famous
pyramids (p125)

Siwa Oasis
The ultimate 'away
from it all' (p305)

Western Desert
Get lost on a desert
safari (p280)

MEDITERRANEAN
SEA

Tobruk
Al-Burdi
Gulf of Sallum
Sidi Barani
Sallum
Sidi Abdel Rahman
Marsa Matruh
El Alamein
Rosetta
Baltim
Alexandria
Damanhur
Mansura
Tanta
Benha
CAIRO
Wadi Natrun
Libyan Plateau
Jaghbub
Qara Oasis
Siwa Oasis
Pyramids of Giza
Giza
Qattara Depression
Al-Fayoum Oasis
Lake Qarun
Siwa
Medinat al-Fayoum
Beni Suef
LIBYA
Great Sand Sea
Bawiti
Bahariya Oasis
Gebel az-Zuqaq
Gebel Gala Siwa
Black Desert
Minya
Mallawi
Deir Mawas
White Desert National Park
Qasr al-Farafra
Asyut
Western (Libyan) Desert
Farafra Oasis
Abu Minqar
Ghard Abu Muharriq
Al-Qasr
Dakhla Oasis
Al-Kharga
Mut
Al-Kharga Oasis
Baris

ELEVATION
1500m
1000m
500m
200m
100m
0

N 0 — 200 km
0 — 100 miles

Gilf Kebir
Gebel Uweinat

SUDAN

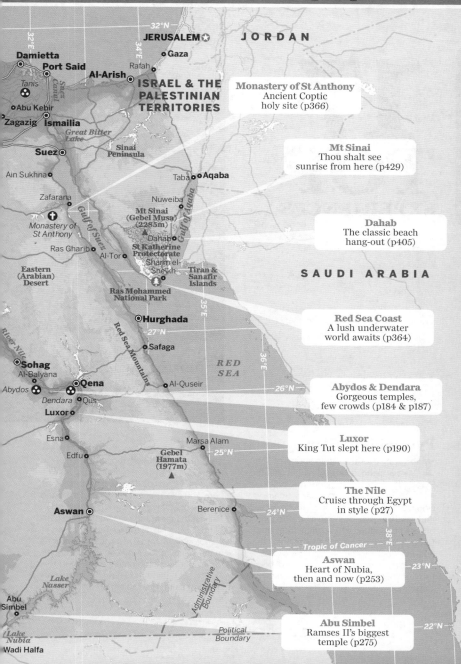

JERUSALEM ⊙

JORDAN

Gaza

Rafah

Damietta
Port Said
Al-Arish

Tanis ☢

ISRAEL & THE
PALESTINIAN
TERRITORIES

Abu Kebir

Zagazig **Ismailia**

Suez ⊙

Ain Sukhna

Great Bitter
Lake

Sinai
Peninsula

Taba ● **Aqaba**

Nuweiba

Monastery of St Anthony
Ancient Coptic
holy site (p366)

Mt Sinai
Thou shalt see
sunrise from here (p429)

Zafarana

Monastery of
St Anthony

Ras Gharib ●

Mt Sinai
(Gebel Musa)
(2285m)

Dahab ●
St Katherine
Protectorate

Sharm el-
Sheikh

Tiran &
Sanafir
Islands

Dahab
The classic beach
hang-out (p405)

SAUDI ARABIA

Eastern
(Arabian)
Desert

Al-Tor ●

Ras Mohammed
National Park

⊙ **Hurghada**

Red Sea Coast
A lush underwater
world awaits (p364)

Safaga ●

Sohag ⊙
Al-Balyana

Abydos ☢

Qena

Dendara ● Qus

Luxor ●

Al-Quseir ●

RED
SEA

Red Sea Mountains

Esna ●

Edfu ●

Marsa Alam

Gebel
Hamata
(1977m) ▲

Abydos & Dendara
Gorgeous temples,
few crowds (p184 & p187)

Luxor
King Tut slept here (p190)

River Nile

Aswan ⊙

Berenice ●

The Nile
Cruise through Egypt
in style (p27)

Tropic of Cancer

Aswan
Heart of Nubia,
then and now (p253)

Administrative Boundary

Lake
Nasser

Abu
Simbel

Lake
Nubia

Wadi Halfa

Political
Boundary

Abu Simbel
Ramses II's biggest
temple (p275)

17
TOP
EXPERIENCES

Pyramids of Giza

1 Towering over the urban sprawl of Cairo and the desert plains beyond, the Pyramids of Giza (p125) and the Sphinx are at the top of every traveller's itinerary. Bring lots of water, an empty memory card and plenty of patience! You'll have to fend off lots of people pushing horse rides and Bedouin headdresses in order to enjoy this ancient funerary complex, but no trip to Egypt is complete without a photo of you in front of the last surviving ancient wonder of the world.

Luxor

2 With the greatest concentration of ancient Egyptian monuments anywhere in Egypt, Luxor (p190) rewards time spent here. You can spend days or weeks around this town, walking through the columned halls of the great temples on the east bank of the Nile, such as the Ramesseum, or climbing down into the tombs of pharaohs in the Valley of the Kings on the west bank. Time spent watching the sun rise over the Nile or set behind the Theban hills are some of Egypt's unforgettable moments. Memorial Temple of Hatshepsut (p219)

Cruising the Nile

3 The Nile is Egypt's lifeline, the artery that runs through the entire country, from south to north. Only by setting adrift on it can you appreciate its importance and its beauty, and more practically, only by boat can you see some archaeological sites as they were meant to be seen. Sailing is the slowest and most relaxing way to go, but even from the deck of a multistorey floating hotel you're likely to glimpse the magic. For tips on choosing a cruise, see p27.

Mt Sinai

4 It may not be the highest of Sinai's craggy peaks, but Mt Sinai (p429) is the peninsula's most sacred. A place of pilgrimage for Jews, Christians and Muslims alike, the summit affords the magnificent spectacle of light washing over the sea of surrounding mountaintops. Down below, tucked into the mountain's base, is the St Katherine's Monastery (p428). Its sturdy Byzantine fortifications are built over the spot where Moses is believed to have witnessed the burning bush. St Katherine's Monastery

Dahab

5 Laid-back Dahab (p405), a midsized town near the southern tip of the Sinai, is Egypt's version of a chill pill, the place for ruin-fatigued travellers to cast off the history lessons and recuperate in one of the small-scale beachfront hotels. Once your batteries have recharged, dive into Dahab's famous underwater world or organise some desert adventure fun. Though you may find you're also seduced by the joy of doing nothing for a few more days.

Desert Safaris

6 Whether you travel by 4WD, camel or foot, for a couple of hours or a couple of weeks, you'll be able to taste the simple beauty and isolation of wildest Egypt. The highlights of an excursion in Egypt's Western Desert include camping among the surreal formations of the White Desert (p296), crossing the mesmerising dunes of the Great Sand Sea (p316) and heading deep into the desert to live out *English Patient* fantasies at the remote Gilf Kebir (p280). White Desert National Park

Souqs

7 The incessant salesmanship of Egyptians makes more sense when you see it at work in Egypt's historic heart, the souq. Here vendors are set up cheek by jowl, all hawking their wares in their set district, cajoling and haggling and sometimes just shouting louder than the competition. Visit a centuries-old souq such as Cairo's famous Khan al-Khalili (p74) first, and you'll see its pattern at work even in ad hoc modern markets such as the Souq al-Gomaa (p114). Along the way, pick up dusty antiques, King Tut kitsch ... or even a donkey. Khan al-Khalili

Oasis Life

8 It's impossible not to relax in an oasis – here, with the endless desert shimmering on the horizon, you can float in hot springs or explore the remains of ancient Roman outposts and tribal villages. In Siwa (p304), the Dahab of the desert, cold springs and palm groves keep you cool during the day. In Da-khla, the restored mud-brick town of Al-Qasr (p292) gives a glimpse of centuries-old oasis living. It's easy to spend enough time out here to make the long drive worth it. Siwa Oasis

Red Sea Diving

9 Egypt's Sinai and Red Sea coastlines are the doorstep to a wonderland that hides below the surface. Whether you're a seasoned diving pro or a first-timer, Egypt's underwater world of coral cliffs, colourful fish and spookily beautiful wrecks is just as staggeringly impressive as the sights above. Bring out your inner Jacques Cousteau by exploring the enigmatic wreck of WWII cargo ship the *Thistlegorm* (p43), a fascinating museum spread across the sea bed. Elphinstone Reef on the Red Sea coast

SARA-JANE CLELAND / LONELY PLANET IMAGES ©

MARK WEBSTER / LONELY PLANET IMAGES ©

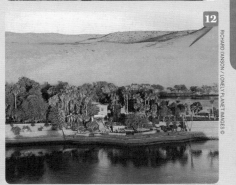

Abu Simbel

10 Ramses II built Abu Simbel (p275) a long way south of Aswan, along his furthest frontier and just beyond the Tropic of Cancer. But these two enormous temples are a marvel of modern engineering as well: in the 1960s they were relocated, block by block, to their current site to protect them from the flooding of Lake Nasser. To appreciate the isolation, spend the night at Abu Simbel, either on a boat on the lake or at Nubian cultural centre and ecolodge Eskaleh (p277).

Abydos & Dendara

11 Time is short and everyone wants to see the Pyramids, Tutankhamun's gold and the Valley of the Kings. But some of the most rewarding moments are to be had away from the crowds in the less visited monuments, where you can contemplate the ancients' legacy in peace. Nowhere is this truer than at Abydos (p184), one of the most sacred spots along the Nile, and Dendara (p187), one of the world's best-preserved ancient temples. They're north of Luxor – the opposite direction from the tour buses. Abydos

Aswan Sunset

12 Watch the sun set over Aswan (p253), frontier of the ancient Egyptian empire and southernmost outpost for the Romans. It's still the gateway to Nubia, where cultures blend to create a laid-back place that values time to enjoy the view. There is something about the way the river is squeezed between rocks, the proximity of the desert, the lonely burial places of the Aga Khan and of forgotten ancient princes that makes the end of the day more poignant here than anywhere else along the Egyptian Nile.

Coptic Sites

13 It was to the barren mountains and jagged cliffs of the sprawling desert that the first early ascetics came, even then seeking an escape from Egypt's hubbub. Today Coptic monasteries such as those of St Anthony and St Paul (p366), where the tradition of Christian monasticism began, still play an important role in the modern Coptic faith. Visit the four monasteries of Wadi Natrun (p163), or walk on the walls of St Anthony's and ponder the impressive faith that took men away from the ease of the towns and into the harsh wilderness to start anew. Deir Anba Bishoi, Wadi Natrun

Ahwas

14 Though the ahwa gets its name from the Arabic word for coffee, *shai* (tea) is much more common at this traditional cafe that's a major centre of Egyptian social life. With your drink on a tiny tin-top table, a backgammon board in front of you and perhaps a bubbling sheesha (water pipe) to one side, you'll slip right into the local groove. These days, ahwas can be sawdust-strewn, men-only joints or a chic lounge with a mixed crowd and fruit-flavoured tobaccos. For tips on finding your scene, see p108.

HANS GEORG ROTH/CORBIS ©

MARCO DI LAURO/GETTY IMAGES ©

Relax in a Mosque

15 The quiet, shady arcades of a medieval mosque are the perfect place to take a break from modern Cairo. Far from being austere places of worship, many mosques also function as public break rooms – people drop in for a quiet chat or to read a book. Al-Azhar Mosque (p80) bustles with theological students, the isolated Mosque of Amr ibn al-As (p73) has plenty of room, and the Mosque of Al-Maridani (p84) is filled with trees. Kick your shoes off and stay a while. Al-Azhar Mosque

Alexandria

16 Flaunting the pedigree of Alexander the Great and the powerful queen Cleopatra, Egypt's second-largest city is rich in history, both ancient and modern. Visit the Bibliotheca Alexandrina (p327), the new incarnation of the ancient Great Library, or any number of great small museums around town. Walk the souqs of atmospheric Anfushi (p325), the oldest part of the city, and be sure to feast on fresh seafood with a Mediterranean view (p334). Bibliotheca Alexandrina

Egyptian Museum

17 The scale of the Egyptian Museum (p136) is simply overwhelming. More than a hundred rooms are packed to the rafters with some of the most fascinating treasures excavated in Egypt: glittering gold jewellery, King Tut's socks and mummies of the greatest pharaohs, plus their favourite pets. On top of it all, very few of the objects are labelled. Don't push yourself to see it all, and do hire a guide for an hour or two to unlock some of the storehouse's secrets.

need to know

Currency
» Egyptian pound (E£)

Language
» Arabic

When to Go

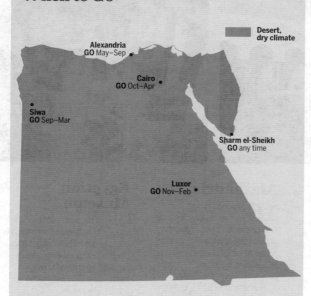

Desert, dry climate

Alexandria GO May–Sep

Cairo GO Oct–Apr

Siwa GO Sep–Mar

Sharm el-Sheikh GO any time

Luxor GO Nov–Feb

High Season (Oct–Feb)

» Egypt's 'winter' is largely sunny and warm, with very occasional rain (more frequent on the Mediterranean).

» Be prepared for real chill in unheated hotels, especially in damp Alexandria.

Shoulder (Mar–May, Sep–Oct)

» Spring brings occasional dust storms disrupting flights.

» Heat can extend into October, when crowds are lighter.

» Warm seas and no crowds at Mediterranean spots in autumn.

Low Season (Jun–Aug)

» Scorching summer sun means only the hardiest sightseers visit Upper Egypt.

» Avoid the Western Desert.

» High season on the Mediterranean coast.

Your Daily Budget

Budget less than

E£300

» Dorm bed: E£70

» *Fiteer* (Egyptian pizza): E£10

» Fresh produce for pennies

» Major sites are pricey

» Day train to Luxor: E£90

Midrange

E£300 –1000

» Hotel with air-con: E£180

» Two sit-down meals: E£80

» Car and driver: E£300

» Sleeper to Luxor: E£360

Top End over

E£1000

» Luxury hotel room: US$200

» Two meals: E£180

» Personal tour guide/ driver: E£75 per hour

» Flight to Luxor: US$120

Money

» ATMs common in cities. Credit cards accepted at higher-end businesses. Shortage of small change so can be difficult to break large bills.

Visas

» Required for most visitors; usually possible to buy at airport on arrival. Typically valid for 30 days and can be extended.

Mobile Phones

» Egypt uses the same frequency as Europe and Australia. Local SIM cards can be used in all multiband phones.

Transport

» Buses or shared minivans are the most common transport. Reasonably good trains connect Cairo with Alexandria and Upper Egypt.

Websites

» **Lonely Planet** (www.lonelyplanet. com/egypt) Destination information, hotel bookings, traveller forum.

» **Egypt Tourism** (www.egypt.travel) Official tourism site with trip-planning tools.

» **Daily News Egypt** (www.thedaily newsegypt.com) English newspaper.

» **Egypt Independent** (www.almasryalyoum. com/en) Respected online news.

» **Theban Mapping Project** (www.theban mappingproject.com) Archaeological database.

Exchange Rates

Australia	A$1	E£6.5
Canada	C$1	E£6
Europe	€1	E£7.9
Israel	1NIS	E£1.60
Japan	¥100	E£7.8
Jordan	JD1	E£8.5
New Zealand	NZ$1	E£5
UK	£1	E£9.5
USA	US$1	E£6

For current exchange rates see www.xe.com.

Important Numbers

Drop the 0 from the area code when dialling from abroad.

Ambulance	☑123
Country code	☑20
Fire	☑180
International access code	☑00
Tourist police	☑126

Arriving in Egypt

See also Getting Around in destination chapters.

» **Cairo International Airport**

Taxi – Prearrange pickup (E£100–120) or bargain on arrival (E£80–100); one hour to centre

Buses – E£2; up to two hours to centre

» **Sharm el-Sheikh**

Taxi – Bargaining required, ideally E£20-25

» **Alexandria Burg al-Arab**

Taxi – Bargain on arrival (E£100–150) Bus – E£6, plus E£1 per bag

Egypt after the Revolution

The 2011 revolution that ousted longtime president Hosni Mubarak also disrupted security, and at the time of writing, the political situation was still unstable, with the ruling military council issuing occasional violent crackdowns on protests against the murky elections process. It is important to emphasise, however, that this is extremely localised activity, centred on Midan Tahrir in Cairo. The rest of the country is generally calm.

Incidents of petty crime have been on the rise as well, but are still rare compared even with European capitals; see p515 for more. The biggest risk for tourists still remains the extremely talented touts and scammers who are a daily nuisance – see boxed text p517, for tips on dealing with their attentions.

On the plus side, old security restrictions on tourists have been lifted, making it much easier to explore Egypt independently.

what's new

For this new edition of Egypt, our authors have combed the country for new places to eat, drink, sleep and to get to know Egyptian culture and history. We're even pretty excited about some infrastructure improvements.

Egyptian Textile Museum, Cairo

1 This collection of fabrics from Pharaonic times to the present is small but very well presented. Bonus: it's in the attractively redone medieval avenue, Sharia Muizz li-Din Allah. (p77)

Museum of Islamic Art, Cairo

2 Reopened after a years-long renovation, this treasure trove shows off ceramic tiles, carpets, illuminated manuscripts and plenty more. (p82)

Dina's Hostel, Cairo

3 Your stay at this woman-owned budget hotel might coincide with an art installation or a dance performance. Dina's is a great place to tap into contemporary Cairo cool. (p94)

Fasahat Soumaya, Cairo

4 Soumaya herself cooks home-style Egyptian food for what feels like all her friends, in this tiny below-ground restaurant downtown. (p101)

Baladi Bars, Cairo

5 Cairo's local drinking scene used to be thoroughly seedy and often depressing, but a gentle scrubbing, courtesy of beer maker Stella, has given these bars fresh life. (p110)

Sofitel Old Cataract Hotel & Spa, Aswan

6 Upper Egypt's finest historic hotel has reopened after a top-to-bottom overhaul by Sofitel, keeping the old-world glamour but modernising the rooms. (p261)

Siwa-Bahariya Road, Western Desert

7 Repaving this desert highway has cut the drive between the oases down from ten hours to five, so it's a real (if pricey) alternative to backtracking to the cities. (p315)

Sinai Old Spices, Sharm el-Sheikh

8 A proper (and cheap!) B&B in a beach town where the more typical lodgings are vast resort palaces. (p399)

Bedouin Bus

9 A new local initiative providing a much-needed transport link between St Katherine's Monastery and the coastal towns of Dahab and Nuweiba. (p416)

Wilderness Ventures Egypt, Sinai

10 Learn Bedouin lore – like what the stars mean and how to really ride a camel – with this excellent tour operator that works with the Jabaliyya Bedouin. (p434)

Al-Karm Ecolodge, Sinai

11 This candlelit lodge, run by the local Bedouin, is set in a peaceful, secluded patch of desert in the peninsula interior. (p434)

Trains to Upper Egypt

12 Security policies used to restrict tourists to travel only on night trains to Upper Egypt. Those rules are abolished, and now you can ride by day and enjoy the view. (p529)

if you like...

Wildlife

Along the Nile, in the lush river delta and in sprawling salt lakes, bird life flourishes. Underwater coral reefs teem with color. Even Egypt's arid deserts host a surprising array of plants and critters.

Aswan Get up before dawn to spot herons, hoopoes and more with expert birders (p260)

Wadi Rayyan The brackish lake, not far from where the ancients worshipped crocodiles, is a lifeline for migrating birds – take your binocs on a rowboat (p158)

Shiatta Gazelles and flamingos frolic at this salt lake in the desert west of Siwa (p308)

Lake Nasser Take a tour with African Angler to snare some fish for dinner – or just enjoy the view (p30)

Marsa Alam Reefs off the coast here are home to mantas, spinner dolphins and even sharks (p382)

Islamic Architecture

Most of the gems of Egypt's Islamic era, from the 8th century to late Ottoman times, are in Cairo, so aficionados should plan for extra time there. But other gorgeous examples of building craft can be found elsewhere in the country.

Bein al-Qasreen A string of the finest buildings from the Mamluk era, now restored as an open-air museum (p74)

Mosque of Qaitbey Trek to Cairo's not-actually-that-spooky City of the Dead to admire the most beautiful stone dome in Cairo (p88)

Al-Qasr This oasis town was built in the Ottoman era, starting in the 16th century – check the beautifully carved lintels over the doorways (p292)

Rosetta's Ottoman Houses Try to find the secret staircase to the women's gallery in one restored residential compound, and admire the millworks at another (p344)

Al-Quseir The old Hajj port is a tumble of Ottoman-era buildings that seem lost in time (p379)

Deserts

Seeking blissful isolation? The desert landscape in Egypt is vast and surprisingly varied. And there's just as much variety in how you can explore it.

White Desert National Park For a truly mind-bending experience, schedule your overnight trip to this eerie landscape during the full moon (p296)

Great Sand Sea These picture-perfect dunes extend hundreds of miles into Libya, but you can get a taste of the emptiness even on a short trip (p316)

Monastery of St Simeon For desert beauty without the days-long trek, visit this Coptic site in Aswan (p259

St Katherine Protectorate The epicentre of Bedouin-run hiking and camel treks in the Sinai (p428

Daraw Head south from Kom Ombo to this desert settlement that hosts a twice-weekly camel market when beasts arrive from the Sudan (p252)

» Hot-air balloons over Luxor's west bank (p227)

Beaches

There's no shortage of sand in Egypt – the desert extends even to the shores. Whether you're on the Red Sea or the Mediterranean coast, you'll find fresh air and stellar scenery – with the bonus of underwater life on the Red Sea's reefs.

Sinai Beach Camps North of Nuweiba lie a string of low-tech bungalows where pure vegging out is the order of the day (p426)

Sidi Abdel Rahman A bijou resort spot on the Mediterranean (p347)

Marsa Matruh Cairo's main beach escape is a cultural experience in summer high season, and a spooky ghost town any other time (p348)

Sharm el-Sheikh Egypt's most fully developed resort, Sharm welcomes sun-worshippers of all stripes, with lively nightlife as well (p395)

Local Food

Egypt's cuisine may not be as renowned as others in the Middle East, but that doesn't mean you won't eat well here. Expect hearty, cheap and fresh dishes, exceptional summer mangoes and, in the autumn, fresh dates in a dozen varieties.

Sofra Great traditional dishes, such as varied *tagens* (meat-and-vegetable stews) are served at this old-fashioned Luxor restaurant (p233)

Backpacker Concierge This tour operator periodically runs an organised culinary trip and can connect you with cheesemakers and more (p528)

Seafood in Alexandria Cruise the heaving fish market at the port, then dig in to freshly grilled goodies straight from the Mediterranean (p333)

Siwa Oasis Some of Egypt's best olives, dates and pomegranates come from this western oasis, which also has its own distinctive Berber-influenced cuisine (p304)

Juice stands Slurp down freshly pressed orange, mango, pomegranate and more. The frothy green *qasab* (sugarcane) is a local favourite (p498)

Souqs & Shopping

Whether you're just browsing or searching for gifts for everyone on your list, Egypt's souqs are the perfect destination, with as much entertainment as actual products – not to mention more offers of tea than you could ever drink.

Khan al-Khalili Cairo's medieval trading zone is still a commercial hub for souvenirs like a gold cartouche necklace – the perfect place to polish your haggling skills (p74)

Souq al-Gomaa Get in the scrum at this weekly Cairo junk swap, and you might come out with new clothes…or old taxidermy (p114)

Birqash Camel Market What to get the person who has everything (p165)

Anfushi Pick up some fresh fish, new underwear and a smart set of buttons at Alexandria's distinctly local old souq (p338)

Attareen Antique Market Another Alexandria trove, where you can find some mid-20th-century gems (p339)

Aswan Souq Nibble fresh peanuts and compare prices on Nubian talismans (p253)

If you like...faded grandeur,
Port Said's waterfront is a daydream of dilapidated grand facades which hark back to the days when this was every sailor's sin city (p355)

Adventure

Egypt isn't a high-adrenaline destination – the desert heat has a way of slowing things down. But these more active outings can still inspire. In addition, of course, divers can enjoy all kinds of underwater thrills.

Hot-air ballooning Get a bird's-eye view of the tombs at Luxor (p227)

Sandboarding Who needs snow? Try this dusty sport near Al-Fayoum, after spotting whale fossils (p162)

Sunset horse riding The best way to admire the Pyramids of Giza (p131)

Hiking in the Sinai Start with Mt Sinai, a well-trod path, and trek further from there (p429)

Tuk-tuks Hop in one of these tiny auto-rickshaws for a quick careen around a village, accompanied by the latest pop hits from giant speakers (p527)

Long-term safaris Pack up and head out for a week or more – we tell you how (p280)

Relaxation

Cairo, 20 million strong, gives Egypt a reputation for hectic noise and chaos. But beyond the city – and even within it – are plenty of places to enjoy some peace and quiet.

Andalus Garden These pretty manicured gardens by the Nile are a favourite spot for young Cairene couples to take some fresh air (p91)

Felucca Sail the Nile as in centuries past, on a creaky wooden boat. A sunset cruise in Cairo is a perfect respite from the din (p92); a multiday trip in Upper Egypt really unplugs you from the world (p32)

Hot springs The Western Desert is dotted with nature's answer to modern stress – float and contemplate the stars (p291)

Dahab It's as if the proverbial chill pills were dispensed over the counter at this mellow beach town on the Sinai. Guaranteed you'll stay longer than planned (p405)

Ancient Traces

Given Egypt's Pharaonic riches, you could flip to any page in this book and find something with a story thousands of years old. These are some of the more out-of-the-way sites to add to your itinerary.

Medinet Madi You need a 4WD to get here, but the sight of sphinxes half-buried in drifting sand is exactly what archaeology buffs come to Egypt for (p160)

Red Pyramid At Dahshur, south of Cairo, you'll likely be the only visitor to this enormous monument, making the climb inside its tunnels all the more exciting (p154)

Deir al-Muharraq In Egyptian terms, Christianity is relatively new history – but this Coptic monastery claims the world's oldest church, from 60 AD (p179)

Sikait The Roman-era emerald mines in the Eastern Desert exude an eerie atmosphere of abandoned dreams (p386)

If you like...odd museums
Cairo's Agricultural Museum is state-of-the-art, c 1930, when these wax models and dioramas were lovingly crafted (p92)

If you like...alternative healing treatments
Sink into a hot sand bath near Gebel Dakrur – allegedly good for all that ails you (p309)

Traditional Arts

In some villages, women still bake bread in the shapes the pharaohs ate, and old Bedouin, Nubian and Berber wisdom is still alive and well. Cairo's independent music venues have fostered traditional talents, and tour operators offer chances to learn directly from locals.

Fair Trade Egypt This shop in Cairo is a good starting point for finding Egyptian traditional crafts (p114)

Makan This intimate space in Cairo hosts an intense Nubian musical ritual called a *zar* (p111)

El Tanboura Hall Another traditional-music incubator in Cairo, this space sees regular shows by Suez Canal–area artists and others (p111)

Eskaleh This Nubian cultural centre and hotel offers guests a chance to immerse in local food and music (p277)

Bedouin knowledge Wilderness Ventures Egypt teaches local star lore, as well as herbal medicine on nature walks (p433)

Vintage Tourism

For those who long for the age of steamer trunks, pith helmets and softly scudding overhead fans, Egypt delivers. You may have to squint to see the sepia tone, but the country's long history of tourism means there's plenty of yesteryear left.

Dahabiyyas Cruise the Nile as 19th-century adventurer Amelia Edwards did, on one of these elegant sailboats (p33)

Mena House Oberoi Splash out in the Pyramids-view suites, or just sip a beer amid the luxury enjoyed by Khedive Ismail (p132)

Pension Roma A bargain way to live in the past, this Cairo hotel has antique furniture and original details like privacy screens (p94)

Sofitel Old Cataract Hotel One of Agatha Christie's favourites, and a great place to watch the sun set (p261)

Trains Egypt's trains have seen better days, but they're still a relaxing way to see parts of the country, especially on the route to Aswan (p528)

Cafe Culture

Sipping tea is a national pastime. The big cities, where this break is most needed, are best, but even in the hinterlands you'll find a convivial ahwa, as Egyptians call their coffee-houses.

Wel3a This hip Cairo cafe specialises in the finest sheesha – sweetened tobacco sucked through a water pipe (p110)

Amphitrion The best place in Heliopolis to watch the world go by, this was once a hangout for British officers (p134)

Fishawi's The ahwa in Cairo's Khan al-Khalili has been open for centuries, and some regulars look like they've been smoking sheesha here almost as long (p109)

Tea on safari Proof you don't need the physical trappings of a cafe to enjoy its pleasures: hunker in the shade of your jeep, sip your scalding tea and have a chat

Trianon Alexandria is known for its cafes where legendary writers have taken a breather. This one was Cavafy's favourite (p337)

month by month

January

Winter in most of Egypt means balmy days, perfect for sightseeing, but chilly nights, especially in unheated hotel rooms. Alexandria and the Mediterranean coast can be a bit rainy, but otherwise precipitation is still rare.

Cairo International Book Fair

Held at the Cairo opera grounds in the last week of January and the first of February (see www.cairobookfair.org for dates), this is one of the city's major cultural events. But most of the lectures and other events (and the books themselves) are in Arabic only.

Moulid al-Nabi

The prophet Mohammed's birthday is a nationwide celebration with sweets and new clothes for kids. In Cairo, the week before is an intense Sufi scene at Midan al-Hussein. For more on *moulid*s (religious festivals), see p484. For dates, see p515.

Egyptian Marathon

Endurance runners take to the west bank of the Nile near Luxor, starting from in front of the Temple of Hatshepsut. The race takes place in late January or early February, followed by a half-marathon in Sharm el-Sheikh in March. For dates, see www.egyptianmarathon.com.

February

The winter chill continues, though it's the perfect time of year in the south. Tourists think so too, and Aswan and Luxor are packed, as are the beaches.

Ascension of Ramses II

Takes place on 22 February. One of the two dates each year (the other is in October) when the sun penetrates the inner sanctuary of the temple at Abu Simbel, illuminating the statues of the gods within. Draws a big crowd of theorists of all kinds.

International Fishing Tournament

Held at Hurghada on the Red Sea; attended by anglers from all over the world.

March

With warmer days come winds, especially the khamsin, a hot current that causes periodic, intense sandstorms lasting a few hours and often grounding flights. Bear this in mind when booking trips through to early May.

April

The khamsin carries on, and on days when it's not blowing, the air is pleasantly fresh. This is the shoulder season for tourism, and archaeological sites begin to empty out.

Dahab Festival

A mash-up of windsurfing contest, divers' meet, DJ party and Bedouin culture show, this weeklong get-together is as groovy as its host town of Dahab. Oh, and camel races too! Details at www.dahabfestival.info.

Shamm al-Nassim

The Monday after Coptic Easter (6 May 2013, 21 April 2014, 13 April 2015). Literally 'sniffing the breeze', this spring ritual came from Pharaonic tradition via the Copts. It's celebrated by all Egyptians, who picnic in parks, on riverbanks and even on traffic islands.

El-Limbo
Egypt's Suez Canal area has many distinct folk traditions, including this effigy-burning party held every year in Port Said, right before Shamm al-Nassim. Rooted in 19th-century protests against the British, the conflagration feels both pagan and modern, as today's effigies are contemporary celebrities and politicos.

May
You won't meet a lot of 17-year-olds – they're all indoors studying for the nationwide final exam all secondary-school students take before graduation.

June
Egypt lets out a collective sigh of relief after exams, and summer ramps up. The heat is in full force by the end of the month.

Moulid of Abu al-Haggag
In the third week of the Islamic month of Sha'aban (early July 2012, June in subsequent years), this Sufi festival in Luxor offers a taste of rural religious tradition. Some villages have *moulid*s around the same time; see p484

July
Extreme summer heat doesn't deter Muslims observing Ramadan. During the holy month of fasting, daytime activity slows down even more than it usually does in hot weather.

Ramadan
The ninth month of the Islamic calendar is dedicated to fasting by day and feasting by night. Foodies will love a visit during this time; ambitious sightseers may be frustrated. For more practicalities, see p516 and p515 for dates.

Eid al-Fitr
The feast that marks the end of Ramadan lasts three days and, if it's possible, involves even more food than the past month put together.

August
This is a major Egyptian vacation period. Expect beach zones, especially in the Mediterranean, to be thronged. Anywhere else is so hot you can feel your eyeballs burn. Life generally takes place after sundown.

September
The barest respite from the heat.

October
As the summer heat finally breaks, students head back to school and the cultural calendar revs up again, especially in Cairo.

An ideal time for travelling, with manageable weather and few other visitors.

Birth of Ramses
On 22 October; the second date in the year when the sun's rays penetrate the temple at Abu Simbel.

International Festival for Experimental Theatre
A long-running event held at venues all over Cairo, from standard stages to antiques shops. Shows can be hit or miss, but many are very tourist-friendly as you don't have to speak Arabic to enjoy them. See www.cdf-eg.org for the line-up.

Siyaha
An oasis-wide celebration of the date harvest, Siwa's annual get-together takes place around the full moon this month. Much like a *moulid*, though not as raucous, there's Sufi chanting and plenty of food.

Moulid of Al-Sayyed Badawi
In the last week of October, close to a million pilgrims throng the city of Tanta in the Nile Delta, where a 13th-century mystic founded an important Sufi order. Part family fun fair, part intense ritual, it's worth a trip if you don't mind crowds.

Eid al-Adha
For the Feast of the Sacrifice, a four-day Islamic (and national) holiday, families slaughter sheep and goats at home, even in densest Cairo. There's literally blood in the streets, and the air smells of roasting meat. In short, not for vegetarians. For dates, see p515.

November

With a light chill in the air, restaurants start serving up heartier stews, while visitors start trickling in to enjoy ruins and beaches at a moderate temperature.

⭐ Arab Music Festival

Early in the month, 10 days of classical, traditional and orchestral Arabic music held at the Cairo Opera House and other venues. See www.cairoopera.org for schedules, and buy tickets in person at the main hall.

⭐ Cairo International Film Festival

From the last weekend in November into December, this 10-day event shows recent films from all over the world, all without censorship. Anything that sounds like it might contain scenes of exposed flesh sells out immediately. Schedules at www.cairofilmfest.org.

◉ Cairo Biennale

This fairly conservative government-sponsored show doesn't fully reflect the contemporary Egyptian art scene, but it's worth checking out if you're here. Opens in December 2012 and 2014, until mid-February. Go to www.cairobiennale.gov.eg.

December

Not much is on the calendar in Egypt, but this is when winter tourism starts in earnest, as visitors flood in for winter beach breaks. There's a surprising amount of Santa Claus kitsch to be seen.

itineraries

Whether you've got six days or 60, these itineraries provide a starting point for the trip of a lifetime. Want more inspiration? Head online to lonelyplanet.com/thorntree to chat with other travellers.

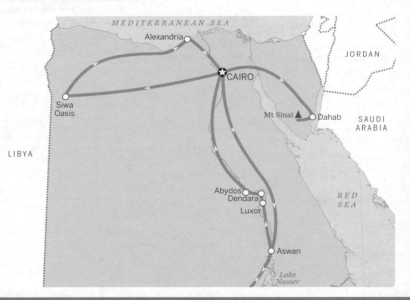

Four Weeks
Egypt Bottom to Top

In a month you can cover most of Egypt's main sights – a trip of nearly 2000km.

Head south from Cairo on the sleeper train to **Aswan**, where you can soak up Nubian culture and make the side trip to the awesome **Abu Simbel**. Sail back down the Nile to **Luxor** on a felucca. If you want to skip the crowds at the big sites, take a boat to **Dendara** and **Abydos** instead.

When you've had your fill of ancient ruins, make your way back to the modern metropolis of **Cairo**. Along with the top sites, make time to sit in one of the city's bustling ahwas (cafes), wreathed in sweet sheesha (water pipe) smoke.

After Cairo, take the bus to **Siwa Oasis**, one of Egypt's most idyllic spots. After hanging out in this tranquil haven, and perhaps going on a desert safari, backtrack along the Mediterranean coast to **Alexandria** and spend a couple of days in its wonderful cafes and museums.

Finally, head for **Dahab** to recharge and enjoy the laid-back Bedouin vibe, pausing only to arrange the obligatory dive trip and to hike up **Mt Sinai**.

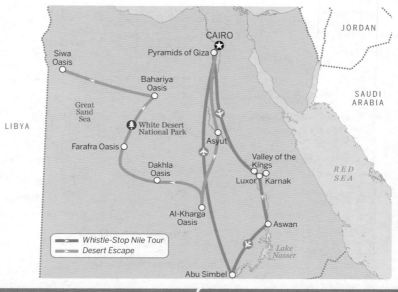

One–Two Weeks
Whistle-Stop Nile Tour

If you pay for domestic plane tickets, one week is enough time to sample Egypt's top sights. With two weeks, you can extend your trip to Aswan.

Three days in **Cairo** will allow you to see the astounding **Pyramids of Giza**, seek out the treasures of the Egyptian Museum and explore the medieval souq of Khan al-Khalili. Then fly to **Luxor**. In three days you can visit most major sights, including the **Valley of the Kings**, the Valley of the Queens and Deir al-Bahri on the west bank of the Nile, as well as the spectacular temples of **Karnak** and **Luxor** on the east bank.

If you can add another week to your trip, or even a few days, you can head further south. The long, relaxing version is to spend four days sailing up the Nile to **Aswan** on a budget-friendly felucca or a luxurious cruiser; the shorter version is to hop on the morning train. From Aswan, you absolutely must visit **Abu Simbel**, the grandest of all Pharaonic monuments, perched on the edge of Lake Nasser. Fly there, then to Cairo and home.

One–Two Weeks
Desert Escape

Inspired by *Lawrence of Arabia* and *The English Patient* scenery, would-be desert rovers can get sand-happy in the amazing Western Desert.

Begin a bus from **Cairo** or **Asyut** to **Al-Kharga Oasis**, the southernmost oasis in the Western Desert loop. Spend a day here exploring the Al-Kharga Museum of Antiquities as well as the Graeco-Roman temples, tombs and other interesting traces of the trade routes that flourished here during the Roman Empire.

From Al-Kharga, make your way northwest to **Dakhla Oasis** to see the fascinating hivelike, mud-walled settlements of Balat and Al-Qasr. Next, hop north to either **Farafra Oasis** or **Bahariya Oasis**, where you can make a two- or three-day camp in the stunning **White Desert National Park**.

If you have closer to two weeks, then you can strike west across several hundred kilometres of open sands to **Siwa Oasis**. You'll need to go as part of an organised desert tour, or hire a 4WD to drive the remote desert highway, one of the most surreal spots in the entire country. Perched on the edge of the **Great Sand Sea**, Siwa is renowned for its dates and olives and is a great base for additional dune exploration, should you need it.

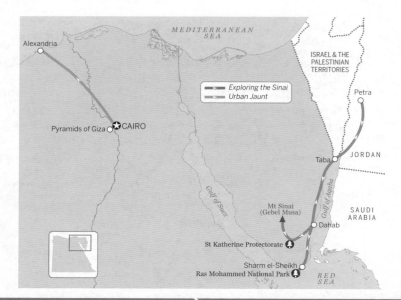

10–14 Days
Exploring the Sinai

One Week
Urban Jaunt

To sample all the peninsula has to offer, spend up to two weeks in its incredible desert landscapes and serene underwater world. You'll also have time to hop across the border to Petra, in Jordan.

From **Sharm el-Sheikh**, arrange a trip to the spectacular reefs of **Ras Mohammed National Park**. Divers will want to head on to the Thistlegorm, a sunken British supply ship that many consider the world's best wreck dive. For those who prefer snorkelling, there are fine reefs close to shore (and in Sharm as well).

Then hop on a bus to **Dahab**, a laid-back town dubbed the 'Ko Samui of the Middle East'. From here, you can arrange camel and jeep safaris to such natural wonders as the Coloured Canyon.

After a few days' beach time, lace up your boots and head to the **St Katherine Protectorate** for a trek with a Bedouin guide, as well as a night-time ascent of **Mt Sinai** (Gebel Musa) to catch a sunrise of biblical proportions.

In your last few days, take the ferry and bus to the ancient city of **Petra**. Return, after two nights, to fly out of Sharm el-Sheikh.

Get a taste of contemporary Egypt in its two largest cities. First thing in Cairo, head to the **Pyramids of Giza**, on the city's western edge. Not only will you check these sightseeing biggies off your list, you'll get a sense of the scale of this megalopolis. Spend the next day wandering Islamic Cairo and Al-Azhar Park, on the city's east edge. For contrast on your third day, take the metro to Coptic Cairo and the excellent Coptic Museum. Nearby Souq al-Fustat makes for easy, attractive souvenir shopping. In the evening, ride a felucca on the Nile. On your last day, cafe-hop in leafy Zamalek and the Cairo Opera grounds. At sunset, take the elevator up the Cairo Tower for a final view.

The next morning, take the express train to **Alexandria**, rich with Graeco-Roman history. The stunning modern Bibliotheca Alexandrina hints at the glory of the ancient library here – stop here and at the excellent Alexandria National Museum. On your second day, indulge in Alexandria nostalgia: ride the creaking streetcar and tour cafes where the city's literati sipped coffee and scribbled. Thanks to the new airport, you can fly directly out of Alex.

Cruising the Nile

Where & How to Cruise

Want to get on the river but are unsure where to go or how to do it? Our guide to the basics will help you make your choice.

Cruise Length

Short cruise Three or four days
Sailing cruise Five to six days
Cairo to Aswan At least a week

Best for Adventure

A **felucca** is the most likely way to find adventure. An open-top sailing boat without cabins or facilities, it is best taken from south to north – if the wind fails, you can always float downriver.

Made for Romantics

Dahabiyyas – the name translates as 'the golden one' – will waft you back into the 19th century, when these large and luxurious sailing boats were the only viable form of transport for visitors.

Most Popular Route

Between Luxor and Aswan, although this is also the busiest part of the river and you might find yourself in a long line of boats.

Far from the Crowds

Lake Nasser is the place to go if you would rather see empty landscapes and the odd wild animal than crowds of tourists.

A cruise on the Nile River has always ranked among the world's most exciting and most romantic travel experiences. The combination of the world's longest river and its extraordinary monuments, the stunningly fertile valley and the barren beauty of the surrounding desert, the light, the heat and the joy of slow travel in a superfast world: it all adds up to one of the highlights of any trip to Egypt.

Rain seldom falls on this part of the Nile Valley, so without the river, the country would simply not exist. Ancient Egyptians recognised this fact when they likened their land to a lotus – the delta was the flower, the oasis of Al-Fayoum the bud, and the river and its valley the stem that supported them all.

But rather than the practical use of the waterway, the Nile's beauty strikes travellers most: the soft light of its mornings, the lushness of the plants and trees that grow along its banks, the thrill of flights of birds that shuttle up- or downriver on their migrations, the patience of fishermen, rowing out in the morning to cast their nets, the greatness of it all.

Cruise Tips

When to travel Summer (June to August) can be extremely hot (and is therefore the cheapest season to cruise). Christmas and Easter are usually the busiest (and most expensive). Spring and autumn are ideal, with the light being particularly good in October and November.

Where to start Most cruises starting from Luxor are a day longer than those starting from Aswan, partly because they are going against the Nile's

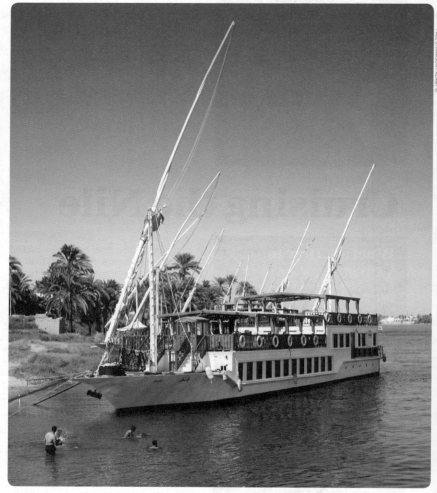

» (above) A dahabiyya sailing the Nile near Luxor
» (left) Felucca boatmen on the Nile

strong current. If you want to spend longer in Luxor or are concerned about cost, start from Aswan and head north.

Cabin choice On cruisers, try to avoid the lowest deck. Most boats listed on p34-5 have decent views from all cabins, but the banks of the Nile are high (and get higher as the river level drops) and you want to see as much as possible. Ask for a deck plan when booking.

Sailing time Many passengers on Nile cruisers are surprised by how little time is spent cruising – the boats' large engines cover distances relatively quickly and cruise times are often only four hours per day.

Itineraries & Sites

Large cruisers stick to rigid itineraries on the busy Luxor–Aswan stretch of the Nile. On these trips, generally lasting from three to six nights, days are spent visiting monuments, and relaxing by the pool or on deck. By night there is a variety of entertainment: cocktails, dancing and fancy-dress parties – usually called a *galabeya* (man's robe) party, as passengers are encouraged to 'dress like an Egyptian' – are all part of the fun. Actual sailing time is minimal on most of these trips – often as little as four hours each day, depending on the itinerary.

Feluccas and dahabiyyas determine their own schedules and do not need special mooring spots, so can stop at small islands or antiquities sites often skipped by the big cruisers. But even these boats usually have preferred mooring places. Because they use sail power instead of large engines, a far greater proportion of time is spent in motion. Night-time entertainment is more likely to be stargazing, listening to the sounds of the river, and occasionally riverbank fireside music from the crew or villagers.

The stretch of the Nile between Luxor and Aswan has the greatest concentration of well-preserved monuments in the country, which is why it also has the greatest number of boats and tourists (sailing in both directions). No boats have cruised between Cairo and Luxor since the 1990s, but this is now due to change.

Feluccas and dahabiyyas rarely sail between Luxor and Esna because police permits are difficult to get and because the big cruisers usually have priority using the busy Esna lock. Dahabiyya operators

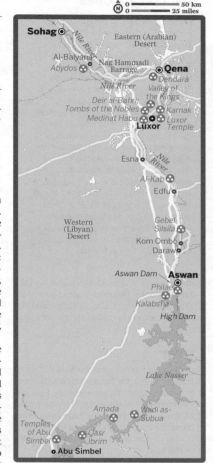

Cruising the Nile

will bus passengers to Esna from Luxor. Felucca trips generally start in Aswan and end south of Esna; captains can arrange onward transport to Luxor, but this often costs extra.

The following are the most common stops on itineraries.

Cairo to Luxor

This stretch of the river has mostly been excluded from cruise itineraries since attacks on boats in the 1990s. The archaeological sites at **Dendara** (p187) and **Abydos** (p184) have been on some tour schedules for the

ANCIENT BARQUES

River travel was so central to the ancient Egyptian psyche that it seemed perfectly obvious that the sun god Ra travelled through the sky in a boat and that the dead would sail to the afterlife. The earliest boats are likely to have been simple skiffs made of papyrus bundles, best for hunting and travelling short distances. Ancient Egyptians then developed elaborate wooden boats powered by multiple sets of oars, a long narrow sail and a steering oar that later evolved into a rudder. The most elaborate surviving example of an ancient boat was among Pharaoh Khufu's funerary goods and can be seen at the Cheops Boat Museum (p126) at the Pyramids of Giza. Numerous models of simpler boats have been found in tombs.

past few years – it is also possible to take a day cruise to Dendara from Luxor (see p227). Cruises from Cairo to Luxor and Aswan are expected to restart in the very near future.

Luxor

The capital of Egypt's glorious New Kingdom pharaohs, home to Tutankhamun, Ramses II and many other famous names, Luxor is blessed with many remarkable monuments. Most cruises only cover the bare minimum, so if you are interested in seeing the sights, it pays to spend an extra day or two here away from the boat.

Highlights include the temples of **Karnak** (p194), **Luxor Temple** (p194), the **Luxor Museum** (p203), the **Valley of the Kings** (p209), the **Tombs of the Nobles** (p207), **Deir al-Bahri** (p219) and **Medinat Habu** (p207).

Between Luxor & Aswan

This most famous stretch of the river is studded with stunning architecture and varied scenes of great natural beauty. All cruisers stop to visit the Ptolemaic temples of **Esna** (p245), **Edfu** (p247) and **Kom Ombo** (p251). On the shorter cruises, all three sites are visited in a single day. While none of the sites is so large that this is unrealistic, exploring three great temples is a lot to jam into one day and the rushed visit means that you will be moored longer at Luxor or Aswan.

Dahabiyyas and feluccas take longer to cover the distance between the three temples, usually seeing only one a day. Most dahabiyyas (and some feluccas) also stop at the rarely visited and highly recommended sites of **Al-Kab** (p246) and **Gebel Silsila** (p250). Cruisers do not have moorings here, so visitors may be limited to your fellow passengers, giving a taste of how it might have been for 19th-century travellers.

Aswan

The Nile is squeezed between rocks and a series of islands at Aswan, which makes it particularly picturesque, especially with the desert crowding in on both sides of the river. If you embark here you will probably spend only one night in town, but some cruisers stay moored for two nights. Most itineraries include a visit to **Philae** (p267), site of the Temple of Isis; the **High Dam** (p269); and the Northern Quarries, site of the **Unfinished Obelisk** (p255). Occasionally cruisers offer a felucca ride around **Elephantine Island** (p256) as an excursion; if not, it is worth organising your own. Some also offer an optional half-day tour (generally by plane) to **Abu Simbel** (p275).

Lake Nasser

The lake was created when the High Dam was built near Aswan, and covers much of Egyptian Nubia, once home to hundreds of

NILE FACTS

As the world's longest river, the Nile cuts through 11 countries and an incredible 6680km of Africa as it winds its way north towards the Mediterranean Sea. It has two main sources: Lake Victoria in Uganda, out of which flows the White Nile; and Lake Tana in the Ethiopian highlands, from which the Blue Nile emerges. The two rivers meet at Khartoum in Sudan. Some 320km further north, they are joined by a single tributary, the Atbara. From here, the river flows northwards to its end without any other source and almost no rain adding to its waters.

» (above) Sailing past the Aga Khan Mausoleum in Aswan
» (left) The *Prince Abbas* cruise ship on Lake Nasser

tombs, temples and churches (see p270 for details of Nubian history and culture). Some monuments were moved from their original sites prior to the building of the dam and are grouped together at four locations: **Kalabsha** (p273), **Wadi as-Subua** (p274; accessible only by boat), **Amada** (p274; accessible only by boat) and, of course, **Abu Simbel** (p275).

Because so few cruisers sail on Lake Nasser, moorings are never crowded and monuments – with the exception of the Temple of Ramses II at Abu Simbel – are not overrun. Itineraries are generally three nights/four days from Aswan to Abu Simbel, or four nights/five days from Abu Simbel to Aswan.

Sailing a Felucca

For many travellers, the only way to travel on the Nile is slowly, on board a traditional felucca (Egyptian sailing boat). Except for swimming, this is as close as you can get to the river. Read on to make sure that this is for you and that you avoid the pitfalls.

A Slow Journey

Most felucca trips begin at Aswan; the strong northward current means that boats are not marooned if the wind dies. Trips go to Kom Ombo (two days/one night), Edfu (three days/two nights – the most popular option) or Esna (four days/three nights).

Feluccas are not allowed to sail after 8pm, so most stop at sunset and set up camp on the boat or on shore. Night-time entertainment ranges from stargazing and the crew singing to partying, depending on you and your fellow passengers.

Find the Captain

With so many feluccas (hundreds, thousands?) and so many touts in Aswan, arrang-

---

THE BEST OF THE NILE

Close to the Nile in luxury Enjoying a private cruise on a dahabiyya (p33).

Economy cruise Taking a felucca trip from Aswan to Edfu (p32).

Nubian adventure Safarai to Abu Simbel on African Angler's *Ta Seti* (p35).

Nostalgia trip Reliving Agatha Christie's Egypt on the Nile's last steamer, the *Sudan* (p34).

Five-star plutocracy Style and luxury on Oberoi's award-winning *Philae* (p35).

Family fun Combining luxury cruising and sightseeing with kid-friendly cooking on the *Sun Boat III* (p35).

---

ing a felucca trip can be daunting. Small hotels can be just as aggressive in trying to rope you in. To be sure of what you're getting, it's best to arrange things yourself.

Many of the better felucca captains can be found having a sheesha or a drink in Nileside restaurants such as the Aswan Moon (p264); Emy, near the Panorama restaurant (p264); or on Elephantine Island (p256). Meet a few captains – and inspect his boat – before choosing one you get on with well. Women alone or in a group should try to team up with a few men if possible, as some women travellers have reported sailing with felucca captains who had groping hands. There have been some rare reports of assault.

Officially, feluccas can carry a minimum of six passengers and a maximum of eight. Fares are open to negotiation and dictated by demand. Expect to pay at least E£100 per person from Aswan to Kom Ombo, E£130 to Edfu and E£160 to Esna, including food. On top of this you need to add E£5 to E£10 per person for the captain to arrange the police registration. You can get boats for less, but take care; if it's much cheaper you'll either have a resentful captain and crew, or you'll be eating little more than bread and *fuul* (fava bean paste) for three days. Do not hand out the whole agreed amount until you get to your destination because there have been several reports of trips being stopped prematurely for a so-called breakdown.

If you do have problems, the tourist police or the tourist office should be the first port of call.

PARKED UP

In Aswan and Luxor, the mooring scene can become very crowded, often with eight or 10 boats tied up together. For most people this means that the view from your cabin might be someone else's cabin. With the wide choice of hotels, particularly in Luxor, it makes sense to keep 'parked up' time to a minimum.

Dahabiyyas, the Golden Boats

'The choice between a dahabiyya and a steamer is like the choice between travelling with post-horses and travelling by rail. One is expensive, leisurely, delightful; the other is cheap, swift, and comparatively comfortless.'

When the 19th-century traveller Amelia Edwards wrote these lines in *A Thousand Miles Up the Nile,* package tours by steamer were already crowding dahabiyyas off the Nile. But they have made a comeback in the past few years and dozens of them are now afloat. We have listed four companies with boats that are beautifully appointed, with an antique feel, tasteful decor and double lateen sails. With such small numbers of passengers, this is the most luxurious way to see the monuments without crowds. As most dahabiyyas have flexible itineraries and personalised service, it is also the best way to feel truly independent while still travelling in comfort, although often at considerably more expense than on feluccas or cruisers. Prices include all meals and usually also transfers to and from airports/train stations. Some include entrance to monuments and guide fees, but you should check when booking your trip. Trips are best arranged before you depart for Egypt.

Meroe

(☑0100 657 8322; www.nourelnil.com; 5-night trip per person from €1700; ❋@) A replica of a 19th-century dahabiyya indistinguishable from the original, the beautifully finished *Meroe* is the coolest dahabiyya currently on the Nile and is rare for being owner-operated. It has room for 20 passengers in 10 comfortable, stylish white cabins with private bathroom, and large windows overlooking the Nile. Because it is newly built, plumbing and water filtration are good, and there is plenty of storage for clothes and suitcases. During the day, when not visiting an ancient site or a local market, there is plenty of space on deck to read in your own corner, to watch the scenery or to dive off and swim in the strong current of the Nile. The chef buys from farmers and markets on the way, so the food is simple but totally fresh and delicious: plenty of fresh vegetables, farm-bred chicken, duck and fish. This tailor-made trip, with moorings at small islands and outside villages, is a unique way to see the Nile, reminiscent of another age. If there is no wind, the dahabiyya is towed by a motor boat. The same owners have three other boats, *Malouka, El Nil* and *Assouan*, whose cabins are significantly less expensive. All boats only run from Esna to Aswan (five nights).

La Flâneuse du Nil

(☑in France 01 42 86 16 00; www.la-flaneuse-du-nil.com, in French; 4-night trip per person in a double cabin from €875; ❋) *La Flâneuse* has been quickly picked up by several upmarket British tour operators and with good reason: the

---

PLANNING YOUR FELUCCA TRIP

Toilet facilities There are no onboard toilet facilities, so you will need to go to the toilet overboard or find somewhere private when you stop on shore.

Ensure that your boat is riverworthy Check that the captain has what appears to be a decent, riverworthy boat, and the essential gear: blankets (it gets cold at night), cooking implements and a sunshade. If a different boat or captain is foisted on you at the last minute, be firm in refusing.

Establish whether the price includes food To be sure you're getting what you paid for, go with whoever does the shopping.

Agree on the number of passengers beforehand Ask to meet fellow passengers, because you are going to be sharing a small space.

Decide on the drop-off point before you set sail Many felucca captains stop 30km south of Edfu in Hammam, Faris or Ar-Ramady.

Don't hand over your passport Captains can use a photocopy to arrange the permit.

Bring comfort essentials It can get bitterly cold at night, so bring a sleeping bag. Insect repellent is a good idea. A hat, sunscreen and plenty of bottled water are essential.

Take your rubbish with you Wherever you stop, be sure to clean up after yourself.

TRAVEL ACCOUNTS ON THE NILE

» **Sensual and spiritual** *A Winter on the Nile* by Lonely Planet author Anthony Sattin – Sattin tells the parallel stories of Florence Nightingale and Gustave Flaubert, who both sailed up the Nile in 1849. While Nightingale was fascinated by the spirituality of ancient Egypt, Flaubert found his pleasures in the brothels.

» **Classical Egyptology** *A Thousand Miles Up the Nile* by Amelia B Edwards – Edwards was so absorbed by the remains of ancient Egyptian civilisation she came across on her journey that she founded the London-based Egypt Exploration Fund, which still finances archaeological missions today.

» **Ancient encounter** *The Histories* by Herodotus – Egyptian customs, curious manners, tall tales and a few facts from a curious Greek historian in the 5th century BC.

» **The long journey** *Old Serpent Nile: A Journey to the Source* by Stanley Stewart – a view from the ground as Stewart travels from the Nile Delta to its source in the Mountains of the Moon, in Uganda, during the late 1980s.

boat is well fitted and well run. Like original dahabiyyas, it relies on sails (or tugs) to move, but does have air-con in the seven cabins. Tours are shorter than some, taking four nights from Esna to Aswan and three nights from Aswan back to Esna.

Lazuli

(☏0100 877 7115; www.lazulinil.com; 5-night trip per person from €990; ✳) There are now three *Lazulis* on the Nile, one with five cabins and two with six. The long, elegant boats have two lateen sails, a spacious deck with deck chairs, cushions and a long table at which most meals are served. The cabins are comfortable with compact but modern private bathrooms and solar-power energy.

The Orient

(☏02-2395 9124; www.nile-dahabiya.com; 4-night trip per person s/d from €1100/700; ✳) With four double cabins and one suite, the *Orient* is smaller than many dahabiyyas but none the worse for that. Well turned out, run by Egyptians who also own one of our favourite restaurants in Luxor (Sofra; p233), this and its sister ship *Zekrayaat* are good midrange choices. The *Orient* leaves Esna each Saturday, the *Zekrayaat* each Monday.

Cruisers

There are as many as 300 cruisers plying the waters between Aswan and Luxor. Like hotels, they range from slightly shabby to sumptuous, but almost all have some sort of pool, a large rooftop area for sunbathing and watching the scenery, a restaurant, a bar, air-con, TV, minibars and en suite bathrooms.

A cruise remains the easiest way to see the Nile in comfort on a midrange budget and can be ideal for families with older children who want to splash in a pool between archaeological visits, or for people who want to combine sightseeing with relaxation. The downside is that monuments are almost always seen with large groups and the itineraries are generally inflexible. Boats are almost always moored together, and the sheer volume of traffic means that generators and air-con units overwhelm the peace of the river. The consensus from our research is that scrimping on cruises means substandard hygiene, no pool, cubby-hole cabins and lots of hidden extras, which makes a felucca trip a far better option.

The only way around this is to book an all-inclusive package to Egypt. Not only are the prices usually lower but, in the case of cut-price cruises, the agency guarantees the reliability of the boat. The best deals are from Europe. Avoid booking through small hotels in Egypt: the hotels are not licensed as travel agencies so you will have no recourse if there are problems. The following are some of the most noteworthy boats. With the uncertain state of tourism at the time of writing, prices, which include all meals, entrance to monuments and guides, varied considerably. As such, we have not included prices: please check with the company before you book.

Between Luxor & Aswan

M/S Sudan

(☏in France 01 73 00 81 88; www.steam-ship-sudan. com; ✳) The *Sudan* was built as part of Thomas Cook's steamer fleet in 1885 and was once owned by King Fouad. It was also used as a set in the film *Death on the Nile*. It has been refurbished and offers 23 cabins, all with private bathroom, air-con and access to the deck. It's unusual in that it has no pool, but it's also unique because it has so much history and character, something sorely missing on most cruisers. Its configuration means it cannot moor to other cruisers, so night-time views are good. There is a choice of three- and four-night cruises. Note that the management does not accept children under seven.

M/S Sun Boat III

(www.abercrombiekent.co.uk; ❋🏠🏊) Abercrombie & Kent's most intimate cruiser, the beautiful *Sun Boat III* has 14 cabins and four suites decorated in contemporary Egyptian style, straight out of a magazine. The seven-night itinerary includes visits to Dendara and Abydos. Dinner on board is à la carte or a set menu with two European choices and one Egyptian. There's also the option of in-room dining. The boat is impeccably run and operates a no-mobile-phone policy in public areas. Facilities include a pool and exercise machines. The company also operates the 40-cabin, deluxe M/S *Sun Boat IV* and the 32-cabin *Nile Adventurer*, back in service after a complete refit. All A&K boats have excellent Egyptologists as guides and private mooring docks in Luxor, Aswan and Kom Ombo.

M/S Philae

(www.oberoihotels.com; ❋🏠🏊) Designed to resemble a Mississippi paddle boat, the award-winning *Philae* runs four- and six-night cruises. Its interior is filled with wood panelling and antiques, and all rooms have a balcony. The old-world feel is backed up by state-of-the-art water filtration, a library and all the comforts of a good five-star hotel. Prices more than double in high season around Christmas, Easter and the autumn/winter school holidays.

M/S Nile Goddess

(www.sonesta.com/nilecruises; ❋@🏊) One of the top boats of the Sonesta's five cruisers, the *Nile Goddess* is a large, plush, five-star vessel with lots of marble and gilt. Sonesta's sister ship, the M/S *Sun Goddess*, is slightly cheaper; the M/S *Moon Goddess* and *Star Goddess* are even plusher and more expensive.

M/S Beau Soleil

(www.msbeausoleil.com; ❋🏊) The five-star *Beau Soleil* is more reasonably priced than many others and recommended for its good service and facilities. The smallest cabins are 15 sq metres (large for such a boat) and many of the cabins have their own balcony from where you can watch the scenery go by.

M/S Darakum

Not a boat you can book direct, but one that is offered by a number of international agencies. New, spacious and top-end, if not super-luxurious, the *Darakum* has 44 cabins and eight suites, plus a swimming pool. The decor is more 1970s than New Kingdom and you have to be quick to get a sunbed, but prices come right down out of the autumn/winter school holidays.

Lake Nasser

Of the handful of boats currently cruising on Lake Nasser, a few stand out above the rest.

Ta Seti

(📞097-230 9748; www.african-angler.net) Something different: Tim Baily worked in safaris south of the Sahara before setting up African Angler, the first company to run Lake Nasser safaris. He has a staff of skilled guides, expert in the flora, fauna and fish life of the lake, and owns several styles of small boat. Two-cabin houseboats have toilet and shower, the two-bunk safari boats are more basic, while the mothership carries the kitchen and supplies. Cruises can be from one to seven nights and can start from Aswan or Abu Simbel.

Kasr Ibrim

(📞02-2516 9653/4/6; www.kasribrim.com.eg; ❋) The *Kasr Ibrim* and its twin the *Eugénie* were the brainchild of Mustafa al-Guindi, a Cairene of Nubian origin who is almost single-handedly responsible for getting Lake Nasser opened to tourists. The boats are stunningly designed and each has a pool, a hammam (bathhouse) and French cuisine.

Nubiana

(📞0122 104 0255; www.lakenasseradventure.com; ❋) The *Nubiana* is a small motorboat with three small cabins, a suite and a shared shower. Above is a lounge and sun deck. A speedboat can also be arranged for fishing trips or waterskiing. The same company also organises five-day boat trekking trips from Aswan to Abu Simbel.

Prince Abbas

(📞02-2690 1797; www.moevenpick-hotels.com; ❋🏊) A five-star deluxe ship operated by the Swiss chain Mövenpick, it has a library, gym, sun deck with a plunge pool and a Jacuzzi. The spacious cabins have TV, music system, minibar, picture windows and private bathroom.

Diving the Red Sea

Best Diving Intro Experience

Gently submerging into Dahab's sloping **Lighthouse Reef** (p408), and discovering a colourful world of darting, curious fish only a few steps from the shore.

Best Famous Dive Site Experience

Plunging into the **Blue Hole** (p410).

Best Wreck-Diving Experience

Exploring the underwater museum of the *Thistlegorm* (p43), the WWII supply ship first discovered by Jacques Cousteau.

Best Marine-Life Experience

Coming face to face with hammerheads and mantas, passing by large shoals of tuna, while spotting emperor angelfish and turtles at world renowned **Elphinstone Reef** (p382).

Best Off-the-Beaten-Track Experience

Bucking the diving trend of heading to Dahab or Sharm el-Sheikh and instead venturing to the far south near **Marsa Alam** (p382), where the pristine reefs of the Fury Shoals can be accessed as day trips.

It's not hard to see why the Red Sea boasts such a legendary reputation among diving enthusiasts. Under the surface of this 1800km-long body of water lurks a completely different world. Once submerged, you'll find a startling fantasia of coral mountains and shallow reefs swarming with brightly coloured fish. You can explore sheer drop-offs disappearing into un-plumbed depths and coral-encrusted shipwrecks bathed in an ethereal blue hue. It's not just diver hyperbolic spin either. In 1989 a panel of scientists and conservationists chose the northern section of the Red Sea as one of the Seven Underwater Wonders of the World.

The two jewels in the Red Sea's crown are Ras Mohammed National Park, home to the 'Holy Trinity' of Shark Reef, Eel Garden and the *Jolanda*, and the WWII wreck of the *Thistlegorm*, a British warship first discovered in the 1950s by Jacques Cousteau. Whichever reefs you decide to dive, you'll soon discover that the sights below Egypt's waters are just as magnificent as those above.

The strongest appeal of the Red Sea is that you can tailor your diving holiday to your own travelling style. Independent travellers spend more time than they planned in the backpacker-friendly village of Dahab, while package tourists enjoy the creature comforts in the resort towns of Sharm el-Sheikh and El-Gouna. For those who want to seriously maximise their underwater time, there's no better option than a week on a live-aboard. Regardless of your travelling style, the Red Sea never fails to impress and is one of the top highlights of any trip to Egypt.

When to Dive

The Red Sea can be dived year-round, though diving conditions are at their peak during the summer months of July to September. Despite this, if you're not great at dealing with heat you should try to avoid booking a dive holiday in August, when land temperatures regularly skyrocket to over 40°C.

Most Popular Period

» **July–September** The best time to dive the Red Sea is in Egypt's summer months, when calm sea conditions, sea temperatures averaging 26°C, and excellent visibility make for astonishingly good diving conditions.

Quietest Period

» **December–January** During winter, rough seas and strong winds can make access to some dive sites difficult and even impossible, though if you're happy to stick to shore dives you shouldn't have a problem. Visibility does take a hit during this period and sea temperatures also drop substantially. The plus side is that, unlike in summer, you'll be diving without the crowds.

Other Seasonal Considerations

» If you are planning to dive in the Red Sea's southernmost sections (Marsa Alam and beyond), take into account that a plankton bloom reduces visibility for a few weeks during April and May and so is best avoided.

Where to Dive

Diving tends to be concentrated at the northern end of the Egyptian Red Sea, although increasing numbers of advanced divers are pushing further south. The most popular sites are around the southern tip of the Sinai Peninsula, most famously the thin strip of land that juts out into the sea and forms **Ras Mohammed National Park** (p393).

Another major diving area is in the **Straits of Tiran**, which form the narrow entrance to the Gulf of Aqaba. The currents sweeping through the deep channel allow coral to grow prolifically, attracting abundant marine life. The reefs further north

---

> **RED SEA STATS**
>
> **Depth**
> » 4m to 40m
>
> **Visibility**
> » 15m to 40m
>
> **Water Temperature**
> » Averages 21°C to 30°C, with January the coldest month and August the warmest.
>
> **Access**
> » Shore, boat and live-aboard

---

along the shores of the Gulf of Aqaba are also popular.

On the western side of the Sinai Peninsula lay the **Straits of Gubal**, a series of coral pinnacles just beneath the surface of the sea, famous for snagging ships trying to navigate north to the Suez Canal. This is where the majority of Egypt's shipwrecks, including the *Thistlegorm*, lie.

Heading south, the best reefs are found around the many offshore islands. Although most reefs near Hurghada have been damaged by uncontrolled tourist development, there is a plethora of pristine dive sites further south.

With so many dive sites and operators to choose from, it can be difficult for first-time Red Sea divers to know where to base themselves. The following are our tips from north to south.

Nuweiba

This major port town (p416) serves as the departure point for ferries to Jordan and attracts significantly fewer divers than its more famous cousins in Sinai. However there are a handful of excellent dive sites in the area (although the diving here is not as rich and as varied as other spots in Sinai and the Red Sea) and is a suitable base for independent-minded divers looking for low-key ambience and minimal crowds. For an even more relaxed experience, you could also base yourself at one of the beach camps on the Nuweiba–Taba coastal highway.

Dahab

The preferred base for independent travellers, this laid-back village (p405) is surround-

Diving the Red Sea

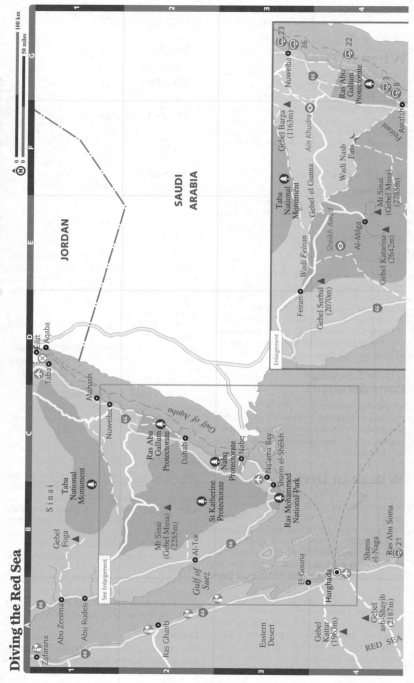

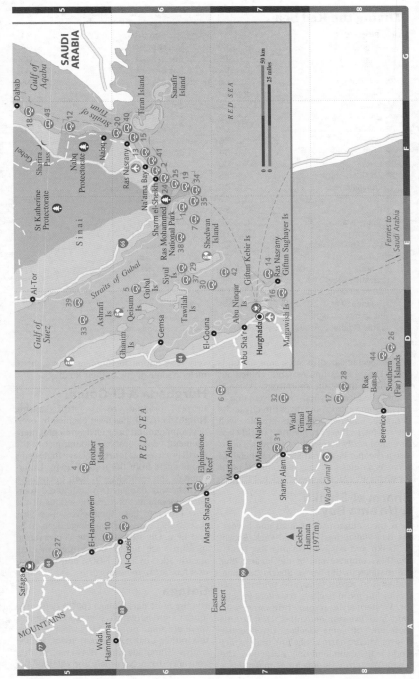

Diving the Red Sea

ed by spectacular dive sites, and abounds with cheap guesthouses and chilled-out restaurants lining the shorefront. Dahab is a fantastic place for first-time divers due to having some great shore dives directly on its doorstep. Experienced divers are also well catered for, as there are plenty of world-class dive sites easily accessed from town. This is also a cheaper base than Sharm el-Sheikh to serve as a quick and easy jumping-off point for diving Ras Mohammed National Park.

Sharm el-Sheikh & Na'ama Bay

Near the southern tip of Sinai and bordering Ras Mohammed National Park, Sharm el-Sheikh and adjacent Na'ama Bay (p395) together comprise one of the busiest dive destinations in the world. Sharm has gone high-end in recent years and primarily caters to European package travellers looking for Western-style resorts brimming with four- and five-star amenities. Despite this there are still some excellent diver-centric resorts where Sharm el-Sheikh's underwater world is the main, and only, attraction. The town's Western-style amenities make this a

very easy option for families who want to include some diving in their holiday.

Hurghada & El-Gouna

Egypt's original resort strip, ageing Hurghada (p370) has been plagued by over-development and poor environmental management, while glossy El-Gouna just to the north is a five-star tourist enclave that seems aeons apart from the rest of Egypt. Unfortunately the reefs close to both towns have been heavily damaged by unfettered tourist development. As a result, serious divers now prefer to base themselves elsewhere, though there are cheap package deals to be had here. On a positive note, conservation measures are finally being implemented, spearheaded by local NGOs, and the situation has begun to improve.

Safaga

For the most part, Safaga (p378) defies the tourist hordes, which is a good thing as there are some pristine reefs offshore from this rather unattractive port town. Unlike nearby Hurghada and El-Gouna, resorts here are extremely low-key, and cater almost exclusively to dedicated divers from overseas rather than families and package travellers.

Al-Quseir

A historic trade and export hub with a history stretching back centuries, the sleepy town of Al-Quseir (p379) holds a charm absent from other Red Sea destinations. The comparative lack of tourist development means that the offshore dive sites here are generally empty, though you will have to contend with strong winds and rough seas.

Marsa Alam

The closest base to the south-coast dive sites, Marsa Alam (p381) still manages to hold on to its remote-outpost ambience despite the resort construction drive of recent years. It's great if you want to experience some of Egypt's most far-flung dives without the cost of a live-aboard. The reefs along this southernmost stretch of the coast lack the crowds further north, though be aware that high winds and strong currents make many of the dives more suitable for experienced divers. Veteran divers of these parts will tell you, once you've dived here nothing else will compare.

Live-Aboards

The vast majority of larger dive operators in Egypt can organise dive safaris to remote sites ranging from one night to two weeks' duration. The cost of these live-aboard dive safaris (also known as marine safaris) varies according to the boat and the destination, with the more-remote sites in the far south generally the most expensive. While you won't see much of terrestrial Egypt, they allow you to access a greater range of dive sites, including many more-distant areas that are too far to explore as day trips.

As a general rule, you should always ask to see the boat before agreeing to sail on it. Also, if a trip is very cheap, check whether the costs of diving and food are included. Furthermore, check that your live-aboard complies with the following two rules:

» There should be a diver-guide ratio of one guide to every 12 divers (or every eight divers in marine park areas).

» Divers on live-aboards entering marine park areas must be experienced, with a minimum of 50 logged dives, as well as insurance coverage.

While it's quite possible to book yourself a basic package on a live-aboard after arriving in Egypt, there are numerous agencies that specialise in Red Sea diving holidays. Here is a small sampling:

Crusader Travel (✉in UK 020-8744 0474; www.divers.co.uk) Diving packages in the Red Sea, including diving for people with disabilities.

Maadi Divers (✉02-2519 8644; www.maadi-divers.com) A friendly local outfit run by owner Magdy El-Araby and his wife, Barbara, Maadi Divers offers affordable trips in Egyptian waters.

Oonasdivers (✉in UK 01323-648924; www.oonasdivers.com) Diving tours based at Na'ama Bay, Red Sea diving safaris from the Marsa Alam region and live-aboard trips.

Thomson (✉in UK 0845-644 7090; www.thomson.co.uk/explorers) Diving packages and live-aboards around Sharm el-Sheikh, Dahab and elsewhere in the northern Red Sea.

What You'll See

The Red Sea is teeming with more than a thousand species of marine life, and is an amazing spectacle of colour and form. Fish, sharks, turtles, stingrays, dolphins, corals, sponges, sea cucumbers and molluscs all thrive in these waters. Around 20% of the

---

ACCESSING THE OFFSHORE MARINE PARK ISLANDS

Accessing the waters of Egypt's far south is strictly regulated. Divers must have completed a minimum of 50 dives before entering; night diving or landing on the islands is prohibited; and fishing, spear fishing and the use of gloves are banned.

Due to these restrictions, permission must be given for each trip, and a park ranger will often accompany boats to ensure that the rules are being enforced. In order to carry divers, boats must have special safety equipment, which national park and Red Sea governorate officials inspect before each trip.

If you've been offered a trip to these remote areas, it's worth checking to see that the boat is licensed. If you are caught on an unlicensed boat you could have your own equipment or belongings confiscated and find yourself in custody.

» (above) Ras Um Sid dive site at Sharm el-Sheikh (p397)
» (left) Fan coral in the Straits of Gubal (p37)

THISTLEGORM: THE RED SEA'S BEST WRECK DIVE

Built by the North East Marine Engineering Company, the 129m-long cargo ship christened the *Thistlegorm* was completed and launched in 1940 in Sunderland, England. Prior to setting out from Glasgow in 1941, she had previously made several successful trips to North America, the East Indies and Argentina. However, with a cargo full of vital supplies destined for North Africa, where British forces were preparing for Operation Crusader (the relief of Tobruk against the German 8th Army), the *Thistlegorm* met her end at 2am on 6 October 1941.

While the ship was waiting in the Straits of Gubal for a call sign to proceed up the Gulf of Suez, four German Heinkel He 111s that were flying out of Crete mounted an attack. The planes were returning from an armed reconnaissance mission up the Sinai coast, and targeted the ship to offload their unused bombs. One bomber scored a direct hit on the No 4 hold, which tore the ship in two and sent the two railway locomotives that the vessel was carrying hurtling through the air. Incredibly, they landed upright on the seabed, one on either side of the wreck. In less than 20 minutes, the ship sank to the ocean floor, taking with it nine sailors out of a crew of 49.

The *Thistlegorm* lay undisturbed until 1956 when legendary French diver Jacques Cousteau located the wreck, lying at a depth of 17m to 35m to the northwest of Ras Mohammed. Cousteau found a cache of WWII cargo packed in the hold, including a full consignment of armaments and supplies, such as Bedford trucks, Morris cars, BSA 350 motorbikes and Bren gun carriers. Although Cousteau took the ship's bell, the captain's safe and a motorbike, he left the wreck as he found it, and proceeded to keep its location secret. However, it was rediscovered in 1993 when some divers stumbled upon its location, and it has since become one of the world's premier wreck-dive sites.

The *Thistlegorm* (location: Sha'ab Ali; depth: 17m to 30m; rating: intermediate to advanced; access: boat) is best dived on an overnight trip since it takes 3½ hours each way from Sharm el-Sheikh by boat; dive operators throughout Sinai can easily help you arrange this. On your first dive, you will do a perimeter sweep of the boat, which is highlighted by a swim along the soldier walkways on the side of the vessel. On your second dive, you will penetrate the ship's interior, swimming through a living museum of WWII memorabilia.

fish species to be found in the Red Sea are endemic to the region.

» **Coral** This is what makes a reef a reef – though thought for centuries to be some form of flowering plant, it is in fact an animal. Both hard and soft corals exist, their common denominator being that they are made up of polyps, which are tiny cylinders ringed by waving tentacles that sting their prey and draw it into their stomach. During the day corals retract into their tube, only displaying their real colours at night.

» **Fish** Most of the bewildering variety of fish species in the Red Sea – including many that are found nowhere else – are closely associated with the coral reef, and live and breed in the reefs or nearby seagrass beds. These include such commonly sighted species as the grouper, wrasse, parrotfish and snapper. Others, such as tuna and barracuda, live in open waters and usually only venture into the reefs to feed or breed.

» **Manta rays** Spotting the graceful, frolicking form of a manta during a Red Sea dive is a major highlight for any diver lucky enough to have this experience. Mantas are easily recognisable for their pectoral 'wings' and huge bulk. They can grow to nearly 7m and can weigh up to 1400kg. They are usually sighted near the surface, where they feed on the plankton present there.

» **Sharks** When diving, the sharks you're most likely to encounter include white- or black-tipped reef sharks. Tiger sharks, as well as the enormous, plankton-eating whale sharks, are generally found only in deeper waters. If you're skittish about these apex predators, you can take comfort in the fact that shark attacks in the Red Sea are rare (though not unheard of).

» **Turtles** The most common type of turtle found in these waters is the green turtle, although the leatherback and hawksbill are occasionally sighted. Turtles are protected in Egypt, and although they're not deliberately hunted, they are sometimes caught in nets and end up on

THE RED SEA'S DUGONG

Little is known about the distribution and numbers of these enigmatic marine mammals in the Red Sea. Weighing up to 500kg, the dugong are easily recognisable for their fusiform shape and dolphin-like tail. These gentle herbivores' natural habitat is shallow coastal waters where they feed on seagrass and other plant forms. This makes them especially vulnerable to coastal degradation and pollution. Most dugong sightings in Egypt have occurred at sites along the coast south of Hurghada, with the Marsa Abu Dabab dive site (to the north of Marsa Alam) becoming famous for dugong-spotting. To help preserve the area and protect the resident dugong of the bay, zoning laws and access restrictions have now been put in place around this dive site.

menus in restaurants in Cairo and along the coasts.

» **Marine life you're better off avoiding** As intriguing as they may seem, there are some creatures that should be given a wide berth, especially moray eels, sea urchins, fire coral, blowfish, triggerfish, feathery lionfish, turkeyfish and stonefish. To help protect yourself, it's a good idea to familiarise yourself with pictures of all these creatures before snorkelling or diving – single-page colour guides to the Red Sea's common marine hazards can be bought in hotel bookshops around diving areas.

Responsible Diving

The Red Sea's natural wonders are just as magnificent as the splendours of Egypt's Pharaonic heritage, and appear all the more stunning when contrasted with their barren desert backdrop. However, care is needed if the delicate world of coral reefs and fish is not to be permanently damaged. Almost the entire Egyptian coastline in the Gulf of Aqaba is now a protectorate, as is the Red Sea coast from Hurghada south to Sudan. Divers and snorkellers should heed the requests of instructors *not* to touch or tread on coral – if you kill the coral, you'll eventually kill or chase away the fish, too.

Overall, the paramount guideline for preserving the ecology and beauty of reefs is to take nothing with you, leave nothing behind. Other considerations:

» Never use anchors on the reef, and take care not to ground boats on coral.

» Avoid touching or standing on living marine organisms or dragging equipment across the reef. Polyps can be damaged by even the gentlest contact. If you must hold on to the reef, only touch exposed rock or dead coral.

» Be conscious of your fins. Even without contact, the surge from fin strokes near the reef can damage delicate organisms. Take care not to kick up clouds of sand, which can smother organisms.

» Practise and maintain proper buoyancy control. Major damage can be done by divers descending too fast and colliding with the reef.

» Take great care in underwater caves. Spend as little time within them as possible as your air bubbles may be caught within the roof and thereby leave organisms high and dry. Take turns to inspect the interior of a small cave.

» Resist the temptation to collect or buy corals or shells or to loot marine archaeological sites (mainly shipwrecks).

» Ensure that you take home all your rubbish and any litter you may find as well. Plastics in particular are a serious threat to marine life.

» Do not feed fish, and minimise your disturbance of marine animals.

Learning to Dive

Most dive clubs in Egypt offer **PADI** (www. padi.com) certification, though you'll occasionally find **NAUI** (www.naui.org), **SSI** (www. divessi.com), **CMAS** (www.cmas2000.org) and **BSAC** (www.bsac.com) as well.

Generally, PADI Open Water dive courses take five (intensive) days and cost between €275 and €320. When comparing prices, check to see whether the certification fee and books are included.

Beginner courses are designed to drum into you things that have to become second nature when you're underwater. They usually consist of classroom work, where you learn the principles and basic knowledge needed to dive, followed by training in a confined body of water, such as a pool, before heading out to the open sea. If you've never dived before and want to give it a try before you commit yourself, all dive clubs offer introductory dives for between €50 and €95, including equipment.

In addition to basic certification, most of the well-established clubs on the coast offer a variety of more advanced courses as well as professional-level courses or training in technical diving.

Choosing a Dive Operator

Whether you choose to plunge into the Red Sea with a small local shop, an established resort or a live-aboard, you will have no problem finding a dive operator. Almost all of the large resorts and hotels along the Red Sea have attached dive centres, and there are a vast number of smaller, independent dive centres in the main coastal towns. Some centres and live-aboards are laid-back and informal, while others are slick and structured. Regardless of which diving style you choose, you're going to get wet – and love every minute of it.

Obviously, with diving a huge cash-cow in this area, there are invariably a few fly-by-night outfits. Avoid them by doing your research first. Look for a dive operator that has a high PADI rating or equivalent, and ask other divers for recommendations. When deciding which dive centre to use, among the considerations should be the operator's attention to safety and its sensitivity to environmental issues.

The **Chamber of Diving and Watersports** (CDWS; www.cdws.travel) is Egypt's only legal dive centre licensing agency. Check the validity date of your dive centre's CDWS licence before choosing to dive with them.

RESEARCHING BEFORE YOU GO

» **The Chamber of Diving and Watersports** (CDWS; www.cdws.travel) Egyptian licensing body for dive operators. Its website provides a list of reputable dive centres in Egypt.

» **Dive Site Directory** (www.divesitedirectory/red_sea.html) Reviews of dive sites throughout the Red Sea.

» **Hurghada Environmental Protection & Conservation Association** (HEPCA; www.hepca.com) This local NGO is extremely active in promoting conservation issues throughout the Red Sea region and also publishes a guide to Red Sea dive sites. For more, see p372.

» **Red Sea Virtual Dive Center** (www.touregypt.net/vdc/) A good starting point for general information on diving the Red Sea.

Accidents still occasionally happen and are usually the result of neglect and negligence. Before making any choices, consider the following factors.

» Take your time when choosing clubs and dive sites, and don't let yourself be pressured into accepting something, or someone, you're not comfortable with.

» Don't choose a club based solely on cost. Safety should be the paramount concern; if a dive outfit cuts corners to keep prices low, you could be in danger.

MARE ROSTRUM

Surrounded by desert on three sides, the Red Sea was formed some 40 million years ago when the Arabian Peninsula split from Africa, allowing the waters of the Indian Ocean to rush in. Bordered at its southern end by the 25km Bab al-Mandab Strait, the Red Sea is the only tropical sea that is almost entirely closed. No river flows into it and the influx of water from the Indian Ocean is slight. These unique geographical features, combined with the arid desert climate and high temperatures, make the sea extremely salty. It is also windy – on average the sea is flat for only 50 days a year.

In regard to its name (the Red Sea is in fact deep blue), there are two competing schools of thought regarding etymology. Some believe that the sea was named after the surrounding red-rock mountain ranges. Others insist it was named for the periodic algae blooms that tinge the water a reddish-brown. Whatever the spark, it inspired ancient mariners to dub these waters *Mare Rostrum* – the Red Sea.

» (above) Dolphin diving off the coast of Nuweiba (p417)
» (left) Red Sea anemonefish

READING UP

» **Red Sea Diver's Guide from Sharm El Sheikh to Hurghada** by Shlomo and Roni Cohen has excellent maps and descriptions of sites around Ras Mohammed, the Straits of Gubal and Hurghada.

» **Sinai Dive Guide** by Peter Harrison has detailed maps and explanations of the main Red Sea sites.

» **Sharm el-Sheikh Diving Guide** by Alberto Siliotti has maps and ratings of numerous sites around Sharm el-Sheikh and Ras Mohammed National Park.

» **Red Sea Diving Guide** by Andrea Ghisotti and Alessandro Carletti covers Egyptian sites, as well as others in Sudan, Israel and Eritrea.

» **The Red Sea: Underwater Paradise** by Angelo Mojetta is one of the better glossy coffee-table books, with beautiful photos of the flora and fauna of Egypt's reefs.

» **The Official HEPCA Dive Guide** produced by the Hurghada Environmental Protection & Conservation Association (HEPCA) details 46 sites with artists' drawings and a small fish index. Proceeds from the sale of this guide go towards maintaining mooring buoys on the Red Sea. For more on HEPCA, see Rescuing the Red Sea, p372.

» If you haven't dived for more than three months, take a check-out dive. This is for your own safety and all reputable operators will make this a requirement. The cost is usually applied towards later dives.

» If you're taking lessons, ensure that the instructor speaks your language well. If you can't understand them, you should request another.

» Check that all equipment is clean and stored away from the sun, and check all hoses, mouthpieces and valves for cuts and leakage.

» Confirm that wetsuits are in good condition. Some divers have reported getting hypothermia because of dry, cracked suits.

» Check that there is oxygen on the dive boat in case of accidents.

» If you're in Sinai, ask if the club donates US$1 per diver each day to the hyperbaric chamber; this is often a reflection of the club's safety consciousness.

Safe Diving

The most important thing to remember when diving in the Red Sea is to use common sense. More often than not, most diving fatalities are caused by divers simply forgetting (or disregarding) some of the basic rules.

In Dahab, where the majority of accidents have occurred, drink and drugs have often played a starring role in these tragic and largely avoidable deaths. Many of those who lose their lives are experienced divers who should have known better than to go beyond safety limits or dive under the influence. Others are divers who were not experienced enough for the situations they found themselves in. The next time you complain about having to take a test dive, remember that dive clubs have a good reason to be cautious.

The following are some common-sense tips for safe diving:

» Possess a current diving certification card from a recognised scuba-diving instructional agency.

» Be sure you are healthy and feel comfortable diving.

» Don't drink and dive. Alcohol dehydrates, especially in a dry climate such as Egypt's, and increases your susceptibility to decompression sickness.

» If you are taking prescription drugs, inform your medical examiner that you intend to go diving. Sometimes diving can affect your metabolism and your dosage might need to be changed.

» Dive within your scope of experience. The Red Sea's clear waters and high visibility often lull divers into going too deep. The depth limit for sports divers is 30m. Stick to it.

» Do not fly within 24 hours of diving. You also shouldn't climb above 300m, so don't plan a trip to St Katherine's Monastery or into the Eastern Desert mountains for the day after a dive.

» Be aware that underwater conditions vary tremendously from site to site, and that both daily and seasonal weather and current changes can significantly alter any site and dive

CLIMBING & DIVING: A WORD OF CAUTION

Altitude can kill, particularly if your body is full of residual nitrogen. If you've been diving recently, be advised that Mt Sinai is high enough to induce decompression sickness. As a general rule, avoid climbing the mountain for 12 hours after one dive, or 18 hours if you've been on multiple dives. Although this may complicate your travel plans, trust us – you'll be delayed a lot longer if you end up confined in a hyperbaric chamber. And, of course, decompression sickness is anything but fun.

conditions. These differences influence not only which sites you can dive on any particular day, but also the way you'll need to dress for a dive and the necessary dive techniques.

» Be aware of local laws, regulations and etiquette about marine life and the environment.

» Make sure you recognise your boat from the water. Some dive sites get crowded and boats can look similar from underneath. It's not unknown for divers to get left behind because they didn't realise their boat had left without them.

» Be insured. If something happens to you, treatment in the hyperbaric chamber can cost thousands. The most reputable clubs will make insurance a condition for diving with them. If you hadn't planned to dive before arriving in Egypt, many of the better clubs can provide insurance.

Travel with Children

Best Regions for Kids

Cairo
Intensely crowded Cairo isn't obviously kid-scale, but kids may delight at donkey carts in medieval alleys. In mosques, they're welcome to roam barefoot on carpets (but not yell). For more kid activities, see p93

Nile Valley
All of Upper Egypt, from Luxor south, is straight out of picture books: temples, camels and old-timey boats.

Western Desert
The slow pace of the oases is well suited to children. Aside from in Bawiti, there's virtually no hassle, and out in the dunes, kids can make as much noise as they like.

Red Sea Coast
The Sinai may have better beaches, but Egyptian families fill the resorts on the coast here, so older kids may make friends. Teens can learn to dive here (or in the Sinai).

The Sinai
The interior offers some unforgettable treks. On the beaches, there are wild beach camps or the comfort of Sharm el-Sheikh.

Visiting Egypt with children can be a delight. For them, seeing ancient monuments – or even a camel – up close can be a fantasy made real. For you, the incredibly warm welcome towards young ones can smooth over many small practical hassles.

Egypt for Kids
Attitudes
What Egypt lacks in kiddie infrastructure like playgrounds and nappy-changing tables, it more than makes up for in its loving attitude to little ones. In all but the finest restaurants, waiters are delighted to see kids – don't be surprised if your baby even gets passed around the place for everyone to hug and kiss, or your toddler is welcomed onto laps and fed sweets. (Yes, probably right before bedtime. Egyptian kids don't know the concept of 'bedtime'.)

Teenagers are less subject to this kind of attention, though their Egyptian counterparts will likely seem a bit younger and more sheltered. By adolescence, separation of the sexes is more typical, so teens should abide by grown-up etiquette when meeting Egyptians of their age.

Practicalities
Safety standards may make visitors nervous: don't expect car seats (or even seat belts, for that matter) in taxis or private cars, or child-size life preservers on boats.

Hygiene in food preparation can be inconsistent, so be prepared for diarrhoea or other stomach problems (and have a plan for when you're struck down and the kids are still raring to go). Rehydration salts, available very cheaply at all pharmacies (ask for Rehydran), can be a life-saver, as children can lose fluid rapidly in Egypt's hot, dry climate.

Keep kids away from stray animals, which can spread disease – street cats in particular are everywhere and liable to scratch if approached.

Formula is readily available, as are disposable nappies. High-chairs are often available in restaurants. Babysitting facilities are usually available in top-end hotels. Nutritious snacks like peanuts, sesame-seed bars, dried fruit and dates are common; stock up for outings, though, as it's possible to wind up somewhere with no other services than someone selling Coke and potato chips.

If you need more enticements during your trip, stop by the bookshop in any five-star hotel – they're usually stocked with good Egypt-theme books and toys.

For more practical advice, pick up a copy of Lonely Planet's *Travel with Children,* written by a team of parent-authors.

Children's Highlights

There's plenty more to do in Egypt than look at pyramids and ride camels – though these are pretty fun too. Here are some tips for child-friendly fun in the desert, on the water and at some ancient sites.

Desert Life

» Bundle into a jeep for a Western Desert excursion, especially the otherworldly terrain of the White Desert.

» Siwa's mellow atmosphere is perfect for kids, though the bus ride is very long. Once there, they can dive-bomb into springs and graze on fresh dates.

» Getting to the Birqash camel market is an adventure in itself. Once there, older kids will be awed, especially budding photographers. (But little ones are a liability, given the camels' propensity to bolt in unexpected directions.)

» Wilderness Adventures Egypt in Sinai runs a camel riding school (much better than just posing on one for a snapshot) and a stargazing class, to make sense of the glimmering sky in the Sinai.

» How did a whale wind up in the desert? Find out in Wadi al-Hittan, where fossils are set in the sand. Trips here often include sandboarding on nearby dunes.

Ancient & Awesome

» Older children will be astounded to enter the Great Pyramid of Cheops at Giza – though test for a tendency for claustrophobia beforehand.

» Devise a virtual treasure hunt for children at the Egyptian Museum. Can they find King Tut's wig box? How many miniature oarsmen row a miniature boat? Where are the baboon mummies?

» At the Bibliotheca Alexandrina, bookworms can inspect antique manuscripts, while science fans

---

PLANNING

Before You Go

If they're not already, get kids reading about ancient Egypt. As a starter, Zilpha Keatley Snyder's classic fantasy *The Egypt Game* may get tweens hooked. For budding Egyptologists, the British Museum's website www.ancientegypt.co.uk is loaded with games and other material; www.greatscott.com introduces hieroglyphics.

For modern Egypt, look for *The Day of Ahmed's Secret,* by Florence Parry Heide and Judith Heide Gilliland, a wonderful picture book set in one of Cairo's poor neighbourhoods. Teens may like *Aunt Safiyya and the Monastery,* by Bahaa' Taher; *Life Is More Beautiful than Paradise,* by Khaled al-Berry; or *I Want to Get Married!* by Ghada Abdel Aal.

Also make sure children are up-to-date with routine vaccinations, and discuss possible travel vaccinations with your doctor well before departure.

What to Pack

See p511 for first-aid kit suggestions, and don't skimp on the sunscreen. For infants, you'll want a chest or back carrier – outside of well-paved Sharm el-Sheikh, strollers will get you nowhere.

can explore the science museum. And everyone loves the planetarium.

All Aboard!

» Whether you go for an evening in Cairo or a multiday trip in Upper Egypt, a felucca ride is an excellent place to play pirate.

» Egypt's trains are seldom crowded in first class, making a trip into the Delta region – perhaps to Tanta, famous for its sweets – a low-stress half-day out.

» On a Friday, join Egyptian families on the boat to Qanater, the Nile Barrages just outside of Cairo.

» The trek up Mt Sinai, if taken slowly, isn't terribly strenuous, and teens especially will delight at being out in the middle of the night.

» Hop on a bike on Luxor's west bank – it's a great way to catch a breeze.

» Ride the tram in Alexandria from end to end for a cheap, low-stress view of the city.

» Ride a horse at sunset by the Pyramids of Giza. Stables here have helmets in all sizes.

On the Water

» Snorkelling in the Red Sea is a dazzling introduction to the underwater world. Seek out sites where kids can drift along the side of a reef, rather than directly over it.

» The Alexandria ship yards are where boats of all sizes get worked on. Ask aspiring captains which they'd like to helm. Round it out with a visit to the fish market, then dinner at one of the family-friendly restaurants.

» For shipping on an even larger scale, stop in Port Said and watch the massive freighters go through the Suez Canal.

regions at a glance

Cairo

Entertainment ✓✓✓
History ✓✓✓
Shopping ✓✓✓

Watching
Cairo is the very model of a modern megalopolis, and just watching the human parade can easily take up an evening. You could hit the town to see belly dancers in a dive like Palmyra or a luxury-hotel cabaret, or embark on a Downtown bar crawl or a cocktail cruise in Zamalek. But it's worth planning your evenings around the schedule of great live music, whether at the swish Cairo Opera House or at a casual place such as After Eight or Makan.

p58

More than Pyramids
Thanks to the Pyramids alone, on the west edge of the city at Giza, Cairo is a required stop. But then there's the Egyptian Museum, so crammed with thrilling artefacts that it gets a whole separate chapter in this book (p136). Fast-forward a bit through time to visit Coptic Cairo, a maze of early churches and a fine museum, and of course the medieval city, spiked with minarets, that was for a time the capital of the Islamic Empire.

Souqs & Boutiques
Heaving with commerce for more than a millennium, the souq of Khan al-Khalili is a great browse even if you're not in the mood to buy. If nothing strikes your fancy there, head to one of the city's many boutiques for stylish souvenirs, from vintage movie posters to leather-bound books.

Cairo Outskirts & the Delta

Ancient History ✓✓
Rural Life ✓✓
Sufi Tradition ✓

The Other Pyramids
The vast complex of Saqqara, the centrepiece of which is Zoser's experimental step pyramid, is a full-day outing from Cairo, south into the desert. Dedicated Egyptomaniacs can also visit Tanis, a ruined city set between lush fields and desert sand.

Oases & Farms
Just an hour from Cairo is the semi-oasis of Al-Fayoum, where the arts colony of Tunis harbours ceramicists and other creative types. North of the city, in the fertile Nile Delta, there are few tourist sites, but the view looks good from a train window.

Sufi Tradition
The birthday of 13th-century religious leader al-Sayyed Ahmed al-Badawi draws up to a million people each year to the town of Tanta.

p146

Nile Valley: Beni Suef to Qena

Ancient History ✓
Coptic Heritage ✓✓✓
Urban Charm ✓

Temples & Tombs

For years this area of Egypt was all but closed to foreign visitors so many of the fine temples and tombs – such as Beni Hasan and Tell al-Amarna – are still well off the tourist trail. The temples at Abydos and Dendara are more accessible, by a scenic boat trip.

Coptic Churches

At Deir al-Muharraq monks conduct Mass in the Coptic language and the church here is thought to be the oldest in the world. At the Red Monastery, near Sohag, the walls still display 4th-century frescoes.

Minya

Minya, the official gateway to Upper Egypt, is a surprisingly elegant mid-size city with faded early-20th-century architecture. When the Akhenaten Museum opens it may be a destination in itself; until then, it's a nice place to pause between Cairo and Luxor.

p169

Nile Valley: Luxor

Ancient History ✓✓✓
More History ✓✓✓
Museums ✓✓

Luxor & Karnak

Luxor has the highest concentration of ancient Egyptian tombs, temples and more: Karnak, with its towering papyrus-look columns, the astonishingly large Ramesseum, and Luxor Temple, which is open till 10pm for atmospheric sightseeing. And that's just on the east bank of the Nile.

Valley of the Kings

On the west bank, it just gets better: the Valley of the Kings, of King Tut fame; the Temple of Hatshepsut, cut out of the cliffs; and, oh, the 1,000-tonne Colossi of Memnon just standing by.

Luxor Museum

More than just a means to enjoy the air-conditioning, Luxor Museum has an excellent collection of finds from nearby temples – including two royal mummies, displayed unwrapped. Follow up with a trip to the Mummification Museum, which explains the whole process.

p190

Nile Valley: Esna to Abu Simbel

Ancient History ✓✓✓
Wilderness ✓✓
Nubian Heritage ✓✓

Tremendous Temples

The Temple of Horus at Edfu is one of the best preserved in Egypt, and just down the river are the quarries of Gebel Silsila, where so many ancient building projects got their start. But the biggest attraction of all – literally and figuratively – is the mammoth Ramses II temple at Abu Simbel.

Lake Nasser & Aswan

A cruise along Lake Nasser's banks reveals crocodiles and gazelles – board a dahabiyya boat for a few days to really settle in. Around Aswan in winter, the birdwatching is exceptional.

Nubian Heritage

Trancelike folk music, elegant mud-brick architecture and distinctive clothing are characteristics of the unique culture in this part of Egypt. Stay the night at Eskaleh, a cultural centre in Abu Simbel, to get the full flavour.

p242

Siwa Oasis & the Western Desert

Ancient History ✓
Wilderness ✓✓✓
Ecotourism ✓✓

Graeco-Roman Traces
Ruined garrisons at Qasr ad-Dush and Qasr al-Ghueita hint at the lively trade routes that criss-crossed the desolate sands during the glory days of the Roman Empire. Well before that, the Oracle of Amun foretold destruction in the 6th century BC.

Wild Deserts
'Desert' doesn't convey the full variety of wild land here: soak in hot springs or cold pools such as the famous Cleopatra's Bath. The White Desert gleams like a snow field in the full moon.

Ecotourism
Few trips are lower impact than a camel safari under the stars. Round out the adventure with a stay at one of several exceptional lodges designed to integrate seamlessly with the desert landscape and the date-palm groves of the oases.

p278

Alexandria & the Mediterranean Coast

Nostalgia ✓✓✓
Ancient History ✓✓✓
Fun in the Sun ✓

Alexandria Cafes
Traces of Alexandria's cosmopolitan glamour, at its height in the early 20th century, can still be found in scores of old cafes where writers Lawrence Durrell, Constantine Cavafy and others once mused.

Port-City History
The Bibliotheca Alexandrina may have opened in 2002 but its model is the ancient library that once drew scholars from all over the Mediterranean and beyond. For a portrait of the city from Graeco-Roman times on, visit the excellent Alexandria National Museum.

Fun in the Sun
Seafront pleasures here include fresh fish dinners on Alexandria's corniche and beaches strung out to the west, mobbed in summer as Egyptians escape the heat. One nicer spot is Sidi Abdel Rahman, near the WWII battleground of El Alamein.

p317

Suez Canal

Nostalgia ✓✓✓
Ancient History ✓
Industry ✓✓✓

Ismailia & Port Said
Squint just right in downtown Ismailia and Port Said, and you can almost see the be-fezzed pashas and European dandies who built the canal, strolling in front of the decaying French-colonial buildings. With hotels of the same vintage, these cities are like museums you can sleep in too.

Ancient Waterways
Before the British and French opened up the shipping channel between Africa and Asia, the pharaohs and the Greeks dug waterways here. See the archaeological traces at the Ismailia Museum.

Cruise the Canal
Watch global commerce in action as giant container ships transit through the canal. In Port Said stroll the waterside boardwalk then hop a free ferry to cruise the canal yourself and get a glimpse of the action.

p353

Red Sea Coast

Fun in the Sun ✓
Ancient History ✓
Wilderness ✓✓

Resorts & Beach Camps

The rather concrete resort towns of Hurghada and El-Gouna are offset by simpler pleasures such as the beach camps around Marsa Alam and, if you're a kitesurfer, the windy coast at Safaga.

Historic Outposts

The Coptic monasteries of St Anthony and St Paul are landmarks, both for their status as the first Christian hermitages and for the 13th-century wall paintings. In the photogenically crumbling port of Al-Quseir, visit a 16th-century Ottoman fortress.

Eastern Desert

Tourist infrastructure in the Eastern Desert is sparse but with a guide you can trek to abandoned Roman mines, spot migratory birds and even visit a remote camel market. Divers in the know head to the reefs near Marsa Alam.

p364

Sinai

History ✓
Fun in the Sun ✓✓✓
Wilderness ✓✓✓

Mt Sinai

God allegedly gave Moses the law here at Mt Sinai, a popular hike for religious and secular travellers alike. At St Katherine's Monastery at the base of the peak, admire rare early Byzantine icons.

Beach Camps & Resorts

The laid-back beach camp – thatch roof, candlelight, barefoot bliss – is perfected along the coast between Taba and Nuweiba and in backpacker-built Dahab. At the other end of the scale, Sharm el-Sheikh serves up a glitzy holiday scene, beautiful reefs and good eats.

Deserts & Reefs

If it's desert you're after, the interior of the Sinai is the place for starlit treks with Bedouin guides. You can spot flocks of flamingos in the Zerenike Protectorate or, for even more colour, explore the coral wonderland of Ras Mohammed National Park.

p387

> Every listing is recommended by our authors, and their favourite places are listed first

> Look out for these icons:

 Our author's top recommendation

 A green or sustainable option

 No payment required

On the Road

Cairo

Best Places to Eat

» At-Tabei ad-Dumyati (p101)
» Fasahat Soumaya (p101)
» Sudan Restaurant (p102)
» Farahat (p105)
» Citadel View (p105)

Best Places to Stay

» Pension Roma (p94)
» Dina's Hostel (p94)
» Hotel Royal (p94)
» Cairo Marriott (p90)
» Mena House Oberoi (p132)

Why go?

First, the drawbacks: Cairo's crowds make Manhattan look like a ghost town, papyrus sellers hound you at every turn, and your snot will run black from the smog.

But it's a small price to pay to tap into the energy of the place Egyptians call *Umm ad-Dunya* – the Mother of the World. This urban buzz is a product of 20-or-so million inhabitants simultaneously crushing the city's infrastructure under their collective weight and lifting its spirit up with their exceptional charm and humour. One taxi ride can pass resplendent mosques built at the pinnacle of the Islamic empire, grand avenues, and 19th-century palaces. The Pyramids of Giza hulk on the western edge, past Nasser-era concrete towers. A caked-on layer of beige sand unifies the mix of eras and styles.

Blow your nose, crack a joke and look through the dirt to see the city's true colours. If you love Cairo, it will love you back.

When to go

Cairo

°C/°F Temp — Rainfall inches/mm

	J	F	M	A	M	J	J	A	S	O	N	D

Mar-May In khamsin season the city gets choked with dust.

Jun-Aug Ramadan is a feast every night. Boiling in the daytime.

Oct-Jan Best time to visit: cooler days, lots of cultural events.

How to Blend In

Even if your skin colouring allows it, it's next to impossible to 'pass' as a native Cairene. But you can look more like a resident expat, thus deflecting hustler attention onto the more obvious tourists walking behind you and leaving you free to enjoy the good things about Cairo. Here's how:

» Carry your stuff in a plastic shopping bag or a generic tote. Nothing screams 'tourist' like a multipocketed, zippered, heavy-duty-nylon backpack with visible water bottle.

» Wear impractical shoes. This is a city. Fashion counts.

» Cover your legs – this goes for men and women. Islamic rules aside, Egyptians have a higher level of modesty, and it's clear you haven't been here long if you don't feel embarrassed to show your knees in public.

» Carry a copy of the *Al-Ahram Weekly* – or the Arabic *Al-Ahram*, if you want to go deep undercover.

» Learn and use the local nonverbal cues (see boxed text, p481).

PLAYING CHICKEN

It may sound silly, but the greatest challenge most travellers face in Cairo is crossing the street. Traffic seldom stops, so you have to trust the cars will avoid you. Our advice: position yourself so that one or more locals forms a buffer between you and oncoming traffic, then cross when they do – they usually don't mind being used as human shields. Never, ever hesitate or turn back once you've stepped off the sidewalk, and cross as if you own the road. But do it fast!

Top Tips

» Early-morning, late-night and Friday-afternoon arrivals/departures at Cairo airport are preferable (to avoid traffic).

» Keep small coins and bills (E£5 and under) for change and tips in an easily accessible pocket. See p514 for suggested tip amounts.

» Strangers who approach you around Midan Talaat Harb, the Egyptian Museum and Khan al-Khalili almost certainly want to sell you something. See p517 for advice on touts.

» Most Cairo residents drink the tap water. If your system can handle it, help yourself to cold water outside mosques to cut down on plastic-bottle use.

BIG MANGO NIGHTS

Check **Cairo Live Events Guide** (cairoliveeventsguide.blogspot.com) to see what's on when you're in town. Great regular gigs: Al-Tannoura Sufi dancers at Wikalat al-Ghouri and folk music at Makan (p111).

Fast Facts

» **Area** 86,369 sq km
» **Population** more than 20 million
» **Area code** ☏02

City Reads

» *Cairo: The City Victorious,* by Max Rodenbeck
» *Cairo's Street Stories,* by Lesley Lababidi
» *Understanding Cairo: The Logic of a City out of Control,* by David Sims
» *Taxi,* by Khalid Al-Khamissy

Resources

» Cairo 360 (www.cairo360.com) City listings and reviews
» Yallabina (www.yallabina.com) Movie and events listings
» Cairobserver (www.cairobserver.com) Smart articles on Cairo's urban fabric
» Egy.com (www.egy.com) 19th- and 20th-century Cairo history

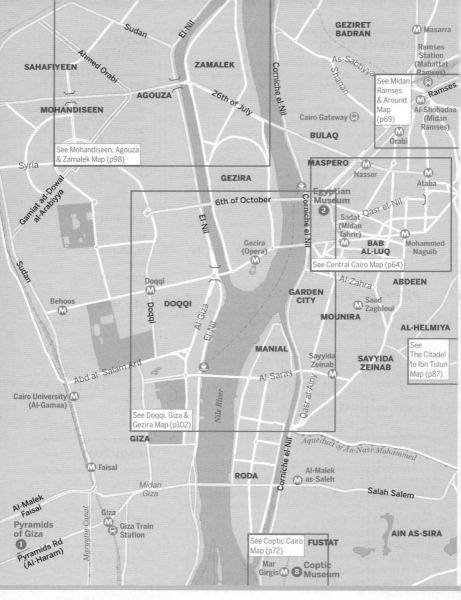

Cairo Highlights

1 Tip your head back and gape at the **Pyramids of Giza** (p125)

2 Give your regards to Tutankhamun and his cohorts in the mazelike **Egyptian Museum** (p136)

3 Stroll the beautifully restored stretch of medieval street known as **Bein al-Qasreen** (p74)

4 Escape the city noise in the greenery of **Al-Azhar Park** (p83)

5 Admire the skills of centuries of weavers,

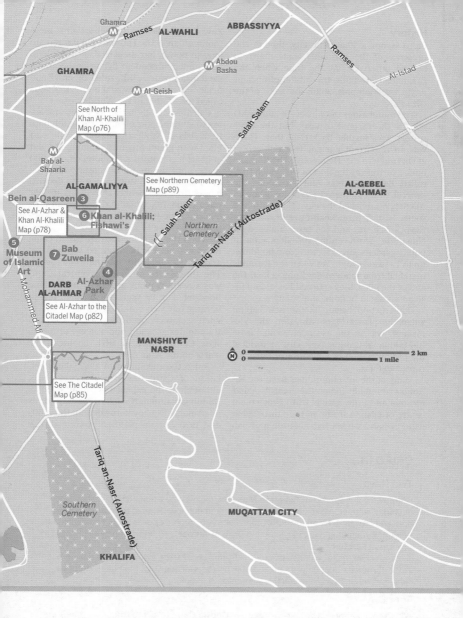

Ghamra
M
Ramses AL-WAHLI ABBASSIYYA

GHAMRA

M Abdou Basha

Ramses Al-Istad

M Al-Geish

Salah Salem

See North of Khan Al-Khalili Map (p76)

M Bab al-Shaaria

AL-GAMALIYYA

See Northern Cemetery Map (p89)

AL-GEBEL AL-AHMAR

Bein al-Qasreen ③

See Al-Azhar & Khan Al-Khalili Map (p78)

⑥ Khan al-Khalili; Fishawi's

Salah Salem

Northern Cemetery

Tariq an-Nasr (Autostrade)

⑤ Museum of Islamic Art

⑦ Bab Zuweila

DARB AL-AHMAR

④ Al-Azhar Park

Mohammed Ali

See Al-Azhar to the Citadel Map (p82)

MANSHIYET NASR

See The Citadel Map (p85)

Ⓝ 0 —————— 2 km
0 —————— 1 mile

Tariq an-Nasr (Autostrade)

Southern Cemetery

MUQATTAM CITY

KHALIFA

calligraphers and more at the **Museum of Islamic Art** (p80)

⑥ Trawl **Khan al-Khalili** (p74) for deals, then recharge at the venerable ahwa (coffeehouse) **Fishawi's** (p109)

⑦ Climb the minarets at **Bab Zuweila** (p80)

⑧ Admire the beautiful syncretic artistic styles at the **Coptic Museum** (p71)

⑨ Ditch the guidebook and just **walk** (see boxed text, p63) – maybe even get a little lost

History

Cairo is not a Pharaonic city, though the presence of the Pyramids leads many to believe otherwise. At the time when the Pyramids were built, the capital of ancient Egypt was Memphis, 20km southeast of the Giza Plateau.

The foundations of Cairo were laid in AD 969 by the Fatimid dynasty, but the city's history goes further back than that. There was an important ancient religious centre at On (modern-day Heliopolis). The Romans built a fortress at the port of On, which they called Babylon, while Amr ibn al-As, the general who conquered Egypt for Islam in AD 642, established the city of Fustat to the south. Fustat's huge wealth was drawn from Egypt's rich soil and the taxes imposed on Nile traffic. Tenth-century travellers wrote of public gardens, street lighting and buildings up to 14 storeys high. Yet when the Fatimids marched from modern-day Tunisia near the end of the 900s, they spurned Fustat and instead set about building a new city.

Construction began on the new capital when the planet Mars (Al-Qahir, 'the Victorious') was in the ascendant; thus arose Al-Madina al-Qahira, 'the city victorious', the pronunciation of which Europeans corrupted to Cairo.

Many of the finest buildings from the Fatimid era remain today: the great Al-Azhar Mosque and university is still Egypt's main centre of Islamic study, and the three great gates of Bab an-Nasr, Bab al-Futuh and Bab Zuweila straddle two of Islamic Cairo's main thoroughfares. The Fatimids did not remain long in power, but their city survived them and, under subsequent dynasties, became a capital of great wealth, ruled by cruel and fickle sultans. This was the city that was called the Mother of the World.

Cairo eventually burst its walls, spreading west to the port of Bulaq and south onto Roda Island, while the desert to the east filled with grand funerary monuments. But at heart it remained a medieval city for 900 years, until the mid-19th century, when Ismail, grandson of Mohammed Ali, decided it was time for change. During his 16-year reign (1863–79), Ismail did more than anyone since the Fatimids to alter the city's appearance.

When the French-educated Ismail came to power, he was determined to build yet another city, one with international cachet. The future site of modern central Cairo was a swampy plain subject to annual Nile flooding. For 10 years the former marsh became one vast building site as Ismail invited architects from Belgium, France and Italy to design and build a new European-style Cairo, which earned the nickname 'Paris on the Nile'.

Since the revolution of 1952, the population of Cairo has grown spectacularly, although at the expense of Ismail's vision. Building maintenance fell by the wayside as apartments were overcrowded. In the 1960s and 1970s, urban planners concreted over

CAIRO IN...

Two Days

Start with the magnificent **Egyptian Museum**, followed by a quick and delicious lunch at **Gad** downtown. Make your way to the restored medieval Islamic **Bein al-Qasreen** area and browse in **Khan al-Khalili**, then compare purchases over tea at **Fishawi's**. Wander through the back alleys around **Darb al-Ahmar**, and finish with dinner of stuffed pigeons at **Farahat**.

On day two make an early start for the **Pyramids of Giza**, followed by a relaxing late lunch at **Andrea**. Just before sunset, stroll through **Garden City**, then take a **felucca ride**. For dinner, head to a stylish restaurant in Zamalek.

Four Days

With a couple more days, take the metro to **Coptic Cairo** to see the museum there, and save some shopping time for the tasteful **Souq al-Fustat** and the hip Egyptian boutiques of Zamalek. Plunge back into the maze of Islamic Cairo with a visit to the **Mosque of Ibn Tulun** and nearby monuments, and try to catch a Sufi dance performance at the **Wikala of al-Ghouri**. Other nightlife musts: the chic weekend scene at **Arabesque**, or the seedier one at downtown bars and nightclubs such as **Shahrazad**. Finally, treat yourself to the green respite of **Al-Azhar Park**.

DIY WALKING CAIRO

Contrary to first impressions, Cairo is an excellent city for walking. The terrain is level, the scenery changes quickly, and you'll never accidentally wander into a 'bad' neighbourhood. We encourage stowing the guidebook and getting a little lost in Cairo's back lanes, and, at least once, accepting a stranger's invitation to tea. These are some of the best places to stroll over the course of a day.

Islamic Cairo in the Morning

Start before 7am with tea at Fishawi's cafe and watch the khan slowly wake up. Take a quick peek at Bein al-Qasreen (p75) to admire the buildings without the crush of commerce, then head south: take the small alley on the south side of Al-Azhar Mosque, heading toward Al-Azhar Park, then turn south, roughly following the old walls built by Saladin, in the Darb al-Ahmar district. Tiny workshops here produce shoes, parquet flooring, mother-of-pearl inlay boxes and more. But it's also a residential district, where families on upper floors run baskets down to the *ba'al* (grocer) for supplies, and knife-sharpeners and junk traders (the men who shout 'Beee-kya!') roll through the lanes. Keeping your bearings with the park to your left, you can wander all the way to the Citadel. To loop back to Sharia al-Azhar, go via Sharia al-Khayamiyya.

Garden City at Twilight

The interlocking circles that form the streets of Garden City (p70) are maddening if you want to get anywhere, but they're perfect for admiring the crumbling mansions in this colonial-era district. The best time to visit is the hour before sundown, when the dust coating the architectural curlicues turns a warm gold and the starlings shrill in the trees.

Start at the north end (get the brutalist concrete Canadian embassy behind you right away!), keeping an eye out for wrought-iron dragons on cobwebbed gates, a rare Turkish-style wood-front home and the last real garden in Garden City, behind the Four Seasons hotel. Nearby at 10 Sharia Tulumbat is Grey Pillars, the British residency during WWII, with a beautiful birdcage elevator inside. You wind up, conveniently, near the Dok Dok felucca landing stage for a sailboat ride.

Downtown after Midnight

A jaunt Downtown (p66) is less walking than cafe-hopping. Here the air is cool and the streets are thronged. Start at Midan Orabi, where you can perch on any random planter and someone will come and sell you tea. From here Sharia Alfy and the smaller streets on either side are your playground for snacking, sheesha-smoking and maybe even some lavish tipping of belly dancers (see p112). For a younger scene, head to the pedestrian streets around the stock exchange. No matter how late you're out, you can wind up the night at the 24-hour Odeon Palace Hotel bar (p108).

---

the sparsely populated west bank of the Nile so they could build desperately needed new suburbs.

In more recent decades, growth has crept beyond Muqattam Hills on the east and the Pyramids on the west. Luxe gated communities, sprawling housing blocks and full satellite cities, complete with malls and megastores, spring up from the desert every year: communities like 6th of October City, New Cairo and others are the new Egyptian dream. Whether the desert and the economy can sustain them remains to be seen.

⊙ Sights

Cairo's sights are spread all over the city, so it makes sense to do things in one area before moving on to the next – but don't try to cram too much into one day, or you'll soon be overwhelmed. The awe-inspiring but cluttered Egyptian Museum requires at least half a day, and ideally two or three shorter visits. Khan al-Khalili and most of the medieval monuments are in Islamic Cairo, and you'll need a full day or several visits at different times of the day. Definitely allow a few hours of aimless wandering in this area (even if it comes at the expense of 'proper'

Central Cairo

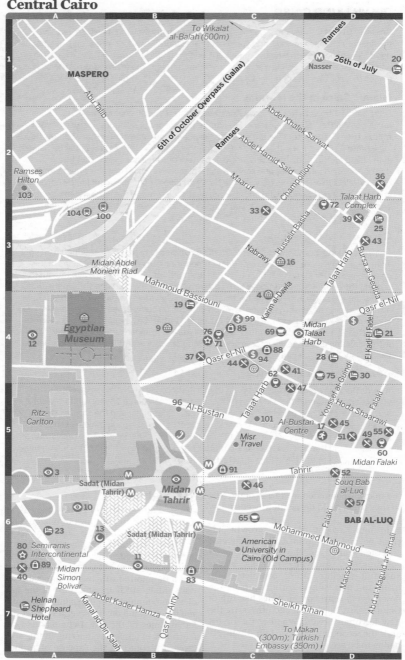

CAIRO

To Wikalat al-Balah (500m)

Ramses

MASPERO

Abu Talib

6th of October Overpass (Galaa)

Ramses

Abdel Khalek Sarwat

M Nasser 26th of July 20

Ramses Hilton 103

Maaruf

Abdel Hamid Said

Champollion

36

104 100

Talaat Harb Complex

33

72

39 25

Nabrawy 16

Hussein Bashi

43

Midan Abdel Moniem Riad

Mahmoud Bassiouni

Karim al-Dawla

Talaat Harb

Bursa al-Gedida

Qasr el-Nil

19

4

9

99 85

76 71

69

Midan Talaat Harb

El Kadi El Fadel

21

12

Egyptian Museum

37 Qasr el-Nil

88

28

Ritz-Carlton

44 94

@

62 41

75 30

47

Talaat Harb

Youssef al-Gundi

Hoda Shaarawi

Falaki

96 Al-Bustan

101

Al-Bustan Centre

17 45

49 55

51 60

Misr Travel

Midan Falaki

3

Sadat (Midan Tahrir)

91

Tahrir

52

10

Midan Tahrir

46

Souq Bab al-Luq 57

13

65

BAB AL-LUQ

23

Sadat (Midan Tahrir)

Mohammed Mahmoud

80 Semiramis Intercontinental

11

American University in Cairo (Old Campus)

@

40 89

Midan Simon Bolivar

83

Mansour

Abd al-Magid ar-Rimali

Helnan Shepheard Hotel

Kamal ad-Din Salah

Abdel Kader Hamza

Qasr al-Ainy

Sheikh Rihan

Falaki

To Makan (300m); Turkish Embassy (350m)

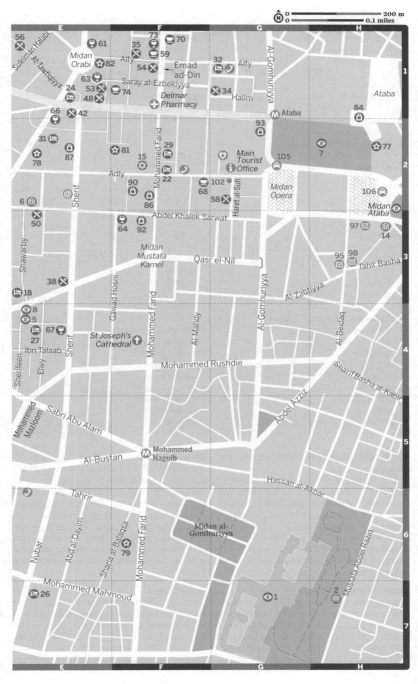

Central Cairo

sightseeing), as the back lanes give the truest sense of the city.

The Pyramids of Giza can be visited in four or five hours, but with the 10km trip to the edge of the city and back, it's inevitably a full-day outing. Coptic Cairo can be toured in a morning – made especially easy by metro access – and you'll likely soak up Downtown's atmosphere just by going to and from your hotel, or by hanging out there in the evenings.

DOWNTOWN CAIRO

Though the Egyptian Museum is found here, the part of town between Midan Ramses and Midan Tahrir, which locals call Wust al-Balad, is better known for its practical offerings: budget hotels, eateries and a dazzling stream of window displays. (Don't rely on that shoe store/lingerie shop/prosthetic-limbs dealer as a landmark – there's another one just a block away.) Occasionally try to look away from the traffic and fluorescent-lit shops and up at the dust-caked but elegant Empire-style office and apartment buildings that drip faded glamour (or is that an air-conditioner leaking?). It's a wonderful part of town to explore – just be prepared for sensory overload and loads of perfume-shop touts.

Midan Tahrir
SQUARE.

The world learned the name Midan Tahrir (Liberation Sq) in early 2011, when millions of Egyptians converged here in a peaceful revolution to oust then-president Hosni Mubarak. On a regular day, it's just your average giant traffic circle, albeit one where half-a-dozen major arteries converge, and one that's still occasionally taken over by demonstrations.

One of the most distinctive orientation aids is the erstwhile Nile Hilton, currently being renovated as the Ritz-Carlton. The modernist slab, with its mod hieroglyphic facade, was built in 1959. Due north is Mubarak's National Democratic Party (NDP) headquarters, torched during the revolution and, at least as of late 2011, still a blackened shell; many activists were advocating that it remain so, as a reminder of the old regime's failures. Just across the road, by contrast, is the neoclassical, lurid pink bulk of the Egyptian Museum (p136), unscathed during the uprising because activists formed a human chain around the place to protect it.

South of the hotel, the **Arab League Building** (Map p64) is the occasional gathering place of leaders from around the Middle East, and now often the site of smaller demonstrations. South across Sharia Tahrir you'll see the ornate white palace of the **Ministry of Foreign Affairs**, and the adjacent **Omar Makram Mosque** (Map p64), where anybody who's anybody has their funeral. The rest of the south side is occupied by the monstrous **Mogamma** (Map p64), home to 18,000 civil servants and notorious nationwide for its infernal bureaucracy. Comedian Adel Imam lampooned the place in his classic 1992 film *Irhab wal-Kabab* (Terrorism and Kabab), in which his frustrated character takes everyone in the building hostage.

The next building around, across the four-lane Qasr al-Ainy, has quite a different reputation: it's the old campus of the elite **American University in Cairo** (AUC; Map p64), the college of choice for the sons and daughters of Egypt's stratospherically wealthy. Most have decamped to a new campus opened in an eastern suburb, but that hasn't stopped average Egyptians from imagining the Western-inspired debauchery that goes on behind the tall fences.

Midan Talaat Harb   SQUARE

Downtown's two main streets, Sharia Talaat Harb and Sharia Qasr el-Nil, intersect at the traffic circle of Midan Talaat Harb, where cars whiz around a statue of tarboosh-sporting Mr Harb, founder of the national bank. On the square is **Groppi's** (p109), in its heyday one of the most celebrated patisseries this side of the Mediterranean and *the* venue for ritzy society functions and concert dances. Gold mosaics around the doorway are, alas, the only remaining glitter.

Just south of the square on Sharia Talaat Harb, **Café Riche** (p104), established in 1908, was once the main hang-out for Egyptian writers and intellectuals. Nasser allegedly met with his collaborators here while planning the 1952 Revolution.

North of the square, shops along Sharia Qasr el-Nil sell the equivalent of a drag queen's dream of footwear. The street itself boasts some particularly fine architecture, notably the **Italian Insurance building** (Map p64), on the corner of Qasr el-Nil and Sharia Sherifeen, and the **Cosmopolitan Hotel** (p96), a short block off Qasr el-Nil. The area around the hotel and the neighbouring **Cairo Stock Exchange** (Map p64) has been pedestrianised and is packed with lively cafes popular with the city's young activists.

Midan Ataba   SQUARE

This traffic-clogged area of park, markets and transit hub is the transition point from European-built Cairo, particularly its theatre and entertainment district, to the medieval Cairo of Saladin (Salah ad-Din), the Mamluks and the Ottomans. You'll likely find yourself here because it's a convenient walk from here to Islamic Cairo.

Ezbekiyya

By night the crowded stalls of the **Ezbekiyya Book Market** (Map p64) are busy with browsers. By day **Ezbekiyya Gardens** (Map p64; admission E£2) are a dusty urban respite. The famous Shepheard's Hotel, the preferred accommodation of the British colonists, was once located opposite – it was destroyed by

Black Saturday rioters in 1952 (see p456). Next to the gardens, Midan Opera marks the site of the old opera house, which burnt down in 1971, and was rebuilt as a towering car park.

Post Office

On the southwest side of Midan Ataba, past the flyovers, the domed **main post office** (Map p64) has a pretty courtyard. A window immediately on your right is where you buy tickets to the neighbouring **Postal Museum** (Map p64; 2nd fl, Midan Ataba; admission E£2; ☺8am-3pm Sun-Fri), a beautifully maintained collection of stamps, uniforms and even tiny scale models of great post offices throughout Egypt.

Shar Hashamaim   SYNAGOGUE

(Map p64; 17 Sharia Adly; 10am-3pm Mon-Thu & Sat, 10am-5pm Fri) One of the few remaining testaments to Cairo's once-thriving Jewish community, this art-nouveau-meets-ancient-Egypt synagogue is now seldom used, and the heavy police presence makes for a rather tense scene. The interior is theoretically open to visitors, but the rigorous security check is often scrapped in favour of full closure.

Abdeen Palace   MUSEUM

(Qasr Abdeen; Map p64; ☑2391 0042; Midan al-Gomhuriyya; adult/student E£10/5; ☺9am-2.45pm Sat-Thu) Worth visiting only if you're in the area, Abdeen Palace is partially open to visitors as a military museum that also displays a tedious assortment of gifts to various Egyptian presidents. Its story is more remarkable. Begun in 1863, the palace was a centrepiece of Khedive Ismail's plan for a modern Cairo, inspired by Paris' then-recent makeover; the khedive even called in mastermind French planner Baron Haussmann as a consultant. He wanted the palace finished for the 1869 opening of the Suez Canal, to impress visiting dignitaries, but its 500 rooms weren't completed until 1874. It was the royal residence until the monarchy was abolished in 1952. Enter the museum at the back (east) side.

MIDAN RAMSES

The northern gateway into central Cairo, Midan Ramses is a byword for bedlam. The city's main north–south access collides with overpasses and arterial roads to swamp the square with an unchoreographed slew of vehicles. Commuters swarming from the train station add to the melee.

Midan Ramses & Around

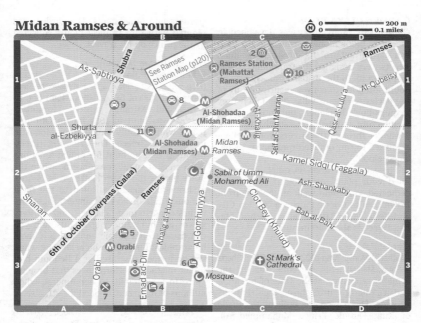

Midan Ramses & Around

◎ Sights
1 Al-Fath Mosque.. B2
2 Egyptian National Railways
   Museum... C1
3 Studio Emad Eddin.................................. B3

🛏 Sleeping
4 African House Hostel.............................. B3
5 Capsis Palace... B3
6 Victoria Hotel.. B3

✖ Eating
7 At-Tabei ad-Dumyati.............................. A3

ℹ Transport
8 Microbuses for Alexandria &
   Delta... B1
9 Microbuses for Suez & Sinai................. B1
10 Trams for Heliopolis.............................. C1
11 Ulali Bus Station.....................................B2

The eponymous Ramses, a multistorey Pharaonic colossus of red granite, stood amid the traffic until 2006, when he was removed, with much complex machinery and road closures, to stand sentry at the yet-to-be-built Grand Egyptian Museum. He now stands swaddled in plastic wrap on the edge of the desert north of the city, perhaps missing his old view over the action.

Ramses Station ARCHITECTURE, MUSEUM
(Mahattat Ramses; Map p69) Cairo's main train station, built in its current style in 1892, is an attractive marriage of Islamic style and industrial-age engineering – or at least it is on the outside. Its interior was redone with gaudy Dubai-mall aesthetics in 2011. At its eastern end it houses the **Egyptian National Railways Museum** (Map p69), which was getting a much-needed overhaul at the time of research. Its collection includes a supremely elegant train car built for Empress Eugénie on the occasion of the opening of the Suez Canal.

Al-Fath Mosque MOSQUE
(Map p69) On the south side of the square is Cairo's pre-eminent orientation aid, **Al-Fath Mosque**. Completed in the early 1990s, the mosque's minaret is visible from just about anywhere in central and Islamic Cairo.

GARDEN CITY & RODA

Garden City (Map p102) was developed in the early 1900s along the lines of an English garden suburb. Its curving, tree-lined streets were designed for tranquillity, while its proximity to the British embassy was no doubt intended to convey security. Many of the enclave's elegant villas have fallen prey to quick-buck developers, but enough grand architecture and lush trees survive to make a wander through the streets worthwhile – at sunset, the air of faded romance is palpable (see p63).

The island of Roda is quiet, its banks lined with plant nurseries. If you're very dedicated, you could walk all the way from Downtown to Coptic Cairo via Garden City and Roda. From Midan Talaat Harb to Manial Palace is about 40 minutes.

Manial Palace   MUSEUM

(Mathaf al-Manial; Map p102; ☎2368 7495; Sharia al-Saray, Manial) This museum was on the brink of reopening at the time of research, and it's one of Cairo's most eccentric tourist sites. The palace was built by the uncle of King Farouk, Prince Mohammed Ali, in the early 20th century. Apparently he couldn't decide which architectural style he preferred, so he went for the lot: Ottoman, Moorish, Persian and European rococo. The palace contains, among other things, Farouk's horde of hunting trophies and the prince's collection of medieval manuscripts,

clothing and other items. The gardens are planted with rare tropical plants collected by the prince on his travels.

Umm Kolthum Museum
& Monastirli Palace   MUSEUM

(Map p72; ☎2363 1467; Sharia al-Malek as-Salih, Roda; adult/student E£2/1; ◷9am-4pm) Set in a peaceful Nileside garden, **Monastirli Palace** was built in 1851 for an Ottoman pasha whose family hailed from Monastir, in northern Greece. The *salamlik* (greeting area) that he built for public functions is an elegant venue for concerts, while the other part is the **Umm Kolthum Museum**, a shrine-like space dedicated to the most famous Arab diva. The singer's signature rhinestone-trimmed glasses and glittery gowns are hung under spotlights, and you can listen to her music and watch a short biographical film, from the beginning when she performed disguised as a Bedouin boy, to her magnetic performances that brought Cairo to a standstill, to her funeral, when millions of mourners flooded the streets.

Nilometer   NOTABLE BUILDING

(Map p72; Sharia al-Malek as-Salih, Roda; admission E£10; ◷9am-4pm) At the very southern tip of Roda, inside the Monastirli Palace compound, the Nilometer was constructed in AD 861, like others built millennia before (see boxed text p271), to measure the rise and fall of the river, and thus predict the fortunes of the annual harvest. If the water rose

DOWNTOWN ARTS

Cairo's art scene is more active and diverse than ever, and much of the action is Downtown. In addition to these arts spaces, the city's cultural centres (p116) often mount interesting shows, and Darb 17 18 (p73) is worth a trip.

Cairo Atelier (Map p64; ☎2574 6730; 2 Sharia Karim al-Dawla; ◷10am-1pm & 5-10pm Sat-Thu) Off Sharia Mahmoud Bassiouni, as much a clubhouse as an exhibition space.

Contemporary Image Collective (Map p64; ☎2396 4272; www.ciccairo.com; 4th fl, 22 Abdel Khalek Sarwat; ◷noon-8pm Tue-Sat) Excellent photo exhibits documenting Egyptian life, plus film and photo workshops.

Mashrabia Gallery (Map p64; ☎2578 4494; www.mashrabia.org; 8 Sharia Champollion; ◷11am-8pm Sat-Thu) A bit cramped but represents the bigger names in painting and sculpture.

Studio Emad Eddin (SEE; Map p69; ☎2576 3850; www.seefoundation.org; 18 Sharia Emad al-Din) Rehearsal and workshop space for performing artists; check the website for events.

Townhouse Gallery (Map p64; ☎2576 8086; www.thetownhousegallery.com; 10 Sharia Nabrawy; ◷10am-2pm & 6-9pm Sat-Wed, 6-9pm Fri) Set amid car-repair shops, Townhouse has launched many international Egyptian artists. Its workshop space, Rawabet, across the street, hosts performances.

to 16 cubits (a cubit is about the length of a forearm) the harvest was likely to be good, inspiring one of the greatest celebrations of the medieval era. Any higher, though, and the flooding could be disastrous, while lower levels presaged hunger. The Turkish-style pencil-point dome is a Farouk-era reconstruction of an earlier one wrecked by Napoleon's troops. The measuring device, a graduated column, sits below the level of the Nile at the bottom of a flight of precipitous steps, which the guard will cheerfully let you descend for a little baksheesh.

COPTIC CAIRO

A maze of ancient and modern churches and monasteries, set within the bounds of a former Roman fortress, Coptic Cairo is a fascinating counterpoint to the rest of the city, and holds a beautiful museum. You can visit the oldest mosque and the oldest synagogue in Cairo, as well as a dynamic arts centre and the quality shopping complex of Souq al-Fustat.

There are three entrances to the Coptic compound: a sunken staircase across from the footbridge over the metro gives access to a section of narrow cobbled alleyways, most churches and the synagogue; the main gate in the centre is for the Coptic Museum; and another doorway further south leads to the Hanging Church. At one time there were more than 20 churches clustered within less than 1 sq km; more survive than are listed here.

Coptic Museum   MUSEUM
(Map p72; ✆2363 9742; Sharia Mar Girgis; adult/student E£50/25, audio guide E£10; ☺9am-4pm) This museum, founded in 1908, houses Coptic art from the earliest days of Christianity in Egypt up through early Islam. It is a beautiful place, as much for the elaborate woodcarving in all the galleries as for the treasures they contain. These include a sculpture that shows obvious continuity from the Ptolemaic period, rich textiles and whole walls of monastery frescoes. Allow at least a couple of hours to explore the 1200 or so pieces on display.

Hanging Church   CHURCH
(Al-Kineesa al-Mu'allaqa; Map p72; Sharia Mar Girgis; ☺Coptic Mass 8-11am Wed & Fri, 9-11am Sun) Just south of the museum on Sharia Mar Girgis (the main road parallel with the metro), a stone facade inscribed with Coptic and Arabic marks the entrance to the 9th-century (some say 7th-) Hanging Church, so named

ℹ COPTIC CAIRO PRACTICALITIES

» Mar Girgis metro station is directly in front of the compound.

» Visitors must have shoulders and knees covered to enter churches or mosques.

» Churches have Mass on Sunday, and some on Friday as well.

» Bring small money for church donation boxes.

» A few basic cafes, with restrooms, are scattered among the churches.

» For cheap street snacks, cross the metro tracks to the west side.

» See boxed text p367 for more details on Coptic art.

» For variety, take the bus back to Tahrir. It goes from the terminal by the Mosque of Amr ibn al-As, so you can be sure of a seat.

because it is suspended over the Water Gate of Roman Babylon. Still in use, it is equally crowded with tourists and parishioners who come to pray over a collection of saints' relics and an icon of Mary. Steep stairs lead to a 19th-century facade topped by twin bell towers. In a small inner courtyard, vendors sell taped liturgies and videos of the Coptic pope, Shenouda III.

With its three barrel-vaulted, wooden-roofed aisles, the interior of the church feels like an upturned ark. Ivory-inlaid screens hiding the altar have intricate geometric designs that are distinguishable from Islamic patterns only by the tiny crosses worked into them. Between the pews, a fine pulpit used only on Palm Sunday stands on 13 slender pillars that represent Christ and his disciples; one of the pillars, darker than the rest, is said to symbolise Judas. In the baptistry, off to the right, a panel has been cut out of the floor to reveal the Water Gate below.

Church of St Sergius & Bacchus   CHURCH
(Abu Serga; Map p72; ☺8am-4pm) This is the oldest church inside the walls, built in the 11th century with 3rd- and 4th-century pillars. It honours two Syrian saints and is built over a cave where Joseph, Mary and the infant Jesus are said to have taken shelter after fleeing to Egypt to escape persecution from

Coptic Cairo

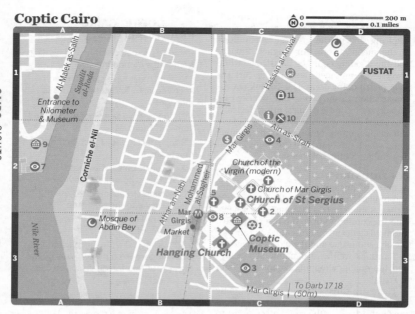

Coptic Cairo

King Herod of Judea, who had embarked upon a 'massacre of the first born'. The cave in question, now a crypt, is reached by descending steps in a chapel to the left of the altar (usually locked). Every year, on 1 June, a special mass is held here to commemorate the event. To get here, walk down the central lane (Haret Al-Kidees Girgis), turning right at the T, then left as it jogs; stairs lead down to the entrance, below street level.

Roman Towers ARCHITECTURE
(Map p72) In AD 98, the Roman emperor Trajan established a fortress here, called Babylon, likely a corruption of Per-hapi-en-on (Estate of the Nile God at On), a Pharaonic name for the area. What remains are two round towers of Babylon's western gate. These were part of riverfront fortifications: at the time, the Nile would have lapped right up against them. Visitors can peer down around the southern tower, where excavations have revealed part of the ancient quay, several metres below street level. The Greek Orthodox Monastery and Church of St George sit on top of the northern tower.

**Greek Orthodox Monastery
& Church of St George** CHURCH
(Map p72; 8am-4pm) The first doorway north of the museum gate leads to the Greek Orthodox Monastery and Church of St George. St George (Mar Girgis) is one of the region's most popular Christian saints. A Palestinian conscript in the Roman army, he was

executed in AD 303 for resisting Emperor Diocletian's decree forbidding the practice of Christianity. There has been a church dedicated to him in Coptic Cairo since the 10th century; this one dates from 1909. The interior has been gutted by fires, but the stained-glass windows and blue-green tile ceiling remain bright. The neighbouring monastery is closed to visitors. The Coptic *moulid* (saints' festival) of Mar Girgis is held here on 23 April. There is a small cafe next to the monastery.

Church of St Barbara
CHURCH
(Map p72) At the corner past Abu Serga, the Church of St Barbara is dedicated to a martyr who was beaten to death by her father for trying to convert him to Christianity. Her supposed relics rest in a small chapel left of the altar, along with a few other saints' remains. Beyond the church an iron gate leads to the large, peaceful (if a bit litter-strewn) Coptic cemetery (Map p72).

FREE Ben Ezra Synagogue
SYNAGOGUE
(Map p72; donations welcome) In the opposite direction from the Church of St Barbara, just outside the walls, the 9th-century synagogue occupies the shell of a 4th-century Christian church. In the 12th century the synagogue was restored by Abraham Ben Ezra, rabbi of Jerusalem. Tradition marks this as the spot where the prophet Jeremiah gathered the Jews in the 6th century after Nebuchadnezzar destroyed the Jerusalem temple. The adjacent spring is supposed to mark the place where the pharaoh's daughter found Moses in the reeds, and where Mary drew water to wash Jesus. In 1890, a cache of more than 250,000 papers, known as the Geniza documents, was uncovered in the synagogue. From them, researchers have been able to piece together details of the life of the North African Jewish community from the 11th to 13th centuries.

Mosque of Amr ibn al-As
MOSQUE
(Map p72; Sharia Sidi Hassan al-Anwar, Old Cairo) The first mosque built in Egypt, this structure was established in AD 642 by the general who conquered Egypt for Islam. On the site where Ibn al-As pitched his tent, the original structure was only palm trunks thatched with leaves. It expanded to its current size in AD 827, and has been continuously reworked since then – most recently, a wood roof was installed to mimic the original style more closely. The oldest section is

to the right of the sanctuary; the rest of the mosque is a forest of some 200 different columns, the majority taken from ancient sites. There's little else to see, but the vast space is a pleasant place to rest. To reach it, head north on Sharia Mar Girgis, beyond the Coptic compound and past Souq al-Fustat, a covered market with quality craft shops and a cafe.

Darb 17 18
ARTS CENTRE
(off Map p72; ☎ 2361 0511; off Sharia Qasr al-Shama; 10am-10pm Sat-Wed, 4-10pm Fri) This cool creative space aims to be a 'trampoline' for contemporary art, which gives you an idea what fun you might find here – there's usually an art show on, and occasional movies or performances at night. Around the corner is El Nafeza, a paper-making workshop that uses traditional techniques (and of course sells the results). To reach Darb, walk south on Sharia Mar Girgis and follow the road as it bears left. At the end of the street, turn left on Sharia Qasr al-Shama, then turn right two streets on – Darb 17 18 is at the end.

ISLAMIC CAIRO
Despite the number of minarets on the skyline in this part of the city, 'Islamic' Cairo is a bit of a misnomer, as this area is not significantly more religious than other districts. But for many centuries it was one of the power centres of the Islamic empire, and its monuments are some of the most resplendent architecture inspired by Islam. Today, traditional *galabeya* (men's full-length robes) still outnumber jeans, buildings and crowds press closer, and the din comes less from car traffic and more from the cries of street vendors and the clang of small workshops. Here the streets are a warren of blind

HAVE YOUR SAY

Found a fantastic restaurant that you're longing to share with the world? Disagree with our recommendations? Or just want to talk about your most recent trip?

Whatever your reason, head to lonelyplanet.com, where you can post a review, ask or answer a question on the Thorntree forum, comment on a blog, or share your photos and tips on Groups. Or you can simply spend time chatting with like-minded travellers. So go on, have your say.

ISLAMIC CAIRO: PLANNING A WALK

The district is quite large and packed with notable buildings, so we've subdivided it into several smaller areas:

Midan al-Hussein & Around (p74) Includes Khan al-Khalili, Bein al-Qasreen and the northern walls and gates.

Al-Azhar to the Citadel (p80) Monuments on the south side of Sharia al-Azhar, such as the Al-Ghouri buildings.

Darb al-Ahmar (p83) Between the street of the same name and Al-Azhar Park.

The Citadel to Ibn Tulun (p84) The hillside Ottoman military compound, plus the mosques of Sultan Hassan and Ibn Tulun.

Northern Cemetery (p88) East of the ring road, including the best Mamluk dome.

Each area is good for a half-day wander, and ideally you'll visit several times, perhaps once on a weekday to feel the throng of commerce and again on a Friday morning, when most shops are shut and it's easier to admire architectural details.

There are many more medieval buildings than we can identify here. For more detail, pick up the guide-maps published by the Society for Preservation of the Architectural Resources of Egypt (SPARE), on sale at the AUC Bookstore (p113).

There are several good approaches. One is to come on foot from Downtown, so you can see the transition from the modern city; from Midan Ataba, bear east on the market street of Sharia al-Muski. (To bypass this and cut straight to the Khan al-Khalili, hail a taxi and ask for 'Al-Hussein' or hop on a microbus at Ataba.) The Bab al-Shaaria metro stop deposits you on the northwest edge of the medieval city – walk due east on Sharia Emir al-Guyush al-Gawani, and you'll reach the northern stretch of Sharia al-Muizz li-Din Allah.

Another strategy is to start at Al-Azhar Park, where you get a good view over the district, then exit through the downhill park gate and head north through Darb al-Ahmar. Finally, for a taste of purely residential Islamic Cairo, see p63 for a possible route.

alleys, and it's easy to lose not just a sense of direction but also a sense of time.

An ambitious restoration program is making over monuments as well as streets and everyday buildings, with fresh paint and turned-wood window screens. Return visitors may be shocked at the changes – some parts of the district now almost resemble Damascus's old city in their tidiness. But the changes have, for the most part, greatly benefited residents. Vast Al-Azhar Park, once an enormous rubbish heap, is hard to argue with as an improvement.

MIDAN AL-HUSSEIN & AROUND

Midan al-Hussein   SQUARE

(Map p78) The square between the two venerated mosques of Al-Azhar and Sayyidna al-Hussein was one of the focal points of Mamluk Cairo and remains an important space at feast times, particularly on Ramadan evenings and during the *moulids* (see boxed text p484) of Hussein and the Prophet Mohammed. The square is a popular meeting place, and the ahwas with outdoor seating at the entrance to the khan are often packed with equal parts locals and tourists.

Mosque of Sayyidna al-Hussein   MOSQUE

(Map p78) One of the most sacred Islamic sites in Egypt, this mosque is the reputed burial place of the head of Hussein, the grandson of the Prophet whose death in Karbala, Iraq, cemented the rift between the Sunni and Shia branches of Islam. Never mind that the Umayyad Mosque in Damascus claims the same Shiite relic, and that both mosques were established by Sunnis – the site is still so holy that non-Muslims are not allowed inside. Most of the building dates from about 1870, except for the beautiful 14th-century stucco panels on the minaret. The modern metal sculptures in front are elegant Teflon canopies that expand to cover worshippers during Friday prayers.

Khan al-Khalili   MARKET

(Map p78) It's easy to dismiss Khan al-Khalili as a tourist trap, what with all the heavy-pressure touts and made-in-China trinkets. But Cairenes have plied their trades here since the khan was built in the 14th century, and parts of the market, such as the gold district, are still the first choice for thousands of locals to do business.

Shopping

Open from early morning to sundown (except Friday morning and Sunday), the agglomeration of shops – many arranged around small courtyards, a sort of medieval 'minimall' – stock everything from soap powder to semiprecious stones, not to mention toy camels and alabaster pyramids. The khan used to be divided into fairly rigid districts, but the only distinct areas are now the gold sellers, the coppersmiths and the spice dealers. Apart from the clumsy 'Hey mister, look for free' touts, the merchants of Khan al-Khalili are some of the greatest smooth-talkers you will ever meet. Almost anything can be bought here and if one merchant doesn't have what you're looking for, he'll happily find somebody who does. For general shopping tips, see p113.

Landmarks

One of the few specific things to see in the khan, the historic ahwa **Fishawi's** (Map p78) is in an alley one block west of Midan al-Hussein. The other landmark, on the southwest side of the khan, is **Midaq Alley** (Zuqaq al-Midaq; Map p78), the setting for one of Naguib Mahfouz' best-known works. The tiny stepped alley may not be populated with the same colourful characters as the novel, but the way of life here is little changed from the author's 1940s depiction. Such is the al-

ley's fame that the street sign is kept in the coffeehouse at the foot of the steps and produced only on payment of baksheesh.

Bein al-Qasreen STREET
(Palace Walk; Map p76; Sharia al-Muizz li-Din Al-lah) The part of Sharia al-Muizz just north of Khan al-Khalili's gold district is known as Bein al-Qasreen, a reminder of the great palace complexes that flanked the street during the Fatimid era. The palaces fell into ruin and were replaced by the works of subsequent rulers. Today three great abutting Mamluk complexes line the west of the street, providing one of Cairo's most impressive assemblies of minarets, domes and striped-stone facades. They're easy to visit, as you don't have to remove your shoes. Admission is free, but tip the caretakers.

Madrassa & Mausoleum of as-Salih Ayyub

(Map p76) In Mamluk times, this complex was essentially the high court, as the theological school it housed produced the most influential judges. It was built earlier, however, in 1247, in the era of the Ayyubids, the ruling dynasty established by Saladin (Salah ad-Din). The adjoining tomb, where Sultan Ayyub resides, was built by his Turkic wife, Shagarat al-Durr (Tree of Pearls), in 1250, well after the sultan's death, which she had concealed to keep the French crusader armies in Damietta from sensing weakness. Shagarat al-Durr managed to defeat the crusaders, then ruled on as sultana and ushered in the Mamluk era, when the Turkic janissaries took power.

VISITING ISLAMIC CAIRO

» Appropriate dress is not just polite but necessary if you want to enter mosques; legs and shoulders must be covered. Wear sturdy shoes that can be easily slipped off.

» Caretakers are usually around from 9am until early evening. Mosques are often closed to visitors during prayer times.

» Bring small change to tip caretakers at mosques – a bit of baksheesh for pointing out details or climbing a minaret is typical. (See boxed text p514 for typical amounts.) But be firm and don't pay more than you wish.

» With the exception of Sultan Hassan and Ar-Rifai, all mosques are free to enter, but some caretakers will claim an admission fee. If you're not sure, ask if there is a ticket ('fee taz-*kar*-a?') and politely refuse payment if there is none.

» In ticketed monuments, some guards will attempt to resell a previous visitor's ticket (cadged by another guard inside, assuring the visitor it's 'normal' to hand it over). If it is not torn out of the book in front of you, it's reused.

» Some caretakers have even claimed guidebooks aren't permitted in mosques, to prevent you from reading these very warnings.

Madrassa & Mausoleum of Qalaun
(Map p76) Completed in 1279 after little more than a year's work, this madrassa is the most

North of Khan al-Khalili

splendid of the three monuments here. The mausoleum, on the right, is a particularly intricate assemblage of inlaid stone and stucco, patterned with stars and floral motifs and lit by stained-glass windows. The complex also includes a *maristan* (hospital), which Qalaun ordered built after he visited one in Damascus, where he was cured of colic. The Moroccan traveller and historian Ibn Battuta, who visited Cairo in 1325, was impressed that Qalaun's hospital contained 'an innumerable quantity of appliances and medicaments'. He also described how the mausoleum was flanked by Quran reciters day and night chanting requiems for the dead within.

Madrassa & Mausoleum of An-Nasir Mohammed
(Map p76) Sultan An-Nasir ('the Victor'), son of Qalaun, was both despotic and exceedingly accomplished. His madrassa was built in 1304 in part with a Gothic doorway An-Nasir plundered from a church in Acre (now Akko, Israel) after he and his army ended Crusader domination there in 1290. Note how the word *Allah* has been inscribed at the point of the arch. The lacy pattern on the carved stucco minaret, a North African style, reveals more foreign influence. Buried in the mausoleum (on the right as you enter but usually locked) is An-Nasir's mother and favourite son; the sultan himself is next door in the mausoleum of his father, Qalaun.

Madrassa & Mausoleum of Barquq
(Map p76) Barquq seized power in 1382, when Egypt was reeling from plague and famine;

North of Khan al-Khalili

LOCAL KNOWLEDGE

MOHAMED ELSHAHED, CAIROBSERVER.COM

Some of urban-planning expert Elshahed's favourite places in Cairo:

Green space Giza Zoo (p93) has a deservedly bad reputation for animal conditions, but it's a gem of 19th-century placemaking, with a wonderful lion's house, a Gustav Eiffel bridge and a Japanese pavilion.

Mosque Al-Hakim Mosque (p79) is one of the oldest in Cairo, but its pure form and all-white wash gives it a modern feel. One of the most calming spaces to relax or even read a book. It feels very secular, because of the mix of people.

Church St Joseph's Cathedral (Map p64) was built in 1909 in a Florentine style, as a little piece of Italy in Cairo for a large Italian congregation. Another peaceful space to sit for a few minutes.

Museum Mahmoud Mukhtar Museum (p91) is a beautiful little 1960s building. The famous sculptor is buried in the basement. While you're here visit the park next door and the opera grounds, built in 1936 by father of modern Egyptian architecture, Mustafa Fahmy.

View Southern tip of Roda Island (p70), where you can get a sweeping view of the Nile and also visit the Nilometer and the Umm Kolthum museum, and peek at the Minasterli Palace.

---

his Sufi school was completed four years later. Enter through the bold black-and-white marble portal into a vaulted passageway. To the right, the inner court has a lavish blue-and-gold ceiling supported by four porphyry Pharaonic columns. Barquq's daughter is buried in the splendid domed tomb chamber; the sultan himself preferred to rest in the Northern Cemetery (see p89), surrounded by Sufi sheikhs.

Sabil-Kuttab of Abdel Rahman Katkhuda

(Map p76) Where the road splits, the Sabil-Kuttab of Abdel Rahman Katkhuda is one of the iconic structures of Islamic Cairo, depicted in scores of paintings and lithographs. Building this fountain-school combo was an atonement for sins, as it provided two things commended by the Prophet: water for the thirsty and enlightenment for the ignorant. This one was built in 1744 by an emir notorious for his debauchery. There's nice ceramic work inside.

Down the little alley to the east, **Qasr Beshtak** (Palace of Amir Beshtak; Map p76) is a rare example of 14th-century domestic architecture, originally five floors high. It has been nicely restored and is open periodically as a concert venue. Inside is a small shop selling classical Arabic music and other items.

Egyptian Textile Museum   MUSEUM
(Map p76; Sharia al-Muizz li-Din Allah; adult/student E£20/10; ◉9am-4.30pm) The collection starts at the beginning, with Pharaonic diapers,

and moves on through beautifully embroidered Coptic tunics and great embroidered *qiswat* (the panels that adorn the Kaaba in Mecca). It's a small museum, but well worth a peek for anyone with an affinity for weaving and fabric.

Sharia al-Muski   MARKET, STREET
(Map p78) Congested and fabulous, the market street known as Sharia al-Muski begins in the khan (where it's formally called Sharia Gawhar al-Qaid) and runs parallel to Sharia al-Azhar to Midan Ataba. It's the 'real life' counterpoint to Khan al-Khalili's touristy maze, lined with carts selling cheap shoes, plastic toys, fireworks, bucket-sized bras and some truly shocking lingerie.

Sharia al-Gamaliyya   STREET
(Map p76) From Midan al-Hussein, walk up the road that leads along the west side of the mosque. Stick to it as it doglegs left. This avenue, Sharia al-Gamaliyya, was the heart of a trading district in medieval Cairo, and a major thoroughfare. Today it looks more like a back alley, with many of the Mamluk-era buildings obscured by webs of restorers' wooden scaffolding. One completed project: the 1408 **Mosque of Gamal ad-Din** (Map p76), cleaned up to reveal a row of shops below, the rent from which contributed to the mosque's upkeep. Street-food adventurers should keep an eye out for *masmats* – specialists in innards who make tasty rice sausage.

Al-Azhar & Khan al-Khalili

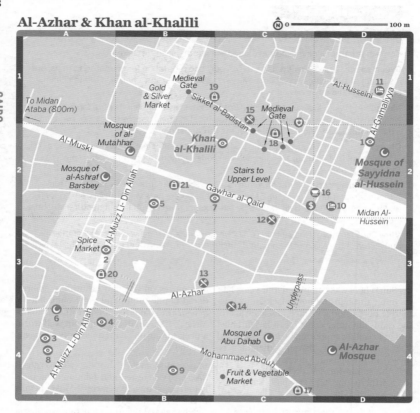

N 0 ▬▬▬▬▬ 100 m

Al-Azhar & Khan al-Khalili

Khanqah & Mausoleum of Sultan Beybars al-Gashankir
MOSQUE, TOMB

(Map p76) Built in 1310, this *khanqah* (Sufi monastery) is one of the city's first. It's distinguished by its stubby minaret, topped with a small ribbed dome. Thanks to a multipart 'baffled' entrance that orients the rooms away from the street, it is serene inside. Mamluk sultan Beybars al-Gashankir is entombed in a room that shimmers with black-and-white marble panelling and light from stained-glass windows. He ruled for only a year, then wound up strangled – his name was excised from the building facade by order of his successor.

Wikala al-Bazara
ARCHITECTURE

(Map p76; Sharia al-Tombakshiyya; adult/student E£20/10; ☉8am-5pm) This is one of about 20 remaining *wikala* (merchants' inn) in the medieval city, down from about 360 in the 17th century, when this one was built. All were built to the same plan: storerooms and stables surrounding a courtyard, with guestrooms for traders on the upper floors. Now the rooms are used as offices – computers and phones look incongruous. Heavy front gates (check out the inlaid-wood door lock – and the anachronistic Lancashire fire badge) protected the merchandise at night. Make the most of your entrance fee by using the restroom, and climbing up to the roof for a good view.

Northern Walls & Gates
GATE

The square-towered **Bab an-Nasr** (Gate of Victory; Map p76) and the rounded **Bab al-Futuh** (Gate of Conquests; Map p76) were built in 1087 as the two main northern entrances to the walled Fatimid city. Despite the gates' dramatic names, they never needed to repel a military attack. That is, until the French arrived, and widened the arrow slits to accommodate cannons for their attack on the feisty Husayniyya neighbourhood to the north. Napoleon's commanders took the liberty of naming Bab an-Nasr's towers after themselves – you can see the carved names if you climb the stairs.

As you walk through Bab an-Nasr and along the imposing outer wall to Bab al-Futuh, look closely at the stones – many were repurposed from Pharaonic sites. And don't miss the delicate carved stone arch at Bab al-Futuh, by Syrian artisans – still some of the finest stonework in the country.

Mosque of Al-Hakim
MOSQUE

(Map p76) Built into the northern walls, this mosque is the work of the sixth Fatimid ruler of Egypt, who took the throne at the age of 11 and whose tutor nicknamed him 'Little Lizard' because of his frightening looks and behaviour. His 24-year reign was marked by violence and behaviour that went far beyond the usual court intrigues; modern historians speculate he may simply have been insane. Those nearest to him lived in constant fear for their lives. He had his nicknaming tutor killed, along with scores of others. A victorious general rushing unannounced into the royal apartments was confronted by a bloodied Hakim standing over a disembowelled page boy. The general was beheaded.

Hakim reputedly often patrolled the streets in disguise, riding a donkey. Most notoriously, he punished dishonest merchants by having them dealt with by a well-endowed black servant. His death was as bizarre as his life. On one of his solitary nocturnal jaunts up onto the Muqattam Hills, Hakim simply disappeared; his body was never found. To one of his followers, a man called Al-Darizy, this was proof of Hakim's divine nature. From this seed Al-Darizy founded the sect of the Druze that continues to this day.

Completed in 1013, the vast Mosque of Al-Hakim is one of Cairo's older mosques but it was rarely used for worship. Instead it functioned as a Crusaders' prison, a stable, a warehouse, a boys' school and, most appropriately considering its notorious founder, a madhouse. An Ismaili Shiite group restored the mosque in the 1980s, but with its open-plan square and spare decoration, it's not nearly as interesting as the man behind it. The real masterpieces are the two stone minarets, the earliest surviving in the city (thanks in part to a post-earthquake restoration in 1304 by Beybars al-Gashankir).

Sharia al-Muizz li-Din Allah
STREET

(Map p78) Sharia al-Muizz, as it's usually called, takes its name from the Fatimid caliph who conquered Cairo in AD 969. It is the former grand thoroughfare of medieval Cairo, once chock-a-block with storytellers, entertainers and food stalls. These days the street has been redone, from new pavement to the tips of the minarets of the monuments along its length. During morning vehicle-free hours, visitors may comfortably gawk at the sites without fear of being flattened by traffic. First-timers will likely be impressed by the streetscape; return visitors may be taken aback at the extent of the changes.

One stretch of the street is occupied by small places selling sheeshas, braziers and pear-shaped cooking pots for fuul (fava beans). Soon the stock expands to crescent-moon minaret tops, coffee ewers and other copper products, hence its more popular name, Sharia an-Nahaseen (Street of the Coppersmiths).

On the right, about 200m south, is the **Mosque of Suleiman Silahdar** (Map p76), which was built comparatively late, in 1839, during the reign of Mohammed Ali. It has a thin, Turkish-inspired minaret and graceful, curvaceous lines along its facade, with a rounded *sabil-kuttab* (public fountain and Quranic school) on the corner.

Beit el-Suhaymi   HOUSE
(Map p76; Darb al-Asfar; adult/student E£30/15; ⊘9am-4.30pm) Just south of Suleiman's *sabil*, the narrow lane Darb al-Asfar runs to the east. With its new paving stones and elaborate *mashrabiyya* (wooden lattice screens), it conjures up the Middle Ages – if the Middle Ages were clean. The first few buildings you pass are part of Beit el-Suhaymi, a family mansion and caravanserai built in the 17th and 18th centuries. After jogging through a narrow hall, you arrive at a peaceful courtyard surrounded by reception halls, storerooms and baths. It has been thoroughly restored, though barely furnished (the fire extinguishers, a precaution required by the extensive new woodwork, are the most prominent item on display). As a result it can feel a bit ghostly.

The changes on Darb al-Asfar have been heavily debated, as they displaced at least 30 families in the name of restoration. One definite benefit has been that the street has been reclaimed for residents. Many of the ground-floor spaces used to be small workshops and factories – noisy and sometimes unsafe for kids. Now those who still live here, at least, can enjoy the privacy of the lane as it was originally built.

Mosque of al-Aqmar   MOSQUE
(Map p76; Sharia al-Muizz li-Din Allah) This petite mosque, the oldest in Egypt with a stone façade, was built in 1125 by one of the last Fatimid caliphs. Several features appear here that became part of the mosque builders' essential vocabulary, including *mu-*

qarnas vaulting (stalactite-like decorative stone) and the ribbing in the hooded arch. If you climb to the roof, you'll have a great view along Bein al-Qasreen.

AL-AZHAR TO THE CITADEL
South of Sharia al-Azhar, Sharia al-Muizz li-Din Allah continues as a market street 400m down to the twin-minareted gate of Bab Zuweila. From there, you can carry on south through Sharia al-Khayamiyya another 40 minutes or so to the main entrance of the Citadel.

Al-Azhar Mosque   MOSQUE
(Gami' al-Azhar; Map p78; Sharia al-Azhar; ⊘24hr) Founded in AD 970 as the centrepiece of the newly created Fatimid city, Al-Azhar is one of Cairo's earlier mosques, and its sheikh is considered the highest theological authority for Egyptian Muslims.

A madrassa was established here in AD 988, growing into a university that is the world's second-oldest educational institution (after the University of al-Kairaouine in Fez, Morocco). At one time the university was one of the world's pre-eminent centres of learning, drawing students from Europe and all over the Islamic empire. The large modern campus (due east) is still the most prestigious place to study Sunni theology.

The building is a harmonious blend of architectural styles, the result of numerous enlargements over a thousand years. The central courtyard is the earliest part, while from south to north the three minarets date from the 14th, 15th and 16th centuries; the latter, with its double finial, was added by Sultan al-Ghouri, whose mosque and mausoleum stand nearby. The tomb chamber, located through a doorway on the left just inside the entrance, has a beautiful mihrab (a niche indicating the direction of Mecca) and should not be missed.

Beit Zeinab al-Khatoun   HOUSE
(House of Zeinab Khatoun; Map p82; ☑2735 7001; Sharia Mohammed Abduh; admission E£15; ⊘9am-5pm) Leaving Al-Azhar Mosque, turn left and then left again into an alley between the southern wall of the mosque and a row of shops housed in the vaults of a 15th-century merchants' building. At the top of this road, on a peaceful little plaza, lies this small but interesting Ottoman-era house with a rooftop affording superb views of the surrounding minaret-studded skyline.

Across the plaza, **Beit al-Harrawi** (Map p82; ☑2510 4174; admission E£15; ⊗9am-5pm) is another fine 18th-century mansion, but its sparse interior isn't worth the entry fee. Both houses are often used as concert venues, and Beit al-Harrawi is home to the Arabic Oud House, a music school; at night it's often open and you can wander in for free.

Mausoleum of Al-Ghouri　　MOSQUE, TOMB
(Map p78; Sharia al-Muizz li-Din Allah; adult/student E£25/15; ⊗9am-5pm) On the south side of Sharia al-Azhar, opposite the khan, two buildings loom over Sharia al-Muizz, together forming an exquisite monument to the end of the Mamluk era. Both were built by Qansuh al-Ghouri, the penultimate Mamluk sultan, who ruled for 16 years. At the age of 78, he rode to Syria at the head of his army to meet the Ottoman Turks at the battle of Marj Dabiq. Betrayed by one of his own emirs, Al-Ghouri was beheaded, and his body was never recovered. The elegant mausoleum, dating from 1505, actually contains the body of Tumanbey, his short-lived successor, hanged by the Turks at Bab Zuweila when they claimed the city in 1517. The building hosts a weekly musical event on Sundays at 9pm: usually Nubian drumming or Sufi chanting (not to be confused with the Sufi dancing at the Wikala of al-Ghouri up the street).

Mosque-Madrassa of Al-Ghouri
(Map p78) Across Sharia al-Muizz to the west, Al-Ghouri's mosque's interior is small but beautifully decorated, with soaring ceilings. It's also possible to climb the red-chequered minaret (for baksheesh; ignore claims of 'tickets').

Wikala of Al-Ghouri　　ARCHITECTURE
(Map p78; adult/student E£20/10; ⊗9am-8pm Sat-Thu) Another of the doomed sultan's legacies lies 100m east of Sharia al-Muizz, halfway to Al-Azhar. Similar to the Wikala al-Bazara, north of Midan al-Hussein, but more sympathetically restored, this *wikala*'s upper rooms are artists' ateliers while the former stables are craft shops. The courtyard serves as a theatre for the free Sufi dance performances by Al-Tannoura Egyptian Heritage Dance Troupe (p111), which is a good time to see the interior, rather than pay the admission fee.

Carpet & Clothes Market　　MARKET
(Map p78) The street between al-Ghouri's mosque and the mausoleum, as well as the alleys just west and south, were historically the city's silk market, and the small passageways are still filled with carpet sellers. While it isn't a particularly great place to buy anything, it's still worth walking through for its atmosphere. Less than 50m south of the mosque on n the west side of Sharia al-Muizz, is Cairo's last **tarboosh (fez) maker** (Map p78), who shapes the red felt hats on heavy brass presses. Once worn by every *effendi* (gentleman), the tarboosh is now mainly bought by hotels and tourist restaurants. They sell for between E£15 and E£60. Continuing south into the district called Al-Ghouriyya, Sharia al-Muizz becomes a busy market for household goods and cheap clothing.

Sabil of Muhammed Ali Pasha　　ARCHITECTURE
(Map p82; Sharia al-Muizz li-Din Allah; admission E£10; ⊗8.30am-5pm) Further down on the left is this delicate 1820 *sabil*, the first in Cairo to have gilded window grilles and calligraphic panels in Ottoman Turkish. It has been meticulously restored, with interesting displays about Muhammed Ali, who had the complex built to honor his son Tusun, who died of plague. Nifty details include access to the cistern below and desks in the *kuttab* (schoolroom) upstairs, which welcomed students until 1992.

Bab Zuweila　　GATE
(Map p82; adult/student E£15/8; ⊗8.30am-5pm) Built at the same time as the northern gates (11th century), beautiful Bab Zuweila is the only remaining southern gate of medieval Al-Qahira. Visitors may climb the ramparts, where some intriguing exhibits about the gate's history are in place. The two minarets atop the gate, also open to visitors, offer one of the best available views of the area. In Mamluk times, the space in front of the gate was the site of executions, a popular form of street theatre, with some victims being sawn in half or crucified. The spirit of a healing saint was (and still is) said to reside behind one towering wooden door, which supplicants have studded with nails and teeth as offerings over the centuries.

Mosque of Al-Mu'ayyad Shaykh　　MOSQUE
(Map p82; Sharia al-Muizz li-Din Allah) Built into the Fatimid walls between 1415 and 1421, the red-and-white-striped **Mosque of Al-Mu'ayyad Shaykh** was laid out on the site of a prison where its patron Mamluk sultan had earlier languished. Its entrance portal,

CAIRO SIGHTS

Al-Azhar to the Citadel

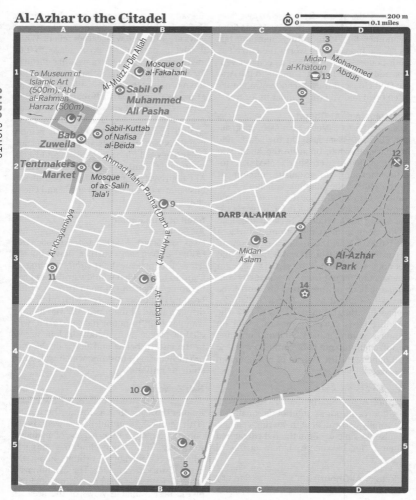

dripping with stalactite vaulting, is particularly grand. The enormous bronze door is thought to have been pilfered from the Mosque of Sultan Hassan.

Museum of Islamic Art   MUSEUM
(off Map p82; ✆2390 1520; Sharia Bur Said; admission E£50; ⊙9am-5pm Sat-Thu, 9am-noon & 2-5pm Fri) Recently renovated, this museum on the edge of the medieval city holds one of the world's finest collections of Islamic applied art. In the interest of not overwhelming the visitor, what's on display is only a sliver of the 80,000 objects the museum owns, and

unfortunately, English signage is somewhat limited. Still, the selected items are stunning, and the best works speak for themselves, so you can easily spend a couple of hours here.

To the right as you enter are architectural details – frescoes, carved plaster so fine it looks like lace, an intricate inlaid-wood ceiling – and ceramics grouped by dynasty. A surprising amount of figurative work is on view, and not all of it strictly Islamic – a shard of an Ayyubid bowl shows Mary holding a crucified Christ. To the left, pieces are grouped by function and medium: medical

Al-Azhar to the Citadel

tools, astrolabes, some breathtaking carpets, illuminated Qurans, even headstones.

The museum is 500m due west from Bab Zuweila. Coming from Midan Ataba, the museum is 700m southeast, straight down Sharia al-Qala'a; the entrance is on the back side of the building, around the corner. Midan Tahrir is 1.6km west along Sharia Sami al-Barudi (passing the Mohammed Naguib metro station en route).

Tentmakers Market   MARKET

(Sharia al-Khayamiyya; Map p82) The 'Street of the Tentmakers' is one of the remaining medieval speciality quarters – it takes its name from the artisans who produce the bright fabrics used for the ceremonial tents at wakes, weddings and feasts. They also make appliqué wall hangings and bedspreads, and print original patterns for tablecloths. The highest concentration of artisans is directly after Bab Zuweila, in the covered tentmakers market. About 800m south, Sharia al-Khayamiyya intersects Sharia Mohammed Ali; a left turn here will take you directly to the Mosque-Madrassa of Sultan Hassan and to the Citadel.

DARB AL-AHMAR

In its heyday in the 14th and 15th centuries, Darb al-Ahmar ('Red Rd') and neighbouring alleys and cul-de-sacs had a population of about 250,000, and the district is still nearly as dense. It is also dense with historic monuments, most from the late Mamluk era, as the city expanded outside the Fatimid gates. As part of the Al-Azhar Park project, this neighbourhood has in parts been beautifully restored, along with various social programs to boost income in this long-poor area. It's a fascinating jumble and rewarding for an aimless wander. The historic street itself is now known as Ahmad Mahir Pasha on the north end and At-Tabana in its southern stretch.

Al-Azhar Park   PARK

(Map p82; ☏2510 7338; www.alazharpark.com; Sharia Salah Salem; admission Mon-Wed/Thu-Sun E£5/7; ⊙10am-10pm) Cairo's eastern horizon changed substantially when this green space opened in 2005. With funds from the Aga Khan Trust for Culture, what had been a mountain of garbage, amassed over centuries, was transformed into the city's first (and only) park of significant size. A profusion of gardens, emerald grass, even a lake (part of a larger public water-supply system) cover the grounds, while ambient Arabic music drifts softly from speakers and fountains bubble in front of sleek modern Islamic architecture. It's most fun on weekends, when families make a day out with picnics.

Bab al-Mahruq

(Map p82) Depending on your outlook, the park is a gorgeous respite or a weirdly isolated elite playground. This was offset slightly when the Bab al-Mahruq entrance, through a medieval gate in the old Ayyubid walls, finally opened in 2009. This granted easier access for residents of the lower-income Darb al-Ahmar district. You can enter here before 6pm, but after dark you can only exit through the main park gates on Sharia Salah Salem (taxis wait but overcharge; microbuses go to Ataba for E£2).

Technically entry at Bab al-Mahruq is only E£2, but you'll have a hard time convincing the guard you deserve the subsidised 'downhill' price. While you're down here, check out the ongoing excavations of the Ayyubid walls – one major achievement was the rediscovery of Bab al-Barqiya, which had long ago been lost under the trash heap.

Restaurants

In addition to a couple of small cafes and the open-air theatre El Genaina, there's an excellent restaurant here, Citadel View (p105), capitalising on the park's views across the medieval city and beyond. For a less substantial investment, **Alain Le Notre** (dishes E£40-50) serves salads, wraps and ice cream, and the **Lakeside Restaurant** (dishes E£18-32), on the other side of the park, serves more modest food like fuul (fava bean) and Lebanese *manaeesh* (flat bread).

Mosque of Aslam al-Silahdar   MOSQUE
(Map p82; Midan Aslam) As the closest monument to the Bab al-Mahruq entrance to Al-Azhar Park, this mosque makes a good landmark for finding your way there. The 14th-century structure is distinguished by beautiful stone-inlay floors, intricate carved-stucco medallions in the walls and a beautiful tiled dome. Across the square is a gallery selling neighbourhood handicrafts. Coming from Bab Zuweila, to find the mosque (and Bab al-Mahruq) walk east behind the Mosque of Qijmas al-Ishaqi.

Mosque of Qijmas al-Ishaqi   MOSQUE
(Map p82; Sharia Ahmad Mahir Pasha) One of the best examples from this period is this 1481 mosque, at the north end of the street on the east side. Don't be deceived by the plain exterior: inside are beautiful stained-glass windows, inlaid marble floors and stucco walls.

Mosque of Al-Maridani   MOSQUE
(Map p82; Sharia Ahmad Mahir Pasha) About 150m further on the right of the Mosque of Qijmas al-Ishaqi, this 1339 building incorporates architectural elements from several different periods: eight granite columns were taken from a Pharaonic monument; the arches contain Roman, Christian and Islamic designs; and the Ottomans added a fountain and wooden housing. Trees in the courtyard, attractive *mashrabiyya* and a lack of visitors make this a peaceful place to stop.

Mosque-Madrassa of Umm Sultan Sha'aban   MOSQUE
(Map p82; Sharia At-Tabana) With its towering red-and-white-striped façade and entrance trimmed with an atypical triangular arrangement of muqarnas vaulting, this complex is more interesting on the outside than in. But it is worth entering briefly, through a long hallway, to see how the interior of the building is oriented away from the street, to align properly with Mecca. It was built in 1369 by Khawand Baraka, the mother of the reigning Mamluk, to commemorate her completion of the hajj.

Blue Mosque   MOSQUE
(Mosque of Aqsunqur; Map p82; Sharia At-Tabana) Built in 1347, this building is highly touted by would-be guides, but it's nothing like its Istanbul namesake. It's classic Mamluk architecture throughout, except for one wall of flowery blue Ottoman tiles, looking a bit out of place, as they were installed 300 years later. The minaret affords an excellent view of the Citadel, though, as well as the remains of Saladin's city walls, to the east behind the mosque.

Khayrbek Complex   MOSQUE, TOMB
(Map p82; Sharia At-Tabana) Emir Khayrbek was governor of Aleppo under Sultan al-Ghouri, but defected to the Ottoman side in the 1516 battle of Marj Dabiq, which effectively ended Mamluk rule. Khayrbek returned to Cairo in the company of the new Ottoman ruler, Selim I, and took over the governorship of Egypt. Khayrbek's mausoleum (which he savvily had built years before his treachery) and a mosque are the anchors of this clutch of buildings, but what's interesting is how other structures – the 13th-century Alin Aq Palace, plus several later Ottoman houses – are all interconnected. The mosque's brick minaret sits on a Pharaonic stone block.

THE CITADEL TO IBN TULUN

South of Darb al-Ahmar, the late-Ottoman-era Citadel complex watches over the city and draws tourists in droves. At its base, on Midan Salah ad-Din and along Sharia al-Salbiyya, is another especially historic quarter, including two of Cairo's largest mosques, plus several other smaller monuments. Though overall, in contrast with historic quarters further north, this area has yet to see much revitalisation.

The Citadel   FORTRESS
(Al-Qala'a; Map p85; ☑2512 1735; Sharia Salah Salem; adult/student E£50/25; ☉8am-4pm, mosques closed during Fri prayers) Sprawling over a limestone spur on the eastern edge of the city, the Citadel was home to Egypt's rulers for 700 years. Their legacy is a collection of three very different mosques, several palaces (housing some underwhelming museums; admission fee included) and a couple of terraces with views over the city. This is

The Citadel

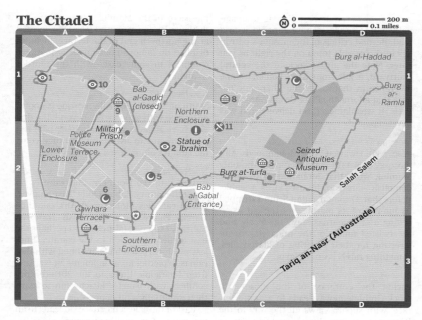

The Citadel

one of the most popular tourist attractions in Cairo, though the slight hassle of getting here detracts a bit from its appeal.

Saladin began building the Citadel in 1176 to fortify the city against the Crusaders, who were then rampaging through Palestine. Following their overthrow of Saladin's Ayyubid dynasty, the Mamluks enlarged the complex, adding sumptuous palaces and harems. Under the Ottomans (1517–1798) the fortress expanded westwards and a new main gate,

the Bab al-Azab, was added, while the Mamluk palaces deteriorated. Even so, when Napoleon's French expedition took control in 1798, the emperor's savants regarded these buildings as some of the finest Islamic monuments in Cairo.

This didn't stop Mohammed Ali – who rose to power after the French – from drastically remodelling, and crowning the complex with the Turkish-style mosque that dominates Cairo's eastern skyline. After Mohammed Ali's grandson Ismail moved his residence to the Abdeen Palace (p68), the Citadel became a military garrison. The British army was barracked here during WWII, and Egyptian soldiers still have a small foothold, although most of the Citadel has been given over to tourists.

Mosque of Mohammed Ali

(Map p85) Modelled on classic Turkish lines, with domes upon domes upon domes, the mosque took 18 years to build (1830-48) and its interior is all twinkling chandeliers and luridly striped stone, the main dome a rich emerald green. Perhaps the most evocative description of it is in Olivia Manning's *The Levant Trilogy*: 'Above them Mohammed Ali's alabaster mosque, uniquely white in this sand-coloured city, sat with minarets pricked, like a fat, white, watchful cat'. Other writers, however, have called it unimaginative and graceless and compared it to a toad. Beyond criticism, the mosque's patron lies in the marble tomb on the right as you enter. Note the glitzy clock in the central courtyard, a gift from King Louis-Philippe of France in thanks for the Pharaonic obelisk that adorns the Place de la Concorde in Paris. It was damaged on delivery and was never repaired.

Mosque of An-Nasir Mohammed

(Map p85) Dwarfed by Mohammed Ali's mosque, this 1318 constructure is the only Mamluk work that Mohammed Ali didn't demolish – instead, he used it as a stable. Before that, Ottoman sultan Selim I stripped its interior of its marble, but the old wood ceiling and muqarnas show up nicely, and the twisted finials of the minarets are interesting for their covering of glazed tiles, something rarely seen in Egypt.

Police Museum Terrace

Facing the entrance of the mosque, a mock-Gothic gateway leads to a grand terrace, with superb views all the way to the Pyramids at Giza. Immediately below, in the Citadel's Lower Enclosure (closed to the public), the steep-sided roadway leading to Bab al-Azab was the site of the infamous

massacre of the Mamluks (see p451). The flyblown **Police Museum** (Map p85), located at the northern end of the terrace, includes displays on famous political assassinations, complete in some cases with the murder weapon.

Gawhara Terrace

South of Mohammed Ali's mosque is another terrace with good views. Beyond, the dull **Gawhara Palace & Museum** (Map p85) is a lame attempt to evoke 19th-century court life, and it's often closed anyway.

Northern Enclosure

Entrance to the Northern Enclosure is via the 16th-century Bab al-Qulla. Past an overpriced cafe lies Mohammed Ali's one-time Harem Palace, now the lavish **National Military Museum** (Map p85) and perhaps the best-tended exhibition in the country. Endless plush-carpeted halls are lined with dioramas depicting great moments in warfare, from Pharaonic times to the 20th-century conflicts with Israel – kitschy fun to start, then eventually a bit depressing.

East of the cafe, a narrow road leads to an area with a few smaller museums, along the humble lines of the dull **Carriage Museum** (Map p85), which displays various royal carriages. Devotees of Islamic architecture might appreciate the 1528 **Mosque of Suleiman Pasha** (Map p85), a far more tasteful example of the Ottoman-style domed mosque.

Mosque-Madrassa of Sultan Hassan

MOSQUE

(Map p87; Midan Salah ad-Din; admission E£25; ⊙8am-5pm) Massive yet elegant, this great structure is regarded as the finest piece of early-Mamluk architecture in Cairo. It was built between 1356 and 1363 by the troubled Sultan Hassan, a grandson of Sultan Qalaun; he took the throne at the age of 13, was deposed and reinstated no less than three times, then assassinated shortly before the mosque was completed. Tragedy also shadowed the construction when one of the minarets collapsed, killing some 300 onlookers. Beyond the striking, recessed entrance, a dark passage leads into a square courtyard whose soaring walls are punctured by four *iwans* (vaulted halls), one dedicated to teaching each of the four main schools of Sunni Islam. At the rear of the eastern *iwan,* an especially beautiful mihrab is flanked by stolen Crusader columns. To the right, a bronze door leads to the sultan's mausoleum.

ℹ️ TO AND FROM THE CITADEL

Walking from Midan Ataba is feasible, but long: to the Citadel's entrance gate, it's almost 4km through the furniture and musical-instruments districts along Sharia al-Qala'a and its continuation, Sharia Mohammed Ali. At Midan Salah ad-Din, walk along Sharia Sayyida Aisha to Sharia Salah Salem, where you turn left to reach the main gate. Alternatively, minibus 150 (E£1) runs from Midan Ataba to Midan Salah ad-Din, still a 15-minute walk from the entrance; a second microbus can take you from Salah ad-Din to Sayyida Aisha at Salah Salem. Taking a taxi is only marginally quicker due to the complicated traffic-flow on Salah Salem.

Leaving the Citadel, if you want to take a taxi, walk downhill and away from the main entrance to hail a cab, where you're less likely to encounter a driver who refuses to use his meter.

The Citadel to Ibn Tulun

Opposite the grand mosque, the **Mosque of Ar-Rifai** (Map p87; admission E£25) is constructed on a similarly grand scale, begun in 1869 and not finished until 1912. Members of modern Egypt's royal family, including Khedive Ismail and King Farouk, are buried inside, as is the last shah of Iran. Their tombs lie to the left of the entrance.

FREE **Amir Taz Palace** HOUSE
(Map p87; 17 Sharia Suyufiyya; admission free; ☺8am-4pm) Walking west along busy Sharia al-Saliba eventually leads to the Mosque of Ibn Tulun. A short detour north on Sharia Suyufiyya brings you to this restored home of one of Sultan al-Nasir Muhammad's closest advisers, who later controlled the throne through Sultan Hassan. Now used as a cultural centre, the home is not as extensive as Beit el-Suhaymi, but admission is free, and it's less cluttered than the Gayer-Anderson Museum, so you can see the structure of the place. There are a couple of small exhibits, a beautiful wood ceiling in the loggia, as well as clean bathrooms.

FREE **Museo Mevlevi** RELIGIOUS
(Sama'khana; Map p87; Sharia Suyufiyya; ☺8am-4pm) A little further down the street from the Amir Taz Palace, behind a green door with an Italian Institute sign, this museum is essentially a meticulously restored Ottoman-era theatre for whirling dervishes. Hidden behind stone facades, the beautiful wood structure feels like a little jewel box. Downstairs, see the remains of the madrassa that forms the building's foundation; the

The Citadel to Ibn Tulun

thorough notes are a rare model of thoughtful excavation.

Mosque of Ibn Tulun MOSQUE
(Map p87; Sharia al-Saliba; ☺8am-4pm) The city's oldest intact, functioning Islamic monument is easily identified by its high walls topped with neat crenulations that resemble a string of paper dolls. It was built between AD 876 and 879 by Ibn Tulun, who was sent to rule the outpost of Al-Fustat in the 9th century by the Abbasid caliph of Baghdad. It's also one of the most beautiful mosques in Cairo, despite a rather ham-fisted restoration using cement on the mud-brick-and-timber structure. Ibn Tulun drew inspiration from his homeland, particularly the ancient Mosque of Samarra (Iraq), on which the spiral minaret is modelled. He also added some innovations of his own: according to architectural historians, this is the first structure to use the pointed arch, a good 200 years before the European Gothic arch. The mosque

covers 2.5 hectares, large enough for the whole community of Al-Fustat to assemble for Friday prayers.

The mosque's geometric simplicity is best appreciated from the top of the minaret, which also has magnificent views of the Citadel. Reach the tower from the outer, moat-like courtyard, originally created to keep the secular city at a distance, but at one time filled with shops and stalls.

Gayer-Anderson Museum MUSEUM

(Beit al-Kritliyya, the House of the Cretan Woman; Map p87; Sharia ibn Tulun; adult/student E£35/20, video E£20; ⏱9am-4pm) Through a gateway to the south of the main entrance of the Mosque of Ibn Tulun, this quirky museum gets its current name from John Gayer-Anderson, the British major and army doctor who restored the two adjoining 16th-century houses between 1935 and 1942, filling them with antiquities, artworks and knick-knacks acquired on his travels in the region. On his death in 1945, Gayer-Anderson bequeathed the lot to Egypt. The puzzle of rooms is decorated in a variety of styles: the Persian Room has exquisite tiling, the Damascus Room has lacquer and gold, and the Queen Anne Room displays ornate furniture and a silver tea set. The enchanting *mashrabiyya* gallery looks down onto a magnificent *qa'a* (reception hall) which has a marble fountain, decorated ceiling beams and carpet-covered alcoves. The rooftop terrace has been lovingly restored, with more complex *mashrabiyya*. You may find the interior familiar – the museum was used as a location in the James Bond film *The Spy Who Loved Me*. Across

the street, Khan Misr Touloun (see p114) is a good handicrafts emporium.

From here, it's rewarding to keep walking another 750m west to the popular quarter of Sayyida Zeinab, where there's a metro station.

NORTHERN CEMETERY

The Northern Cemetery is half of a vast necropolis called Al-Qarafa or, more common among tourists, the City of the Dead. The titillating name conjures a vision of morbid slums, of tomb structures bursting with living families. But the area is more 'town' than 'shanty', complete with power lines, a post office and multistorey buildings. Thanks to a near complete absence of cars, it's also a fairly peaceful part of the city, with a friendly neighbourhood feel and some flawless Mamluk monuments.

The easiest way to the Northern Cemetery is walking east from Midan al-Hussein along Sharia al-Azhar. At Sharia Salah Salem, cross via the overpass. In addition to the three main monuments we list here, several others have been well restored, but are not reliably open.

Mosque of Qaitbey MOSQUE

(Map p89) Sultan Qaitbey, a prolific builder, was the last Mamluk leader with any real power in Egypt. He ruled for 28 years and, though he was as ruthless as any Mamluk sultan, he was also something of an aesthete. It was in the construction of some 80 buildings in his name that the Mamluk style was truly refined. His mosque, completed in 1474 as part of a much larger complex,

---

THE CITY OF THE DEAD

Some estimates put the number of living Cairenes in the Northern and Southern Cemeteries at half a million; others, perhaps more realistic, guess only 50,000. As Max Rodenbeck notes in *Cairo: The City Victorious,* some of the tomb dwellers, especially the paid guardians and their families, have lived here for generations. Others have moved in more recently – there was a spike in 1992, following the earthquake that flattened cheaply built high-rises, and others may have opted for a more central Qarafa home over forced relocation to a bleak low-income suburb. On Fridays and public holidays visitors flock here to picnic and pay their respects to the dead – a lively time to visit.

The cemetery first appealed to Mamluk sultans and emirs because it afforded ample building space. The vast mausoleums they built were more than just tombs; they were also meant as places for entertaining – a continuation of the Pharaonic tradition of picnicking among the graves. Even the humblest family tombs included a room for overnight visitors. The dead hoped they would be remembered; the city's homeless thanked them for free accommodation. This coexistence of the living and the dead was happening as far back as the 14th century, though these days in some tomb-houses, cenotaphs serve as tables and washing is strung between headstones.

Northern Cemetery

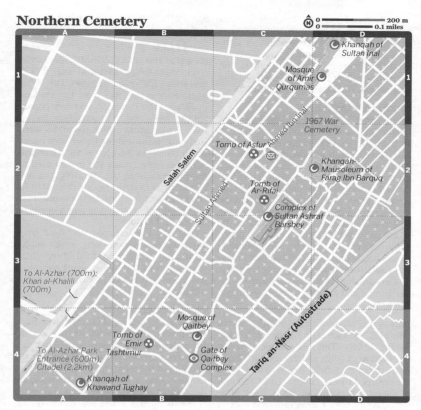

is widely agreed to mark the pinnacle of Islamic building in Cairo.

Behind the boldly striped facade, the interior has four *iwans* around a central court lit by large, lattice-screened windows. Panelled in cool marble with a mesmerising decorative wood ceiling, it's one of the most pleasant places in Cairo to sit and relax. The adjacent tomb chamber contains the cenotaphs of Qaitbey and his two sisters.

The true glory, however, is above, where the exterior of the dome is carved with interlaced star and floral designs; its intricacy and delicacy were never surpassed in Cairo or anywhere else in the Islamic world – climb the minaret for the best view.

Khanqah-Mausoleum of Farag Ibn Barquq
RELIGIOUS

(Map p89) Built by a son of Sultan Barquq, whose great madrassa and mausoleum stand on Bein al-Qasreen, this tomb complex was completed in 1411 because Farag's father had wished to be buried near some particular illustrious Sufi sheikhs. The *khanqah,* a sort of monastery for a Sufi order, is a fortress-like building with high, sheer facades and twin minarets and domes, the largest stone domes in Cairo. In the courtyard, monastic cells lead off the arcades. Inside the two domed tomb chambers (one for women, one for men), the ceilings are painted in mesmerising red-and-black geometric patterns.

Complex of Sultan Ashraf Barsbey
RELIGIOUS, TOMB

(Map p89) Enclosed by a stone wall midway between Barquq's tomb and the Mosque of Qaitbey, this is the third significant building in the cemetery, but beyond the mosque-madrassa, the rest of the compound, which included student housing and a smaller Sufi school, is crumbling. Barsbey, who ruled from 1422 to 1438, is buried here; he also built a mosque on Sharia al-Muizz, at the corner of Sharia al-Muski. The dome under which he rests is carved with a beautiful star pattern, somewhere between older chevron patterns and the sinuous elegance of Qaitbey's dome. Inside is some fine marble flooring and an ivory-inlay minbar (pulpit). The guard will let you in for baksheesh (ask the ever-present children if he's not around).

GEZIRA & ZAMALEK

Uninhabited until the mid-19th century, Gezira (Arabic for 'island') was a narrow strip of alluvial land rising up out of the Nile. After he built modern-day Downtown, Khedive Ismail dedicated his energy to a great palace on the island, with the rest of the land as a royal garden. During the development boom of the early 20th century, the palace grounds were sold off, while the palace was made into a hotel. Much of the island is occupied by sports clubs and parks, while the northern third is stylish Zamalek, a leafy neighbourhood of old embassy mansions and 1920s apartment blocks. It has few tourist sites, but it's a pleasant place to wander around and an even better place to eat, drink and shop.

Museum of Modern Egyptian Art   MUSEUM
(Map p102; admission E£10; ☉10am-2pm & 5-9pm Tue-Thu, Sat & Sun) This vast – perhaps too vast – collection of 20th- and 21st-century Egyptian art can be difficult to appreciate, given the cramped rooms, collected dust and lack of signage. Nonetheless, it's a good place for a respite from Cairo's din, as it's set in the green, well-groomed Gezira Exhibition Grounds (Map p102), across from the Cairo Opera House.

The museum's prizes are all on the ground floor: Mahmoud Mukhtar's deco-elegant bronze *Bride of the Nile* is here, along with Mahmoud Said's painting *Al Madina* (The City, 1937). Though Said has a slew of kitschy imitators, he was one of the first artists to depict folk life in vivid colour, and he inspired Naguib Mahfouz to pursue his own career in writing. Throughout the museum are examples of how Western trends such as pop art have manifested themselves in Egypt – almost always with a much sharper social or political message.

Other Arts Venues
Elsewhere in the exhibition grounds, the Hanager Arts Centre (Map p102; ☎2735 6861; admission free; ☉10am-9pm Tue-Sun) and the Palace of Arts (Map p102; ☎2737 0603, 736 7627; admission free; ☉10am-1.30pm & 5.30-

9pm Sat-Thu) host rotating exhibits and performances.

Cairo Tower   VIEWPOINT
(Burg Misr; Map p102; ☎2736 5112; www.cairotower.net; Sharia el-Borg; adult/child under 6 E£70/free, video E£20; ☉8am-midnight) This 187m-high tower is the city's most famous landmark after the Pyramids, and very popular with Cairenes and Arab sightseers. Built in 1961, the structure, which resembles a stylized lotus plant with its latticework casing, was a thumb to the nose at the Americans, who had given Nasser the money used for its construction to buy US arms. The 360-degree views from the top are clearest in the late morning, after the haze burns off, or late afternoon. You might encounter a queue for the elevator at dusk.

The Sky Garden cafe, one floor down from the observation deck, serves not-too exorbitant drinks and food (beer E£20, sandwiches E£45). The revolving restaurant just below that is a bit pricier, with a E£150 minimum.

Cairo Marriott   PALACE
(Map p98; Sharia Saray al-Gezira) Never mind that this is a luxury hotel: its core is a lavish palace built by Khedive Ismail to house Empress Éugenie when she visited for the opening of the Suez Canal in 1869. A stroll through gives a sense of its original grandeur. Head straight through and down the stairs to further grand old sitting rooms, then out into the garden and right to the next entrance to find the fantastic former ballroom, with triple-height ceilings and an enormous staircase for making a dramatic entrance.

Museum of Islamic Ceramics   MUSEUM
(Map p98; ☎2737 3298; 1 Sharia Sheikh al-Marsafy, Zamalek; adult/student E£25/15; ☉10am-1.30pm & 5.30-9pm Sat-Thu) This beautiful small museum was closed for renovation at the time of research (admission and hours are approximate). But when it reopens, it's worth a peek for its collection of colourful plates, tiles and even 11th-century hand grenades. Equally appealing is the gorgeous 1924 villa it's housed in.

What is still open: the garden and back of the building, which are given over to the Gezira Art Centre (Map p98), with several galleries hosting rotating contemporary exhibitions.

Andalus Garden GARDENS
(Hadeeqat al-Andalus; Map p102; Sharia Saray al-Gezira; admission E£2; ☺7am-10pm) One of several formal gardens in the area that are popular strolling spots for couples in the evening. This one's small, but adjacent to the Nile, and also nice during the day as it has plenty of shade from palm trees and vine-covered pergolas. Across Midan Saad Zaghloul, on the southwest side, is the entrance to the grandly named Garden of Freedom and Friendship (Map p102; admission E£2; ☺7am-10pm), much larger but without the river views.

Mahmoud Mukhtar Museum MUSEUM
(Map p102; ☎2735 2519; Sharia Tahrir; admission E£5; ☺10am-1.30pm & 5-10pm Tue-Sun) This museum was closed for renovation at the time of research, but if it has reopened, it is certainly worth a visit (hours and admission price approximate). Mukhtar (1891–1934) was the sculptor laureate of independent Egypt, responsible for Saad Zaghloul on the nearby roundabout and the *Egypt Reawakening* monument outside the Giza Zoo. Collected in this elegant, little-visited museum, his work ranges from tiny caricatures (look for *Ibn al-Balad,* a spunky city kid) to life-size portraits. Mukhtar's tomb sits in the basement. Egyptian architect Ramses Wissa Wassef (1911–74) designed the building – originally open, to capture natural light, but this was changed presumably to keep the cleaning budget down.

MOHANDISEEN, AGOUZA & DOQQI
A map of Cairo in Baedecker's 1929 guide to Egypt shows nothing on the Nile's west bank other than a hospital and the road to the Pyramids. The hospital is still there, set back from the corniche, but it's now hemmed in on all sides by midrise buildings. This is the sprawl of Giza governorate – in administrative terms, not even part of Cairo at all – and it reaches all the way out to the foot of the Pyramids (they're not isolated in the desert, as you might have imagined). In the 1960s and 1970s, the neighbourhoods of Mohandiseen, Agouza and Doqqi, the closest areas to the Nile, were created to house Egypt's emerging professional classes. They remain middle-class bastions, home to families who made good under Sadat's open-door policy – though some pockets of Mohandiseen are Cairo's ritziest.

Unless you happen to find concrete and traffic stimulating, the main reason to come here are some good restaurants, a few embassies and upscale shopping on Sharia Suleiman Abaza and Sharia Libnan.

What little history there is since the pharaohs floats on the river in the form of houseboats moored off Sharia el-Nil just north of Zamalek Bridge in Agouza. These floating two-storey structures once lined

---

> WORTH A TRIP

'GARBAGE CITY'

Looking around some parts of Cairo, you might think garbage is never collected – but it certainly is, by tens of thousands of people known as *zabbaleen*. The *zabbaleen* are Coptic Christians, and their district at the base of the Muqattam Hills contains one of the most surprising churches in the country. The Church of St Simeon the Tanner (Kineesat Samaan al-Kharraz; ☎2512 3666; Manshiyet Nasr), on a ridge above 'Garbage City', seats 5000 and is ringed with biblical scenes carved into the rock. Look over the ridge and you can see the whole sprawling city; look down, and you see all the city's refuse, sorted into recyclable bits.

But this church is not old, nor are any of the others in the complex, though some are tucked in spooky hermits' caves. Completed in 1994, St Simeon is a belated honour for a 10th-century ascetic who prayed to make Muqattam move at the behest of Fatimid caliph Al-Muizz li-Din Allah (per Matthew 17:20: 'If ye have faith as a grain of mustard seed, ye shall say unto this mountain, Remove hence to yonder place; and it shall remove...'). Today the church is a major site of Coptic pilgrimage.

Tell your taxi driver 'Manshiyet Nasr' or 'Madeenat az-Zabbaleen'. After turning off the highway toward Muqattam, make the first left, going slightly uphill. Once you're in the *zabbaleen* district, anyone you pass will wave you in the right direction – they all know where you're headed.

For food out this way, visit the nearby branch of Andrea (see p133; ☎2250 57920; Rd 52, Muqattam; ☺noon-2am).

the Nile all the way from Giza to Imbaba. During the 1930s some boats became casinos, music halls and bordellos. Many of the surviving residences still have a bohemian air, as chronicled in Naguib Mahfouz' novel *Adrift on the Nile*.

Agricultural Museum
MUSEUM

(Al-Mathaf al-Zirai; Map p102; ☏3761 6785; off Sharia Wizarat al-Ziraa, Doqqi; admission E£3, camera E£10; ☺9am-2pm Sun-Thu) Built in 1930 in the most expansive British colonial style, this whole museum should be in a museum. Only two buildings of a much larger complex are still open, and they're a bit decrepit, but they still pack in amazing amounts of information: dioramas depict traditional weddings, glass cases are packed with wax cucurbits, and scale models demonstrate the wheat-threshing process. Dusty and a bit spooky, it's a true hall of wonders.

Mr & Mrs Mahmoud Khalil Museum
MUSEUM

(Map p102; ☏3338 9720; 1 Sharia Kafour, Doqqi) This museum was closed for renovation at the time of research, but if it has reopened, definitely make the trek, even if you didn't come to Egypt to see 19th- and 20th-century European and Japanese art. In fact, Mahmoud and the missus, Emiline Lock, hobnobbed with European artists at the turn of the last century and amassed an impressive collection: Delacroix, Gauguin, Toulouse-Lautrec, Monet and more. The museum is just a few minutes' walk south from the Cairo Sheraton.

🏃 Activities

Also see p131 for details on horse riding by the Pyramids.

Boat Rides

One of the most pleasant things to do on a warm day is to go out on a felucca, Egypt's ancient broad-sail boat, with a supply of beer and a small picnic just as sunset approaches. Because it's near a wider spot in the river, the best spot for hiring is the **Dok Dok landing stage** (Map p102), and the dock just to the south, on the corniche in Garden City, across from the Four Seasons. Subject to haggling, a boat and captain should cost between E£50 and E£70 per hour; your captain will appreciate additional baksheesh.

Once night falls, light-festooned **party boats** crowd the docks near Maspero, the east bank of the Nile north of 6th of October Bridge. A 45-minute or hour-long ride usually costs E£6 or so per person, and boats go whenever they're full.

Swimming

Finding a place to cool off in the city can be difficult. Cairenes who can afford it swim in members-only clubs. Some hotels do allow day use for nonguests, at a price. The best bargains are in Mohandiseen, where a minimum charge at the cafes at **Atlas Zamalek Hotel** (Map p98; ☏3346 7230; 20 Sharia Gamiat ad-Dowal al-Arabiyya; E£60 minimum) and **Nabila Hotel** (Map p98; ☏3303 0302; 4 Sharia Gamiat ad-Dowal al-Arabiyya; E£40 minimum; ☺10am-6pm) give you access to their small rooftop pools.

For a bigger day outing, **Mohamed Ali Club** (☏3345 0228; Km 13, Upper Egypt Agriculture Rd; day use E£100) is a major social scene – a mix of expats and Egyptians – with house music, good Lebanese food (E£20 to E£40) and beers (E£28). It's located 3km south on the west bank, about even with Ma'adi. For a similar price, you can rent a room for the day at **Cataract Pyramids Resort** (☏3771 8060; www.cataracthotels.com; Harraniyya Rd, Giza; day use d E£200). Located due east of the Pyramids on the road to Saqqara.

Courses

For language schools, see p513.

Belly-Dancing Lessons

The more service-minded tourist hotels can arrange classes, and this is the most flexible option. Some of the city's gyms and health centres offer group courses: try **Tawazon Studio** (Map p64; ☏0109 555 7266; 5 Sharia Youssef al-Guindi), where drop-in classes cost E£60 when they're running, and **Samia Allouba Dance & Fitness Centre** (Map p98; ☏3302 0572; www.samiaalloubacenter.com; 6 Sharia Amr, Mohandiseen). If you're experienced, contact **Mme Raqia Hassan** (☏3748 2338; www.raqiahassan.net), the grande dame of Egyptian belly dance. She runs a small studio in her Doqqi apartment, where either she or one of her protégés will give you (or a group, if you can get one together) lessons.

Tours

Numerous companies and individuals offer tours of sights within and around Cairo. For private outings to ancient sites, we recommend **Hassan Saber** (☏0100 515 9857; has sansaber@hotmail.com), whose years of experience include an appearance on Anthony

CAIRO FOR CHILDREN

Cairo can be exhausting for kids, but there is much they will enjoy. Most children will like an excursion on a Nile **felucca** (p92) or a night-time party boat, gawking at Tut's treasures in the **Egyptian Museum** (p136) and investigating the **Pyramids at Giza** (p125), as well as the mazelike market of **Khan al-Khalili** (p74). Also check out smaller, uncrowded attractions like the **Agricultural Museum** (p92) and the **Postal Museum** (p68).

Overlooking Islamic Cairo, **Al-Azhar Park** (p83) has one of the few children's playgrounds in the central city, though the gardens in **Gezira** (p90) and **Ezbekiyya** (p68) also give room to run. When only bribery will help, try **Mandarine Koueider** (p106) for delectable, distracting ice cream. Or cut straight to toys at **Mom & Me** (Map p98; ☑2736 5751; 20A Sharia Mansour Mohammed, Zamalek). If you're staying a while, it's worth buying *Cairo, the Family Guide*, by Lesley Lababidi and Lisa Sabbahy (AUC Press, E£100), revised in 2010.

A few more ideas:

Cairo Puppet Theatre (Masrah al-Ara'is; Map p64; ☑2591 0954; Ezbekiyya; admission E£15; ⏱6pm Thu-Sun) Shows are in Arabic, but colourful and animated enough to entertain all ages.

National Circus (Map p98; ☑3347 0612; Balloon Theatre, Sharia el-Nil, Agouza; admission E£30-50; ⏱box office 11am-10pm, performances 10pm-midnight) Traditional one-ring show with clowns, acrobats, lions and lots of glitter, usually running during the cooler months. Go early to get good seats at this one-ring show with clowns, acrobats, lions and lots of glitter. It's very traditional (including in its use of animals), and usually runs during the cooler months.

Giza Zoo (Guineenet al-Haywanat; Map p102; ☑3570 8895; Midan al-Gamaa, Giza; admission E£20; ⏱9am-4pm) In rather sorry shape these days, you're going not for the animals, but for a chance to mingle with local children.

Dr Ragab's Pharaonic Village (☑3568 8601; www.pharaonicvillage.com; 3 Sharia al-Bahr al-Azam, Moneib; admission from E£158; ⏱9am-10pm) Full-tilt tourist trap, and a little tattered, but good for sparking the imagination about what life in ancient Egypt was like. Ticket window closes at 5pm. On the west bank of the Nile, 3.5km south of the Giza Zoo.

Bourdain's *No Reservations*. Witty and enthusiastic **Ahmed Seddik** (☑0100 676 8269; www.ahmedseddik.com; day-long tour E£200) runs a busy itinerary of group tours; check his website for the schedule. He's strongest on the Egyptian Museum and Saqqara. **Samo Tours** (☑2299 1155; www.samoegypttours.com) is also reliable, with excellent English-speaking guides, Egyptologists and drivers.

To hire a taxi for the day and dispense with a guide, try **Aton Amon** (☑0100 621 7674; aton_manos@yahoo.com; full day E£300), who speaks English and French; he also does airport pickups. Friendly **Fathy el-Menesy** (☑2486 4251; full day E£300) speaks English and owns a well-maintained Peugeot.

Drivers (and sometimes guides) will often try to push you into shopping add-ons – the spurious perfume store that claims to supply the Body Shop; the illustrious papyrus 'museum' – for which they'll receive a commission. Many drivers factor this into their daily earnings, so it can be hard to dissuade them. Be firm, and if you're truly desperate, offer to pay the difference yourself. It may be the only way to convey the message that tourists are often happier without these shopping detours.

⭐ Festivals & Events

For more information on festivals and public holidays see p21.

Moulid of Sayyidna al-Hussein FESTIVAL
On the square in front of the Mosque of al-Hussein, this Sufi gathering celebrates the birthday of the prophet's grandson. If the crowds get too intense, you can watch from one of the rooftop cafes. It's near the end of the Islamic month of Rabei al-Tani (early March 2013, late February 2014 and 2015). For more on *moulids*, see p484.

Moulid of Sayyida Zeinab FESTIVAL
The last week of the Islamic month of Ragab (early June 2013, late May in 2014 and 2015),

this veneration of the prophet's granddaughter is a great neighbourhood event, behind the mosque of the same name.

Ahlan wa Sahlan FESTIVAL
(www.raqiahassan.net) Belly-dancing convention in June – fun even for beginners, but it's a participant event, not for spectators.

Sleeping

Cairo is chock-a-block with budget crash pads, including a few exceptionally good ones, but midrange gems are rarer. On the upper end, impressive luxury hotels line the banks of the Nile. If your wallet has adequate padding, this is one city where you may want to enjoy these establishments. (At some point in 2013, the Ritz-Carlton will join the party, in the refurbished Nileside property that was once the Hilton, on Midan Tahrir.) At least feel free to treat these hotels as locals do: as places of respite from the city din, with clean bathrooms and other comforts. Rates at the high end fluctuate according to season, and rarely include taxes or breakfast.

It pays to make reservations in advance, at least for your first night or two. Cairo is no place to haul your luggage around while comparing room rates.

DOWNTOWN

This is primarily budget territory, though there are a few noteworthy upper-end sleeps. Either way, you'll be in the thick of things and near great cheap eateries. Most hotels are located on or around Sharia Talaat Harb in old apartment blocks. Don't be alarmed by grimy stairs and shaky elevators – they aren't necessarily a reflection of the hotels above. Many have balconies and windows overlooking noisy main streets; request a rear room if you're a light sleeper, with earplugs as backup.

TOP CHOICE Pension Roma HOTEL $
(Map p64; 2391 1088; www.pensionroma.com. eg; 4th fl, 169 Sharia Mohammed Farid; s/d with fan E£80/127; s/d with air-con E£165/253; ❈ ☗) Run by a French-Egyptian woman with impeccable standards, the Roma brings dignity, even elegance, to the budget-travel scene. You'll never be pressured to buy a tour here (they're not even an option), and the towering ceilings, antique furniture and filmy white curtains create a feeling of timeless calm. Book ahead, as the place is popular with repeat guests, many of whom could af-

ford more expensive digs but prefer the old-Cairo atmosphere here. Most rooms have shared bath, though a few newer rooms have private facilities, and some rooms have shower cubicles.

TOP CHOICE Dina's HOSTEL $
(Map p64; 2396 3902; www.dinashostel.com; 5th fl, 42 Sharia Abdel Khalek Sarwat; dm E£45, s/d with shared bath E£110/140; s/d with air-con E£140/200; ❈ ☗) Tranquil and tidy, Dina's is a welcome addition to Cairo's hostel scene, not least because it's woman-owned and low on pressure tactics. It's also easy on the eyes, with warm colors, Egyptian appliqué pillows and soaring ceilings. The place has more private rooms than dorm beds, but it stays true to hostel roots with a gleaming shared kitchen. The building entrance is down a passage just east of Stephenson's pharmacy.

Hotel Royal BOUTIQUE HOTEL $$
(Map p64; 2391 7203; www.cairohotelroyal.com; 1st fl, 10 Sharia Elwy; s/d US$30/40; ❈ ☗) The Royal's owner lived in Norway for years and brought back a minimalist all-white Scandinavian sensibility that's brightened with just a touch of Egyptian glitzy gold trim. All rooms have niceties like minifridges, comfy office-style desk chairs and bunches of flowers on bedside tables. It's smack in the middle of a lively late-night cafe scene, but away from main-street traffic noise.

Hotel Luna HOTEL $
(Map p64; 2396 1020; www.hotellunacairo. com; 5th fl, 27 Sharia Talaat Harb; s/d with shared bathroom E£100/140; s/d from E£150/200; ❈ ☗) Modern, backpacker-friendly Luna offers three options: simple, slightly aged rooms with shared bath; basic private-bath rooms; and the quieter 'Bella Luna' rooms with thicker mattresses and soothing pastel colour combos. Regardless, the fastidious owner has provided many small comforts, such as bedside lamps and bathmats. Resident tour organiser Sam gets high marks from readers, and there's an excellent shared kitchen.

Berlin Hotel HOTEL $
(Map p64; 2395 7502; berlinhotelcairo@hotmail. com; 4th fl, 2 Sharia Shawarby; s/d with aircon E£147/177, s/d with fan E£100/130; ❈ ☗) Among Cairo regulars, there are Roma loyalists and Berlin loyalists. Like Pension Roma, Berlin

CAIRO HOTEL SCAMS

In short, all scams are attempts to distract you from your lodging of choice. Hotels do not open and close with any great frequency in Cairo, and if it's listed in this book it is very unlikely to have gone out of business by the time you arrive.

At the airport, you may be approached by a man or woman with an official-looking badge, claiming to be government tourism representatives. (There are no such true reps at the airport.) They'll ask if you've booked a hotel, then offer to call to confirm that a room is waiting for you. Of course, they don't call the hotel – they call a friend, who says there is no booking and that his establishment is full. Concerned, the tout will offer to find you an alternative...

Some taxi drivers will stall by saying they don't know where your hotel is. In that case tell them to let you out at Midan Talaat Harb – from here it's a short walk to most budget hotels. Other lines include telling you the hotel you're heading for is closed/very expensive/horrible/a brothel and suggesting a 'better' place, for which they earn a commission, which will then be added to your bill.

The most elaborate scam is when a stranger (often on the airport bus) chats you up and asks your name and where you're staying. Then the person says goodbye and isn't seen again. What they next do is call a friend, who goes and stands outside the hotel you've booked. When you arrive, he or she will ask 'Are you...?', using the name you volunteered back at the airport. Then you'll be told that the hotel has been closed by the police/flooded due to plumbing issues/totally booked out and that the owners have organised a room for you elsewhere.

Finally, when checking in without a prior reservation, never pay for more than a night in advance. No decent hotel will ask for more, and this gives you recourse if the place doesn't meet your needs.

is pleasantly old-fashioned and very low on pressure tactics. Here, though, the knowledgeable owner can arrange airport pickup and reasonably priced tours. Most of the 11 colour-saturated rooms (green! pink!) have air-con and private showers (but shared toilets); three rooms have fan only. There's a shared kitchen too, and good long-stay rates.

Hotel Osiris HOTEL $$
(Map p64; ☎2794 5728; http://hotelosiris.over-blog.com; 12th fl, 49 Sharia Nubar; s/d from €25/40; ❄☎) On the top floor of a commercial building, the Osiris' rooms enjoy views across the city. The French-Egyptian couple who run the place keep the tile floors and white walls spotless, and the pretty hand-sewn appliqué bedspreads tidily arranged on the plush mattresses. Breakfast involves fresh juice, crepes and omelettes. Its location in Bab al-Luq is quiet at night.

Cairo City Center HOTEL $$
(Map p64; ☎0127 777 6383; www.cairocitycenter hotel.com; 14 Sharia Champollion; s/d US$30/40; ❄☎) Don't judge it by the dingy, claustrophobic lobby – rooms here are fine, with high ceilings, shiny tile floors, new bathrooms and good-quality mattresses. The

sitting area has a beautiful terrace looking straight down Sharia Mahmoud Bassiouni.

Sara Inn Hostel HOSTEL $
(Map p64; ☎2392 2940; www.sarainnhostel.com; 21 Sharia Youssef al-Guindi; dm E£50, with shared bathroom E£80/115; s/d from E£125/175; ❄☎) This is another decent option offering both dorms and private rooms for shoestring travellers. The Sara Inn is a small but personable place where you can easily get to know the staff. Plenty of well-strewn rugs and tapestries give a relaxed and cosy feel.

African House Hostel HOSTEL $
(Map p69; ☎2591 1744; www.africanhousehostel.com; 3rd fl, 15 Sharia Emad ad-Din; s/d/tr with shared bathroom US$17/19/25; s US$22; ☎) The African House offers an affordable way to stay in one of the city's most gorgeous mid-19th-century buildings. Rooms on the 4th floor have dimmer halls, but big balconies. The shared kitchen is a bit grotty, and the toilets occasionally run, but the staff are very nice.

Windsor Hotel HOTEL $$
(Map p64; ☎2591 5277; www.windsorcairo.com; 19 Sharia Alfy; s/d with shower & hand basin US$37/48, s/d full bathroom from US$46/59; ❄☎) Rooms

at the Windsor are dim, many with low ceilings and noisy air-conditioners, and management is prone to adding surprise extra charges. But with the beautifully maintained elevator, worn stone stairs and a hotel restaurant where the dinner bell chimes every evening at 7.30pm, the place is hard for nostalgia buffs to resist. The entrance is around the back, in the narrow street just south of Sharia Alfy.

Grand Hotel
HOTEL $$

(Map p64; ☑2575 7700; grandhotel@link.net; 17 Sharia 26th of July; s/d E£284/381; ❋☎) This busy seven-storey palace managed to survive conversion to a midrange place without losing too much old-fashioned flair. The hundred or so rooms still have good parquet floors, and there a few remaining art-deco flourishes, though the shiny white-tile bathrooms are a wonderful modern addition. Entry is around the back in a tiny plaza.

Victoria Hotel
HOTEL $$

(Map p69; ☑2589 2290; www.victoriahotel-egypt. com; 66 Sharia al-Gomhuriyya; s/d from €40/54; ❋☎) Not far from Ramses Station, the Victoria is a grand old palace with the happy addition of silent air-con, as well as comfy beds and satellite TV. Off long halls lined with clouded mirrors, the rooms have antique furniture and nice high ceilings. Two hitches: internet access isn't free, and the only nearby restaurant is At-Tabei ad-Dumyati. But you're very close to the Orabi metro stops.

Meramees Hostel
HOSTEL $

(Map p64; ☑2396 2318; www.merameeshotel.com; 5th fl, 32 Sharia Sabri Abu Alam; s/d with shared bathroom E£75/110; ❋☎) This well-positioned hostel is easy-going, and the rooms have high ceilings, wooden floorboards, large windows and balconies – though those on the 5th floor are noticeably better kept than on the 6th. Communal bathrooms and a kitchen are kept clean, and the management seems to have travellers' interests in mind.

Capsis Palace
BUSINESS HOTEL $$

(Map p69; ☑2575 4029; 117 Sharia Ramses; s/d US$28/41; ❋☎) Run by the same owners as the Victoria, the Capsis is a thoroughly modern place with smallish but nicely kept rooms. By far the best option close to the train station. No wi-fi in rooms, though, and it costs to use it in the lobby.

Carlton Hotel
HOTEL $$

(Map p64; ☑2575 5022; www.carltonhotelcairo. com; 21 Sharia 26th of Jul; s/d half board from US$38/58; ❋☎) If you get one of the renovated ('class A') rooms, this is a gem with a whiff of yesteryear, with the perk of an excellent rooftop bar. If you get stuck with an old room, it's not worth half the price.

Talisman Hotel
BOUTIQUE HOTEL $$$

(Map p64; ☑2393 9431; www.talisman-hotel.com; 5th fl, 39 Sharia Talaat Harb; s/d from US$85/95; ❋☎) The boutique Talisman has great style – jewel-tone rooms with a dash of Oriental kitsch – but its rooms aren't as well kept as they ought to be. But the cocooning silence afforded by double-pane windows counts for a lot.

Cosmopolitan Hotel
HOTEL $$

(Map p64; ☑2392 3845; 1 Sharia Ibn Taalab; s/d US$59/67; ❋) Gloomy dark furniture, mysteriously spotted carpeting and reports of surly service would normally get this art-nouveau place dropped from the list. But its prime location, on a pedestrian street in Downtown, is tough to beat. If you could choose anywhere in Cairo, this might not be it – but if it's already booked as part of a package, you could do worse.

GARDEN CITY

Just south of Midan Tahrir, this area is a lot quieter and much less congested, but there aren't many hotels to choose from.

Hotel Juliana
HOTEL $$

(Map p102; ☑0122 424 9896; www.juliana-hotel. com; 3rd fl, 8 Sharia Ibrahim Naguib; s/d E£170/250; ❋☎) Not quite as sleek as its website suggests, but still showing a bit of style, with a red-and-gold colour scheme and balconies off every room. Perks include fridges and a small but functional shared kitchen. With only 18 rooms, it fills up fast – book ahead. Finding it in Garden City's web is a bit tricky – turn off Sharia Qasr el-Aini at the Co-op petrol station, and make the first left, and the next soft left after that. The hotel is in the same building as the Arab-African Bank.

Four Seasons at Nile Plaza
LUXURY HOTEL $$$

(Map p102; ☑2791 7000; www.fourseasons.com/ caironp; 1089 Corniche el-Nil; r from US$240; ❋☎▨) Of the two Four Seasons in Cairo (the other is in Giza), this one has a more modern vibe (cool Omar Nagdi painting behind reception), and a handier location, 15 minutes' walk from the Egyptian Museum.

The impeccable rooms have windows that actually open (unfortunately rare in luxury hotels). Plus: three (!) swimming pools.

Kempinski Nile
LUXURY HOTEL **$$$**
(Map p102; ☑2798 0000; www.kempinski.com; 12 Sharia Ahmed Ragab; r from US$239; ❄☞🏊) Opened in 2010, this Nileside tower nearly rivals its neighbour, the Four Seasons, for comfort. Rooms are a bit smaller, though, and the bathrooms not quite so opulent. But all rooms have balconies, and internet access is free.

Garden City House
PENSION **$$**
(Map p64; ☑2794 8400; 23 Sharia Kamal ad-Din Salah; s/d with shared bathroom from E£97/143, s/d E£151/206; ❄) This pension is untouched by time – not great in some ways (rooms could use a fresh coat of paint), but a boon in others, such as the gentlemanly staff. The cheapest, fan-only rooms are small and stifling; those with en-suite bath are more spacious. Dinner is an option. The handy location is steps from Tahrir.

ISLAMIC CAIRO
The negatives: no immediate metro access, touts like locusts, nowhere to get a beer and more than the usual number of mosques with loudspeakers. But this is the place to plunge in at Cairo's deep end.

Arabian Nights
HOTEL **$$**
(☑2589 4230; www.arabiannights.hostel.com; 10 Sharia al-Addad; s/d E£140/160; ❄☞) On a relatively quiet street east of Midan al-Hussein, this midrange hotel is distinctly out of the tourist fray. Some rooms are quite dark and you need to check that the air-con works, but standards are generally good. The challenge is finding it: turn north on Sharia al-Mansouria (east along Sharia al-Azhar from Midan Hussein); 300m on, turn left at the ruined shell of a cinema (the Kawakeb cited as a landmark on the hotel's map).

El-Malky Hotel
HOTEL **$$**
(Map p78; ☑2589 0804; sales@malky.com; 4 Sharia al-Husseini; s/d E£130/170; ❄) Rooms at this place favoured by Arab tourists are varied: some have balconies, while a few much cheaper ones are concrete prisons with no windows. The rooftop views here are impressive, and it's cleaner than its neighbour, El Hussein.

El Hussein
HOTEL **$$**
(Map p78; ☑2591 8089; Midan al-Hussein; s/d E£155/180; ❄) Off either side of an open-ended hallway where street noise reverberates, the rooms here are dreary. But front-facing ones with balconies afford mesmerising people-watching on the square below. There's a top-floor restaurant too. Entrance is in the back alley, one block off the square.

Le Riad
BOUTIQUE HOTEL **$$$**
(Map p76; ☑2787 6074; www.leriad-hoteldecharme.com; 114 Sharia al-Muizz li-Din Allah; ste from €240; ❄☞) Le Riad wouldn't be out of place in Damascus or Marrakech. In Cairo, though, it's alone in its amazing style – and, it must be said, its price. Nonetheless, the rooms are marvellous confections of Egyptian folk and Oriental fantasy, with rich colours, eye-popping fabrics and beaded lamps galore. Perks such as laptops in every room, DVDs of Egyptian films and a pretty rooftop terrace add a bit to the value.

ZAMALEK & GEZIRA
The relatively quiet enclave of Zamalek offers the best night's sleep in the city, if not the cheapest. Many of Cairo's best restaurants, shops, bars and coffee shops are here, but sights are a taxi ride away over traffic-jammed bridges.

Cairo Marriott
LUXURY HOTEL **$$$**
(Map p98; ☑2728 3000; www.marriott.com/caieg; 16 Sharia Saray al-Gezira; r from US$219; ❄☞🏊) Historic atmosphere is thick in the the lobby and other public areas, which all occupy a 19th-century palace. The rooms are all in two modern towers, and many have tiny bathrooms, but touches like plasma-screen TVs and extra-plush beds make up for it. It also has a popular garden cafe and a great pool.

Hotel Longchamps
HOTEL **$$**
(Map p98; ☑2735 2311; www.hotellongchamps.com; 5th fl, 21 Sharia Ismail Mohammed; s/d from US$66/84; ❄☞) The old-European-style Hotel Longchamps has a residential feel. Rooms are spacious and well maintained, and guests gather to chat on the greenery-covered, peaceful rear balcony around sunset, or lounge in the restaurant. If you want your own balcony and a small bathtub, get an 'executive' room. Book well ahead.

Novotel Cairo El Borg
BUSINESS HOTEL **$$$**
(Map p102; ☑2735 6725; www.novotel.com; 3 Sharia Saray al-Gezira; r from US$138; ❄☞🏊) Convenient location, sparkling new facilities and a pool are the selling points here, and more than make up for the somewhat

Mohandiseen, Agouza & Zamalek

Mohandiseen, Agouza & Zamalek

generic chain feel. Midan Tahrir is just over the bridge; a metro stop is around the corner; and some of Gezira's prettiest gardens are just across the road.

Golden Tulip Flamenco Hotel HOTEL **$$**
(Map p98; ☎2735 0815; www.flamencohotels.com; 2 Sharia Gezirat al-Wusta; s/d from US$89/99; ❋☎) This popular place is a reasonable alternative to five-star heavyweights. Rooms

are comfortable and well equipped, if slightly cramped in standard configuration. The extra US$10 for 'superior' class gives you interior space and a balcony overlooking the houseboats on the Nile.

Sofitel El Gezirah LUXURY HOTEL **$$$**
(Map p102; ☎2737 3737; www.sofitel.com; Sharia al-Orman; r from US$209; ❋☎❄) Tired from long travels? Rest up here in a sumptuous

room with superb views, and let the staff look after you. But if you're planning a lot of sightseeing, go elsewhere – the location, at the southern tip of Gezira, is frustrating.

Mayfair Hotel HOTEL **$**
(Map p98; ☏2735 7315; www.mayfaircairo.com; 2nd fl, 9 Sharia Aziz Osman; s/d with shared bathroom E£150/170, s/d from E£220/250; ✷🤝) The cheapest sleep in the neighbourhood, on a quiet street, with a fine large terrace. Double rooms are clean and good-size, with balconies, TVs and fridges. But many single rooms are cramped, and the young staff perfectly nice but perhaps a tad too attentive to female guests.

DOQQI
An upscale option, the Cairo Sheraton, was undergoing renovation at the time of research; it's set to reopen in late 2012.

El Tonsy HOTEL **$$**
(Map p102; ☏3337 6908; tonsihotelcairo@gmail. com; 143 Sharia Tahrir; s/d US$45/60; ✷🤝) Opened in 2011, this smart modern place is often used by groups, but it's also handy for the independent traveller who prefers to stay in a less touristy neighbourhood. The carpeted rooms are a little spare, but some have huge balconies (with Nile views for US$10 more), and there's a great terrace bar from which you can spy the Pyramids. The restaurant is a bit expensive, but there are plenty of dining options along this street and nearby.

🍴 Eating

In Cairo, you can spend E£5 or E£250 on dinner. At one end of the spectrum are the street carts, *kushari* counters, and fruit-and-veg markets where the majority of Cairenes feed themselves. One step up are the Egyptian fast-food operations – forget 'Kentucky' and Pizza Hut – that serve some of the most delicious and cheap meals you'll have. See the boxed text p497 for some of the standards. As with the hotel scene, reliable midrange options are in short supply, but the few good ones offer great value, especially for traditional food.

At the upper end, Cairo dining can be quite cosmopolitan, with the chefs usually imported straight from the relevant country, along with all the ingredients. Dinner reservations are generally recommended.

Many restaurants double as bars and nightclubs, with guests proceeding from multicourse meals into boozing and grooving. If a place like this has notable food, we list it here, but if the scene's more the thing, it's under Drinking.

Too tired to leave the hotel? You can get just about anything delivered, and even order online through **Otlob.com** (www.otlob. com), with service from more than 60 of the city's most popular restaurants.

DOWNTOWN
This is predominantly cheap-and-cheerful territory, plus a few nostalgic favourites. It's by far the best place to get good authentic Egyptian food.

TOP CHOICE
At-Tabei ad-Dumyati EGYPTIAN FAST FOOD **$**
Orabi (Map p69; 31 Sharia Orabi; dishes E£3-14; ⏱7am-1am); Talaat Harb (Map p64; Talaat Harb Complex, Sharia Talaat Harb; dishes E£3-10; 9am-midnight) About 200m north of Midan Orabi, this place offers some of the cheapest meals in Cairo – and also some of the freshest and most delicious. Start by picking four salads from a large array, then order shwarma or ta'amiyya, along with some lentil soup or fuul. The entrance to the sit-down Orabi restaurant is set back from the street and signed only in Arabic; immediately north is the constantly thronged takeout window, where just about anything is available that can be stuffed into a pita pocket. A branch in the basement food court of the Talaat Harb mall has a more limited menu.

Gomhouriya EGYPTIAN **$$**
(Map p64; 42 Sharia Falaki; pigeons E£30; ⏱noon-midnight) Roast, stuffed pigeon is the star of the show here – just tell the waiter how many birds you want, and they arrive crisp and hot, along with salad and all-you-can-drink mugs of peppery, lemony broth. The small English sign says 'Shalapy'.

Fasahat Soumaya EGYPTIAN **$**
(Map p64; ☏0100 9873 8637; 15 Sharia Youssef al-Guindi; mains E£15-30; ⏱1-10.30pm; 🖋) Down a little pedestrian alley is this sweet restaurant with only a few tables. All the staples are here, prepared like an Egyptian mom would make: various stuffed veggies, hearty stews and extra odd bits (rice sausage, lamb shanks) on Thursdays. The sign is in Arabic only, green on a white wall, with a few steps down to the basement space.

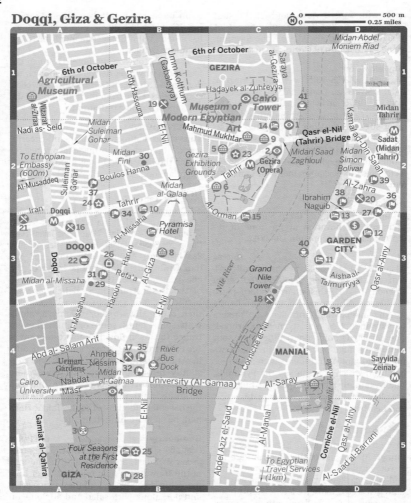

CAIRO EATING

Hati al-Geish   GRILL **$$**

(Map p64; 23 Sharia Falaki; mains E£25-60; ⊘11am-11pm) Carnivores will salivate upon entering this place, where the air is heavy with the smell of charcoal-cooked meat. The *kastileeta* (lamb chops) are splendid, and the tender *moza* (shanks) good for gnawing – the *moza fatta,* with a side of rice-and-pita casserole, is very good. Even items listed as 'Appetizers' are substantial. No beer, but fresh juices come dressed up with pink sugar rims, and the waiters are quite dapper too.

Sudan Restaurant   SUDANESE **$**

(Map p64; Haret al-Sufi; dishes E£6-17; ⊘10am-10pm) One of several Sudanese restaurants and cafes in this alley, this is the tidiest and perhaps serves the most delicious dishes. Try *salata iswid* ('black salad'), a spicy mix of eggplant and peanuts, and *qarassa,* stew served in a bread bowl, among other treats. It's in the alley connecting Sharia Adly and Sharia Abdel Khalek Sarwat, in a courtyard off the southern end. Sign is Arabic only – yellow letters on a red background.

Doqqi, Giza & Gezira

Artine 2000   EGYPTIAN $$
(Map p64; 26 Sharia Sherif; mains E£30-45; ◷10am-8pm, to 2pm Fri) Simple home-style Egyptian food at this little upstairs-downstairs restaurant. *Mulukhiyya*, the garlicky green soup is a must, with rabbit or meatballs. *Tagen*s (stews) are hearty, and fried eggplant with loads of garlic starts the meal right. The only English on the sign is the '2000' – look for it in the courtyard of the building at the corner with Qasr el-Nil.

Arabesque   EGYPTIAN $$
(Map p64; ☏2574 8677; www.arabesque-eg.com; 6 Qasr el-Nil; dishes E£20-70; ◷noon-3pm & 7pm-2am) Chic locals consider this place, bedecked with Stella-bottle chandeliers, primarily a bar and lounge, but the food is very good too. There are full classic mains such as stuffed pigeon, but it's just as rewarding to make a meal of generous-size hot and cold mezze: zingy pickled eggplant, delicate vine leaves and even cute little shwarma 'sliders'. Make reservations on the weekend.

Gad   EGYPTIAN FAST FOOD $$
(sandwiches E£2-15, mains E£20-50 ◷9am-2am) 26th of July (Map p64; 13 Sharia 26th of Jul); Sarwat (Map p64; Sharia Abdel Khalek Sarwat at Shawarby); Falaki (Map p64; North side Midan Falaki) Gad's lighthouse logo is fitting: it's a beacon in the night for hungry Cairenes. The ground floor is for takeaway, and arranged by type of food: *fiteer* (flaky pizza) dough being stretched here, shwarma being sliced there, salads at yet another counter. Order and pay at the till first, then take the receipts to the relevant counters. You can also sit upstairs, away from the crowds, and order off the menu. The one on Sarwat is typically less crowded.

Abou Tarek   EGYPTIAN FAST FOOD $
(Map p64; 40 Sharia Champollion; dishes E£3-10; ◷8am-midnight; ☏) 'We have no other

branches!' proclaims this temple of *kushari*. No, the place has just expanded, decade by decade, into the upper storeys of its building, even as it has held onto the unofficial Best Kushari title. It's worth eating in to check out the elaborate decor upstairs. You must pay in advance, either at the till downstairs (for takeaway) or with your waiter.

El-Abd
BAKERY **$**

(Map p64; pastries E£1-6; ☺8.30am-midnight) Talaat Harb (35 Sharia Talaat Harb); 26th of July (25 Sharia Talaat Harb) For pastries head for Cairo's most famous bakery, easily identified by the crowds of people outside tearing into their croissants, sweets and savoury pies. It's a great place to augment your ho-hum hotel breakfast.

Akher Sa'a
EGYPTIAN FAST FOOD **$**

(Map p64; dishes E£2-10; ☺24hr) Alfy (8 Sharia Alfy); Sarwat (14 Sharia Abdel Khalek Sarwat) A frantically busy fuul and ta'amiyya takeaway joint with a no-frills cafeteria next door, Akher Sa'a has a limited menu but its food is fresh and good. The Sarwat branch has a fast-food-style set-up downstairs (note the genius giant-ta'amiyya 'burger') but glacial table service upstairs.

Koshary Goha
EGYPTIAN FAST FOOD **$**

(Map p64; 4 Sharia Emad ad-Din; kushari E£3, pasta E£12; ☺10am-midnight) Solid *kushari* in a gorgeous vintage-Cairo setting. But the real treat is the *makaroneh bi-lahm,* a baked pasta casserole with spicy tomato sauce. The staff sometimes calls it lasagne.

Fatatri at-Tahrir
EGYPTIAN FAST FOOD **$**

(Map p64; 166 Sharia Tahrir; dishes E£9-15; ☺7am-1am) This tiny place just off Midan Tahrir has been serving sweet and savoury *fiteer* to Downtown residents and legions of backpackers for decades. It's reliable and delicious, though it can get very crowded in the afternoon.

Hawawshi Eid
EGYPTIAN FAST FOOD **$**

(Map p64; Sharia Saray al-Ezbekiyya; hawawshi E£6-8.50; ☺10am-4am) Just a few pounds gets you a huge round of bread filled with meat (spicy if you like) and baked in a paper wrapper until molten and delicious, plus pickles galore. There's no English sign – look for the oven out front, to the right of the counter.

Estoril
EGYPTIAN **$$**

(Map p64; ☎2574 3102; off Sharia Talaat Harb; mezze E£10-35, mains E£35-65; ☺noon-midnight) It's sometimes hard to get the attention of

a waiter at Estoril (in an alley next to the Amex office), through clouds of cigarette smoke and tables crammed with Cairo's arts-and-letters set. But once seated, you'll feel like one of the club, scooping up simple mezze and ordering beer after beer. It's not uncommon to see women alone here, and the bar in the back is a good place to perch too.

Café Riche
EGYPTIAN, EUROPEAN **$$**

(Map p64; 17 Sharia Talaat Harb; dishes E£15-50; ☺10am-midnight; ☑) This narrow restaurant, allegedly the oldest in Cairo, was the favoured drinking spot of the intelligentsia. The action has shifted elsewhere now, but a certain old guard still sits under the ceiling fans, along with tourists who like the historic ambience. It's a reliable and nostalgic spot to enjoy a cold beer (E£12) and a meal of slightly Frenchified Egyptian dishes, including a page of veg options, or even a Euro-style breakfast.

Abu al-Hassan al-Haty
GRILL **$$**

(Map p64; 3 Sharia Halim; mains E£20-45) With its foggy mirrors, dusty chandeliers and waiters who look older than the building itself, this is a beautiful relic of Downtown – it's often used as a set for period TV shows. The food (mostly grilled items) is a bit secondary, but perfectly palatable.

Felfela Restaurant
EGYPTIAN **$$**

(Map p64; 15 Sharia Hoda Shaarawi; dishes E£20-45; ☺8am-midnight; ☑) Attracting tourists, coach parties and locals since 1963, Felfela is an institution that can deliver a reliable, if not wildly delicious, meal with good service. A bizarre jungle theme rules the decor, but the food is straight-down-the-line Egyptian and consistently decent, especially the mezze and grilled chicken.

Le Bistro
FRENCH **$$**

(Map p64; 8 Sharia Hoda Shaarawi; mains E£30-55; ☺noon-11pm) Tucked away below street level, Le Bistro is a surprisingly chic outpost Downtown. The food may not quite match its European ideal, but Cairenes love it, and steak *frites* can make a nice change from kebab. The restaurant entrance is to the right; you can also order off the food menu at the bar (enter to the left).

Self-catering

Souq at-Tawfiqiyya
MARKET

(Map p64; Sharia at-Tawfiqiyya) Blocks-long fruit-and-veg market, open late. Good dairy store at corner with Talaat Harb selling fresh cheese.

Souq Bab al-Luq MARKET
(Map p64; Midan Falaki) Big indoor neighbourhood market with produce and meat; surrounding shops sell dry goods.

GARDEN CITY

This is the place to come for a formal feast. The luxury hotels lining the banks of the Nile here have some truly excellent restaurants.

Mahrous EGYPTIAN $
(Sharia al-Haras; meals E£15; ⊙4pm-4am; ✐) Perhaps Cairo's best fuul, worth elevating to dinner status (note the atypical hours). With each plate of beans, you get a big spread of extra salads and fresh potato chips. It's just a tiny stand on a residential block. Turn in to Garden City at the Co-op gas station, make the first left, then a hard left at the next intersection.

Osmanly TURKISH $$$
(Map p102; ✐2798 0000; Kempinski Nile, Corniche el-Nil; mezze E£40; mains E£110-240; ⊙noon-midnight; ✐) Exceptionally good Turkish food, served with elan, starting with handwashing in jasmine-scented water and moving on to a dazzling selection of cold mezze, and impeccably grilled meat. The four-course set menu is a relative steal at E£315.

Sabaya LEBANESE $$$
(Map p64; ✐2795 7171; Semiramis InterContinental, Corniche el-Nil; mezze E£25-50, mains E£70-140; ⊙7.30pm-1am) Diverse and delicate mezze come with fresh-baked pillows of pita, and mains such as *fatta* are served in individual cast-iron pots. The setting is very sleek, but considering portion sizes are generous and sharing is the norm, the prices are not as high as you would expect.

Taboula LEBANESE $$
(Map p102; ✐2792 5261; 1 Sharia Latin America; mezze E£12-35, mains E£35-65; ⊙noon-1am) The Lebanese food at this basement joint isn't as good as Sabaya's, but the atmosphere is more fun – here it's all big groups of Cairenes celebrating birthdays around giant communal tables, with lots of cocktails to go around. Mezze like the *tomiyya* (garlic sauce) are your best bet, but skip the meatballs.

Bird Cage THAI $$$
(Map p64; ✐2795 7171; Semiramis InterContinental, Corniche el-Nil; mains E£65-115; ⊙noon-midnight)

This soothing, wood-panelled space is a favourite with wealthy Cairenes. Grilled foods don't have the proper char, but other preparations, such as whole sea bass wrapped in banana leaves, are good and beautifully presented. The chef will make it truly Thai-spicy if you ask.

Revolving Restaurant FRENCH $$$
(Map p102; ✐2365 1234; Grand Nile Tower, Manial; entrées E£75-145, mains E£180-260; ⊙7pm-midnight) Start with *terrine de foie gras* as you peer at the Pyramids from the 41st floor. By the time your *filet d'agneau* with tomato confit and a sweet garlic doughnut arrives, you'll be looking east to the Citadel. Sure, it's a gimmick, but the Revolving Restaurant at least has good French haute cuisine as well. And, unlike in the rest of this Saudi-run hotel, alcohol is served.

COPTIC CAIRO

Elfostat Tivoli EGYPTIAN $$
(Map p72; Sharia Hassan al-Anwar; entrées E£5-16, mains E£30-45 ⊙9:30am–7pm) The best place to rest up after a Coptic Cairo tour, though no real local feel as it's part of the built-for-tourists Souq al-Fustat complex. Still, prices are reasonable considering the garden setting.

ISLAMIC CAIRO

There are plenty of fast-food joints around Midan al-Hussein but the restaurants in this part of town are limited – you really have to like grilled meat, and not be too squeamish about hygiene.

Farahat EGYPTIAN $$
(Map p78; 126A Sharia al-Azhar; pigeon E£30; ⊙noon-midnight) In an alley off Sharia Al-Azhar, this place is legendary for its pigeon, available stuffed or grilled. It doesn't look like much – just plastic chairs outside – but once you start nibbling the succulent, spiced birds, you'll believe the hype.

Citadel View MIDDLE EASTERN $$
(✐2510 9151; Sharia Salah Salem; entrées E£18-26, mains E£45-90; ⊙noon-midnight) Eating at this gorgeous restaurant in Al-Azhar Park – on a vast multilevel terrace, with Cairo's elite seated around you and the whole city sprawled below – feels almost like visiting a luxury resort. Fortunately the prices are not so stratospheric, and the food is good, with dishes like spicy sausage with pomegranate syrup and grilled fish with tahini. On Friday,

only a buffet (E£150) is on offer, and not the best value. No alcohol.

Gad
EGYPTIAN FAST FOOD **$**

(Map p78; Sharia al-Azhar; sandwiches E£2-15, mains E£20-50 ☺9am-2am) A branch of the Downtown snack experts.

Al-Halwagy
EGYPTIAN **$**

(Map p78; Midan al-Hussein; dishes E£6-30; ☺24hr) Not directly on the square, but just behind a row of buildings, this good ta'amiyya, fuul and salad place has been around for nearly a century. You can eat at pavement tables or hide away upstairs.

Khan el-Khalili Restaurant & Mahfouz Coffee Shop
EGYPTIAN **$$**

(Map p78; ☎2590 3788; 5 Sikket al-Badistan; snacks E£12-40, mains E£30-60; ☺10am-2am) The luxurious Moorish-style interiors of this restaurant and adjoining cafe are a popular haven from the khan's bustle. The place may be geared to tourists but the food is reasonably good, the air-con is strong and the toilets are clean. Look for the metal detector in the lane, immediately west of the medieval gate.

ZAMALEK

Zamalek has some of Cairo's best and most stylish restaurants. Cheap dining is not one of the island's fortes but there are a few possibilities, such as the Baraka shwarma stand (Map p98) on Sharia Brazil.

Didos Al Dente
ITALIAN **$$**

(Map p98; 26 Sharia Bahgat Ali; pasta E£32-47; ☺11am-2am) A noisy, crowded pizza-and-pasta joint with a small outdoor space, Didos rings with the clatter of dishes and often has crowds waiting out front for a table. It's popular with students from the nearby AUC dorm. No alcohol.

Maison Thomas
EUROPEAN **$$**

(Map p98; 157 Sharia 26th of Jul; sandwiches E£33-58, pizzas E£40-65; ☺24hr) A little slice of the Continent, with loads of brass and mirrors, and waiters in long white aprons serving crusty baguette sandwiches. But this institution is best known for its pizza, with generous toppings. There's a branch in Heliopolis (Map p134).

La Mezzaluna
ITALIAN **$$**

(Map p98; Sharia Aziz Osman; pastas E£28-44, mains E£42-66; ☺8am-11pm) Head down a tiny alley to find this funky bi-level space that's frequented by Cairo bohemians. The menu is roughly Italian, from conventional combos such as tomato and basil to others like dill-and-salmon ravioli. Salads are enormous. No alcohol is served, but the little patio out front is a quiet place to take coffee.

L'Aubergine
BISTRO **$$**

(Map p98; ☎2738 0080; 5 Sharia Sayyed al-Bakry; entrées E£16-30, mains E£32-72; ☺noon-2am; ☕) This snug, white-walled, candlelit restaurant devotes half its menu to global vegetarian dishes, such as Turkish stewed aubergine and gnocchi with blue cheese. You can't go wrong with most of the cheesier, creamier items, and the chill-out soundtrack is a nice respite from Cairo street noise.

Mandarine Koueider
ICE CREAM **$**

(Map p98; ☎2735 5010; 17 Sharia Shagaret ad-Durr; per scoop E£5; ☺9am-11pm) The place to get your fix of delectable ice cream and sorbet. Definitely try the *zabadi bi-tut* (yoghurt with blackberry). There's another branch in Heliopolis (Map p134).

Nawab
INDIAN **$$**

(Map p98; ☎2736 0433; 21B Sharia Bahgat Ali; mains E£41-68; ☺noon-10pm; ☕) If you want some Indian spice without the trek to the Mena House Oberoi in Giza, come to this good-value neighbourhood spot for butter chicken, lamb korma and a solid vegetarian selection.

La Taverna
CAFE **$$**

(Map p98; 140 Sharia 26th of Jul; mains E£12-38; ☺8am-midnight) Thanks to its proximity to El Sawy cultural centre, there's usually an interesting crowd of Egyptians at this casual restaurant, and a buzz of big concepts being discussed. The food itself (club sandwiches, pastas) isn't astounding, but it's reasonably priced for Zamalek, and there's outside seating or cool air-con indoors.

Abou El Sid
EGYPTIAN **$$**

(Map p98; ☎2735 9640; 157 Sharia 26th of Jul; mezze E£12-25, mains E£25-70; ☺noon-2am) Cairo's first hipster Egyptian restaurant (and now a national franchise), Abou El Sid is as popular with tourists as it is with upper-class natives. You can get better *molokhiyya* (garlicky leaf soup) elsewhere, but here you wash it down with a cocktail and lounge on kitschy gilt 'Louis Farouk' furniture. The entrance is down a street off 26th of July, on the west side of the Baehler's Mansions complex; look for the tall wooden doors. Reservations are a good idea.

La Bodega
MEDITERRANEAN **$$$**

(Map p98; ☑2735 0543; www.labodegaegypt.com; 1st fl, Baehler's Mansions, 157 Sharia 26th of Jul; mains E£75-120; ⊘noon-2am) Make a reservation a few days in advance if you want to score a table at this perpetual hot spot – otherwise, go early in the week and take your chances at the door. The menu leans toward Italian and Greek seafood, and there's also a vegetarian tasting menu (E£62). But given the eye candy that dines in this sumptuous colonial-style room, you might not notice the food.

Five Bells
EGYPTIAN **$$**

(Map p98; 13 Sharia Ismail Mohammed; mezze E£17-33; ⊘12.30pm-1am) A pretty place to rest up after a long stroll through Zamalek, this garden restaurant serves traditional Egyptian mezze to a soundtrack of Edith Piaf and other wistful European tunes. Snack on hot meatballs, fresh fried potato crisps and cold beer (E£17).

Self-catering

Several shops on 26th of July sell very good-quality produce.

Alfa Market
SUPERMARKET

(Map p98; ☑2737 0801; 4 Sharia al-Malek al-Afdal) Local foods and imported items.

Sekem
GROCERIES

(Map p98; ☑2738 2724; Sharia Ahmed Sabry) Organic products and tofu.

MOHANDISEEN & DOQQI

These concrete suburbs look bland and flavourless, but it's possible to find some excellent restaurants – and don't discount the Nile views.

Yemen Restaurant
YEMENI **$**

(Map p102; 10 Sharia Iran, Doqqi; dishes E£10-30; ⊘24hr) This fluorescent-lit place has all the ambience of a car showroom, but great authentic Yemeni dishes, served without cutlery, with huge rounds of flaky flatbread for scooping. Everything-in-the-pot *salta* is standard, but most everything on the cryptic menu is richly spiced, even the 'choped meat'. Sharia Iran is one block north of Midan Doqqi, running west.

Cedars
LEBANESE **$$**

(Map p98; 42 Sharia Geziret al-Arab, Mohandiseen; mezze E£10-25, mains E£45-75; ⊘noon-1am) This chic Lebanese restaurant is a favourite with Mohandiseen's lunching ladies, then with a younger crowd later in the evening. Rattan chairs dot the spacious terrace, where there's sheesha along with the better-than-average food: peppery *mouhamarra* (walnut and pomegranate syrup dip), fresh and salty *ayran* (yoghurt drink) and big sandwiches stuffed with French fries. You can also get full meals from the grill.

TOP CHOICE At-Tabei ad-Dumyati
EGYPTIAN FAST FOOD **$**

(Map p98; 17 Sharia Gamiat ad-Dowal al-Arabiyya; 7am-2am) A branch of the Downtown fast-food experts.

Sea Gull
SEAFOOD **$$**

(Map p102; 106 Sharia el-Nil, Doqqi; meals E£100-140; ⊘noon-midnight) There's no real menu at this Nileside restaurant – you just select which fish you like from the iced-down display, then retire to your table to admire the view and tuck into a spread of salads while everything is grilled. The crowd is almost entirely Egyptian families, perhaps drawn by the waiters in their smart national-flag uniforms. Outside seating is great on a balmy night; there's air-con inside if you want it. On the street, look for the neon fish and crabs on the fence.

Abu Ammar al-Suri
SYRIAN **$**

(Map p98; 8 Sharia Surya, Mohandiseen; sandwiches E£12-17, mains E£27-50; ⊘11am-2am) At this thronged fast-food operation, pantalooned men work the shwarma skewers, folding meat slices into huge pieces of Syrian-style *saj* flatbread. It has good lentil soup too.

Makani
SUSHI, CAFE **$$**

(sandwiches E£19-30, sushi rolls E£48-60; ⊘8am-2am) Mohandiseen (Map p98; 9 Sharia Amr); Zamalek (Map p98; 118 Sharia 26th of Jul) Sushi and croissants aren't a standard combo, but both the Japanese flavours and the sandwiches are quite good, and the atmosphere is good for either hanging out over coffee and great carrot cake or for a longer meal.

Al-Sudan al-Sharqi
SUDANESE **$**

(Map p102; Sharia al-Nagar, Doqqi; meals E£25; ⊘noon-11pm) Very bare bones, and some Arabic is required, but the reward is richly spiced meat or veg stews and huge rounds of spongy Eritrean *injera* bread. Look on the east side of the short street: the sign is only in Arabic, red on a white background; you go up a few steps to enter.

FIND YOUR OWN AHWA

Cairo's ahwas – traditional coffeehouses – are essential places to unwind, chat and breathe deeply over a sheesha. Dusty floors, rickety tables and the clatter of dominoes and *towla* (backgammon) define the traditional ones. But newer, shinier places – where women smoke as well – have expanded the concept, not to mention the array of sheesha flavours, which now include everything from mango to bubblegum.

There's an ahwa for every possible subculture. We list a couple of the most famous ones here but half the joy of the ahwa is discovering 'yours'. Look in back alleys all over Downtown. Sports fans gather south of Sharia Alfy; intellectuals at Midan Falaki. There's a nice traditional joint down the lane behind Al-Azhar Mosque, and a cool mixed crowd next to Townhouse Gallery. Young activists have claimed the pedestrian streets around the stock exchange. Even some mall food courts can be surprisingly fun. Most ahwas are open from 8am to 2am or so, and you can order a lot more than tea and coffee: try *karkadai* (hibiscus, hot or cold), *irfa* (cinnamon), *kamun* (cumin, good for colds), *yansun* (anise) and, in winter, hot, milky *sahlab*.

El-Mashrabiah
EGYPTIAN $$
(Map p102; ☑3748 2801; 4 Sharia Ahmed Nessim, Giza; mains E£30-60; ☺noon-1am) Excellent Egyptian food is served with formality at this intimate eatery. Located a few steps below street level, the dining room is further darkened by ornate carved panelling, deep leather banquettes and waiters dressed in sombre suits. The kofta and *tagen* (stew cooked in a deep clay pot) are good, as is the rabbit with *molokhiyya* and the duck with starchy taro root. But vegetarians don't get much to work with. No alcohol

Al-Omda
EGYPTIAN FAST FOOD $
(Map p98; 6 Sharia al-Ghazza, Mohandiseen; dishes E£8-30; ☺noon-2am) A mini-empire taking up the better part of a block, Al-Omda offers numerous ways to put grilled meats into your system. At the takeout joint on the corner, get a *shish tawouq* sandwich with spicy pickles. Or else you can sit down in the old-style 'Oriental' restaurant around the corner to your left, or head upstairs to the neon-lit cafe and get a sheesha with the trendy crowd.

🍷 Drinking

Cairo isn't a 'dry' city, but locals tend to run on caffeine by day, available at both traditional ahwas and European-style cafes. Drinking beer or spirits typically doesn't start till the evening hours, and then it's limited to Western-style bars, most with a lot of expats mixed in, and some cheaper, more locals-only dives (see boxed text, p110). For the former, Zamalek is the best place to go boozing; the latter are all Downtown.

Liquor is expensive and wine is barely drinkable, but beer is widely available and cheap. Beers range from around E£10 to E£25, cocktails are typically only at more upscale bars and range from E£40 to E£60. The fancier places can have door policies as strict as the nightclubs, so dress well and go in mixed groups. Many places also have full menus, so you can snack as you go.

DOWNTOWN

Zahret al-Bustan
COFFEEHOUSE
(Map p64; Sharia Talaat Harb; tea & sheesha E£9; ☺8am-2am) This traditional ahwa is a bit of an intellectuals' and artists' haunt, though also firmly on many backpackers' lists, so be alert to scam artists. It's in the lane just behind Café Riche.

Jungle Land
COFFEEHOUSE
(Map p64; Sharia Mohammed Farid; sheesha E£7, tea E£6; ☺24hr) A distinctly new-fangled sort of ahwa, with an overwhelming 'exotic Africa' theme, complete with a life-size plaster elephant. At night there's live music, though it's surprisingly busy in the daytime too – maybe due to the luxurious air-con.

Soma Caffe
COFFEEHOUSE
(Kawkab al-Sharq; Map p64; 11 Sharia Saray al-Ezbekiyya; ☺24hr) A slightly more modern ahwa dedicated to the 'Star of the Orient', Umm Kolthum. Look for the huge busts of the singer out front. Complement it with a visit to **Al-Andaleeb** (Map p64), dedicated to singer/composer Mohammed Abd al-Wahhab, down the block at the corner with Sharia Mohammed Farid.

Odeon Palace Hotel
BAR
(Map p64; 6 Sharia Abdel Hamid Said; beer E£12, ☺24hr) Its fake turf singed from sheesha coals, this slightly dilapidated rooftop bar is

favoured by Cairo's heavy-drinking theatre and cinema clique, and is a great place to watch the sun go down (or come up).

Le Grillon BAR
(Map p64; 8 Sharia Qasr el-Nil) Nominally a restaurant, this bizarre faux patio is all about beer, sheesha and gossip about politics and the arts scene. The illusion of outdoors is created with wicker furniture, fake vines and lots of ceiling fans. The entrance is in the back of a courtyard between two buildings.

Windsor Bar BAR
(Map p64; 19 Sharia Alfy; ☺6pm-1am) Alas, most of the Windsor's regular clientele has passed on, leaving a few hotel guests, a cordial, polyglot bartender and a faint soundtrack of swing jazz and Umm Kolthum. Colonial history has settled in an almost palpable film on the taxidermist's antelope heads, the barrel-half chairs and the dainty wall sconces. Solo women will feel comfortable here.

Groppi's CAFE
(Map p64; Midan Talaat Harb; coffee & pastries from E£7; ☺8am-11pm) Distinctly *not* part of the new coffee wave, Groppi's high point was more than 50 years ago when it was one of the most celebrated patisseries this side of the Mediterranean. Today, the offerings are poor and overpriced, and the tearoom reeks of cheap tobacco, but it nevertheless continues to appeal to hardcore nostalgia buffs.

Groppi Garden CAFE
(Map p64; Sharia Adly; coffee & pastries from E£7; ☺8am-11pm) Same bland coffee and uninteresting pastries as the other Groppi, but the garden terrace here is a peaceful place for a cup of tea and a sheesha. The cafe was the city's first outdoor cinema, and a favoured relaxation spot for Allied troops in WWII, who mixed easily with the local ladies.

Cilantro CAFE
(Map p64; 31 Sharia Mohammed Mahmoud; coffees & teas E£8-35, sandwiches E£12-45; ☺9am-2am; ☎) Egypt's answer to Starbucks and Costa, this popular chain does all the usual coffee drinks, teas and juices, plus packaged sandwiches and cakes. If it weren't for the gaggles of headscarf-wearing teenage girls who crowd the banquettes after school, it would be easy to forget you're in Egypt. There are other branches just about everywhere you turn: Zamalek (Map p98; 157 Sharia 26th of July), Heliopolis (Map p134; 4 Sharia Ibra-

him) and Doqqi (Map p102; Midan al-Missaha), to name a few. All offer free wi-fi, strong air-con and usually clean restrooms.

Orfanidis & Sons LIQUOR STORE
(Map p64; cnr Sharia Mohammed Farid & Sharia Alfy) Sign in Arabic only; entrance screened with a sheet. Cold beer from E£5 per can.

Drinkies LIQUOR STORE
(Map p64; ☎19930; 41 Sharia Talaat Harb) Spiffy modern booze sellers; no need to sneak behind a curtain, and even offers delivery.

ISLAMIC CAIRO

Fishawi's COFFEEHOUSE
(Map p78; off Midan al-Hussein; tea & sheesha around E£10; ☺24hr, during Ramadan 5pm-3am) Probably the oldest ahwa in the city, and certainly the most celebrated, Fishawi's has been a great place to watch the world go by since 1773. Despite being swamped by foreign tourists and equally wide-eyed out-of-town Egyptians, it is a regular ahwa, serving up *shai* (tea) and sheesha to stallholders and shoppers alike. Unfortunately, prices seem to vary without rhyme or reason, so confirm early with your waiter, and also brace yourself for a parade of roaming salesmen hawking wallets, pistol-shaped cigarette lighters and packet after packet of tissues.

Coffeeshop Al-Khatoun COFFEEHOUSE
(Map p82; Midan Al-Khatoun; tea & sheesha E£15; ☺3pm-1am) Tucked away in a quiet square behind Al-Azhar, this modern outdoor ahwa is a great place to rest up after a walk, with tea and snacks and comfortable pillow-strewn benches. In the evenings it attracts an arty crowd – students from the oud school on the square and others.

ZAMALEK & GEZIRA

Simonds CAFE
(Map p98; 112 Sharia 26th of Jul, Zamalek; coffees & pastries from E£7; ☺7am-10pm) The recent overhaul of this century-old French-style cafe has divided locals: some say it's been thoroughly sterilised, while others welcome the fresh coat of paint. Regardless, it's still a Cairene tradition to sit on a rickety chair and read the morning paper over a flaky, buttery pastry. Order and pay at the cash register, then take your ticket to the barista.

Arabica CAFE
(Map p98; 20 Sharia al-Marashly, Zamalek; cappuccino E£8, breakfast E£10-15, fiteer E£15-30; ☺10am-midnight) Funky and lived-in, this upstairs cafe hosts a young crowd who doodle on the

BALADI BAR CRAWL

Bar-hopping in Cairo typically takes you to Western-style lounges. But there's a parallel drinking culture in cheaper *baladi* (local) bars. These 'cafeterias', as they're often signed, have a slightly seedy, old-fashioned air. Renovations funded by beer company Stella have taken a layer of grime off a few, and now there's even an online guide at www. baladibar.com. Entrances are often hidden or screened off. Beers cost E£8 to E£12, and waiters expect tips. A few Downtown classics:

Cafeteria El Horreya (Map p64; Midan Falaki; ☺8am-2am) A Cairo institution, and quite wholesome as it's big, brightly lit and welcoming to women. No beer served on the side with the chessboards.

Cafeteria Stella (Map p64; cnr Sharia Hoda Shaarawi & Sharia Talaat Harb; ☺1pm-midnight) Ceilings are higher than the room is wide, with tables crammed with a mix of characters from afternoon on. Look for the entrance behind a kiosk. Free nibbles are served with beer.

Cap d'Or (Map p64; Sharia Abdel Khalek Sarwat) Quite run-down and lit with fluorescent bulbs. The staff are used to seeing foreigners, but usually male-only.

Cafeteria Port Tawfiq (Map p64; Midan Orabi) Tiny, dark and reasonably inviting.

Cairo (Map p64; 3 Sharia Saray al-Ezbekiyya) Walk through the grill restaurant to the 1st-floor bar. The sign is in Arabic only, blue letters on a red background.

Gemaica (Map p64; 16 Sharia Sherif) That's Egyptian for 'Jamaica'. In the pedestrian area around the stock exchange.

paper-topped tables. Unlike at slicker competitors, you can actually get some Egyptian food here along with your latte: fuul and *shakshuka* (scrambled eggs, peppers and tomatoes) for breakfast, and *fiteer* anytime.

Wel3a COFFEEHOUSE
(Map p98; 177 Sharia 26th of Jul, Zamalek; sheesha E£18-25, pot of tea E£22; ☺24hr) A very upmarket ahwa specialising in the finest sheesha tobacco, imported from Jordan, the Gulf and beyond. Nice selection of sandwiches and snacks too.

Sequoia LOUNGE
(Map p98; ☎2735 0014; www.sequoiaonline.net; 53 Sharia Abu al-Feda, Zamalek; beer E£28, cocktails E£20-40, mezze E£20-40, minimum Sun-Wed E£125, Thu-Sat E£150; ☺11am-1am) At the very northern tip of Zamalek, this sprawling Nileside lounge is a swank scene, with low cushions for nursing a sheesha, snacking on everything from Egyptian-style mezze to sushi and sipping a cocktail. We don't recommend it for main meals. Bring an extra layer – evenings right on the water can be surprisingly cool.

Garden Café CAFE
(Map p98; Cairo Marriott, 16 Sharia Saray al-Gezira, Zamalek; ☺6.30am-10pm) The Marriott's garden terrace is one of the most comfortable spots in town to relax over a drink. Big cane chairs, fresh air and good-quality wine and beer make it deservedly popular. The food is pricey and not very special.

La Bodega BAR
(Map p98; ☎2735 0543; 1st fl, Baehler's Mansions, 157 Sharia 26th of Jul, Zamalek; beer E£20, cocktails E£40; ☺noon-2am) This vast, amber-lit lounge doubles as a restaurant, but it's the long brass-top bar and original cocktails that garner most of the attention. The place draws Cairo celebs, who look gorgeous against the belle-époque backdrop. Reservations are recommended.

Deals BAR
(Map p98; 2 Sharia Sayyed al-Bakry, Zamalek; ☺4pm-2am) A small cellar bar that never looks open actually gets too packed for comfort late in the evening and at weekends. It's pleasant enough at quieter times.

Buddha Bar LOUNGE
(Map p102; Sofitel Gezira, Sharia al-Orman, Gezira; minimum E£250; ☺5pm-2am) The Cairo outpost of the world-famous Buddha Bar is where you can party with the beautiful people while sipping lychee martinis and listening to chill-out beats.

Drinkies LIQUOR STORE
(Map p98; ☎19330; 157 Sharia 26th of Jul, Zamalek) Cold beer and more.

☆ Entertainment

Cairenes thrive after sundown, so it's no surprise there's a lot of nightlife: clubs, lounges, a growing live-music scene and plenty of belly dancing. Not that you need to go inside – street life can be entertainment enough. See p63 for a suggested Downtown stroll, and also check out the Nile corniche downtown and Qasr el-Nil bridge.

Clubs & Live Music

Many venues are eclectic, changing musical styles and scenes every night. Many also start as restaurants and shift into club mode after midnight, at which point the door policy gets stricter. Big packs of men (and sometimes even single men) are always a no-no – go in as mixed a group if you can, and ideally make reservations.

Cairo Jazz Club   JAZZ, DJ
(Map p98; ☑3345 9939; www.cairojazzclub.com; 197 Sharia 26th of Jul, Agouza; ◑5pm-3am) The city's liveliest stage, with modern Egyptian folk, electronica, fusion and more seven nights a week, usually starting around 10pm. You must book a table ahead (online is easiest), and no one under 25 is admitted.

After Eight   JAZZ, DJ
(Map p64; ☑2574 0855, 0100 339 8000; www. after8cairo.com; 6 Sharia Qasr el-Nil, Downtown; minimum Wed-Sun E£60, Thu-Sat E£100; ◑8pm-4am) A funky, poorly ventilated venue that gets packed for everything from Nubian jazz to the wildly popular DJ Dina, who mixes James Brown, '70s Egyptian pop and the latest cab-driver favourites on Tuesdays; the clientele is equally eclectic. Reserve online (the website's style in no way reflects the club's).

Cairo Opera House   CLASSICAL MUSIC, JAZZ
(Map p102; ☑2739 0144; www.cairoopera.org; Gezira Exhibition Grounds) Performances by the Cairo Opera and the Cairo Symphony Orchestra are held in the 1,200-seat Main Hall, where jacket and tie are required for men (travellers have been known to borrow them from staff). The Small Hall is casual. Check the website for the schedule; note that some events are at a theatre near Abdeen Palace, or in Alexandria.

El Sawy Culture Wheel   JAZZ, PERFORMING ARTS
(El Sakia; Map p98; ☑2736 8881; www.culturewheel. com; Sharia 26th of Jul, Zamalek; ◑9am-9pm) The most popular young Egyptian rock and jazz bands play at this lively complex of a dozen performance spaces and galleries tucked under a bridge overpass. The main entrance is on the south side of 26th of July; there's a nice outdoor cafe by the Nile too.

El Genaina   CONCERT VENUE
(Map p82; ☑2362 5057; www.mawred.org; Sharia Salah Salem, Islamic Cairo) Al-Azhar Park's 300-seat open-air theatre hosts touring Western artists, stars from the Middle East and locals. Shows are often free (though you must pay the park entrance fee).

TOP CHOICE Makan   TRADITIONAL MUSIC
(off Map p64; ☑2792 0878; www.egyptmusic.org; 1 Sharia Saad Zaghloul, Mounira) The Egyptian Centre for Culture & Art runs this intimate space dedicated to folk music. Don't miss the traditional women's *zar*, a sort of musical trance and healing ritual (Wednesday, 9pm; E£20); Tuesday is usually Nass Makan, an Egyptian-Sudanese jam session. To find the space, walk south on Sharia Mansour.

FREE Al-Tannoura Egyptian Heritage Dance Troupe   TRADITIONAL MUSIC
(Map p78; ☑2512 1735; ◑8pm Mon, Wed & Sat) Egypt's only Sufi dance troupe – more raucous and colourful than white-clad Turkish dervishes – puts on a mesmerising performance at the Wikala of Al-Ghouri near Al-Azhar, and occasionally other venues. It's a great opportunity to see one of the medieval spaces in use; arrive about an hour ahead to secure a seat.

El Tanboura Hall   TRADITIONAL MUSIC
(Map p64; ☑2392 6768; www.elmastaba.org; 30A Sharia al-Balaqsa, Abdeen) Regular shows by Rango, a trance-y Sudanese folk group (Thursday, 9.30pm, E£20), and El Tanboura Band (Friday, 9.30pm, E£20), playing *simsimiyya*, a musical style from the Suez Canal region.

Tamarai   CLUB, LOUNGE
(☑2456 6666; www.tamarai-egypt.com; Nile City Towers, 2005C Corniche el-Nil; minimum E£250 Thu-Sat) Strawberry-guava martinis, gorgeous lighting, an edgy pharaonic-goes-industrial interior and even alleged Paris Hilton sightings have put this restaurant/lounge/dance palace at the top of the nightlife list. Seeing and being seen are top activities, but this is also the best house music in the city. Definitely book ahead. It's on the

east bank of the Nile, about even with the north end of Zamalek.

Club 35
CLUB, LOUNGE

(Map p102; ☑3573 8500; Four Seasons at the First Residence, 35 Sharia al-Giza, Giza; ☺7pm-3am) If you go before midnight, the place doesn't look all that promising, as it's still in soft-jazz Asian-fusion-bistro mode. But later, a mixed crowd packs in for dancing...even though there's no actual dance floor.

Belly Dancing

If you see only one belly dancer in your life, it had better be in Cairo, the art form's true home. The best dancers perform at Cairo's five-star hotels, usually to an adoring crowd of wealthy Gulf Arabs. Shows typically begin around midnight, although the star might not take to the stage until 2am or later. Admission is steep; expect to pay upwards of E£250, which includes food but not drinks. Cairo's divas are often getting in tiffs with their host hotels or their managers, so their venues may change from what's given below.

At the other end of the scale, you can watch a less nuanced expression of the art form for just a few pounds at several clubs around Sharia Alfy in Downtown. They're seedy (prostitution is definitely a sideline), the mikes are set on the highest reverb, and most of the dancers have the grace of amateur wrestlers. But it can be fun, especially if you can maintain enough of a buzz to join in the dancing onstage (a perk if you shower the dancer and the band with enough E£5 notes), but not so fun if you fall for the myriad overcharging tactics, such as fees for unordered snacks and even napkins (expect to pay about E£15 to E£20 for a Stella, after about E£5 to E£10 cover charge). As at the hotels, nothing happens till after midnight.

Haroun al-Rashid
CABARET

(Map p64; ☑2795 7171; Semiramis InterContinental, Corniche el-Nil, Garden City; ☺11pm-4am Tue-Thu & Sun) This old-fashioned-looking five-star club – all red curtains and white marquee lights – is where the famous Dina has been known to undulate.

TOP CHOICE Shahrazad
CABARET

(Map p64; 1 Sharia Alfy, Downtown; admission E£5) Worth visiting for the gorgeous interior alone, this old-school hall got a makeover in recent years, and its Orientalist fantasia, complete with red velvet drapes, feels substantially less seedy than other downtown dives. This doesn't necessarily inspire a classier air in the patrons, however. Occasionally the venue hosts a DJ night for an artier crowd.

Palmyra
CABARET

(Map p64; off Sharia 26th of Jul, Downtown) The furthest on the 'other end of the scale' is Palmyra, a cavernous, dilapidated 1950s dancehall in an alley off Sharia 26th of July. It has a full Arab musical contingent, belly dancers who get (marginally) better the more money is thrown at them, and an occasional singer or acrobat. In addition to a cover charge of E£6, there's a minimum of E£30, which basically covers a beer and a sheesha. It's in a courtyard behind shopfronts; once back there, go under the marquee marked 'Meame' (they mean Miami). Palmyra is on the left after the hotel; Miami bar is at the end.

Nile Maxim
CABARET, CRUISE

(Map p98; ☑2728 3000; opposite Cairo Marriott, Sharia Saray al-Gezira, Zamalek; minimum charge E£180; ☺sailings at 7.30pm & 10.45pm) The best of the Nile cruise boats, run by the Marriott, is a relatively economical way to see a big-name star such as Randa or Asmahan, along with an à la carte menu. Go for the later sailing, as the show is less rushed.

Arabesque
CLUB, LOUNGE

(Map p64; ☑2574 8677; www.arabesque-eg.com; 6 Qasr el-Nil, Downtown; ☺7pm-2am) Book in advance for a table late on Thursday or Friday, when a belly dancer performs. Other nights this upper-crust place segues from tasty restaurant to chilled-out club with a house-music soundtrack.

Cinema

Cairo is the centre of film production for the Middle East, so there's quite a lot on. Check listings in *Al-Ahram Weekly* or online at www.yallabina.com. Tickets typically cost around E£25 and can be cheaper at daytime sessions (when more women attend shows at the lower-rent places). Also check schedules at the many cultural centres (p116). The following regularly screen English-language films:

Cinema Metro
CINEMA

(Map p64; 35 Sharia Talaat Harb, Downtown) Once Cairo's finest, this 1930s palace has been spruced up enough to show 3D blockbuster movies.

CAIRO CRAFTS: WHAT & WHERE

In addition to shops, these are the best districts for certain goods.

Gold and silver Head to the gold district on the west end of Khan al-Khalili.

Backgammon and sheesha pipes Shops that stock ahwas line Sharia al-Muizz around Bein al-Qasreen. Another set of sheesha dealers are just east and west of Bab Zuweila.

Appliqué Best buys are at the Tentmakers Bazaar (Sharia al-Khayamiyya), south of Bab Zuweila.

Carpets The carpet bazaar south of the Mosque of al-Ghouri has imports; flat-weave Bedouin rugs are the only local style.

Spices Most dealers in the Khan are more trouble than they're worth. Try Abd al-Rahman Harraz or shops around Midan Falaki.

Perfume In addition to the southwest corner of Khan al-Khalili, try shops around Midan Falaki.

Inlay Artisans in Darb al-Ahmar sell out of their workshops.

Muski glass Available everywhere, but interesting to see the glassblowing studios in the district north of Bab al-Futuh.

Cinema Tahrir
CINEMA

(Map p102; ☎3335 4726; 122 Sharia Tahrir, Doqqi) Comfortable, modern cinema where single females shouldn't receive hassle.

Citystars Centre
CINEMA

(off Map p64; ☎2480 2013; Sharia Omar ibn Khattab, Nasr City) Megaplex at the mall.

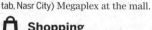

Shopping

Faced with the mountains of chintzy souvenirs and the over-eager hustlers trying to sell them to you over endless glasses of tea, it's tempting to keep your wallet firmly shut in Cairo. But then you'd be missing out on some of Egypt's most beautiful treasures. The trick is knowing where to look.

Though they're touristy and stocked with goods from China, the tiny shops of Khan al-Khalili do yield a few specific finds. Downtown along Sharia Qasr el-Nil has cheap, mass-market fashion. Sharia al-Marashly and Sharia Mansour Mohammed in Zamalek have some gem boutiques for housewares and clothing, and not all of them are as expensive as you'd expect. For everything else, head to Citystars, Cairo's best mall (p135).

DOWNTOWN & GARDEN CITY

Oum El Dounia
HANDICRAFTS

(Map p64; 1st fl, 3 Sharia Talaat Harb, Downtown; ☺10am-9pm) At a great central location, Oum El Dounia sells an exceptionally tasteful selection of locally made glassware, Bedouin jewellery, cotton clothes and other

interesting trinkets. Illustrated postcards by cartoonist Golo make a nice change. Not especially cheap, but very good work, and open every day of the year.

American University in
Cairo Bookstore
BOOKS

(Map p64; ☎2797 5370; Sharia Sheikh Rihan, Downtown; ☺10am-6pm Sat-Thu) The best English-language bookshop in Egypt, with two floors of material on the politics, sociology and history of Cairo, Egypt and the Middle East. Plenty of guidebooks and maps, and some fiction.

Wikalat al-Balah
CLOTHING, MARKET

(Souq Bulaq, Bulaq Market; off Map p64; north of Sharia 26th of Jul, Bulaq) This street market specialises in secondhand clothing, mostly well organised, clean and with marked prices (especially on Sharia al-Wabur al-Fransawi). It starts a few blocks west of the 6th of October overpass.

Sono Cairo
MUSIC

(Sawt al-Qahira; Map p64; Midan Opera, Downtown; ☺10am-11pm) In an arcade set back from Sharia al-Gomhurriya; stocks the classic Arab crooners on CD and cassette.

Ezbekiyya Book Market
BOOKS

(Map p64; Ezbekiyya Gardens, Downtown) The 50 or so stalls here yield occasional finds, and some stock fun gift items such as Arabic alphabet posters.

Lehnert & Landrock BOOKS
(Map p64; 44 Sharia Sherif, Downtown; ⏱10am-7pm Mon-Sat) Old maps, books about Cairo and Egypt (some secondhand), vintage postcards and reprints of old photographs.

Kartmo SOUVENIRS
(Map p64; 13 Sharia Mahmoud Bassiouni, Downtown) In the passage cutting through to Sharia Qasr el-Nil, this enamel-sign maker sells snazzy 'Midan Tahrir' street plaques for E£200 – a nice revolutionary souvenir. You can also order custom designs, which take about a week.

Leather Home SHOES
(Map p64; Semiramis Inter-Continental, Corniche el-Nil, Garden City) For emergency sandals, or even something longer-wearing, the Egypt-made men's and women's shoes here are fairly priced.

COPTIC CAIRO

Souq al-Fustat HANDICRAFTS, MARKET
(Map p72; Sharia Mar Girgis, Old Cairo; ⏱8am-4pm) A new market built for tourists, this is nonetheless a nice collection of shops, with respectable vendors of antique carpets, modern ceramics, spices, richly embroidered *galabiyyas* and wooden toys along with a branch of Abd El Zaher. Prices are marked (though occasionally negotiable), and sales pressure is pleasantly low.

ISLAMIC CAIRO

TOP CHOICE **Abd El Zaher** GIFTS
(Map p78; 31 Sharia Mohammed Abduh; ⏱9am-11pm) Cairo's last working bookbinder also makes beautiful leather- and oil-paper-bound blank books, photo albums and diaries. Gold monogramming is included in the prices, which are heartbreakingly low considering the work that goes into them. Getting your own books bound starts around E£15 and takes a few days.

Abd al-Rahman Harraz FOOD
(off Map p82; 1 Midan Bab al-Khalq; ⏱10am-10pm) Established 1885, this is one of the most esteemed spice traders in Cairo, with a brisk business in medicinal herbs as well (upstairs, herbalists diagnose and prescribe). There's no English sign: look for dioramas of Egyptian village life in the corner shop windows. It's about 450m west of Bab Zuweila, and a couple blocks east of the Museum of Islamic Art.

Souq al-Gomaa MARKET
(Friday Market; Southern Cemetery; ⏱6am-noon Fri) South of the Citadel, this sprawling weekly market is all the craziness of a medieval bazaar in a modern setting: under a highway flyover, expect new bicycles, live donkeys, toilets and broken telephones. Savvy pickers can find some great antiques and vintage clothes. Go before 10am to avoid the overwhelming crush of people. Tell the taxi driver 'Khalifa', the name of the neighbourhood.

Atlas CLOTHING, HANDICRAFTS
(Map p78; Sikket al-Badistan) In business since 1948, the Atlas family specialises in silk kaftans and slippers. You can also order the fabric by the yard, or in custom-tailored clothing.

Khan Misr Touloun HANDICRAFTS
(Map p87; Midan ibn Tulun; ⏱10am-5pm Mon-Sat) This shop opposite the Mosque of Ibn Tulun is stacked with a desirable jumble of reasonably priced wooden chests, jewellery, pottery, puppets and scarves. Closes for vacation in August.

Mahmoud Abd El Ghaffar ACCESSORIES
(Al Wikalah; Map p78; 73 Sharia Gawhar al-Qaid; ⏱11am-11pm) One of the best dealers in belly-dancing outfits in the city; the really nice stuff is upstairs. Look for the entrance at the end of a short lane just off the main street.

Karama BEAUTY
(Map p78; 112 Sharia al-Azhar) Very popular with Cairenes for scent copies as well as its own blends and basic essences; look for the open-sided corner shop at the corner of Sharia al-Muizz.

ZAMALEK

TOP CHOICE **Fair Trade Egypt** HANDICRAFTS
(Map p98; 1st fl, 27 Sharia Yehia Ibrahim; ⏱9am-8pm Sat-Thu, 10am-6pm Fri) Crafts sold here are produced in income-generating projects throughout the country. Items for sale include Bedouin rugs, hand-woven cotton, pottery from Al-Fayoum and beaded jewellery from Aswan. The cotton bedcovers and shawls are particularly lovely, and prices are very reasonable.

Nomad HANDICRAFTS, JEWELLERY
(Map p98; 1st fl, 14 Sharia Saray al-Gezira; ⏱9am-8pm) Specialists in jewellery and traditional Bedouin crafts and costumes. Items include appliqué tablecloths and cushion covers, dresses made in the oases, woven baskets,

ANTIQUES ROADSHOW: CAIRO EDITION

Evidence of Cairo's glam years can be found in dusty warehouses and glittery shops. These are some of the best.

Ahmed El Dabba & Sons (Map p78; 5 Sikket al-Badistan, Islamic Cairo) The most respected antiques dealer in Khan al-Khalili, filled with Louis XV furniture, jewellery and snuff boxes.

Amgad Naguib (☎0128 668 0908) Make an appointment to visit Amgad's dusty treasure house Downtown. Along with vintage sunglasses, movie posters and groovy glass, you get some great stories.

Kerop (Map p64; 116 Mohammed Farid, Downtown; ⊙9am–1pm Mon–Fri) Vintage Cairo photos, from original plates, in a time-warp office.

King Saleh Bazaar (Map p76; 80 Sharia al-Muizz li-Din Allah, Islamic Cairo) Immediately south of the Madrassa & Mausoleum of Qalaun. The more you look through the dust, the more pops out.

Nostalgia (Map p98; 6 Sharia Zakaria Rizk, Zamalek) From framed Arabic ad prints to escargot forks.

L'Orientaliste (Map p64; 15 Sharia Qasr el-Nil, Downtown; ⊙10am-8pm Mon-Sat, 10am-5pm Sun) FInd rare books on Egypt and the Middle East, as well as lithographs, maps and engravings.

---

silk slippers and chunky silver jewellery. To find it, go past the Egyptian Water Works office to the 1st floor and ring the bell. There is a smaller branch in the Cairo Marriott (Map p98).

Diwan BOOKS, MUSIC
(Map p98; ☎2736 2578; 159 Sharia 26th of Jul; ⊙9am-11.30pm) Fabulous: English, French and German titles, from novels to travel guides to coffee-table books. It also has a kids' section, a large music wing and a small cafe.

Sami Amin ACCESSORIES, HOMEWARES
(Map p98; 15A Sharia Mansour Mohammed; ⊙10.30am-10pm Mon-Sat) Cool chunky brass-and-enamel jewellery as well as various leather goods for the home. Just down the street, at number 13, are leather bags, belts and other accessories, many imprinted with tribal patterns, and all very well priced.

Balady HANDICRAFTS
(Map p98; 13 Sharia Mansour Mohammed; ⊙10.30am-10pm) Great assortment of hip gift items: Umm Kolthum laptop cases, handmade soaps, good-quality essential oils.

Home & Beyond HOMEWARES, BEAUTY
(Map p98; 17 Sharia Mansour Mohammed) Stocks Arabic house-number tiles, striped lamp-

shades and blocks of fragrant *ambar* – a musky moisturizer.

Loft ANTIQUES, HOMEWARES
(Map p98; 1st fl, 12 Sharia Sayyed al-Bakry; ⊙10am-10pm Mon-Sat) In a rambling apartment, this eclectic store stocks local regional curiosities from small brass candlesticks to antique divans, as well as large painted tabletop trays as seen in chic restaurants around town. On Friday, they serve free tea and crepes.

Mobaco CLOTHING
(Map p98; 8 Sharia Ahmed Sabry) Sporty designs, inexpensive and with a great range of colours. There's always a flattering long skirt available, and men can choose from a rainbow of polo shirts sporting a camel logo. There are stores throughout the city, including at the Semiramis Intercontinental (Map p64).

Dina Maghawry JEWELLERY
(Map p98; 2nd fl, 16 Sharia Sayyed al-Bakry; ⊙11am-9pm Sat-Thu) Delicate cascading necklaces trimmed with semiprecious stones and other elegant but modern pieces. Not cheap, but gorgeous work.

Mix & Match CLOTHING
(Map p98; 11 Sharia Brazil; ⊙10am-8pm) Well made and locally designed, these separates for women in wool, silk and cotton are reasonably priced and often feature subtle Middle

Eastern details. A branch two blocks south, at 11 Sharia Hassan Sabry, stocks larger sizes.

Wady Craft Shop
HANDICRAFTS

(Map p98; 5 Sharia Michel Lutfallah; ⏱9am-1pm & 2-5pm) This charity store run by the Anglican church sells work done by refugee organisations: cotton bags, aprons, tablecloths, inlay coasters and silk-screened tea towels. Enter the church complex on Michel Lutfallah, and head to the northeast corner.

Mounaya Gallery
HOMEWARES, CLOTHING

(Map p98; 1st fl, 14 Sharia Montazah; ⏱11am-8pm Mon-Thu & Sat, noon-8pm Fri; ⏱11am-8pm Sat-Thu, noon-8pm Fri) Chic Cairene couples do their wedding registries at this swank shop. Buy goods like gorgeous embroidered bed linens and robes from Malaika – an exception to the general rule that little Egyptian cotton is turned into quality products domestically.

DOQQI

Nagada
CLOTHING, CERAMICS

(Map p102; www.nagada.net; 13 Sharia Refa'a; ⏱10am-6.30pm) Handwoven, colour-saturated silks, cottons and linens are the mainstay of this luxe shop. Buy by the yard, or in boxy, drapey women's and men's apparel. There's also very pretty pottery from Al-Fayoum.

ℹ Information

Cultural Centres

British Council & Library (www.britishcouncil.org.eg) Agouza (Map p98; ☎3300 1666; 192 Sharia el-Nil; ⏱8am-8pm); Heliopolis (☎19789; 4 Sharia el-Minia, off Sharia Nazih Khalifa; ⏱9am-7pm Sat-Thu) Organises performances, exhibitions and talks and has a useful library.

Centre Français de Culture et de Coopéra-tion Heliopolis (☎2419 3857; 5 Sharia Shafik al-Dib, Ard al-Golf; ⏱10am-10pm Sun-Thu); Mounira (☎2794 7679; 1 Sharia Madrassat al-Huquq al-Fransiyya; ⏱11am-7pm Sun-Tue, Thu & Fri, 11am-8pm Wed; Ⓜ Saad Zaghloul) Regular films, lectures and exhibitions.

Goethe Institut (www.goethe.de) Doqqi (Map p102; ☎3748 4501; 13 Sharia Hussein Wassef); Downtown (Map p64; ☎2575 9877; 5 Sharia al-Bustan; ⏱library 1-7pm Sun-Wed) Seminars and lectures in German on Egyptology and other topics, plus visiting music groups, art exhibitions and film screenings. The library has more than 15,000 (mainly German) titles. The Doqqi location focuses on language classes.

Instituto Cervantes (Map p102; ☎3760 1746; www.elcairo.cervantes.es; 20 Sharia Boulos Hanna, Doqqi; ⏱9am-4pm Sun-Thu) Spanish language and cultural institute, screening films and organising lectures.

Istituto Italiano di Cultura (Map p98; ☎2735 8791; www.iiccairo.esteri.it; 3 Sharia Sheikh al-Marsafy, Zamalek; ⏱library 10am-4pm Sun, Tue & Thu) A busy program of films and lectures (sometimes in English) and art exhibitions, plus a library.

Netherlands-Flemish Institute (NVIC; Map p98; ☎2738 2520; www.nvic.leidenuniv.nl; 1 Sharia Mahmoud Azmy, Zamalek; ⏱9am-2pm Sun-Thu) This centre hosts art exhibitions and

---

SHARP DRESSED: CUSTOM TAILORS

With cheap, skilled labor at hand, Cairo is a good place to get a bespoke suit. Bring magazine clips of looks you like, as local tailors aren't always up on trends. You may also need to bring your own fabric (at least 3m for a jacket and a pair of pants, plus another metre for extra pants). The best material is at Salem, listed below; cheaper shops on Midan Opera sell Egyptian-made textiles. Allow a week, plus another day for final adjustments.

Samir El Sakka (Map p64; 31 Sharia Abdel Khalek Sarwat, Downtown; ⏱10am-1.30pm & 5.30-8.30pm Mon-Fri) This old-school tailor trained in Rome; he stocks a small selection of fabrics. Suit prices start around E£1000.

Orange Square (Map p98; 4A Sharia Ibn al-Nabieh, Zamalek; ⏱noon-8pm) With books to select designs from and a decent stock of fabric, this trendy operation is the easiest place to get a suit made. But it's not the cheapest: suits start at E£1500; shirts at E£450.

Osman Ahmed (Map p64; ☎0122 331 8622; 18 Sharia Adly, Downtown; ⏱10am-2pm, 4-8pm Mon-Sat) As he doesn't speak English or stock fabrics, Mr Ahmed is the least convenient option, but his skills transcend the language barrier. He's used to foreign customers, and can work off a magazine photo.

Salem (off Map p98; ☎3345 2232; 30 Sharia Libnan, Mohandiseen; ⏱11am-6pm) The finest suit fabrics from England and Italy are available here.

is well regarded for its weekly lectures and film series, almost always in English.

Dangers & Annoyances

Despite a rise in petty crime following the 2011 revolution, Cairo is still a very safe city, with crime rates likely much lower than where you're visiting from. You can safely walk around just about any neighbourhood until at least 1am or 2am.

THEFT There have been incidents of bag theft; see p515. Pickpockets are rare, but do sometimes operate in crowded spots such as Khan al-Khalili, the metro and buses. If anything does get stolen go straight to the tourist police.

BOGUS TOURS Cairo's worst scams are associated with tours. Rather than making arrangements in Cairo, you are almost always better off booking tours in the place you'll be taking them. Stick with reputable agencies. Even your hotel is not a good place to book anything but typical day-trips from Cairo. Never book with a random office Downtown (many are fronts) or with the help of someone you meet on the street.

STREET HASSLE Contrary to media reports, women are generally safe walking alone in Cairo. After about 11pm, however, it's preferable to have some male accompaniment, and at all times avoid the cheapest buses (notorious for frottage, to female commuters' chagrin) and large groups of aimless men: political demonstrations and any kind of football-related celebration can bring out the testosterone. Also be a bit wary of men (or boys) who want to escort you across a street – it's a prime groping opportunity.

Emergency

In case of an accident or injury, call the As-Salam International Hospital (p117). For anything more serious, contact your embassy (see p510).

Ambulance (☏123)

Fire service (☏180)

Police (☏122)

Tourist police (☏126)

The **main tourist police office** (Map p64; ☏2390 6028; Sharia Alfy) is on the 1st floor of a building in the alley just left of the main tourist office in Downtown. Come here first for minor emergencies, including theft; there are other offices by the Pyramids, across from Mena House (Map p126) and in Khan al-Khalili (Map p78).

Internet Access

The most conveniently located, all charging about E£5 per hour:

Concord (Map p64; 28 Sharia Mohammed Mahmoud, Downtown; ⊙10am-2am) Handy for southern Downtown.

InterClub (Map p64; 12 Sharia Talaat Harb, Downtown; ⊙8am-2am) Printing, faxing and scanning services; in alley next to Estoril restaurant.

Intr@net (Map p64; 1st fl, 36 Sharia Sherif, Downtown; ⊙24hr) Full service; walk back into the shopping arcade and upstairs.

Sigma Net (Map p98; Sharia Gezirat al-Wusta, Zamalek; ⊙24hr) Opposite Golden Tulip Flamenco Hotel. Good air-con.

Zamalek Center (Map p98; 25 Sharia Ismail Mohammed, Zamalek; ⊙24hr) Best rates in the area; other business services too.

Media

NEWS-STANDS One on the corner of Sharia 26th of July and Hassan Sabry in Zamalek (Map p98) has by far the best stock. All the major hotels have decent shops.

Medical Services

HOSPITALS Many of Cairo's hospitals suffer from antiquated equipment and a cavalier attitude to hygiene, but there are several exceptions. Your embassy should be able to recommend doctors and hospitals. Other options:

As-Salam International Hospital (☏2524 0250, emergency 19885; www.assih.com; Corniche el-Nil, Ma'adi) In the southern suburb of Ma'adi.

Badran Hospital (off Map p102; ☏3337 8823; www.badranhospital.com; 3 Sharia al-Ahrar, Doqqi) Just northwest of 6th of October in Doqqi.

PHARMACIES These pharmacies operate 24 hours, have English-speaking staff and will deliver to your hotel.

Al-Ezaby (Map p98; ☏19600; 46 Sharia Bahgat Ali, Zamalek)

Ali & Ali Downtown (☏2365 3880); Mohandiseen (☏3302 1421) Delivery-only.

Delmar (Map p64; ☏2575 1052; cnr Sharia 26th of Jul & Sharia Mohammed Farid, Downtown)

New Victoria Pharmacy (Map p98; ☏2735 1628; 6 Sharia Brazil, Zamalek)

Seif Pharmacy (☏19199)

Money

For general information about money, see p513. For banking hours, see p510. Hotel bank branches can change cash, but rates are slightly better at independent exchange bureaus, of which there are several along Sharia Adly in Downtown and on Sharia 26th of July in Zamalek. These tend to be open from 10am to 8pm Saturday to Thursday. ATMs are numerous, except in Islamic Cairo – the most convenient machine here is below El Hussein hotel (Map p78) in Khan al-Khalili.

American Express (Amex; www.americanexpress.com.eg; ⊙9am-3pm Sat-Thu) Downtown (Map

BUSES FROM CAIRO GATEWAY

DESTINATION	COMPANY	PRICE	DURATION	TIMES
Alexandria	West & Mid Delta	E£30	3hr	Hourly 4.45am–1.15am
Al-Arish	East Delta	E£30–35	5hr	7.30am, 4pm
Al-Kharga	Upper Egypt Travel	E£65	8–10hr	9.30pm, 10.30pm
Al-Quseir	Upper Egypt Travel	E£60–80	10hr	6.30am, 11pm, 1.30am
Bahariya (Bawiti)	Upper Egypt Travel	E£30	4–5hr	7am, 8am
Dahab	East Delta	E£90	9hr	8am, 1.30pm, 7.30pm, 11.45pm
Dakhla	Upper Egypt Travel	E£75	8–10hr	7.30pm, 8.30pm
Farafra	Upper Egypt Travel	E£45	8–10hr	7am, 8am
Hurghada	SuperJet	E£65	6hr	7.30am, 2.30pm, 11.10pm
Ismailia	East Delta	E£15	4hr	Every 30min 6am-7pm
Luxor	Upper Egypt Travel	E£100	11hr	9pm
Marsa Matruh	West & Mid Delta	E£60–70	5hr	6.45am, 8.45am, 11am, 4.30pm, 7.45pm, 10pm, 11.30pm
Port Said	East Delta	E£20–25	4hr	Hourly 6.30am–9.30pm
Sharm	East Delta	E£60–80	7hr	6.30am, 10.30am, 4.30pm, 11pm, 1am
Sharm	SuperJet	E£85	7hr	7.30am, 1.15pm, 10.45pm
Siwa	West Delta	E£70	11hr	7.45pm, 11.30pm
St. Katherine's	East Delta	E£50	7hr	11am
Suez	East Delta	E£15–20	2hr	Every 30min 6am–7pm
Taba & Nuweiba	East Delta	E£60–100	8hr	6am, 9.30am, 11.30pm

p64; ☑2574 7991; 15 Sharia Qasr el-Nil); Heliopolis (☑2480 1530; Citystars Centre)

Citibank (☑16644; www.citibankegypt.com; ☺8.30am-5pm Sun-Thu) Garden City (Map p102; ☑2795 1873; 4 Sharia Ahmad Pasha); Zamalek (Map p98; ☑2736 5622; 4A Sharia al-Gezira)

Thomas Cook (☑emergency 0100 140 1367; www.thomascookegypt.com; ☺8am-4.30pm Sat-Thu) Airport (☑2265 4447); Downtown (Map p64; ☑2574 3776; 17 Sharia Mahmoud Bassiouni); Heliopolis (Map p134; ☑2416 4000; 7 Sharia Baghdad, Korba); Heliopolis (☑0122 773 4609; Sheraton Heliopolis, 1229 Sharia al-Sheikh Ali Gad al-Haqq); Mohandiseen (Map p98; ☎3344 0008; 10 Sharia 26th of Jul); Zamalek (Map p98; ☎2696 2101; 3A Sharia Ismail Mohammed)

Post

Marked with green-and-yellow signs, post offices are numerous, though not all have signs in English explaining which window is meant for what business.

Main post office (Map p64; Midan Ataba; ⊙9am-6pm Sat-Thu) Stamps and letters at front entrance; parcels at the back entrance.

Poste restante and parcels (Map p64; ⊙9am-2pm Sat-Thu) On the back end of the main post office. Mail is held for three weeks; take your passport. For parcels, leave your package unsealed for inspection; the staff will tape it up. Boxes are for sale; rates for slowest service are E£150 for the first kilo, E£40 for each thereafter.

Post traffic centre (Map p69; Midan Ramses; ⊙9am-2pm Sat-Thu) Another place to mail packages.

Express mail (EMS; Map p64; ⊙24hr) The main office is near the Ataba central office.

Telephone

Telephone centrales Downtown (Map p64; fax 2578 0979; 13 Midan Tahrir; ⊙24hr); Downtown (Map p64; fax 2393 3903; 8 Sharia Adly; ⊙24hr); Downtown (Map p64; fax 2589 7635; Sharia Alfy; ⊙24hr); Downtown (Map p64; Sharia Tahrir; ⊙24hr); Zamalek (Map p98; Sharia 26th of Jul)

Toilets

Clean toilets in Cairo are a bit hard to come by, though most large museums and monuments have passable facilities. In Khan al-Khalili, head for the Naguib Mahfouz restaurant. You can also nip in to fast-food places like Gad, where the toilets usually have an attendant; tip E£1 or E£2.

Tourist Information

Ministry of Tourism Downtown (Map p64; ☎2391 3454; 5 Sharia Adly; ⊙9am-6pm); Pyramids (Map p126; ☎3383 8823; Pyramids Rd; ⊙8.30am-5pm) Opposite Mena House Oberoi; Ramses Station (Map p120; ☎2492 5985; ⊙9am-7pm).

Travel Agencies

The streets around Midan Tahrir teem with travel agencies, but watch out for dodgy operators (see p117). Along with Amex and Thomas Cook (see p117), these are reliable:

Backpacker Concierge (☎0106 350 7118; www.backpackerconcierge.com) Culturally and environmentally responsible desert trips and Nile cruises, plus more focused custom trips such as food tours. No walk-in office, but can

BUS STATION SNACK

If you're just passing through Cairo Gateway bus station and need a meal, take a short walk to **Hamada** (Sharia al-Sahafa; kushari from E£3) for exceptionally good *kushari*. Turn right out the front of the bus station, then make a left at the first intersection; Hamada is on the right, midway down, with a red sign.

communicate via phone, email, Facebook and Twitter.

Egypt Panorama Tours (☎2359 0200; www.eptours.com; 4 Rd 79, Ma'adi; ⊙9am-5pm) Opposite Ma'adi metro station, this is one of the best-established agencies in town. It will book tickets, tours and hotel rooms and courier the documents to you, if necessary. It's good for four- and five-star hotel deals and tours within Egypt and around the Mediterranean. Note that separate departments handle flights and excursions.

Lovely Bazaar (Map p98; ☎2737 0223, 0111 861 2219; www.egyptbargaintours.com; Sharia Gezirat al-Wusta, Zamalek) Ibrahim's bargain tours in Cairo and beyond come recommended by travellers.

Misr Travel (Map p64; ☎2393 0010; www.misrtravel.net; 1 Sharia Talaat Harb, Downtown) The official Egyptian government travel agency, which also has offices in most of the luxury hotels.

Getting There & Away

Air

For international and domestic airfares, see the Transport chapter (p521).

CAIRO INTERNATIONAL AIRPORT For information on the airport see p121. For flight information call ☎0900 77777 from a landline in Egypt or ☎27777 from a mobile phone.

EGYPTAIR OFFICES Airport Terminal 3 (☎2696 6798); Downtown (Map p64; ☎2393 0381; cnr Sharia Talaat Harb & Sharia al-Bustan); Downtown (Map p64; ☎2392 7680; 6 Sharia Adly)

Bus

The main bus station, for all destinations in the Suez Canal area, Sinai, the deserts, Alexandria and Upper Egypt, is **Cairo Gateway** (Map p60; Mina al-Qahira, Turgoman Garage; Sharia al-Gisr, Bulaq; MOrabi), 400m west of the Orabi metro stop.

Tickets are sold at different windows according to company and destination. Suez and Sinai tickets are to the right; Alexandria and towns in Upper Egypt to the left. It is advisable to book most tickets in advance, particularly for popular routes such as Sinai, Alexandria and Marsa Matruh in summer. Companies don't offer student discounts. Companies operating here are **East Delta Travel Co** (☏3262 3128) for Suez and the Sinai; **West & Mid Delta Bus Co** (☏2432 0049) for Alexandria, Marsa Matruh and Siwa; **Super Jet** (☏2290 9017) for some Sinai resort towns; and **Upper Egypt Travel Co** (☏2576 0261) to Western Desert oases and Luxor (though for the latter, the train is better). For information about buses to Libya, Israel and Jordan see p522.

A few smaller bus stations run more frequent service. Head here if the Cairo Gateway departure times aren't ideal.

Abbassiyya (Sinai Station; Sharia Ramses, Abbassiyya; Ⓜ Abbassiyya) A few buses from Sinai still terminate here, 4km northeast of Ramses; take the nearby metro to the centre.

Abboud (Khazindar; Sharia al-Tir'a al-Boulaqia, Shubra; Ⓜ Mezallat) Services to the Delta and Wadi al-Natrun, 5km north of Ramses. Walk east from metro, about 800m.

Al-Mazah (Sharia Abou Bakr al-Siddiq, Heliopolis) Some international services, 3.5km northwest from the Korba area of Heliopolis; take a taxi.

Ulali (Map p69; Sharia Shurta al-Ezbekiyya, Ramses; Ⓜ Al-Shohadaa) No bus-station structure, just a ticket window for East Delta services to Tanta, Zagazig and canal zone cities, and summer departures for Sinai, plus plenty of microbuses.

Microbus & Servees

You can get a seat in a shared van or taxi to most destinations from the blocks between Ramses Station and Midan Ulali (see Map p69).

For al-Fayoum and the western oases, head to Moneib, on Sharia el-Nil in Giza, under the ring road overpass (take a taxi or walk 800m east from the Sakkiat Mekki metro stop). Midan al-Remaya in Giza, near the Pyramids, is another starting pointing for al-Fayoum and western Delta town; hop on a microbus from the Giza metro station. For details, see specific destinations chapters.

Train

Trains to Alexandria, Upper Egypt and major towns in the Delta are the most efficient and comfortable. Train travel to smaller towns is recommended for rail-fans only, as it's often quite slow and scruffy. **Ramses Station** (Mahattat Ramses; ☏2575 3555; Midan Ramses) is Cairo's main train station. It was under renovation at the time of research, but should have a **left luggage office** (per piece per day E£2.50; ⊙24hr), a **post office** (⊙8am-8pm), ATMs and a **tourist information office** (⊙9am-7pm).

Secondary stations include Giza (Map p60), for the sleeper to Upper Egypt; Giza Suburban (Map p60), next to the metro stop of the same name, for Al-Fayoum; and Ain Shams, in the northeast part of the city, for Suez.

For general details about the types of trains and tickets, see p528. For first-class services, visit www.enr.gov.eg, where you can check schedules and purchase first-class tickets for trains on the main Alexandria–Aswan line. Purchasing tickets at Ramses requires getting to the right set of windows for your destination and knowing the time and/or train number you want. Confirm at the information desk, where the clerk can write your preference in Arabic to show the ticket seller.

ALEXANDRIA The best trains are the Special and Spanish trains, which make fewer stops than the French ones. First class (ula) gets you

Ramses Station

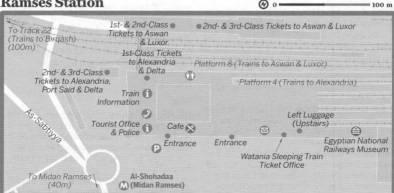

◉ 0 ————— 100 m

- To Track 22 (Trains to Birqash) (100m)
- 1st- & 2nd-Class Tickets to Aswan & Luxor
- 2nd- & 3rd-Class Tickets to Aswan & Luxor
- 1st-Class Tickets to Alexandria & Delta
- Platform 8 (Trains to Aswan & Luxor)
- 2nd- & 3rd-Class Tickets to Alexandria, Port Said & Delta
- Platform 4 (Trains to Alexandria)
- Train ℹ Information
- Tourist Office & Police ℹ
- Cafe ✕
- Left Luggage (Upstairs)
- Entrance
- Entrance
- Egyptian National Railways Museum
- Watania Sleeping Train Ticket Office
- As-Sabtiyya
- To Midan Ramses (40m)
- Al-Shohadaa Ⓜ (Midan Ramses)

MAJOR TRAINS FROM CAIRO

Prices are for first-class service, all with air-con, unless otherwise noted.

DESTINATION	STATION	PRICE	DURATION	TIMES
Alexandria (direct)	Ramses	E£50	2½hr	8am, 9am, 11am, noon, 2pm, 6pm, 7pm, 9pm, 10.30pm
Alexandria (stopping)	Ramses	E£35	3–3½hr	8 daily, 6am–8.15pm
Aswan	Ramses	E£109	14hr	8am, noon, 7pm, 8pm, 1am
Ismailia	Ramses	E£15	3hr	6.15am, 1pm, 1.45pm, 2.45pm, 5.45pm, 7.50pm, 10pm
Luxor & Aswan (sleeper)	Giza	US$60/E£360	9½hr (Luxor), 13hr (Aswan)	8pm, 8.40pm
Luxor	Ramses	E£90	10½hr	8am, noon, 7pm, 8pm, 1am
Marsa Matruh (sleeper)	Giza	US$43/E£252	7hr	11pm Sat, Mon, Wed, mid-Jun–mid-Sep
Port Said	Ramses	E£21	4hr	6.15am, 1.45pm, 7.50pm
Suez (2nd class, fan only)	Ain Shams	E£15–18	2¼hr	6.15am, 9.20am, 1.10pm, 4.15pm, 6.45pm, 9.45pm
Tanta	Ramses	E£35–50	1–1½hr	6am, 8.15am, 10am, 11am, noon, 2.10pm, 3.10pm, 4pm, 5.15pm
Zagazig	Ramses	E£15	1½hr	5.15am, 6.15am, 1pm, 1.45pm, 3.40pm, 7.50pm, 10pm

a roomier, assigned seat and usually a much cleaner bathroom.

LUXOR & ASWAN Tourists used to be restricted to travelling on only a few trains to Upper Egypt, but this appears to have been lifted. If you do encounter a desk clerk who does not want to sell you a ticket, you can always purchase a ticket on board from the conductor, for a small additional fee, or in advance online.

The overnight wagon-lits service to Luxor and Aswan is operated by a private company, **Watania** ([☎]3748 9488; www.wataniasleepingtrains. com). You can purchase tickets at the point of departure, Giza Station (Map p60), in the trailer to the right of the entrance, or at Ramses in the larger **sleeping train ticket office** (Map p120; [⏰]9am-8pm), which keeps longer hours and can take credit cards (for a surcharge), as well as cash in euros, dollars or Egyptian pounds. Book

before 6pm for the same day, but in high season (October to April), book several days in advance.

MARSA MATRUH Watania runs a train to the Mediterranean coast three times a week during the summer season.

SUEZ CANAL Delays on this route are common; going by bus is more efficient. If you're determined to travel by train, the best option is to Ismailia.

 Getting Around

To/From the Airport

Cairo International Airport (www.cairo-airport. com) is 20km northeast of the centre. The terminology is a bit confusing: **Terminal 1** ([☎]2265 5000) is three buildings, all within view of each other, though only arrival halls 1 and 3 receive commercial flights. Opened in 2009, **Terminal 3**

(al-Matar al-Gideed; ☎ 2266 0508) is 2km south. Terminal 2 is being renovated, slated for completion in late 2013. A blue-and-white shuttle bus connects Terminals 1 and 3, though a shuttle train (called the APM) was scheduled to go into service soon after this book went to print.

There's no left-luggage service, but there is free wi-fi. You can pick up a SIM card in Terminal 3 at the Vodafone kiosk, or inside the convenience store, both to the far right as you come out of customs.

BUS Don't believe anyone who tells you there is no bus to the city centre. Air-con bus 27 or 356 (E£2, plus E£1 per large luggage item, one hour) runs at 20-minute intervals from 7am to midnight between Midan Abdel Moniem Riad (behind the Egyptian Museum) in central Cairo and the airport. After hours, the only option is bus 400 (50pt). Minibus 324 (50pt) goes to Midan Ramses. And, should you need them, buses depart for Alexandria hourly (E£35 to E£42, 4hr).

Blue shuttle buses connect air terminals and the bus station. At Terminal 1, arrivals 1, the shuttle stops in the first lane of the car park, a little to your right as you come out the doors. In arrivals 3, bear left outside – the shuttle stops in the outer lane, under the skybridge to the Air Mall. The shuttle stops across the road from the bus complex just after you turn right at the petrol station. In Terminal 3, bear right out the doors, to the far end of the outer lane. From here, the shuttle drives straight into the bus terminal.

TAXI The going rate to central Cairo is about E£75; metered cabs (p124) are seldom seen at this end, so you'll need to negotiate with one of the mob of drivers clustered around the door when you exit. It's better to get away a bit before starting negotiations, as just walking can some-times bring the price down. Triple-check the agreed fare, as there is an irritating tendency for drivers to nod at what you say and claim a higher fare later. (Heading to the airport from the centre, you can easily get a meter taxi; you'll have to pay E£5 to enter the airport grounds.)

For a smoother arrival, arrange a car through your hotel, or call **Cairo Airport Shuttle Bus** (☎ 0128 911 1777; www.cairoshuttlebus. com; E£100 to Downtown), which runs small vans and has a desk at Terminal 1, arrivals 1 (though it can pick you up anywhere). In Terminal 1, arrivals 3, at the car-rental desk in the centre, **Star Choice** (☎ 0100 313 0020) offers rides for E£110. In Terminal 3, look for the limo desk to the right, near the convenience store; the companies here typically charge E£100.

In the traffic-free early hours of the morning, the journey to central Cairo takes 20 minutes. At busier times of the day it can take more than an hour.

METRO Perhaps during the life of this book, the metro line between the airport and central Cairo will open, but don't hold your breath.

Bus & Minibus

Cairo is thoroughly served by a network of lumbering sardine-cans-on-wheels and smaller, shuttle-size minibuses (on which, theoretically, there's no standing allowed), but visitors will find only a few uses for them: they're good for a slow but cheap trip to the Pyramids or from the airport, but elsewhere you can travel more efficiently and comfortably by metro and/or taxi. Signs are in Arabic only, so you'll have to know your numerals. There is no known map of any of the city's bus routes. Just hop on and pay the conductor when he comes around selling tickets, which cost between 50pt and E£2 depending on distance and whether there's air-con

CAIRO AIRPORT TERMINALS AND AIRLINES

TERMINAL	AIRLINES	SERVICES
Terminal 1, Arrivals 1	Al-Masria, British Airways, Emirates, Etihad, Kenya, Nile Air, Qatar, Royal Air Maroc, Sudan, Yemenia	ATM before immigration and to right just before exit doors; shuttle service to right after customs
Terminal 1, Arrivals 3	Alitalia, Air France, Delta, Eritrean, Ethiopian, KLM, Kuwait Airlines, Middle East Airlines, Oman Air, Royal Jordanian, Saudi Arabia	ATM to left; info desk to right; limo service straight ahead
Terminal 3	Aegean, Austrian, BMI, Egypt Air (domestic and international), Lufthansa, Singapore, Swiss, Turkish Airlines	ATMs to right; info desk in centre by escalators; car desks to right

(mint-green buses sometimes have it, as do the big white CTA buses).

Major bus hubs are Midan Abdel Moniem Riad, behind the Egyptian Museum and Midan Ataba (both Map p64).

Car

Driving in Cairo can't be recommended – not only is it harrowing, but you're only contributing to the hideously clogged streets. Lane markings are ignored and traffic lights are discretionary unless enforced by a policeman.

At night some drivers use their headlights exclusively for flashing oncoming vehicles. But Cairo drivers do have road rules: they look out for each other and are tolerant of driving that elsewhere might provoke road rage. Things only go awry when an inexperienced driver – like an international visitor, perhaps – is thrown into the mix.

For more information about cars and driving in Egypt see p525.

HIRE The only reason we expect you might rent a car is to drive directly out of the city. Finding a cheap deal with local operators is virtually impossible; you're much better off organising ahead via the web. The major options:

Avis (www.avisegypt.com) Airport (☑2265 2429); Garden City (☑2793 2400; 11 Sharia Kamal ed-Din Salah)

Budget (☑2265 2395; www.budget.com; Terminal 1, Cairo Airport)

Europcar (☑0106 6611027; www.europcar. com/car-EGYPT.html; Terminal 1, Cairo Airport)

Hertz (www.hertzegypt.com) Airport (☑0128 000 0823); Downtown (Map p64; ☑2575 8914; Ramses Hilton, Corniche el-Nil)

Metro

The metro is blissfully efficient, inexpensive and, outside rush hours (7am to 9am and 3pm to 6pm), not too crowded. Given the impossible car traffic in Cairo, if you can make even a portion of your journey on the metro, you'll save time and aggravation. Three lines are now in operation. Line 1 stretches 43km along the east bank of the Nile. Line 2 crosses to the west bank, passing through Downtown and across Gezira en route. Long-awaited Line 3, set to open at press time in early 2012, runs from Ataba to Abbassiya, and will eventually extend to Imbaba on the west bank and to the airport. See the Cairo Metro map, p124.

Metro stations have signs with a big red 'M' in a blue star. Tickets cost E£1 to any stop; keep yours handy to feed into the turnstile on the way out. At the time of research, a stored-value card was in the works to replace tickets. Trains run every five minutes or so from around 6am until 11.30pm.

USEFUL METRO STATIONS

Ataba Convenient for Downtown.

Bab al-Shaaria Closest to Islamic Cairo, on the north side.

Gezira (Opera) By the Cairo Opera House, closest to Zamalek.

Giza Next to Giza train station, handy for buses to the Pyramids.

Mar Girgis In the middle of Coptic Cairo.

Mohammed Naguib Close to Abdeen Palace and the Museum of Islamic Art.

Al-Shohadaa Beneath Midan Ramses and Ramses Railway Station.

Nasser Sharia 26th of July and Sharia Ramses; closest to Downtown nightlife.

Sadat Beneath Midan Tahrir, close to the Egyptian Museum.

Two carriages in the centre of each train are reserved for women. Look for the blue 'Ladies' signs on the platform marking where you should stand.

Microbus

Cairenes use the private microbus (meekrobas) – a small van with 12 or so seats – as much as the public bus. No destinations are marked, which can make them hard to use at first. But they're quite useful for major routes: from the Giza metro to near the Pyramids and Midan al-Remaya for long-distance microbuses, and from Ataba to Sayyida Aisha for the Citadel. Locals use coded hand gestures to communicate their destination to passing microbuses; if the van has a free seat, it will stop. Fares vary according to distance, from 50pt to E£3, paid after you take your seat. This often requires passing your money to passengers ahead and receiving your change the same way (which is always done scrupulously).

River Bus

It's of limited utility, but it's scenic; the river bus runs from the Corniche near Downtown Cairo to Giza by the zoo and Cairo University. The Downtown terminal is located at Maspero, 250m north of the Ramses Hilton, in front of the big round TV building. Boats depart every 15 minutes for Giza from near the zoo (Map p102). The trip takes 30 minutes and the fare is E£1.

Cairo Metro

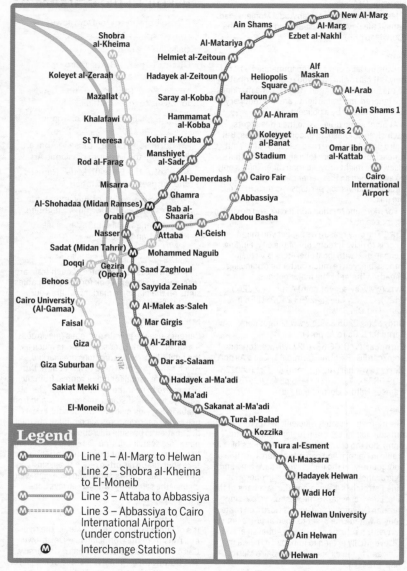

New Al-Marg
Al-Marg
Ezbet al-Nakhl
Ain Shams
Al-Mataryia
Alf Maskan
Helmiet al-Zeitoun
Shobra al-Kheima
Koleyet al-Zeraah
Hadayek al-Zeitoun
Heliopolis Square
Al-Arab
Mazallat
Saray al-Kobba
Haroun
Ain Shams 1
Khalafawi
Hammamat al-Kobba
Al-Ahram
Ain Shams 2
St Theresa
Kobri al-Kobba
Koleyyet al-Banat
Omar ibn al-Kattab
Rod al-Farag
Manshiyet al-Sadr
Stadium
Misarra
Al-Demerdash
Cairo Fair
Cairo International Airport
Ghamra
Al-Shohadaa (Midan Ramses)
Abbassiya
Orabi
Bab al-Shaaria
Abdou Basha
Nasser
Attaba
Al-Geish
Sadat (Midan Tahrir)
Mohammed Naguib
Doqqi
Gezira (Opera)
Saad Zaghloul
Behoos
Sayyida Zeinab
Cairo University (Al-Gamaa)
Al-Malek as-Saleh
Faisal
Mar Girgis
Giza
Al-Zahraa
Giza Suburban
Dar as-Salaam
Nile
Sakiat Mekki
Hadayek al-Ma'adi
El-Moneib
Ma'adi
Sakanat al-Ma'adi
Tura al-Balad
Kozzika
Tura al-Esment
Al-Maasara
Hadayek Helwan
Wadi Hof
Helwan University
Ain Helwan
Helwan

Legend

Line 1 – Al-Marg to Helwan
Line 2 – Shobra al-Kheima to El-Moneib
Line 3 – Attaba to Abbassiya
Line 3 – Abbassiya to Cairo International Airport (under construction)
Interchange Stations

Taxi

Outside the mid-afternoon rush, taxis are readily available and will come to a screeching halt with the slightest wave of your hand. The whole Cairo cab experience has been transformed by new white taxis with meters and even, on occasion, air-con. Older unmetered, black-and-white taxis still ply the streets, but although there's potential for getting a cheaper fare in them, the discomfort and near-inevitable argument at the end make them not worth your while.

Meter rates start at E£2.50, plus E£1.25 per kilometre and E£0.25 waiting. A tip of 10% or so is very much appreciated, and it's good to have small change on hand, as drivers are often short of it. Some people have reported taxis with suspiciously fast-running meters, or drivers who claim the meter is broken. If you encounter either situation, simply stop the car, get out and flag down another – the vast majority are legitimate and won't give you trouble.

Hiring a taxi for a longer period runs from E£25 to E£35 per hour, depending on your bargaining skills; E£300 for a full day is typical. One excellent service is **Blue Cab** (☑3760-9716, 0100 442 2008), which can be booked ahead – very reliable for early-morning airport departures, for instance, or trips out of town.

Tram

Rattly old-fashioned trams ('slow metros', in local parlance) run from the north side of Midan Ramses (see Map p69) to Heliopolis (50pt, 45 minutes). The line goes close to Midan Roxy on the southern edge of Heliopolis (see Map p134), where it divides into two: Nouzha (through central Heliopolis on Sharia al-Ahram; sign written in red) and Abdel Aziz Fahmy (west side; sign in green or blue). The third line, to Al-Mirghani in the east, has been dismantled to construct the new underground metro line.

GREATER CAIRO

Giza

Technically all of Cairo on the west bank of the Nile is Giza, though the name is inextricably linked with the Pyramids, 9km from the river, on the edge of the desert. Truly mercenary sightseers could conceivably stay out here and bypass Cairo entirely, but that's missing a lot of the fun. More realistically, you'll probably come out here on a day outing. Pyramids Rd leads straight to the site, and the village of Nazlet as-Samaan at its base and south of Pyramids Rd.

Pyramids of Giza   ARCHAEOLOGICAL SITE
(Map p126; adult/student E£60/30; ☉8am-4pm)
For nearly 4000 years, the extraordinary shape, impeccable geometry and sheer bulk of the Giza Pyramids have invited the obvious question: 'How were we built, and why?'

Centuries of research have given us parts of the answer. We know they were massive tombs constructed on the orders of the pharaohs by teams of workers tens-of-thousands strong. This is supported by the discovery of a pyramid-builders' settlement, complete with areas for large-scale food production

and medical facilities. Ongoing excavations on the Giza Plateau have provided more evidence that the workers were not the slaves of Hollywood tradition, but an organised workforce of Egyptian farmers. During the flood season, when the Nile covered their fields, the same farmers could have been redeployed by the highly structured bureaucracy to work on the pharaoh's tomb. In this way, the Pyramids can almost be seen as an ancient job-creation scheme. And the flood waters made it easier to transport building stone to the site.

But despite the evidence, some still won't accept that the ancient Egyptians were capable of such achievements. So-called pyramidologists point to the carving and placement of the stones, precise to the millimetre, and argue the numerological significance of the structures' dimensions as evidence that the Pyramids were constructed by angels or aliens. It's easy to laugh at these out-there ideas, but when you see the monuments up close, especially inside, you'll better understand why so many people believe such awesome structures must have unearthly origins.

Great Pyramid of Khufu (Cheops)

(Map p126; adult/student E£100/50; ☉8am-noon, 1-6pm) The oldest pyramid in Giza and the largest in Egypt, Khufu's Great Pyramid stood 146m high when it was completed around 2570 BC. After 46 windy centuries, its height has been reduced by 9m.

There isn't much to see inside the pyramid, but the experience of climbing through the ancient structure is unforgettable – though impossible if you suffer the tiniest degree of claustrophobia. The elderly and unfit should not attempt the climb, as it is very steep.

First you clamber up the face of the pyramid a bit, up rudimentary stairs to the left of the entrance. Leave your camera with the guard if you have one, then crouch down to enter. At a juncture in the tunnel, a passage descends to an unfinished tomb (usually closed) about 100m along and 30m deep in the bedrock. From here, another passage, 1.3m high and 1m wide, ascends for about 40m to reach the Great Gallery, an impressive narrow space 47m long and 8.5m high. At the start of the gallery, a small horizontal passage leads into the so-called Queen's Chamber.

As you climb up through the Great Gallery, notice how precisely the blocks in the

The Giza Plateau

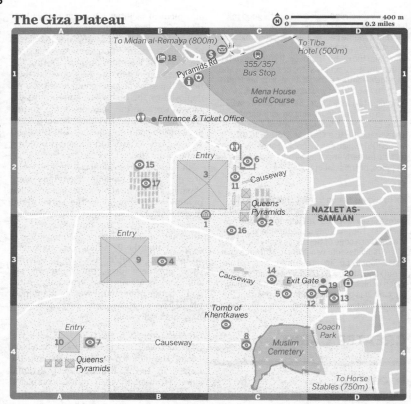

To Midan al-Remaya (800m)

To Tiba Hotel (500m)

Pyramids Rd

355/357 Bus Stop

Mena House Golf Course

Entrance & Ticket Office

Entry

Causeway

Queens' Pyramids

NAZLET AS-SAMAAN

Entry

Causeway

Exit Gate

Entry

Causeway

Queens' Pyramids

Tomb of Khentkawes

Muslim Cemetery

Coach Park

To Horse Stables (750m)

ceiling fit together. In the 10m-long King's Chamber at the end, the walls are built of red granite blocks. The ceiling itself consists of nine huge slabs of granite, which weigh more than 400 tonnes. Above these slabs, four more slabs are separated by gaps, which are designed to distribute the enormous weight away from the chamber. Good airflow from the modern ventilation system (built into two ancient tiny air shafts) will help you breathe easier as you contemplate the tremendous weight suspended above you.

East of the pyramid is a ruin of a different era: **King Farouk's rest house**, a grand neo-Pharaonic structure built in 1946 by Mustafa Fahmy. It's now an unfortunate shambles, but there's a good view of the city from the adjacent yard.

Along the pyramid's east face, three small structures some 20m high resemble piles of rubble. These are the **Queens' Pyramids** (Map p126), the tombs of Khufu's wives and sis-

ters. You can enter some of them, but they're quite steamy inside. In the **eastern cemetery** (Map p126) behind, one or two tombs are occasionally open, and you can still see the perfectly smooth limestone facing along the bases of some structures. Note also the **solar barque pits** (Map p126) between the pyramids, which held giant ritual boats.

Cheops Boat Museum

(Map p126; adult/student E£50/25; ⊙9am-4pm Oct-May, 9am-5pm Jun-Sep) Immediately south of the Great Pyramid is this fascinating museum with exactly one object on display. Five pits near the Great Pyramid of Khufu contained the pharaoh's solar barques (boats), which may have been used to convey the mummy of the dead pharaoh across the Nile to the valley temple, from where it was brought up the causeway and into the tomb chamber. The boats were then buried around the pyramid to provide transport for the pharaoh in the next world.

The Giza Plateau

CAIRO GIZA

One of these ancient wood vessels, possibly the oldest boat in existence, was unearthed in 1954. The enormous structure was carefully restored from 1200 pieces of Lebanese cedar and encased in this museum to protect it from the elements. Visitors to the museum must help this process by donning protective footwear to keep sand out.

Pyramid of Khafre (Chephren)
(Map p126; adult/student E£30/15; ⊙8am-4pm when open to visitors) Southwest of the Great Pyramid, Khafre's pyramid seems larger than that of his father, Khufu. At just 136m high, it's not, but it stands on higher ground and its peak is still capped with the original polished limestone casing. Originally all three pyramids were totally encased in this smooth white stone, which would have made them gleam in the sun. Over the centuries, this casing has been stripped for use in palaces and mosques, exposing the softer inner-core stones to the elements.

At the time of research, the interior of the pyramid was closed; it usually alternates opening with the Pyramid of Menkaure. The chambers and passageways of this pyramid are less elaborate than those in the Great Pyramid, but are almost as claustrophobic. The entrance descends into a passage and then across to the burial chamber, which still contains Khafre's large granite sarcophagus.

Back outside, to the east of the pyramid, are the substantial remains of **Khafre's funerary temple** (Map p126) and the flagged paving of the causeway that provided access from the Nile to the tomb.

Pyramid of Menkaure (Mycerinus)
(Map p126; adult/student E£30/15; ⊙8am-4pm when open to visitors) At 62m (originally 66.5m), this pyramid is the smallest of the trio, only about one-tenth the bulk of the Great Pyramid. The pharaoh Menkaure died before the structure was finished – around the bottom are several courses of granite facing that was never properly smoothed.

The pyramid alternates opening with the Pyramid of Khafre. Inside, you descend into three distinct levels – the largest surprisingly vast – and you can peer into the main tomb. Outside the pyramid you'll see the excavated remains of **Menkaure's funerary temple** and, further east, the ruins of his **valley temple**. To the south is another set of **Queens' Pyramids**. If you hike this far, horse and camel touts will want to lure you out in the desert for better photo ops of all three pyramids. If you go, keep your general-admission ticket handy in case police ask for it when you return.

Khafre's Valley Temple
(Map p126) You approach the Sphinx through this temple that once sat at the edge of a small artificial lake, connected to the Nile by a canal – it was in this way that construction materials were brought to the area at the start, and later, worshippers came to visit the temple. The sturdy building is filled with beautiful pink granite columns and alabaster floors. Look in the corners, where the pink granite facing stones are fit together like pieces of a jigsaw puzzle. The temple originally held 23 statues of Khafre, which were illuminated with the ancient version

The Pyramids of Giza

Constructed more than 4000 years ago, the Pyramids are the last remaining wonder of the ancient world. The giant structures – the **Great Pyramid of Khufu 1**, the smaller **Pyramid of Khafre 2** and the **Pyramid of Menkaure 3** – deservedly sit at the top of many travellers' to-do lists. But the site is challenging to explore, with everything, including the smaller **Queens' Pyramids 4** and assorted tombs such as the **Tomb of Senegemib-Inti 5**, spread out in the desert under the hot sun. And it all looks, at first glance, a bit smaller than you might have thought.

It helps to imagine them as they were: originally, the Pyramids gleamed in the sun, covered in a smooth white limestone casing. These enormous mausoleums, each devoted to a single pharaoh, were part of larger complexes. At the east base of each was a 'funerary temple', where the pharaoh was worshipped after his demise, with daily rounds of offerings to sustain his soul. In the ground around the pyramids, wooden boats – so-called solar barques – were buried with more supplies to transport the pharaoh's soul to the afterlife (one of these has been reconstructed and sits in the **Cheops Boat Museum 6**). From each funerary temple, a long stone-paved causeway extended down the hill.

At the base of the plateau, a lake covered the land where the village of Nazlet as-Samaan is now – this was fed by a canal and enlarged with flood waters each year. At the end of each causeway, a 'valley temple' stood at the water's edge to greet visitors. Next to Khafre's valley temple, the lion-bodied **Sphinx 7** stands guard.

So much about the Pyramids remains mysterious – including the whereabouts of the bodies of the pharaohs themselves. But there's still plenty for visitors to see. Here we show you both the big picture and the little details to look out for, starting with the **ticket booth and entrance 8**.

ZORA O'NEILL

Pyramid of Khafre
Khufu's son built this pyramid, which has some surviving limestone casing at the top. Scattered around the base are enormous granite stones that once added a snappy black stripe to the lowest level of the structure.

Khafre's Valley Temple

7

Eastern Cemetery

The Sphinx
This human-headed beast, thought to be a portrait of Khafre, guards the base of the plateau. The entrance is only through Khafre's valley temple. Come early or late in the day to avoid the long queue.

Cheops Boat Museum
Preserved in its own modern tomb, this 4500-year-old cedar barge was dug up from in front of the Great Pyramid and reassembled by expert craftsmen like a 1224-piece jigsaw puzzle.

ZORA O'NEILL

ZORA O'NEILL

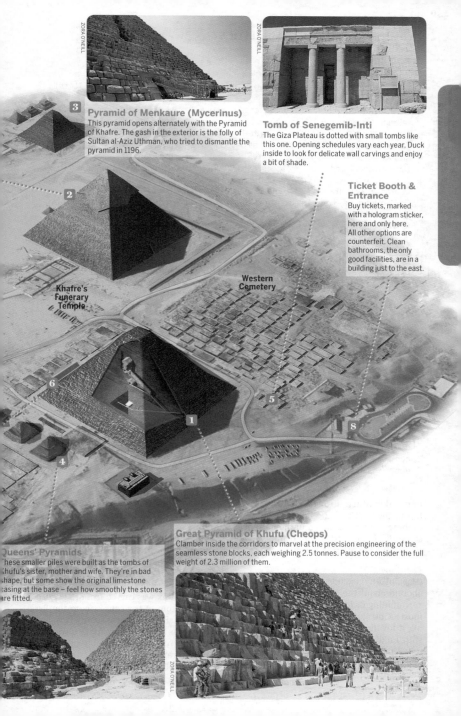

Pyramid of Menkaure (Mycerinus)
This pyramid opens alternately with the Pyramid of Khafre. The gash in the exterior is the folly of Sultan al-Aziz Uthman, who tried to dismantle the pyramid in 1196.

Tomb of Senegemib-Inti
The Giza Plateau is dotted with small tombs like this one. Opening schedules vary each year. Duck inside to look for delicate wall carvings and enjoy a bit of shade.

Ticket Booth & Entrance
Buy tickets, marked with a hologram sticker, here and only here. All other options are counterfeit. Clean bathrooms, the only good facilities, are in a building just to the east.

Khafre's Funerary Temple

Western Cemetery

Queens' Pyramids
These smaller piles were built as the tombs of Khufu's sister, mother and wife. They're in bad shape, but some show the original limestone casing at the base – feel how smoothly the stones are fitted.

Great Pyramid of Khufu (Cheops)
Clamber inside the corridors to marvel at the precision engineering of the seamless stone blocks, each weighing 2.5 tonnes. Pause to consider the full weight of 2.3 million of them.

ZORA O'NEILL

PYRAMIDS PRACTICALITIES

Entrance & Tickets

The main **entrance** is at the end of Pyramids Rd (Sharia al-Haram), though if you come on a tour bus, you may enter through a gate below the Sphinx, in the village of Nazlet as-Samaan; you can also exit here on foot.

Additional tickets are required for the Cheops Boat Museum and the pyramid interiors. The Great Pyramid is always open, along with one of the other two (they alternate every year or so). Pyramid interior tickets are purchased at the main entrance. Secondary-pyramid tickets are sold all day, but Great Pyramid tickets (300 available in summer, 500 in winter) are sold in two lots, first thing in the morning and at 1pm. In winter, you may need to queue, especially on Wednesday and Thursday, when tour groups come from the Red Sea. If you exit the site to purchase afternoon interior tickets, let the guards know so there's no trouble when you come back through.

Cameras are allowed all over the site, including in the museum, but not inside pyramids and tombs. Guards will watch your camera at the pyramid entrances, in exchange for E£2 or so baksheesh; some will also permit photos inside tombs for a tip.

Facilities & Food

Clean **bathrooms** are outside the main entrance (tip the attendant E£1 or E£2). On the plateau, there's one decent one in the Cheops Boat Museum, and another in a dodgy trailer near the Great Pyramid. At the base of the Sphinx, the open-air **cafe** (Map p126; drinks E£20, sandwiches E£25-55) also has some. For food, it's grossly overpriced, and the waiters are easily 'confused' when making change. For the same amount, you can refresh at the nearby Pizza Hut or far lovelier **Mena House Oberoi** (see p132), though this means a hike back up the hill to the main entrance. For **cheap eats**, walk a bit northeast on the main road through Nazlet as-Samaan, and you'll pass various snack options.

Horses & Camels

Considering the pressure, it's tempting to ignore the camel touts; however, the distance between the three pyramids is significant, so the service is a real one. 'Official' prices (E£35 per hour) exist, but, as one tourist police officer said with an apologetic shrug, 'You're still expected to bargain'. Realistically, you can't ride an animal any distance for less than E£50, and E£20 is the minimum for a short trot and photo op. Choose only healthy-looking animals, and if you're asked to pay more than agreed before you're let down, call over the nearest tourist police, or go to the office by the Mena House and complain. For longer rides, hiring a horse from one of the village stables is a far better option than taking one at the Pyramids. See p131 for recommended stables.

of mood lighting, through slits between the top of the wall and the flat roof. Only one of these statues, all carved in the hard black stone diorite, has been found intact – it is now in the Egyptian Museum.

The Sphinx

(Map p126) Legends and superstitions abound about the Sphinx, and the mystery surrounding its long-forgotten purpose is almost as intriguing as its appearance. On seeing it for the first time, many visitors agree with English playwright Alan Bennett, who noted in his diary that seeing the Sphinx is like meeting a TV personality in the flesh: he's smaller than one had imagined.

Known in Arabic as Abu al-Hol (Father of Terror), the feline man was dubbed the Sphinx by the ancient Greeks because it resembled the mythical winged monster with a woman's head and lion's body who set riddles and killed anyone unable to answer them. (It even has a little tail, daintily curled over its back right paw.)

The Sphinx was carved from the bedrock at the bottom of the causeway to the Pyramid of Khafre; geological survey has shown that it was most likely carved during this pharaoh's reign, so it probably portrays his features, framed by the *nemes* (striped head-cloth worn by royalty).

As is clear from the accounts of early Arab travellers, the nose was hammered off sometime between the 11th and 15th centuries, although some still like to blame Napoleon for the deed. Part of the fallen beard was carted off by 19th-century adventurers and is now on display in the British Museum in London. These days the Sphinx has potentially greater problems: pollution and rising groundwater are causing internal fractures, and it is under a constant state of repair.

Cemeteries & Tombs

Private cemeteries are tucked into the hill alongside the causeways, as well as arrayed in neat rows around the Pyramids in a grid pattern – the **eastern cemetery** next to the Great Pyramid, as well as the **western cemetery** (Map p126). Only a few of the tombs are open to the public at any given time, but the **tomb of Seshemnufer IV** (Map p126), just southeast of the Great Pyramid, is almost always open. Just inside the columned entrance, carved deer adorn the walls of the entrance room, and there's a burial chamber you can climb down into. At the north end of the western cemetery, the **Tomb of Senegemib-Inti** (Map p126), contains interesting inscriptions, including a rather vicious-looking hippopotamus, rippling with muscle.

Wissa Wassef Art Centre   WEAVING STUDIOS
(☎3381 5746; www.wissawassef.com; Saqqara Rd, Harraniyya; ⊙10am-5pm daily, studios closed Fri)
Along the Maryutia Canal south of Pyramids Rd (turn south below the massive flyover), in a stretch of half-developed green farmland, this mudbrick complex is the work of architect Ramses Wissa Wassef. It won an Aga Khan prize for its refined traditional style. The artisans who work here in open studios are known for their distinctive tapestries depicting rural scenes. Crude imitations are standard in souvenir shops; the ones for sale and on display in the museum here are in a completely different class, like paintings in wool. There's pottery and batik fabric, done to equally good effect. The place has the feeling of a sanctuary – quiet and refreshingly green, especially after a dusty Pyramids visit.

To get here, take a Saqqara-bound microbus (E£1) or taxi from Pyramids Rd at Maryutia Canal – a giant flyover runs above it. Get off when you see the blue 'Harraniyya' sign, after about 3.5km, and about 600m after the

flyover turns away. The centre is by the canal on the west side of the road.

Kerdassa   SHOPPING CENTRE
(Tir'at al-Maryutia) We mention this spot only because it is sometimes pushed as an insider shopping destination where you can buy scarves and *galabiyyas* direct from the 'factory'. But the dismal setting of semi-rural poverty adjacent to a new strip mall, plus the price of a taxi ride (at least E£20 from the Pyramids), cancels out the minor savings. The village is about 5.5km north of Pyramids Rd (roughly 15 minutes).

 Activities

Horse Riding

There's only one thing to do around the Pyramids, and you'll never stop hearing about it. But a desert horse ride at sunset, with the Pyramids as a background, is unforgettable.

All of the stables are strung along the road south of the coach park by the Sphinx gate. General expat opinion holds that some of the best stables are **NB** (☎3382 0435), owned by Naser Breesh, who's praised for his healthy steeds and good guides; his place is just behind the Sphinx Club, further south than the others. **FB** (☎0106 507 0288) is also recommended.

Expect to pay around E£100 per person per hour at a good place; a reputable operation won't ask for money till the end of the ride. Others may charge less, but often their horses are very poorly kept. Tip your guide an additional E£5 or E£10, and keep your Pyramids site ticket or you'll be charged again to enter. Moonlight rides around the Pyramids are another favourite outing but

---

ⓘ THE PYRAMIDS AFTER DARK

Narrated by the Sphinx, the **sound and light show** (Map p126; ☎3386 3469; www.soundandlight.com.eg; admission E£75, plus E£10 for translation headset; ⊙7pm & 8pm) is a rather dated spectacular. It's not worth a special trip, but fine if you're in the area – it is neat to see the Pyramids so dramatically lit. Though there's officially no student discount, some readers report negotiating a small one. The first show is typically in English; the second varies. The entrance is on the Sphinx side.

THE PYRAMIDS HUSTLE

Crammed with buses, postcard vendors and gargling camels, the Pyramids is an intense tourist scene, and many visitors find it the most gruelling part of their trip. Unfortunately, until the site is better managed and the people in the village by the Pyramids have some other income besides selling horse and camel rides, there is no way to avoid the sales pressure and scam attempts. It does help, however, to know what you're up against.

The hustle can start before you even leave your hotel, where someone tries to sell you a 'sunrise tour' of the Pyramids: really just a way of delivering you early to the horse touts, as you can't enter the site before 8am. En route, someone will chat you up at the Giza metro, or a man will jump in your taxi while it's stuck in traffic on Pyramids Rd. The road ahead is closed, he warns, and the best way to proceed is on a horse. (The road *is* closed, sort of; about 1km from the site, all outbound traffic must detour north on Sharia al-Mansouria. Don't panic – you'll loop back to the Pyramids soon.) Nearer the gate, others will try to convince you the entrance has moved, or point you to a secret back route. Counterfeit tickets aren't unheard-of – buy yours only from the ticket windows at the main gate.

Once through the turnstiles, police might direct you to a waiting man, or men will ask for your ticket in an official tone. Ignore them, as they're just attempting to become your guide. You need only show your additional tickets at the Great Pyramid and whichever secondary pyramid is open (and guards should take only half the ticket, not the whole thing). Guards also usually check your general ticket at the Sphinx to make sure you haven't slipped in the downhill gate. Attendants at smaller tombs will ask for a ticket, hoping you'll assume you need to buy one – flash your general ticket, and you should be fine.

Even knowing all this won't stop touts from approaching you, and no matter how tersely and frequently you say no, these guys won't stop – it's the only job they've got. So it's key for your own happiness not to snap, but to smile and just keep walking. It also helps to remember that the Pyramids have been attracting tourists since day one, and a local was probably already waiting to sell a souvenir.

under new regulations you can't ride very close to the site after 6pm.

🛏 Sleeping

A Pyramids-area hotel may appeal if you want to get an early start out there, and treat yourself a bit while you're at it. Plus, the only camping option in the Cairo area is out this way.

Mena House Oberoi　LUXURY HOTEL **$$$**
(Map p126; ☑3377 3222; www.menahouse oberoi.com; Pyramids Rd; s/d garden wing from €160/180, r palace wing from €280; 🕸🎧🌊) Built in 1869 as Khedive Ismail's hunting lodge, Mena House dazzles with intricate gold decoration and air that perpetually smells of jasmine. The grandest palace-wing rooms are borderline-kitschy Arabian Nights style, with whimsical tapestry bedspreads and opulent mirrors. Rooms in the garden wing are more typically modern. The swimming pool is suitably capacious.

Barceló　HOTEL **$$**
(☑3582 3300; www.barcelo.com; 229 Pyramids Rd; r from US$59; 🕸🎧🌊) Well placed – and well priced – for a strategic visit to the Pyramids, without totally giving up on the city. The Giza metro stop is about 3km away, and the Pyramids are 4km. It's a standard chain, but all new as of 2010, with good breakfast and a nice rooftop pool.

Salma Motel　CAMPGROUND **$**
(☑0100 487 1300; salma.camp@yahoo.com; Saqqara Rd, Harranniya; camping per person E£25, cabins E£90) The only camping option in Cairo is miles from the centre, adjacent to the Wissa Wassef Art Centre (p131) on the Maryutia Canal. To get here, take a microbus or taxi from Pyramids Rd in the direction of Saqqara and get off when you see the blue 'Harranniya' sign. Coming by car, take the Ring Rd freeway west, then exit at Maryutia Rd and head south.

Tiba Hotel　HOTEL **$$**
(off Map p126; ☑3385 1659; www.tibapyramidshotel.com; Pyramids Rd; r from €32; 🕸🎧) The best deal

within walking distance of the Pyramids, though still not great quality. The traffic noise is intense as it's at a major intersection. Only stay here if you're on a budget and planning a surgical strike on the Pyramids.

Eating

Andrea EGYPTIAN $$
(☑3383 1133; 59 Tir'at al-Maryutia; entrées E£7-20, mains E£30-35; ◷10am-midnight) Take a trip to the country at this garden restaurant located 1.5km north of Pyramids Rd on the west side of Maryutia Canal (you must drive north about 2km, below the flyover, then loop around to come down the other side of the canal; if you reach onramps to the elevated highway above, you've gone plenty far). At the entrance women pat out bread dough and tend the spit-roasted chicken the place is justly famous for. It makes a great post-Pyramids lunch with salads and a few cold Stellas. (Make sure your driver doesn't take you to the unrelated Andrea Gardenia, south of Pyramids Rd.)

Moghul Room INDIAN $$$
(Map p126; ☑3377 3222; Mena House Oberoi, Pyramids Rd; mains E£95-170; ◷7-11.45pm daily & 12.30-2.45pm Fri) Cairo's best Indian restaurant specialises in mild North Indian-style curries and kebabs, with an emphasis on tandoori dishes. Though it's a long taxi ride from Downtown, the opulent decor, good food and live sitar music make it worthwhile. There's a wide range of vegetarian options (from E£60 to E£65) and an extensive wine list.

Khan al-Khalili EGYPTIAN, EUROPEAN $$
(Map p126; Mena House Oberoi, Pyramids Rd; mains E£60-95; ◷24hr) The casual restaurant at Mena House has huge windows opening onto the Pyramids – a great place to rest up after a day of sightseeing, even if the food is a bit bland. But the menu is broad enough – from spaghetti to Indian dishes – that it's a crowd pleaser. A Stella costs E£25.

🔒 Shopping

Lehnert & Landrock BOOKS
(Map p126; ◷9am-10pm) By the Sphinx-side gate, with old maps, books about Cairo and Egypt, plus vintage postcards and reprints of old photographs.

① Information

Emergency
Tourist Police (Map p126; ☑126; Pyramids Rd) Across from Mena House.

Tourist Information
Ministry of Tourism (Map p126; ☑3383 8823; Pyramids Rd; ◷8.30am-5pm) Across from Mena House.

① Getting There & Away

The most efficient traffic-beating way is to go via metro to Giza, then by taxi (about E£15), microbus or bus.

Microbuses cluster at the bottom of the westside stairs from the metro (drivers are yelling 'Haram'). The fare is E£3. You can get off where the van turns off Pyramids Rd (at Sharia al-Mansouria, with the Tiba Hotel on the southeast corner), and walk 1km straight to the entrance.

Buses (usually E£1) stop on the north side of Pyramids Rd, just west of the underpass. Hop any headed for Midan al-Remaya and get off at Sharia al-Mansouria, or look out for 355 or 357, which terminate in front of Mena House Oberoi, about 250m from the site entrance.

Returning to Cairo, taxis will try to convince you to go for a flat fare, rather than on the meter. Walking out further helps. You could also take a tuk-tuk from the Sphinx side out to Pyramids Rd for about E£3.

Heliopolis

This suburb shows a different, more relaxed side of the city. Coupled with a ride on the creaky old 'slow metro' (tram), the pretty district is a nice antidote to central Cairo's tourist pressure. With all its trees and outdoor cafes, it's a pleasant place for an evening's wander. Many Egyptians think so too, as Heliopolis has become 'downtown' for people living in dull satellite cities further east. It's also reasonably close to the airport, so you can get a taste of Cairo even if you're just on a pit stop in an airport-area hotel before an early flight.

Belgian industrialist and baron Édouard Empain laid out Heliopolis in the early 20th century as a 'garden city' for the colonial officials who ruled Egypt. Its whitewashed Moorish-style buildings with dark wood balconies, grand arcades and terraces are the European vision of the 'Orient' set in stone. Since the 1950s, overcrowding has filled in the green spaces between the villas with apartment buildings festooned with

Heliopolis

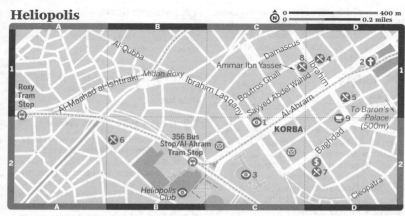

Heliopolis

satellite dishes, but the area still has a relaxed, vaguely Mediterranean air.

Sharia al-Ahram runs through Korba, 'downtown' Heliopolis. At the south end, **Uruba Palace** (Map p134) was once a grand hotel graced by the likes of King Albert I of Belgium and then appropriated as the presidential offices – at least until Mubarak got the boot in 2011. From the palace, at the first intersection with Sharia Ibrahim Laqqany (detour left for some pretty arcades), is the open-air cafeteria **Amphitrion** (Map p134), as old as Heliopolis itself and a popular watering hole for Allied soldiers during the world wars. At the end of the street, the **Basilica** (Map p134) is a miniature version of Istanbul's famous Aya Sofya, dubbed the 'jelly mould' by local expats. Baron Empain is buried here.

Empain lived in a fantastical Hindu-look mansion, bedecked with geishas, elephants and serpents. The so-called **Baron's Palace** (Qasr al-Baron; Map p134) is due east from the basilica, on Sharia al-Uruba (Airport Rd). It's not worth a dedicated trip, as you can't enter, but keep an eye out for it on your way to or from the airport. It has been locked tight since 1997, when 'Satanists' were allegedly holding rituals here – turns out they were a bunch of upper-class teenage metalheads.

Some might say similar delusions surround the **October War Panorama** (☎2402 2317; Sharia al-Uruba; admission E£20; ☺shows 9.30am, 11am, 12.20pm, 6pm & 7.30pm Wed-Mon), a commemoration of the 1973 'victory' over Israel, built with slightly sinister flair by North Korean artists. A large circular mural and diorama depicts the Egyptian forces breaching of the Bar Lev Line on the Suez Canal, while a stirring commentary (in Arabic only) recounts the heroic victories. It neatly skips over the successful Israeli counterattacks. The exhibition is about 2.5km southwest of the Baron's Palace, on the same road; you can flag down a bus on Sharia al-Uruba or get a taxi.

✖ Eating

In addition to the Amphitrion (p133), where you can have a beer and sheesha and use the wi-fi, the following places are good.

Mangiamo   EGYPTIAN, ITALIAN $$
(Map p134; 100 Sharia Ammar Ibn Yasser; mains E£20-60; ☺10am-2am) Tucked away on a residential corner, Mangiamo feels a little like a private club, and its garden is a lovely quiet

place to sit, with all the Heliopolis ladies out for lunch. The menu does all the Egyptian staples, plus good pizza and pasta.

Abu Ammar al-Suri   SYRIAN **$**
(Map p134; 19 Sharia Ibrahim; sandwiches E£12-17, mains E£27-50; ☺11am-2am) A branch of the tasty operation in Mohandiseen. Look for the light-up plastic shwarma on the corner.

Arabiata   EGYPTIAN FAST FOOD **$**
(Map p134; Sharia Ibrahim; dishes E£5-15; ☺8am-2am) One of the most popular cheap snack places in Heliopolis, with takeout or seats upstairs.

 Shopping

Citystars Centre   SHOPPING CENTRE
(Sharia Omar ibn Khattab, Nasr City; ☺11am-1am) Cairo's most lavish mall is the current landing spot for every new international chain, from Starbucks to Wagamama. There's a kids' theme park and a big cinema. It's about 12km east of Downtown. Just hop in a taxi and say, 'Citystars'.

❶ Getting There & Away

The fastest route is the metro to Saray al-Kobba (exit on the east side of the tracks), then a taxi; tell the driver 'Korba'. But Cairo's vintage trams are a more scenic option – though likely slower and definitely quite a bit dirtier. Get off where the line branches, just before Midan Roxy; on a good day, the ride takes about 30 minutes from Midan Ramses. Also, airport bus 356 goes from Midan Abdel Moniem Riad. The ride takes about 45 minutes. Get off outside the Heliopolis Club (the first stop after reaching the street with tram tracks). Trams and buses usually run every 20 minutes.

Egyptian Museum

One of the world's most important collections of ancient artefacts, the Egyptian Museum takes pride of place in Downtown Cairo, on the north side of Midan Tahrir. Inside the great domed, oddly pinkish building, the glittering treasures of Tutankhamun and other great pharaohs lie alongside the grave goods, mummies, jewellery, eating bowls and toys of Egyptians whose names are lost to history. To walk around the museum is to embark on an adventure through time.

This is in part due to the museum structure itself. There's nary an interactive touch-screen to be found; in fact many of the smaller items are in the same vitrines in which they were first placed when the museum opened in 1902. The lighting is so poor in some halls that by late afternoon you have to squint to make out details and read the words on the cryptic, typed display cards placed on a few key items.

In this way, the Egyptian Museum documents not just the time of the pharaohs, but also the history of Egyptology. Some display cards have turned obsolete as new discoveries have busted old theories. And the collection rapidly outgrew its sensible layout, as, for instance, Tutankhamun's enormous trove and the tomb contents of Tanis were both unearthed after the museum opened, and then had to be shoehorned into the space. Now more than 100,000 objects are wedged into about 15,000 sq m.

All this makes the Egyptian Museum somewhat challenging to visit. One of the most rewarding strategies is simply to walk around and see what catches your eye. But it's hard to shake the sense that something even more stunning is waiting in the next room. We recommend some highlights – they're easy enough to spot because they usually have crowds around them – but be sure to stop and see some of the lesser items, as they often do just as well if not better in bringing the world of the pharaohs back to life.

History

The current museum has its origins in several earlier efforts at managing Egypt's ancient heritage, beginning in 1835, when Egyptian ruler Mohammed Ali banned the export of antiquities. Not that anyone heeded this – French archaeologist Auguste Mariette was busy shipping his finds from Saqqara to the Louvre when he was empowered to create the Egyptian Antiquities Service in 1858.

Mariette's growing collection, from some 35 dig sites, bounced around various homes in Cairo until 1902, when the current building was erected, in a suitably prominent position in the city. There it has stood, in its original layout, a gem of early museum design. But the lack of upkeep, and the ever-expanding field of Egyptology, has strained the place. For decades, the museum's basement store was a notorious morass, as neglected sculptures sank into the soft flooring and needed to be excavated all over again.

Until 1996, museum security involved locking the door at night. When an enterprising thief stowed away overnight and helped himself to treasures, the museum authorities installed alarms and detectors, at the same time improving the lighting on many exhibits. During the 2011 revolution, the museum was broken into and a few artefacts went missing. To prevent further looting, activists formed a human chain around the building to guard its contents. By most reports, they were successful.

MUSEUM TOUR: GROUND FLOOR

Before entering the museum, wander through the garden. To your left lies the tomb of Auguste Mariette (1821–81), with a statue of the archaeologist, arms folded, shaded under a spreading tree. Mariette's tomb is overlooked by an arc of busts of two dozen Egyptological luminaries including Jean-François Champollion, who cracked the code of the hieroglyphs; Gaston Maspero, Mariette's successor as director of the Egyptian Antiquities Service; and Karl Lepsius, the pre-eminent 19th-century German Egyptologist.

The ground floor of the museum is laid out roughly chronologically in a clockwise fashion starting at the entrance hall. For room numbers see Map p139.

Room 43 – Atrium

The central atrium is filled with a miscellany of large and small Egyptological finds. In the area before the steps lie some of the collection's oldest items. In the central cabinet No

8, the double-sided Narmer Palette, found at the Temple of Horus in Kom al-Ahmar near Edfu, is of great significance. Dating from around the 1st dynasty, it depicts Pharaoh Narmer (also known as Menes, c 3100 BC) wearing, on one side, the crown of Upper Egypt and, on the other side, the crown of Lower Egypt, suggesting the first union of Upper and Lower Egypt under one ruler. Egyptologists take this as the birth of ancient Egyptian civilisation and Narmer's reign as the first of the 1st dynasty. This, then, is the starting point of more than 3000 years of Pharaonic history in which more than 170 rulers presided over 30 dynasties and produced almost everything in this building. In this sense, the Narmer Palette is the foundation stone of the Egyptian Museum.

Room 48 – Early Dynastic Period

In glass cabinet No 16 is the limestone statue of Zoser (Djoser; 2667–2648 BC), the 3rd-dynasty pharaoh whose chief architect Imhotep designed the revolutionary Step Pyramid at Saqqara. The statue, discovered in 1924 in its serdab (cellar) in the northeastern corner of the pyramid, is the oldest statue of its kind in the museum. The seated, near-life-size figure has lost its original inlaid eyes but is still impressive in a tight robe and striped head cloth over a huge wig.

Rooms 47 & 46 – Old Kingdom

Look for the three exquisite black schist triads that depict the pharaoh Menkaure (Mycerinus; 2532–2503 BC), builder of the smallest of the three Pyramids of Giza, flanked either side by a female figure. The hardness of the stone makes the sculptor's skill all the greater and has helped ensure the triads' survival through the ages. The figure to the pharaoh's right is the goddess Hathor, while each of the figures on his left represents a nome (administrative division) of Egypt, the name of which is given by the symbol above their head. These triads (plus one other than is not held by this museum) were discovered at the pharaoh's valley temple, just east of his pyramid at Giza.

ℹ MUSEUM PRACTICALITIES

Entrance & Tickets

Getting into the **Egyptian Museum** (Map p139; ☏2579 6948; www.egyptianmuseumcairo. org; Midan Tahrir, Downtown; adult/student E£60/30; ⊘9am-6pm Sat-Thu, 9am-4pm Fri) is an exercise in queuing: at peak times, you'll wait to have your bag x-rayed, to buy tickets, to check your camera, to pass the turnstiles and to have your bag checked again. And a line forms at the exit (off the northwest corner) at closing time. Last tickets are sold one hour before closing time.

Additional tickets for the **Royal Mummies Halls** (adult/student E£100/60) are purchased upstairs near Room 56.

Cameras must be checked at the front gate, in the kiosk adjacent to the first X-ray machine. A small tip (E£1 or E£2) is nice when you claim your items. Return promptly at closing time, or you may find the room locked up.

Timing

The museum is very crowded through most of the winter and on all public holidays. The only minor respite is around lunchtime and late afternoon, when larger groups have gone. Friday afternoons, when the museum closes earlier, are also quieter. The museum can be quite dim near dusk; you may want to bring a small torch.

Guides

Official guides troll for business in the garden area and will take you around for upwards of E£60 per hour. For those with more than a passing interest in Egyptology, a visit in the company of Ahmed Seddik or Hassan Saber (p92) is highly recommended.

Facilities & Food

Restrooms are on the mezzanine of each southern staircase. A sign says tips are not accepted but, well, they are – E£1 or E£2 is good. The plaza on the west side of the building holds a basic **cafe**, with cold drinks, ice cream (E£15) and basic sandwiches. You can only re-enter the museum at the front, and with much sweet-talking of the guards. A formal sit-down **restaurant** is used only by occasional tour groups.

Rooms 42, 37 & 32 – Masterpieces of the Old Kingdom

In the centre of Room 42 is one of the museum's masterpieces, a smooth, black **statue of Khafre** (Chephren; 2558–2532 BC). The builder of the second pyramid at Giza sits on a lion throne, and is protected by the wings of the falcon god Horus. The use of the stone diorite, which is harder than marble or granite, suggests the pharaoh's power. In fact, Khafre had 23 identical pieces carved for his valley temple at the Giza Plateau, though this is the only survivor.

Slightly to the left in front of Khafre, the core of the stunning **wooden statue of Ka-Aper** (No 40) was carved out of a single piece of sycamore (the arms were ancient additions; the legs, modern restorations). The sycamore was sacred to the goddess Hathor,

while Ka-Aper's belly suggests his prosperity. His eyes are amazingly lifelike, set in copper lids with whites of opaque quartz and corneas of rock crystal, drilled and filled with black paste to form the pupils. When this statue was excavated at Saqqara in 1870, local workmen named him Sheikh al-Balad (Headman), for his resemblance to their own local leader. Behind you, to the left of the door, sits the **Seated Scribe** (No 44), a wonderful painted limestone figure, hand poised as if waiting to take dictation, his inlaid eyes set in an asymmetrical face giving him a very vivid appearance.

Room 32 is dominated by the beautiful **statues of Rahotep and Nofret** (No 27), a noble couple from the 4th-dynasty reign of Sneferu, builder of the Bent and the Red Pyramids at Dahshur. Almost life-size with well-preserved painted surfaces, the limestone sculptures have simple lines making them seem almost contemporary, despite

Egyptian Museum

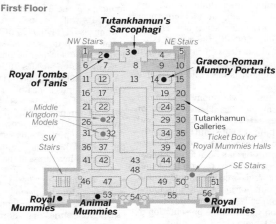

First Floor

NW Stairs — NE Stairs

Tutankhamun's Sarcophagi

Royal Tombs of Tanis

Graeco-Roman Mummy Portraits

Middle Kingdom Models

Tutankhamun Galleries

SW Stairs

Ticket Box for Royal Mummies Halls

SE Stairs

Royal Mummies   **Animal Mummies**   **Royal Mummies**

Ground Floor

Amarna Room

NW Stairs — NE Stairs

Exit

Gift Shop (Closed)

Outdoor Café

Restaurant — Meidum Geese

Statue of Khafre (Chephren)

Atrium

SE Stairs

Clinic

Tourist Police

SW Stairs — Narmer Palette — Entrance

---

having been around for a staggering 4600 years.

In a cabinet off to the left, a limestone group shows **Seneb**, 'chief of the royal wardrobe', and his family (No 39). Seneb is notable for being a dwarf: he sits cross-legged, his two children strategically placed to cover his short legs. His full-size wife Senetites places her arms protectively and affectionately around his shoulders. Redis-covered in their tomb in Giza in 1926, the happy couple and their two kids were more recently used in Egyptian family-planning campaigns.

Also here is a **panel of Meidum geese** (No 138), part of an extraordinarily beautiful wall painting from a mudbrick mastaba (bench above a tomb) at Meidum, near the oasis of Al-Fayoum (see p160). Though painted around 2500 BC, the pigments remain vivid and the degree of realism, even within the distinct Pharaonic style, is astonishing – ornithologists have had no trouble identifying the species.

Room 37, entered via Room 32, contains furniture from the Giza Plateau **tomb of Queen Hetepheres**, wife of Sneferu and mother of Khufu (Cheops), including a carrying chair, bed, bed canopy and a jewellery box. Her mummy has not been found but her shrivelled internal organs remain inside her Canopic chest. A glass cabinet holds a miniature ivory statue of her son Khufu, found at Abydos. Ironically, at under 8cm, this tiny figure is the only surviving representation of the builder of Egypt's Great Pyramid.

Room 26 – Montuhotep II

The seated statue in the corridor on your right, after leaving Room 32, represents Theban-born **Montuhotep II** (2055–2004 BC; No 136), first ruler of the Middle Kingdom period. He is shown with black skin (representing fertility and rebirth) and the red crown of Lower Egypt. This statue was discovered by Howard Carter under the forecourt of the pharaoh's temple at Deir al-Bahri in Thebes in 1900, when the ground gave way under his horse – a surprisingly common means of discovery in the annals of Egyptology.

Rooms 21 & 16 – Sphinxes

These **grey-granite sphinxes** are very different from the great enigmatic Sphinx at Giza – they look more like the Cowardly Lion from *The Wizard of Oz,* each with a fleshy human face surrounded by a great shaggy mane and big ears. Sculpted for Pharaoh Amenemhat III (1855–1808 BC) during the 12th dynasty, they were moved to Avaris by the Hyksos and then to the Delta city of Tanis (see p167) by Ramses II. Also here, in Room 16, is an extraordinary wood figure of the ka (spirit double) of the 13th-dynasty ruler Hor Auibre.

Room 12 – Hathor Shrine

The centrepiece of this room is a remarkably well-preserved vaulted **sandstone chapel**, found near the Theban temple of Deir al-Bahri. Its walls are painted with reliefs of Tuthmosis III (1479–1425 BC), his wife Meritre and two princesses, making offerings to Hathor, who suckles the pharaoh. The life-size cow statue suckles Tuthmosis III's son and successor Amenhotep II (1427–1400 BC), who also stands beneath her chin.

Hatshepsut (1473–1458 BC), who was coregent for part of Tuthmosis III's reign, eventually had herself crowned as pharaoh. Her life-size **pink granite statue** stands to the right of the chapel. Although she wears a pharaoh's headdress and a false beard, the statue has definite feminine characteristics. In the corridor outside this room, the large reddish- painted limestone head is also of Hatshepsut, taken from one of the huge Osiris-type statues that adorned the pillared facade of her great temple at Deir al-Bahri. Also in Room 12, on the north wall, are decorations from the same temple showing the famed expedition to Punt, which scholars posit may be current-day Somalia or perhaps the Arabian Peninsula.

Room 3 – Amarna Room

Akhenaten (1352–1336 BC), the 'heretic pharaoh', did more than build a new capital at Tell al-Amarna, close the temples of the traditional state god Amun and promote the sun god Aten in his place. He also ushered in a period of great artistic freedom, as a glance around this room will show. Compare these great torsos with their strangely bulbous bellies, hips and thighs, their elongated faces and thick lips, with the sleek, hard-edged Middle Kingdom sculpture of previous rooms.

Perhaps most striking of all is the **unfinished head of Nefertiti** (No 161, in the left alcove), wife of Akhenaten. Worked in brown quartzite, it's an incredibly delicate and sensitive portrait and shows the queen to have been extremely beautiful – unlike some of the relief figures of her elsewhere in the room, in which she appears with exactly the same strange features as her husband. The masterpiece of this period, the finished bust of Nefertiti, can be seen in the Neues Museum in Berlin.

HIGHLIGHTS OF THE EGYPTIAN MUSEUM

The following are our favourite, must-see exhibits, for which you need at least half a day but preferably a little more.

Tutankhamun Galleries (1st fl; p142) Top on everyone's list, King Tut's treasures occupy a large chunk of the museum's upper floor. Go first to Room 3 to see his sarcophagi while the crowds are light.

Old Kingdom Rooms (Ground fl, Rooms 42, 37 & 32; p138) After peeking at Tutankhamun, return to the ground floor for a chronological tour. Look out for the statue of well-muscled Khafre – you may also recognise him from the Sphinx.

Amarna Room (Ground fl, Room 3; p140) Stepping into this room feels like visiting another museum entirely – the artwork commissioned by Akhenaten for his new capital at Tell al-Amarna, is dramatically different in style from his predecessors. Say hi to his wife, Nefertiti, while you're here.

Royal Tombs of Tanis (1st fl, Room 2; p144) While everyone else is gawking at Tutankhamun's treasure down the hall, this room of gem-encrusted gold jewellery, found at the largest ruined city in the Nile Delta, is often empty.

Graeco-Roman Mummy Portraits (1st fl, Room 14; p144) An odd interlude in mummy traditions, from very late in the ancient Egypt game, these wood panel portraits were placed over the faces of embalmed dead, staring up in vividly realistic style.

Animal Mummies (1st fl, Rooms 53 & 54; p145) Tucked in an odd corner of the museum, this long, dim room contains the bundled remains of the ancients' beloved pets, honoured gods and even their last meals.

Middle Kingdom Models (1st fl, Rooms 32 & 27; p145) When you've had your fill of gold and other royal trappings, stop in these rooms to get a picture of common life in ancient Egypt, depicted in miniature dioramas made to accompany the pharaoh to the other world.

Royal Mummies Halls (1st fl, Rooms 56 & 46; p142) Visit these around lunch or near closing time to avoid the crowds – they don't require more than half an hour, but they do put a human face on all the stunning objects you've seen.

Room 10 – Ramses II

At the foot of the northeast stairs is a fabulous large, **grey-granite representation of Ramses II** (1279–1213 BC), builder of the Ramesseum and Abu Simbel. But here in this statue he is tenderly depicted as a child with his finger in his mouth nestled against the breast of a great falcon, in this case the Canaanite god Horus.

Room 34 – Graeco-Roman Room

It is best to visit these last rooms after seeing the first floor, because this is the end of the ancient Egyptian story. By the 4th century BC, Egypt had been invaded by many nations, most recently by the Macedonian Alexander the Great. Egypt's famously resistant culture had become porous, as will be obvious from the **statue** situated immediately to the left as you enter this room: a typically Greek face with curly beard and locks, but wearing a Pharaonic-style headdress.

Nearby on the right-hand wall, you'll see a large **sandstone panel** inscribed in three languages: official Egyptian hieroglyphics; the more popularly used demotic; and Greek, the language of the new rulers. This trilingual stone is similar in nature to the more famous Rosetta Stone (see p345) that is now housed in London's British Museum. A **cast of the Rosetta Stone** stands near the museum entrance (Room 48).

MUSEUM TOUR: FIRST FLOOR

Exhibits here are grouped thematically and can be viewed in any order, but if you come up the southeast stairs, you'll enter the

Tutankhamun Galleries at Room 45 and experience the pieces in roughly the same order that they were laid out in the tomb (a poster on the wall outside Room 45 illustrates the tomb and treasures as they were found). But first, directly above the stairs, are the Royal Mummies Halls.

Rooms 56 & 46 – Royal Mummies Halls

These rooms house the remains of some of Egypt's most illustrious pharaohs and queens from the 17th to the 21st dynasties, 1650 to 945 BC. They lie in individual glass showcases (kept at a constant 22°C) in two rooms at either corner of the museum. The mood is suitably sombre, and talking above a hushed whisper is forbidden (somewhat counterproductively, a guard will bellow 'silence' from time to time). Tour guides are not allowed to enter, although some do.

Displaying dead royalty has proved controversial. Late President Anwar Sadat took the royal mummies off display in 1979 for political reasons, but the subsequent reappearance of 11 of the better-looking mummies in 1994 did wonders for tourism figures, inspiring the opening of a second mummy room with second-tier but no less interesting personages. The ticket price is steep, but you certainly won't see so many mummies in any other single museum, nor get to peer at them so closely. Parents should be aware that the mummies can be a frightening sight for young children.

ROOM 56

Take time to study some of the first room's celebrated inmates, beginning with the brave Theban pharaoh **Seqenenre Taa II** who died violently, possibly during struggles to reunite the country at the end of the Second Intermediate Period, around 1560 BC. His wounds are still visible beneath his curly hair, and his twisted arms reflect his violent death. The perfectly wrapped mummies of **Queen Merit Amun** and **Amenhotep I** (1525–1504 BC) show how all royal mummies would once have looked, bedecked with garlands.

On the opposite side of the room, **Tuthmosis II** (1525–1504 BC) lies next to his sister-wife, **Hatshepsut** – the great queen and female pharaoh, rendered so grandly in stone in Room 12, is here reduced to an 'obese female with bad teeth', according to the descriptive text. Their son, **Tuthmosis III** (1479–1425 BC) occupies the last case, look-

ing not too bad considering he'd been severely damaged by grave robbers centuries ago.

In the centre of the room, **Ramses II** is strikingly well preserved, his haughty profile revealing the family's characteristic curved nose, his grey hair tinged with henna and his fingernails long. By contrast, his 13th son and successor, **Merenptah** (1213–1203 BC), has a distinctly white appearance caused by the mummification process. **Amenhotep II** rests in the next case, finally settled after a particularly tumultuous century of being shipped up and down the Nile and stolen from his tomb in the Valley of the Kings. **Tuthmosis IV** (1400–1390 BC) sports beautifully styled hair; he was also the first pharaoh to have his ears pierced. With his smooth black skin and square chin, **Seti I** (1294–1279 BC) rivals Ramses II in flawless preservation.

ROOM 46

The second mummy room (same ticket) is located across the building, off Room 46. The corridor display relates some of the most famous mummy discoveries, including the 1881 Deir al-Bahri cache, and displays the body of **Queen Tiy**, with long flowing hair. Many of the mummies in this section date from the 20th and 21st dynasties, the end of the New Kingdom and the start of the Third Intermediate Period (c 1186–945 BC). You first pass **Ramses III** (1184–1153 BC) **and IV** (1153–1147 BC), and around the corner, the face of **Ramses V** (1147–1143 BC) is marked with small raised spots, likely caused by smallpox. In the centre of the room, **Nedjmet** (c 1070–946 BC) wears a lavish curly wig and has black-and-white stones for eyes. Next to her, **Queen Henettawy** (c 1025 BC), in a linen shroud painted with an image of Osiris, is a product of modern restorers, who repaired her cheeks, which had burst from overpacking by ancient embalmers. In the final section, the mummy of **Queen Nesikhonsu** still conveys the queen's vivid features, while **Queen Maatkare** lies with her pet baboon.

Tutankhamun Galleries

The treasures of the young New Kingdom pharaoh Tutankhamun, who ruled for only nine years during the 14th century BC (1336–1327 BC), are among the world's most famous antiquities. English archaeologist Howard Carter unearthed the tomb in 1922. Its well-hidden location in the Valley of the Kings, below the much grander but ransacked tomb of Ramses VI, had long prevented its discovery (see p211). Many archaeologists now believe that up to 80% of these extraordinary treasures were made for Tutankhamun's predecessors, Akhenaten and Smenkhkare – some still carry the names of the original owners. Perhaps with Tutankhamun's death everything connected with the Amarna Period was simply chucked in with him to be buried away and forgotten.

About 1700 items are spread throughout a series of rooms on the museum's 1st floor, and although the gold shines brightest, sometimes the less grand objects give more insight into the pharaoh's life. The following are some of the highlights.

ROOM 45
Flanking the doorway as you enter are two life-size **statues of Tutankhamun**, found in the tomb antechamber. The statues are made of wood coated in bitumen, their black skin suggesting an identification with Osiris and the rich, black river silt, symbolising fertility and rebirth.

ROOMS 35 & 30
The **pharaoh's lion throne** (No 179) is one of the museum's highlights. Covered with sheet gold and inlaid with lapis, cornelian and other semiprecious stones, the wooden throne is supported by lion legs. The colourful tableau on the chair back depicts Ankhesenamun applying perfume to her husband, under the rays of the sun (Aten), the worship of which was a hangover from the Amarna period. And evidence of remodelling of the figures suggests that this was actually the throne of Akhenaten, Tutankhamun's father and predecessor. The royals' robes are modelled in beaten silver, their hair of glass paste.

Opposite the throne, on the east wall, **Tutankhamun's wig box** is made of dark wood, with strips of blue and orange inlay. The mushroom-shaped wooden support inside once held the pharaoh's short curly wig.

Many **golden statues** were placed in the tomb to help the pharaoh on his journey in the afterlife, including a series of 28 gilt-wood protective deities and 413 shabti, attendants who would serve the pharaoh in the afterlife. Only a few of them are displayed here.

ROOM 20
This room contains exquisite **alabaster jars** and **vessels** carved into the shape of boats and animals. Some critters have lifelike

EXTRA GUIDANCE
To make the most of an Egyptian Museum visit, stop by the AUC Bookstore (p113) and pick up *The Illustrated Guide to the Egyptian Museum in Cairo*, edited by Alessandro Bongioanni and Maria Croce Sole (E£180). It's packed with colour photographs and varied itineraries.

pink tongues sticking out – as if the artist just wanted to show he could render such a thing in stone.

ROOMS 10 & 9
The eastern end of this gallery is filled with the pharaoh's three elaborate **funerary couches**, one supported by the cow-goddess Mehetweret, one by two figures of the goddess Ammit, 'the devourer' who ate the hearts of the damned, and the third by the lioness god Mehet. The huge **bouquets** of persea and olive leaves in Room 10, near the top of the stairs, were originally propped up beside the two black and gold guardian statues in Room 45. A cross-section plan on the wall next to the stairs shows how all the furniture was arranged in the tomb.

At the west end of Room 9, an alabaster chest contains four **Canopic jars**, the stoppers of which are in the form of Tutankhamun's head. Inside these jars, four miniature gold coffins (now in Room 3) held the pharaoh's internal organs. The chest was placed inside the golden Canopic shrine with the four gilded goddesses: Isis, Neith, Nephthys and Selket, all portrayed with protective outstretched arms.

Most people walk right past Tutankhamun's amazing **wardrobe**, laid out along the south wall. The pharaoh was buried with a range of sumptuous tunics covered in gold discs and beading, ritual robes of 'fake fur', a large supply of neatly folded underwear and split-toe socks to be worn with the 47 pairs of flip-flop–type sandals. From these and other objects, the Tutankhamun Textile Project has worked out that the pharaoh's vital statistics were: chest 79cm (31in), waist 74cm (29in) and hips 109cm (43in).

ROOMS 8 & 7
These galleries just barely accommodate four massive **gilded wooden shrines**. These fitted one inside the other, like a set of

Russian dolls, encasing at their centre the sarcophagi of the boy pharaoh.

ROOM 3

Everybody wants to see this room as it contains the pharaoh's golden sarcophagus and jewels; at peak times, prepare to queue. Tutankhamun's astonishing **death mask** has become an Egyptian icon. Made of solid gold and weighing 11kg, it covered the head of the mummy, and lay inside a series of three sarcophagi. The mask is an idealised portrait of the young pharaoh; the eyes are fashioned from obsidian and quartz, while the outlines of the eyes and the eyebrows are delineated with lapis lazuli. No less wondrous are the two **golden sarcophagi**, the inner two of the burial. The outermost coffin, along with the pharaoh's mummy, remains in his tomb in the Valley of the Kings. The smallest coffin is, like the mask, cast in solid gold and inlaid in the same fashion. It weighs 110kg. The slightly larger coffin is made of gilded wood.

Room 4 – Ancient Egyptian Jewellery

Even after Tutankhamun's treasures, this stunning collection of **royal jewellery** takes the breath away. The collection covers the period from early dynasties to the Romans and includes belts, inlaid beadwork, necklaces, semiprecious stones and bracelets. Among the most beautiful is a piece from the Pyramid of al-Lahun: the **diadem of Queen Sit-Hathor-Yunet**, a golden headband with a rearing cobra inset with semiprecious stones. Also of note is Pharaoh Ahmose's gold dagger and Seti II's considerable gold earrings.

Room 2 – Royal Tombs of Tanis

This glittering collection of gold- and silver-encrusted objects came from six intact 21st- and 22nd-dynasty tombs unearthed at the Delta site of Tanis (p167) by the French in 1939. The tombs rivalled Tutankhamun's in riches, but news of the find was overshadowed by the outbreak of WWII. The gold **death mask of Psusennes I** (1039–991 BC), with thick black eyeliner, is shown alongside his silver inner coffin and another silver coffin with the head of a falcon belonging to the pharaoh Shoshenq II (c 890 BC).

Room 14 – Graeco-Roman Mummy Portraits

This room contains a small sample of the stunning portraits found on Graeco-Roman

---

KING TUT GOES TO THE LAB

Though we have much concrete evidence of the pharaoh Tutankhamun, in the form of his tomb contents, the boy king still remains elusive in some ways. How did he die? Who were his parents? Who was his wife? Advances in DNA analysis finally inspired a test of Tut and other mummies thought to be his relatives, and the results were revealed in 2010.

The DNA tests confirmed the predominant theory that Tut's grandparents were Amenhotep III and Queen Tiy. This in turn showed that Tut's father was almost certainly the 'heretic' pharaoh Akhenaten. Finally, the team was able to confirm that another unidentified mummy was Tut's mother – as well as Akhenaten's sister.

The researchers also looked for congenital disease markers. Had Tut and his forebears suffered from an ailment that caused the distorted face shape and androgynous look depicted so famously in Akhenaten's portraiture? In fact, the DNA showed no such abnormality – so Akhenaten's odd appearance may have been just a stylistic choice.

But Tutankhamun was likely affected by inbreeding all the same. Two mummified foetuses buried with him are almost certainly his unborn daughters. And a separate theory posits that his wife was Ankhesamun, his half-sister. This all suggests the foetuses were too deformed to live.

Finally, while preparing Tutankhamun's mummy for the DNA analysis, a CT scan revealed a club foot and necrosis in one toe – which accounts for the numerous canes found in his tomb, despite his death at age 19. The samples also tested positive for parasites associated with malaria, which may have killed him.

So not every mystery is yet solved – but researchers are still at work on other mummies, which may untangle more of Tutankhamun's complex family history.

mummies, popularly known as the **Fayoum Portraits** (see boxed text, p161). Painted on wooden panels, often during the subject's life, and placed over the mummies' embalmed faces, these portraits express the personalities of their subjects better than the stylised elegance of most other ancient Egyptian art, and are recognised as the link between ancient art and the Western portrait tradition.

Room 34 – Pharaonic Technology

Interesting for gadget buffs, this room contains a great number of everyday objects that helped support ancient Egypt's great leap out of prehistory. Some, such as the hand tools for farming and, are still in use in parts of Egypt today, and others – needles and thread, combs, dice – look remarkably like our own. **Pharaonic boomerangs** were apparently used for hunting birds.

Room 43 – Yuya & Thuyu Rooms

Before Tutankhamun's tomb was uncovered, the tomb of Yuya and Thuyu (the parents of Queen Tiy, and Tutankhamun's great-grandparents) had yielded the most spectacular find in Egyptian archaeology. Found virtually intact in the Valley of the Kings in 1905, the tomb contained a vast number of treasures, including five ornate sarcophagi and the remarkably well-preserved mummies of the two commoners who became royal in-laws. Among many other items on display is the fabulous gilded and bead-trimmed **death mask of Thuyu**, at the front of the room.

Room 53 – Animal Mummies

Animal cults grew in strength throughout ancient Egypt, as the mummified cats, dogs, crocodiles, birds, monkeys and jackals in Room 53 suggest. Tucked in a dim, dusty wing of the museum, their rigid forms are a bit creepier than their human counterparts. Some edible beasts became 'victual mummies', preserved as food and 'browned' with resin, to offer the pharaoh an eternal picnic.

Room 37 – Model Armies

Discovered in the Asyut tomb of governor Mesheti and dating from about 2000 BC (11th dynasty), these are two sets of 40 **wooden warriors** marching in phalanxes. The darker soldiers (No 72) are Nubian archers from the south of the kingdom, each wearing brightly coloured kilts of varying design, while the lighter-skinned soldiers (No 73) are Egyptian pikemen.

Rooms 32 & 27 – Middle Kingdom Models

These lifelike **models** were mostly found in the tomb of Meketre, an 11th-dynasty chancellor in Thebes, and, like some of the best Egyptian tomb paintings, they provide a fascinating portrait of daily life almost 4000 years ago. They include finely modelled servants (especially in Room 32), fishing boats, kitchens and carpentry and weaving workshops. In Room 27, a model of Meketre's house includes fig trees in the garden, and 1.5m-wide scene shows Meketre sitting with his sons, four scribes and others, counting cattle.

Cairo Outskirts & the Delta

Includes »

Top Tips

» Microbuses and trains are the best way to travel just outside of Cairo.

» See p92 for recommended tour guides and drivers for day trips.

Best Reads

» *The Fayoum: History and Guide* by R Neil Hewison

» *In an Antique Land* by Amitav Ghosh, about life in a Delta village

» *Coptic Monasteries* by Gawdat Gabra

Why Go?

Typical Egypt itineraries rarely take in the area right around Cairo because little of it can honestly be put in the 'must-see' category. But with the exception of the ancient site of Saqqara, which lies on the city's southern edge, and this alone can be a draw. Thanks to speedy microbuses and good trains through the Delta, it's easy to get from Cairo's confines to open green fields; ancient sites you'll have all to yourself; modern Coptic monasteries with roots 17 centuries deep; and the only-in-Africa action of a live camel market. Just as important, if not more so, these spots are places to meet Egyptians who will marvel that you made the journey to their overlooked corner of the country. Every destination in this chapter can be visited as an easy day trip or a leisurely overnight excursion from the capital.

When to Go
Medinat al Fayoum

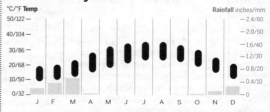

Dec–Feb The best time to visit shadeless Saqqara and other pyramids.

Jun–Aug Summer heat can be paralysing. Cool off at Lake Qarun in Al-Fayoum.

Oct The *moulid* (saints' festival) of al-Sayyed Badawi in Tanta draws a million people.

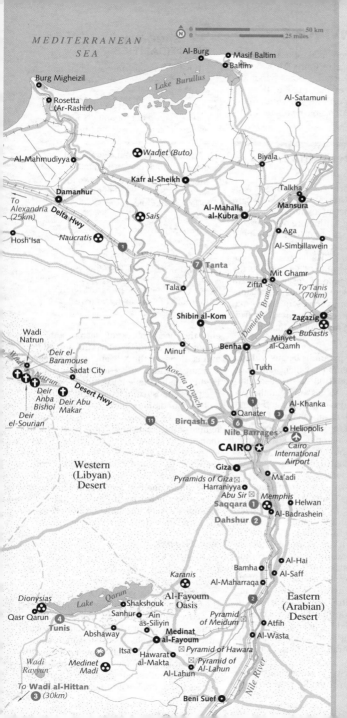

1 Explore the half-buried ruins of sprawling **Saqqara** (p148)

2 Penetrate the heart of the Red Pyramid at **Dahshur** (p154)

3 Go sandboarding and fossil-spotting in the desert sands of **Wadi al-Hittan** (p159)

4 Chill out in the funky arts colony of **Tunis** (p160)

5 Immerse yourself in the sights, sounds and smells of the **Birqash camel market** (p165)

6 Pile on to a merry boat of day trippers to see the **Nile Barrages** at Qanater (p166)

7 Take a comfortable train trip to the Delta city of **Tanta** (p166), just to eat some sweets and enjoy the view

DESERT ENVIRONS

The Western Desert makes a forbidding border on this edge of Cairo. Most people head out this way for the 'other pyramids', the stone structures that predate those at Giza, but it's also worth the trip south to the lakes, dunes and archaeological sites of Al-Fayoum.

Saqqara, Memphis & Dahshur

Although most tourists associate Egypt with the Pyramids of Giza, there are known to be at least 118 ancient pyramids scattered around the country, with more being discovered every few years or so. The majority of these monuments are spread out along the desert between the Giza Plateau and the semi-oasis of Al-Fayoum. They include the must-see Step Pyramid of Zoser at Saqqara and the Red and Bent Pyramids of Dahshur. These three pyramids represent the formative steps of architecture that reached fruition in the Great Pyramid of Khufu (Cheops).

History

The story of these pyramids begins with the ancient city of Memphis, which barely survives today. Around 3100 BC, the legendary pharaoh Narmer (Menes) unified the two lands of Upper and Lower Egypt and founded Memphis, symbolically on the spot where the Nile Delta met the valley. For most of the Pharaonic period Memphis was the capital of Egypt, though the seat of power was later moved to Thebes (now Luxor) during the era of the New Kingdom.

Originally known as Ineb-hedj, meaning 'White walls', the contemporary name of Memphis derives from Men-nefer, meaning 'Established and beautiful'. Indeed, the city was filled with palaces, gardens and temples, making it one of the greatest cities of the ancient world. In the 5th century BC, long after its period of power, Greek historian and traveller Herodotus still described Memphis as 'a prosperous city and cosmopolitan centre'. Even after Thebes became the capital during the New Kingdom, Memphis remained Egypt's second city, and prospered until it was finally abandoned during the first Arab invasions in the 7th century AD.

Although the city was once an area replete with royal pyramids, private tombs

---

ℹ **SAQQARA PRACTICALITIES**

» The main monuments are in an area around the Step Pyramid known as North Saqqara.

» About 1km south of the Step Pyramid is a group of monuments known as South Saqqara, with no official entry fee or opening hours.

» The only toilets at the site are at the main entrance to North Saqqara.

» Pack a lunch, as there are no food outlets at Saqqara aside from people selling cold drinks.

» Check at the ticket office to see which monuments are open – this constantly changes.

» Saqqara is one of the most popular attractions in the Cairo area, and because of the distances involved, independent visitors are rare. See p150 for more tips on timing your visit.

---

and the necropolises of sacred animals, centuries of builders quarrying for stone, annual floods of the Nile and greed-stricken antiquity hunters succeeded where even the mighty Persians failed: the city of Memphis itself has almost completely vanished.

The foundations have long since been ploughed under, and even the enormous temple of the creator god, Ptah, is little more than a few sparse ruins frequently waterlogged due to the high water table. Today, there are few clues as to Memphis' former grandeur and importance and, sadly, it's difficult to imagine that any sort of settlement once stood here. The only solid traces of Memphis remain the funerary complexes – the pyramids – that lie around the fringes.

◉ Sights

Saqqara ARCHAEOLOGICAL SITE
(Map p154 adult/student E£60/30, parking E£2; ⊙8am-4pm, to 3pm during Ramadan) Covering a 7km stretch of the Western Desert, Saqqara, the huge cemetery of ancient Memphis, was an active burial ground for more than 3500 years and is Egypt's largest archaeological site. The necropolis is situated high above the Nile Valley's cultivation area, and is the final resting place for deceased pharaohs and their families, administrators, generals and sacred animals. Old Kingdom pharaohs

were buried within Saqqara's 11 major pyramids, while their subjects were buried in the hundreds of smaller tombs. The name Saqqara is most likely derived from Sokar, the Memphite god of the dead.

Most of Saqqara, except for the Step Pyramid, was buried in sand until the mid-19th century, when the great French Egyptologist Auguste Mariette uncovered the Serapeum. Since then, it has been a gradual process of rediscovery: the Step Pyramid's massive funerary complex was not exposed until 1924, and it is in a constant state of restoration. French architect Jean-Philippe Lauer, who began work here in 1926, was involved in the project for an incredible 75 years until his death in 2001. More recently, there has been a string of new discoveries, including a whole slew of mummies and even a new pyramid. For more information, see boxed text p156.

Imhotep Museum

(Map p154) In the complex at the entrance is this beautiful collection of some of the best finds at Saqqara, and one of the finest small museums in Egypt. It is framed as a tribute to the architect Imhotep, who served the pharaoh Zoser and is credited with creating ancient Egypt's first comprehensive vision of stone architecture (he also happens to be considered the world's first physician). His solid wood coffin is on display in one room.

There's also a good installation of the turquoise-green faience tiles from inside Zoser's pyramid and the striking carvings of starving people, complete with bony ribs and sagging breasts, found on the causeway of Unas. You'll also see some beautifully realistic portrait heads and statues, and a mummy (Merenre I) with his toes and head exposed – the oldest complete royal mummy, from 2292 BC.

As an interesting counterpoint to all the ancient stuff, one room is a recreation of the library of Jean-Philippe Lauer, who spent most of his life excavating Saqqara. 'At times, I spoke to Imhotep,' the archaeologist said of his sometimes-desperate reconstruction process.

Zoser's Funerary Complex

(Map p152) In the year 2650 BC, Imhotep, the pharaoh's chief architect (later deified) built the **Step Pyramid** for Zoser (2667–2648 BC). It is Egypt's (and the world's) earliest stone monument, and its significance cannot be overstated. Previously, temples were

made of perishable materials, while royal tombs were usually underground rooms topped with a mud-brick mastaba (structure in the shape of a bench above tombs that was the basis for later pyramids). However, Imhotep developed the mastaba into a pyramid *and* built it in hewn stone. From this flowed Egypt's later architectural achievements.

The pyramid was transformed from mastaba into pyramid through six stages of construction, the builders gaining confidence in their use of the new medium and mastering techniques required to move, place and secure the huge blocks. This first pyramid rose in six steps to a height of 60m, and was encased in fine white limestone.

The Step Pyramid is surrounded by a vast funerary complex, enclosed by a 1645m-long panelled limestone wall, and covers 15 hectares. Part of the enclosure wall survives today, and a section near the entrance was restored to its original 10m height.

You enter the complex at the southeastern corner via a **colonnaded corridor** and a broad **hypostyle hall**. The 40 pillars in the corridor are 'bundle columns', ribbed to resemble a bundle of palm or papyrus stems. The walls have been restored, but the protective ceiling is modern concrete. After the entrance, you pass through a large, false, half-open ka (attendant spirit) door when you enter – note the stone 'hinge' near the bottom. There were fourteen such doors in the complex, in previous eras made of wood but here carved for the first time from stone and painted to resemble wood. They allowed the pharaoh's ka to come and go at will.

The hypostyle hall leads into the **Great South Court**, a huge open area flanking the south side of the pyramid, with a section of wall featuring a frieze of cobras (the rest are in the Imhotep Museum). The cobra (uraeus) represented the goddess Wadjet, a fire-spitting agent of destruction and protector of the pharaoh. It was a symbol of Egyptian royalty, and a rearing cobra always appeared on the brow of a pharaoh's headdress or crown.

Near the base of the pyramid is an altar, and in the centre of the court are two stone D-shaped boundary markers, which delineated the ritual race the pharaoh had to run, a literal demonstration of his fitness to rule. The race was part of the Jubilee Festival (Heb-Sed), which usually occurred after 30 years' reign and showed the pharaoh's

After the Pyramids of Giza, a trip to Saqqara and the surrounding sites is the most popular day outing from Cairo, and you should have no trouble arranging a tour through your accommodation. For more freedom, simply hire a taxi for the day.

Just getting out of the city can be half the battle, so ideally go on a Friday or Saturday, when the traffic is lighter. In any case get a very early start. In winter, when daytime temperatures are manageable, visit Dahshur first, as it's the furthest away (about an hour in light traffic). Then you reach Saqqara at midday, when many of the tour buses have moved on. But if the day is at all hot, start with Saqqara to avoid the peak heat, and pace yourself.

Pack a picnic lunch (takeaway sandwiches, for instance), as there is no real place to eat; at the end of the day, you can always head to Andrea (p133) for a heartier meal.

symbolic rejuvenation and the recognition of his supremacy by officials from all over Egypt. The construction of the Heb-Sed within Zoser's funerary complex was therefore intended to perpetuate his revitalisation for eternity.

The buildings on the eastern side of the pyramid are also connected with the royal jubilee, and include the **Heb-Sed (Jubilee) Court**. Buildings on the east side of the court represent the shrines of Lower Egypt, and those on the west represent Upper Egypt. All were designed to house the spirits of Egypt's gods when they gathered to witness the rebirth of the pharaoh during his jubilee rituals.

North of the Heb-Sed Court are the **House of the South Court** and **House of the North Court**, representing the two main shrines of Upper and Lower Egypt, and symbolising the unity of the country. The heraldic plants of the two regions were chosen to decorate the column capitals: papyrus for the north and lotus for the south.

The House of the South also features one of the earliest examples of tourist graffiti. In the 47th year of Ramses II's reign, nearly 1500 years after Zoser's death, Hadnakhte, a treasury scribe, recorded his admiration for Zoser while 'on a pleasure trip west of Memphis' in about 1232 BC. His hieratic script, written in black ink, is preserved behind perspex just inside the building's entrance.

A stone structure right in front of the pyramid, the **serdab** (a small room containing a statue of the deceased to which offerings were presented) contains a slightly tilted wooden box with two holes drilled into its north face. Look through these and you'll have the eerie experience of coming face to face with Zoser himself. Inside is a lifelike statue of the long-dead pharaoh, gazing stonily out towards the stars. However, this is only a copy – the original is in Cairo's Egyptian Museum.

The original entrance to the Step Pyramid is directly behind the serdab, and leads down to a maze of subterranean tunnels and chambers quarried for almost 6km through the rock. The pharaoh's burial chamber is vaulted in granite, and others are decorated with reliefs of the jubilee race and feature some exquisite blue faience tile decoration. Although the interior of the pyramid is unsafe and closed to the public, part of the blue-tiled decoration can be seen in the Imhotep Museum at the site entrance.

Pyramid of Userkaf

(Map p152) Northeast of the funerary complex is the Pyramid of Userkaf, the first pharaoh of the 5th dynasty, which is closed to the public for safety reasons. Although the removal of its limestone casing has left little more than a mound of rubble, it once rose to a height of 49m. Furthermore, its funerary temple was once decorated with the most exquisite naturalistic relief carvings, judging from one of the few remaining fragments (now in the Egyptian Museum) showing birds by the river.

Pyramid & Causeway of Unas

(Map p152) What appears to be another big mound of rubble, to the southwest of Zoser's funerary complex, is actually the Pyramid of Unas, the last pharaoh of the 5th dynasty (2375–2345 BC). Built only 300 years after the inspired creation of the Step Pyramid, this unassuming pile of loose blocks and debris once stood 43m high.

From the outside, the Pyramid of Unas is not much to look at, though the interior marked the beginning of a significant development in funerary practices. For the first time, the royal burial chamber was decorated, its ceiling adorned with stars and its white alabaster-lined walls inscribed with beautiful blue hieroglyphs.

The aforementioned **hieroglyphs** are some of the earliest examples of the funerary inscriptions that are now known as the **Pyramid Texts** (later compiled into the Egyptian *Book of the Dead*). Covering the walls of a number of the pyramids at Saqqara, the hieroglyphs are 'spells' to protect the soul of the deceased. Of the 283 separate phrases in Unas' tomb, most are prayers and hymns and lists of items, such as food and clothing the pharaoh would require in the afterlife.

The 750m-long causeway running from the east side of Unas' pyramid to his valley temple (now marked by little more than a couple of stone columns at the side of the road leading up to the site) was originally roofed and decorated with a great range of painted relief scenes, including a startling image of people starving, thought to be due to a famine during Unas' reign. A portion of the relief is on display in the Imhotep Museum.

The two 45m-long boat pits of Unas lie immediately south of the causeway, while on either side of the causeway are numerous **tombs** – more than 200 have been excavated. Of the several better-preserved examples usually open to visitors are the tombs of one of Unas' queens, Nebet, and that of Princess Idut, who was possibly his daughter. There are also several brightly painted tombs of prominent 5th- and 6th-dynasty officials. These include the Tomb of Mehu, the royal vizier (minister), and the Tomb of Nefer, the supervisor of singers.

Several beautiful tombs have been cleared in the area east of the Pyramid of Unas. Although not quite as famous as the tombs north of the Step Pyramid, this set includes a number of interesting Pharaonic attendants. These include the joint Tomb of Niankhkhnum and Khnumhotep, overseers of the royal manicurists to Pharaoh Nyuserra; the Tomb of Neferherenptah, the overseer of the royal hairdressers; and the Tomb of Irukaptah, overseer of the royal butchers.

Around the sides of the Pyramid of Unas are several large **shaft tombs** built much later, in the Saite era (664–525 BC) and the Persian period (525–404 BC). These are some of the deepest tombs in Egypt, although as with just about everywhere else in the country, precautions against grave robbers failed.

However, the sheer size of the tombs and the great stone sarcophagi within, combined with their sophisticated decoration, demonstrate that the technical achievements of the later part of ancient Egyptian history were equal to those of earlier times.

To the north of the pyramid is the enormous tomb shaft of the Saite general Amun-Tefnakht. On the south side of the pyramid is a group of three Persian tombs – the entrance is covered by a small wooden hut to which a guard in the area has the key. If you don't have your own torch, he'll lead you down a 25m-deep winding staircase to the vaulted tombs of three officials: the admiral Djenhebu to the west, chief royal physician Psamtik in the centre and Psamtik's son, Pediese, to the east.

Monastery of St Jeremiah

(Map p152) Uphill from the causeway of Unas, southeast of the boat pits, are the half-buried remains of this Coptic monastery, which dates from the 5th century AD. Unfortunately, little is left of the structure, which was ransacked by invading Arabs in 950. More recently, the wall paintings and carvings were removed to the Coptic Museum in Cairo (p71).

BEST OF SAQQARA

If you keep up a good pace, you can see the high points of Saqqara in about half a day.

» Start with a quick visit to the **Imhotep Museum**, to get the lay of the land.

» Head for **Zoser's funerary complex**, entering through the hypostyle hall, and gaze on the **Step Pyramid**, the world's oldest pyramid.

» Walk south towards the causeway of Unas.

» Drive to the **Pyramid of Teti** to see some of the famous Pyramid Texts inside, and then pop into the nearby **Tomb of Kagemni**.

» End with the most wonderful tomb of all, the **Mastaba of Ti**, with its fascinating reliefs of daily life.

» Revisit the museum to see some of the best items that have been removed from the tombs for protection.

North Saqqara

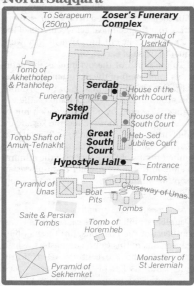

Pyramid of Sekhemket

(Map p152) Closed to the public because of its dangerous condition, the unfinished pyramid of Zoser's successor Sekhemket (2648–2640 BC) is a short distance west of the ruined monastery. The project was abandoned for unknown reasons when the great limestone enclosure wall was only 3m high, despite the fact that the architects had already constructed the underground chambers in the rock beneath the pyramid as well as the deep shaft of the south tomb. An unused travertine sarcophagus was found in the sealed burial chamber, and a quantity of gold and jewellery and a child's body were discovered in the south tomb. Recent surveys have also revealed another mysterious large complex to the west of Sekhemket's enclosure, but this remains unexcavated.

Tomb of Akhethotep & Ptahhotep

(Map p152) Akhethotep and his son Ptahhotep were senior royal officials during the reigns of Djedkare (2414–2375 BC) and Unas at the end of the 5th dynasty. Akhethotep served as vizier, judge, supervisor of pyramid cities and supervisor of priests, though his titles were eventually inherited by Ptahhotep, along with his tomb. The joint mastaba has two burial chambers, two chapels and a pillared hall.

The painted reliefs in Ptahhotep's section are particularly beautiful, and portray a wide range of animals, from lions and hedgehogs to the domesticated cattle and fowl that were brought as offerings to the deceased. Ptahhotep himself is portrayed resplendent in a panther-skin robe inhaling perfume from a jar. Ever the fan of pampering himself, he is having his wig fitted, his feet massaged and his fingers manicured (some Egyptologists prefer to interpret this detail as Ptahhotep inspecting an important document, which would be in keeping with his official status).

Philosophers' Circle

(Map p154) Nearby is this sad-looking group of Greek statues, which are arranged in a semicircle and sheltered by a spectacularly ugly concrete shelter. This is the remnant of a collection of philosophers and poets set up as a wayside shrine by Ptolemy I (323–283 BC) as part of his patronage of learning. From left to right are Plato, Heraclitus, Thales, Protagoras, Homer, Hesiod, Demetrius of Phalerum and Pindar.

Serapeum

(Map p154) The Serapeum, which is dedicated to the sacred Apis bull, is one of the highlights of visiting Saqqara. The Apis bulls were by far the most important of the cult animals entombed at Saqqara. The Apis, it was believed, was an incarnation of Ptah, the god of Memphis, and was the calf of a cow struck by lightning from heaven. Once divinely impregnated, the cow could never again give birth, and her calf was kept in the Temple of Ptah at Memphis and worshipped as a god.

The Apis was always portrayed as black, with a distinctive white diamond on its forehead, the image of a vulture on its back and a scarab-shaped mark on its tongue. When it died, the bull was mummified on one of the large alabaster embalming tables discovered at Memphis, then carried in a stately procession to the subterranean galleries of the Serapeum at Saqqara, and placed in a huge stone sarcophagus.

The first Apis burial took place in the reign of Amenhotep III (1390–1352 BC), and the practice continued until 30 BC. The enormous granite and limestone coffins could weigh up to 80 tonnes each. Until the mid-19th century, the existence of the sacred Apis tombs was known only from classical references. In 1851, Auguste Mariette, after finding a half-buried sphinx at Saqqara, and using the description given by the Greek historian Strabo in 24 BC, uncovered the avenue leading to the Serapeum. However, only one Apis sarcophagus was found intact.

Mastaba of Ti

(Map p154) Northeast of the Philosophers' Circle is the Mastaba of Ti, which was discovered by Mariette in 1865. It is perhaps the grandest and most detailed private tomb at Saqqara, and one of our main sources of knowledge about life in Old Kingdom Egypt. Its owner, Ti, was overseer of the Abu Sir pyramids and sun temples (among other things) during the 5th dynasty. In fact, the superb quality of his tomb is in keeping with his nickname, Ti the Rich.

A life-size statue of the deceased stands in the tomb's offering hall (as with the Zoser statue, the original is in the Egyptian Museum). Ti's wife, Neferhetpes, was priestess and 'royal acquaintance'. Together with their two sons, Demedj (overseer of the duck pond) and Ti (inspector of royal manicurists), the couple appears throughout the tomb alongside detailed scenes of daily life. As men and women are seen working on the land, preparing food, fishing, building boats, dancing, trading and avoiding crocodiles, their images are accompanied by chattering hieroglyphic dialogue, all no doubt familiar to Ti during his career as a royal overseer: 'Hurry up, the herdsman's coming', 'Don't make so much noise!', 'Pay up – it's cheap!'.

Pyramid of Teti

(Map p154) The avenue of sphinxes excavated by Mariette in the 1850s has again been hidden by desert sands, but it once extended to the much earlier Pyramid of Teti (2345–2323 BC). As the first pharaoh of the 6th dynasty, Teti built his pyramid in step form and cased it in limestone. Unfortunately, the pyramid was robbed for its treasure and its stone, and today only a modest mound remains. The interior fared better, and is similar in appearance to that of the Pyramid of Unas. Here you can see portions of the hieroglyphic spells of the Pyramid Texts up close, as well as a shower of stars. Within the intact burial chamber, Teti's basalt sarcophagus is well preserved, and represents the first example of a sarcophagus with inscriptions.

Tomb of Kagemni

A chief justice under Teti, Kagemni appears in his own mastaba tomb as a bit plump (look at the reliefs just inside the door), and if the lively friezes inside reflect his character at all, he enjoyed the riches of the land. Look for catfish and eels thriving in the Nile, cows being milked, men feeding puppies, even dragonflies and other insects. Particularly vivid are the scenes of a crocodile and hippo fighting, and a row of vigorous dancers and acrobats.

Next door, the tombs of Mereruka and Ankhmahor contain similarly precise scenes, but they have since been closed due to deteriorating conditions.

Tomb of Horemheb

(Map p152) Originally designated as the final resting place of General Horemheb, this tomb became irrelevant in 1323 BC when its intended occupant seized power from Pharaoh Ay. Soon afterwards, Pharaoh Horemheb (1323–1295 BC) commissioned the building of a new tomb in the Valley of the Kings. The tomb at Saqqara was never put to use, but it yielded a number of exquisite reliefs that are currently displayed around the world.

South Saqqara

(Map p154) The most remote site in South Saqqara is the unusual funerary complex called the **Mastaba of Al-Faraun**, also called the Pharaoh's Bench. It belongs to the last 4th-dynasty pharaoh, the short-lived Shepseskaf (2503–2498 BC). Shepseskaf was the son of Menkaure (builder of Giza's third great pyramid), though he failed to emulate the glory of his father. Occupying an enclosure once covering 700 sq metres, Shepseskaf's rectangular tomb was built of limestone blocks, and originally covered by a further layer of fine, white limestone and a lower layer of red granite. Inside the tomb, a 21m-long corridor slopes down to storage rooms and a vaulted burial chamber.

Working your way back north, you pass the **Pyramid of Pepi II** (2278–2184 BC). The pharaoh's 94-year reign at the end of the 6th dynasty was probably the longest in Egyptian history. Despite Pepi's longevity, his 52m-high pyramid was of the same modest proportions as those of his predecessor, Pepi I. The exterior is little more than a mound of rubble, but the interior is decorated with more passages from the Pyramid Texts.

South Saqqara is also home to the pyramids of **Djedkare**, **Merenre** and **Pepi I**. Known as the 'Pyramid of the Sentinel', the 25m-high Djedkare pyramid contains the remains of the last ruler of the 5th dynasty, and can be penetrated from the north side.

The pyramids of Merenre and Pepi I are little more than slowly collapsing piles of rock, though the latter is significant as 'Memphis' appears in one of its names.

Dahshur ARCHAEOLOGICAL SITE
(adult/student E£50/25, parking E£2; ⊗8am-4pm, to 3pm during Ramadan) About 10km south of Saqqara lies this impressive 3.5km-long field of 4th- and 12th-dynasty pyramids. Although there were originally 11 pyramids here, only the two Old Kingdom ones remain intact, along with three Middle Kingdom pyramid complexes.

Pharaoh Sneferu (2613–2589 BC), father of Khufu and founder of the 4th dynasty, built Egypt's first true pyramid here, the **Red Pyramid**, as well as an earlier version, the **Bent Pyramid**. These two striking pyramids are the same height, and together are also the third-largest pyramids in Egypt after the two largest at Giza. Before founding the necropolis at Dahshur, Sneferu also began the Pyramid of Meidum in Al-Fayoum.

The pyramids here are just as impressive as their counterparts at Giza, the site is much more peaceful (no camel touts in sight) and the entry fee is cheaper.

The area surrounding the Bent Pyramid is still a militarised zone, so it can only be admired at a distance. Fortunately, the wonderful Red Pyramid is open to visitors, and penetrating its somewhat dank interior is a true Indiana Jones-esque experience.

Tickets are purchased at a small gatehouse on the edge of the site; there are no other facilities.

Red Pyramid

The world's oldest true pyramid is the North Pyramid, better known as the Red Pyramid. It derives its name either from the red tones of its weathered limestone, after the better-quality white limestone casing was removed, or perhaps from the red graffiti and construction marks scribbled on its masonry in ancient times. The architects had learned from their experiences building the rather deformed Bent Pyramid, so carried on where they had left off, building the Red Pyramid at the same 43-degree angle as the Bent Pyramid's more gently inclining upper section.

The entrance – via 125 extremely steep stone steps up, up, up, then down again, plus a 63m-long passage – takes you down to two antechambers with stunning 12m-high **corbelled ceilings** and a 15m-high

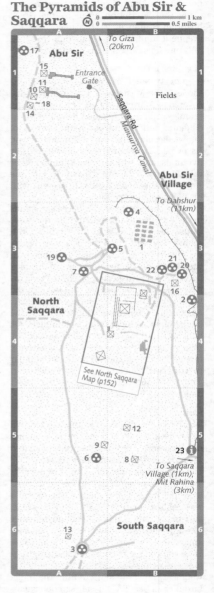

The Pyramids of Abu Sir & Saqqara

corbelled burial chamber in which fragmentary human remains, possibly of Sneferu himself, were found. Also look for charcoal graffiti, left by British explorers in the early 19th century.

See North Saqqara Map (p152)

The Pyramids of Abu Sir & Saqqara

Take your ticket with you up to the entrance, along with a little baksheesh (tip) for the bored attendant.

Bent Pyramid

Experimenting with ways to create a true, smooth-sided pyramid, Sneferu's architects began with the same steep angle and inward-leaning courses of stone they used to create step pyramids. When this began to show signs of stress and instability around halfway up its eventual 105m height, they had little choice but to reduce the angle from 54 degrees to 43 degrees and begin to lay the stones in horizontal layers. This explains why the structure has the unusual shape that gives it its name. Most of its outer casing is still intact, and inside (closed to visitors) are two burial chambers, the highest of which retains its original ancient scaffolding of great cedar beams to counteract internal

instability. There is also a small subsidiary pyramid to the south as well as the remains of a small funerary temple to the east. About halfway towards the cultivation to the east are the ruins of Sneferu's valley temple, which yielded some interesting reliefs.

Black Pyramid

You can only peer at this structure from the parking area by the Bent Pyramid. The oddly shaped, towerlike pyramid was built by Amenemhat III (1855–1808 BC), and appears to have completely collapsed in medieval times due to its limestone outer casing being pilfered. But the mud-brick remains contain a maze of corridors and rooms designed to deceive tomb robbers. Thieves did manage to penetrate the burial chambers but left behind a number of precious funerary artefacts that were discovered in 1993.

Mit Rahina   MUSEUM
(Memphis; adult/student E£35/20, parking E£2; ⏱8am-4pm, to 3pm during Ramadan) The only remaining evidence of Memphis is this noteworthy open-air museum, built around a magnificent fallen colossal limestone **statue of Ramses II**. Its position on its back gives a great opportunity to inspect the carving up close – even the pharaoh's nipples are very precise. It was one of a pair that flanked the temple of Ptah here. Its twin is the statue that stood in Midan Ramses in Cairo until 2006, until it was moved to the desert near Giza, to stand guard by the Grand Egyptian Museum construction site.

Other highlights of the museum include an alabaster sphinx of the New Kingdom, two statues of Ramses II that originally adorned Nubian temples, and the huge stone beds on which the sacred Apis bulls were mummified before being placed in the Serapeum at Saqqara.

Abu Sir   ARCHAEOLOGICAL SITE
(Map p154; off Saqqara Rd; admission free; ⏱8am-4pm) Lying between Giza and Saqqara and surrounded by sand dunes, the pyramids of Abu Sir form the necropolis of the 5th dynasty (2494–2345 BC). Unfortunately, most of the remains have not withstood the ravages of time as well as their bigger, older brethren at Giza, and today the pyramids are slumped and lack geometric precision.

Appreciating Abu Sir is all about expectations – if you arrive with grand visions, you're going to be severely disappointed. But

ARCHAEOLOGY IN ACTION

If you thought major Egyptological discoveries were a thing of the past, think again. Saqqara, perhaps more than any other site in Egypt, keeps revealing stunning finds.

In 2005, Egyptian archaeologists unearthed a 2300-year-old mummy buried in sand at the bottom of a 6m shaft. The perfectly preserved mummy was wearing a golden mask and encased in a wooden sarcophagus covered in brightly coloured images of gods and goddesses. Describing the find, Dr Zahi Hawass, then-secretary-general of Egypt's Supreme Council of Antiquities, said: 'We have revealed what may be the most beautiful mummy ever found in Egypt.'

In 2006, the graves of three royal dentists were discovered after the arrest of tomb raiders led archaeologists to the site. Just two months later, the mummified remains of a doctor were found alongside surgical tools dating back more than 4000 years.

In 2007, archaeologists unveiled the tombs of a Pharaonic butler and a scribe that had been buried for more than 3000 years. The scribe's mud-brick tomb contained several wooden statues and a door with intricate hieroglyphics, while the butler's limestone grave contained two painted coffins. Of particular interest were the blue and orange painted murals that adorned the butler's tomb, and depicted scenes of people performing rituals and monkeys eating fruit.

In 2008, Saqqara made global headlines following the discovery of a new pyramid. Although little remains aside from the 3m-tall, square-shaped foundation, it's estimated that the pyramid once reached a height of approximately 15m, and may be more than 4300 years old.

A year after uncovering the pyramid, archaeologists entered for the first time and found the mummy of Queen Sesheshet. The mother of Teti, first pharaoh of the 6th dynasty, Sesheshet ruled Egypt for just over a decade and was one of just a handful of female pharaohs. Although the burial chamber had been raided in antiquity, the mummy survived along with its coverings of linen, pottery and gold leaf.

Archaeologists have been excavating Saqqara for more than a century, but it's estimated that only one-third of the total site has been uncovered. In fact, Dr Hawass believes that some 70% of Egypt's ancient monuments remain buried – which means plenty more news to come.

come if you're interested in visiting one of the prominent necropolises of the Old Kingdom, and you'll be surprised by the relative calmness of the archaeological site and the nearby dunes. With virtually no other tourists (or touts) to contend with, you can enjoy a moment of peace at the humble ruins, and revel in the serene desolation of the surrounding desert.

There is an official gatehouse at the site, but no set ticket price. In lieu of this, ad hoc guides lounge out front and will show you around for baksheesh. Don't count on a toilet here – there is one, but there's no guarantee it's working or that you'll be allowed to use it.

Of the four pyramid complexes at Abu Sir – Sahure, Nyuserra, Neferirkare and Raneferef – Sahure's is the most complete. Head here first if your time is limited. Alternatively, if you pass through here on a horse ride to Saqqara, you'll get a good sense of the place.

Pyramid of Sahure
Sahure (2487–2475 BC) was the first of the 5th-dynasty pharaohs to be buried at Abu Sir. His pyramid, originally 50m high, is now badly damaged. The entrance corridor is only half a metre high, and slopes down to a small room. From there, you can walk through a 75m-long corridor before crawling 2m on your stomach through Pharaonic dust and spiderwebs to reach the burial chamber.

The better-preserved remains of Sahure's funerary temple complex stand east of the pyramid. This must have been an impressive temple, with black-basalt-paved floors, red-granite date-palm columns and walls decorated with 10,000 sq metres of superbly detailed reliefs (some of these are now in the museums of Cairo and Berlin). It was connected by a 235m-long causeway to the valley temple, which was built at the edge of the cultivation and bordered by water. From the pyramid, on a clear day you can see some 10 other pyramids stretching out to the horizon.

Pyramid of Nyuserra

The most dilapidated of the finished pyramids at Abu Sir belonged to Nyuserra (2445–2421 BC). Originally some 50m high, this pyramid has been heavily quarried over the millennia. In fact, Nyuserra reused his father Neferirkare's valley temple, and then redirected the causeway to lead not to his father's pyramid, but to his own.

Pyramid of Neferirkare

Neferirkare (2475–2455 BC) was the third pharaoh of the 5th dynasty and Sahure's father. His burial place originally resembled the Step Pyramid at Saqqara. However, the present-day complex is only the core as the original outer casing has been stripped away, reducing the pyramid from its original planned height of 72m to today's 45m.

In the early 20th century in Neferirkare's funerary temple, archaeologists found the so-called **Abu Sir Papyri**, an important archive of Old Kingdom documents written in hieratic script, a shorthand form of hieroglyphs. They relate to the cult of the pharaohs buried at the site, recording important details of ritual ceremonies, temple equipment, priests' work rotas and the temple accounts.

South of Neferirkare's pyramid lies the badly ruined **Pyramid of Queen Khentkawes II**, wife of Neferirkare and mother of both Raneferef and Nyuserra. In her nearby funerary temple, Czech archaeologists discovered another set of papyrus documents. In addition, two virtually destroyed pyramids to the south of the queen's pyramid may have belonged to the queens of Nyuserra.

Pyramid of Raneferef

On a diagonal, just west of Neferirkare's pyramid, are the remains of the unfinished Pyramid of Raneferef (2448–2445 BC; also known as Neferefre), who is believed to have reigned for four years before Nyuserra. However, work was so little advanced at the time of his death that the tomb was only completed as a mastaba.

In the adjoining mud-brick cult building, Czech archaeologists found fragments of statuary, including a superb limestone figurine of Raneferef protected by Horus (now in the Egyptian Museum) along with papyrus fragments relating to the Abu Sir temple archives.

Royal Sun Temples of Abu Ghorab

Just northwest of the Abu Sir pyramids lies the site of Abu Ghorab, which is home to two temples dedicated to the worship of Ra, the sun god of Heliopolis. The Abu Sir Papyri describe six such temples but only two, built for Pharaohs Userkaf (2494–2487 BC) and Nyuserra, have ever been discovered.

Both of these temples follow the traditional plan of a valley temple, and contain a causeway and a large stone enclosure. This enclosure contains a large limestone **obelisk** standing some 37m tall on a 20m-high base. In front of the obelisk, the enormous alabaster altar can still be seen. Made in the form of a solar disc flanked by four 'hotep' signs (the hieroglyphic sign for 'offerings' and 'satisfied'), the altar itself reads: 'The sun god Ra is satisfied.'

Tours

For experienced riders, a popular outing is horse or camel ride from Giza to Saqqara, a trip of about three hours – see p130 for more details.

At Saqqara, it's also possible to hire a camel, horse or donkey from near the Serapeum to take you on a circuit of the sites for between E£25 and E£50. You'll need to pay more the further into the desert away from North Saqqara you go.

ℹ Getting There & Away

You can reach Saqqara and Mit Rahina by public transport, but only with a great deal of trouble; Dahshur and Abu Sir are not at all accessible this way. For this reason, the area is typically visited as part of an organised tour or with a private taxi from Cairo hired for the day (about E£300, plus parking at each site). Moreover, the sites of Saqqara and Dahshur are quite vast, and it's an asset to have a car to drive you around them. (For more logistical concerns, see boxed text p150).

For the truly determined: take a microbus or bus down Pyramids Rd in Cairo to Maryutia Canal (under the ring-road flyover), then hop a microbus bound for Saqqara village; ask to be let off at 'Haram Saqqara'. It's a 1.5km walk to the ticket office, though you may be able to get a tuk-tuk to take you there, and even down the road to Mit Rahina.

Al-Fayoum

✔ 084 / POP 2.5 MILLION

This large fertile basin, about 70km wide and 60km long, is often referred to as an oasis, though technically it's watered not by springs but by the Nile via hundreds of capillary canals, many dug in ancient times. The area harbours a number of important archaeological sites, as the pharaohs built pleasure palaces here and the Greeks, who believed the crocodiles in Lake Qarun were sacred, built temples where pilgrims could feed the beasts. The region is famous for its lush fields and orchards, so it's a good place to revel in fresh produce, and the lake is a popular weekend spot for vacationing Cairenes.

As a visitor, you'll deal primarily with two towns in the oasis. Medinat al-Fayoum, a city of half a million, is built along one of the largest canals and offers the usual Egyptian urban chaos. It's the main transit hub and has all the services you might need, including hotels. The downtown area is along the Bahr Yusuf, the main canal through the oasis. The village of Tunis, an arts colony on the west edge of Al-Fayoum, is the more typical place to spend the night – or on the nearby shores of Lake Qarun.

◉ Sights

Lake Qarun   LAKE

Prior to the 12th-dynasty reigns of Sesostris III and his son Amenemhat III, the area that's now known as Al-Fayoum was entirely covered by Lake Qarun. In an early effort at land reclamation, both pharaohs dug a series of canals linking Qarun to the Nile, and drained much of the lake. Over the past few centuries, the lake has regained some of its former grandeur due to the diversion of the Nile to create more agricultural land, and it now stretches for 42km. However, since it presently sits at 45m below sea level, the water has suffered from increasing salinity. Remarkably, the wildlife has adapted, and today the self-proclaimed 'world's most ancient lake' supports a unique ecosystem. There's a good chance you'll spot countless varieties of birds here including a large colony of flamingos.

Qarun is a popular weekend spot for Cairenes looking to cool down, and the lake edge is dotted with cafes and wedding pavilions. It's not a big swimming spot, but even the sight of an expansive lake on the edge of the desert is refreshing, and makes a nice diversion from a morning spent pyramidhopping.

Ptolemaic Temple

At the western end of Lake Qarun, just east of the village of Qasr Qarun, are the ruins of ancient Dionysias, once the starting point for caravans to the Western Desert oasis of Bahariya. Although little remains of this historic settlement, a **Ptolemaic temple** (adult/student E£25/15; ⊙8am-4pm), built in 4 BC and dedicated to Sobek, the crocodileheaded god of Al-Fayoum, is still standing. If you're feeling adventurous, you can go down to the **underground chambers** (beware of snakes), and up to the roof for a view of the desert, the sparse remains of Ptolemaic and Roman settlements, and the oasis.

Wadi Rayyan Protected Area   PARK

(admission per person E£15 plus per vehicle E£5, camping per person E£10) In the 1960s, Egyptian authorities created three lakes in the Wadi Rayyan depression, southwest of Lake Qarun, to hold excess water from agricultural drainage. This was intended to be the first step in an ambitious land-reclamation project, though not everything went to plan when the water started to become increasingly brackish. On the bright side, Wadi Rayyan is particularly conducive to large colonies of birds, and today the entire depression is administered as a quasi-national park.

The area is a major nesting ground for both endemic and migrating birds, though it's also something of a weekend picnic spot for escaping Cairenes, especially near 'the

---

SECURITY IN AL-FAYOUM

Al-Fayoum was long notorious for its heavy-handed security for independent travellers. In recent years, however, this seems to have lifted, and few travellers have reported issues. The exception is Americans, who are obliged to travel with a police escort. The easy way around this is simply to claim you're from somewhere else. Police at checkpoints seldom inspect passports (though you should carry yours just in case), and often if you're a lone tourist in a microbus full of Egyptians, you're waved on through without question. Of course if you check in to a hotel, you'll need to show a passport, and then the jig is up. Police escorts are not the end of the world, though they may insist on setting your itinerary. Otherwise, they're just looking for a little entertainment and a complimentary lunch.

Medinat al-Fayoum

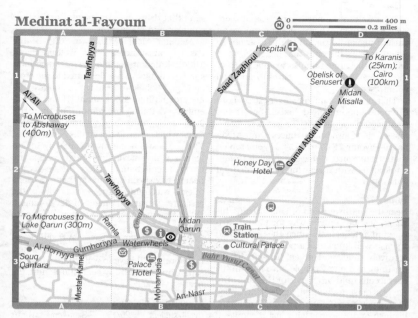

Waterfalls' where one lake drains into the other. The falls aren't as dramatic as the name suggests, but they're the only ones in Egypt. Along the main lakefront, you'll also find a visitors centre, toilets and a couple of cafes serving cold drinks and light meals.

For fun, you can be taken out in a big wooden rowboat, for about E£50 for a one-hour trip out to the middle of the lake and then back up close to the falls.

Wadi al-Hittan   PARK

Some 55km further south from Wadi Rayyan (and part of the park's protected area) is Wadi al-Hittan (Valley of the Whales), where more than 400 skeletons of primitive whales have been lying for about 40 million years. These are the fossilised remains of the basilosaurus, some up to 18m long, and the smaller dorodontus, both rather fierce water predators. They show the clear evolution of land-based mammals into sea-going ones, as they have vestigial front and back legs. The sands are also studded with the remains of manatees, big bony fish and plenty of shark teeth – which look very out of place in what is now a vast desert.

The Valley of the Whales is crisscrossed by a small network of walking tracks leading out to more than a dozen skeletons, in addition to a wilderness campground complete with basic toilets and fire pits. It doesn't sound like much, but the desert setting is dramatic, and it's a great destination for a day or overnight outing, usually combined with Wadi Rayyan – see Tours (p162) for possible organisers.

Karanis   ARCHAEOLOGICAL SITE

(adult/student E£25/15; ☺8am-4pm) At the edge of the oasis depression, 25km north of Medinat al-Fayoum on the road to Cairo, lie the ruins of ancient Karanis. Founded by Ptolemy II's mercenaries in the 3rd century BC, the town was once a mud-brick settlement with a population in the thousands.

Today, little of the ancient city remains intact aside from a few walls, though Karanis is home to two well-preserved **Graeco-Roman temples**. The larger and more interesting temple was built in the 1st century BC and is dedicated to two local crocodile gods, Pnepheros and Petesouchos. In front of the east entrance is a large square container – essentially a giant swimming pool for the holy crocs. Inside, niches in the wall are where crocodile mummies would've been stowed, and a block-like structure was the 'house' for the gods. The temple is also adorned with inscriptions dating from the reigns of the Roman emperors Nero, Claudius and Vespasian.

It's a trek to the north temple, and there is far less structure here – but you can see an ancient pigeon tower, off to the east, not so different from the ones that dot Al-Fayoum today. In the ruined domestic area north of the temple, you'll find a bathtub adorned with frescos.

There's a museum on-site, next to Lord Cromer's onetime field house, but it has been closed indefinitely. To get here, catch one of the Cairo-bound buses from Medinat al-Fayoum (E£5 to E£7). If you stop en route from Cairo, it may be difficult to find a microbus with a seat for you to Medinat al-Fayoum.

Tunis   VILLAGE

Near the southwest end of Lake Qarun, this village has been a getaway for Cairene artists and intellectuals since the 1970s, and it's also well known as a pottery centre. It's relatively quiet and green (though hardly pristine), and many people have built in the curvaceous mud-brick style of Hassan Fathy, Egypt's most influential modern architect. Even if you stop in for just a couple of hours, it's lush and relaxing, with just a couple of minor things to do besides hang out.

Fayoum Pottery School

(☎682 0405; ⊙10am-6pm daily) Established in the 1970s by a Swiss artist, Evelyne Porret, this school, which trains children and adults in the local potting traditions, is set in a beautiful mud-brick compound. Its architecture – very much in the Egyptian vernacular style – is as attractive as the students' creations from clay, which are on sale here. From the school, ask for directions to the workshop of **Ahmed Abou Zeid**, another noted local potter.

Fayoum Art Centre

(☎682 0083; www.fayoumartcenter.com) This project run by painter Mohamed Abla hosts classes and resident artists from around the world. Also on the grounds is the **Caricature Museum**, a great collection of Egyptian political cartoons – interesting if you can read Arabic. Still, pop in just for the feel of the place – like the pottery school, it's a beautiful space, and you never know what you'll find here.

Medinet Madi   ARCHAEOLOGICAL SITE

This ancient city is one of the most isolated in Al-Fayoum, but this is also part of its appeal, as you're often alone out in the blowing sand that drifts over the heads of the stone sphinxes and other ruins.

Medinet Madi (Arabic for 'City of the Past') is most noted for a well-preserved Middle Kingdom temple, few of which have survived in Egypt. It is dedicated to the crocodile god Sobek and the cobra goddess Renenutet, built by Amenemhat III and Amenemhat IV. Italian excavations in the early 20th century uncovered an archive of Greek texts, which refer to the city as Narmouthis. The site is still being investigated by Italian teams, which have uncovered a separate crocodile-cult temple where the beasts appear to have been bred in captivity – a cache of eggs was found, along with bodies of the creatures in various stages of development. Often they were sacrificed when still quite young.

Visiting really requires a 4WD vehicle, as there is no real track to the site. If you take a taxi here, you'll have to walk 2km across the sand from the highway near Abu Gandir, the nearest village.

Pyramid of Meidum   ARCHAEOLOGICAL SITE

(adult/student E£25/15; ⊙8am-4pm) About 30km northeast of Medinat al-Fayoum is the ruin of the first true pyramid attempted by the ancient Egyptians. It began as an eight-stepped structure, with the steps later filled in and an outer casing added to form the first pyramid shell. However, there were serious design flaws and, sometime after completion (possibly as late as the last few centuries BC), the pyramid's own weight caused the sides to collapse. Today, only the core stands, though it is still an impressive sight.

Pharaoh Huni (2637–2613 BC) commissioned the pyramid, although it was his son Sneferu who was responsible for the actual building. Sneferu's architects then went on to build the more successful Bent and Red Pyramids at Dahshur.

The guard will unlock the entrance of the pyramid, from where steps lead down 75m to the empty burial chamber. Near the pyramid are the large mastaba tombs of some of Sneferu's family and officials, including his son Rahotep and wife Nofret.

The pyramid is perhaps a bit too difficult to reach, considering its current appearance. The best option is to hire a taxi and visit as part of a larger tour. You could conceivably take any microbus running between Cairo and Beni Suef, and ask to be dropped off at the Meidum turn-off (E£13 to E£15), but you

PORTRAITS OF THE PAST

Al-Fayoum may not be famous for much these days, but it was here that caches of what are some of the world's earliest portraits were found. These extraordinarily lifelike representations, known as the Fayoum Portraits, were painted on wooden panels and put over the faces of mummies, or painted directly onto linen shrouds covering the corpses. This fusion of ancient Egyptian and Graeco-Roman funerary practices laid the foundation for the Western tradition of realistic portraiture.

Dating from between 30 BC and AD 395, the paintings were executed in a technique involving a heated mixture of pigment and wax. Remarkable for the skill of the anonymous artists who painted them, the realistic and eerily modern-looking faces bridge the centuries. The haunting images are made all the more poignant by their youth (some are only babies) – a reflection of the high infant-mortality rates at the time.

More than a thousand of these portraits have been found, not just in Al-Fayoum but also throughout Egypt. They now reside in numerous museums around the world, including the Egyptian Museum in Cairo (see p144).

would then still have about 6km to go, and it can be difficult to get a lift.

Pyramid of Hawara ARCHAEOLOGICAL SITE
(adult/student E£25/15; ⊙8am-4pm) About 8km southeast of Medinat al-Fayoum, on the north side of the Bahr Yusuf, the canal that connects the Al-Fayoum to the Nile, stands the dilapidated second pyramid of Amenemhat III, built at a gentler angle than his first one (the towerlike Black Pyramid at Dahshur).

Although the Pyramid of Hawara was originally covered with white limestone casing, sadly only the mud-brick core remains today, and even the once-famous temple has been quarried. Herodotus described this temple (300m by 250m) as a 3000-room labyrinth that surpassed even the Pyramids of Giza. Strabo claimed it had as many rooms as there were provinces, so that all the pharaoh's subjects could be represented by their local officials in the presentation of offerings. The interior of the pyramid, now closed to visitors, revealed several technical developments: corridors were blocked using a series of huge stone portcullises; the burial chamber is carved from a single piece of quartzite; and the chamber was sealed by an ingenious device using sand to lower the roof block into place.

The Greeks and Romans also used the area as a cemetery: the dead were mummified in an Egyptian way, but the mummies' wrappings incorporated a portrait-style face (see boxed text p161).

Microbuses between Medinat al-Fayoum and Beni Suef pass through the town of Hawarat al-Makta. From there, it is just a short walk to the pyramid. Alternatively, you can visit in a taxi as part of a circuit.

Pyramid of Al-Lahun ARCHAEOLOGICAL SITE
(adult/student E£25/15; ⊙8am-4pm) About 10km southeast of Hawara are the ruins of this mud-brick pyramid, built by Pharaoh Sesostris II (1880–1874 BC). As you can't get inside the structure, it's not worth a separate trip. But if you're driving by, keep an eye out for its strangely lumpen shape, set on an existing rock outcropping for extra stature. Ancient tomb robbers stripped it of all its rock and treasures, except for the amazing solid-gold cobra that is now displayed in the jewellery room (Room 4) of the Egyptian Museum in Cairo.

If you're a true pyramid completist, take any service taxi or bus running between Cairo and Beni Suef, and ask to be dropped off at the village of Al-Lahun. From here, you will have to walk for another 2km. You can also visit via private taxi.

Waterwheels LANDMARK
(Map p159; Bahr Yusuf, Medinat al-Fayoum) The whole oasis of Al-Fayoum is famous for its waterwheels, which number more than 200 and have become a prominent symbol of the town and the oasis. The Greeks invented the waterwheel, and the first depictions of them are seen in Ptolemaic Egyptian sources, so it's quite likely that since Pharaonic times, these devices have kept the town well irrigated despite its irregular topography of rolling hills and steep depressions. Although some of the rickety waterwheels (such as the ones at the centre of Medinat al-Fayoum) look as if they were built thousands

READING THE PHARAONIC SCENES DR JOANN FLETCHER

When visiting temples and tombs, the endless scenes of pharaohs – standing sideways, presenting a never-ending line of gods with the same old offerings – can start to get a bit much. Look closer, however, and these scenes can reveal a few surprises.

As the little figures on the wall strike their eternal poses, a keen eye can find anything from pharaohs ploughing fields to small girls pulling at each other's hair. A whole range of activities that we consider modern can be found among the most ancient scenes, including hairdressing, perfumery, manicures and even massage – the treasury overseer Ptahhotep (p152) certainly enjoyed his comforts. There are similar scenes of pampering elsewhere at Saqqara, with a group of men in the Tomb of Ankhmahor enjoying both manicures and pedicures.

With the title 'overseer of royal hairdressers and wigmakers' commonly held by the highest officials in the land, hairdressing scenes can also be found in the most unexpected places. Not only does Ptahhotep have his wig fitted by his manservants, similar hairdressing scenes can even be found on coffins, as on the limestone sarcophagus of 11th-dynasty Queen Kawit (in Cairo's Egyptian Museum), which shows her wig being deftly styled.

Among its wealth of scenes, the Theban Tomb of Rekhmire, on Luxor's West Bank, shows a banquet at which the female harpist sings, 'Put perfume on the hair of the goddess Maat.' And nearby in the Deir al-Medina tomb of the workman Peshedu, his family tree contains relatives whose hair denotes their seniority: the eldest shown has the whitest hair.

As in many representations of ancient Egyptians, black eye make-up is worn by both male and female, adult and child. As well as its aesthetic value, it was also used as a means of reducing the glare of the sun – think ancient sunglasses. Even manual workers wore it: the Deir al-Medina Tomb of Ipy once contained a scene in which men building the royal tombs were having eye paint applied while they worked. Difficult to imagine on a building site today!

of years ago, the vast majority are modern constructions.

Tours

Wadi al-Hittan is best visited as part of a tour, as a quality vehicle is required. **Hany Zaki** (☑0100 166 6979) and **Etman Abood** (☑0100 133 3781) are both recommended for day trips, which involve visiting the lake at Wadi Rayyan and going **sandboarding** on the dunes nearby. Both charge about E£350 for four people for the day. They can also provide transport to Medinet Madi.

In Medinat al-Fayoum, you can hire a *hantour* (horse-drawn carriage) for about E£30 for 30 minutes or E£50 for an hour, to visit the city's older mosques, the souq and a smaller set of waterwheels.

🛏 Sleeping & Eating

Bedding down in Medinat al-Fayoum is not the most scenic option, though there are a couple of decent options if this is all your schedule permits. It's far better, though, to head to Lake Qarun or Tunis to really enjoy

Al-Fayoum's rural atmosphere. All the lodges have their own restaurants, and in Medinat al-Fayoum there are plenty of standard Egyptian snack joints, though nothing particularly remarkable.

Helnan Auberge Fayoum   LUXURY HOTEL $$$
(☑698 1200; www.helnan.com; near Shakshouk, Lake Qarun; s/d from US$100/120; ❄🛜🏊) Built in 1937 as King Farouk's private hunting lodge, this hotel was where world leaders met after WWII to decide the borders of the Middle East. These days it remains an elegant refuge, so long as you focus on the colonial glamour and don't expect perfectly suave service.

Sobek Camp   BUNGALOW $$
(☑0100 678 7478; sobekvilla@hotmail.com; Tunis; s/d E£150/200) A few basic rooms, simple but newly built, are part of a larger potters' compound in the village of Tunis, in a nice green spot with plenty of space to lounge around. One major perk is the home-cooked meals.

Zad al-Mosafer
BUNGALOW **$**

(☎0100 639 5590; Tunis; s/d E£85/100, without bathroom E£45/85) The quintessential groovy hang-out in Tunis, this is a somewhat ad hoc 'ecolodge' that's been around for years. It shows its age a bit, and it's on the main Lake Qarun road, so not exactly quiet, but the food and company are excellent.

New Panorama Village
HOTEL **$$**

(☎683 0746; near Shakshouk, Lake Qarun; s/d from E£250/275; ✱@✲) Arguably better value than the Helnan, but lacking the historical flair, this collection of modern balcony-lined chalets looks over the lake. The restaurant specialises in fresh fish and fowl from the area.

Palace Hotel
HOTEL **$$**

(☎631 1222; Bahr Yusuf, Medinat al-Fayoum; s/d E£165/220; ✱) An ageing but well-tended relic, this is a solid option with clean rooms and a little cafeteria on the 1st floor. Look for a yellow building with a sign above street level; the entrance is on the side alley behind a watch kiosk.

Honey Day Hotel
HOTEL **$$**

(☎634 1205; 105 Sharia Gamal Abdel Nasser, Medinat al-Fayoum; s/d from E£180/260; ✱) The Honey Day is near the microbus station, which is convenient if you're hauling heavy bags. Rooms are comfortable, if slightly overfurnished. There is also a small restaurant here.

❶ Information

Al-Fayoum has produced lots of glossy brochures, but it's hard to find someone to speak with. The **Fayoum Tourism Authority** (☎634 2313; Bahr Yusuf, Medinat al-Fayoum) has an office next to the waterwheels in Al-Fayoum's main town, but it's not always staffed; the same goes for a kiosk by the Helnan Auberge Fayoum on Lake Qarun.

❶ Getting There & Away

Microbuses (E£7 to E£10, 1½ to two hours) are the quickest way to travel from Cairo to Al-Fayoum. Catch them at Midan al-Remaya in Giza, from Ulali near Ramses Station or from the ring-road underpass in Moneib. In Medinat al-Fayoum, ask to be dropped at Bahr Yusuf. If you're heading for Lake Qarun or Tunis, take a microbus direct from Midan al-Remaya to Abshaway, just south of the lake; from there you can take another microbus onward.

Returning, microbuses leave Medinat al-Fayoum from north of the train station and head to various main stations in Cairo; the fare depends on the destination.

Trains (E£3.25, 2½ hours) go to Medinat al-Fayoum from Giza (next to the metro stop of the same name) at 9am, 2pm and 5pm. They're slow and quite grubby, but a train nonetheless. They return at 7.15am, noon and 5.30pm.

❶ Getting Around

For the lakes, Tunis and the various archaeological sites, you can hire a taxi in Al-Fayoum for between E£300 and E£400 for the day, in which time you could feasibly visit Karanis, Lake Qarun and Wadi Rayyan, with a short stop in Tunis.

If you want to spend more time in the desert or visit Wadi al-Hittan, you're probably better off going on an organised trip – see Tours (p162) for information.

Microbuses connect most of the smaller villages with Medinat al-Fayoum – you can get to Shakshouk, for instance, the closest settlement to the good hotels on Lake Qarun, for E£1. To reach Qasr Qarun or Tunis, you'll likely have to switch microbuses in Abshaway (E£1).

Within Medinat al-Fayoum, green-and-white minibuses (25pt) cover all areas.

Wadi Natrun

Wadi Natrun, about 100km northwest of Cairo, is known for its Coptic monasteries where thousands of Christians escaped from Roman persecution in the 4th century. Of the 60 or so original compounds in the valley, only four remain. These monastery buildings are impressive, as they were fortified after Arab raids in 817, but the art inside is not as striking as at the Monastery of St Anthony in the Eastern Desert. Your experience will largely depend on when you visit – most days are quiet, but visitors mob the churches on Christian and public holidays, yielding a glimpse into contemporary Coptic traditions. The monastic tradition is thriving, and the Coptic pope is still chosen from the Wadi Natrun monks.

The area was also important to the ancient Egyptians because the valley's salt lakes dry up in the summer and leave natron, a substance crucial to the mummification process. Today, natron is used on a larger scale by the chemical industry.

Wadi Natrun lies on the desert side of the eight-lane Cairo–Alexandria Desert Hwy, which roughly separates the green fields of the Delta and the harsh sands of the Western

Desert, though the area is now dotted with farms and new satellite towns.

⊙ Sights

Deir Anba Bishoi   MONASTERY
(☺9am-6pm) St Bishoi came to the desert in 340 AD and founded two monasteries in Wadi Natrun: this one and neighbouring Deir el-Sourian. Deir Anba Bishoi is built around a church that contains the saint's body, said to be perfectly preserved in its tubelike container. Each year on 15 July, the tube is carried in procession around the church. According to the monks, the bearers clearly feel the weight of a whole body.

The fortified keep is entered via a draw-bridge, passing into an area with a vegetable garden, well, kitchens, two churches and storerooms that can hold provisions for a year. On the roof (men only can climb up), trapdoors open to small cells that acted as makeshift tombs for those who died during frequent sieges. Adjacent is an enormous new **cathedral**. Outside the keep in a separate building is a shop selling monastery products: olive oil, honey, candles and, oddly, cleaning supplies.

Deir el-Sourian   MONASTERY
(☺9am-6pm) About 500m northwest of Deir Anba Bishoi, Deir el-Sourian is the most picturesquely situated of the monasteries. It is named after wandering Syrian monks who bought the monastery from the Copts in the 8th century, though the Copts took it back in the 16th century. Its Church of the Virgin contains **11th-century wall paintings** and older icons with the eyes scratched out, including one saint in a distinctly Pharaonic-looking robe. The church was built around the 4th-century cave where St Bishoi resided and tied his hair to the ceiling to keep himself awake during prayers.

Elsewhere in the compound is a second ancient church, the tamarind tree of St Ephraim, allegedly sprung from the Syrian holy man's cane, and some slightly unfortunate mannequins of monks illustrating daily life at the monastery.

Deir Abu Makar   MONASTERY
(☺9am-6pm, closed during fasting periods) Nearly 20km southeast of Deir Anba Bishoi and Deir el-Sourian, Deir Abu Makar is the most secluded of the monasteries, so it's wise to confirm first at the bigger monasteries that it's open. It was founded around the cell where St Makarios spent his last 20 or so

years. Structurally, it suffered more than other monasteries at the hands of raiding Bedouin, but it is famous as most of the Coptic popes over the centuries have been selected from among its monks. It is the last resting place of many of those popes and also contains the remains of the 49 Martyrs, a group of monks killed by Bedouin in 444.

Deir el-Baramouse   MONASTERY
(☺9am-6pm Fri-Sun, closed during fasting periods) Once quite isolated due to a bad road, Deir al-Baramouse now has more than 100 monks in residence, plus six modern churches in addition to its restored medieval fortress (not open to the public). There are also remnants of **13th-century wall frescos** in its oldest church, the Church of the Virgin Mary.

🏃 Activities
El-Hammra Eco-Lodge's pool is open for day use.

🛏 Sleeping
In addition to the one option below, men are welcome to spend the night at any of the monasteries, but must have written consent from the Cairo offices (see Information). Even if you're not devout, it is good manners to attend religious services, and to leave a generous donation with the monks on departure.

El-Hammra Eco-Lodge   LODGE $$
(☎355 0944 or 0100 660 5060; www.elhammrae co-lodge.com; s/d per person E£150/125, with three meals E£200/175; ✸) With somewhat wind-blown grounds and a view of the industrial silos on one of Wadi Natrun's salt lakes, this collection of rustic cottages isn't as 'green' as some would hope. But it's quiet, the owner is a character, the food is very good (breakfast is included). The pool is open for day use (E£75 for up to four people, including access to a bungalow, or E£80 per person with lunch).

ⓘ Information
Some of the monasteries close during the three major fasting periods: Lent (40 days before Easter Week), Advent (40 days before Christmas) and the Dormition (two weeks in August), so it's worth checking with their Cairo offices:
Deir Abu Makar (☎02-2577 0614; stmacarius@stmacariusmonastery.org)
Deir Anba Bishoi (☎02-2591 4448)
Deir el-Baramouse (☎02-2592 2775)

Deir el-Sourian (☎02-2590 5161; info@st
-mary-alsourian.com)

ⓘ Getting There & Away

Alexandria-bound West & Mid Delta Co buses
from Cairo Gateway can drop you on the Desert
Hwy close to Wadi Natrun (tell the driver you
want to get off at Master Mall and Rest), but
charge the full price to Alex (E£30). Cheaper
are microbuses (E£8, one hour) from Midan
al-Remaya near the Pyramids of Giza, or West
& Mid Delta Co buses from Abboud (E£12); the
buses go into the less-than-lovely town of Wadi
Natrun. Tuk-tuks and taxis wait at the highway
and the bus depot. A tuk-tuk to Deir Anba Bishoi
and Deir el-Sourian (you can walk between the
two), with pickup a couple of hours later, will cost
E£20. To visit all four monasteries, you'll need a
taxi; expect to pay around E£20 per hour.

A taxi from Cairo should cost about E£250
there and back, including a couple of hours driving around to all the monasteries.

THE NILE DELTA

North of Cairo, the Nile River divides into
two branches that enter the Mediterranean
at the old ports of Damietta and Rosetta,
forming one of the most fertile and most
cultivated regions in the world. Laced with
countless waterways, the lush, fan-shaped
Delta region is a relaxing counterpoint to
Cairo's grit and the desert's austerity. Very
few tourists make it here, and there is little infrastructure in the way of hotels and
information offices; police may even be a bit
suspicious of your motives. But just a day
visit on a train or bus can be rewarding for
travellers who prefer aimless exploration to
actual sightseeing.

Birqash Camel Market

Egypt's largest **camel market** (Souq al-Gamaal;
admission E£25, camera E£20; ⏰6am-noon Fri,
Sun & Mon) is held at Birqash (pronounced
Bir'ash), a small village 35km northwest of
Cairo, just on the edge of the Delta's cultivated land. Until 1995 the market was held in
Cairo's western suburb of Imbaba, but when
that land became too precious for camels,
one of Cairo's age-old institutions was relocated. The Birqash camel market is not
for the faint of heart – these beasts are not
treated like beloved pets. But it can make an
unforgettable day trip, especially if you're a
photographer.

Hundreds of camels are sold here every
market day, with the liveliest action between
7am and 10am. Most of the animals are
brought up the Forty Days Rd from western
Sudan to just north of Abu Simbel by camel
herders, and from there to the market in
Daraw in Upper Egypt. Unsold camels are
then hobbled and crammed into trucks for
the 24-hour drive to Birqash. By the time
they arrive, many are emaciated, fit only for
the knacker's yard, and some expire at the
market itself. Traders stand no nonsense
and camels that get out of line are beaten
relentlessly.

In addition to those from Sudan, there are
camels from various parts of Egypt (including Sinai, the west and the south) and sometimes from as far away as Somalia. They are
traded for cash or other livestock, such as
goats, sheep and horses, and sold for farm
work or slaughter. Smaller camels go for as
little as E£600, but bigger beasts can sell for
E£5000 and up.

ⓘ Information

While at the market, watch out for pickpockets.
Women should dress conservatively – the market is very much a man's scene, with the only
female presence being the local tea-lady. But
traders here are accustomed to tourists and are
generally happy to answer questions and have
their photos taken if you ask nicely. Always be
alert to bolting camels – even hobbled, they can
move pretty fast.

ⓘ Getting There & Away

Using public transport, the most convenient
way to get to Birqash involves the chugging old
suburban train (E£1.25, 1½ hours) from Midan
Ramses in Cairo, grubby and littered with peanut
shells but packed with interesting passengers.
Trains depart from track 22 (the far west end
of track 11, around the curve) at 7am and 9am;
buy your ticket on board. When you arrive at
Birqash (signed only in Arabic), cross the canal
on the south side, then flag down any passing
pickup truck, which is almost certainly headed
to the market, about five minutes' drive away.
It's not really walkable, nor scenic. You should
offer to pay the driver E£1 or so, but often he'll
wave it off.

Microbuses and trucks (E£1) also run from the
site of the old camel market at Imbaba. To get to
Imbaba, take a microbus from Midan Abdel Moniem Riad in Downtown Cairo, then ask around for
a connecting service to the old market – Imbaba
airport (matar Imbaba) is the nearest landmark.
Or you could take a taxi to the old market site.

Returning to Cairo, microbuses for Imbaba leave when full. The train runs roughly every 30 minutes until 4pm, and most truck drivers leaving the market are happy to give you a lift back to the station (*mahattat Bir'ash*).

The easiest option is to simply hire a taxi from Cairo, with waiting time – one hour in the market is usually enough for most people. The full trip will cost around E£150. You could also combine this with a trip to the Nile Barrages and have the taxi drop you there, then return on the river bus.

Nile Barrages

Half the appeal of Qanater ('Barrages'), the Cairene equivalent of England's Blackpool or Coney Island in New York, is the ride up and back on the ramshackle river bus. The 90-minute trip is best done on Fridays or public holidays, when large groups of young people and smaller family parties pack the boats and the scraggly public gardens at Qanater, a 1km patch of land between the two branches of the Nile where the 19th-century barrages are handsome pieces of engineering.

On the boats, Arabic pop blares and the younger passengers sing along, clap their hands, dance and decorously flirt. It's an enjoyable, sociable jaunt, though prepare yourself for attention. Tourists are a rare and intriguing sight, and Qanater is a popular destination for young males, who relish cruising the promenade between the two barrages on their motor scooters.

The barrages themselves are a series of basins and locks built to guarantee a year-round flow of water into the Delta region, thus leading to a great increase in cotton production. The barrage on the Damietta branch consists of 71 sluices stretching 521m across the river; the Rosetta Barrage is 438m long with 61 sluices.

ℹ️ Getting There & Away

River buses (E£6) go from the dock in front of the TV building (Maspero), just north of the Ramses Hilton in central Cairo. They depart when full, from 9am to about 11.30am. You can return by microbus (E£6) if the boat departures aren't convenient, or if you need a little quiet. Qanater is very close to Birqash, so you could hire a taxi to drive you to the market, then leave you at Qanater, and take the boat back; pay about E£150.

Tanta

☑️ 040 / POP 429,000

The largest city in the Delta, Tanta is an easy place to sample slower-paced Delta life, as it's accessible by good trains. It's a major centre for Sufism, and home to a large mosque dedicated to al-Sayyed Ahmed al-Badawi, a Moroccan Sufi who fought the Crusaders in the 13th century. The *moulid* (saints' festival; for more on these, see p203) held in his honour follows the cotton harvest, usually the last week in October. It is one of the biggest in Egypt, drawing crowds of more than a million people for the eight days of chanting, rituals and sweets for which Tanta is best known.

If visiting during the *moulid,* prepare yourself for mayhem (women should not go alone) and book accommodation well in advance.

History

This area of the western Delta was once home to the ancient cities of Sais, Naucratis and Wadjet. Although these cities have been wiped off the map, anyone with a historical interest in the Delta region might be interested in knowing where they once stood. A museum in Tanta allegedly holds some treasures, but it is perpetually closed for 'renovation'.

Northwest of Tanta, on the east bank of the Rosetta branch of the Nile, once stood the legendary city of **Sais** (Sa al-Hagar), Egypt's 26th-dynasty capital. Sacred to Neith, goddess of war and hunting and protector of embalmed bodies, Sais dates back to the start of Egyptian history, and was replete with palaces, temples and royal tombs. However, the city was destroyed in 525 BC by the Persian emperor Cambyses, who reportedly exhumed the mummies of previous rulers from the ground and had them publicly whipped and burned.

West of Tanta, more than halfway along the road to Damanhur, is where the city of **Naucratis** once stood. The city was given to the Greeks to settle during the 7th century BC.

Northeast of Damanhur and northwest of Tanta was the Egyptian cult centre of **Wadjet** (known as Buto to the Greeks), which honoured the cobra goddess of Lower Egypt. Cobras were once worshipped here by devout followers.

◎ Sights

The **Mosque of al-Sayyed Ahmed al-Bad-awi** is 300m from the train station – bear right across the parking area in front of the station and then you'll see the mosque at the end of the first major street. Inside the mosque to the left, al-Badawi's shrine is lit with green fluorescent lights and circled by pilgrims snapping photos on their mobile phones. Behind the mosque is Tanta's old **market** district, good for an aimless stroll. The road to the mosque is lined with **sweets-sellers**; the local speciality is a type of nougat studded with nuts or dried chickpeas.

⌂ Sleeping & Eating

Most visitors to Tanta generally pass through by day, though Tanta has a decent range of accommodation. Hotels cluster around the train station, and the best of the lot is the **New Arafa Hotel** (☎340 5040; Midan al-Mahatta; s/d from E£270/420; ❄ ⊛). Arriving passengers are greeted with large, lavishly furnished rooms that are well insulated from the bustling city streets, and there is a decent bar and restaurant on the premises.

❶ Getting There & Away

From Ramses Station in Cairo, a comfortable air-con train (E£35 to E£50, one to 1½ hours) runs to Tanta nine times a day (four morning departures give you time for a day trip) and deposits you directly in the centre. The fastest return trains go at 5pm and 6pm; the last goes at 10pm. This is far preferable to a bus, as it's not subject to traffic whims.

If you do come by bus or microbus (from Turgoman, Midan Ulali or Abboud), you'll be dropped at the Souq al-Gomla station, about 2km northwest of the centre; a taxi is E£2 or E£3. You can hire a driver to take you around the area for about E£50 per hour.

Zagazig & Bubastis

☎055 / POP 279,000

Just outside the city of Zagazig (Egyptians say 'az-za'-a-*zi*') are the ruins of Bubastis, one of the country's most ancient cities. Serious Egyptology buffs will an enjoy a visit to the temple that's dedicated to the resident deity, the elegant cat goddess Bastet. It's an easy outing to combine with the larger Tanis.

◎ Sights

Temple of Bubastis ARCHAEOLOGICAL SITE
(adult/student E£15/10; ◷8am-4pm) Festivals held in Bastet's honour are said to have attracted more than 700,000 revellers to the Temple of Bubastis. They sang, danced, feasted, consumed great quantities of wine and offered sacrifices to the goddess. The temple was begun by the great pyramid builders Khufu and Khafre during the 4th dynasty, and pharaohs of subsequent dynasties made their additions over about 17 centuries. Although this architectural gem once rose above the city, today the temple is just a pile of rubble. However, the **cat cemetery** 200m down the road, which consists of a series of underground galleries where many bronze statues of cats were found, is morbidly fun to explore.

⌂ Sleeping

Zagazig is only 80km northeast of Cairo, and serves as an easy day trip from the capital. If you get stuck, you could try one of the budget hotels around the train station, though they're of questionable cleanliness. A better option is the **Marina** (☎231 3934; 58 Gamal Abdel Nasser; s/d from E£275/300; ❄), a somewhat upmarket affair near Al-Fatr Mosque that caters to local business travellers.

❶ Getting There & Away

Trains running between Cairo and Port Said call in Zagazig (E£15, 1½ hours), though these are some of the older and grubbier trains in the system. Moreover, morning air-con departures are only at 5.15am and 6.15am (the really beat-up trains run a bit later) – not the most flexible for a day trip. Returning trains leave roughly every hour from 4pm to 10pm.

So it can be cheaper and more comfortable, and perhaps faster, to go by bus or microbus. There are frequent departures in both directions between Zagazig's train station and Cairo's Abboud terminal (E£4 to E£6, one to two hours). From the train station in Zagazig, the temple is about 1km southeast along Sharia Farouq. Taxis (E£1) can whisk you away to the site in under a minute.

Tanis

Just outside the village of San al-Hagar, 70km northeast of Zagazig, are the partly excavated ruins of Tanis, a city known as Djanet to the ancient Egyptians and Zoan to the Hebrews. The site rightly falls low on the priority list for Egyptology fans, but it is striking because it sits on the edge of lush green plantations. Some guides call it the Saqqara of the Delta, due to its impressive scale – though it is not so well preserved as the desert ruins.

For several centuries Tanis was one of the largest cities in the Delta, and became a site of great importance after the end of the New Kingdom, especially during the Late Period (747–332 BC). Cinema buffs are also quick to point out that Tanis is where Indiana Jones discovered the 'Lost Ark'. But despite this cameo, you'll probably have the site to yourself; there's no official entry fee.

The earliest buildings at Tanis are from the reign of Psusennes I (1039–991 BC), who surrounded the Temple of Amun with a great enclosure wall. His **royal tomb** and five others from the 21st dynasty were unearthed by the French in 1939, and the treasures are some of the most spectacular ever found in Egypt. The tombs at the site are now quite empty, as the trove, which includes gorgeous jewellery, is on view in the Egyptian Museum (p144).

Psusennes I and later kings reused blocks and statues from earlier eras – so much of the stone actually dates from the Old and Middle Kingdoms. His successors added a temple to Mut, Khons and the Asiatic goddess Astarte, together with a sacred lake, and temple building continued until Ptolemaic times.

❶ Getting There & Away

To reach Tanis, take a microbus or East Delta bus from Ulali or Abboud in Cairo (E£5 to E£10, one to two hours) to the town of Faqus, which is about 35km south of Tanis. From Faqus, take a service taxi or bus (E£1) to the village of San al-Hagar, or alternatively hire a taxi (E£25) to take you to the site.

Alternatively, and much more slowly and with much more dust, the train takes about 3½ hours to get to Abu Kabir (adult/student E£20/15), the nearest station to Faqus. These old, non-air-con trains leave from the far east end of Cairo's Ramses Station (ask for 'Sharq' or 'Limun') approximately every two hours.

If you're coming from Zagazig, the train is slightly more appealing. It takes just 45 minutes to Abu Kabir, and there are more options, with service every hour or so.

Nile Valley: Beni Suef to Qena

Best Places to Eat

» Koshary Nagwa (p174)

» Dahabiyya Restaurant (p174)

» Al-Watania Palace Hotel (p182)

Best Places to Stay

» Al-Safa Hotel (p184)

» Al-Watania Palace Hotel (p181)

» City Center Hotel (p172)

» Horus Resort (p174)

» House of Life (p186)

Why Go?

If you're in a hurry to reach the treasures and pleasures of the south, it is easy to dismiss this first segment of Upper Egypt between Cairo and Luxor. But the less touristed parts of the country almost always repay the effort of a visit.

Much of this part of the valley is less developed than the other valleys – you will see farmers still working by hand, although they're also having to grapple with the issues of modernity, particularly problems with pumps and water shortages.

But however much a backwater this region might seem, it played a key role in Egypt's destiny as its many archaeological sites bear witness – from the lavishly painted tombs of the early provincial rulers at Beni Hasan to the remains of the doomed city of Akhetaten, where Tutankhamun was brought up, and the Pharaonic-inspired monasteries of the early Christian period.

When to Go

Asyut

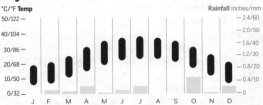

Apr Sham el Nessim, the spring festival is celebrated in style in the region.

Aug Millions of people arrive to celebrate the Feast of the Virgin outside Minya.

Oct-Nov The ideal touring time, with the light being particularly beautiful.

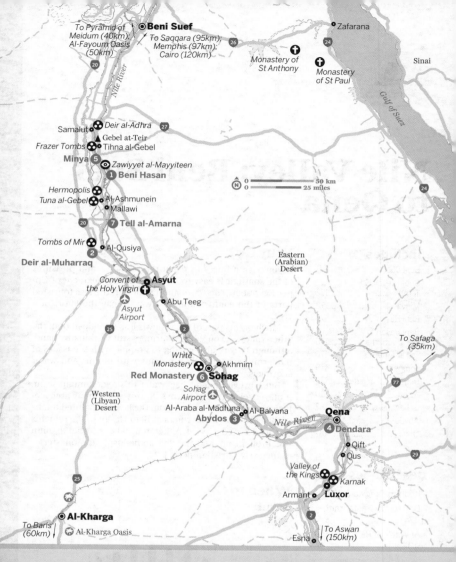

Nile Valley: Beni Suef to Qena Highlights

1 Admire lithe dancers, hunters and even wrestlers in the finely painted tombs at **Beni Hasan** (p175)

2 Visit the Coptic monastery of **Deir al-Muharraq** (p179) to see why Copts claim to be heirs to the ancient Egyptians

3 Gaze upon some of ancient Egypt's finest temple

reliefs at the **Temple of Seti I** (p185) in Abydos

4 Marvel at one of the best-preserved temple complexes in Egypt in Dendara's magnificent **Temple of Hathor** (p187)

5 Hang out in the elegant colonial centre of **Minya** (p172)

6 See the frescoes at the **Red Monastery** (p183), one of the finest buildings from late antiquity

7 Wander through the lush countryside around **Akhetaten** (p179), the doomed city of the heretic king Akhenaten

History

For the ancient Egyptians, Upper Egypt began south of the ancient capital of Memphis, beyond present-day Saqqara.

The ancients divided the area that stretched between Beni Suef and Qena into 15 nomes (provinces), each with its own capital. Provincial governors and notables built their tombs on the desert edge. Abydos, located close to modern Sohag, was once the predominant religious centre in the region as well as one of the country's most sacred sites: Egypt's earliest dynastic rulers were interred there and it flourished well into the Christian era.

The New Kingdom Pharaoh Akhenaten tried to break the power of the Theban priesthood by moving his capital to a new city, Akhetaten (near modern Mallawi), one of the few places along the Nile not already associated with a deity.

Christianity arrived early in Upper Egypt. Sectarian splits in Alexandria and the popularity of the monastic tradition established by St Anthony in the Eastern Desert encouraged priests to settle in the provinces. The many churches and monasteries that continue to function in the area are a testament to the strength of the Christian tradition: this area has the largest Coptic communities outside Cairo.

Dependant on agriculture, much of the area remained a backwater throughout the Christian and Islamic periods, although Qena and Asyut flourished as trading hubs: Qena was the jumping-off point for the Red Sea port of Safaga, while Asyut linked the Nile with the Western Desert and the Darb al-Arba'een caravan route.

Today much of the region remains poor. Agriculture is still the mainstay of the economy, but cannot absorb the population growth. The lack of any real industrial base south of Cairo has caused severe economic hardship, particularly for young people who drift in increasing numbers into the towns and cities in search of work. Resentment at their lack of hope was compounded by the loss of remittances from Iraq: many people from this region had found work there in the 1980s, but lost it with the outbreak of the first Gulf War. Religious militants exploited the violence that exploded in the 1990s and directed it towards the government, in a bid to create an Islamic state. Security forces responded by dishing out some heavy-handed tactics. The violence eventually petered out but the causes of the unrest – poverty and thwarted hopes – remain and will need to be addressed by Mubarak's successors.

Dangers & Annoyances

Ever since the Islamic insurrection in the 1990s, this has been one of the most difficult regions to travel through, with security forces often turning foreigners away. But the situation stabilised many years ago and the security clampdown has gradually been lifted so that it should now be possible to travel without problems. Even Nile cruises through this region, which were stopped in the 1990s, are set to run again.

❶ Getting There & Away

Trains are recommended for getting in and out of this part of the country. There are frequent services heading north to Cairo and south to Luxor and Aswan. At some stations, the old edict that foreigners can only buy tickets for selected services is still enforced. But in practice, if you can't buy a ticket at the station, you ought to be able to buy one on the train. Buses, private vehicles and taxis are alternatives now that security measures have been eased, but it can be very slow to leave Cairo by road.

❶ Getting Around

Trains are the best way of moving between the cities in this part of Egypt, while a good network of buses, servees (service taxis) and pick-up taxis links towns and villages. If the security situation changes, the police may put them off limits to foreigners or you might find yourself being escorted by armed police. If they do, you should try to allow extra time for delays at the checkpoints, where the escort will need to change vehicles.

Beni Suef

☑ 082 / POP 193,535

Beni Suef is a provincial capital, 120km south of Cairo. From antiquity until at least the 16th century it was famous for its linen, and in the 19th century was still sufficiently important to have an American consulate, but there is now little to capture the traveller's interest beyond the sight of a provincial city at work. It is, however, a transport hub between Cairo and Luxor, and the Red Sea and Al-Fayoum.

◎ Sights

Beni Suef Museum   MUSEUM

(adult/student E£15/10; ⊘9am-4pm) Next to the governorate building and behind the zoo, this museum is Beni Suef's main attraction.

There is a small but worthwhile collection of objects from the Old Kingdom to the Mohammed Ali period with good Ptolemaic carvings, Coptic weavings and 19th-century table-settings.

🛏 Sleeping & Eating

There are cheap *kushari,* fuul (fava beans) and ta'amiyya stands around the train station.

City Center Hotel   HOTEL **$$**
(📞236 7273; www.citychotel.com; Midan al-Mahatta; s/d E£140/160; ❄🛜) Around the corner from the forlorn Semiramis Hotel and across the square from the train station is this new three-star, 45-room hotel, popular with managers and white-collar workers. The 6th-floor restaurant serves a mixed menu including pizzas, chicken and pigeons for lunch and dinner.

❶ Information

Bank of Alexandria (Sharia Saad Zaghloul) Just off Midan al-Gomhuriyya.
Post office (Sharia Safiyya Zaghloul)

❶ Getting There & Away

BUS The bus station is along the main road, Sharia Bur Said, south of the town centre. Buses run from about 6am to 6pm to Cairo, Minya and Al-Fayoum. There is also a daily bus to Zafarana (E£35, three to four hours). The bus will stop at the turn-off to the Monastery of St Anthony (p366), about 130km east of Beni Suef. From there it is a further 12km to the monastery.

TRAIN There are frequent train connections north to Cairo and Giza (both E£19.36/31.20 2nd/1st class, 90 minutes to two hours), and south to Minya (E£19.36/31.20, one hour 25 minutes).

Gebel at-Teir & Frazer Tombs

The clifflike Gebel at-Teir (Bird Mountain) rises on the east bank of the Nile, some 93km south of Beni Sueft and 20km north of Minya. **Deir al-Adhra** (Monastery of the Virgin) is perched 130m above the river. The mountain takes its name from a legend that all Egyptian birds paused here on the monastery's annual feast day. The monastery was formerly known as the Convent of the Pulley, a reminder of the time when rope was the only way of reaching the cliff top.

Coptic tradition claims that the Holy Family rested here for three days on their journey through Egypt. A cave-chapel built on the site in the 4th century AD is ascribed to Helena, mother of Byzantine Emperor Constantine. A 19th-century building encloses the cave, whose icon of the virgin is said to have miraculous powers. The monastery, unvisited for most of the year, is mobbed during the week-long Feast of the Assumption, celebrated on the days leading up to 22 August.

You can get to the monastery by public transport (*servees* or microbus from Minya to Samalut and a boat across the river), but a private taxi from Minya shouldn't cost more than E£100 to E£150 for the return trip.

Five kilometres south of Tihna al-Gebel, the **Frazer Tombs** date back to the 5th and 6th dynasties. These Old Kingdom tombs are cut into the east-bank cliffs, overlooking the valley. Only two tombs are open, and both, very simple, contain eroded images and hieroglyphs but no colourful scenes and are likely to appeal only if you have a passion for rarely visited sites.

Minya

📞086 / POP 235.234

Minya, the 'Bride of Upper Egypt' (Arousa as-Sa'id), sits on the boundary between Upper and Lower Egypt. A provincial capital 245km south of Cairo, it was the capital of the Upper Egyptian cotton trade, but its factories now process sugar and produce soap and perfume.

When Minya was caught up in the Islamist insurgency of the 1990s, the government sent tanks and armoured personnel carriers. Some police posts from that period still dot the town centre, but the violence has abated and security stepped down, which is good news for visitors because Minya has some of the most pleasant town centres in Upper Egypt. With broad tree-lined streets, a wide corniche and some great, if shabby, early 20th-century buildings, central Minya has retained the feel of a more graceful era. At the time of our visit, this was one of the most relaxed places to visit between Cairo and Luxor.

◉ Sights

Beyond the pleasure of walking around the town centre and watching the Nile flow against the background of the Eastern Hills,

Minya

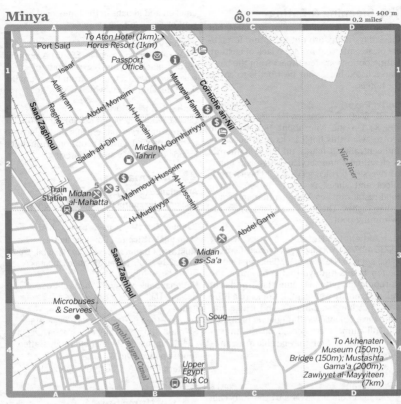

Minya doesn't have many sights. There is a souq (market) at the southern end of the town centre and the streets that run from it to Midan Tahrir are among the liveliest.

Hantours (horse-drawn carriages; E£25 to E£35 per hour) can be rented for a leisurely ride around the town centre or along the Corniche. Feluccas (Egyptian sailing boats; E£30 per hour) can be rented at the landing opposite the tourist office for trips along the river and to Banana Island, which is good for a picnic.

Akhenaten Museum   MUSEUM
The new Akhenaten Museum on the east bank is heading towards completion and was due to open not long after the time of writing. If the Egyptian authorities can swing it, it will be home, for some months at least, to the iconic bust of Queen Nefertiti (now in Berlin) as well as other treasures from nearby Tell al-Amarna.

Minya

🛏 Sleeping
1 Dahabiyya Houseboat & Restaurant	B1
2 King Akhenaton Hotel	C2

🍽 Eating
3 Koshary Nagwa	B2
4 Mohamed Restaurant	C3
5 Savoy Restaurant	A2

Zawiyyet al-Mayyiteen   CEMETERY
On the east bank about 7km southeast of town, a large Muslim and Christian cemetery, called Zawiyyet al-Mayyiteen (Place of the Dead), consists of several hundred mudbrick mausoleums. Stretching for 4km from the road to the hills and said to be one of the largest cemeteries in the world, it is an interesting sight.

🛏 Sleeping & Eating

Minya has a decent selection of hotels, but these days many are not accepting foreigners or are suffering from the lack of custom. Eating options are few. Apart from the basic places listed here, your best bet is to eat in the hotels.

Horus Resort HOTEL $$
(☎231 6660; Corniche an-Nil; s/d US$50/75; ❄🏠♨) On the Nile about 1km from the centre, what this hotel lacks in atmosphere and centrality, it makes up for in standards of cleanliness and service. There is a popular riverside terrace serving cold beers, fresh juices and sheeshas (water pipes), and a good restaurant serving Egyptian and some Italian dishes. There is also a large riverside swimming pool.

King Akhenaton Hotel HOTEL $$
(☎236 4917/8; www.kingakhenaton.com; Corniche an-Nil; s/d with Nile view E£137/195; ❄) One of the few hotels in town that is booming, the 48-room Akhenaton is comfortable and central, and mostly well-kept. Rooms are a little worn, but have satellite TV and fridge and some have Nile views. Buffet-style breakfast and full dinners are served on the upper-floor restaurant. Staff may be able to arrange transport.

Dahabiyya Houseboat & Restaurant FLOATING HOTEL $
(☎236 5596; Corniche an-Nil; s/d E£50/100) This old Nile sailing boat has been moored along the Corniche near the tourist office for many years. Refurbished some five years ago, it is Minya's most unusual address, with a restaurant on the upper deck and accommodation below. The two small cabins have TVs but share a bathroom, and tend to be noisy as the restaurant is open until the last person leaves.

Aton Hotel HOTEL $$
(☎234 2993/4; Corniche an-Nil; ❄♨) Still referred to locally as the Etap (its former incarnation), this was Minya's top hotel until it closed in 2010 for a major renovation. It should reopen in 2012. On the west bank of the Nile, many of the well-equipped bungalow rooms have great river views. There will be two restaurants, a bar and a pool.

Savoy Restaurant EGYPTIAN $
(Midan al-Mahatta; dishes E£5-20) A busy corner restaurant, the Savoy serves good rotisserie

chicken and kebabs in the fan-cooled restaurant or you can take away.

Koshary Nagwa EGYPTIAN FAST FOOD $
(Sharia al-Gomhuriyya; dishes E£5-15) A popular corner place serving big portions of good, basic *kushari* a few steps from the souq. Beware the chili sauce, which is very hot.

Mohamed Restaurant EGYPTIAN $
(Sharia al-Hussaini; dishes E£5-15) This popular restaurant serves basic grills and salads on a street packed with food options, from juice stands to a bakery and patisserie.

ℹ Information

Ambulance (☎123)
Bank of Alexandria (Sharia al-Gomhuriyya) Changes foreign currency.
Banque Misr (Midan as-Sa'a) Has an ATM.
Main post office (off Corniche an-Nil)
Mustashfa Gama'a (University Hospital; ☎236 6743, 234 2505; Midan Suzanne Mubarak/Corniche an-Nil)
National Bank of Egypt (Sharia al-Gomhuriyya) Has an ATM.
Police (☎122)
Tourist office Corniche an-Nil (☎236 0150; ◷9am-3.30pm Sat-Thu); train station (☎234 2044) Supposedly 24 hour but rarely staffed.
Tourist police (☎126)
Western Union (☎236 4905; Sharia al-Gomhuriyya; ◷9am-7pm Sat-Thu)

ℹ Getting There & Away

BUS The **Upper Egypt Bus Co** (☎236 3721; Sharia Saad Zaghloul) has hourly services to Cairo (E£12, four hours) from 6am. Buses leave for Hurghada at 10.30am and 10.30pm (E£50, six hours).

MICROBUS & SERVEES A seat in a microbus or *servees* will cost E£30 to Cairo and E£15 to Asyut.

TRAIN The **tourist office** (☎234 2044) in the station may be able to help with information. Trains to Cairo (1st-/2nd-class E£48/27, three to four hours) have only 1st- and 2nd-class carriages and leave at least every 1½ hours starting at 4.25am. The last one, at 6.40pm, continues on to Alexandria. Trains heading south leave fairly frequently, with the fastest trains departing from Minya between 11pm and 1am. Foreigners can board the two Wagons Lit trains that come from Cairo, but you are likely to need a reservation if you want a couchette. Seven 1st-/2nd-class trains go all the way to Luxor (E£69/37, six to eight hours) and Aswan (E£84/44, eight to 11 hours), stopping at Asyut (E£32/19, two hours),

Sohag (E£48/31, three to four hours) and Qena (E£60/34, five to seven hours).

Beni Hasan

The necropolis of **Beni Hasan** (adult/student E£30/20; ⊙8am-5pm) occupies a range of east-bank limestone cliffs some 20km south of Minya. It is a superb and important location and has the added attraction of a rest house, which may open for drinks. Most tombs date from the 11th and 12th dynasties (2125–1795 BC), the 39 upper tombs belonging to nomarchs (local governors). Many remain unfinished and only four are currently open to visitors, but they are worth the trouble of visiting for the glimpse they provide of daily life and political tensions of the period.

A guard will accompany you from the ticket office, so baksheesh is expected (at least E£10). Try to see the tombs chronologically, as follows.

◉ Sights

Tomb of Baqet (No 15)   TOMB
Baqet was an 11th-dynasty governor of the Oryx nome (district). His rectangular tomb chapel has seven tomb shafts and some well-preserved wall paintings. They include Baqet and his wife on the left wall watching weavers and acrobats – mostly women in diaphanous dresses in flexible poses. Further along, animals, presumably possessions of Baqet, are being counted. A hunting scene in the desert shows mythical creatures among the gazelles. The back wall shows a sequence of wrestling moves that are still used today. The right (south) wall is decorated with scenes from the nomarch's daily life, with potters, metalworkers and a flax harvest, among others.

Tomb of Kheti (No 17)   TOMB
Kheti, Baqet's son, inherited the governorship of the Oryx nome from his father. His tomb chapel, with two of its original six papyrus columns intact, has many vivid painted scenes that show hunting, linen production, board games, metalwork, wrestling, acrobatics and dancing, most of them watched over by the nomarch. Notice the yogalike positions on the right-hand wall, between images of winemaking and herding. On the west-facing wall are images of 10 different trees.

Tomb of Amenemhat (No 2)   TOMB
Amenemhat was a 12th-dynasty governor of Oryx. His tomb is the largest and possibly the best at Beni Hasan and, like that of Khnumhotep, its impressive facade and interior decoration mark a clear departure from the more modest earlier ones. Entered through a columned doorway and with its six columns intact, it contains beautifully executed scenes of farming, hunting, manufacturing and offerings to the deceased, who can also be seen with his dogs. As well as the fine paintings, the tomb has a long, faded text in which Amenemhat addresses the visitors to his chapel: 'You who love life and hate death, say: Thousands of bread and beer, thousands of cattle and wild fowl for the ka of the hereditary prince...the Great Chief of the Oryx Nome...'

Tomb of Khnumhotep (No 3)   TOMB
Khnumhotep was governor during the early 12th dynasty, and his detailed 'autobiography' is inscribed on the base of walls that contain the most detailed painted scenes. The tomb is famous for its rich, finely rendered scenes of plant, animal and bird life. On the left wall farmers are shown tending their crops while a scribe is shown recording the harvest. Also on the left wall is a representation of a delegation bringing offerings from Asia – their clothes, faces and beards are all distinct.

Speos Artemidos
(Grotto of Artemis)   MONUMENT
If the guardian agrees, you can follow a cliffside track that leads southeast for about 2.5km, then some 500m into a wadi to the rock-cut temple of Speos Artemidos (Grotto of Artemis). Known locally as Istabl Antar (Stable of Antar, an Arab warrior-poet and folk hero), it deserves neither its Greek nor Arab names for it dates back to the 18th dynasty. Started by Hatshepsut (1473–1458 BC) and completed by Tuthmosis III (1479–1425 BC), it was dedicated to the lion-goddess Pakht. There is a small hall with roughly hewn Hathor-headed columns and an unfinished sanctuary. On the walls are scenes of Hatshepsut making offerings and, on its upper facade, an inscription describing how she restored order after the Hyksos, even though she reigned long after the event. Expect to be accompanied by a police escort and a guard (who will want baksheesh).

ℹ Getting There & Away

It may be possible to take a microbus from Minya to the east bank and then another heading south to Beni Hasan, but as elsewhere, this will take time. A taxi from Minya will cost anything from E£100 to E£200, depending on your bargaining skills and how long you stay at the site.

Beni Hasan to Tell al-Amarna

Forty kilometres south of Minya, near the town of Al-Ashmunein, **Hermopolis** (Map p177; admission free) is the site of the ancient city of Khemenu. Capital of the 15th Upper Egyptian nome, its name (Eight Town) refers to four pairs of snake and frog gods that, according to one Egyptian creation myth, existed here before the first earth appeared out of the waters of chaos. This was also an important cult centre of Thoth, god of wisdom and writing, whom the Greeks identified with their god Hermes, hence the city's Greek name, 'Hermopolis'.

Little remains of the wealthy ancient city, the most striking ruins being two colossal 14th-century-BC quartzite statues of Thoth as a baboon. These supported part of Thoth's temple, which was rebuilt throughout antiquity. A Middle Kingdom temple gateway and a pylon of Ramses II, using stone plundered from nearby Tell al-Amarna, also survive. The most interesting ruins are from the Coptic basilica, which reused columns and even the baboon statues, though first removing their giant phalluses.

Several kilometres south of Hermopolis and then 5km along a road into the desert, **Tuna al-Gebel** (Map p177; adult/student E£15/10; ⏱8am-5pm) was the necropolis of Hermopolis. Given the lack of tourists in the area, check with the Minya tourist office that the site is open.

At one time Tuna al-Gebel belonged to Akhetaten, the short-lived capital of Pharaoh Akhenaten, and along the road you pass one of 14 stelae marking the boundary of the royal city. The large stone stele carries Akhenaten's vow never to expand his city beyond this western limit of the city's farmlands and associated villages, nor to be buried anywhere else, although it seems he was eventually buried in the Valley of the Kings at Luxor. To the left, two damaged statues of the pharaoh and his wife Nefertiti hold offering tables; the sides are inscribed with figures of three of their daughters.

South of the stele, which is located about 5km past the village of Tuna al-Gebel, are the **catacombs** (Map p177) and tombs of the residents and sacred animals of Hermopolis. The dark catacomb galleries once held millions of mummified ibis, the 'living image of Thoth', and thousands of mummified baboons, sacrificed and embalmed by the Ptolemaic and Roman faithful. The subterranean cemetery extends for at least 3km, perhaps even all the way to Hermopolis. You need a torch to explore the galleries.

The nearby **Tomb of Petosiris** (Map p177) was built by a high priest of Thoth from the early Ptolemaic period. His temple-like tomb, like his sarcophagus in the Egyptian Museum in Cairo, shows early Greek influence. The wonderful coloured reliefs of farming and the deceased being given offerings also show Greek influence, with the figures wearing Greek dress.

The guard may open several other tombs (for a baksheesh), the most interesting being the **Tomb of Isadora** (Map p177), a wealthy woman who drowned in the Nile during the rule of Antoninus Pius (AD 138–161). The tomb has few decorations, but does contain the unfortunate woman's **mummy**, its teeth, hair and fingernails clearly visible.

The slow village service from Minya stops at Mallawi and from there, a network of microbuses runs around the villages here. But unless you have time to burn, the only viable way to get around these sites is by taxi from Minya, perhaps continuing on to Asyut. Expect to pay E£100 to E£200, depending on the time you want to spend and your bargaining skills.

Tell al-Amarna

In the fifth year of his reign, Pharaoh Akhenaten (1352–1336 BC) and his queen Nefertiti abandoned the gods and priests of Karnak and established a new religion based on the worship of Aten, god of the sun disc.

They also built a new city, Akhetaten (Horizon of the Aten), on the east bank of the Nile, in the area now known as Tell al-Amarna, a beautiful yet solitary crescent-shaped plain, which extends about 10km from north to south. Bounded by the river and backed by a bay of high cliffs, this was the capital of Egypt for some 30 years.

Akhetaten was abandoned for all time after Akhenaten's death. His successor, a son by a minor wife, changed his name from

Hermopolis, Tuna al-Gebel & Tell al-Amarna

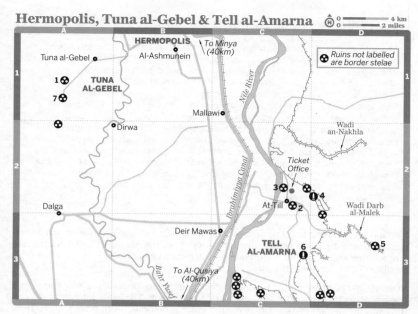

Tutankhaten to Tutankhamun (1336–1327 BC), moved the capital back to Thebes, re-established the cult of Amun at Thebes, restored power to the Theban priesthood and brought an end to what is known as the Amarna Period. Akhetaten fell into ruin, its palaces and temples quarried during the reign of Ramses II for buildings in Hermopolis and other cities.

Archaeologists value the site because, unlike most places in Egypt, it was occupied for just one reign. Many visitors are attracted by the romance of Akhenaten's doomed project but the ruins, scattered across the desert plain, are hard to understand, the tombs nowhere near as interesting or well preserved as others along the Nile (although the remains of the north palace and the Great Temple of Aten can still be identified), and the visit can be disappointing.

◉ Sights

Two groups of cliff tombs, about 8km apart, make up the **Tell al-Amarna necropolis** (Map p177; adult/student E£25/15; ◷8am-4pm Oct-May, to 5pm Jun-Sep), which features some coloured, though defaced, wall paintings of life during the Aten revolution. Remains of temples and private or administrative build-

Hermopolis, Tuna al-Gebel & Tell al-Amarna

ings are scattered across a wide area: this was, after all, an imperial city.

There used to be a bus for touring the site but it was not running at the time of our visit. As the site is so large, the only viable way of visiting is to come by private taxi or with your own car.

In all, there are 25 tombs cut into the base of the cliffs, numbered from one to six in the north, and seven to 25 in the south. Not all are open to the public and only five (Nos 3 to 6 and the royal tomb) currently have light. Even if you have transport, the guards may be unwilling to open the unlighted tombs and the lighted tombs contain some of the best reliefs. You will be expected to tip the guards (at least E£10 per person). Many visi-

KING LISTS DR JOANN FLETCHER

Ancient Egyptians constructed their history around their pharaohs. Instead of using a continuous year-by-year sequence, events were recorded as happening in a specific year of a specific pharaoh: at each pharaoh's accession they started at year 1 until the pharaoh died, then began again with year 1 of the next pharaoh.

So it was vital to have reliable records listing each reign. While a number of so-called 'king lists' can be seen in the Egyptian Museum in Cairo, the Louvre in Paris and the British Museum in London, the only one remaining in its original location was created by Seti I in his Abydos Temple. With an emphasis on the royal ancestors, Seti names 75 of his predecessors beginning with the semi-mythical Menes (usually regarded as Narmer), yet in typical Egyptian fashion he rewrites history by excluding those considered 'unsuitable', from the foreign Hyksos pharaohs of the Second Intermediate Period and the female pharaoh Hatshepsut to the Amarna pharaohs: Amenhotep III is immediately followed by Horemheb, and thus Akhenaten, Smenkhkare, Tutankhamun and Ay are simply erased from the record.

tors find the southern tombs a disappointment after the hassle of getting there. Be sure to bring water as there is currently no possibility of buying any at the site.

NORTHERN TOMBS

Tomb of Huya (No 1)   TOMB
Huya was the steward of Akhenaten's mother, Queen Tiye, and relief scenes to the right and left of the entrance to his tomb show Tiye dining with her son and his family. On the right wall of this columned outer chamber, Akhenaten is shown taking his mother to a small temple he has built for her and, on the left wall, sitting in a carrying chair with Nefertiti.

Tomb of Meryre II (No 2)   TOMB
Meryre II was superintendent of Nefertiti's household, and to the left of the entrance, you will find a scene that shows Nefertiti pouring wine for Akhenaten.

Tomb of Ahmose (No 3)   TOMB
Ahmose's title was 'Fan-Bearer on the King's Right Hand'. Much of his tomb decoration was unfinished: the left-hand wall of the long corridor leading to the burial chamber shows the artists' different stages. The upper register shows the royal couple on their way to the Great Temple of Aten, followed by armed guards. The lower register shows them seated in the palace listening to an orchestra.

Tomb of Meryre I (No 4)   TOMB
High priest of the Aten, Meryre is shown, on the left wall of the columned chamber, being carried by his friends to receive rewards from the royal couple. On the right-hand

wall, the royal couple are shown making offerings to the Aten disc; note here the rare depiction of a rainbow.

Tomb of Pentu (No 5)   TOMB
Pentu, the royal physician, was buried in a simple tomb. The left-hand wall of the corridor is decorated with images of the royal family at the Great Temple of Aten and of Pentu being appointed their physician.

Tomb of Panehsy (No 6)   TOMB
The tomb of Panehsy, chief servant of the Aten in Akhetaten, retains the decorated facade most others have lost. Inside, scenes of the royal family, including Nefertiti driving her chariot and, on the right wall of the entrance passage, Nefertiti's sister Mutnodjmet, later married to Pharaoh Horemheb (1323–1295 BC), with dwarf servants. Panehsy appears as a fat old man on the left wall of the passage between the two main chambers. Two of the first chamber's four columns were removed by the Copts, who added a nave to the inner wall and created a chapel – the remains of painted angel wings can be seen on the walls.

SOUTHERN TOMBS

Tomb of Mahu (No 9)   TOMB
This is one of the best preserved southern tombs. The paintings show interesting details of Mahu's duties as Akhenaten's chief of police, including taking prisoners to the vizier (minister), checking supplies and visiting the temple.

Tomb of Ay (No 25)   TOMB
This is the finest tomb at Tell al-Amarna. Ay's titles were simply 'God's Father' and

'Fan-Bearer on the King's Right Hand' and he was vizier to three pharaohs before becoming one himself (he succeeded Tutankhamun and reigned from 1327 to 1323 BC). His wife Tiyi was Nefertiti's wet nurse. The images here reflect the couple's importance, with scenes including Ay and Tiyi worshipping the sun and Ay receiving rewards from the royal family, including red-leather riding gloves. Ay wasn't buried here, but in the west valley beside the Valley of the Kings (p218) at Thebes.

ROYAL TOMB OF AKHENATEN

Akhenaten's own **tomb** (Map p177; additional ticket adult/student E£20/10) is in a ravine about 12km up the Royal Valley (Wadi Darb al-Malek), the valley that divides the north and south sections of the cliffs and where the sun was seen to rise each dawn. A well-laid road leads up the bleak valley. The guard will need to start up the tomb's generator. Very little remains inside. The right-hand chamber has damaged reliefs of Akhenaten and his family worshipping Aten. A raised rectangular outline in the burial chamber once held the sarcophagus, which is now in the Egyptian Museum in Cairo (after being returned from Germany). Akhenaten himself was probably not buried here, although members of his family certainly were. Some believe he was buried in KV 55 in Luxor's Valley of the Kings, where his sarcophagus was discovered. The whereabouts of his mummy remains are a mystery.

❶ Getting There & Away

Even if the security situation allows it, getting to Tell al-Amarna by public transport remains a challenge, and until the site bus starts running, it's pointless: the site is so large that it is impossible to visit on foot. So for now you need to take a taxi from Asyut, Minya or Mallawi and cross on the irregular car ferry (E£15 per car). Expect to pay as much as E£150 to E£250 depending on where you start and how long you want to stay. Be sure to specify which tombs you want to visit or your driver may refuse to go to far-flung sites.

Tombs of Mir

The necropolis of the governors of Cusae, the **Tombs of Mir** (adult/student E£25/15; ⊙9am-5pm Sat-Wed), as they are commonly known (sometimes also Meir), were dug into the barren escarpment during the Old and Middle Kingdoms. Nine tombs are deco-

rated and open to the public; six others were unfinished and remain unexcavated.

Tomb No 1 and the adjoining tomb No 2 are inscribed with 720 Pharaonic deities, but as the tombs were used as cells by early Coptic hermits, many faces and names of the gods were destroyed. In tomb No 4 you can still see the original grid drawn on the wall to assist the artist in designing the layout of the wall decorations. Tomb No 3 features a cow giving birth.

About 50 minutes' drive from Asyut towards Minya, the bus will drop you at Al-Qusiya. Few vehicles from Al-Qusiya go out to the Tombs of Mir, so you'll have to hire a taxi to take you there. Expect to pay at least E£50, depending on how long you spend at the site. A taxi from Asyut to Mir will cost E£70 to E£100. Ideally, you could combine this with a visit to Deir al-Muharraq.

Deir al-Muharraq

Deir al-Muharraq (Burnt Monastery), an hour's drive northwest of Asyut, is a place of pilgrimage, refuge and vows where the strength of Coptic traditions can be experienced. The 120 resident monks believe that Mary and Jesus inhabited a cave on this site for six months and 10 days after fleeing from Herod. This was their longest stay at any of the numerous places where they are said to have rested in Egypt. Coptic tradition claims the **Church of al-Azraq** (Church of the Anointed) sits over the cave and is the world's oldest Christian church, consecrated around AD 60. More certain is the presence of monastic life here since the 4th century. The current building dates from the 12th to 13th centuries. Unusually, the church contains two iconostases. The one to the left of the altar came from an Ethiopian Church of Sts Peter and Paul, which used to sit on the roof. Other objects from the Ethiopians are displayed in the hall outside the church.

The **keep** beside the church is an independent 7th-century tower, rebuilt in the 12th and 20th centuries. Reached by drawbridge, its four floors can serve as a mini-monastery, complete with its own small **Church of St Michael**, a refectory, accommodation and even burial space behind the altar.

Monks believe the monastery's religious significance is given in the Book of Isaiah.

In that day there will be an altar to the Lord in the midst of the land of Egypt, and a pillar to the Lord at its border. It will be a sign and a witness to the Lord of Host in the land of Egypt; when they cry to the Lord because of oppressors he will send them a saviour, and will defend and deliver them. And the Lord will make himself known to the Egyptians; and the Egyptians will know the Lord in that day and worship with sacrifice and burnt offering, and they will make vows to the Lord and perform them.

Isaiah 19:19-21

The monastery has done much to preserve Coptic tradition: monks here spoke the Coptic language until the 19th century (at that time there were 190 of them) and while other monasteries celebrate some of the Coptic liturgy in Arabic (for their Arabic-speaking congregation), here they stick to Coptic.

Also in the compound, the **Church of St George** (Mar Girgis) was built in 1880 with permission from the Ottoman sultan, who was still the official sovereign of Egypt. It is decorated with paintings of the 12 apostles and other religious scenes, its iconostasis is made from marble, and many of the icons are in Byzantine style. Tradition has it that the icon showing the Virgin and Child was painted by St Luke.

Remember to remove shoes before entering either church and respect the silence and sanctity of the place. For a week every year (usually 21–28 June), thousands of pilgrims attend the monastery's annual feast, a time when visitors may not be admitted.

You will usually be escorted around the monastery and, while there is no fee, donations are appreciated. Visits sometimes finish with a brief visit to the new church built in 1940 or the nearby gift shop or, sometimes, with a cool drink in the monastery's reception room.

About 50 minutes' drive from Asyut towards Minya, the bus will drop you at Al-Qusiya. From there, you may be able to get a local microbus (E£4) to the monastery.

Asyut

📞 088 / POP 389,307

Asyut, 375km south of Cairo, was settled during Pharaonic times on a broad fertile plain bordering the west bank of the Nile and has preserved an echo of antiquity in its name. As Swaty, it was the ancient capital of the 13th nome of Upper Egypt. Surrounded by rich agricultural land and sitting at the end of one of Africa's great caravan routes, from sub-Saharan Africa and Sudan to Asyut via Al-Kharga Oasis (see boxed text p283), it has always been important commercially, if not politically. For centuries one of the main commodities traded here was slaves: caravans stopped here for quarantine before being traded, a period in which slavers used to prepare some of their male slaves for the harem.

Much of modern Asyut is an agglomeration of high-rises that carry no trace or reminder of the ancient Egyptian entrepôt. In the late 1980s this was one of the earliest centres of Islamist fomentation. In the summer and autumn of 2000, it was also the scene of an apparition in which the Virgin Mary appeared to Copts and Muslims, in the words of one witness, 'with flashes of heavenly lights and spiritual doves'.

The choice of hotels and transport links make it the best overnight stopover between Minya and Luxor, as does its reputation for fruit and juices. And at least some of its citizens heed the governor's call that 'cleanliness is a civilised behaviour.'

⊙ Sights

For a city of such history, Asyut has surprisingly little to show for itself, partly because most of the city still remains unexcavated and the ancient tombs in the hills on the edge of the irrigation are currently unvisited.

Asyut Barrage   LANDMARK
Until the Nile-side **Alexan Palace**, one of the city's finest 19th-century buildings, has been renovated and re-opened, the most accessible monument to Asyut's period of wealth is the Asyut Barrage. Built over the Nile between 1898 and 1902 to regulate the flow of water into the Ibrahimiyya Canal and assure irrigation of the valley as far north as Beni Suef, it also serves as a bridge across the Nile. As the barrage still has strategic importance, photography is forbidden, so you should keep your camera out of sight.

Banana Island   ISLAND
(Gezirat al-Moz) Banana Island, to the north of town, is a shady, pleasant place to picnic. You'll have to bargain with a felucca captain for the ride: expect to pay around E£40 an hour.

Convent of the Holy Virgin CONVENT

At Dirunka, some 11km southwest of Asyut, this convent was built near a cave where the Holy Family are said to have taken refuge during their flight into Egypt. Some fifty nuns and monks live at the convent, built into a cliff situated about 120m above the valley. One of the monks will be happy to show you around. During the Moulid (saints' festival) of the Virgin (held in the second half of August), up to a million pilgrims come to pray, carrying portraits of Mary and Jesus. You will need to go by taxi (E£15 to E£30).

🛏 Sleeping

As a large provincial centre, Asyut has a selection of hotels but many are overpriced and noisy.

Al-Watania Palace Hotel HOTEL $$

(📞228 7981; Sharia al-Gomhuriyya; s/d US$60/80; 🕸🛜) The newest, smartest and largest hotel in Asyut has spacious rooms, an impressive lobby, various function rooms and more stars than anywhere else around. There is a choice of restaurants, although at the time of our visit, only the rooftop grill was operating. What you lose in location and atmosphere is made up for with comfort and service.

Partner Tut Hotel FLOATING HOTEL $$

(📞02 3761 2478; Corniche an-Nil (Thawra); s/d US$100/130; 🕸🛜) What to do with a decommissioned cruise boat? Moor it down river and turn it into a hotel, of course. One of several tied up between Cairo and Luxor, the Tut has 49 rooms and a top-deck restaurant. On the Nile about a kilometre from the centre, it's rooms are a little sterile but scrupulously clean. There is a popular riverside terrace serving cold beers, fresh juices and water pipes, and a good restaurant serving Egyptian and some Italian dishes.

Assiutel Hotel HOTEL $$

(📞231 212; 146 Corniche an-Nil (Thawra); s US$47 & 67, d US$66 & 86; 🕸) Overlooking the Nile and the noisy corniche, this was long the best place in town. It has two levels of rooms, neither particularly welcoming, the cheaper ones more worn, but all with satellite TV, fridge and private bathroom. There is a dull restaurant (mains E£15 to E£30) and one of Asyut's only bars.

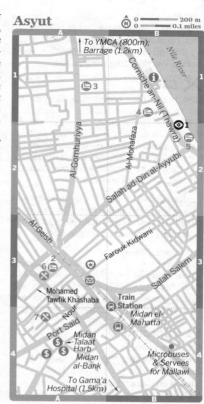

Asyut

◎ Sights
1 Alexan Palace B2

🛏 Sleeping
2 Akhenaten Hotel A3
3 Al-Watania Palace Hotel A1
4 Assiutel Hotel B1
5 Partner Tut Hotel B2

✕ Eating
Al-Watania Palace Hotel .... (see 3)
Assiutel Hotel .... (see 4)
6 Casablanca Sweet Restaurant........... A3
7 Kushari Galal A4

Akhenaten Tourist Hotel HOTEL $$

(📞233 1600; Sharia Mohamed Tawfik Khashaba; s/d E£120/200; 🕸🛜) The Akhenaten is an old-timer that has recently been overhauled. Same old friendly welcome at reception.

YMCA
HOSTEL $

(📞230 3018; Sharia el-Nemis; s/d E£30/50; ❄) This place offers basic rooms (with fridges) that get booked out by Egyptian youth groups. Worth calling ahead to book.

🍴 Eating

Most hotels have restaurants, the best being the mid-priced rooftop restaurant at Al-Watania Palace Hotel, although the Assiutel is currently the only place in town serving alcohol. There are the usual fuul and ta'amiyya stands around the train station and some more upmarket options along the Nile and a very friendly cafe.

Kushari Galal
EGYPTIAN FAST FOOD $

(Sharia Talaat Harb; dishes from E£5) The most reliable carbohydrate intake place in town – delicious, convenient and open late.

Casablanca Sweet Restaurant
EGYPTIAN FAST FOOD $

(Sharia Mohamed Tawfiq Khashba; dishes E£7-12) Come here for savoury *fiteer* (Egyptian pancakes), pizzas (though nothing to do with the Italian variety) and sweet crêpes.

ℹ Information

Ambulance (📞123)

Bank of Alexandria (Sharia Port Said; ⏱9am-2pm & 6-8pm Sun-Thu) Has an ATM.

Banque du Caire (Midan Talaat Harb) Has an ATM.

Banque Misr (Midan Talaat Harb) Has an ATM.

Gama'a Hospital (📞233 4500; University of Asyut)

Main post office (Sharia al-Geish)

Police (📞122)

Tourist office (📞231 0010; 1st fl, Governorate Bldg, Corniche an-Nil (Thawra); ⏱8.30am-3pm Sun-Thu) The very welcoming staff at the tourist office can provide maps of the city and help arrange onward travel.

Tourist police (📞126)

ℹ Getting There & Away

Asyut is a major hub for all forms of transport, although if you want to go by road to Luxor and the south you will have to change at Sohag.

AIR Asyut's airport, 35km west of the city, has been reopened and there are now several flights a week to Cairo and Kuwait.

BUS The **bus station** (📞233 0460) near the train station has services to Cairo (E£40), Sharm el-Sheikh (E£80), west to Dakhla (E£30) and elsewhere in the New Valley, and an 11am service to Hurghada (E£40).

SERVEES & TAXI There is no *servees* to Luxor, but there is to Mallawi (E£10). A private taxi to Luxor will cost around E£150 each way.

TRAIN There are several daytime trains to Cairo (1st-/2nd-class E£61/34, four to five hours) and Minya (E£32/19, one hour), and about 10 daily south to Luxor (E£53/30, five to six hours) and Aswan (E£74/41, eight to nine hours). All stop in Sohag (E£25/17, one to two hours) and Qena (E£41/25, three to four hours).

Sohag

📞093 / POP 189,638

The city of Sohag, 115km south of Asyut, is one of the major Coptic Christian areas of Upper Egypt. Although there are few sights in the city, the nearby White and Red Monasteries, and the town of Akhmim across the river, are all of interest.

◉ Sights

At the time of writing the new **Sohag Museum** was still not open but it will eventually display local antiquities, including those from ongoing excavations of the temple of Ramses II in Akhmim. Until then, apart from the weekly Monday morning livestock market, there is little in town to delay visitors.

Currently the best reason to stop at Sohag is to visit two early Coptic monasteries nearby, which trumpet the victory of Christianity over Egypt's pagan gods. To get to the monasteries you'll have to take a taxi (about E£25 per hour).

White Monastery
MONASTERY

(Deir al-Abyad; ⏱7am-dusk) On rocky ground above the old Nile flood level, 12km northwest of Sohag, this monastery was founded by St Shenouda around AD 400 and dedicated to his mentor, St Bigol. White limestone from Pharaonic temples was reused, and ancient gods and hieroglyphs still look out from some of the blocks. It once supported a huge community of monks and boasted the largest library in Egypt, but today the manuscripts are scattered around the world and the monastery is home to 23 monks. The fortress walls still stand though they failed to protect the interior, most of which is in ruins. Nevertheless, it is easy to make out the plan of the church inside the enclosure walls. Made of brick and measuring 75m by 35m, it follows a basilica plan, with a nave, two side aisles and a triple apse. The nave and apses are intact, the domes decorated with the Dormition of the Virgin and Christ Pantocrator. Nineteen columns, taken from an earlier structure, separate the side chapels from the nave. Visitors wanting to assist in services may arrive from 4am.

Red Monastery
MONASTERY

(Deir al-Ahmar; ⊙7am-midnight) The Red Monastery, 4km southeast of the White Monastery and hidden at the rear of a village, is even more extraordinary. Founded by Besa, a disciple of Shenouda who, according to legend, was a thief who converted to Christianity, it was dedicated to St Bishoi. The older of the monastery's two chapels, the Chapel of St Bishoi and St Bigol, dates from the 4th century AD and some 80% of its surfaces are still covered with painted plaster and frescoes. At the time of writing these were being restored by a team sponsored by the American Research Center in Egypt and USAID. While some of the chapel is hidden by scaffolding, many of the frescoes are now visible. The quality and extent of the surviving work has led this chapel to be likened to the Hagia Sophia in İstanbul as one of the great surviving monuments of late antiquity. The chapel of the Virgin, across the open court, is a more modern and less interesting structure.

Akhmim
TOWN

The satellite town of Akhmim, on Sohag's east bank, covers the ruins of the ancient Egyptian town of Ipu, itself built over an older predynastic settlement. It was dedicated to Min, a fertility god often represented by a giant phallus, equated with Pan by the Greeks (who later called the town Panopolis). The current name contains an echo of the god's name, but more definite links to antiquity were uncovered in 1982 when excavations beside the Mosque of Sheikh Naqshadi revealed an 11m-high **statue of Meret Amun** (adult/student E£20/10; ⊙8am-6pm). This is the tallest statue of an ancient queen to have been discovered in Egypt. Meret Amun (Beloved of the Amun) was the daughter of Ramses II, wife of Amenhotep and priestess of the Temple of Min. She is shown here with flail in hand, wearing a ceremonial headdress and large earrings. Nearby, the remains of a seated statue of her father still retains some original colour.

Little is left of the temple itself, and the statue of Meret Amun now stands in a huge excavation pit, among the remains of a Roman settlement and houses of the modern town. Another excavation pit has been dug across the road and a more extensive excavation is underway nearby.

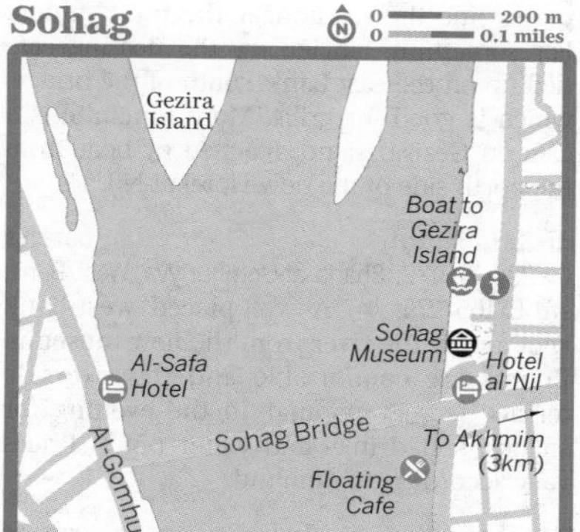

Akhmim was famed in antiquity for its textiles – one of its current weavers calls it 'Manchester before history'. The tradition continues today and opposite the statue of Meret Amun, across from the post office, a green door leads to a small **weaving factory** (knock if it is shut). Here you can see weavers at work and buy hand-woven silk and cotton textiles straight from the bolt (silk E£65 to E£75 per metre, cotton E£30) or packets of ready-made tablecloths and serviettes.

A taxi to Akhmim should cost around E£30 per hour. The microbus costs E£4 and takes 15 minutes.

🛏 Sleeping & Eating

Sohag doesn't have the charm of Minya or the facilities of Luxor, but it does have a good hotel. The best food options are in the two main hotels. Budget *kushari,* fuul and ta'amiyya

Sohag

Gezira Island

Boat to Gezira Island

Sohag Museum

Al-Safa Hotel

Hotel al-Nil

Sohag Bridge

To Akhmim (3km)

Floating Cafe

Al-Gomhuriyya

Saqqafa

To White Monastery (12km); Red Monastery (16km)

Train Station

Al-Mahatta

Al-Qute

To Moghaf Qena Service Taxi Station (2km)

Nile River

Midan el-Aref

places line the roads near the train station. For something fancier, try the floating cafe tied up on the east bank, south of the bridge, which is good for grills. More romantic is a cafe on Gezira Island, reached by boat from the north side of the new Hotel al-Nil.

Al-Safa Hotel HOTEL $$
(☑230 7701/2; Sharia al-Gomhuriyya, West Bank; s/d E£165/275; 🕸) A well-placed west-bank spot across the river from the new museum. Rooms are comfortable and the riverside terrace is very popular in the evening for snacks, soft drinks and water pipes. Prices vary according to demand.

Hotel al-Nil HOTEL $$
(☑460 6253; Sharia al-Gamah, East Bank; s/d E£200/300; 🕸) The newest hotel in town, on the east bank near the new museum and across the water from Al-Safa. Rooms are well equipped and most have views of the Nile, but the new floors are unlikely to add to the pleasure of staying here.

ℹ Information

Bank of Alexandria (Sharia al-Gomhuriyya; 🕙9am-2pm & 6-8pm Sun-Thu) Has an ATM; changes cash and travellers cheques.
Banque du Caire (Sharia al-Gomhuriyya) Has an ATM; changes cash and travellers cheques.
Post office (Sharia al-Gomhuriyya)

Tourist office (☑460 4913; Governorate Bldg; 🕙8.30am-3pm Sun-Thu) This helpful office, in the building beside the new museum on the east bank, can help arrange visits to the monasteries.
Tourist police (☑460 4800)

ℹ Getting There & Away

Train and private taxi remain the easiest way of moving around.

AIR Since 2010, Sohag has also had an international airport, with direct flights to Cairo and Kuwait.

MICROBUS Microbus services are an option to the north and to Qena (E£13), but the station (ask for 'Moghaf Qena') is out of the centre and hard to find. You will need to change in Qena to get to Luxor. There are also microbuses from here to Al-Balyana (E£3).

TRAIN There is frequent train service north and south along the Cairo–Luxor main line, with a dozen daily trains to Asyut (E£25/17, one to two hours) and Luxor (E£21/13, three to four hours). The service to Al-Balyana (3rd-class only, E£5.50, one to two hours) is very slow.

Abydos

As the main cult centre of Osiris, god of the dead, **Abydos** (ancient name Ibdju; adult/student E£30/15; 🕙8am-5pm) was *the* place to

Abydos

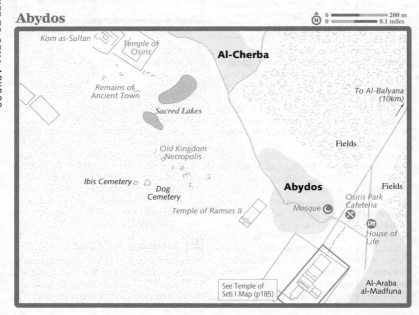

be buried in ancient Egypt. It was used as a necropolis from predynastic to Christian times (c 4000 BC–AD 600), more than 4500 years of constant use. The area now known as Umm al-Qa'ab (Mother of Pots) contains the mastaba tombs of the first pharaohs of Egypt, including that of the third pharaoh of the 1st dynasty, Djer (c 3000 BC). By the Middle Kingdom his tomb had become identified as the tomb of Osiris himself.

Although there were shrines to Osiris throughout Egypt, each one the supposed resting place of another part of his body, the temple at Abydos was the most important, being the home of his head. It was a place that most Egyptians would try to visit in their lifetime – or have themselves buried here. Failing that, they would be buried with small boats to enable their souls to make the journey after death.

One of the temple's more recent residents was Dorothy Eady. An Englishwoman better known as 'Omm Sety', she believed she was a reincarnated temple priestess and lover of Seti I. For 35 years she lived at Abydos and provided archaeologists with information about the working of the temple, in which she was given permission to perform the old rites. She died in 1981 and was buried in the desert.

◎ Sights

Temple of Seti I   MONUMENT

The first structure you'll see at Abydos is the striking Cenotaph or Great Temple of Seti I, which, after a certain amount of restoration work, is one of the most complete temples in Egypt. This great limestone structure, unusually L-shaped rather than rectangular, was dedicated to the six major gods – Osiris, Isis and Horus, Amun-Ra, Ra-Horakhty and Ptah – and also to Seti I (1294–1279 BC) himself. In the aftermath of the Amarna Period, it is a clear statement of a return to the old ways. As you roam through Seti's dark halls and sanctuaries an air of mystery surrounds you.

The temple is entered through a largely destroyed **pylon** and two **courtyards**, built by Seti I's son Ramses II, who is depicted on the portico killing Asiatics and worshipping Osiris. Beyond is the **first hypostyle hall**, also completed by Ramses II. Reliefs depict the pharaoh making offerings to the gods and preparing the temple building.

The **second hypostyle hall**, with 24 sandstone papyrus columns, was the last

Temple of Seti I

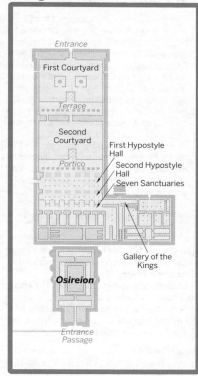

part of the temple to have been decorated by Seti, although he died before the work was completed. The reliefs that were finished are of the highest quality. Particularly outstanding is a scene on the rear right-hand wall showing Seti standing in front of a shrine to Osiris, upon which sits the god himself. Standing in front of him are the goddesses Maat, Renpet, Isis, Nephthys and Amentet. Below is a frieze of Hapi, the Nile god.

At the rear of this second hypostyle hall are **sanctuaries** for each of the seven gods (right to left: Horus, Isis, Osiris, Amun-Ra, Ra-Horakhty, Ptah and Seti), which once held their cult statues. The Osiris sanctuary, third from the right, leads to a series of inner chambers dedicated to the god, his wife and child, Isis and Horus, and the ever-present Seti. More interesting are the chambers off to the left of the seven sanctuaries: here, in a group of chambers dedicated to the mysteries of Osiris, the god is shown mummified

THE CULT OF OSIRIS

The most familiar of all ancient Egypt's myths is the story of Isis and Osiris, preserved in the writings of the Greek historian Plutarch (c AD 46–126) following a visit to Egypt. According to Plutarch, Osiris and his sister-wife Isis ruled on earth, bringing peace and prosperity to their kingdom. Seething with jealousy at their success, their brother Seth invited Osiris to a banquet and tricked him into climbing inside a chest. Once Osiris was inside, Seth sealed the coffin and threw it into the Nile, drowning his brother. Following the murder, the distraught Isis retrieved her brother-husband's body, only to have it seized back by Seth who dismembered it, scattering the pieces far and wide. But Isis refused to give up and, taking the form of a kite, searched for the separate body parts, burying each piece where she found it, which explains why there are so many places that claim to be Osiris' tomb.

Another version of the story has Isis collecting the parts of Osiris and reassembling them to create the first mummy, helped by Anubis, god of embalming. Then, using her immense magic, she restored Osiris to life for long enough to conceive their son Horus. Raised to avenge his father, Horus defeated Seth. While Horus ruled on earth, represented by each pharaoh, his resurrected father ruled as Lord of the Afterlife. A much-loved god, Osiris came to represent the hope for salvation after death, a concept as important to life-loving ancient Egyptians as it was to early Christians.

with the goddess Isis hovering above him as a bird, a graphic depiction of the conception of their son Horus.

Immediately to the left of this, the corridor known as **Gallery of the Kings** is carved with the figures of Seti I with his eldest son, the future Ramses II, and a long list of the pharaohs who preceded them (see p178).

Temple of Ramses II   MONUMENT
Just northwest of Seti I's temple is the smaller and less well preserved structure built by his son Ramses II (1279–1213 BC). Although following the rectangular plan of a traditional temple, it has sanctuaries for each god Ramses considered important, including Osiris, Amun-Ra, Thoth, Min, the deified Seti I and, of course, Ramses himself. Although the roof is missing, the reliefs again retain a significant amount of their colour, clearly seen on figures of priests, offering bearers and the pharaoh anointing the gods' statues. You may not be allowed to visit this site.

🛏 Sleeping & Eating

There are a couple of hotels and cafes in Al-Araba al-Madfuna, the village in which the temples stand.

House of Life   HOTEL $$
(☏0102 2733 0071; www.houseoflife.info; full board per person in old/new house E£150/400; @) The only hotel functioning at the time of our visit, this simple Dutch-, Egyptian- and US-run house overlooking the Temple of Seti I has

six rooms, sharing three bathrooms. There's a big terrace, and guests can access the internet and washing machine. The partners have also constructed another building nearby – three four-bedroom apartments – and are in the process of putting up a 37-room hotel. You could just stay the night, or you could take part in their rituals of massage and ancient Egyptian healing. Essential oils and other products are on sale. Desert trips can be arranged.

Osiris Park Cafeteria   CAFE $
(☉7am-10pm) Right in front of the Temple of Seti I, this is the only reliable option within sight of the temple. The food is overpriced and consists mostly of snacks, although chicken meals (E£40) are sometimes available, and the welcome is friendly and the drinks cold. There is also a surprisingly good range of books and brochures about the temple.

ℹ Getting There & Away

Al-Araba al-Madfuna is 10km from the nearest train station, at Al-Balyana, but most people arrive on a day-trip from Luxor. Many companies in Luxor offer coach tours. A private taxi from Luxor should cost around E£300 return, depending on how long you want at the temple. A train leaves Luxor at 8.25am (1st/2nd-class E£34/21, three hours). A private taxi from Al-Balyana to the temple will cost about E£50 including wait time. A microbus from Al-Balyana costs E£2. There is a train back to Luxor at 3.20pm, and another at 5pm (3rd class only, E£8).

Qena

📱096 / POP 201,191

Ninety-one kilometres east of Al-Balyana, and 62km north of Luxor, Qena sits on a huge bend of the river and at the intersection of the main Nile road and the road running across the desert to the Red Sea towns of Port Safaga and Hurghada. A market town and provincial capital, it was off-limits for a long time. Security restrictions have been lifted, making it a useful junction for a visit to the spectacular temple complex at Dendara, located just outside the town. It's also the place to be on the 14th of the Islamic month of Sha'ban, when the city's 12th-century patron saint, Abdel Rehim al-Qenawi, is celebrated.

👁 Sights

Dendara   TEMPLE COMPLEX
Although built at the very end of the Pharaonic period, the **Temple of Hathor** (adult/student E£35/20; ⊙8am-5pm) at her cult site of Dendara is one of the iconic Egyptian buildings, mostly because it remains virtually intact, with a great stone roof and columns, dark chambers, underground crypts and twisting stairways all carved with hieroglyphs.

Dendara was an important administrative and religious centre as early as the 6th dynasty (c 2320 BC). The goddess Hathor had been worshipped here since the Old Kingdom. But this great temple was only begun in the 30th dynasty, with much of the building undertaken by the Ptolemies and completed during the Roman period.

Few deities have such varied characteristics. Hathor was the goddess of love and sensual pleasures, patron of music and dancing: the Greeks appropriately associated her with their goddess Aphrodite. Like most Egyptian gods, Hathor was known by a range of titles, including 'the golden one', 'she of the beautiful hair' and 'lady of drunk-

Dendara

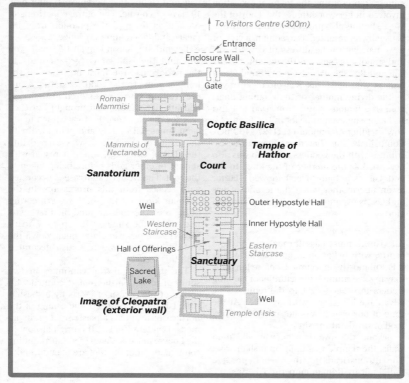

DON'T MISS

THE OSIREION

Directly behind the Temple of Seti I, the Osireion is a weird and wonderful building that continues to baffle Egyptologists, though it is usually interpreted as a cenotaph to Osiris. Originally thought to be an Old Kingdom structure, on account of the great blocks of granite used in its construction, it has now been dated to Seti's reign; its design is believed to be based on the rock-cut tombs in the Valley of the Kings. At the centre of its columned 'burial chamber', which lies at a lower level than Seti's temple, is a dummy sarcophagus. This chamber was originally surrounded by water, but thanks to a rising water table, the entire structure is now flooded, making inspection of the funerary and ritual texts carved on its walls hazardous.

enness', representing the joyful intoxication involved in her worship. As the 'Lady of the West' she was also protector of the dead. She is usually represented as a woman, a cow, or a woman with a headdress of cow's horns and sun disc, as she was the daughter of the sun-god Ra. She was also a maternal figure and as wife of Horus was often portrayed as the divine mother of the reigning pharaoh. In a famous statue from Deir al-Bahri in Luxor she even appears in the form of a cow suckling Amenhotep II (1427–1400 BC). Confusingly, she shared many of these attributes with the goddess Isis, who was also described as the mother of the king. In the end Isis essentially overshadowed Hathor as an ubermother when the legend of Isis and Osiris expanded to include the birth of Horus.

Touring the Temple

All visitors must pass through the visitors centre, with ticket office and bazaar. While it is still mostly unoccupied, before long this may involve running the gauntlet of hassling traders in order to get to the temple. One advantage is a clean, working toilet. At the time of our visit it was not possible to buy food or drinks at the site.

Beyond the towering gateway and mud walls, the temple was built on a slight rise. The entrance leads into the **outer hypostyle hall**, built by Roman emperor Tiberius, the first six of its 24 great stone columns adorned on all four sides with Hathor's head, defaced by Christians but still an impressive sight. The walls are carved with scenes of Tiberius and his Roman successors presenting offerings to the Egyptian gods: the message here, as throughout the temple, is the continuity of tradition, even under foreign rulers. The ceiling at the far left and right side of the hall is decorated with zodiacs. One section has now been cleaned and the colours are very bright.

The inner temple was built by the Ptolemies. The smaller **inner hypostyle hall** again has Hathor columns and walls carved with scenes of royal ceremonials, including the founding of the temple. But notice the 'blank' cartouches that reveal much about the political instability of late Ptolemaic times – with such a rapid turnover of pharaohs, the stonemasons seem to have been reluctant to carve the names of those who might not be in the job for long. Things reached an all-time low in 80 BC when Ptolemy XI murdered his more popular wife and stepmother Berenice III after only 19 days of co-rule. The outraged citizens of Alexandria dragged the pharaoh from his palace and killed him in revenge.

Beyond the second hypostyle hall, you will find the **Hall of Offerings** leads to the **sanctuary**, the most holy part of the temple, home to the goddess' statue. A further Hathor statue was stored in the crypt beneath her temple, and brought out each year for the New Year Festival, which in ancient times fell in July and coincided with the rising of the Nile. It was carried into the Hall of Offerings, where it rested with statues of other gods before being taken to the roof. The western staircase is decorated with scenes from this procession. In the open-air kiosk on the southwestern corner of the roof, the gods awaited the first reviving rays of the sun-god Ra on New Year's Day. The statues were later taken down the eastern staircase, which is also decorated with this scene.

The theme of revival continues in two suites of rooms on the roof, decorated with scenes of the revival of Osiris by his sister-wife, Isis. In the centre of the ceiling of the northeastern suite is a plaster cast of the famous 'Dendara Zodiac', the original now in the Louvre in Paris. Views of the surrounding countryside from the roof are magnificent.

The **exterior walls** feature lion-headed gargoyles to cope with the very occasional rainfall and are decorated with scenes of pharaohs paying homage to the gods. The most famous of these is on the rear (south) wall, where Cleopatra stands with Caesarion, her son by Julius Caesar.

Facing this back wall is a small **temple of Isis** built by Cleopatra's great rival Octavian (the Emperor Augustus). Walking back towards the front of the Hathor temple on the west side, the palm-filled Sacred Lake supplied the temple's water. Beyond this, to the north, lie the mudbrick foundations of the **sanatorium**, where the ill came to seek a cure from the goddess.

Finally there are the two **mammisi** (birth houses), the first built by the 30th-dynasty Egyptian pharaoh, Nectanebo I (380–362 BC), and decorated by the Ptolemies, the one nearest the temple wall built by the Romans and decorated by Emperor Trajan (AD 98–117). Such buildings celebrated divine birth, both of the young gods and of the pharaoh himself as son of the gods. Between the *mammisi* lie the remains of a 5th-century-AD **Coptic basilica**.

Dendara is 4km southwest of Qena on the west side of the Nile. Most visitors arrive from Luxor. A return taxi from Luxor will cost you about E£200. There is also a day cruise to Dendara from Luxor (see p229). If you arrive in Qena by train, you will need to take a taxi to the temple (E£40 to the temple and back with some waiting time).

🛏 Sleeping & Eating

Qena is close enough to Luxor for most people not to need to stay over, but there is one obvious choice if you need to stay. Food choices beyond the hotel have improved, and downtown and around the train station there are restaurants and cafes serving fuul, *kushari* and pizza.

Basma Hotel   HOTEL **$$**
(☎533 2779; Sharia el-Mina el-Nahry; s/d E£250/300; ❄) Reputed to be owned by the security forces, this is the newest and cleanest hotel in Qena, with a huge riverside terrace good for soft drinks and a quiet dinner. The odd tour boat that comes this far is obliged to dock here.

❶ Information

Bank of Alexandria (off Sharia Luxor; ◷8.30am-2pm & 6-8pm Sun-Thu)
Banque du Caire (Sharia Luxor)

❶ Getting There & Away

Train or private taxi are the best ways of travelling independently.
BUS The **Upper Egypt Bus Co** (☎532 5068; Midan al-Mahatta), at the bus station opposite the train station, runs regular services to Cairo (E£60), Hurghada (E£25) and Suez (E£60).
MICROBUS From the microbus station, 1km inland from the bridge, you can get south to Luxor (E£4) and Aswan (E£20), east to Hurghada (E£20), Marsa Alam (E£40) and Suez (E£60), and north to Nag Hamadi (E£4), Sohag (E£15) and Asyut (E£20).
TRAIN All main north–south trains stop at Qena. There are 1st-/2nd-class air-con trains to Luxor (E£21/14, 40 minutes) and trains to Al-Balyana (2nd/3rd class E£15/8, two hours).

❶ Getting Around

Your best option is to travel by private taxi. Expect to pay at least E£40 for the ride to Dendara.

Nile Valley: Luxor

Best Places to Eat

» Sofra (p233)

» Al-Moudira (p235)

» Silk Road (p234)

» Nile Valley Hotel (p236)

» As-Sahaby Lane (p234)

Best Places to Sleep

» Al-Moudira (p231)

» Hilton Luxor Resort & Spa (p229)

» Nefertiti Hotel (p229)

» Beit Sabée (p231)

» La Maison de Pythagore (p229)

Why Go?

Luxor is often called the world's greatest open-air museum, but that comes nowhere near describing this extraordinary place. Nothing in the world can compare to the grandeur of ancient Thebes.

The setting is still breathtakingly beautiful, the Nile flowing between the modern town and the west-bank necropolis, backed by the enigmatic Theban escarpment. Scattered across the landscape is an embarrassment of riches, from the temples of Karnak and Luxor on its east bank to the many tombs and temples on the west bank.

Thebes' wealth and power, already legendary in antiquity, began to lure Western travellers from the end of the 18th century. Today's traveller risks being surrounded by coachloads of tourists herded through the main sights, but with a little planning it is possible to avoid the crowds and get the most from the magic of the Theban landscape and its unparalleled archaeological heritage.

When to go
Luxor

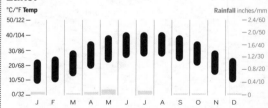

Apr–May, Oct–Nov Some of the best months to visit with the richest light.

Jun/Jul Sha'aban, the month when the city celebrates its holy man, Youssef Abu al-Haggag.

26 Nov The day Howard Carter opened the tomb of Tutankhamun in 1922.

One City, Two Banks

The monuments of Luxor are divided over both banks of the Nile. The **east bank** (Map p196), has the city of Luxor, the Temple of Luxor, the museums, and the temple complex at Karnak. Just south of the town is Sharia Khaled Ibn Walid, 'Little Britain', with many resort hotels in all price categories, and mostly British-run restaurants and pubs. The more rural **west bank** (Map p206) is scattered with the monuments and necropolis of ancient Thebes. It offers smaller and quieter accommodation, mostly in and around the village of Al-Gezira, near the ferry landing, while the monuments are strung out at the edge of the desert.

DON'T MISS

With so many world-class monuments it is easy to lose sight of contemporary Luxor, particularly when time is limited. Take some time to stroll through the Luxor **souq** (Map p196), and venture beyond the tourist bazaar just off Sharia al-Mahatta, where locals shop for fabrics, food and household goods. There you get a glimpse into a world, far away from the temples. On the west bank, **Souq at Talaat** (Map p206) is a very authentic weekly market, little visited by tourists, held on Tuesday mornings in Taref near the Temple of Seti I. Instead of taking a taxi across the bridge, head for the local ferry opposite Luxor Temple to go across, and take a taxi or a bicycle near the ferry landing on the west bank.

Tackling the West Bank

Take more than a day to visit the west bank. Plan your day in advance as tickets for most sights must be bought from the central ticket office (Map p206), and are only valid for that day. Early morning visits are ideal, but that is unfortunately when most tour groups visit the **Temple of Deir al-Bahri** or the **Valley of the Kings**. So leave these two to the afternoon to avoid the crowds and visit other sights such as **Tombs of the Nobles** or the **Ramesseum** in the morning.

AVENUE OF SPHINXES

A 3km-long alley of sphinxes connecting Luxor and Karnak is being excavated. The buildings covering the sphinxes are being destroyed, leaving an artery of road works right through town.

Need to know

» **Telephone code** 095
» **Population** 484,132
» **Opening hours** Sights on West Bank, 6am-5pm daily

Top Tip

Large numbers of coach-loads of day trippers from the Red Sea arrive in Luxor around 10am, heading either for the Valley of the Kings or the Temple of Karnak, so avoid those sights late morning if you don't like being overrun.

Resources

» Luxor travel guide (www. luxoregypt.org, www.luxor -on-line.com) has information on Luxor

» Theban Mapping Project (www.thebanmapping project.com) is an-depth look at the Valley of the Kings

» Flat rental (www. flatsinluxor.com) Accommodation, guide and tour bookings

History

Thebes (ancient Waset) became important in the Middle Kingdom period (2055–1650 BC). The 11th-dynasty Theban prince Montuhotep II (2055–2004 BC) reunited Upper and Lower Egypt, made Thebes his capital and increased Karnak's importance as a cult centre to the local god Amun with a temple dedicated to him. The 12th-dynasty pharaohs (1985–1795 BC) moved their capital back north, but much of their immense wealth from expanded foreign trade and agriculture, and tribute from military expeditions made into Nubia and Asia, went to Thebes, which remained the religious capital. This 200-year period was one of the

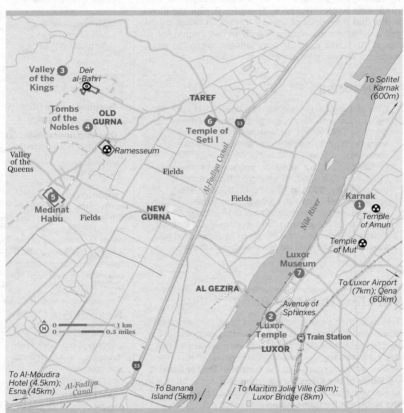

Nile Valley: Luxor Highlights

❶ Wander around the exotic stone garden of gigantic papyrus-shaped stone columns in the great hypostyle hall at **Karnak** (p201).

❷ Marvel at the stunning architecture of the **Luxor Temple** (p201) and return later at night to see the beautifully lit carvings on the walls.

❸ Like the pharaoh, be led by the Gods into the Afterworld in the **Valley of the Kings** (p209).

❹ Glimpse the good life of an ancient Egyptian aristocrat on his tomb walls in the **Tombs of the Nobles** (p207).

❺ Wander through the best-preserved Theban temple, **Medinat Habu** (p221), in the soft, late-afternoon light.

❻ Sense the spirituality of the rarely visited **Temple of Seti I** (p217).

❼ Visit the numerous treasures of the compact **Luxor Museum** (p203).

richest times throughout Egyptian history, which witnessed a great flourishing of architecture and the arts, and major advances in science.

It was the Thebans again, under Ahmose I, who, after the Second Intermediate Period (1650–1550 BC), drove out the ruling Asiatic Hyksos and unified Egypt. Because of his military victories and as the founder of the 18th dynasty, Ahmose was deified and worshipped at Thebes for hundreds of years. This was the beginning of the glorious New Kingdom (1550–1069 BC), when Thebes reached its apogee. It was home to tens of thousands of people, who helped construct many of its great monuments.

The greatest contributor of all to Thebes was probably Amenhotep III (1390–1352 BC). He made substantial additions to the temple complex at Karnak, and built his great palace, Malqata, on the west bank, with a large harbour for religious festivals and the largest memorial temple ever built. Very little of the latter is left beyond the so-called Colossi of Memnon, the largest monolithic statue ever carved. His son Amenhotep IV (1352–1336 BC), who later renamed himself Akhenaten, moved the capital from Thebes to his new city of Akhetaten (Tell al-Amarna), worshipped one god only (Aten the solar god), and brought about dramatic changes in art and architecture. After his death, the powerful priesthood was soon reinstated under Akhenaten's successor, Tutankhamun (1336–1327 BC), who built very little but became the best-known pharaoh ever when his tomb was discovered full of treasure in 1922. Ramses II (1279–1213 BC) may have exaggerated his military victories, but he too was a great builder and added the magnificent hypostyle hall to Karnak, other halls to Luxor Temple, and built the Ramesseum and two magnificent tombs in the Valley of the Kings for himself and his many sons.

The decline of Pharaonic rule was mirrored by Thebes' gradual slide into insignificance: when the Persians sacked Thebes, it was clear the end was nigh. Mudbrick settlements clung to the once mighty Theban temples, and people hid within the stone walls against marauding desert tribes. Early Christians built churches in the temples, carved crosses on the walls and scratched out reliefs of the pagan gods. The area fell into obscurity in the 7th century AD after the Arab invasion, and the only reminder of

THE GREAT PLAN

Mass tourism has definitely arrived in Luxor, and tourism is now arguably the greatest threat to the city's, and the country's, monuments. Dr Zahi Hawass, the former head of the Supreme Council of Antiquities, has stated that if nothing is done, the monuments will be destroyed in less than 100 years. Before the 2011 revolution, there was a plan to turn Luxor into the largest open-air museum in the world, but at the time of writing most of the work had been stalled due to lack of government funds. On both banks, huge swathes of houses and entire villages have been demolished to clear the areas around the historical sites. On a positive note, visitors centres are being built at the main sights and replicas of some of the most beautiful but fragile tombs are planned.

its glorious past was the name bestowed on it by its Arab rulers: Al-Uqsur (The Fortifications), giving modern Luxor its name. By the time European travellers arrived here in the 18th century, Luxor was little more than a large Upper Egyptian village, known more for its 12th-century saint, Abu al-Haggag, buried above the mound of Luxor Temple, than for its half-buried ruins.

The growth of Egyptomania changed that. Napoleon arrived in 1798 wanting to revive Egypt's greatness and, with the publication of the *Description de l'Egypte,* did manage to revive interest in Egypt. European exhibitions of mummies, jewellery and other spectacular funerary artefacts from Theban tombs (often found by plundering adventurers rather than enquiring scholars) made Luxor an increasingly popular destination for travellers. By 1869, when Thomas Cook brought his first group of tourists to Egypt, Luxor was one of the highlights. Mass tourism had arrived and Luxor regained its place on the world map.

⊙ Sights

Luxor sights are spread on the east and west banks of the Nile. Start on the east bank, where visitors will find most of the hotels, the modern town of Luxor and the temple complexes of Luxor and Karnak. The west bank, traditionally the 'side of the dead', is

LUXOR IN...

Two days

If you've only got two days in Luxor, your schedule will be full on. Spend the first day on the east bank, starting early morning with a visit of the **Temple of Karnak**. After Karnak stroll along the Corniche to the **Luxor Museum**. After a late lunch at **Sofra**, visit the Temple of Luxor in the golden glow of the afternoon sun. Return after dinner to see the temple floodlit. The next day take a taxi for a day to the west bank, and start early again to avoid the crowds at the **Valley of the Kings**. On the way back visit the newly opened **Howard Carter's House** and the **Temple of Deir al-Bahari**. After lunch visit the **Tombs of the Nobles**, or the wonderful temple of Ramses III at **Medinet Habu**.

Four days

Four days allows for a more leisurely schedule. Allow one extra day on the west bank to visit **Tombs of the Nobles**, the **Ramesseum** and the **Temple of Seti**, and take a day trip to the amazing **temples of Denderah** and **Abydos**.

where the mortuary temples and necropolis are located.

EAST BANK
Temples of Karnak

More than a temple, Karnak (off Map p196; Sharia Maabad al-Karnak; adult/student E£65/40; ☉6am-6pm) is an extraordinary complex of sanctuaries, kiosks, pylons and obelisks dedicated to the Theban gods and the greater glory of pharaohs. Everything is on a gigantic scale: the site covers over 2 sq km, large enough to contain about 10 cathedrals, while its main structure, the Temple of Amun, is one of the world's largest religious complexes. This was where the god lived on earth, surrounded by the houses of his wife Mut and their son Khonsu, two other huge temple complexes on this site. Built, added to, dismantled, restored, enlarged and decorated over nearly 1500 years, Karnak was the most important place of worship in Egypt during the New Kingdom. It was called Ipet-Sut, meaning 'The Most Esteemed of Places'; Karnak is its Arabic name meaning 'fortified settlement'. New Kingdom records show that the priests of the Temple of Amun had 81,000 people working in or for the temple, owned 421,000 head of cattle, 65 cities, 83 ships and 276,400 hectares of agricultural land, giving an idea of its economic, as well as spiritual, significance.

The most important place of worship was the massive Amun Temple Enclosure (Precinct of Amun; Map p200), dominated by the great Temple of Amun-Ra, which contains the famous hypostyle hall, a spectacular forest of giant papyrus-shaped columns. On its southern side is the Mut Temple

Enclosure, once linked to the main temple by an avenue of ram-headed sphinxes. To the north is the Montu Temple Enclosure, which honoured the local Theban war god. The 3km paved avenue of human-headed sphinxes that once linked the great Temple of Amun at Karnak with Luxor Temple is now again being cleared. Most of what you can see was built by the powerful pharaohs of the 18th to 20th dynasties (1570–1090 BC), who spent fortunes on making their mark in this most sacred of places. Later pharaohs extended and rebuilt the complex, as did the Ptolemies and early Christians. Basically the further into the complex you venture, the older the structures.

Wandering through this gigantic complex is one of the highlights of any visit to Egypt. The light is most beautiful in the early morning, and the temple is quieter then, as later in the morning the tour groups and loads of day trippers from Hurghada arrive. It pays to visit more than once, to make sense of the overwhelming jumble of ancient remains.

Amun Temple Enclosure   TEMPLE
The Quay of Amun was the dock where the large boats carrying the statues of the gods moored during the festivals. From tomb paintings such as those in the Tomb of Nakht (p208) we know that there were palaces to the north of the quay surrounded by lush gardens. On the east side is a ramp sloping down to the processional avenue of ram-headed sphinxes, which leads to the massive unfinished first pylon, built by Nectanebo I of the 30th dynasty. On the inside is a massive mudbrick construction

NILE VALLEY: LUXOR SIGHTS

ramp, onto which the blocks of stone for the pylon were dragged up with rollers and ropes. When Napoleon's expedition visited there were still blocks on the ramp.

Great Court

Behind the first pylon lies the Great Court, the largest area of the Karnak complex. To the left is the **Temple of Seti II** with three small chapels that held the sacred barques of Mut, Amun and Khonsu during the lead-up to the Opet Festival. In the southeastern corner (far right) is the well-preserved **Temple of Ramses III**, a miniature version of the pharaoh's temple at Medinat Habu. The temple plan is simple and classic: pylon, open court, vestibule with four Osirid columns and four columns, hypostyle hall with eight columns and three barque chapels for Amun, Mut and Khonsu. At the centre of the court are two rows of five columns. Only one still stands, 21m tall with a papyrus-shaped capital, and a small alabaster altar at the middle: all that remains of the **Kiosk of Taharka**, the 25th-dynasty Nubian pharaoh.

The **second pylon** was begun by Horemheb, the last 18th-dynasty pharaoh, and continued by Ramses I and Ramses II, who also raised three colossal red-granite **statues** of himself on either side of the entrance; one is now destroyed.

Great Hypostyle Hall

Beyond the second pylon is the awesome **Great Hypostyle Hall** (Map p200), one of the greatest religious monuments ever built. Covering 5500 sq metres – enough space to contain both Rome's St Peter's Basilica and London's St Paul's Cathedral – the hall is an unforgettable forest of 134 towering papyrus-shaped stone pillars. It symbolised a papyrus swamp, of which there were so many along the Nile. Ancient Egyptians believed that these plants surrounded the primeval mound on which life was first created. Each summer when the Nile began to flood, this hall and its columns were under several feet of water. Originally, it would have been brightly painted – some colours remain – and roofed, making it pretty dark away from the lit main axis. The size and grandeur of the pillars and the endless decorations are overwhelming: take your time, sit for a while and stare at the dizzying spectacle.

The hall was planned by Ramses I and built by Seti I and Ramses II. Note the difference in quality between the delicate raised relief in the northern part, by Seti I, and the

much cruder sunken relief work, added by Ramses II in the southern part of the hall. The cryptic scenes on the inner walls were intended for the priesthood and the royalty who understood the religious context, but the outer walls are easier to comprehend, showing the pharaoh's military prowess and strength, and his ability to bring order to chaos.

On the back of the **third pylon**, built by Amenhotep III, to the right the pharaoh is shown sailing the sacred barque during the Opet Festival (see boxed text p199). Tuthmosis I (1504–1492 BC) created a narrow court between the third and fourth pylons, where four obelisks stood, two each for Tuthmosis I and Tuthmosis III (1479–1425 BC). Only the bases remain except for one, 22m high, raised for Tuthmosis I.

Inner Temple

Beyond the **fourth pylon** is the Hypostyle Hall of Tuthmosis III built by Tuthmosis I in precious wood, and altered by Tuthmosis III with 14 columns and a stone roof. In this court stands one of the two magnificent 30m-high obelisks erected by Queen Hatshepsut (1473–1458 BC) to the glory of her 'father' Amun. The other is broken but the upper shaft lies near the sacred lake. The **Obelisk of Hatshepsut** is the tallest in Egypt, its tip originally covered in electrum (a commonly used alloy of gold and silver). After Hatshepsut's death, her stepson Tuthmosis III eradicated all signs of her reign (see boxed text p220) and had them walled into a sandstone structure.

The ruined **fifth pylon**, constructed by Tuthmosis I, leads to another colonnade now badly ruined, followed by the small **sixth pylon**, raised by Tuthmosis III, who also built the pair of red-granite columns in the vestibule beyond, carved with the lotus and the papyrus, the symbols of Upper and Lower Egypt. Nearby are two huge statues of Amun and the goddess Amunet, carved in the reign of Tutankhamun.

The original **sacred barque sanctuary** of Tuthmosis III, the very core of the temple where the god Amun resided, was replaced by a granite one, that was built and decorated with well-preserved painted reliefs by Alexander the Great's successor and half-brother, the fragile, dim-witted Philip Arrhidaeus (323–317 BC).

East of the shrine of Philip Arrhidaeus, is the oldest known part of the temple, the **Middle Kingdom Court**, where Sesostris I

Luxor – East Bank

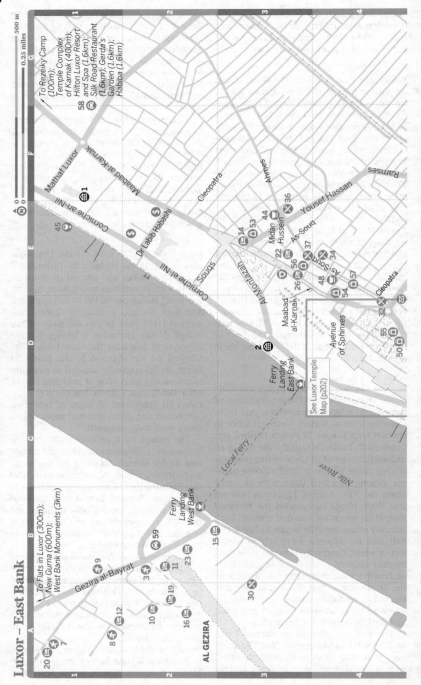

0 0.25 miles
0 500 m

To Rezeiky Camp (100m); Temple Complex of Karnak (400m); Hilton Luxor Resort and Spa (1.6km); Silk Road Restaurant (1.6km); Gerda's Garden (1.6km); Habiba (1.6km)

To Flats in Luxor (300m); New Gurna (600m); West Bank Monuments (3km)

AL GEZIRA

Gezira al-Bayrat

Nile River

Ferry Landing East Bank

Ferry Landing West Bank

Local Ferry

See Luxor Temple Map (p202)

Avenue of Sphinxes

Maabad al-Karnak

Corniche an-Nil
Corniche el-Nil
Mathaf Luxor
Maabad al-Karnak
Dr Labib Habashi
Sphinx
Al-Montazah

Cleopatra
Ahmes
Ramses
Yousef Hassan
As-Souq
Midan Hussein
Cleopatra

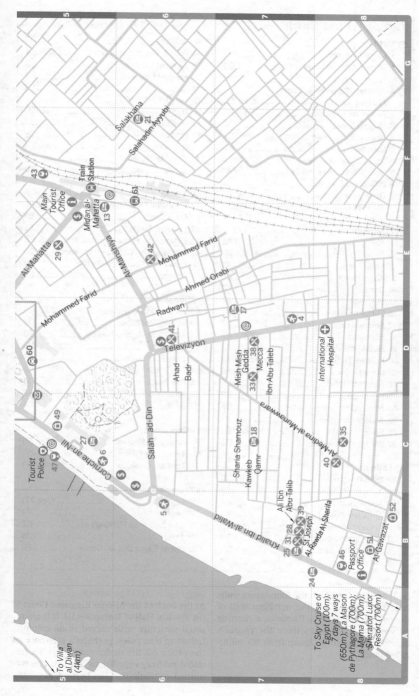

Luxor – East Bank

built a shrine, of which the foundation walls have been found. On the northern wall of the court is the **Wall of Records**, a running tally of the organised tribute the pharaoh exacted in honour of Amun from his subjugated lands.

Great Festival Hall of Tuthmosis III
At the back of the Middle Kingdom Court is the Festival Hall of Tuthmosis III. It is an unusual structure with carved stone columns imitating tent poles, perhaps a reference to the pharaoh's life under canvas on his frequent military expeditions abroad. The columned vestibule that lies beyond, generally

THE BEAUTIFUL FESTIVAL OF THE OPET

The most important annual religious festival in Thebes and Egypt was the Opet Festival, when the barque shrines of the Theban triad Amun, Mut and Khonsu were taken in a procession from Karnak Temple to their home at Luxor Temple. The festival lasted two to four weeks during the summer, the second month of the Nile flood, and was particularly important during the New Kingdom. The cult images were carried on the shoulders of the priests along the avenue of sphinxes, stopping for ceremonies and to rest at six barque shrines on the way, or taken by boat up the Nile, as seen on the reliefs in Amenhotep III's Colonnade in Luxor Temple and the outer wall of the Temple of Ramses III in the Great Court in Karnak. The statue of Amun was reunited with his ithyphallic form Amenemopet, symbolising fertility and rejuvenation. The ceremony reaffirmed the pharaoh's authority and his close ties with the 'King of Gods' Amun. The pharaoh, after all, was the living embodiment of the god Horus on earth. Now, during the *moulid* (saint's festival) of Abu al-Haggag (see boxed text p203), one of the highlights of this three-day festival is a felucca pulled in procession through town and circling the temple, a modern survival of the ancient Opet Festival.

referred to as the **Botanical Gardens**, has wonderful, detailed relief scenes of the flora and fauna that the pharaoh had encountered during his campaigns in Syria and Palestine, and had brought back to Egypt.

Secondary Axis of the Amun Temple Enclosure

The courtyard between the Hypostyle Hall and the **seventh pylon**, built by Tuthmosis III, is known as the **cachette court**, as thousands of stone and bronze statues were discovered here in 1903. The priests had the old statues and temple furniture they no longer needed buried around 300 BC. Most statues were sent to the Egyptian Museum in Cairo, but some remain, standing in front of the seventh pylon, including four of Tuthmosis III on the left.

The well-preserved **eighth pylon**, built by Queen Hatshepsut, is the oldest part of the north–south axis of the temple, and one of the earliest pylons in Karnak. Carved on it is a text she falsely attributed to Tuthmosis I, justifying her taking the throne of Egypt.

East of the seventh and eighth pylons is the **sacred lake** (Map p200), where, according to Herodotus, the priests of Amun bathed twice daily and nightly for ritual purity. On the northwestern side of the lake is part of the **Fallen Obelisk of Hatshepsut** showing her coronation, and a **Giant Scarab** in stone dedicated by Amenhotep III to Khepri, a form of the sun god.

In the southwestern corner of the enclosure is the **Temple of Khonsu**, god of the moon, and son of Amun and Mut. It can be reached from a door in the southern wall of the Hypostyle Hall of the Temple of Amun, via a path through various blocks of stone. The temple, mostly the work of Ramses III and enlarged by later Ramesside rulers, lies north of Euergetes' Gate and the avenue of sphinxes leading to Luxor Temple. The temple pylon leads via a peristyle court to a hypostyle hall with eight columns carved with figures of Ramses XI and the High Priest Herihor, who effectively ruled Upper Egypt at the time. The next chamber housed the sacred barque of Khonsu.

Mut Temple Enclosure   TEMPLE

From the 10th pylon an avenue of sphinxes leads to the partly excavated southern enclosure – the Precinct of Mut (closed to the public). The badly ruined Temple of Mut was built by Amenhotep III and consists of a sanctuary, a hypostyle hall and two courts. Amenhotep also set up more than 700 black granite statues of the lioness goddess Sekhmet, Mut's northern counterpart, which are believed to form a calendar, with two statues for every day of the year, receiving offerings each morning and evening.

Montu Temple Enclosure   TEMPLE

A gate, usually locked, on the wall near the Temple of Ptah (in the Amun Temple Enclosure) leads to the Montu Temple Enclosure. Montu, the falcon-headed warrior god, was one of the original deities of Thebes. The main temple was built by Amenhotep III and modified by others. The complex is very dilapidated.

Open-Air Museum   MUSEUM

(Map p200; tickets at main ticket office, adult/ student E£25/15; ⊙6am-5.30pm summer, 6am-

Amun Temple Enclosure

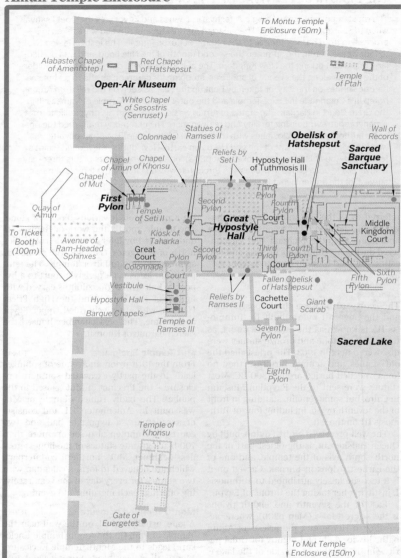

To Montu Temple Enclosure (50m)

Alabaster Chapel of Amenhotep I

Red Chapel of Hatshepsut

Open-Air Museum

Temple of Ptah

White Chapel of Sesostris (Senruset) I

Statues of Ramses II

Colonnade

Reliefs by Seti I

Obelisk of Hatshepsut

Wall of Records

Hypostyle Hall of Tuthmosis III

Sacred Barque Sanctuary

Chapel of Amun   Chapel of Khonsu

Chapel of Mut

Third Pylon

First Pylon

Temple of Seti II

Second Pylon

Great Hypostyle Hall

Fourth Pylon

Court

Middle Kingdom Court

Quay of Amun

→ To Ticket Booth (100m)

Avenue of Ram-Headed Sphinxes

Kiosk of Taharka

Great Court

Pylon   Second Pylon

Third Pylon

Fourth Pylon

Fifth Pylon

Sixth Pylon

Court

Colonnade

Court

Vestibule

Hypostyle Hall

Barque Chapels

Temple of Ramses III

Reliefs by Ramses II

Fallen Obelisk of Hatshepsut

Cachette Court

Giant Scarab

Sacred Lake

Seventh Pylon

Eighth Pylon

Temple of Khonsu

Gate of Euergetes

To Mut Temple Enclosure (150m)

4.30pm winter) Off to the left (north) of the first court of the Amun Temple Enclosure is Karnak's open-air museum. This museum is missed by most visitors but is definitely worth a look. The well-preserved chapels include the **White Chapel of Sesostris I**, one of the oldest and most beautiful monuments in Karnak, which has wonderful Middle Kingdom reliefs; the **Red Chapel of Hatshepsut**, its red quartzite blocks reassembled in 2000; and the **Alabaster Chapel of Amenhotep I**. The museum also contains a

& 10.30pm summer) This highly kitsch sound and light show is a 1½-hour Hollywood-style extravaganza that recounts the history of Thebes and the lives of the many pharaohs who built here in honour of Amun. It's worth a visit particularly for the walk through the beautifully lit temple at night.

DAY	SHOW 1	SHOW 2	SHOW 3
Monday	English	Spanish	
Tuesday	English	French	
Wednes-day	English	Spanish	
Thursday	English	French	Arabic
Friday	English	French	
Saturday	English	Italian	
Sunday	English	German	

Luxor Temples & Museums

Luxor Temple
TEMPLE

(Map p202; Corniche an-Nil; adult/student E£50/30; ⊙6am-9pm Oct-Apr, to 10pm May-Sep) Largely built by the New Kingdom pharaohs Amenhotep III (1390–1352 BC) and Ramses II (1279–1213 BC), this temple is a strikingly graceful monument in the heart of the modern town. Visit early when the temple opens, before the crowds arrive, or later at sunset when the stones glow. Whenever you go, be sure to return at night when the temple is lit up, creating an eerie spectacle as shadow and light play off the reliefs and colonnades.

The temple, also known as the Southern Sanctuary, was once the dwelling place of Amenemopet, the ithyphallic Amun of the Opet, and was largely built for the Opet celebrations, when the statues of Amun, Mut and Khonsu were annually reunited during the inundation season with that of Amun of Opet (see boxed text p199). Amenhotep III greatly enlarged an older shrine built by Hatshepsut, and rededicated the massive temple as Amun's southern *ipet* (harem), the private quarters of the god. The structure was further added to by Tutankhamun, Ramses II, Alexander the Great and various Romans. The Romans constructed a military fort around the temple that the Arabs later called Al-Uqsur (The Fortifications), giving modern Luxor its name.

In ancient times the temple would have been surrounded by a warren of mudbrick houses, shops and workshops, which now

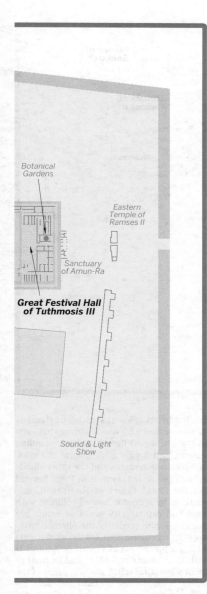

Botanical Gardens

Eastern Temple of Ramses II

Sanctuary of Amun-Ra

Great Festival Hall of Tuthmosis III

Sound & Light Show

collection of statuary found throughout the temple complex.

Sound & Light Show
SHOW

(Map p201; ☎238 6000, 238 2777; www.soundand light.com.eg; adult/student E£100/60, video camera E£35; ⊙6.30pm, 7.45pm & 9pm winter, 8pm, 9.15pm

Luxor Temple

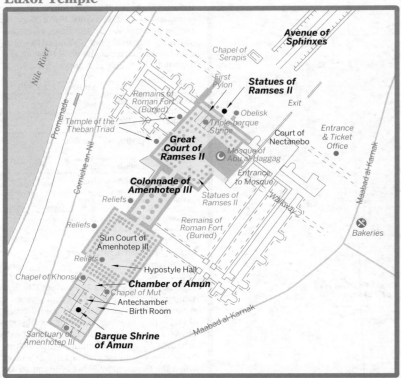

Avenue of Sphinxes

Chapel of Serapis

Nile River

First Pylon

Statues of Ramses II

Remains of Roman Fort (Buried)

Exit

Promenade

Temple of the Theban Triad

Obelisk

Triple-barque Shrine

Entrance & Ticket Office

Entrance

Great Court of Ramses II

Court of Nectanebo

Mosque of Abu al-Haggag

Corniche an-Nil

Entrance to Mosque

Colonnade of Amenhotep III

Statues of Ramses II

Reliefs

Walkway

Maabad al-Karnak

Reliefs

Remains of Roman Fort (Buried)

Bakeries

Sun Court of Amenhotep III

Reliefs

Chapel of Khonsu

Hypostyle Hall

Chamber of Amun

Chapel of Mut

Antechamber

Birth Room

Maabad al-Karnak

Sanctuary of Amenhotep III

Barque Shrine of Amun

lie under the modern town, but after the decline of the city people moved into the – by then – partly covered temple complex and built their city within it. In the 14th century, a mosque was built in one of the interior courts for the local sheikh (holy man) Abu al-Haggag. Excavation works, begun in 1885, have cleared away the village and debris of centuries to uncover what can be seen of the temple today, but the mosque remains and has recently been restored after a fire.

The temple is less complex to understand than Karnak, but here again you walk back in time the deeper you go into it. In front of the temple is the beginning of the **avenue of sphinxes** that ran all the way to the temples at Karnak 3km to the north, and is now being entirely excavated.

The massive 24m-high **first pylon** was raised by Ramses II and decorated with reliefs of his military exploits, including the Battle of Kadesh. The pylon was originally fronted by six colossal **statues of Ramses II**, four seated and two standing, but only two of the seated figures and one standing remain, and a pair pink granite **obelisks**, of which one remains and the other stands in the Place de la Concorde in Paris. Beyond lies the **Great Court of Ramses II**, surrounded by a double row of columns with lotus-bud capitals, the walls of which are decorated with scenes of the pharaoh making offerings to the gods. On the south (rear) wall is a procession of 17 sons of Ramses II with their names and titles, and in front of them a beautiful relief, the first pylon of the temple with statues, obelisks and flags, reliefs of his military successes. In the northwestern corner of the court is the earlier **triple-barque shrine** built by Hatshepsut and usurped by her stepson Tuthmosis III for Amun, Mut and Khonsu. Over the southeastern side hangs the 14th-century **Mosque of Abu al-Haggag**, dedicated to a local sheikh, entered from Sharia Maabad al-Karnak, outside the temple precinct.

Beyond the court is the older splendid Colonnade of Amenhotep III, built as the grand entrance to the Temple of Amun of the Opet. The walls behind the elegant open papyrus columns were decorated during the reign of the young pharaoh Tutankhamun and celebrate the return to Theban orthodoxy following the wayward reign of the previous pharaoh, Akhenaten. The Opet Festival is depicted in lively detail, with the pharaoh, nobility and common people joining the triumphal procession. Look out for the drummers and acrobats doing back bends.

South of the Colonnade is the Sun Court of Amenhotep III, once enclosed on three sides by double rows of towering papyrus-bundle columns, the best preserved of which, with their architraves extant, are those on the eastern and western sides. In 1989 workmen found here a cache of 26 statues, buried by priests in Roman times, now moved to the Luxor Museum.

Beyond lies the Hypostyle Hall, the first room of the original Opet temple, with four rows of eight columns each, leading to the temple's main rooms. The central chamber on the axis south of the Hypostyle Hall was the cult sanctuary of Amun, stuccoed over by the Romans in the 3rd century AD and painted with scenes of Roman officials. Through this chamber, either side of which are chapels dedicated to Mut and Khonsu, is the four-columned antechamber, where offerings were made to Amun, and immediately behind it the Barque Shrine of Amun, rebuilt by Alexander the Great, with reliefs portraying him as an Egyptian pharaoh.

To the east a doorway leads into two rooms. The first is Amenhotep III's birth room with scenes of his divine birth. You can see the moment of his conception, when the fingers of the god touch those of the queen and 'his dew filled her body', according to the accompanying hieroglyphic caption. The Sanctuary of Amenhotep III is the last chamber; it still has the remains of the stone base on which Amun's statue stood, and although it was once the most sacred part of the temple, the busy street that now runs directly behind it makes it less atmospheric.

TOP CHOICE Luxor Museum   MUSEUM
(Map p196; Corniche an-Nil; adult/student E£80/40; ⊙8.30am-2pm). This wonderful museum has a beautifully displayed collection, from the end of the Old Kingdom right through to the Mamluk period, mostly gathered from the Theban temples and necropolis.

MOULIDS AROUND LUXOR

In the Sufi tradition, a *moulid* is a birthday celebration for a holy man or saint, mostly dead but occasionally still alive. Some *moulids* attract up to a million visitors receiving *baraka* (blessings); others are very local village affairs. A carnival spirit is in the air, people are dressed up for the occasion, there is a big market, you can see Sufis of different orders entranced by repeating the name of God, hear real folk music and see *tahtib*, a male dance performed with wooden staves.

The largest *moulid* in the area is that of Abu al-Haggag (see boxed text p199), Luxor's patron saint, who is believed to have brought Islam to Luxor eight centuries ago. The streets around Luxor Temple and his mosque are lined with stalls selling sweets and toys, and there is an impressive procession of craftspeople carrying models of their trade up to the mosque. Abu al-Haggag is celebrated in the middle of the month of Sha'aban, the month before Ramadan, when most *moulids* take place.

There are several smaller *moulids* around Luxor: Abu'l Gumsan, named after a religious man who died in 1984, on 27 Sha'aban near the West Bank village of Taref; Sheikh Musa and Abu al-Jud in the sprawling village of Karnak; Sheikh Hamid on 1 Sha'aban and Sheikh Hussein a couple of days later.

The week-long Coptic *moulid* of Mar Girgis (St George) takes place at the monastery of the same name at the village of Razagat, culminating on 11 November. This area is officially forbidden to foreigners, but the service taxis that ferry the hundreds of people to the *moulid* often avoid the checkpoint by taking a desert track.

Women attending *moulids* should dress very conservatively and preferably be accompanied by a man, as groping and harassment does occur.

Ask at the tourist office (p239) for exact dates.

The ground-floor gallery has several masterpieces including a well-preserved limestone **relief of Tuthmosis III** (No 140), an exquisitely carved **statue of Tuthmosis III** in greywacke from the Temple of Karnak (No 2), an alabaster **figure of Amenhotep III** protected by the great crocodile god Sobek (No 155) and, one of the few examples of Old Kingdom art found at Thebes, a **relief of Unas-ankh** (No 183), found in his tomb on the west bank.

A new wing was opened in 2004, dedicated to the glory of Thebes during the New Kingdom period. The highlight, and the main reason for the new construction, is the two **royal mummies**, Ahmose I (founder of the 18th dynasty) and the mummy some believe to be Ramses I (founder of the 19th dynasty and father of Seti I), beautifully displayed without their wrappings in dark rooms. Other well-labelled displays illustrate the military might of Thebes during the New Kingdom, the age of Egypt's empire-building, including chariots and weapons. On the upper floor the military theme is diluted with scenes from daily life showing the technology used in the New Kingdom. **Multimedia displays** show workers harvesting papyrus and processing it into sheets to be used for writing. Young boys are shown learning to read and write hieroglyphs beside a display of a scribe's implements and an architect's tools.

DON'T MISS

THE BEST TOMBS

With so many tombs to choose from, these are the highlights of the Theban necropolis:

Valley of the Kings
» Tuthmosis III (p216)
» Amenhotep II (p215)
» Horemheb (p215)

Valley of the Queens
» Amunherkhepshef (p225)

Tombs of the Nobles
» Nakht (p208)
» Sennofer (p209)
» Ramose (p208)

Deir al-Medina
» Sennedjem (p221)

Back in the old building, moving up via the ramp to the 1st floor, you come face to face with a seated **granite figure** of the legendary scribe Amenhotep (No 4), son of Hapu, the great official eventually deified in Ptolemaic times and who, as overseer of all the pharaoh's works under Amenhotep III (1390–1352 BC), was responsible for many of Thebes' greatest buildings. One of the most interesting exhibits is the **Wall of Akhenaten**, a series of small sandstone blocks named *talatat* or 'threes' by workmen – probably because their height and length was about three hand lengths – that came from Amenhotep IV's contribution at Karnak before he changed his name to Akhenaten and left Thebes for Tell al-Amarna. His building was demolished and about 40,000 blocks used to fill in Karnak's ninth pylon were found in the late 1960s and partially reassembled here. The scenes showing Akhenaten, his wife Nefertiti and temple life are a rare example of decoration from a Temple of Aten. Further highlights are treasures from Tutankhamun's tomb, including *shabti* (servant) figures, model boats, sandals, arrows and a series of gilded bronze rosettes from his funeral pall.

A ramp back down to the ground floor leaves you close to the exit and beside a black-and-gold wooden head of the cow deity Mehit-Weret, an aspect of the goddess Hathor, which was also found in Tutankhamun's tomb.

On the left just before the exit is a small hall containing 16 of 22 statues that were uncovered in Luxor Temple in 1989. All are magnificent examples of ancient Egyptian sculpture but pride of place at the end of the hall is given to an almost pristine 2.45m-tall quartzite statue of a muscular Amenhotep III, wearing a pleated kilt.

Mummification Museum   MUSEUM
(Map p196; ☑238 1501; Corniche an-Nil; adult/student E£50/25; ◎9am-2pm) Housed in the former visitors centre on Luxor's Corniche, the small Mummification Museum has well-presented exhibits explaining the art of mummification. On display are the well-preserved mummy of a 21st-dynasty high priest of Amun, Maserharti, and a host of mummified animals. Vitrines show the tools and materials used in the mummification process – check out the small spoon and metal spatula used for scraping the brain out of the skull. Several artefacts that were crucial to the mummy's journey

MAKING MUMMIES *DR JOANN FLETCHER*

Although the practice of preserving dead bodies can be found in cultures across the world, the Egyptians were the ultimate practitioners of this highly complex procedure that they refined over a period of almost 4000 years. Their preservation of the dead can be traced back to the very earliest times, when bodies were simply buried in the desert away from the limited areas of cultivation. In direct contact with the sand that covered them, the hot, dry conditions allowed the body fluids to drain away while preserving the skin, hair and nails intact. Accidentally uncovering such bodies must have had a profound effect upon those who were able to recognise people who had died sometimes years before.

A long process of experimentation to preserve the bodies without burying them in the sand began. It wasn't until around 2600 BC that internal organs, which is where putrefaction actually begins, began to be removed. As the process became increasingly elaborate, all the organs were removed except the kidneys, which were hard to reach, and the heart. The heart was considered the source of intelligence rather than the brain, which was generally removed by inserting a metal probe up the nose and whisking to reduce it to a liquid that could be easily drained away. All the rest – lungs, liver, stomach, intestines – were removed through an opening cut in the left flank. Then the body and its separate organs were covered with piles of natron salt and left to dry out for 40 days, after which they were washed, purified and anointed with a range of oils, spices and resins. All were then wrapped in layers of linen, with the appropriate amulets set in place over the various parts of the body as priests recited the incantations needed to activate the protective functions of the amulets.

With each internal organ placed inside its own Canopic jar, the wrapped body complete with its funerary mask was placed inside its coffin. It was then ready for the funeral procession to the tomb, where the vital Opening of the Mouth ceremony reanimated the soul and restored its senses; offerings were given, while wishing the dead 'a thousand of every good and pure thing for your soul and all kinds of offerings on which the gods live'.

to the afterlife have also been included, as well as some picturesque painted coffins. Presiding over the entrance is a beautiful little statue of the jackal god, Anubis, the god of embalming who helped Isis turn her brother-husband Osiris into the first mummy.

WEST BANK

The west bank is a world away from the noise and bustle of Luxor town on the east bank. Taking a taxi across the bridge, 6km south of the centre, or crossing on the old ferry, you are immediately in the lush countryside, with bright green sugarcane fields along irrigation canals and clusters of colourful houses, all against the background of the desert and the Theban hills. Coming towards the end of the cultivated land you start to notice huge sandstone blocks lying in the middle of fields, gaping black holes in the rocks and giant sandstone forms on the edge of the cultivation below. Magnificent memorial temples were built on the flood plains here, where the illusion of the pharaoh's immortality could be perpetuated

by the devotions of his priests and subjects, while his body and worldly wealth, and the bodies of his wives and children, were laid in splendidly decorated hidden tombs excavated in the hills.

From the New Kingdom onwards, the necropolis also supported a large living population of artisans, labourers, temple priests and guards, who devoted their lives to the construction and maintenance of this city of the dead, and who protected the tombs full of treasure from eager robbers. The artisans perfected the techniques of tomb building, decoration and concealment, and passed the secrets down through their families. They all built their tombs here.

Until a generation ago, villagers used tombs to shelter from the extremes of the desert climate and, until recently, many lived in houses built over the Tombs of the Nobles. These beautifully painted houses were a picturesque sight to anyone visiting the west bank. However, over the past 100 years or so the Supreme Council of Antiquities has been trying to relocate the inhab-

Luxor – West Bank

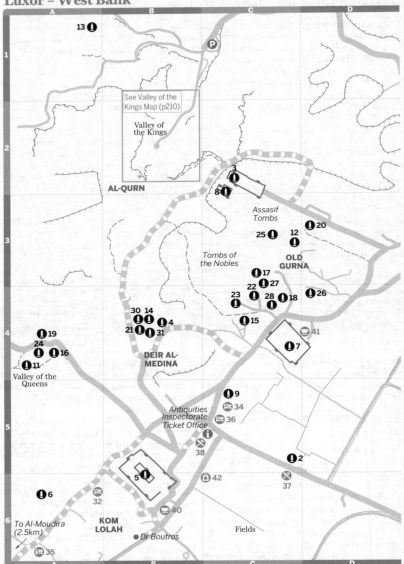

itants of Al-Gurna. In spring 2007 their houses were demolished, and the families were moved to a huge new village of small breeze-block houses 8km north of the Valley of the Kings.

Tickets

It is planned that every site will have its own visitors centre and ticket office, but at the time of writing the **Antiquities Inspectorate ticket office** (Map p206; main road, 3km inland from ferry landing; ☺6am-5pm), near

Medinat Habu, still provided all tickets except for the Temple at Deir al-Bahri, the Assasif tombs (available at Deir al-Bahri ticket office), the Valley of the Kings and the Valley of the Queens. Check there first to see which tickets are available, and which tombs are open. All sites are officially open from 6am to 5pm. Photography is not permitted in any tombs and guards may confiscate film or memory cards.

Tickets are valid only for the day of purchase and no refunds are given. Prices (adult/student):

Dra Abu'l Naga (Roy & Shuroy) E£15/10

Deir al-Medina Temple & Tombs (except Peshedu) E£30/15

Medinat Habu (Temple of Ramses III) E£30/15

Ramesseum E£35/20

Temple of Merenptah E£15/10

Temple of Seti I E£30/15

Tomb of Ay (Western Valley) E£25/15

Tomb of Peshedu (Deir al-Medina) E£15/10

Tombs of the Nobles E£15/10 to E£30/10 per group of tombs

Tombs of the Nobles   TOMBS
(Map p206; ⊙6am-5pm) The tombs in this area are some of the best, but least visited, attractions on the west bank. Nestled in the foothills opposite the Ramesseum, there are more than 400 tombs belonging to nobles from the 6th dynasty to the Graeco-Roman period. Where the pharaohs decorated their tombs with cryptic passages from the Book of the Dead to guide them through the afterlife, the nobles, intent on letting the good life continue after their death, decorated their tombs with wonderfully detailed scenes of their daily lives.

Only 15 or so tombs are open to the public – they are divided into five groups and each requires a separate ticket from the Antiquities Inspectorate ticket office near Medinat Habu.

Tombs of Khonsu, Userhet & Benia (Nos 31, 51 & 343)

(Map p206) Khonsu was First Prophet in the memorial temple of Tuthmosis III (1479–1425 BC). Inside the first chamber of Khonsu's tomb are scenes of the Montu festival at Armant, about 20km south of Luxor, the festival of the god of war over which he presided. The sacred barque with the shrine of Montu is towed by two smaller boats. The gods Osiris and Anubis are also honoured, and in many scenes Khonsu is seen making offerings to them. The ceiling is adorned with images of ducks flying around and nests

Luxor – West Bank

with eggs. Next door is the less preserved tomb of Userhet, a priest during the time of Seti I (1294–1279 BC).

The **Tomb of Benia**, just behind that of Khonsu, is even more colourful. Benia was a boarder in the Royal Nursery and chief treasurer also during the reign of Tuthmosis III. There are many scenes of offering tables piled high with food and drinks overlooked by Benia, and sometimes by his parents. In a niche cut out at the end of the tomb is a statue of Benia flanked by his parents, all three with destroyed faces.

Tombs of Menna & Nakht (Nos 52 & 69)

(Map p206) The beautiful and highly colourful wall paintings in the **Tomb of Menna** and the **Tomb of Nakht** emphasise rural life in 18th-dynasty Egypt. Menna was an estate inspector and Nakht was an astronomer of Amun. Their finely detailed tombs show scenes of farming, hunting, fishing and feasting. The Tomb of Nakht has a small museum area in its first chamber. Although this tomb is so small that only a handful of visitors are able to squeeze in at a time, the walls have some of the best-known examples of Egyptian tomb paintings.

Tombs of Ramose, Userhet & Khaemhet (Nos 55, 56 & 57)

(Map p206) The **Tomb of Ramose**, a governor of Thebes under Amenhotep III and Akhenaten, is fascinating because it is one of the few monuments dating from that time, a period of transition between two different forms of religious worship. The exquisite paintings and low reliefs show scenes in two different styles from the reigns of both pharaohs, depicting Ramose's funeral and his relationship with Akhenaten. The tomb was never actually finished, perhaps because Ramose died prematurely.

Next door is the **Tomb of Userhet** (Map p206), one of Amenhotep II's royal scribes, with fine wall paintings depicting daily life. Userhet is shown presenting gifts to Amenhotep II; there's a barber cutting hair on another wall; other scenes include men making wine and people hunting gazelles from a chariot.

The **Tomb of Khaemhet** (Map p206), Amenhotep III's royal inspector of the granaries and court scribe, has scenes on the walls showing Khaemhet making offerings, the pharaoh depicted as a sphinx, the funeral ritual of Osiris and images of daily country life as well as official business.

Tombs of Sennofer & Rekhmire (Nos 96 & 100)

(Map p206) The most interesting parts of the **Tomb of Sennofer**, overseer of the Garden of Amun under Amenhotep II, are to be found deep underground, in the main chamber. The ceiling there is covered with clear paintings of grapes and vines, while most of the vivid scenes on the surrounding walls and columns depict Sennofer and all the different women in his life, including his wife and daughters and his wet nurse. The guard usually has a kerosene lamp, but bring a torch (flashlight) just in case.

The **Tomb of Rekhmire**, governor under Tuthmosis III and Amenhotep II, is one of the best preserved in the area. In the first chamber, to the extreme left, are scenes of Rekhmire receiving gifts from foreign lands. The panther and giraffe are gifts from Nubia; the elephant, horses and chariot are from Syria; and the expensive vases come from Crete and the Aegean Islands. Beyond this is the unusual chapel. The west wall shows Rekhmire inspecting the production of metals, bricks, jewellery, leather, furniture and statuary, while the east wall painting shows banquet scenes, complete with lyrics (the female harpist sings 'Put perfume on the hair of the goddess Maat').

Tombs of Neferronpet, Dhutmosi & Nefersekheru (Nos 178, 295 & 296)

(Map p206) Discovered in 1915, the highlight of the brightly painted **Tomb of Neferronpet** (also known as Kenro), the scribe of the treasury under Ramses II, is the scene showing Kenro overseeing the weighing of gold at the treasury. Next door, the **Tomb of Nefersekheru**, an officer of the treasury during the same period, is similar in style and content to his neighbours. The ceiling is decorated with a huge variety of elaborate geometric patterns. From this long tomb, a small passage leads into the **Tomb of Dhutmosi**, which is in poor condition.

WHAT TO BRING

When visiting the west bank sights, bring plenty of water (though it is available at some of the sights) and a sun hat. Small change for baksheesh is much needed too, as guardians rely on tips to augment their pathetic salaries; a few Egyptian pounds should be enough for them to either leave you in peace, or to open a door or reflect light on a particularly beautiful painting. A torch (flashlight) can come in handy.

Valley of the Kings   TOMBS

(Wadi Biban al-Muluk; Map p210; www.thebanmappingproject.com; adult/student for 3 tombs excl Ramses VI, Ay & Tutankhamun E£80/40, Tomb of Ramses VI E£50/25, Tomb of Tutankhamun E£100/50; ⊙6am-4pm; Tomb of Ay tickets available from the Antiquities Inspectorate office near Medinat Habu E£25/15) Once called the Great Necropolis of Millions of Years of Pharaoh, or the Place of Truth, the Valley of the Kings has 63 magnificent royal tombs from the New Kingdom period (1550–1069 BC), all very different from each other. The west bank had been the site of royal burials from the First Intermediate Period (2160–2025 BC) onwards. At least three 11th-dynasty rulers built their tombs near the modern village of Taref, northeast of the Valley of the Kings. The 18th-dynasty pharaohs, however, chose the isolated valley dominated by the pyramid-shaped mountain peak of Al-Qurn (The Horn). The secluded site enclosed by steep cliffs was easy to guard and, when seen from the Theban plain, appears to be the site of the setting sun, associated with the afterlife by ancient Egyptians.

The tombs have suffered great damage from treasure hunters, floods and, in recent years, from mass tourism: carbon dioxide, friction and humidity produced by the average of 2.8g of sweat left by each visitor have affected the reliefs and the pigments of the wall paintings. The Department of Antiquities has installed dehumidifiers and glass screens in the worst-affected tombs, and introduced a rotation system for opening some tombs to the public while restoring others. Lighting in the tombs was being installed at the time of writing so visitors will be able to visit at night, thus avoiding the heat of the day. Three replica tombs are planned in the near future: the tomb of Tutankhamun, Seti I

Valley of the Kings

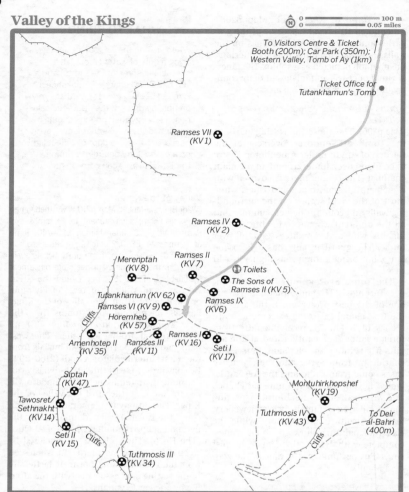

and Nefertari (in the Valley of the Queens; see p225).

The road into the Valley of the Kings is a gradual, dry, hot climb, so be prepared, especially if you are riding a bicycle. The air-conditioned **visitors centre** (off Map p210) has a good model of the Valley, a movie about Carter's discovery of the Tomb of Tutankhamun, and toilets. Soft drinks, ice creams and snacks are available from the stalls at the tourist bazaar near the entrance. A *tuf-tuf* (a little electrical train) ferries visitors between the visitors centre and the tombs (it can be hot during sum-

mer). The ride costs E£10. It's worth having a torch to illuminate badly lit areas.

Most of the tombs described here are usually open to visitors and are listed in the order that they are found when entering the site.

Tomb of Ramses VII (KV 1)

(Map p210) Near the main entrance is the small, unfinished **tomb of Ramses VII** (1136–1129 BC). Only 44.3m long – short for a royal tomb because of Ramses' sudden death – it consists of a corridor, a burial chamber and an unfinished third chamber.

His architects hastily widened what was to have been the tomb's second corridor, making it a burial chamber, and the pharaoh was laid to rest in a pit covered with a sarcophagus lid. Niches for Canopic jars are carved into the pit's sides, a feature unique to this tomb. Walls on the corridor leading to the chamber are decorated with fairly well preserved excerpts from the Book of Caverns and the Opening of the Mouth ritual, while the burial chamber is decorated with passages from the Book of the Earth.

Tomb of Ramses IV (KV 2)

(Map p210) The **tomb of Ramses IV** was already known in Ptolemaic times, evident from the graffiti on the walls dating back to 278 BC. Ramses IV (1153–1147 BC) died before the tomb was completed. The paintings in the burial chamber have deteriorated, but there is a wonderful image of the goddess Nut, stretched across the blue ceiling, and it is the only tomb to contain the text of the Book of Nut, with a description of the daily path taken by the sun every day. The red-granite sarcophagus, though empty, is one of the largest in the valley. The discovery of an ancient plan of the tomb on papyrus (now in the Turin Museum) shows the sarcophagus was originally enclosed by four large shrines similar to those in Tutankhamun's tomb. The mummy of Ramses IV was later reburied in the Tomb of Amenhotep II (KV 35), and is now in the Egyptian Museum in Cairo.

Tomb of Ramses IX (KV 6)

(Map p210) Opposite Ramses II is the most visited tomb in the valley, the Tomb of Ramses IX (1126–1108 BC), with a wide entrance, a long sloping corridor, a large antechamber decorated with the animals, serpents and demons from the Book of the Dead, and then a pillared hall and short hallway before the burial chamber. On either side of the gate on the rear wall are two figures of Iunmutef priests, both dressed in priestly panther-skin robes and sporting a ceremonial side lock. The walls of the burial chamber feature the Book of Amduat, the Book of Caverns and the Book of the Earth; the Book of the Heavens is represented on the ceiling. Although it is unfinished, it was the last tomb in the valley to have so much of its decoration completed, and the paintings are relatively well preserved.

Tomb of Ramses II (KV 7)

(Map p210) As befits the burial place of one of Egypt's longest-reigning pharaohs (67 years, from 1279 to 1213 BC), KV 7 is one of the biggest tombs in the valley. However, flash floods destroyed much of what must have been spectacular decoration, so it is unlikely to open anytime soon. Based on the decorative scheme in his father Seti I's superb tomb, the walls of Ramses II's tomb would once have been just as brightly coloured, featuring scenes from the Litany of Ra, Book of Gates, the Book of the Dead and other sacred texts. In one of the side chambers off the burial chamber is a statue of Osiris similar to one found by Dr Kent Weeks in KV 5 (see boxed text, p214), giving him yet more evidence for his theory that KV5 belongs to the many sons of Ramses.

Tomb of Merenptah (KV 8)

(Map p210) Ramses II lived for so long that 12 of his sons died before he did, so it was finally his 13th son Merenptah (1213–1203 BC) who succeeded him in his 60s. The second-largest tomb in the valley, Merenptah's tomb has been open since antiquity and has its share of Greek and Coptic graffiti. Floods have damaged the lower part of the walls of the long tunnel-like tomb, but the upper parts have well-preserved reliefs. The corridors are decorated with the Book of the Dead, the Book of Gates and the Book of Amduat. Beyond a shaft is a false burial chamber with two pillars decorated with the Book of Gates. Although much of the decoration in the burial chamber has faded, it remains an impressive room, with a sunken floor and brick niches on the front and rear walls.

The pharaoh was originally buried inside four stone sarcophagi, three of granite (the lid of the second still in situ, with an effigy of Merenptah on top) and the fourth, innermost, sarcophagus of alabaster. In a rare mistake by ancient Egyptian engineers, the outer sarcophagus did not fit through the tomb entrance and its gates had to be hacked away.

Tomb of Tutankhamun (KV 62)

(Map p210) The story of the celebrated discovery of the famous tomb and all the fabulous treasures it contained far outshines its actual appearance, and it is one of the least impressive tombs in the valley. Tutankhamun's tomb is small and bears all the signs of a rather hasty completion and inglorious

Luxor

There's usually no way around the crowds of visitors and hawkers in the Valley of the Kings, but try to go early, before it gets hot. Stop off at the **Colossi of Memnon** 1 as you pass them, taking a look at the ongoing excavation of the ruins of the Temple of Amenhotep III, whose entrance they once flanked. From the royal tombs, drive around the hillside to visit the massive terraced **Temple of Hatshepsut** 2, almost entirely reconstructed but still good to see as it is the best surviving example of classical-style Egyptian architecture in Luxor.

The Theban hillside further to the south is pitted with thousands of tomb openings. The Tombs of the Nobles in what was **Gurna Village** 3 and the nearby **Workers' Tombs** 4 at Deir al-Medina are very different in style and construction from the royal burials. In some ways, their views of everyday life are more impressive than the more orthodox scenes on the walls of the royal tombs.

In the afternoon, drop down towards the line between desert and agriculture to see two royal temples. The Ramesseum is dedicated to the memory of Ramses II and contains the upper half of a massive statue of the pharaoh. In midafternoon, when the light starts to soften, head over to **Medinet Habu** 5, the temple of Ramses III. The last of the great imperial temples built during the New Kingdom, the temple has retained much of its grandeur, as well as extensive (and often exaggerated) records of the king's reign.

TOP TIPS

» Allow at least one day.
» Tickets for everything except the Valley of the Kings must be bought at the ticket office.
» Bring a hat, sunscreen and plenty of water.
» Photography is not allowed inside the tombs, but there is plenty to see – and photograph – outside.

Medinet Habu
Original paintwork, applied more than 3000 years ago, can still be seen on lintels and inner columns. Some of this was preserved by the mudbrick houses and chapels of early Christians (since destroyed).

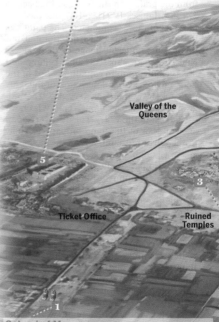

Valley of the Queens

Ticket Office

Ruined Temples

Colossi of Memnon
Although the Greeks called him Memnon, the colossi were built for Pharaoh Amenhotep III, who built the largest of all funerary temples here on the west bank (its ruins are only now being excavated).

Workers' Tombs (Deir al-Medina)
What to do with your spare time if you were an ancient Egyptian tomb worker? Cut a tomb and decorate it with things you didn't have in this life, including ceilings decorated with rug patterns.

Temple of Hatshepsut
Hatshepsut's funerary temple is unlike any other in Luxor. Built on three terraces with its back to the hill that contains the Valley of the Kings, it was once as grand as the pharaoh-queen.

Valley of the Kings

2

Tombs of the Nobles (all this hillside)

Ramesseum (Temple of Ranses II)

Gurna Village
Rumours of treasure beneath houses in Gurna led the government to move the villagers and demolish their houses in the early 2000s. Some Gurna houses dated back to at least the beginning of the 19th century.

THE GREATEST FIND SINCE TUTANKHAMUN

In May 1995, American archaeologist Dr Kent Weeks discovered the largest tomb in Egypt, believed to be the burial place of the many sons of Ramses II. It was immediately hailed as the greatest find since that of Tutankhamun, or as one London newspaper put it: 'The Mummy of all Tombs'.

In 1987 Weeks located the entrance to tomb KV 5, which Howard Carter had uncovered but dismissed as destroyed. Weeks' team cleared the entrance chambers, finding pottery, fragments of sarcophagi and wall decorations, which led him to believe it was the Tomb of the Sons of Ramses II.

Then in 1995 Weeks unearthed a doorway leading to an incredible 121 chambers and corridors, making the tomb many times larger and more complex than any other found in Egypt. Clearing the debris from this unique and enormous tomb is a painstaking and dangerous task. Not only does every bucketful have to be sifted for fragments of pottery, bones and reliefs, but major engineering work has to be done to shore up the tomb's structure. Progress is slow but Weeks speculates that it has as many as 150 chambers, and each year brings discovery of more chambers or new corridors. Progress of the excavation can be followed on the excellent website www.thebanmappingproject.com, or in Weeks' fascinating account in his book *The Lost Tomb*.

burial. The son of Akhenaten and one of Akhenaten's sisters, he ruled briefly (1336–1327 BC) and died young, with no great battles or buildings to his credit, so there was little time to build a tomb.

The Egyptologist Howard Carter slaved away for six seasons in the valley, believing that he would find the tomb of Tutankhamun intact with all its treasures. The first step was found on 4 November 1922, and on 5 November the rest of the steps and a sealed doorway came to light. Carter wired Lord Carnarvon to join him in Egypt immediately for the opening of what he believed was the completely intact Tomb of Tutankhamun.

The tomb's priceless cache of treasures, although it had been partially robbed twice in antiquity, vindicated Carter's dream beyond even his wildest imaginings. Four chambers were found crammed with jewellery, furniture, statues, chariots, musical instruments, weapons, boxes, jars and food. Even the later discovery that many had been stuffed haphazardly into the wrong boxes by necropolis officials 'tidying up' after the ancient robberies does not detract from their dazzling wealth. Some archaeologists believe that Tutankhamun was perhaps buried with all the regalia of the unpopular Amarna royal line, as some of it is inscribed with the names of his father Akhenaten and the mysterious Smenkhkare (1388–336 BC), who some Egyptologists believe was Nefertiti ruling as pharaoh.

Most of the treasure is in the Cairo Museum, a few pieces are in Luxor Museum, and

only Tutankhamun's mummy in its gilded wooden coffin is in situ. The burial chamber walls are decorated by chubby figures of the pharaoh before the gods, painted against a yellow-gold background. The wall at the foot end of the sarcophagus shows scenes of the pharaoh's funeral; the 12 squatting apes from the Book of Amduat, representing the 12 hours of the night, are featured on the opposite wall.

Tomb of Ramses VI (KV 9)

(Map p210) The intactness of Tutankhamun's tomb is largely thanks to the existence of the tomb of Ramses VI. The tomb was actually begun for the ephemeral Ramses V (1147–1143 BC) and continued by Ramses VI (1143–1136 BC), with both pharaohs apparently buried here; the names and titles of Ramses V still appear in the first half of the tomb. Following the tomb's ransacking a mere 20 years after burial, the mummies of both Ramses V and Ramses VI were moved to Amenhotep II's tomb where they were found in 1898 and taken to Cairo.

Although the tomb's plastering was not finished, its fine decoration is well preserved, with an emphasis on astronomical scenes and texts. Extracts from the Book of Gates and the Book of Caverns cover the entrance corridor. These continue into the midsection of the tomb and well room, with the addition of the Book of the Heavens. Nearer the burial chamber the walls are decorated with extracts from the Book of Amduat. The burial chamber is beautifully decorated, with a superb double image of Nut framing the Book of the Day and Book of the Night on the ceiling. This nocturnal landscape in black and gold shows the sky goddess swallowing the sun each evening to give birth to it each morning in an endless cycle of new life designed to revive the souls of the dead pharaohs. The walls of the chamber are filled with fine images of Ramses VI with various deities, as well as scenes from the Book of the Earth, with scenes that show the sun god's progress through the night, the gods who help him and the forces of darkness trying to stop him reaching the dawn; look out for the decapitated, kneeling figures of the sun god's enemies around the base of the chamber walls and the black-coloured executioners who turn the decapitated bodies upside down to render them as helpless as possible.

Tomb of Ramses III (KV 11)

(Map p210) Ramses III (1184–1153 BC), the last of Egypt's warrior pharaohs, built one of the longest tombs in the Valley of the Kings. His tomb, started but abandoned by Sethnakht (1186–1184 BC), is 125m long, much of it still beautifully decorated with colourful painted sunken reliefs featuring the traditional ritual texts (Litany of Ra, Book of Gates etc) and Ramses before the gods. Unusually here are the secular scenes, in the small side rooms of the entrance corridor, showing foreign tributes such as highly detailed pottery imported from the Aegean, the royal armoury, boats and, in the last of these side chambers, the blind harpists that gave the tomb one of its alternative names: 'Tomb of the Harpers'.

In the chamber beyond is an aborted tunnel where ancient builders ran into the neighbouring tomb. They shifted the axis of the tomb to the west and built a corridor leading to a pillared hall, with walls decorated with scenes from the Book of Gates. There is also ancient graffiti on the rear right pillar describing the reburial of the pharaoh during the 21st dynasty (1069–945 BC). The remainder of the tomb is only partially excavated and structurally weak.

Ramses III's sarcophagus is in the Louvre in Paris, its detailed lid is in the Fitzwilliam Museum in Cambridge and his mummy – found in the Deir al-Bahri cache – was the model for Boris Karloff's character in the 1930s film *The Mummy*. The mummy is now in Cairo's Egyptian Museum.

Tomb of Horemheb (KV 57)

(Map p210) This tomb was discovered filled with ransacked pieces of the royal funerary equipment, including a number of wooden figurines that were taken to the Egyptian Museum in Cairo. Horemheb (1323–1295 BC), a general and military strongman under Tutankhamun, brought stability after the turmoil of Akhenaten's reign. He had already built a lavish tomb in Saqqara, but abandoned it for this tomb. The various stages of decoration in the burial chamber give a fascinating glimpse into the process of tomb decoration.

From the entrance, a steep flight of steps and an equally steep passage leads to a well shaft decorated with superb figures of Horemheb before the gods. Notice Hathor's blue-and-black striped wig and the lotus crown of the young god Nefertum, all executed against a grey-blue background. The six-pillared burial chamber decorated with part of the Book of Gates remains partially unfinished, showing how the decoration was applied by following a grid system in red ink over which the figures were drawn in black prior to their carving and painting. The pharaoh's empty red-granite sarcophagus carved with protective figures of goddesses with outstretched wings remains in the tomb; his mummy is missing.

Tomb of Amenhotep II (KV 35)

(Map p210) One of the deepest structures in the valley, this tomb has more than 90 steps down to a modern gangway, built over a deep pit designed to protect the inner, lower chambers from both thieves (which it failed to do) and the water from flash floods.

Stars cover the entire ceiling in the huge burial chamber and the walls feature, as if on a giant painted scroll, text from the Book of Amduat. While most figures are of the same sticklike proportions as in the tomb of Amenhotep's father and predecessor Tuthmosis III, this is the first royal tomb in the valley to also show figures of more rounded proportions, as on the pillars in the burial chamber showing the pharaoh before Osiris, Hathor and Anubis. The burial chamber is also unique for its double level; the top level was filled with pillars, the bottom contained the sarcophagus.

Although thieves breached the tomb in antiquity, Amenhotep's (1427–1400 BC) mummy was restored by the priests, put back in his sarcophagus with a garland of flowers around his neck, and buried with

13 other royal mummies in the two side rooms, including Tuthmosis IV (1400–1390 BC), Amenhotep III, Merenptah, Ramses IV, V and VI and Seti II (1200–1194 BC), most of which are now at the Egyptian Museum.

Tomb of Tuthmosis III (KV 34)
(Map p210) Hidden in the hills between high limestone cliffs and reached only via a steep staircase that crosses an even steeper ravine, this tomb demonstrates the lengths to which the ancient pharaohs went to thwart the cunning of the ancient thieves.

Tuthmosis III (1479–1425 BC), an innovator in many fields, and whose military exploits and stature earned him the description 'the Napoleon of ancient Egypt', was one of the first to build his tomb in the Val-

TOMB BUILDING DR JOANN FLETCHER

Tombs were initially created to differentiate the burials of the elite from the people whose bodies were placed directly into the desert. By about 3100 BC the mound of sand heaped over these elite graves was replaced by a more permanent structure of mudbrick, whose characteristic bench shape is known as a 'mastaba' after the Arabic word for bench.

As stone replaced mudbrick, the addition of further levels to increase height gave birth to the pyramid, whose first incarnation at Saqqara is also the world's oldest monumental structure. Its stepped sides soon evolved into the more familiar smooth-sided structure, of which the Pyramids of Giza are the most famous examples.

It was only when the power of the monarchy broke down at the end of the Old Kingdom that the afterlife became increasingly accessible to those outside the royal family, and as officials became increasingly independent they began to opt for burial in their home towns. Yet the narrow stretches of fertile land that make up much of the Nile Valley generally left little room for grand superstructures, so an alternative type of tomb developed, cut tunnel-fashion into the cliffs that border the valley and which also proved more resilient against robbery. Most were built on the west side of the river, the traditional place of burial where the sun was seen to sink down into the underworld each evening.

These simple rock-cut tombs consisting of a single chamber gradually developed into more elaborate structures complete with an open courtyard, offering chapel and entrance facade carved out of the rock with a shaft leading down into an undecorated burial chamber. The most impressive rock-cut tombs were those built for the pharaohs of the New Kingdom (1550–1069 BC), who relocated the royal burial ground south to the remote valley now known as the Valley of the Kings. New evidence suggests that the first tomb in the valley may have been built for Amenhotep I (1525–1504 BC; KV 39). The tomb intended for his successor, Tuthmosis I (KV 20), demonstrated a radical departure from tradition: the offering chapel that was once part of the tomb's layout was built as a separate structure some distance away in an attempt to preserve the tomb's secret location. The tombs themselves were designed to resemble the underworld, with a long, inclined rock-hewn corridor descending into either an antechamber or a series of sometimes pillared halls, and ending in the burial chamber.

The tomb builders lived in their own village of Deir al-Medina and worked in relays. The duration of the ancient week was 10 days (eight days on, two days off) and the men tended to spend the nights of their working week at a small camp located on the pass leading from Deir al-Medina to the eastern part of the Valley of the Kings. Then they spent their two days off at home with their families.

Once the tomb walls were created, decoration could then be added; this dealt almost exclusively with the afterlife and the pharaoh's existence in it. The tombs were decorated with texts from the Book of the Dead and with colourful scenes to help guide the pharaoh on his or her journey through the afterlife. The Book of the Dead is the collective modern name for a range of works that deal with the sun god's nightly journey through the darkness of the underworld, the realm of Osiris and home of the dead. The Egyptians believed that the underworld was traversed each night by Ra, and it was the aim of the dead to secure passage on his sacred barque to travel with him for eternity.

ley of the Kings. As secrecy was his utmost concern, he chose the most inaccessible spot and designed his burial place with a series of passages at haphazard angles and fake doors to mislead or catch potential robbers.

The shaft, now traversed by a narrow gangway, leads to an antechamber supported by two pillars, the walls of which are adorned with a list of more than 700 gods and demigods. As the earliest tomb in the valley to be painted, the walls appear to be simply giant versions of funerary papyri, with scenes populated by stick men. The burial chamber has curved walls and is oval in shape; it contains the pharaoh's quartzite sarcophagus that is carved in the shape of a cartouche.

Tomb of Siptah (KV 47)

(Map p210) Discovered in 1905, the tomb of Siptah (1194–1188 BC) was never completed but the upper corridors are nonetheless covered in fine paintings. The tomb's entrance is decorated with the sun disc, and figures of Maat, the goddess of truth, kneel on each side of the doorway. There are further scenes from the Book of Amduat, and figures of Anubis, after which the tomb remains undecorated.

Tomb of Tawosret/Sethnakht (KV 14)

(Map p210) Tawosret was the wife of Seti II and after his successor Siptah died she took power herself (1188–1186 BC). Egyptologists think she began the tomb for herself and Seti II but their burials were removed by her successor, the equally short-lived Sethnakht (1186–1184 BC), who completed the tomb by adding a second burial chamber for himself. The change of ownership can be seen in the tomb's decoration; the upper corridors show the queen, accompanied by her stepson Siptah, in the presence of the gods. Siptah's cartouche was later replaced by Seti II's. But in the lower corridors and burial chambers images of Tawosret have been plastered over by images or cartouches of Sethnakht.

The tomb has been open since antiquity and although the decoration has worn off in some parts, the colour and state of the burial chambers remains good, with astronomical ceiling decorations and images of Tawosret and Sethnakht with the gods. The final scene from the Book of Caverns adorning Tawosret's burial chamber is particularly impressive, showing the sun god as a ram-headed figure stretching out his wings to emerge from the darkness of the underworld.

Tomb of Seti II (KV 15)

(Map p210) Adjacent to the tomb of Tawosret/Sethnakht is a smaller tomb where it seems Sethnakht buried Seti II (1200–1194 BC) after turfing him out of KV 14. Open since ancient times judging by the many examples of classical graffiti, the tomb's entrance area has some finely carved relief scenes, although the rest was quickly finished off in paint alone. The walls have extracts from the Litany of Ra, the Book of Gates and the Book of Amduat and, unusually, on the walls of the well room, images of the type of funerary objects used in pharaohs' tombs, such as golden statuettes of the pharaoh within a shrine.

Tomb of Ramses I (KV 16)

(Map p210) Ramses I (1295–1294 BC) only ruled for a year so his tomb is a very simple affair. His tomb has the shortest entrance corridor leading to a single, almost square, burial chamber, containing the pharaoh's open pink granite sarcophagus. Only the chamber is superbly decorated, very similar to Horemheb's tomb (KV 57), with extracts from the Book of Gates, as well as scenes of the pharaoh in the presence of the gods, eg the pharaoh kneeling between the jackal-headed 'Soul of Nekhen' and the falcon-headed 'Soul of Pe', symbolising Upper and Lower Egypt.

Tomb of Seti I (KV 17)

(Map p210) As befits such an important pharaoh, Seti I (1294–1279 BC), son and heir of Ramses I, has one of the longest (137m) and most beautiful tombs in the valley. Its discovery by Giovanni Belzoni in 1817 generated almost the same interest as the discovery of Tutankhamun's tomb a century later. As the first royal tomb to be decorated throughout, its raised, painted relief scenes are similar to those found in the pharaoh's beautifully decorated temple at Abydos (p184) and the quality of the work is superb. Two of its painted reliefs showing Seti with Hathor are now in the Louvre in Paris and Florence's Archaeological Museum, while Seti's alabaster sarcophagus was bought by Sir John Soane, and it can still be seen in the basement of his London house-turned-museum.

The tomb is indefinitely closed for restoration (ongoing since 1991), but soon there should be a replica of this tomb, including

THE RETURN OF THE MUMMY

In 1881 Egypt's antiquities authority made the greatest mummy find in history: the mummies of 40 pharaohs, queens and nobles, just south of Deir al-Bahri in tomb No 320. It seems that 21st-dynasty priests had them moved as a protection against tomb robbers to this communal grave, after 934 BC. The mummies included those of Amenhotep I, Tuthmosis I, II and III, Seti I and Ramses II and III, many of which are now on display at the Egyptian Museum in Cairo. Their removal from the tomb and procession down to the Nile, from where they were taken by barge to Cairo, was accompanied by the eerie sound of black-clad village women ululating to give a royal send-off to the remains. The episode makes for one of the most stunning scenes in Shadi Abdel Salam's 1969 epic *Al-Mummia* (*The Mummy*), one of the most beautiful films made in Egypt.

However, the cache had already been found a decade earlier by the Abdel Rassoul family from Gurna, who were making a tidy sum by selling contents from it. Mummies, coffins, sumptuous jewellery and other artefacts made their way to Europe and North America. One of the mummies ended up in a small museum in Niagara Falls, Canada, until the late 1990s, when the crossed arms and excellent state of the body were recognised by an Egyptologist as signs of possible royalty. When the museum closed in 1999, the mummy was acquired by the Michael Carlos Museum in Atlanta. CT scans, X-rays, radiocarbon dating and computer imaging attempted to identify the mummy, and although they could only suggest that it was from later than the Ramesside period, an uncanny resemblance to the mummified faces of Seti I and Ramses II was seized upon by some Egyptologists as proof that this was the missing mummy of Ramses I. As a gesture of goodwill, the museum returned the mummy to Egypt in 2003, and it is now in the Luxor Museum.

the missing parts that are now held in foreign museums.

Tomb of Montuhirkopshef (KV 19)

(Map p210) The tomb of Ramses IX's son (c 1000 BC), whose name translates as 'The Arm of Montu is Strong', is located high up in the valley's eastern wall. It is small and unfinished but has fine paintings and few visitors. Its entrance corridor is adorned with life-size reliefs of various gods, including Osiris, Ptah, Thoth and Khonsu, receiving offerings from the young prince, who is shown in all his finery, wearing exquisitely pleated fine linen robes and a blue-and-gold 'sidelock of youth' attached to his black wig – not to mention his gorgeous make-up (as worn by both men and women in ancient Egypt).

Tomb of Tuthmosis IV (KV 43)

(Map p210) The tomb of Tuthmosis IV (1400–1390 BC) is one of the largest and deepest tombs constructed during the 18th dynasty. It is also the first in which paint was applied over a yellow background, beginning a tradition that was continued in many tombs. It was discovered in 1903 by Howard Carter, 20 years earlier than the tomb of Tuthmosis IV's great-grandson, Tutankhamun. It is accessed by two long flights of steps leading down and around to the burial chamber where there's an enormous sarcophagus covered in hieroglyphs. The walls of the well shaft and antechamber are decorated with painted scenes of Tuthmosis before the gods, and the figures of the goddess Hathor are particularly fetching in a range of beautiful dresses decorated with beaded designs.

On the left (south) wall of the antechamber there is a patch of ancient Egyptian graffiti dating back to 1315 BC, written by government official Maya and his assistant Djehutymose and referring to their inspection and restoration of Tuthmosis IV's burial on the orders of Horemheb following the first wave of robbery in the eighth year of Horemheb's reign, some 67 years after Tuthmosis IV died.

Tomb of Ay (KV 23)

(Map p206) Although he succeeded Tutankhamun, Ay's brief reign from 1327 to 1323 BC tends to be associated with the earlier Amarna period and Akhenaten (some Egyptologists have suggested he could have been the father of Akhenaten's wife Nefertiti). Ay abandoned a grandiose tomb in Amarna (see p178) and took over another in the West Valley here. The West Valley played an important part in the Amarna story, as it was chosen as a new burial ground by Amenhotep III for his own enormous tomb (KV 22, partway up the valley), and his son and successor Akhenaten also began a tomb here, before he relocated the capital at Amarna, where he was eventually buried. It seems Tutankhamun too planned to be buried in the West Valley, until his early death saw his successor Ay 'switch' tombs. Tutankhamun was buried in a tomb (KV 62) in the traditional section of the Valley of the Kings, while Ay himself took over the tomb Tutankhamun had begun at the head of the West Valley. The tomb is accessed by a dirt road leading off from the car park at the Valley of the Kings that winds for almost 2km up a desolate valley past sheer rock cliffs. Recapturing the atmosphere (and silence) once found in the neighbouring Valley of the Kings makes it worth the visit.

Although only the burial chamber is decorated, it is noted for its scenes of Ay hippopotamus hunting and fishing in the marshes (scenes usually found in the tombs of nobles not royalty) and for a wall featuring 12 baboons, representing the 12 hours of the night, after which the West Valley or Wadi al-Gurud (Valley of the Monkeys) is named.

Memorial Temple of Hatshepsut TEMPLE
(adult/student E£30/15; ⊙6am-5pm) At Deir al-Bahri, the eyes first focus on the dramatic rugged limestone cliffs that rise nearly 300m above the desert plain, a monument made by nature, only to realise that at the foot of all this immense beauty lies a man-made monument even more extraordinary, the dazzling Temple of Hatshepsut. The almost modern-looking temple blends in beautifully with the cliffs from which it is partly cut; a marriage made in heaven.

Continuous excavation and restoration since 1891 have revealed one of ancient Egypt's finest monuments, but it must have been even more stunning in the days of Hatshepsut (1473–1458 BC), when it was approached by a grand sphinx-lined causeway instead of today's noisy tourist bazaar, and when the court was a garden planted with exotic trees and perfumed plants. Called *Djeser-djeseru* (Most Holy of Holies), it was designed by Senenmut, a courtier at Hatshepsut's court and also thought to have been her lover. If the design seems unusual, note that it did in fact feature all the things a memorial temple usually had, including the rising central axis and a three-part plan, but had to be adapted to the chosen site almost exactly on the same line with the Temple of

NILE VALLEY: LUXOR SIGHTS

Memorial Temple of Hatshepsut

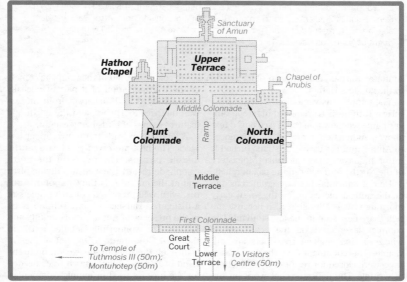

FEMALE PHARAOHS

Pharaoh was an exclusively male title and in early Egyptian history there was no word for a Queen regent, but records show there actually were a few female pharaohs. From early dynastic times it seemed common practice that on the death of the pharaoh, if his heir was too young to rule or there was no heir, his wife, often also his stepsister or sister, would be appointed regent. It's not clear if this role was limited to a regency, or if they were created pharaoh, but what is sure is that they were often buried with all the honours reserved for a pharaoh.

The first queen to have ruled independently is thought to have been Merneith, who was the wife of the 1st-dynasty Pharaoh Djer (c 3000 BC), and mother of Den who ruled after her. Her name was found on a clay seal impression with all the names of the early kings, and she was buried with full royal honours at Abydos. Almost every dynasty had a woman who ruled for a short while under the title of 'King's Mother'. The 12th-dynasty Sobeknofru, daughter of Amenemhat III and wife and half-sister of Amenhotep IV, is thought to have ruled Egypt from 1799 to 1795 BC, and her titles included Female Horus, King of Upper and Lower Egypt, and Daughter of Ra.

Hatshepsut is the most famous of Egypt's female pharaohs. When her husband and half-brother Tuthmosis II died in 1479 BC, Hatshepsut became regent with her stepson Tuthmosis III. Later, with the support of the Amun priesthood, she declared herself pharaoh, and her rule (1473–1458 BC) marked a period of peace and internal growth for Egypt. Sometimes she is shown in the regalia of the male pharaoh, including the false beard, sometimes she is clearly female. When Tuthmosis III finally took control in 1458 BC, he ordered all reference to her be wiped from Egyptian history, so her mummy has never been found, and her name and images were almost all erased.

Nefertiti, wife of the rebel pharaoh Akhenaten, was clearly involved in her husband's policies and is often depicted wearing kingly regalia. Some believe that she was in fact the mysterious Smenkhkare, known to have ruled for a few years after Akhenaten's death in 1336 BC. After Seti II died, his wife Tawosret became co-regent with her stepson Siptah, and later proclaimed herself pharaoh (1188–1186 BC). She was buried in the Valley of the Kings (see p217).

About 1000 years later Cleopatra came to the throne at the age of 17, in 51 BC. It's thought that she first ruled jointly with her father Ptolemy XII and, after his death, with her younger brother Ptolemy XIII. To keep Egypt independent, she allied herself with the Roman Julius Caesar, whom she married and whose son she bore. After Caesar's death, she famously married another powerful Roman, Marc Antony, and fell with him to the might of Augustus Caesar.

Amun at Karnak, and near an older shrine to the goddess Hathor.

The temple was vandalised over the centuries: Tuthmosis III removed his stepmother's name whenever he could (see boxed text above), Akhenaten removed all references to Amun, and the early Christians turned it into a monastery, Deir al-Bahri (Monastery of the North), and defaced the pagan reliefs.

Deir al-Bahri has been designated as one of the hottest places on earth, so an early morning visit is advisable, also because the reliefs are best seen in the low sunlight. The complex is entered via the **great court**, where original ancient tree roots are still visible. The colonnades on the **lower terrace** were closed for restoration at the time of writing. The delicate relief work on the south colonnade, left of the ramp, has reliefs of the transportation of a pair of obelisks commissioned by Hatshepsut from the Aswan quarries to Thebes, and the north one features scenes of birds being caught.

A large ramp leads to the two upper terraces. The best-preserved reliefs are on the **middle terrace**. The reliefs in the north colonnade record Hatshepsut's divine birth and at the end of it is the **Chapel of Anubis**, with well-preserved colourful reliefs of a disfigured Hatshepsut and Tuthmosis III in the presence of Anubis, Ra-Horakhty and Hathor. The wonderfully detailed reliefs in the **Punt Colonnade** to the left of the entrance tell the story of the expedition to the Land of Punt to collect myrrh trees needed for the incense used in temple ceremonies.

There are depictions of the strange animals and exotic plants seen there, the foreign architecture and strange landscapes as well as the different-looking people. At the end of this colonnade is the **Hathor Chapel**, with two chambers both with Hathor-headed columns. Reliefs on the west wall show, if you have a torch, Hathor as a cow licking Hatshepsut's hand, and the queen drinking from Hathor's udder. On the north wall is a faded relief of Hatshepsut's soldiers in naval dress in the goddess' honour. Beyond the pillared halls is a three-roomed chapel cut into the rock, now closed to the public, with reliefs of the queen in front of the deities, and with a small figure behind the door of Senenmut, the temple's architect and some believe Hatshepsut's lover.

The **upper terrace**, restored by a Polish-Egyptian team over the last 25 years, had 24 colossal Osiris statues, some of which are left. The central pink granite doorway leads into the **Sanctuary of Amun**, which is hewn out of the cliff.

On the south side of Hatshepsut's temple lie the remains of the **Temple of Montuhotep**, built for the founder of the 11th dynasty and one of the oldest temples so far discovered in Thebes, and the **Temple of Tuthmosis III**, Hatshepsut's successor. Both are in ruins.

Deir al-Medina   TEMPLE

(Monastery of the Town; Map p206; adult/student E£30/15, extra ticket for Tomb of Peshedu adult/student E£15/10; ⊗6am-5pm) About 1km off the road to the Valley of the Queens and up a short, steep paved road is Deir al-Medina, named after a temple that was occupied by early Christian monks. The small Ptolemaic-era temple of Deir al-Medina, measuring only 10m x 15m, was built between 221 and 116 BC, and it was dedicated to Hathor, the goddess of pleasure and love, and to Maat, the goddess of truth and personification of cosmic order.

Near the temple is a unique ruined settlement, the **Workmen's Village**. Many of the workers and artists who created the royal tombs lived and were buried here. Archaeologists have uncovered more than 70 houses in this village and many tombs, the most beautiful of which are now open to the public.

The beautifully adorned **Tomb of Inherka** (No 359) belonged to a 19th-dynasty servant who worked in the Place of Truth, the Valley of the Kings. The one-room tomb

has magnificent wall paintings, including the famous scene of a cat (representing the sun god Ra) killing a snake (representing the evil serpent Apophis) under a sacred tree, on the left wall. There are also beautiful domestic scenes of Inherka with his wife and children. Right next to it is the **Tomb of Sennedjem** (No 1), a stunningly decorated 19th-dynasty tomb that contains two small chambers and some equally exquisite paintings. Sennedjem was an artist who lived during the reigns of Seti I and Ramses II and it seems he ensured his own tomb was as finely decorated as those of his masters. Due to the popularity and small size of both these tombs, only 10 people at a time are allowed inside; it's likely you'll find yourself in a queue.

While you wait, take a look at the 19th-dynasty **Tomb of Peshedu** (No 3) just up the slope from the other two tombs. Peshedu was another servant in the Place of Truth and can be seen in the burial chamber praying under a palm tree beside a lake.

Close by is the **Tomb of Ipy** (No 217), a sculptor during the reign of Ramses II. Here scenes of everyday life eclipse the usual emphasis on ritual, with scenes of farming and hunting, and a depiction of Ipy's house in its flower- and fruit-filled garden.

Medinat Habu   TEMPLE

(Map p222; adult/student E£30/15; ⊗6am-5pm) Ramses III's magnificent memorial temple of Medinat Habu is perhaps one of the most underrated sites on the west bank. With the Theban mountains as a backdrop and the sleepy village of Kom Lolah in front, it is a wonderful place to spend a few hours late afternoon.

The site was one of the first places in Thebes to be closely associated with the local god Amun. Although the complex is most famous for the funerary temple built by Ramses III, Hatshepsut and Tuthmosis III also constructed buildings here. They were later added to and altered by a succession of rulers through to the Ptolemies. At Medinat Habu's height there were temples, storage rooms, workshops, administrative buildings and accommodation for priests and officials. It was the centre of the economic life of Thebes for centuries and was still inhabited as late as the 9th century AD, when a plague was thought to have decimated the town. You can still see the mudbrick remains of the medieval town that gave the

Medinat Habu

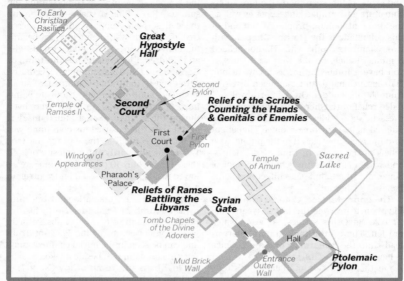

site its name (medina means 'town' or 'city') on top of the enclosure walls.

The original **Temple of Amun**, which was built by Hatshepsut and Tuthmosis III, was later completely overshadowed by the enormous **Funerary Temple of Ramses III**, the dominant feature of Medinat Habu.

Ramses III was inspired in the construction of his shrine by the Ramesseum of his illustrious forebear, Ramses II. His own temple and the smaller one dedicated to Amun are both enclosed within the massive outer walls of the complex.

Also just inside, to the left of the gate, are the **Tomb Chapels of the Divine Adorers**, which were built for the principal priestesses of Amun. Outside the eastern gate, one of only two entrances, was a landing quay for a canal that once connected Medinat Habu with the Nile.

You enter the site through the unique **Syrian Gate**, a large two-storey building modelled after an Asiatic fortress. If you follow the wall to the left you will find a staircase leading to the upper floors. There is not much to see in the rooms but you'll get some great views out across the village in front of the temple and over the fields to the south.

The well-preserved **first pylon** marks the front of the temple proper. Ramses III

is portrayed in its reliefs as the victor in several wars. Most famous are the fine **reliefs** of his victory over the Libyans (who you can recognise by their long robes, sidelocks and beards). There is also a gruesome scene of scribes tallying the number of enemies killed by counting severed hands and genitals.

To the left of the **first court** are the remains of the **Pharaoh's Palace**; the three rooms at the rear were for the royal harem. There is a window between the first court and the Pharaoh's Palace known as the **Window of Appearances**, which allowed the pharaoh to show himself to his subjects.

The reliefs of the **second pylon** feature Ramses III presenting prisoners of war to Amun and his vulture-goddess wife, Mut. Colonnades and reliefs surround the **second court**, depicting various religious ceremonies.

If you have time to wander about the extensive ruins around the funerary temple you will see the remains of an **early Christian basilica** as well as a small **sacred lake**.

The Ramesseum
TEMPLE

(Map p223; adult/student E£35/20; ⏰6am-5pm) Ramses II called his massive memorial temple 'the Temple of Millions of Years of User-Maat-Ra'; classical visitors called it the

Tomb of Ozymandias; and Jean-François Champollion, who deciphered hieroglyphics, called it the Ramesseum. Like other memorial temples it was part of Ramses II's funerary complex. His tomb was built deep in the hills, but his memorial temple was on the edge of the cultivation on a canal that connected with the Nile and with other memorial temples.

Unlike the well-preserved structures that Ramses II built at Karnak and Abu Simbel, his memorial temple has not survived the times very well. It is mostly in ruins, despite extensive restoration – a fact that would no doubt disappoint Ramses II. The Ramesseum is famous for the scattered remains of fallen statues that inspired the English poet Shelley's poem 'Ozymandias', using the undeniable fact of Ramses' mortality to ridicule his aspirations to immortality.

Although it is more elaborate than other temples, the fairly orthodox layout of the Ramesseum, consisting of two courts, hypostyle hall, sanctuary, accompanying chambers and storerooms, is uncommon in that the usual rectangular floor plan was altered to incorporate an older, smaller temple – that of Ramses II's mother, Tuya – off to one side.

The entrance is through a doorway in the northeast corner of the enclosure wall, which leads into the second court, where one should turn left to the **first pylon**. The **first** and **second pylons** measure more than 60m across and feature reliefs of Ramses' military exploits, particularly his battles against the Hittites. Through the first pylon are the ruins of the huge **first court**, including the double colonnade that fronted the royal **palace**.

Near the western stairs is part of the **Colossus of Ramses II**, the Ozymandias of Shelley's poem, lying somewhat forlornly on the ground, where it once stood 17.5m tall. The head of another granite **statue of Ramses II**, one of a pair, lies in the **second court**. Twenty-nine of the original 48 columns of the **great hypostyle hall** are still standing. In the smaller hall behind it, the roof, which features astronomical hieroglyphs, is still in place.

Colossi of Memnon   MONUMENTS
(Map p206) The two faceless Colossi of Memnon that rise majestically about 18m from the plain are the first monuments tourists see when they visit the west bank. The enthroned figures have kept a lonely vigil over the changing landscape, and few visitors have any idea that these giants were only a tiny element of what was once the largest temple built in Egypt, the memorial

The Ramesseum

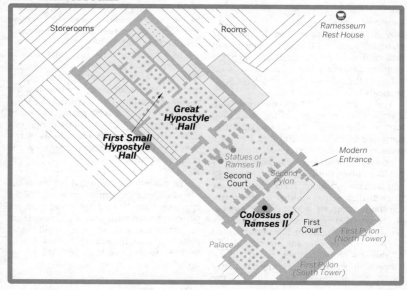

SHELLEY'S 'OZYMANDIAS'

I met a traveller from an antique land

Who said: Two vast and trunkless legs of stone

Stand in the desert...Near them, on the sand,

Half sunk, a shattered visage lies, whose frown,

And wrinkled lip, and sneer of cold command,

Tell that its sculptor well those passions read

Which yet survive, stamped on these life-less things,

The hand that mocked them, and the heart that fed:

And on the pedestal these words – appear:

'My name is Ozymandias, king of kings:

Look on my works, ye Mighty, and despair!'

Nothing beside remains. Round the decay

Of that colossal wreck, boundless and bare

The lone and level sands stretch far away.

temple of Amenhotep III, believed to have covered an area larger than Karnak. The pharaoh's memorial temple has now all but disappeared. Some tiny parts of the temple remain and more is being uncovered by excavation; the colossi are the only large-scale elements to have survived.

The magnificent colossi, each cut from a single block of stone and weighing 1000 tonnes, were already a great tourist attraction during Graeco-Roman times, when the statues were attributed to Memnon, the legendary African king who was slain by Achilles during the Trojan War. The Greeks and Romans considered it good luck to hear the whistling sound emitted by the northern statue at sunrise, which they believed to be the cry of Memnon greeting his mother Eos, the goddess of dawn. She in turn would weep tears of dew for his untimely death. All this was probably due to a crack in the colossus' upper body, which appeared after the 27 BC earthquake. As the heat of the morning sun baked the dew-soaked stone, sand particles would break off and resonate inside the cracks in the structure. After Septimus Severus (193–211 AD) repaired the statue in the 3rd century AD, Memnon's plaintive greeting was heard no more.

The temple was filled with thousands of statues (including the huge dyad of Amenhotep III and his wife Tiy that now dominates the central court of the Egyptian Museum in Cairo), most of which were later dragged off by other pharaohs. A stele, also now in the Egyptian Museum, describes the temple as being built from 'white sandstone, with gold throughout, a floor covered with silver, and doors covered with electrum'. Other statues and fragments of wall reliefs can be seen at the nearby Temple of Merenptah.

The colossi are just off the road, before you reach the Antiquities Inspectorate ticket office, and are usually being snapped and filmed by an army of tourists. A new archaeological project is salvaging what remains of the temple.

Temple of Seti I   TEMPLE
(Map p206; adult/student E£30/15; ⊙6am-5pm)
At the northern end of the Theban necropolis lies the Temple of Seti I. Seti I, who also built the superbly decorated temple at Abydos and Karnak's magnificent hypostyle hall, died before this memorial temple was finished, so it was completed by his son Ramses II. The temple sees few visitors, despite its picturesque location near a palm grove and recent restoration after being severely damaged by floods in 1994.

The entrance is through a small door in the northeast corner of the reconstructed fortresslike enclosure wall. The first and second pylons and the court are in ruins, but recent excavations have revealed the foundations of the pharaoh's palace, just south of the court. The earliest found example of a palace within a memorial temple, its plan is similar to the better-preserved palace at the memorial temple of Ramses III at Medinat Habu.

The walls of the columned portico at the west facade of the temple, and those of the hypostyle court beyond it, contain some superbly executed reliefs. Off the hypostyle are six shrines and to the south is a small chapel dedicated to Seti's father, Ramses I, who died before he could build his own mortuary temple.

Carter's House
MUSEUM

(Map p206; adult/student E£20/15; ⊙8am-5pm) Surrounded by a garden on what is otherwise a barren hill, where the road from Deir al-Bahri to the Valley of the Kings meets the road from Seti I's temple, stands the domed house where Howard Carter lived during his search for Tutankhamun's tomb (p211). The house has been decorated with pictures and tools of the excavation. A cafe is expected to open shortly, making this a peaceful place to stop for refreshment.

Assasif Tombs
TOMBS

This group of tombs, located near Deir al-Bahri, belongs to 18th-dynasty nobles and 25th- and 26th-dynasty nobles under the Nubian pharaohs. The area is under excavation by archaeologists, but of the many tombs here only some are open to the public, including the **Tombs of Kheruef** and of **Mntophaat** (Map p206; adult/student E£30/15; ⊙6am-4.30pm Oct-Apr, to 5pm May-Sep) and of **Pabasa** (Map p206; adult/student E£25/15; ⊙6am-5pm); tickets are available at the ticket office of Deir al-Bahri (Temple of Hetshepsut). The tomb of Kheruef is the largest 18th-dynasty noble's tomb here in Thebes, and it has some of the finest examples of New Kingdom relief, but unfortunately it is in poor condition. The tomb of Pabasa, a 26th-dynasty priest, has wonderful scenes of agriculture, hunting and fishing.

Dra Abu'l Naga
TOMBS

(Map p206; adult/student E£15/10; ⊙6am-5pm) Hidden in the desert cliffs north of Deir al-Bahri lies yet another necropolis, Dra Abu'l Naga, with 114 tombs of rulers and officials, most dating from the 17th dynasty to the late period (about 1550–500 BC). The area has

---

ⓘ RAMESSEUM REST HOUSE

After visiting the tombs of the Nobles or the Ramesseum, take a break on the terrace of the resthouse restaurant right next to the Ramesseum temple that is called, not surprisingly, **Ramesseum Rest House** (Map p223; mains from E£20, drinks E£5-10). It is a great place to relax and have a cool drink, even a beer, or something simple to eat. You can leave your bike here while exploring the surroundings.

---

been extensively plundered but two tombs escaped with their paintings mostly intact.

The **Tomb of Roy** (No 234; Map p206), a royal scribe and steward of Horemheb, is small with scenes of funerary offerings and agriculture, and a beautifully painted ceiling. A few metres away, the T-shaped **Tomb of Shuroy** (No 13; Map p206) contains some finely executed, but in places heavily damaged, paintings of Shuroy and his wife making offerings to the gods and a funeral procession led by a child mourner.

Valley of the Queens
TOMBS

(Biban al-Harim; Map p206; adult/student E£35/20; ⊙6am-5pm) There are at least 75 tombs in the Valley of the Queens. They belonged to queens of the 19th and 20th dynasties and other members of the royal families, including princesses and the Ramesside princes. Only two were open at the time of writing, and the Tomb of Nefertari is closed for the foreseeable future but a replica will be built.

Tomb of Nefertari (No 66)

(Map p206) Hailed as the finest tomb in the Theban necropolis – and in all of Egypt for that matter – the Tomb of Nefertari was completely restored and reopened, but closed again until further notice.

Nefertari was one of the five wives of Ramses II, the New Kingdom pharaoh known for his colossal monuments, but the tomb he built for his favourite queen is a shrine to her beauty and, without doubt, an exquisite labour of love. Every centimetre of the walls in the tomb's three chambers and connecting corridors is adorned with colourful scenes of Nefertari in the company of the gods and with associated text from the Book of the Dead nearby. Invariably, the 'Most Beautiful of Them', as Nefertari was known, is depicted wearing a divinely transparent white gown and a golden headdress featuring two long feathers extending from the back of a vulture. The ceiling of the tomb is festooned with golden stars.

Like most of the tombs in the Valley of the Kings, this one had been plundered by the time it was discovered by archaeologists. Only a few fragments of the queen's pink granite sarcophagus remained, and of her mummified body, only traces of her knees were left.

Tomb of Amunherkhepshef (No 55)

(Map p206) The valley's showpiece is now the Tomb of Amunherkhepshef, with its beauti-

WEST BANK TRANSPORT

Most tourists cross to the west bank by bus or taxi via the bridge, about 7km south of town. But the river remains the quickest way to go. The *baladi* (municipal) ferry costs E£1 for foreigners and leaves from a dock in front of Luxor Temple. Small motor launches (locally called *lunches*) also leave from wherever they can find customers and will take you across for E£10 to E£20 for a small group.

On the west bank, the taxi lot is near the ferry landing. Voices call out the destinations of *kabouts* (pick-up trucks). If you listen out for Gurna you'll be on the right road to the ticket office (50pt). Pick-ups run back and forth between the villages, so you can always flag one down on your way to one of the sites, although you will have to walk from the main road to the entrance, which, in the case of the Valley of the Kings or Queens is quite far. If you want to have an entire pick-up for yourself, it'll cost around E£10. The driver is likely to stick to his normal route.

To hire a private taxi for the day, expect to pay between E£150 and E£250 per day, depending on the season, the state of tourism and your bargaining skills. Past the taxi lot are bicycles for rent for E£15/20 per day.

Donkeys and camels with guides can also be rented at the landing, but it's safer to rent them from a recognised stable (see p227).

For an idea of the distances involved, from the local ferry landing it is 3km straight ahead to the ticket office, past the Colossi of Memnon; 4km to the Valley of the Queens; and 8km to the Valley of the Kings.

---

ful, well-preserved reliefs. Amunherkhepshef, the son of Ramses III, was in his teens when he died. On the walls of the tomb's vestibule, Ramses holds his son's hand to introduce him to the gods that will help him on his journey to the afterlife. Amunherkhepshef wears a kilt and sandals, with the sidelock of hair typical of young boys.

The mummified five-month-old foetus on display in the tomb is the subject of many an inventive story, among them the suggestion that the foetus was aborted by Amunherkhepshef's mother when she heard of his death. It was actually found by Italian excavators in a valley to the south of the Valley of the Queens.

Tomb of Khaemwaset (No 44)

(Map p206) Another son of Ramses III, Khaemwaset died young; there is little information about his age or cause of death. His tomb is filled with well-preserved, brightly coloured reliefs. Like Amunherkhepshef's tomb, it follows a linear plan, and is decorated with scenes of the pharaoh introducing his son to the gods, and scenes from the Book of the Dead. The vestibule has an astronomical ceiling, showing Ramses III in full ceremonial dress, followed by his son wearing a tunic and the sidelock of hair signifying his youth.

Tomb of Titi (No 52)

(Map p206) Egyptologists are not sure which Ramesside pharaoh Titi was married to; in her tomb she is referred to as the royal wife,

royal mother and royal daughter. Some archaeologists believe she was the wife of Ramses III, and her tomb is in many ways similar to those of Khaemwaset and Amunherkhepshef, perhaps her sons. The tomb has a corridor leading to a square chapel, off which is the burial chamber and two other small rooms. The paintings are faded but you can still make out a winged Maat kneeling on the left-hand side of the corridor, and the queen before Toth, Ptah and the four sons of Horus opposite. Inside the burial chamber are a series of animal guardians: a jackal and lion, two monkeys and a monkey with a bow.

New Gurna   VILLAGE

(Map p206; www.fathyheritage.com) Hassan Fathy's mudbrick village lies just past the railway track on the road from the ferry to the Antiquities Inspectorate ticket office. It was built to rehouse the inhabitants of Old Gurna, who lived on and around the Tombs of the Nobles.

The buildings were stunning, with Hassan Fathy's signature domes and vaults, thick mudbrick walls and natural ventilation, but today much of the village is in tatters, although the beautiful mudbrick mosque and theatre survive. Unesco has recognised the need to safeguard the village, but has stalled its plans since the 2011 revolution. Rumour has it the architect Ramez Azmy, who built the Adrére Amellal hotel in Siwa (p312), is planning a hotel in New Gurna.

⚹ Activities

Ballooning

Hot-air ballooning to see the sun rise over the ancient monuments on the west bank and Theban mountains is a great way to start the day. **Horus** (☎228 2670/0111 015 12 41; www. horusballoon.com), **Hod Hod Suleiman** (Map p196; ☎227 1116/0122 115 8593; Sharia Omar Ali, off Sharia Televizyon), **Sky Cruise of Egypt** (☎237 6515/236 0407; Sharia Khaled Ibn al-Walid) and **Sindbad Balloons** (☎227 0437/0100 330 7708; www.sindbadballoons.com) all offer morning flights at varying prices, often depending on how many people are on board. Expect to pay from €80 to €150 per person, although it is possible to bargain, particularly out of season.

Donkey, Horse & Camel Rides

Riding a horse, a donkey or a camel through the fields and seeing the sunset behind the Theban hills is wonderful. Boys at the local ferry dock on the west bank offer donkey and camel rides for about E£30 to E£40 for an hour. There are many reports of women getting hassled, and of overcharging at the end. The west bank hotels also offer camel trips, which include visits to nearby villages for a cup of tea, and donkey treks around the west bank. These trips, which start at around 7am (sometimes 5am) and finish near lunchtime, cost a minimum of about E£50 per person.

Excellent horses can be found at **Nobi's Arabian Horse Stables** (Map p196; ☎231 0024, 0100 504 8558; www.luxorstables.com; approx per hr E£30; ☉7am-sunset), which also provides riding hats, English saddles and insurance. Nobi also has 25 camels and as many donkeys at the same price, and organises longer horse riding and camping trips into the desert or a week from Luxor to Kom Ombo along the west bank. Call ahead to book, and he can arrange a hassle-free transfer to make sure you arrive at the right place, as often taxi drivers will try and take you to a friend's stable instead. Around the corner is **Pharaoh's Stables** (Map p196; ☎231 2263/0100 632 4961; ☉7am-sunset) with horses, donkeys and camels (all E£30 to E£40 per hour).

Volunteering

Those distressed by the state of the horses in Luxor streets may like to visit **ACE** (Animal Care in Egypt; off Map p196; ☎928 0727; www.ace -egypt.org.uk; at the start of Sharia al-Habil, near traffic police; donations welcome; ☉8am-noon & 1-5pm). It's a veterinary hospital and animal welfare centre seeing up to 200 animals a day. Treatment for the working animals of Egyptians, particularly donkeys and horses, is free. The centre also runs an education program receiving 80 local children a day, aiming to impart a love and care for animals. Children can spend the day at the centre to help care for the animals. Volunteers are welcome.

Felucca Rides

As elsewhere in Egypt, the nicest place to be late afternoon is on the Nile. Take a felucca from either bank, and sail for a few hours, catching the soft afternoon light and the sunset, cooling in the afternoon breeze and calming down after sightseeing. Felucca prices range from E£30 to E£50 per boat per hour, depending on your bargaining skills.

A popular felucca trip is upriver to Banana Island, a tiny isle dotted with palms about 5km from Luxor. The trip takes two to three hours. Plan it in such a way that you're on your way back in time to watch a brilliant Nile sunset from the boat. Be sure to agree in advance exactly what is included. Beware that some captains have been charging a fictitious 'entry fee' to the island (it's free).

Swimming

After a hot morning of tombs and temples, a dip in a pool can be heavenly. Most bigger hotels and some budget places have swimming pools. The **Iberotel Luxor** (Map p196; Sharia Khaled Ibn Walid) has a great pool on a pontoon on the Nile that can be used for E£100. The Hilton will usually allow you to swim if you are staying for lunch (check beforehand). The St Joseph and Domina Inn Emilio hotels have small rooftop pools that you can use for E£20. In the current downturn, most other east bank hotels will also allow access for a small fee. On the west bank the **Al-Moudira Hotel** (Map p196; ☎0122 325 1307; www.moudira. com; Daba'iyya) has a wonderful pool set in a peaceful garden on the edge of the desert; nonresidents can use it for E£75.

☞ Tours

Because of the bargaining and hassle involved, some people may find independent travel challenging at times, and a day tour in an air-conditioned tour bus, taking in the main sights, might be just the thing. These tours offer a good introduction to the city.

Most small budget hotels aggressively promote their own tours. Some of these are better than others and there have been complaints from a number of travellers that they ended up seeing little more than papyrus shops and alabaster factories from a sweaty car with no air-con. If you do decide to take one of these tours, expect to pay about E£75 to E£100 per person.

Several of the more reliable travel agents are all next to each other, next door to the Winter Palace Hotel. All offer the same kind of tours, so you can easily compare the prices.

Aladin Tours   CULTURAL TOUR
(Map p196; ☑237 2386, 0100 601 6132; http:// nefertitihotel.com/tours; Nefertiti Hotel, Sharia as-Sahbi) This very helpful travel agency, run by the young, energetic Aladin, organises sightseeing tours in Luxor and around as well as in the Western Desert, plus boat trips and ferry tickets to Sinai.

American Express   CULTURAL TOUR
(Map p196; ☑237 8333; www.americanexpress. com/egypt; Corniche an-Nil, next to Winter Palace Hotel; ⊙8am-8pm) Offers a large menu of tours in and around Luxor. Prices range from E£250 to E£400 per person for a half day.

Jolley's Travel & Tours   CULTURAL TOUR
(Map p196; ☑237 2262; www.jolleys.com; ⊙9am-10pm) This reputable company, next to the Old Winter Palace Hotel, also runs day trips to the main sites.

QEA Travel Agency   CULTURAL TOUR
(Map p196; ☑0100 2943169; Gezira al-Bayrat; http://questforegyptianadventure.com) A different approach from this British-run agency that runs tailor-made tours in and around Luxor, as well as further afield to the Red Sea or the Western Desert. A percentage of its profits go towards charitable projects in Egypt.

Thomas Cook   CULTURAL TOUR
(Map p196; ☑237 2402; www.thomascookegypt. com; ⊙8am-8pm) Next to the Old Winter Palace, and offers an array of tours. Prices range from E£250 to E£400 per person for a half-day.

The **Nefertiti Hotel** (Map p196; ☑010 601 6132; www.nefertitihotel.com/tours; Sharia Sahbi) also organises day cruises to Dendara from E£460 per person. Cairo-based **Min Travel** (☑Cairo 02-2632 5987; www.min-travel.com) organises felucca day trips to Dendara from US$70 per person and offers the possibility of booking by email before you arrive in Egypt.

★ Festivals & Events

The town's biggest traditional festival is the **Moulid of Abu al-Haggag**. One of Egypt's largest *moulid*s (saints' festivals), it is held in honour of Luxor's patron sheikh, Yousef Abu al-Haggag, a 12th-century Iraqi who settled in Luxor. The *moulid* takes place around the Mosque of Abu al-Haggag, the town's oldest mosque, which is built on top of the northeastern corner of Luxor Temple. It's a raucous five-day carnival that takes place in the third week before Ramadan. See the boxed text p203 for details of other *moulid*s.

In late January or early February each year a **marathon** (☑02-2260 6930, 0122 214 8839; www.egyptianmarathon.com) is held on the west bank. It begins at Deir al-Bahri and loops around the main antiquities sites before ending back where it began.

🛏 Sleeping

Luxor has a wide range of hotels for all budgets. Most package-tour hotels are on the east bank, and so are the shops, restaurants and the hectic town life. The west bank is developing at a fast rate and is certainly no longer as rural as it once was. But it is still a tranquil place, where the pace of life is much slower and where evenings are more often than not blissfully quiet. After the revolution of January 2011 the numbers of tourists to Luxor have dropped dramatically. By late 2011 several places, particularly foreign-owned ones, had closed their doors, perhaps waiting for the good times to return soon. Prices for the ones that remained open have dropped. We have listed high-season prices, so be prepared to bargain.

At all costs avoid the hotel touts who may pounce on you as you get off the train or bus; they will get a 25% to 40% commission for bringing you into the hotel, but that will be added to your bill. Many hotels in the budget and midrange bracket offer free or cheap transfers from the airport or train station, so to avoid touts and bargaining with taxi drivers call ahead and arrange to be picked up.

Luxor has a good selection of budget places. Many boast both roof gardens and washing machines. The budget hotels on the west bank are particularly good value, much quieter and often offering a more authentic meeting with locals.

Luxor has an ever-growing selection of midrange hotels on both banks, often catering to families. If you are looking for a hotel with character, then check out the small mudbrick, traditional-style hotels on the west bank. The east bank hotels are often slick, modern places, popular with budget and adventure tour groups. There are some excellent bargains in this category, with good facilities at attractive rates. Out of season some incredibly cheap packages can be found, including flights from the UK.

EAST BANK

TOP CHOICE La Maison de
Pythagore   GUESTHOUSE $$
(off Map p196; ☏0100 535 0532, 00 32 496 559 255 (in Belgium); www.lamaisondepythagore.com, in French; Al-Awamiya; s/d/tr €35/50/60; ✻@) This small guesthouse with seven rooms in a traditional Egyptian house is tucked away in a tiny village behind the Sheraton Hotel, close to the tourist facilities and the Nile, but a world away from Luxor's humdrum. Run by the Belgian Anne and her son Thomas, it's a great place to stay for a few days. The soft traditional architecture encloses simple but cosy rooms, stylishly painted in earthy colours mixed with turquoise and blue. Some rooms have air-con, others fans, but all have large bathrooms. The garden is a small oasis with date palms, flowers, fruit trees, and a fall of bougainvillea. Breakfast is served on the large roof terrace. Lunch (E£40) and dinner (E£55) are made with local seasonal produce. Mother and son are both passionate about Egypt, and run their own tailor-made half-day to one-week tours and adventures for their guests and others.

Hilton Luxor Resort
and Spa   LUXURY HOTEL $$$
(off Map p196; ☏237 4933; www.luxor.hilton.com; New Karnak; r from US$200; ✻@☀☀) The Luxor Hilton is by far the most luxurious resort in Luxor, located 2km north of Luxor centre, past the Karnak Temple and on the Nile. The large rooms are elegant and tastefully decorated in a warm Asian-inspired style with lots of neutral colours and wood. The communal areas exude calm and tranquillity and the spa facilities are impressive – think more Thailand than Egypt. The large grounds include two Nile view infinity swimming pools with submerged sun loungers, a Technogym, and several top-class restaurants, including the Mediterranean Olives and a chic Asian bistro, Silk Road. The staff and management are young, handsome and very hands on.

This hotel is almost a destination in itself, albeit not very family oriented.

Nefertiti Hotel   GUESTHOUSE $$
(Map p196; ☏237 2386; www.nefertitihotel.com; Sharia as-Sahabi, btwn Sharia Maabad al-Karnak & Sharia as-Souq; s/d/tr E£120/160/200, family room E£220; ✻☀) Aladin as-Sahabi runs his family's hotel and the attached Aladin Tours travel agency with great care, offering recently renovated, midrange facilities at budget prices. No wonder this hotel is popular with our readers: the rooms are simple but very cosy, the small private bathrooms are spotless, the breakfast is excellent and served on the roof terrace, and the staff is super friendly. The larger new rooms on the top floors are decorated in local style. The rooftop is great for a drink or a bite, with great views of the west bank and Luxor Temple, both lit up at night. The best budget option!

Winter Palace Hotel   HISTORIC HOTEL $$$
(Map p196; ☏237 1197; www.sofitel.com; Corniche an-Nil; old wing r €180-320, ste €450-900; ✻☀) The Winter Palace was built to attract the aristocracy of Europe and is one of Egypt's most famous historic hotels. A wonderfully atmospheric Victorian pile, it has high ceilings, lots of gorgeous textiles, fabulous views over the Nile, an enormous garden with exotic trees and shrubs, a huge swimming pool, table-tennis tables and a tennis court. The rooms vary in size and decor, but are very comfortable, and the food is excellent, as is the service. The 1960s New Winter Palace has already been demolished, the Pavillion garden wing is about to be, and there are plans to upgrade the old building into a more luxurious version of itself. However, the hotel remains open during all these planned works, so it may be a bit noisier than usual.

Mara House   GUESTHOUSE $$
(Map p196; ☏236 5081, 0100 757 1855; www.egyptwithmara.com; Sharia Salahadin Ayyubi, off Sharia Salakhana; r per person US$50; ✻☀) Irish Mara wanted to open a home for travellers and seems to have succeeded with spacious rooms, each decorated in local style, and including a sitting area and a clean bathroom. Some of the accommodation is small flats, particularly good for families. This is a very popular option so book well ahead in the winter season. The modern house, in a real Egyptian neighbourhood right behind the train station, can be hard to find but call

NILE VALLEY: LUXOR SLEEPING

for instructions or a free transfer. Mara also runs Salahadeen (p234), a popular Egyptian restaurant where the food is served as it is in Egyptian homes.

Fontana Hotel
HOSTEL $

(Map p196; ☑228 0663, 0100 733 3238; www.fontanaluxorhotel.com; Sharia Radwan, off Sharia Televizyon; s/d/tr E£45/60/75, with shared bathroom E£35/50/65; ✳🔊) An old stalwart of the budget-hotel scene, this 25-room hotel has clean rooms, a washing machine for guest use, a luggage storage room, a rooftop terrace and a kitchen. All bathrooms are large and very clean, and toilet paper and towels are provided. The owner Magdi Soliman is always ready to help, and readers have written in to tell us how friendly and helpful his staff are.

Happy Land Hotel
HOSTEL $

(Map p196; ☑227 7922; www.luxorhappyland.com; Sharia Qamr; s/d with shared bathroom E£30/45, s/d/tr with fridge & air-con E£70/80/110; ✳@🔊) The Happy Land, another backpackers' favourite, offers clean rooms and spotless bathrooms, as well as very friendly service, a copious breakfast with fruit and cornflakes and a rooftop terrace. Competition among Luxor's budget hotels is fierce, and the Happy Land comes out well almost every time. It doesn't need to send touts to the station! Bikes can be rented for E£10 per day, and wi-fi and laundry facilities are free. Mr Ibrahim tries his utmost to make everyone appreciate his town. It sells ISIC cards.

St Joseph Hotel
HOTEL $$

(Map p196; ☑238 1707; stjosephhotel@yahoo.com; Sharia Khaled ibn al-Walid; s/d US$25/30; ✳🔊🚦) This popular and well-run three-star hotel has been a favourite with small groups for years thanks to its simple but comfortable rooms with satellite TV, air-con and clean private bathrooms. All rooms have some Nile views, although the front rooms with a full view are quite noisy. There is also a small(heated) rooftop pool, a bar and a restaurant. The breakfast buffet is quite basic.

Sofitel Karnak
RESORT $$$

(☑237 8020; www.sofitel.com; Sharia az-Zinia Gebly, Karnak; r US$110-250; ✳🚦🔊⊖) Quiet and secluded, the enormous Sofitel Karnak has 351 Nubian-style bungalow rooms set in lush Nile-side gardens, 3km north of the Temples of Karnak. The hotel also boasts a very pleasant heated pool, tennis and squash courts and a fitness centre, sauna

and jacuzzi, and it is near an 18-hole golf course. Shuttle buses go to Luxor town.

Sheraton Luxor Resort
RESORT $$$

(off Map p196; ☑227 4544; www.sheratonluxor.com; Sharia Khaled ibn al-Walid; s/d from US$231/271; ✳🔊🚦) This secluded three-storey building is set amid lush gardens at the far southern end of Sharia Khaled ibn al-Walid – close enough to walk to some restaurants but far enough away to avoid any street noise. Rooms are well appointed and those overlooking the Nile have great views, although the run-down garden bungalows should be avoided. The hotel has a shopping arcade and good Italian restaurant, La Mama (p235).

Maritim Jolie Ville
RESORT $$

(☑227 4855; www.jolieville-hotels.com; Kings Island; s/d/tr US$90/120/160; ✳🔊🚦) Set amid lush gardens on Crocodile Island, 4km south of town, this is a great family hotel with a minizoo and playground in addition to the large heated swimming pool, tennis courts and feluccas. There are 320 well-furnished and comfortable, if architecturally unremarkable, bungalow-style rooms, and a hotel motorboat and bus shuttle guests to and from the centre of town. The hotel boasts several good restaurants.

Sonesta St George Hotel
HOTEL $$$

(Map p196; ☑238 2575; www.sonesta.com/egypt_luxor; Sharia Khaled ibn al- Walid; s/d city view US$135/170, Nile view US$250/270; ✳🚦) This 224-room marble-filled hotel, with faux Pharaonic columns and a flame-like fence around the roof, has a kitsch value that should not be overlooked. It is a good, lively place to stay. The hotel is well managed, has friendly staff, recently refurbished and comfortable rooms with great views, a heated swimming pool, a business centre and a good selection of restaurants. Rates are much cheaper when booked via the internet.

Susanna Hotel
HOTEL $$

(Map p196; ☑236 9915; www.susannahotelluxor.com; 52 Sharia Maabad al-Karnak; s/d/tr city view US$30/35/50, Nile view US$40/45/60; ✳🚦) Set between the Luxor Temple and the souq, this modern hotel has 45 spacious rooms with comfortable beds, wi-fi, air-con, satellite TV and great views. There is a good rooftop terrace restaurant with views over Luxor Temple and the Nile, perfect for a sunset drink as alcohol is available.

Domina Inn Emilio
HOTEL $$

(Map p196; ☎237 6666; www.emiliotravel.com; Sharia Yousef Hassan; s/d $40/50; ❄✿🛜🏊) A good midrange hotel, the Emilio has 101 spacious rooms, all fully equipped with minifridge, satellite TV, private bathroom, air-con and 24-hour room service. Other extras include an AstroTurfed roof terrace with plenty of shade and a large pool, a sauna and a business centre.

Anglo Hotel
HOTEL $

(Map p196; ☎238 1679; Midan al-Mahatta; s/d/tr E£70/100/120; ❄🛜) Right next to the train station, so a bit noisy at times, but right in the centre of town. The spacious old-style rooms are excellent value, clean and well maintained, with air-con, satellite TV, private bathroom, telephone and free wi-fi. The bar in the basement is popular with locals.

Rezeiky Camp
CAMPGROUND $

(off Map p196; ☎238 1334; www.rezeikycamp.com. eg; Sharia Maabad al-Karnak; campsite per person E£25, vehicle E£20, s/d with fan E£55/110, with air-con E£65/120; ❄@🏊) Rezeiky Camp is the only place to pitch a tent in town, but it is pleasant enough, with a pool on your doorstep. There is a large garden with a restaurant and bar, and internet access. The motel-style rooms are not nice enough to make up for the inconvenient location, but the place is popular with overland groups, so call ahead to make sure there is space.

WEST BANK

TOP CHOICE Al-Moudira
BOUTIQUE HOTEL $$$

(Map p196; ☎0122 325 1307; www.moudira.com; Daba'iyya; r/ste €220/270; ❄@🏊) Al-Moudira is a true luxury hotel, with an individuality that is missing from so many other hotels in Luxor. A Moorish fantasy of soaring vaults, pointed arches and enormous domes, surrounded by lush green and birdsong, the hotel has 54 rooms grouped together around small courtyards. Each room is different in shape, size (all are very large) and colour, each with its own hand-painted trompe l'oeil theme and with Egyptian antiques. Cushioned benches and comfortable antique chairs invite pashalike lounging and the enormous vaulted bathrooms have the feel of a private hammam (bathhouse). The public spaces are even more spectacular with traditional *mashrabiyya* (wooden lattice) combined with work by contemporary 'orientalist' artists. The staff is friendly and very helpful. Set on the edge of the culti-

vated land and the desert, this hotel is truly spectacular. It's a fairly long way from anywhere, but transport is relatively cheap.

TOP CHOICE Beit Sabée
GUESTHOUSE $$

(Map p206; ☎0100 632 4926, 0100 570 5341; info@beitsabee.com; Kom Lolah; d €40-70, with air-con €50-80; ❄) More like a house than a hotel, Beit Sabée has appeared in design magazines for its cool use of Nubian colours and local furnishings with a twist. Near the farms around Medinat Habu, it offers quiet accommodation and a closer contact with rural Egypt. Set in a traditional-style two-storey mudbrick house, the eight bedrooms with en-suite bathrooms are effortlessly stylish, and breakfast is served in the courtyard or on the roof. A good place to spend a calm few days.

El-Mesala Hotel
GUESTHOUSE $$

(Map p196; ☎231 4004, 0100 441 6741; www.hotel elmesala.com; Al-Gezira, near ferry landing; s/d/tr/ flat €18/28/35/45; ❄🛜) Very welcome newcomer on the scene of small family-oriented hotels in al-Gezira on the west bank. The hotel is on the Nile, a stone's throw from the ferry landing, and therefore perfectly located for visits on both banks. It has 12 immaculate rooms with comfortable beds, and with balconies looking at Luxor Temple and the Nile. The staff and the manager Mr Ahmed are all extremely welcoming, and everything is absolutely spotless. The restaurant is in the front garden, and there's a great rooftop terrace for sun bathing. This hotel comes recommended.

Nile Valley Hotel
HOTEL $$

(Map p196; ☎231 1477, 0122 796 4473; www.nileval ley.nl; Al-Gezira; s/d/tr E£195/255/325, 2-room flat E£510; ❄🏊🛜) Pleasant Dutch-Egyptian-run hotel in a modern block right near the ferry landing. The comfortable rooms almost all have ultraclean private bathrooms, satellite TV and air-con. Some rooms have Nile views but those overlooking the rear garden are quieter and slightly bigger. Upstairs is a good rooftop bar-restaurant with fantastic views of the Nile and Luxor Temple, and there is a pool and children's pool in the garden (E£50 for nonresidents). This hotel is particularly family friendly, and often has families staying here for a week or more.

Amon Hotel
GUESTHOUSE $$

(Map p196; ☎231 0912/0100 639 4585; www. amonhotel.com; Al-Gezira; s/d/tr E£200/250/300;

NILE VALLEY: LUXOR SLEEPING

❋) Charming family-run hotel in a modern building with spotless rooms, a wonderful lush exotic garden where it's pleasant to have breakfast, lunch or a drink, extremely helpful staff and delicious home-cooked meals. In the new wing the rooms are large with private bathrooms, ceiling fans, air-con and balconies overlooking the courtyard. In the old wing, some of the small rooms have private bathrooms, and all have air-con. On the top floor are three triple rooms with an adjoining terrace and stunning views over the Theban Hills and the east bank. This hotel is popular with archaeologists in winter, so book ahead.

Desert Paradise Lodge   LODGE $$
(Map p206; ☎231 3036; www.desertparadiselodge. com; Qabawi; s/d €40/70; ❋@) Far away from the crowds, off the road going to the Valley of the Kings and on the edge of the desert, this is a place for those who want to do the west bank slowly and calmly. This beautiful small lodge, built in traditional style, has spacious domed rooms, lots of communal space, a garden and terraces overlooking the Theban hills. It's 1.5km from the cross-roads to Valley of Kings, on the first left after Carter House.

Al-Fayrouz Hotel   HOTEL $$
(Map p196; ☎231 2709, 0122 277 0565; www.elfay rouz.com; Al-Gezira; s/d/tr/q E£95/150/190/240; ❋🛜) This tranquil hotel with 17 brightly painted rooms, overlooking fields, is a great base for exploring the monuments of the west bank. Under Egyptian-German man-agement, the simple, nicely decorated rooms are spotless and have private bathrooms; some also come with air-conditioning and a balcony with a view. The more expensive rooms are larger, with a sitting area, and have more atmosphere. Meals can be had on the comfortable roof terrace or in the popu-lar garden restaurant.

Hotel Sheherazade   HOTEL $$
(Map p196; ☎231 1228, 0122 212 3719; www.hotel sheherazade.com; Al-Gezira; s/d/tr E£180/250/ 330, flat E£450, 3-course meals per person E£45; ❋) Mohammed Sanusy dreamt of building this place for several years, and he takes great pride in his hotel. The 28 comfortable and spacious rooms are decorated with lo-cal colour and furnishings and all have en-suite bathrooms with water heated by solar panels. The Moorish-style building is sur-rounded by a garden. The large restaurant and garden is at the end of the garden, and now also a small Arabic school (p513). A pool is planned.

El-Nakhil Hotel   HOTEL $$
(Map p196; ☎231 3922, 0122 382 1007; www.el -nakhil.com; Al-Gezira; s/d/tr €25/35/40; ❋❋🛜) Nestled in a palm grove, the Nakhil or 'Palm Tree' is at the edge of Al-Gezira. This resort-style hotel has 17 spotless, well-finished domed rooms, all with private bathrooms and air-con. It also has family rooms, baby cots, and three rooms that can cater for disa-bled guests. There's a large restaurant on the splendid roof terrace with great views over the Nile.

House of Scorpion   GUESTHOUSE $$
(off Map p206; ☎0100 512 8732; tayeb.saket@ yahoo.com; Al-Taref; r E£240-280, ste E£400; ❋🛜) Charming little guesthouse in a mudbrick house with seven different rooms, all large with tiled bathrooms and small salons in Arab style. Tayeb, who runs the place, is very helpful and friendly. Another place away from the crowds that mainly works by word of mouth, but is worth seeking out.

Al-Gezira Hotel   HOTEL $
(Map p196; ☎231 0034; www.el-gezira.com; Gezira al-Bayrat; s/d/tr E£80/120/150; ❋🛜) Different in style, as it is in a modern building over-looking the lush and fertile agricultural land in the village of Gezira al-Bayrat, this hotel is very much a home away from home. It is actually home to quite a few archaeologists during the winter season, and the charming owners really make everyone feel welcome, so much so that the hotel is often full. The 11 cosy and homey rooms are pristine, all with private bathrooms, overlooking the lake or a dried-up branch of the Nile. Management and staff are friendly and efficient, and the upstairs rooftop restaurant, where breakfast is served, has great Nile views as well as cold beer (E£12) and good traditional Egyptian food (set menu E£40).

Kareem Hotel   HOTEL $$
(Map p196; ☎231 3530, 0100 184 2083; www.ho telkareemlxr.com; Al-Gezira; s/d/tr E£100/140/160, 3-room flat per week E£1000; ❋) Newly opened hotel with 12 simple but very clean rooms in a quiet residential area. The owner is young and helpful and keeps the place spotless. The hotel has little character otherwise but offers good value, and has a little garden and a splendid rooftop terrace with a restaurant where the owner's sister cooks dishes and where cool beers are served.

FLAT RENTAL

Families or those planning a prolonged stay in Luxor might consider a self-catering option. Flat rental is mushrooming in Luxor, on both banks; it is cheap, and many foreigners are getting involved in the business. The downside of self-catering is sex tourism, as there is very little control as to whom people can bring in, whereas in hotels foreigners are not allowed to take guests back to their room.

Several companies can arrange flat rentals, including **Flats in Luxor** (off Map p196; ☑ 010 356 4540; www.flatsinluxor.com; per week from £150; ❄ @ ☎), run by a British-Egyptian couple who started renting out their own flats but now also manage others. The websites www.luxor-westbank.com and www.luxor4flats.com also have a wide selection of flats and houses available.

Villa al Diwan (Map p196; ☑ 227 4852, 0100 160 1214; www.al-diwan.fr; Lagalta; from €700 a week; ❄ @ ☎) This wonderful five-bedroom rental villa in traditional style overlooks the Nile and easily accommodates 10 people. The well-appointed rooms are on the first floor, while the ground floor has a kitchen, dining and sitting room and a terrace garden with a new pool. The rooftop terrace is a great place to watch the Nile and the surrounding countryside. It's located on the waterfront on the west bank, about 10 minutes south of the ferry landing.

Marsam Hotel　　　　　　　　GUEST HOUSE **$**
(Map p206; ☑ 237 2403, 231 1603; www.luxor -westbank.com/marsam_e_az.htm; Old Gurna; s/d E£75/150, with shared bathroom E£50/100) Built for American archaeologists in the 1920s, the Marsam, formerly the Sheikh Ali Hotel, is the oldest on the west bank. The hotel is charming, with 30 simple rooms set around a lovely courtyard, with ceiling fans and traditional palm-reed beds. A delicious breakfast with home-baked bread is served in the garden. Atmospheric and quiet, and close to almost all the west bank sights, it is still popular with archaeologists, so you need to book ahead, particularly during the dig season (roughly from October to March).

Nour al-Gurna　　　　　　　　GUEST HOUSE **$$**
(Map p206; ☑ 231 1430, 010 0129 5812; Old Gurna; s E£150, d E£200-250, ste E£300) Set in a palm grove, Nour al-Gurna has large mudbrick rooms, with fans, mosquito nets, small stereos, locally made furniture and tiled bathrooms. Romantic and original, with friendly management, this is a lovely centrally located hotel convenient for visiting west bank sites.

Nour al-Balad　　　　　　　　GUEST HOUSE **$$**
(Map p206; ☑ 242 6111; Ezbet Bisily; s/d/ste E£200/250/300; ❄) The sister hotel to Nour al-Gurna is even quieter and has more spacious rooms. To get there, follow the track behind Medinat Habu for 500m.

✗ Eating

Most people come to Luxor for monuments and not for its fine cuisine – a good thing as most restaurants, particularly in the hotels, are pretty mediocre. However, the food is gradually getting better, with a few restaurants upping the standards by doing what Egyptians do best: cooking honest traditional Egyptian food. Outside of hotels, few places serve alcohol or accept credit-card payment; exceptions are noted in the reviews. Unless otherwise noted, restaurants tend to open from about 9am until midnight.

EAST BANK

TOP
CHOICE **Sofra**　　　　　　　　EGYPTIAN **$$**
(Map p196; ☑ 235 9752; www.sofra.com.eg; Sharia al-Mahdy, 90 Sharia Mohammed Farid; mains E£20-60; ⊙11am-midnight) Sofra remains our favourite restaurant in Luxor. Located in a 1930s house, away from all the tourist tat, it is as Egyptian as can be, in menu and decor, and even in price. The ground floor has three private dining rooms and a salon, giving the feeling of being in someone's home. There is also a wonderful rooftop terrace, which is also a cafe, where you can come for a drink. The house is filled with antique oriental furniture, chandeliers and traditional decorations, all simple but cosy and very tasteful. The menu is large, featuring all the traditional Egyptian dishes such as stuffed pigeon and excellent duck, as well as a large selection of salads, dips (E£4) and mezze. Alcohol is not available, but there are

delicious fresh juices on offer, and sheesha afterwards. It's a real treat, with very friendly staff, and has been recommended by many readers.

Oasis Café
MEDITERRANEAN $$

(Map p196; ☑0111 140 0557; Sharia Dr Labib Habashi; mains E£15-60; ◷10am-10pm; ✱) Originally set in a 1930s building right in the centre of town, the Oasis Café has now moved to a new location off Khaled Ibn Walid. The large room has less character than before, but the menu is the same, offering a regular menu of international dishes, including pastas (E£30 to E£40), grilled meats (E£45 to E£55), filling sandwiches (E£25), daily specials on the blackboard and a wide selection of pastries. This is a good place to recover from the bustle of Luxor town, from the heat or from sightseeing. The dining room is cool, with jazz playing softly, and the *New Yorker* and info about Luxor to read. It's the perfect place for lunch, to linger over a morning latte or to spend the afternoon reading. The place is very Western, but in a nice way like your favourite cafe back home. Beer and wine now available.

As-Sahaby Lane
EGYPTIAN $$

(Map p196; ☑236 5509; www.nefertitihotel.com/sahabi.htm; Sharia as-Sahaby, off Sharia as-Souq; mains E£35-60; ◷9am-11.30pm) Great easygoing alfresco restaurant in the lane running between the souq and the street to Karnak Temple. Fresh and well-prepared Egyptian dishes like *tagen* (stew cooked in earthenware pots) are served as well as good pizzas and salads. The young staff is very friendly, always ready to help or up for a chat. This terrace is a great place to watch the world go by, or relax from shopping in the souq. The same food is served on the hotel's rooftop terrace, with great views over Luxor Temple and the Thebes mountains, both floodlit at night.

Salahadeen
EGYPTIAN $$

(Map p196; ☑0100 757 1855; www.salahadeen.com; Mara Hotel, Sharia Salahadin Ayyubi, off Sharia Salakhana; dishes E£18-60; ◷6pm-midnight; ✱) Salahadeen offers a set menu, 'Salahadeen Feast' (E£100), which includes three courses with 15 dishes of fresh home-cooked Egyptian food to share. Most dishes consist of vegetables, and the vegetarian options are not cooked in a meat broth as in so many other places. The food is served as if it were an Egyptian home – knives and forks are offered but guests are encouraged to eat

in the Egyptian way by dipping bread in the various dishes. Dinner starts promptly at 7pm, but the bar opens for predinner drinks at 6pm; alcohol is also available in the restaurant.

Silk Road
ASIAN $$$

(off Map p196; ☑2374933; www.hilton.co.uk/luxor; New Karnak; dishes E£70-120; ◷Tue-Sun 10am-midnight; ✱) The Silk Road is arguably the most sophisticated dining experience in Luxor, offering an exotic cuisine, rich in spices, sourced from India, Thailand, China and all over Asia and prepared by the wonderful Indian chef. The setting is Asian minimal chic. If you are at a loss with the large-ish menu, ask for a degustation of several dishes (from E£240). Good wine list, and perfect for a romantic dinner.

Puddleduck
EGYPTIAN, EUROPEAN $$

(Map p196; ☑0160 716 8473; junction of Sharia St Joseph & al-Madina; www.puddleduck-restaurant.com; mains E£55-80; ◷5.30-10.30pm, last orders at 9.30pm, closed Wed; ✱) This small restaurant is consistently popular with foreign residents in the area, as well as with visitors, both for its cosy and friendly atmosphere, the personal service of British husband and wife team Jill and Mick, and its excellent food. The menu changes weekly, keeping some of the house favourites like roast beef with Yorkshire pudding, chicken-liver pâté and the notoriously good cheesecake. Dishes are mostly British or European, but the menu features a few well-prepared Egyptian dishes like *tagen*, and fresh fish is a speciality. Book ahead as it is very popular.

Gerda's Garden
EGYPTIAN, EUROPEAN $$

(off Map p196; ☑235 8688, 0122 5348 326; opp Hilton Luxor, New Karnak; www.luxor-german-restaurant.com; dishes E£15-45; ◷6.30-11pm; ✱) German-Egyptian run Gerda's Garden has built up a strong reputation over the last six years, and is very popular with European residents and regular visitors to Luxor. The decor is more provincial European bistro than Egyptian, but the menu features both Egyptian specials like kebab and delicious grilled pigeon, and very European comfort food for those slightly homesick, such as goulash and potato salad.

Jewel of the Nile
BRITISH, EGYPTIAN $$

(Map p196; ☑0106 252 2394; Sharia al-Rawda al-Sherifa, 300m off Sharia Khaled ibn al-Walid; mains E£30-45, set menu E£60-70; ◷10am-midnight winter, 1pm-midnight summer; ✱☏) Laura and

Mahmud offer traditional Egyptian food using organic vegetables from their own farm, as well as well-prepared British food for homesick Brits including steaks, cottage pie, apple crumble and an all-day English breakfast (E£25). On Sundays a traditional lunch is served all day with roast beef and Yorkshire pudding (E£50), and on Saturdays and Wednesdays at 5.30pm there is a popular quiz night in aid of local charities. The menu features a good selection of vegetarian dishes. You can dine in the small outside sitting area or the air-conditioned interior dining room. Alcohol available.

La Mama
ITALIAN **$$**

(off Map p196; ☎237 4544; Sheraton Luxor Resort, Sharia Khaled ibn al-Walid; dishes E£35-90; ☺10.30am-11pm) The Italian restaurant on the terrace overlooking a little pond with wading birds, at the entrance to the Sheraton, is a good bet, particularly if you've got kids in tow. The restaurant is decorated in 1970s style with red-and-white napkins, live Neapolitan music and a good selection of pizzas, pastas and mains, all served in clean five-star surroundings.

1886 Restaurant
MEDITERRANEAN **$$$**

(Map p196; ☎238 0422; Winter Palace Hotel, Corniche an-Nil; mains E£212-240; ☺7-11pm; ✳) The 1886 is the fancy restaurant in the town centre, serving inventive Mediterranean-French food and a few Egyptian dishes with a twist, all in a grand old-style dining room with very formal waiters. Guests are expected to dress up for the occasion – men wear a tie and/or jacket (some are available for borrowing) – and the food is superb and light. The menu changes with the seasons, but expect delicacies such as grilled spine lobster in a butter sauce, or risotto of prawns and truffle. A grand evening out!

A Taste of India
INDIAN **$$**

(Map p196; ☎0109 373 2727; Sharia St Joseph, off Sharia Khaled ibn al-Walid; dishes E£35-70; ☺noon-11pm; ✳) A small British-run Indian restaurant in neutral colours with plain wooden tables and chairs. On the menu are European versions of Indian dishes such as korma, spinach masala and *jalfrezi* (marinated meat curry with tomato, pepper and onion), as well as original Indian specials such as madras and vindaloo curries. For those not too fond of spice, a few international (read British) dishes such as steak and chips are available. The place is popular with expat

Brits and vegetarians who come for spicy vegetable dishes.

Abu Ashraf
EGYPTIAN FAST FOOD **$**

(Map p196; ☎237 5936; Sharia al-Mahatta; dishes E£4-15; ☺8am-11pm) This large, popular restaurant and takeaway is just down from the train station. It serves roasted chicken (E£16), pizzas (E£20), good *kushari* (noodles, rice, black lentils, fried onions and tomato sauce; E£4 to E£10) and kebabs (E£20).

Koshari Elzaeem
EGYPTIAN FAST FOOD **$**

(Map p196; Midan Hussain; ☺24hr) Popular *kushari* restaurant that also serves an Egyptian version of spaghetti (E£8 to E£20). There are a few tables but they fill up fast.

New Mish Mish
EGYPTIAN FAST FOOD **$$**

(☎228 1756, 0100 810 5862; Sharia Telvizyon; dishes E£5-30; ☺8am-midnight; ✳) A long-standing budget-traveller haunt, Mish Mish has a contemporary and air-conditioned fast-food-style interior, serving good sandwiches (E£5 to E£15), salads (E£5 to E£12), grilled meats (E£20 to E£30) including shwarma, mixed grill and stuffed pigeon, and good grilled and fried-fish dishes (E£22 to E£30). There's no alcohol, but there is a selection of fresh fruit juices (E£5).

WEST BANK

TOP CHOICE Al-Moudira
MEDITERRANEAN **$$$**

(off Map p206; ☎0120 325 1307; Daba'iyya; mains E£75-110; ☺8am-midnight) In keeping with its flamboyant decor, Al-Moudira has the most sophisticated and the most expensive food on the west bank, with great salads and grills at lunchtime and a more elaborate menu for dinner with delicious Mediterranean-Lebanese cuisine. This is a great place for a romantic dinner in the courtyard, or by the fire in the winter. Call ahead for reservations.

Restaurant Mohammed
EGYPTIAN **$$**

(Map p206; ☎0120 385 0227; Kom Lolah; set menu E£25-60) With an outdoor terrace and laid-back atmosphere, Mohammed's is the perfect place to recharge batteries in the middle of a day exploring temples and tombs, or to linger in the evening. This is a family affair, the restaurant being attached to the owner's mudbrick house; the charming Mohammed Abdel Lahi serves with his son Azab, while his wife cooks. The menu is small but includes meat grills, delicious chicken and duck as well as stuffed pigeon, served with

LITTLE BRITAIN

The area around the **Sonesta St George Hotel** (Map p196), on Sharia Khaled Ibn Walid, is slightly away from Luxor centre, but it has a large concentration of British pubs and restaurants. Every other restaurant is run by a British-Egyptian couple; most are clean and serve decent British-European food as well as a few Egyptian specialities. If you have had it with *kushari*, kebab or mezze, or are yearning for a good pizza, pasta or steak, then this is the place to head. **Puddleduck** (p234) is a favourite, but they are all quite similar. Roast beef with Yorkshire pudding is on most menus.

fries and excellent simple salads. Stella beer is available (E£12) as well as Egyptian wine. They can organise a picnic in the desert or on a felucca upon demand. Call ahead.

Nile Valley Hotel　　　EGYPTIAN, INTERNATIONAL **$$**
(Map p196; ☏231 1477; Al-Gezira; meals E£35-60; ☺8am-11pm) A popular rooftop restaurant with a bird's-eye view of the action along the west bank's waterfront and Luxor temple, the Nile Valley has a wide-ranging menu of Egyptian and international specialities, but is also a good place to relax with a cold beer (E£16).

Al-Gezira Hotel　　　　　　EGYPTIAN **$$**
(Map p196; ☏231 0034; Al-Gezira; set menu E£35) This comfortable rooftop restaurant serves a set menu with Egyptian specialities, such as the infamous *molokhiyya* (stewed leaf soup) and *mahshi kurumb* (stuffed cabbage leaves cooked with plenty of dill and semna) that must be ordered in advance. There are great views over the Nile and the bright lights of Luxor beyond. Cool beers are on offer (E£12) as well as Egyptian wine (E£85).

Memnon　　　　　　　　　　EGYPTIAN **$$**
(Map p206; ☏012 327 8747; opposite Colossi of Memnon; dishes E£25-50; ☺8am-11pm, later in summer) Excellent, laid-back restaurant with simple but very well-prepared Egyptian fare. If you want a change from that, there are some equally good Indian and Chinese dishes on the menu. Afterwards hang out and stare eternity in the face looking at the Colossi while smoking a sheesha. Leave some

space for the homemade mango sorbet; it's worth it.

Fruit & Vegetable Souq　　　MARKET **$**
(Map p196; Sharia as-Souq) This is the best place for fruit and veg, although the good stuff sells out early in the morning. On either side of the main street are little shops selling produce and groceries throughout the day.

Arkwrights Gourmet Food　　SUPERMARKET **$**
(Map p196; ☏228 2335, 0100 334 5312; Sharia St Joseph, off Sharia Khaled ibn al-Walid, near St Joseph Hotel; ☺6am-midnight) Great food store with fresh fruits and vegetables, freshly made breads and a large selection of Egyptian and imported food products. The quality of the produce is high, and this is the place to stock up for a more sophisticated picnic, as they recently started doing packed lunches – freshly made sandwiches and salads to take away.

Cheap Eats
Luxor has a number of good **bakeries**. Try the ones on Sharia Ahmed Orabi, at the beginning of Sharia Maabad al-Karnak and on Sharia Gedda (both on Map p196). On the west bank try the food and fruit shops on the main street in Al-Gezira, or head for the wonderful weekly market **Souq at-Talaat** (Map p206; ☺Tue mornings), in Taref opposite the Temple of Seti I.

Drinking
EAST BANK
Metropolitan Café & Restaurant　　BAR
(Map p196; lower level, Corniche an-Nil) A pleasant, popular outdoor cafe, right on the Nile, in front of the Winter Palace Hotel. Beers (Stella E£15) and a wide selection of cocktails are available, served on a terrace with rattan furniture and mist machines. The perfect place to enjoy a sundowner, but apart from some snacks with the drinks, the food is pretty mediocre.

New Oum Koulsoum
Coffee Shop　　　　　　　COFFEEHOUSE
(Map p196; Sharia as-Souq; ☺24hr) Pleasant *ahwa* (coffeehouse) right in the heart of the souq, on a large terrace with welcoming mist machines, where you can recover from shopping and haggling and watch the crowds without any hassle. On the menu are fresh juices (E£10 to E£20), hot and cold drinks and a good sheesha (E£10), as well as 'professional Nespresso' coffee (E£15).

Chez Omar
COFFEEHOUSE

(Map p196; Sharia Youssef Hassan) This relaxed cafe terrace in a small garden off the main souq, with bamboo furniture, is perfect to take a break from the buzz around. A good place to have a fresh juice, smoke a sheesha or eat a snack. Inside is Chez Omar II, a cool laid-back eatery with Egyptian dishes like kebab and pigeon stew (E£30).

Kings Head Pub
PUB

(Map p196; ✆228 0489; Sharia Khaled ibn al-Walid; ✼) A relaxed and perennially popular place to have a drink and shoot pool, the Kings Head tries to capture the atmosphere of an English pub without being twee. The laid-back atmosphere also means that women can come here without being harassed.

Cocktail Sunset
COCKTAIL BAR

(Map p196; ✆238 0524; ✼) On a pontoon, which rumour has it once belonged to King Farouk's father, on the Nile, this place is hugely popular for its congenial atmosphere, cocktails and ice-cold beers, particularly at sunset. The Sunset was closed at the time of writing, but said to reopen November 2011.

Al-Ahram Beverages
LIQUOR STORE $

(Map p196; ✆237 2445; Sharia Ramses) This is the Luxor outlet for the country's monopoly beer and wine producer.

WEST BANK
There are no real bars on the west bank; drinking is done at restaurants or not at all.

Maratonga Cafeteria
CAFE

(Map p206; ✆231 0233; Kom Lolah; ⊙6am-11pm) This friendly outdoor cafe-restaurant, in front of Medinat Habu, is the best place to sip a cold drink under a big tree after wandering through Ramses III's magnificent temple, or to have a delicious *tagen* (E£35) or salad for lunch. The view is superlative and the atmosphere is relaxing.

Ramesseum Rest House
CAFE

(Map p206; beside the Ramesseum, Gurna) A friendly, laid-back place to relax after temple viewings. In addition to the usual mineral water and soft drinks, beer is sometimes available.

☆ Entertainment

EAST BANK
With tourism booming in Luxor, the town is busy at night. The Temple of Luxor is open until 10pm and worth seeing at night; the souq is open late as well and more lively at night than in the day. In summer lots of locals stroll along the Corniche. Rumour has it that the sights will soon stay open longer so tourists can avoid the heat of the day for visits.

However, this is not exactly the place for clubbing, even if you're into dancing to outmoded disco music. There are some bars with decent atmosphere, and most of the larger hotels put on a folkloric show several times each week, depending on the season and number of tour groups around.

The discos are at **Tutotel Partner Hotel** (Map p196; ✆237 7990), one of the more popular options, and at **Hotel Mercure** (Map p196; ✆238 0944). They were closed at the time of writing and might reopen when there is more stability.

WEST BANK
If you want to avoid the bright lights of the town, the west bank is the place to be. **Nobi's Arabian Horse Stables** (p227) and **QEA Travel Agency** (p227) arrange evening desert barbecues for groups of 10 or more and sometimes put on a horse-dancing show.

Shopping

A whole range of Egyptian souvenirs are available in Luxor town, but for alabaster it is best to head for the west bank. The alabaster is mined about 80km northwest of the Valley of the Kings, and although the alabaster factories near the Ramesseum and Deir al-Bahri sell cheap handmade cups, vases and lights in the shape of Nefertiti's head, it is possible to find higher-quality bowls and vases, often unpolished, which are great buys. Take care when buying, as sometimes what passes for stone is actually wax with stone chips. Avoid going with a tour guide as his commission will invariably be added to your bill.

The *tagen* (clay pots) that are used in local cooking make a more unusual buy. Very practical, they can be used to cook on top of the stove or in the oven and they look good on the table too. Prices start at E£8 for a very small pot and go up to about E£40. They're on sale on the street just beside the police station in Luxor's east bank.

Habiba
CRAFT

(Map p196; ✆235 7305, 0100 124 2026; www.habibagallery.com; Sharia Sidi Mahmoud, off Sharia as-Souq; ⊙10am-10pm) Run by an Australian woman who loves to travel in Egypt and who wants to promote the best of Egyptian crafts, this tiny shop goes from strength to strength. It sells an ever-expanding selection of Bedouin embroidery, jewellery, leather work, wonderful Siwan scarves, cotton embroidered scarves from Sohag, the best Egyptian cotton towels (usually only for export), mirrors and brass lights – and all at fair-trade fixed prices. A world away from what is available in the nearby souq.

Another **branch** (off Map p196; Sharia Hilton; ◎10am-10pm) has opened in New Karnak near the Luxor Hilton.

Fair Trade Centre CRAFT
(Map p196; ✆236 0870, 0100 034 7900; www.egypt fairtrade.org; Sharia Maabad al-Karnak; ◎9am-10.30pm) A nonprofit shop that markets handicrafts from NGO projects throughout Egypt. It has a good selection of well-priced hand-carved wood and pottery from the nearby villages of Hejaza and Garagos, aromatic oils from Quz, beadwork from Sinai and hand-blown glass, Akhmim table linen, beading from the west bank in Luxor, recycled glass and recycled paper from Cairo. Another **branch** (Map p196; Sharia Maabad Luxor, next to McDonalds; ◎9am-10.30pm) has opened behind Luxor Temple.

Beit al Ayn JEWELLERY
(Map p196; ✆0122 107 9735; Sharia al-Gawazat, off Khaled Ibn Walid; ◎10am-10pm) Large shop filled with a huge selection of silver, mainly unusual tribal Nubian and Bedouin jewellery.

Duty Free Shop Luxor LIQUOR STORE
(Map p196; ✆237 6331; Sharia Yousef Hassan, off Sharia Maabad al-Karnak; ◎10am-2pm & 7-11pm) Shop for cigarettes and alcohol at the downtown duty free, which has a good selection of the main brands. You have to purchase within 48 hours of arrival and have your passport.

Caravanserai CRAFT
(Map p206; ✆0122 327 8771; www.caravan serailuxor.com; Kom Lolah, west bank; ◎8am-10pm) This delightful shop, the only one of its kind on the west bank, is kept by the friendly Hamdi and his family in a beautifully painted mudbrick house near Medinat Habu. He began travelling around Egypt and realised that making crafts was one of the few things poor people could do to earn money, so he decided to set up shop to encourage and help them, the women in particular. Hamdi buys almost everything

people make, telling them what sells well, suggesting ways of improving their goods; above all he loves the people's creativity. The shop has beautiful pottery from the Western Oases, Siwan embroideries, amazing appliqué bags and lots of other crafts that can be found almost nowhere else in Egypt.

AA Gaddis Bookshop SOUVENIRS, BOOKS
(Map p196; ✆238 7042; Corniche an-Nil; www.gad dis-and-co.co.uk; ◎10am-9pm Mon-Sat, 10.30am-9pm Sun, closed Jun & Jul) Next door to the Winter Palace Hotel; extensive selection of books on Egypt, postcards and souvenirs.

Aboudi Bookshop BOOKS
(Map p196; ✆237 2390, 0111 117 4764; www.aboudi -bookstore.com; Sharia Maabad al-Karnak, behind Luxor Temple; ◎9.30am-10pm) Has an excellent selection of guidebooks, English-language books on Egypt and the Middle East, maps, postcards and fiction.

Aboudi Bookshop BOOKS
(Map p196; ✆237 3390, 213 9117; off Sharia Khaled Ibn al-Walid, behind the passport office; ◎9.30am-10pm) Part of the same family as the previous store, this bookshop also has an great selection of English-language books on Egypt and the Middle East, maps and postcards.

❶ Information

Dangers & Annoyances
Luxor is often considered the hassle capital of Egypt, and sadly at the time of writing that is more true than ever, as there is so little business around since the 2011 revolution. The situation was compounded by some hotels warning their clients not to venture outside the hotel. The city's many calèche (horse-drawn carriage) drivers can be particularly aggressive, as there is so little business, and they still need to feed their horses, most of which are quite malnourished. There is no reason not to go out, but it pays to understand the difficult financial situation that Egypt, and particularly Luxor, is in.

The most common scams are asking for extra baksheesh at the monuments, overcharging for a calèche or felucca, charging European prices for taxi rides, and touts in the souq or station targeting new arrivals. A frequent scam is for taxi or calèche drivers to tell tourists there is a local souq that is less touristy than the souq behind the Luxor Temple. They then drive around town and pull up at the same old souq. The tourist office or the tourist police will need a written report from you if anything happens, and will try to take action.

In recent years Luxor has also become a known destination for female sex tourism, popular with some often-older Western women looking for sex with young Egyptians. Individual women travellers looking for nothing more risqué than an ancient temple or a desert sunset can find themselves seriously hassled.

Emergency
Ambulance (⌨123)

Police (Map p196; ⌨122, 237 2350; cnr Sharia Maabad al-Karnak & Sharia al-Matafy)

Tourist police (Map p196; ⌨237 6820; Corniche an-Nil; ⊙8am-3pm, 8pm-midnight) On the walkway below the Corniche, opposite the Winter Palace Hotel.

Internet Access

You can find internet access everywhere in Luxor. Many hotels now also have wi-fi, and it's mostly free in budget and midrange hotels. Prices in internet cafes range from E£4 to E£10 per hour.

Gamil Centre (Map p196; lower level, Corniche an-Nil; ⊙24hr) In front of the Winter Palace Hotel.

Heroes Internet (Map p196; Sharia Televizyon; ⊙24hr)

Lotus Internet Café (Map p196; ⌨238 0419; Sharia as-Souq; ⊙9am-midnight) Located next door to the restaurant.

Salem Net (Map p196; ⌨236 4652; ⊙24hr) Good connection and air-conditioned room next to the train station, opposite the Anglo Hotel.

Medical Services
Dr Boutros (Map p206; ⌨231 0851; Kom Lolah) Excellent English- and French-speaking doctor, who works on the west bank.

Dr Ihab Rizk (⌨0122 216 0846) English-speaking cardiologist, who will come to your hotel, on the east bank.

International Hospital (Map p196; ⌨228 0192/4; Sharia Televizyon) The best place in town.

Money

Most major Egyptian banks have branches in Luxor. Unless otherwise noted, usual opening hours are 8.30am to 2pm and 5pm to 6pm Sunday to Thursday. ATMs can be found all over town, including at most banks and five-star hotels.

American Express (Map p196; ⌨237 8333; Corniche an-Nil; ⊙9am-4.30pm) Beside the entrance to the Winter Palace Hotel.

HSBC (Map p196; Corniche an-Nil) Near Hotel Iberotel.

Banque du Caire (Map p196; Corniche an-Nil) Near the Winter Palace Hotel and Egyptair.

Banque Misr (Map p196; Corniche an-Nil) Near Luxor Hilton Hotel.

Broxelles Exchange (Map p196; ⌨237 1300; Sharia al-Mahatta; ⊙9am-9pm) Better exchange rates than the bank.

National Bank of Egypt (Map p196; Corniche an-Nil) Near the Winter Palace Hotel and Egyptair.

Thomas Cook (Map p196; ⌨237 2196; Corniche an-Nil; ⊙8am-8pm) Below entrance to Winter Palace Hotel.

Post
Main post office (Map p196; Sharia al-Mahatta; ⊙8.30am-2.30pm Sat-Thu)

Telephone

There are card phones scattered throughout the town. Cards are available from kiosks and shops. There are several mobile-phone shops on Sharia al-Mahatta and Sharia Televizyon that sell cheap tourist SIM cards.

Telephone office (Map p196; Corniche an-Nil; ⊙8am-8pm) Below the entrance to Winter Palace Hotel.

Tourist Information
Airport office (off Map p196; ⌨237 2306; ⊙8am-8pm)

Main tourist office (Map p196; Midan al-Mahatta; ⊙8am-8pm) Very helpful and well-informed tourist information opposite the train station. There is also an office for hotel bookings, tours and tickets for the sound and light show in Karnak.

Train station office (Map p196; ⌨237 0259; ⊙8am-8pm)

❶ Getting There & Away
Air
EgyptAir (Map p196; ⌨238 0581; Corniche an-Nil; ⊙8am-8pm) Egypt Air normally operates flights to Cairo, Abu Simbel (via Aswan) and Sharm el-Sheikh. But at the time of writing, due to low volume, there were flights only to Cairo. A one-way ticket to Cairo costs between E£450 and E£720. Even if service is restored, the Abu Simbel flight is hardly worthwhile, as it involves a long wait in Aswan.

Bus
The **ZANAKTA bus station** (⌨237 2118, 232 3218) is out of town on the road to the airport, about 1km from the airport. A taxi from the town to the bus station will cost around E£25 to E£35.

Tickets for the **Upper Egypt Bus Co** (Map p196; ⌨232 3218, 237 2118; Midan al-Mahatta) buses can be bought at its office in town, just south of the train station. Some buses leave from there as well.

Buses heading to Cairo leave at 6.30pm from the town office and 7pm from the bus station (E£100, 10 to 11 hours), but booking ahead is essential.

Five daily buses head from the bus station to Hurghada (E£35 to E£40, five hours) from 8.30am to 8pm. All stop in Qena (E£8, one to two hours) and Safaga (E£30 to E£35, four to 4½ hours) and go on to Suez (E£70 to E£80, 10 hours).

For Al-Quseir and Marsa Alam, change at Safaga. A bus to Sharm el-Sheikh (E£130, 12 hours) and Dahab (E£140, 17 to 16 hours) leaves at 4.30pm from the town office via Suez. It is often full so try to reserve in advance.

There are frequent buses to Qena (E£5 to E£7) between 6.30am and 8pm, but you pay for the taxi to get to the bus station so it's cheaper to take the service taxi. There is a daily bus to Port Said at 7.30pm (E£80, 12 hours) via Ismailia (E£75).

To go to the Western Desert oases take a train to Asyut, from where there are several buses a day to Kharga (E£18) and Dakhla (E£30). At the time of writing there were no buses between Luxor and Aswan.

Super Jet (236 7732) runs buses from Luxor bus station at 8pm to Cairo (E£130, eight to nine hours) via Hurghada (E£45, four hours).

Cruise Ship or Dahabiyya

For information on the many cruise boats and increasing number of dahabiyyas (houseboats) that ply the Nile between Luxor and Aswan see p34 and p33.

Felucca

You can't take a felucca from Luxor to Aswan; most feluccas leave from Esna because of the Esna Lock. But unless you have a strong wind, it can take days to go more than a few kilometres in this direction. For more information, see p32.

Servees & Microbus

The station for service taxis and microbuses (Map p196) on the east bank is behind the train station. Foreigners can take service taxis from Luxor to Aswan (E£18 to E£20) via Esna (E£5), Edfu (E£9), Kom Ombo (E£15), Hurghada (E£20) and Qena (E£4). There is no service to Asyut. The drivers are always ready to privatise the car to make special trips up the Nile to Aswan, stopping at the sights on the way; expect to pay about E£450 to E£500. To Asyut or to Hurghada, the going rate is about E£450. It is possible to take a private service taxi to Kharga via the direct road, avoiding Asyut, at E£700 for the car (maximum seven people).

Train

Luxor Station (Map p196; 237 2018; Midan al-Mahatta) has left-luggage facilities, plenty of cardphones and a post office.

The **Watania Egypt Sleeping Train** (237 2015, in Cairo 02 3748 9488; www.wataniasleep ingtrains.com) goes daily to Cairo at 7.15pm and 10.30pm (single/double including dinner and breakfast US$80/120, child four to 19 years US$45, nine hours). No student discounts; tickets must be paid for in US dollars or euros.

For day trains headed north to Cairo (1st/2nd class E£90/46), the best are 981, at 8.25am, stopping at Qena (for Dendara; 1st/2nd class E£28/19), Balyana (for Abydos; E£34/21, three hours) and Asyut (for the Western Desert; E£53/30).The slower 983 leaves at 10.30am, and the 935 at noon.

There are several trains daily to Aswan (adult 1st/2nd class E£41/25, student 1st/2nd class E£32/20, three hours): the 996 at 7.30am, the 1902 at 9.30am and the 980 at 6pm, as well as to Cairo (1st/2nd class E£90/46): the 981 at 8.45am, the 983 at 10.30am, the 935 at noon, the 887 at 6.25pm, the 977 at 7pm, the 1903 at 7.45pm, the 997 at 11.10pm and the 989 at midnight. All train tickets are best bought in advance, but if you buy your ticket on the train there is a surplus of E£6.

Getting Around

To/From the Airport

Luxor airport is 7km east of town. There is no longer an official price for taxis from Luxor airport into town, so the drivers set their prices, often about E£70 to E£100 or more. Quite often there is not enough work for all the drivers, so when you try and take a taxi, a fight between drivers may erupt. In short, it is a major hassle, so if you want peace of mind ask the hotel to arrange your transfer. There is no bus between the airport and the town.

Bicycle

The compact town lends itself to cycling, and distances on the generally flat west bank are just far enough to provide some exercise but not be exhausting (except when the weather is too hot). Cycling at night is inadvisable given the local habit of leaving car headlights off while driving.

Many hotels rent out bikes. Expect to pay from E£12 to E£15 per day and choose carefully – there's nothing worse than getting stuck with a broken chain halfway to the Valley of the Kings. A good place to rent is from restaurant **7 days 7 ways** (off Map p196; 012 020 1876; www.rentabikeluxor.com/en; Sharia Sheraton; 8am-11pm), which also organises cycling tours around Luxor.

You can take bikes across to the west bank on the *baladi* ferry (p239). If you're based on the west bank, there are several bike rentals near the ferry landing, or ask at your hotel.

Felucca

There is a multitude of feluccas to take you on short trips around Luxor, leaving from various points all along the river. How much you pay depends on your bargaining skills, but expect about E£20 to E£40 for an hour of sailing.

Hantour

Also called a *calèche,* horse-drawn carriages cost about E£20 to E£50 per hour depending on your haggling skills (this is where you really need them). Expect to pay about E£20 to get to Karnak.

Pick-up Taxis

Kabout (pick-up trucks) and microbuses are often the quickest and easiest way to get about in Luxor. They ply fixed routes and will stop whenever flagged down. To get to the Temples of Karnak, take a microbus from Luxor station or from behind Luxor Temple for 50pt. Other routes run inside the town. For information about west bank–bound pick-up trucks, see p239.

Taxi

There are plenty of taxis in Luxor, but passengers still have to bargain hard for trips. A short trip around town is likely to cost at least E£10. Taxis can also be hired for day trips around the west bank; expect to pay E£150 to E£250, depending on the length of the excursion and your bargaining skills.

Nile Valley: Esna to Abu Simbel

Best Places to Stay

» Sofitel Old Cataract Hotel & Spa (p261)
» Eskaleh (p277)
» Philae Hotel (p262)
» Beit al-Kerem (p262)
» Nile Hotel (p262)

Best Activities

» Sail in a dahabiyya (p33)
» Go birdwatching in Aswan (p260)
» Take a felucca trip around the islands in Aswan (p260)
» Visit the camel market in Daraw (p252)
» Go fishing on Lake Nasser (p35)

Why Go

The Nile, south of Luxor, is increasingly hemmed in by the Eastern Desert, its banks lined with grand, well-preserved Graeco-Roman temples at Esna, Edfu and Kom Ombo, its lush fields punctuated by palm-backed villages – it's the ideal place to glide through on a Nile sailing boat. The once-great city of Al-Kab provides the perfect contrast to the grandeur of the temples, while at Gebel Silsila the river passes through a gorge, which made it a sacred site to the ancients, who used the quarry to built the temples in Luxor. Aswan, the ancient ivory-trading post, has a laid-back atmosphere and plenty of things to see.

South of Aswan, the land is dominated by Lake Nasser, the world's largest artificial lake. On its shores is one of ancient Egypt's most awesome structures: the Great Temple of Ramses II at Abu Simbel.

When to Go
Aswan

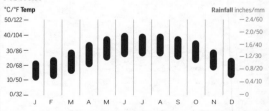

May–mid-Oct The long summers are unbearably hot in Aswan – temperatures soar well above 40°C.

Oct–Nov & Mar–Apr The best months to visit, with warm days and cooler nights.

Dec–Feb Days can occasionally be grey, and it can be too cold at night to make the most of a cruise.

Nile Valley: Esna to Abu Simbel Highlights

❶ Marvel at the perfectly carved walls of the most completely preserved temple in Egypt, at **Edfu** (p247)

❷ Discover where the pharaohs found blocks to build ancient Thebes, at the quarries of **Gebel Silsila** (p250)

❸ Sit on the terrace of Aswan's **Old Cataract Hotel**

and watch the feluccas sail by (p261)

❹ Sense the vanity of Ramses II in the awe-inspiring **Great Temple of Abu Simbel** (p275)

❺ Wander around the little visited ruins of **Abu** on **Elephantine Island** (p256)

❻ Take a boat out to the marvellous **Temple of Isis** at **Philae** (p267)

❼ Stroll through the botanical gardens of **Kitchener's Island** in the afternoon sun (p258)

❽ See the unusual double **Temple of Kom Ombo** in the morning light (p251)

History

The Nile Valley between Luxor and Aswan was the homeland of the vulture and crocodile gods, a place of harsh nature and grand landscapes. Its cult places, centres such as Al-Kab and Kom al-Ahmar, date back to the earliest periods of Egyptian history – it was here that the Narmer Palette, the object around which the origins of the 1st dynasty have been constructed, was found; here that one of the earliest-known Egyptian temples, made of wood not stone, was found; and here that Lascaux-type rock carvings (see boxed text p250) have opened a window onto Egypt's remotest past.

Yet most of what one can see between Luxor and Aswan dates from the last period of ancient Egyptian history, when the country was ruled by the descendants of Alexander the Great's Macedonian general, Ptolemy I (323–283 BC). They ruled for some 300 years, respecting the country's ancient traditions and religion and setting an example to the Romans who succeeded them.

Although they were based in Alexandria and looked out to the Mediterranean, the Ptolemies pushed their way south into Nubia, the land that straddled what is now the border between Egypt and Sudan. They ensured peaceful rule in Upper Egypt by erecting temples in honour of the local gods, building in grand Pharaonic style to appease the priesthood and earn the trust of the people. The riverside temples at Esna, Edfu, Kom Ombo and Philae are as notable for their strategic locations, on ancient trade routes or key commercial centres, as for their artistic or architectural merit.

Aswan's history was always going to be different. However much the rulers in the north, whether Theban or Macedonian, may have wanted to ignore the south, they dared not neglect their southern border. Settlement on Elephantine Island, located in the middle of the Nile at Aswan, dates back to at least 3000 BC. Named Abu (Ivory) after the trade that flourished here, it was a natural fortress positioned just north of the First Nile Cataract, one of six sets of rapids that blocked the river between Aswan and Khartoum. At the beginning of Egypt's dynastic history, in the Old Kingdom (2686–2125 BC), Abu became capital of the first Upper Egyptian nome (province) and developed into a thriving economic and religious centre, its strategic importance underlined by the title accorded to its rulers, Keepers of the Gate of the South. By the end of ancient history, with Egypt part of a larger Roman Empire, the southern frontier town was seen as a place of exile for anyone from the north who stepped out of line.

Climate

Heading south from Luxor, the fertile, green Nile Valley narrows considerably and becomes more and more enclosed by the desert. The climate also changes and becomes increasingly desertlike, with mostly warm, dry days in winter (December to February) – with an average temperature of about 26°C during the day – but often surprisingly cold nights. Summer (June to August) days are dry but often very hot, with temperatures hovering between 38°C and 45°C, making it difficult to visit sights outdoors. At the height of summer, temperatures hardly seem to drop during the night.

❶ Getting There & Away

At the time of research there were no buses between Aswan and Luxor. There are several trains daily between Luxor and Aswan, which preferably should be booked in advance, although tickets are for sale on board for an extra E£6. *Servees* (service taxis) and minibuses run regularly between the two cities and are now the best way of going overland to the places in between. But the most inspiring way of seeing this part of the country is the slow way, sailing a felucca (traditional canvas-sailed boat) or a dahabiyya (houseboat), taking in the sights and the most glorious stretch of river.

There is still a convoy system in place between Aswan and Abu Simbel, and foreigners are only allowed to travel by bus, taxi or minibus in an armed convoy that leaves twice a day. The other option is to fly, or to take a cruise on Lake Nasser.

❶ Getting Around

Foreigners are no longer restricted from travelling between towns in the far south of Egypt, except for Aswan to Abu Simbel. *Servees* and minibuses run between the towns, but the *servees* station is often outside the town, and/or a few kilometres away from the sights. The easiest way to visit the sights between Luxor and Aswan is to either privatise a taxi for a day and visit sights en route, or to privatise a taxi once you are in the town and want to go to the sight. Security tightens inevitably if there has been any kind of incident in the town, even if it's not necessarily related to tourists or terrorism.

SOUTHERN UPPER EGYPT

Esna

📞 095 / POP 67,217

Most visitors come to Esna, 64km south of Luxor on the west bank of the Nile, for the Temple of Khnum, but the busy little farming town itself is quite charming. Beyond the small bazaar selling mainly tourist souvenirs are several examples of 19th-century provincial architecture with elaborate *mashrabiyya* (wooden lattice screens). Immediately north of the temple is the beautiful but run-down **Ottoman caravanserai**, the Wekalat al-Gedawi, once the commercial centre of Esna. Merchants from Sudan, Somalia and central Africa stayed on the 2nd floor here, and a market was held regularly in the courtyard, with Berber baskets, Arab glue, ostrich feathers and elephant tusks all for sale. Opposite the temple is the **Emari minaret** from the Fatimid period, one of the oldest in Egypt, which escaped the mosque's demolition in 1960. An old oil mill, in the covered souq south of the temple, presses lettuce-seed into oil, a powerful aphrodisiac since ancient times.

Esna was until the early 20th century an important stop on the camel-caravan route between Sudan and Cairo, and between the Western Desert oases and the Nile Valley. It is now also known for the two Esna locks on the Nile, where cruise boats have to queue up to pass. The town makes for a pleasant morning excursion from Luxor, or a stop en route from Luxor to Aswan.

The **tourist police office** (📞 240 0686) is in the tourist souq near the temple, and there is a busy **souq**, particularly Monday, beside the canal.

◎ Sights

Temple of Khnum   TEMPLE
(adult/student E£20/15; ◷6am-5pm) The Ptolemaic-Roman Temple of Khnum is situated about 200m from the boat landing, at the end of the tourist souq. The temple today sits in a 9m-deep pit, which represents 15 centuries of desert sand and debris, accumulated since it was abandoned during the Roman period. Most of the temple, which was similar in size to the temples of Edfu and Dendara, is still covered. All that was excavated in the 1840s, what you see now, is the Roman hypostyle hall.

Esna

Esna

◎ Sights

1 19th-Century Houses	B5
2 Caravanserai	B5
3 Emari Minaret	B5
4 Monday Souq	A2
5 Monday Souq	A1
6 Temple of Khnum	B5

◉ Drinking

7 Coffeehouses	B5

BROUGHT BACK TO LIFE

Most Egyptian temples were once as colourful as the tombs in Luxor. Their walls, pillars and ceilings were completely painted. It was long believed that the colours had been lost to time and the abrasive winds. But ongoing work inside the hypostyle hall at the Temple of Khnum shows that the colours are still there. Using a cocktail of chemicals, archaeologists have delicately removed millennia of dust and dirt to confirm that all figures were completely painted and all backgrounds were white. There is now a debate among Egyptologists as to whether the entire temple – and other temples – should be restored, or whether the majority should be left covered, and therefore protected, for future generations.

Khnum was the ram-headed creator god who fashioned humankind on his potter's wheel using Nile clay. Construction of the temple dedicated to him was started, on the site of an earlier temple, by Ptolemy VI Philometor (180–145 BC). The Romans added the hypostyle hall that can be visited today, with well-preserved carvings from as late as the 3rd century AD. A quay connecting the temple to the Nile was built by Marcus Aurelius (AD 161–180).

The central doorway leads into the dark, atmospheric vestibule, where the roof is supported by 18 columns with wonderfully varied floral capitals in the form of palm leaves, lotus buds and papyrus fans; some also have bunches of grapes, a distinctive Roman touch. The roof is decorated with astronomical scenes, while the pillars are covered with hieroglyphic accounts of temple rituals. Inside the front corners, beside the smaller doorways, are two hymns to Khnum. The first is a morning hymn to awaken Khnum in his shrine, and the second is a wonderful 'hymn of creation' that acknowledges him as creator of all, even foreigners: 'All are formed on his potter's wheel, their speech different in every region but the lord of the wheel is their father too.'

On the walls, Roman emperors dressed as pharaohs make offerings to the local gods of Esna. The northern wall has scenes of the ruler catching fish in a papyrus thicket with the god Khnum, and next to this the emperor presents the temple to Khnum.

The back wall, to the northeast, the only remaining part of the original Ptolemaic temple, features reliefs of two Ptolemaic pharaohs, Ptolemy VI Philometor and Ptolemy VIII Euergetes (170–116 BC). A number of Roman emperors, including Septimus Severus, Caracalla and Geta, added their names near the hall's rear gateway.

✖ Eating & Drinking

Few people linger in Esna, as most stop here on the road between Luxor and Aswan. There is nowhere to stay but there are a few ahwas (coffeehouses) with a terrace, serving drinks and some basic food, opposite the temple.

❶ Getting There & Away

Trains are a pain because the train station is on the opposite (east) bank of the Nile, away from the town centre, but kabouts (pickup trucks) go back and forth between the two. The busy kabout station is beside the canal, and a block further north is the servees and minibus station. A seat in a servees or minibus to Luxor is E£5, to Edfu E£4.50 and to Aswan E£12. Arrivals are generally dropped off on the main thoroughfare into town along which hantour (horse-drawn carriage) drivers congregate in the hope of picking up a fare. They ask E£50 for the five- to 10-minute ride to the temple and return.

Al-Kab & Kom al-Ahmar

Between Esna and Edfu are the ruins of two settlements, both dating back more than 3000 years, with traces of even earlier habitation.

Originally known as Nekheb, Al-Kab was one of the most important sites of ancient Egypt as it was the home of Nekhbet, the vulture goddess of Upper Egypt, one of two goddesses who protected the pharaoh right back to the Old Kingdom. The ancient town is still being excavated and recorded, so is off limits, but then there isn't much to see of the town above ground apart from the impressive remains of the 12m-thick mud-brick walls that once surrounded it. The ones that stand now date back to the Late Period (747–332 BC). The oldest of the sandstone temples within the walls, dedicated to the god Thoth, was built by Ramses II (1279–1213

BC) and the adjoining Temple of Nekhbet was built during the Late Period, both reusing blocks from much earlier temples from the Early Dynastic Period (from c 3100 BC) and the Middle Kingdom (2055–1650 BC). To the northwest of the walls is an Old Kingdom cemetery.

Across the road, cut into the hill at the edge of the valley, are the **tombs** (adult/ student E£30/20) of New Kingdom (1550–1069 BC) local governors. The most important is the Tomb of Ahmose (number 2), the 'Captain-General of Sailors', who fought under Pharaoh Ahmose I (1550–1525 BC). Another Ahmose, son of Ebana, left a detailed account of his bravery in the battle against the Hyksos.

From here, if you have transport you can go further east to see several temples dedicated to Nubian gods. A Ptolemaic temple has a staircase going up to two columned vestibules before a chapel carved into the rock. South of there is a small chapel, locally known as Al-Hammam (The Bathhouse), built by Setau, Viceroy of Nubia under Ramses II. At the centre of the wadi is a large vulture-shaped crag covered in inscriptions from predynastic times to the Old Kingdom. Some 3.5km further east into the desert is the small chapel of Nekhbet, built by Amenhotep III (1390–1352 BC) as a way station for the vulture goddess's cult statue when she passed through 'The Valley'. Her protective influence was no doubt appreciated, as this was one of the supply routes to the goldmines that gave Egypt much of its wealth.

Across the river lies **Kom al-Ahmar** (closed to the public), ancient Nekhen or Hierakonpolis, home of the falcon god Nekheny, an early form of Horus. Although little remains of what was one of Egypt's most important cities in predynastic times, recent excavations have revealed a large settlement (with Egypt's earliest brewery!), a predynastic cemetery dating from around 3400 BC with elephant and cattle burials, together with the site of Egypt's earliest-known temple, a large timber-framed structure fronted by 12m-high imported wood pillars. A century ago, within this sacred enclosure, archaeologists discovered a range of ritual artefacts, among them two items of huge historical significance: the Narmer Palette and a superb gold falcon head of the god Horus, both now in Cairo's Egyptian Museum.

❶ Getting There & Away

Al-Kab and Kom al-Ahmar are 26km south of Esna. The best way of seeing Al-Kab is to take a private taxi from Esna or Edfu, or on the way from Luxor to Aswan or vice versa. Dahabiyyas and some feluccas from Aswan to Esna (see p30 for more information) stop here too, but not the bigger cruise boats.

Edfu

☑097 / POP 69,000

Built on a rise above the broad river valley, the Temple of Horus at Edfu, having escaped destruction from Nile floods, is the most completely preserved Egyptian temple. One of the last ancient attempts at building on a grand scale, the temple dominates this west-bank town, 53km south of Esna. The temple's well-preserved reliefs have provided archaeologists with much valuable informa-

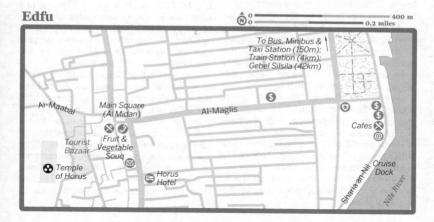

Edfu

tion about the temple rituals and the power of the priesthood. Walking through the large, gloomy chambers, visitors are sometimes overwhelmed by a sense of awe at the mysteries of ancient Egypt.

Modern Edfu, a centre for sugar and pottery, is a friendly, buzzing provincial centre. Although it is an agricultural town, tourism is the biggest money-earner and almost everyone seems to have an interest in the tourist shops, which all visitors must brave in order to reach the temple.

⊙ Sights

Temple of Horus
TEMPLE

(adult/student E£50/25; ⊘7am-7pm) Edfu was a settlement and cemetery site from around 3000 BC onward, as it was the cult centre of the falcon god Horus of Behdet (the ancient name for Edfu), but the Temple of Horus you see today is Ptolemaic. Started by Ptolemy III (246–221 BC) on 23 August 237 BC, on the site of an earlier and smaller New Kingdom structure, the sandstone temple was completed some 180 years later by Ptolemy XII Neos Dionysos, Cleopatra VII's father. In conception and design it follows the general plan, scale, ornamentation and traditions of Pharaonic architecture, right down to the Egyptian attire worn by Greek pharaohs depicted in the temple's reliefs. Although it is much newer than cult temples at Luxor or Abydos, its excellent state of preservation helps to fill in many historical gaps; it is, in effect, a 2000-year-old example of an architectural style that was already archaic during Ptolemaic times.

Two hundred years ago the temple was buried by sand, rubble and part of the village of Edfu, which had spread over the roof. Excavation was begun by Auguste Mariette in the mid-19th century. Today the temple is entered via a long row of shops selling tourist tat, and a new visitors centre with the ticket office, clean toilets, a cafeteria and a room for showing a 15-minute film on the history of the temple in English.

Beyond the Roman *mammisi* (birth house), with some colourful carvings, the massive 36m-high **pylon** (gateway) is guarded by two huge but splendid granite statues of Horus as a falcon. The walls are decorated with colossal reliefs of Ptolemy XII Neos Dionysos, holding his enemies by their hair before Horus and about to smash their skulls; this is the classic propaganda pose of the almighty pharaoh.

Temple of Horus

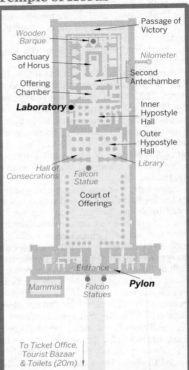

Beyond this pylon, the **court of offerings** is surrounded on three sides by 32 columns, each with different floral capitals. The walls are decorated with reliefs, including the 'Feast of the Beautiful Meeting' just inside the entrance, the meeting being that of Horus of Edfu and Hathor of Dendara, who visited each other's temples each year and, after two weeks of great fertility celebrations, were magically united.

A second set of Horus falcon statues in black granite once flanked the entrance to the temple's first or **outer hypostyle hall**, but today only one remains. Inside the entrance of the outer hypostyle hall, to the left and right, are two small chambers: the one on the right was the temple **library** where the ritual texts were stored; the chamber on the left was the **hall of consecrations**, a vestry where freshly laundered robes and ritual vases were kept. The hall itself has 12 columns, and the walls are decorated with reliefs of the temple's founding.

The **inner hypostyle hall** also has 12 columns, and in the top left part of the hall is perhaps this temple's most interesting room: the temple **laboratory**. Here, all the necessary perfumes and incense recipes were carefully brewed up and stored, their ingredients listed on the walls.

Exit the inner hypostyle hall through the large central doorway to enter the **offering chamber**, or first antechamber, which has an altar where daily offerings of fruit, flowers, wine, milk and other foods were left. On the west side, 242 steps lead up to the rooftop and a fantastic view of the Nile and the surrounding fields. (The roof is closed to visitors.)

The second antechamber gives access to the **sanctuary of Horus**, which still contains the polished-granite shrine that once housed the gold cult statue of Horus. Created during the reign of Nectanebo II (360–343 BC), this shrine, or house of the god, was reused by the Ptolemies in their newer temple. In front of it stands a replica of the wooden barque in which Horus' statue would be taken out of the temple in procession during festive occasions. The original is now in the Louvre, Paris.

On the eastern enclosure wall, look for the remains of the Nilometer, which measured the level of the river and helped predict the coming harvest. For more on Nilometers and their importance in ancient Egypt, see boxed text p271.

🛏 Sleeping & Eating

There is a kebab place on the main square, and several cafeterias on the waterfront, Sharia an-Nil, including internet cafe Koko. At all of these places you should ask how much dishes cost before you order. There is a daily fruit and vegetable souq just off the main square.

Horus Hotel   HOTEL **$$**
(📠471 5284/86; Sharia al-Gumhuriya; s/d/tr without bathroom E£90/170/230; ❄) This hotel, opposite Omar Effendi department store, is the best option in town, but still pretty basic. It's on the upper floors of the building, with clean, bright rooms, with fans or with aircon, and clean, shared bathrooms. The staff are friendly and helpful, and the restaurant (set menu E£40) is one up on other eateries in town.

DON'T MISS

VICTORY PARADE

Exit the hypostyle hall to the east (left) of the sanctuary and you come to a narrow passage between the temple and its outer enclosure wall. This narrow ambulatory, the passage of victory, contains scenes of the dramatic battle between Horus and Seth at the annual Festival of Victory. Throughout the conflict, Seth is shown in the form of a hippopotamus, his tiny size rendering him less threatening.

ℹ Information

As in other Egyptian towns, the main street of Edfu is lined with mobile-phone shops, and the main square (Al Midan), the town's nerve centre, has a few simple but popular cafe-restaurants. A large telephone centrale sits on the southern side of the square and the post office is behind it, just south of here, along the first street off to the left. On the main street, Sharia al-Maglis, is the Banque du Caire, with an ATM.

On the waterfront where the cruise boats dock are some pleasant cafe-restaurants, as well as more bazaars, the Bank of Alexandria, the Bank al-Ahli al-Masri and internet cafe **Koko** (Sharia an-Nil; per hr E£10).

ℹ Getting There & Away

Edfu train station is on the east bank of the Nile, about 4km from the town. There are frequent trains heading to Luxor and Aswan throughout the day, although most are 2nd and 3rd class only.

To get to the town, you must first take a *kabout* from the train station to the bridge, then another into town. Each costs 50pt. Alternatively, hire an entire *kabout* to take you to the main square for about E£20 to E£25.

The bus, minibus and *servees* station can be found at the entrance to town, next to the bridge over the Nile. There are no longer any buses along the Aswan–Luxor road, so the only other option is to buy a seat in a *servees* or minibus: to Luxor (E£7, two hours), Kom Ombo (E£4, 45 minutes), Aswan (E£6, 1½ hours) and Marsa Alam on the Red Sea (E£25, three to four hours). A private minibus to Kom Ombo will cost E£100 per car, to Luxor and Aswan E£150 and to Marsa Alam E£250.

Hantours take passengers from the waterfront to the temple or vice versa for E£20 to E£25, but you will have to bargain.

LASCAUX ON THE NILE

Canadian archaeologists working in the 1960s in the area of Qurta, some 15km north of Kom Ombo, discovered what they thought to be extremely old petroglyphs. Paleolithic, they thought. Ridiculous, said the experts. The matter was dropped, the site forgotten. But the images were rediscovered in 2005 by a team of archaeologists led by Dr Dirk Huyge of the Royal Museum of Art and History, Brussels (Belgium). This time the archaeologists discovered other petroglyphs that were partly covered by sediment and other deposits. These were recently dated in Belgium to the Pleistocene period of rock art, at least 15,000 years old, and therefore both chronologically and stylistically from the same period as the images in Lascaux, France.

The images are carved into the side of huge Nubian sandstone rocks. Most of these fine carvings are of wild horned cows in different positions although there are also gazelles, birds, hippos and fish in a naturalistic style, and a few stylised human figures with pronounced buttocks but no other particular features. These discoveries do not just represent some of the largest and finest examples of rock art ever found in Egypt. They also pose a challenging question. How can there be such similarities between images found in Egypt and France? Was there some sort of cultural exchange between the people of Lascaux and Qurta?

More research is being done at Qurta and no doubt more discoveries will be found. Dr Huyge believes that the Qurta art is part of an evolution and that even older work will be found. The site is guarded but not currently open to the public.

Gebel Silsila

At Gebel Silsila, about 42km south of Edfu, the Nile narrows considerably to pass between steep sandstone cliffs that are cluttered with ancient rock stelae and graffiti. Known in Pharaonic times as Khenu (Place of Rowing), it was an important centre for the cult of the Nile: every year at the beginning of the inundation season, sacrifices were made here to ensure the fertility of the land. The Nile at its height flowing through the narrow gorge must have been a particularly impressive sight, which no doubt explains why the location was chosen as a cult centre. The gorge also marks the change from limestone to sandstone in the bedrock of Egypt. The sandstone quarries here were worked by thousands of men and, judging by the names of pharaohs inscribed in the caves, it seems they were worked from the 18th dynasty or earlier through to the Roman period. The quarries were for centuries the main source in Egypt of sandstone for temple building.

The most attractive monuments are on the west bank, where the rocks are carved with inscriptions and tiny shrines from all periods, as well as adorned with larger chapels. The southern side of the site is marked by a massive pillar of rock, known as the 'Capstan', so called because locals believe there was once a chain – *silsila* in Arabic,

from which the place takes its name – that ran from the east to the west bank. Nearby are the three shrines built by Merenptah, Ramses II and Seti I during the New Kingdom. Further north, the main quarry has clear masons' marks and a group of elaborate private memorial chapels. Several stelae, including a large **Stelae of Shoshenq I**, mark the northern limit of the quarry and lead to the **Speos of Horemheb** (adult/ student E£30/20; ☉7am-8pm), a rock-hewn chapel started by Horemheb (1323–1295 BC) and finished by the officials of the later Ramesside kings.

The more impressive quarries are to be found on the east bank of the river, with several stelae in memory of pharaohs from different periods, and *ex-voto*s. Here one gets a real sense of the grandeur and scale of what the pharaohs undertook, by just looking at the cubist landscape of the gigantic shelves adorned with quarry marks and drawings, left by the removal of the sandstone blocks for the temples.

The best way to get to Gebel Silsila is by felucca or dahabiyya between Aswan and Esna (see p30). You can hire a private taxi from Edfu to take you to the village of Kajuj, 41km south of Edfu, then take the track to the quarries on the east bank of the Nile, in the hope of finding the antiquities department ferry. The small ferry leaves from the east bank right opposite the temple (E£10 per person), but it might take a while to track it down.

Kom Ombo

📞 097 / POP 71,596

The fertile, irrigated sugar-cane fields around Kom Ombo, 65km south of Edfu, support not only the original community of fellaheen (peasant farmers), but also a large population of Nubians displaced from their own lands by the creation of Lake Nasser (see p272). It's a pleasant little place, easily accessible en route between Aswan and Luxor. A huge cattle market is held on the outskirts of town, near the railway line, on Thursday. The main attraction these days, however, is the unique riverside temple to Horus the Elder (Haroeris) and Sobek, about 4km from the town's centre, which stands gloriously on a promontory overlooking the Nile.

In ancient times Kom Ombo was known as Pa-Sebek (Land of Sobek), after the crocodile god of the region. It became important during the Ptolemaic period, when its name was changed to Ombos and it became the capital of the first Upper Egyptian nome during the reign of Ptolemy VI Philometor. Kom Ombo was an important military base and a trading centre between Egypt and Nubia. Gold was traded here, but more importantly it was a market for African elephants brought from Ethiopia, which the Ptolemies needed to fight the Indian elephants of their long-term rivals the Seleucids, who ruled the largest chunk of Alexander's former empire to the east of Egypt.

◎ Sights

Temple of Kom Ombo   TEMPLE
(adult/student E£30/20; ⊙7am-7pm) Standing on a promontory at a bend in the Nile, where in ancient times sacred crocodiles basked in the sun on the riverbank, is the Temple of Kom Ombo. Unique in Egypt, it has a dual dedication to the local crocodile god Sobek and Haroeris, from *har-wer,* meaning Horus the Elder. This is reflected in the temple's plan: perfectly symmetrical along the main axis of the temple, there are twin entrances, two shared hypostyle halls with carvings of the two gods on either side, and twin sanctuaries. It is assumed that there were also two priesthoods. The left (western) side of the temple was dedicated to the god Haroeris, the right (eastern) half to Sobek.

Reused blocks suggest an earlier temple from the Middle Kingdom period, but the main temple was built by Ptolemy VI Philometor, though most of its decoration was completed by Cleopatra VII's father, Ptolemy

Temple of Kom Ombo

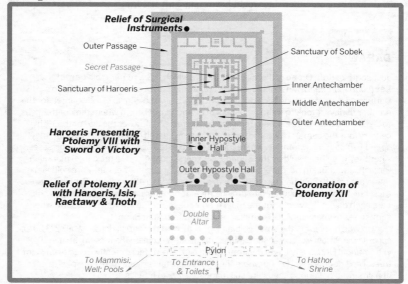

XII Neos Dionysos. The temple's spectacular riverside setting has resulted in the erosion of part of its partly Roman forecourt and outer sections, but much of the complex has survived and is very similar in layout to the other Ptolemaic temples of Edfu and Dendara, albeit smaller.

Passing into the temple's **forecourt**, where the reliefs are divided between the two gods, there is a double altar in the centre of the court for both gods. Beyond are the shared inner and outer hypostyle halls, each with 10 columns. Inside the **outer hypostyle hall**, to the left is a finely executed relief showing Ptolemy XII Neos Dionysos being presented to Haroeris by Isis and the lion-headed goddess Raettawy, with Thoth looking on. The walls to the right show the crowning of Ptolemy XII by Nekhbet (the vulture goddess worshipped at the Upper Egyptian town of Al-Kab) and Wadjet (the snake goddess based at Buto in Lower Egypt), with the dual crown of Upper and Lower Egypt, symbolising the unification of Egypt.

Reliefs in the **inner hypostyle hall** show Haroeris presenting Ptolemy VIII Euergetes with a curved weapon, representing the sword of victory. Behind Ptolemy is his sister-wife and co-ruler Cleopatra II.

From here, three **antechambers**, each with double entrances, lead to the **sanctuaries of Sobek and Haroeris**. The now-ruined chambers on either side would have been used to store priests' vestments and liturgical papyri. The sanctuaries themselves are no longer completely intact, allowing you to see the **secret passage** between them that enabled the priests to give the gods a 'voice' to answer the petitions of pilgrims.

The **outer passage**, which runs around the temple walls, is unusual. Here, on the left-hand (northern) corner of the temple's back wall, is a puzzling scene, which is often described as a collection of '**surgical instruments**'. It seems more probable that these were implements used during the temple's daily rituals.

Near the Ptolemaic gateway on the southeast corner of the complex is a small **shrine to Hathor**, while a small **mammisi** stands in the southwest corner. Beyond this to the north you will find the deep well that supplied the temple with water, and close by is a small pool in which crocodiles, Sobek's sacred animal, were raised.

🛏 Sleeping & Eating

Foreigners are theoretically allowed to stay the night in Kom Ombo now, but there still isn't anywhere worth staying. Snacks and drinks can be bought at the series of cafeterias and tourist bazaars, called Rural Home, in the shade of the trees between the temple and the Nile. **Cafeteria Venus** on the north side of the temple has cold beers in a pleasant garden setting.

WORTH A TRIP

DARAW

Just south of Kom Ombo is the village of Daraw, which has a remarkable **camel market** (souq al-gimaal). Most of the camels are brought up in caravans from Sudan's Darfur and Kordofan along the Forty Days Rd (Darb al-Arba'een; allegedly named for the number of days it took to walk) to just north of Abu Simbel, from where they're trucked to Daraw. Trading caravans were replaced by the faster railway at the end of the 19th century, but the camels still come, except now they are the cargo. Once in Daraw, they spend two days in quarantine, where they are inoculated against a number of diseases. After they have been sold by the Sudanese owners, most go on to the camel market in Birqash, about 35km northwest of Cairo (see p165), and from there they are sold again. Some are sold to Egyptian farmers, others are exported to other Middle Eastern countries, but many are slaughtered to provide meat for poorer Egyptians. Camels are sold here each day of the week, but the main market days are Tuesday and Thursday, when sometimes as many as 2000 camels are brought from Abu Simbel.

Also worth seeing is the small Nubian **Hosh al-Kenzi** (Kenzian House; ☎097 273 0970; opposite Dar Rasoul Mosque, Sharia al-Kunuz; donations welcome; ⊗8am-noon), built in 1912 in traditional Nubian style and decorated with Nubian artefacts mostly made from palm trees. Next door is a workshop where the beaded curtains made from date pips, pieces of palm frond or various seeds are still made for Nubian houses.

🛈 Getting There & Around

The best way to visit the temple is to come on a tour or with a private taxi. A private taxi from Luxor taking in both Edfu and Kom Ombo and returning in the evening can cost from about E£450 to E£700; moving on to Aswan instead of returning to Luxor will cost between E£450 and E£550. A private taxi from Aswan will cost from E£200 to E£250. Alternatively, buy a seat in a *servees* or minibus at E£18 to Luxor or E£8 to Aswan. At the time of reseach, there were no buses between Aswan and Luxor.

Trains are another option, but the train station is some way from the temple.

To get to the temple from the town centre, take a *kabout* to the boat landing on the Nile about 800m north of the temple (50pt), then walk the remainder of the way. *Kabouts* to the boat landing leave from the *servees* station. A private taxi between the town and temple should cost about E£15 to E£20 return.

ASWAN

✓097 / POP 265,004

On the northern end of the First Cataract and marking the country's ancient southern frontier, Aswan has always been of great strategic importance. In ancient times is was a garrison town for the military campaigns against Nubia, its quarries provided the valuable granite used for so many sculptures and obelisks, and it was a prosperous marketplace at the crossroads of the ancient caravan routes. Today, slower than most places in Egypt, laid-back and pleasant, it is the perfect place to linger for a few days, rest and recover from the rigours of travelling along the Nile. The river is wide, languorous and stunningly beautiful here, flowing gently down from Lake Nasser, around dramatic black-granite boulders and palm-studded islands. Colourful, sleepy Nubian villages run down to the water and stand out against the backdrop of the desert on the west bank. Aswan comes as a relief after Luxor, seemingly off the radar in an Egypt that wants to move on with mass tourism.

With so long a history, there is plenty to see in Aswan, but somehow the sightseeing seems less urgent and certainly less overwhelming than elsewhere in Egypt, allowing more time to take in the magic of the Nile at sunset, to stroll in the exotic souq (one of the best outside Cairo), or to appreciate the gentleness of the Nubians. Most tour groups head straight for the Temple of Isis at Philae, taking in the Unfinished Obelisk and the dams on the way, but the rarely visited ruins of ancient Abu and the small Aswan Museum on Elephantine Island are fascinating, as are the exquisite botanical gardens and the Nubia Museum.

The best time to visit Aswan is in winter, when the days are warm and dry. In summer the temperature hovers between 38°C and 45°C; it's too hot by day to do anything but sit by a fan and swat flies, or flop into a swimming pool.

⊙ Sights

Aswan's sights are spread out, mostly to the south and west of the town. The souq cuts right through the centre of town, parallel to the Nile. The Nubia Museum is within walking distance, just, but all other sights require transport. The sites on the islands and on the west bank involve a short boat trip.

TOWN & EAST BANK

Starting from the southern end, **Sharia as-Souq** (Map p256) appears very much like the tourist bazaars all over Egypt, with slightly less persistent traders than elsewhere in the country, trying to lure passers-by into their shops to buy scarves, perfume, spice, and roughly carved copies of Pharaonic statues. But a closer look reveals more exotic elements, with traders selling Nubian talismans for good luck, colourful Nubian baskets and skullcaps, Sudanese swords, African masks, and enormous stuffed crocodiles and desert creatures. Aswan is famous for the quality of its *fuul sudani* (peanuts), henna powder (sold in different qualities) and dried hibiscus flowers, used to make the much-loved local drink *karkadai*. The pace is slow, particularly in the late afternoon, the air has a slight whiff of sandalwood and, as in ancient times, you may feel that Aswan is the gateway to Africa.

Walking along the **Corniche** (Map p256) and watching the sunset over the islands and the desert on the other side of the Nile is a favourite pastime in Aswan. The view from riverside cafe terraces may be blocked by cruise boats, but plans are under way to relocate them all to a dock that is under construction at the northern end of town; for now the best place to watch the sunset is from the Old Cataract Hotel terrace, or from the Sunset restaurant.

Nubia Museum   MUSEUM
(Map p254; Sharia Abtal at-Tahrir; adult/student E£50/25; ⊙9am-5pm) The Nubia Museum is

Aswan

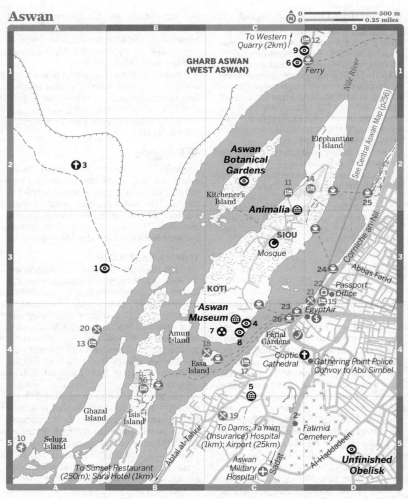

a showcase of the history, art and culture of Nubia and is a real treat. Established in 1997, in cooperation with Unesco, the museum is a reminder of the history and culture of the Nubians, much of which was lost when Lake Nasser flooded their land after the building of the dams (see p272). Exhibits are beautifully displayed in huge halls, where clearly written explanations take you from 4500 BC through to the present day. As it is not on the tour-group circuit, the museum is little-visited.

The exhibits start with prehistoric artefacts and objects from the Kingdom of Kush

and Meroe. Coptic and Islamic art displays lead to a description of the massive Unesco project to move Nubia's most important historic monuments away from the rising waters of Lake Nasser, following the building of the Aswan High Dam. Among museum highlights are 6000-year-old painted pottery bowls and an impressive quartzite statue of a 25th-dynasty priest of Amun in Thebes with distinct Kushite (Upper Nubian) features. The stunning horse armour found in tombs from the Ballana period (5th to 7th centuries BC) shows the sophistication of artisanship during this brief ascendancy. A fascinating

Aswan

display traces the development of irrigation along the Nile River, from the earliest attempts to control the flow of the river, right up to the building of the old Aswan Dam. A model of a Nubian house, complete with old furniture and mannequins wearing traditional silver jewellery, attempts to portray the folk culture of modern Nubia.

Fatimid Cemetery CEMETERY
(Map p254) Behind the Nubia Museum is this vast cemetery; among the modern tombs are some ruined mud-brick domed tombs, some of which go back to the 9th century. The old tombs are covered with domes built on a drum with corners sticking out like horns, a feature unique to southern Egypt. Near the outer edges of the cemetery are tombs decorated with flags, which belong to local saints; you may see Aswanis circumambulating a tomb, praying for the saint's intercession.

The municipality of Aswan has fenced off the Fatimid Cemetery. Enter from the main gate, a 10-minute walk from the Corniche along the road to the airport, and walk right through the cemetery to join the road to the Unfinished Obelisk; just aim for the four-storey building facing the back of the cemetery. The site's caretaker will often accompany you and show you the best-preserved tombs, for which he should be given a baksheesh (tip) of a few pounds.

Unfinished Obelisk ARCHAEOLOGICAL SITE
(Map p254; adult/student E£30/20; ⊙8am-5pm) Aswan was the source of Egypt's finest granite, the hard stone ancient Egyptians used to make statues and embellish temples and pyramids. In the **Northern Quarries**, about 1.5km from town opposite the Fatimid Cemetery, is a huge discarded obelisk. Three sides of the shaft, which is nearly 42m long, were completed except for the inscriptions. At 1168 tonnes, the completed obelisk would have been the single heaviest piece of stone the Egyptians ever fashioned. However, a flaw appeared in the rock at a late stage in the process. So it lies where the disappointed stonemasons abandoned it, still partly attached to the parent rock, with no indication of what it was intended for.

Upon entering the quarry, follow the steps that lead down from the surrounding ramp into the pit of the obelisk, where there are ancient pictographs of dolphins and ostriches or flamingos, thought to have been painted by workers at the quarry.

No *servees* run past the site, but you can get one to the junction on Sharia al-Hadd-

Central Aswan

0   200 m
0   0.1 miles

Central Aswan

adeen and then walk (about 10 minutes). Private taxis will charge about E£15. You can also walk through Fatimid Cemetery to get to it.

THE RIVER

Elephantine Island   ISLAND

(Map p254) Aswan's earliest settlement lies opposite the town centre, just north of the First Cataract. Elephantine Island is the site of ancient **Abu** (meaning both elephant and ivory in ancient Egyptian), both names a reminder of the important role the island once played in the ivory trade. At the beginning of the 1st dynasty (about 3000 BC) a fortress was built on the island to establish Egypt's southern frontier. Abu soon became an important customs point and trading centre. It remained strategically significant throughout the Pharaonic period as a departure point for the military and commercial expeditions into Nubia and the south. During the 6th dynasty (2345–2181 BC) Abu gained its strength as a political and economic centre and, despite occasional ups and downs, the island retained its importance until the Graeco-Roman period.

As well as being a thriving settlement, Elephantine Island was the main cult centre of the ram-headed god Khnum (at first the god of the inundation, and from the 18th dynasty worshipped as the creator of humankind on his potter's wheel), Satet (Khnum's wife, and guardian of the southern frontier) and their daughter Anket. Each year the rushing of the waters of the flood were first heard here on Elephantine Island. Over time religious complexes took over more and more of the island, so residential areas moved either further north on the island or to the east bank. The temple town of Abu received its *coup de grâce* in the 4th century AD, when Christianity was established as the imperial Roman religion. From then on, worship of the ancient gods was gradually abandoned and defensive fortifications were moved to the east bank, today's city of Aswan.

The extensive ruins of Abu take up the southern end of the island. The northern tip is dominated by the large Mövenpick Resort Aswan.

Nubian Villages

Sandwiched between the ruins of Abu and the Mövenpick resort are two colourful Nubian villages, **Siou** and **Koti**. Their shady alleys and gardens make for a tranquil stroll – a north–south path crosses the middle of the island and links the two villages.

Close to the wall separating the Mövenpick resort from Siou village, facing Kitchener's Island, is **Baaba Dool** (Map p254; ✆0100 497 2608; Siou; admission free), a gorgeous painted Nubian house, where the owner Mustapha serves tea, sells Nubian handicrafts and can arrange live music and dancing done by local women. The roof terrace is the perfect place to watch the sunset on the west bank, with a multitude of birds flying around the island opposite.

Western women should be respectful of local tradition and wear modest clothes. More and more visitors prefer to enjoy the traditional set-up of the villages, and rent flats or houses here for a few days (see p263).

Aswan Museum & the Ruins of Abu

(Map p254; adult/student E£30/15; ⏱8am-5pm) The ruins of the original town of Abu and the fascinating **Aswan Museum** lie at the southern end of Elephantine Island. The older part of the museum is housed in the villa of Sir William Willcocks, architect of the old Aswan Dam. Built in 1898, the villa became a museum in 1912. The newer extension was added in 1998.

The main part of the museum houses antiquities discovered in Aswan and Nubia, although most of the Nubian artefacts rescued from the temples flooded by Lake Nasser were moved to the Nubia Museum. The modern annexe has a delightful collection of objects, from weapons, pottery and utensils to statues, encased mummies and sarcophagi from predynastic to late Roman times, found in the excavations on Elephantine Island. The well-displayed objects, with excellent labels in English and Arabic, are organised in separate glass cases, each explaining a particular facet of life on the island in ancient times: death, trade, religion, weaving, hunting, farming, cooking and so on. At the right of the main entrance, in a room by itself, lies the sarcophagus and mummy of a sacred ram, the animal associated with Khnum.

A path through the garden behind the museum leads to the evocative **ruins of ancient Abu**. Numbered plaques and reconstructed buildings mark the island's long history from around 3000 BC to the 14th century AD. The largest structure in the site is the partially reconstructed **Temple of Khnum** (plaque numbers 6, 12 and 13).

DON'T MISS

THE UNOFFICIAL NUBIAN MUSEUM

At **Animalia** (Map p254; ✆231 4152, 0100 545 6420; main street, Siou; admission E£5, incl guided tour E£10; ⏱8am-7pm), Mohamed Sobhi, a Nubian guide, and his family have dedicated part of their large house to the traditions, flora and fauna and the history of Nubia. This small but charming museum has a collection of stuffed animals found in Nubia, samples of sedimentary rocks, great pictures of Nubia before it was flooded by Lake Nasser, a small shop selling Nubian crafts at fixed prices and a lovely roof terrace where drinks and lunch are served overlooking the gardens. Mohamed Sobhi is passionate and knowledgeable about Nubian culture and the natural world, and he also takes people around Elephantine Island, and on early-morning birdwatching trips (see p260).

HENNA TATTOOS

Henna is the natural dye derived from the leaves of the *Lawsonia inermis* shrub, grown in southern Egypt and Nubia for millennia – traces of it have even been found on the nails of mummified pharaohs.

Like their ancestors, Nubian women use henna powder for their hair and also to decorate hands and feet prior to getting married. The intricate red-brown designs adorn the skin for a fortnight or so before fading away.

Women visitors will be offered henna 'tattoos' on their hands (or feet or stomachs, from E£30 per tattoo) at some of the Nubian villages on Elephantine Island or on the west bank of Aswan or in the souq – it looks great and you get to spend time with Nubian women. Always check who will apply the tattoos; this is women's work, but would-be Lotharios see this as a great opportunity to get close to a bit of foreign flesh.

Foreigners tend to prefer black to the traditional red henna tattoos, but beware, as this is in fact natural henna darkened with the very toxic hair dye PPD, which is banned in Europe. Avoid black henna completely, and visit www.hennapage.com to see the damage the dye can cause, from a light allergic reaction to chemical burns and sometimes even death.

Built in honour of the god of inundation during the Old Kingdom, it was added to and used for more than 1500 years before being extensively rebuilt in Ptolemaic times. Other highlights include a small 4th-dynasty **step pyramid**, thought to have been built by Sneferu (2613–2589 BC; father of Khufu of Great Pyramid fame); a tiny **Ptolemaic chapel** (number 15), reconstructed from the Temple of Kalabsha (which is now just south of the High Dam); a reconstructed 18th-dynasty **temple** (number 2), built by Hatshepsut (1473–1458 BC) and dedicated to the goddess Satet; a **cemetery for sacred rams** (number 11), thought to have been the living embodiment of the god Khnum; and the ruins of an **Aramaic Jewish colony** dating from the 5th century BC.

Heavenly portents and priestly prophecies aside, in ancient times only the Nilometer could give a real indication of the likelihood of a bountiful harvest. When the Nilometer here in the southern frontier town recorded a high water level of the river, it meant a good harvest, which in turn meant more taxes. The **Nilometer of the Temple of Khnum** (number 7) is below the southern balustrade of the Khnum temple. Built in the 26th dynasty, its stone stairs lead down to a small basin for measuring the Nile's maximum level. Another stairway, with a scale etched into its wall, leads to the water from the basin's northern end. Descending to the river's edge from beneath a sycamore tree near the museum is the **Nilometer of the Satet Temple** (number 10). Built in late Ptolemaic or early Roman times and restored in the 19th century, its staircase is roofed over and niches in the walls would have had oil lamps to provide light. If you look hard as you descend to the river, you can see the names of Roman prefects carved into the left-hand wall.

Aswan Botanical Gardens   GARDENS
(Map p254; admission E£20; ⊙8am-6pm) To the west of Elephantine Island is Aswan Botanical Gardens, still often referred to by its old name, Kitchener's Island. The island was given to Lord Horatio Kitchener in the 1890s when he was commander of the Egyptian army. Indulging his passion for beautiful palms and plants, Kitchener turned the entire island into a stunning botanical garden, importing plants from the Far East, India and parts of Africa. Covering 6.8 hectares, it is filled with birds as well as hundreds of species of flora. The garden may have lost some of its former glory, but its majestic palm trees are still a stunning sight, particularly just before sunset when the light is softer and the scent of sandalwood floats on the breeze. Avoid coming here on Friday, when the place is invaded by picnicking extended families with stereos.

The island is most easily seen as part of a felucca tour. Alternatively, take the northernmost ferry to Elephantine Island and walk across the village to the other side of the island, where a few little feluccas wait on the island's western edge to take visitors across. Expect to pay at least E£20 to E£25 for a round trip.

WEST BANK

As with the botanical gardens, it is easiest to visit the west bank as part of a felucca tour. The longer way is to take a ferry from Elephantine Island across to the landing for the Monastery of St Simeon. To get to the Tombs of the Nobles, or the Nubian village, take the public ferry that leaves from a landing opposite the train station, on the east bank (Map p256).

Aga Khan Mausoleum

(Map p254; closed to the public) High up on the west bank stands the elegant **Tomb of Mohammed Shah Aga Khan**. The 48th imam (leader) of the Ismaili sect led an illustrious life, was hugely influential in the partition of India and creation of Pakistan, and was father-in-law to Rita Hayworth. The Aga Khan liked to winter in Aswan for his health and was buried here after his death in 1957. His fourth wife, who died in 2000, is also buried here. The family's white villa is in the garden beneath the tomb.

Monastery of St Simeon   MONASTERY

(Map p254; Deir Amba Samaan; adult/student E£25/15; ⊙8am-4pm) The fortress-like 7th-century Monastery of St Simeon was first dedicated to the 4th-century local saint, Anba Hedra, who renounced the world on his wedding day. It was rebuilt in the 10th century and dedicated to St Simeon. From here the monks travelled into Nubia, in the hope of converting the Nubians to Christianity, until Saladin (Salah ad-Din) destroyed the monastery in 1173.

Surrounded by desert sands, the monastery was built on two levels – the lower level of stone and the upper level of mudbrick – surrounded by 10m-high walls. The basilica has traces of frescos, and nearby is the chamber where St Simeon prayed with his beard tied to the ceiling in case he fell asleep. The cells, with their mastaba (bench) beds, once provided accommodation for about 300 resident monks and some 100 pilgrims. The last room on the right still has graffiti from Muslim pilgrims who stayed here en route to Mecca.

Take a private boat to the monastery from the boat landing, scramble up the desert track on foot (about 25 minutes) or hire a camel to take you up (negotiate with the camel drivers but expect to pay about E£30; agree in advance how much time you want to spend). Alternatively, you can take the ferry to the Tombs of the Nobles and ride a

camel or donkey from there, but remember to bring water.

Tombs of the Nobles   TOMBS

(Map p254; adult/student E£25/15; ⊙8am-4pm) The high cliffs opposite Aswan, just north of Kitchener's Island, are honeycombed with the tombs of the governors, the Keepers of the Gate of the South, and other dignitaries of ancient Elephantine Island. Known as the Tombs of the Nobles, six are open to the public. The tombs date from the Old and Middle Kingdoms and most follow a simple plan, with an entrance hall, a pillared room and a corridor leading to the burial chamber. A set of stairs cutting diagonally across the hill takes you up to the tombs from the ferry landing.

The adjoining **tombs of father and son Mekhu and Sabni** (tomb numbers 25 and 26), both governors, date from the long reign of 6th-dynasty Pharaoh Pepi II (2278–2184 BC). The reliefs in Sabni's tomb record how he led his army into Nubia, to punish the tribe responsible for killing his father during a previous military campaign, and to recover his father's body. Upon his return, Pepi II sent him his own royal embalmers and professional mourners, to show the importance accorded to the keepers of the southern frontier. Several reliefs in Sabni's tomb retain their original colours, and there are some lovely hunting and fishing scenes depicting him with his daughters in the pillared hall.

Sarenput was the local governor and overseer of the priesthood of Satet and Khnum under 12th-dynasty Pharaoh Amenemhat II (1922–1878 BC). The **tomb of Sarenput II** (number 31) is one of the most beautiful and best-preserved tombs, its colours still vivid. A six-pillared entrance chamber leads into a corridor with six niches holding statues of Sarenput. The burial chamber has four columns and a niche with wall paintings showing Sarenput with his wife (on the right) and his mother (on the left), as well as hunting and fishing scenes.

The **tomb of Harkhuf** (number 34), governor of the south during the reign of Pepi II, is hardly decorated, except for remarkable hieroglyphic texts about his three trading expeditions into central Africa, right of the entrance. Included here is Pepi II, then only a boy of eight, advising Harkhuf to take extra care of the 'dancing pygmy' he had obtained on his travels, as the pharaoh was very keen to see him in Memphis. 'My

DON'T MISS

BIRDWATCHING

Birdwatchers have long flocked to Aswan to watch birds in the winter period, but to be on the Nile very early in the morning, gliding along the edge of the islands, watching birds and hearing how they fit into ancient Egyptian history or into Nubian traditions, has a much wider appeal, even to non-twitchers. **Mohamed Arabi** (☏0122 324 0132; www.touregypt.net/featurestories/aswanbirding.htm; per person from US$50) is known as the 'Birdman of Aswan' and no bird escapes his eye. He has been taking twitchers and documentary makers for many years, but is also happy to take amateurs out into his small speedboat that glides into the channels between the islands, pointing out the vegetation; sunbirds; hoopoes; purple, squacco, striated and night herons; pied kingfishers; little and cattle egrets; redshanks; and many other birds. Call him direct.

Mohamed Sobhi (☏231 4152, 0100 545 6420) from Animalia (p257) does a similar trip in a normal motor boat for US$25 per person.

majesty desires to see this pygmy more than the gifts of Sinai or of Punt,' Harkhuf writes. Look carefully to see the tiny hieroglyph figure of the pygmy several times in the text.

Hekaib, also known as Pepinakht, was overseer of foreign soldiers during the reign of Pepi II. He was sent to quell rebellions in both Nubia and Palestine, and was even deified after his death, as is revealed by the small shrine of Hekaib built on Elephantine Island during the Middle Kingdom (c 1900 BC). Inside the **tomb of Hekaib** (number 35) there are fine reliefs showing fighting bulls and hunting scenes.

The court of the **tomb of Sarenput I** (number 36), grandfather of Sarenput II and governor during the 12th-dynasty reign of Sesostris I (1965–1920 BC), has the remains of six pillars, decorated with reliefs. On each side of the entrance Sarenput is shown being followed by his dogs and sandal-bearer, his flower-bearing harem, his wife and his three sons.

Qubbet al-Hawa   TOMB
(Map p254) On the hilltop above the Tombs of the Nobles lies this small tomb, constructed for a local sheikh. The steep climb up is rewarded with stunning views of the Nile and the surrounding area.

Nubian Village   VILLAGE
(Map p254) The Nubian village of **Gharb Aswan** (West Aswan) is so far a tranquil affair just north of the Tombs of the Nobles, but things might change soon. A sealed road that peters out in the sand, at the Tomb of the Nobles, announces Aswan's expansion plans on the west bank. For now it's a pleasant place to be, particularly at night, after the souqs near the ferry landing have closed

and most of the tourists have gone back to their hotel on the east bank. Beit al-Kerem (p262) is a wonderful place to stay for a few nights.

Western Quarry   ARCHAEOLOGICAL SITE
Isolated in the desert to the west of the Tomb of the Nobles is the ancient Western Quarry (Gebel Simaan), where stone for many ancient monuments – possibly including the Colossi of Memnon (see p223) – was quarried. The large **unfinished obelisk**, made for Seti I (1294–1279 BC), was decorated on three sides of its apex before it was abandoned. Nearby, the ancient quarry face and marks are clearly visible, along with the tracks on which the huge blocks were dragged down to the Nile.

Expect to pay at least E£90, after bargaining, for the camel ride from the boat landing, half an hour each way. Take plenty of water, and keep an eye out for snakes.

🏃 Activities

Feluccas
The Nile looks fabulous and magical at Aswan, and few things are more relaxing than hiring a felucca before sunset and sailing between the islands, the desert and the huge black boulders, listening to the flapping of the sail and to Nubian boys singing from their tiny dugouts. On days when cruise boats dock together in town, hundreds of feluccas circle the islands, a good time to take a felucca a bit further out towards Seheyl Island (p267). The trustworthy **Gelal** (☏0122 415 4902), who hangs out near Panorama restaurant and the ferry landing, offers hassle-free tours on his family's feluccas at a fixed price (E£30 to E£40 per

boat for an hour, E£35 to E£45 for a motor boat). Gelal is from Seheyl Island and can also arrange a visit to the island and lunch (E£40) in his house, as well as a swim on a safe beach. According to the tourist office, a three- or four-hour tour costs at least E£100 to E£150. A two- to three-hour trip down to Seheyl Island costs about E£120.

For details on taking an overnight felucca trip down the Nile, see p32.

Swimming

Aswan is a hot place, and often the only way to cool down, apart from hiding in your air-conditioned room, is to swim. Joining the local kids splashing about in the Nile is not a good idea (see Schistosomiasis, p512). Schistosomiasis can only be caught in stagnant water; boatmen know where the current is strong enough (but not too strong) for it to be safe for swimming, among them a **beach** (Map p254) on the west bank opposite Seluga Island. To get there rent a motor boat (per person about E£50, and E£30 extra for lunch if you want to spend the day).

Some hotels have swimming pools open to the public, generally from 9am to sunset. The cheapest by far is the Cleopatra Hotel (p263), which costs E£25, but the pool is small and overlooked by other buildings. The Mövenpick resort (p262) charges nonguests E£100 to use its pools, and Isis Aswan (p262) E£50.

☞ Tours

Small hotels and travel agencies arrange day tours of the area's major sights. Half-day guided tours usually include the Temple of Isis at Philae, the Unfinished Obelisk and the High Dam, and start at E£300 (per person with three to five people) with AmEx or Thomas Cook agencies (p265), including admission to all sites. Some budget hotels offer cheaper tours but are not licensed to guide groups. Travel agencies will also arrange felucca trips to Elephantine and Kitchener's Islands for about E£75 to E£100 per person, based on a group of three to five people, but it is cheaper to deal directly with the boatmen.

All travel agencies and most hotels in Aswan offer trips to Abu Simbel, but watch out for huge price differences, and check that the bus is comfortable and has air-con. Thomas Cook charges about E£1000 per person, including a seat in an air-con minibus, admission fees and guide, and E£1400

by air, including transfers, fees and guide. By contrast, budget hotels offer tours for about E£300 to E£400 in a smaller bus, though often not including the entrance fee or guide. For more information about getting to Abu Simbel, see p266.

🛏 Sleeping

Most visitors to Aswan stay on their cruise boats, so there has been little investment in hotels recently, but things are slowly changing. Prices vary greatly depending on the season; the rates mentioned here are high season, which extends from October through to April, but peaks in December and January. In the low season, and even until early November, you'll have no trouble finding a room at lower prices.

Hotel touts at the train station try to convince tired travellers that the hotel they have booked is now closed so that they can take them to another hotel and collect their commission. Ignoring them is the thing to do, as their commission will be added to your bill.

For lodging near Philae, also consider Fekra – see boxed text p270.

TOP CHOICE **Sofitel Old Cataract Hotel & Spa** HISTORIC HOTEL $$$
(Map p254; ☎231 6000; www.sofitel-legend.com; Sharia Abtal at-Tahrir; r/ste from US$368/568; ❄️❄️) The grande dame of hotels on the Nile, the Sofitel Old Cataract is a destination in itself and brings you back to the days of Agatha Christie, who is said to have written part of her novel *Death on the Nile* here (the hotel certainly featured in the movie). The splendid building, surrounded by well-tended exotic gardens on a rock above the river, commands fantastic views of the Nile and several islands, the ruins of Abu and the desert behind. After several years of closure, the Old Cataract reopened at the end of 2011 having been completely refitted. The original building, now known as the Palace Wing, has 76 rooms, of which over half are suites. But the biggest change has been brought to the 1960s annexe, now the Garden Wing, where all rooms have stunning Nile views. The 1902 Restaurant serves some of the finest food in the country, while Kebabgy and Saraya serve simpler food in a more relaxed atmosphere. The infinity pool looks onto the river and ruins of Elephantine Island, while the two-floor spa has fitness centre, hammam, sauna and Thai therapists.

TOP CHOICE **Philae Hotel** HOTEL $$

(Map p256; ☎231 2090; philaehotel@gmail.com; 79 Corniche an-Nil; s/d/tr/f apt US$60/70/90/250; ❄️🛜) This well-established hotel has had a serious revamp, and it is now by far the best midrange hotel in town. The Egyptian owner returned from Germany and went on a shopping spree in Cairo to furbish his hotel. The tasteful and cosy rooms are decorated with fabrics full of Arabic calligraphy and elegant local furnishings. The hotel restaurant serves mainly vegetarian organic food from its own gardens at very reasonable prices (mains E£20 to E£40). The great rooms are no longer a secret, so book ahead as they fill up really quick.

Bet al-Kerem GUESTHOUSE $$

(Map p254; ☎0109 239 9443, 0122 384 2218; www.betelkerem.com; Gharb Aswan, west bank; s/d/f r without bathroom €35/45/50; ❄️) This modern hotel overlooking the desert and the Tomb of the Nobles is a great find, offering eight quiet and comfortable rooms with very clean shared bathrooms. The hotel boasts a wonderful rooftop terrace overlooking the Nile and Nubian village, and has a good restaurant (meals €7 to €11). The staff are very friendly and proud to be Nubian. Call ahead and Shaaban will come and fetch you or explain how to get there.

Nile Hotel HOTEL $$

(Map p254; ☎231 4222; www.nilehotel-aswan.com; Corniche an-Nil; s/d/tr US$40/55/73; ❄️🛜) A very welcome new hotel in this price range, offering 40 well-appointed rooms with spotless private bathrooms, satellite TV and minibar, all with a window or balcony overlooking the Nile. The staff speak English and are very friendly and helpful. There is a restaurant, a small library with foreign novels and books about Egypt, and a business centre. Recommended.

Mövenpick Resort Aswan RESORT $$$

(Map p254; ☎230 3455; www.moevenpick-aswan.com; Elephantine Island; s/d from US$170/230; ❄️@🏊) Hidden in a large garden, the Mövenpick dominates the northern end of Elephantine Island. The hotel recently had a total makeover and has simple but very comfortable rooms, decorated in Nubian style and colours. It is set in lush, tranquil gardens and has a great swimming pool. Guests are transported to and from the town centre by a free ferry. There are better rates when booked via website.

Baaba Dool B&B $

(Map p254; ☎0100 497 2608; Siou, Elephantine Island; r without bathroom per person €10) A great place to unwind for a few days. A few rooms in this beautiful mud-brick house are painted in Nubian style, and have superb views over the Nile and the botanical gardens. Rooms are very basic but clean (bring a sleeping bag) and there are shared hot showers. Mustapha can arrange meals. Book ahead.

Keylany Hotel HOTEL $$

(Map p256; ☎231 7332; www.keylanyhotel.com; 25 Sharia Keylany; s/d/tr US$24/34/45; ❄️🛜🏊) This great little hotel used to come at budget prices, but recently prices have gone up. It has simple but comfortable rooms furnished with pine furniture, and spotless bathrooms with proper showers and hot water. The management and staff are friendly and endlessly helpful. The roof terrace has no Nile views but there is a burlap sunshade and furniture made from palm fronds, and it is a great place to hang out.

Sara Hotel HOTEL $$

(Map p267; ☎232 7234; www.sarahotel-aswan.com; s/d/ste US$75/100/141; ❄️🏊) Built on a clifftop overlooking the Nile about 2km beyond the Nubia Museum, the Sara is isolated but has fantastic views over the First Cataract and the Western Desert. It's worth putting up with the kitsch pastel decor for the spotlessly clean rooms with satellite TV, friendly staff and a good-sized pool overlooking the Nile. Corner rooms have huge balconies. The cafeteria is hugely popular with Aswanis. A shuttle bus runs into town hourly. If you want to stay in Aswan for a few days of peace and quiet, the Sara is a good choice.

Isis Aswan HOTEL $$

(Map p256; ☎231 5100; www.pyramisaegypt.com; Corniche an-Nil; s/d US$100/120; ❄️🏊) Built right on the riverbank, the Isis Aswan has a prime location in the centre of town. The 100 chalet-style rooms in the garden are clean and comfortable, popular with budget tour groups. The hotel has a reasonably good Italian restaurant, a great Nileside bar-terrace and a great figure-eight-shaped pool.

Nuba Nile Hotel HOTEL $

(Map p256; ☎231 3267; www.nubanile.com; Sharia Abtal at-Tahrir; s/d E£60/75; ❄️🛜🏊) This friendly family-run hotel has clean, comfortable rooms, conveniently located just north of the square in front of the train station and beside a popular ahwa and internet cafe. Check the room before you agree, as they vary considerably: some are tiny, others have no windows or hot water, but all have private bathrooms, and all have air-con.

Pyramisa Isis Island Resort & Spa HOTEL $$
(Map p254; ☎231 7400; www.pyramisaegypt. com; r garden/Nile view €110/149; ✳@☒) An imposing four-star resort hotel on its own island (there are regular free shuttle boats to town) with big, well-appointed rooms overlooking the Nile or the garden. Popular with tour groups, it has two huge swimming pools and several restaurants, usually with long queues at the enormous buffets. Very friendly staff.

Marhaba Palace Hotel HOTEL $$
(Map p256; ☎233 0102; www.marhaba-aswan. com; Corniche an-Nil; s/d US$60/80; ✳) The Marhaba has small but cosy, tastefully decorated rooms, with comfortable beds, sumptuous bathrooms (for this price range) and satellite TV. Bright and welcoming, it overlooks a park on the Corniche and has two restaurants, friendly staff and a roof terrace with excellent Nile views.

Hathor Hotel HOTEL $
(Map p256; ☎231 4580; www.hathorhotel.com; Corniche an-Nil; s/d/tr E£85/110/140; ✳☎☒) The 36 spotless rooms vary in size and some are gloomy, but all have a private bathroom and most have air-con (which is controlled at reception), offering good value for money. The great rooftop terrace has a small swimming pool with a few poolside chairs and spectacular Nile views.

Memnon Hotel HOTEL $
(Map p256; ☎230 0483, 0100 193 5639; www. memnonhotel-aswan.com; Corniche an-Nil; s/d E£70/100; ✳☒) The Memnon has been around for a few years and it shows, but the clean, good-sized rooms have great Nile views. The rooftop has a small, not-very-attractive pool and no shade. The shabby hotel entrance is easily missed, on a dusty street off the Corniche, south of the Aswan Moon Restaurant.

Cleopatra Hotel HOTEL $$
(Map p256; ☎231 400; Sharia as-Souq; s/d US$50/70; ✳@☒) Very central and well kept, the Cleopatra has 109 spacious, clean, albeit rather dark, rooms, in need of some update.

It is popular with groups on cut-price package tours because of its convenient location and the reasonably sized (but overlooked) rooftop pool.

Rentals
A number of flats are for rent on the west bank of Aswan, or on Elephantine Island, offering a good-value option for a longer stay, or even just for a night. Walk around on Elephantine Island and you will be offered houses for rent. If you want to book ahead, check **Beit al-Kerem** (p262) for Nubian houses, or Mohamed Sobhi at **Animalia** (see p257). **Mohamed Arabi** (see p260) has four amazing **houses** (Map p254; ☎0122 324 0132; per night from €100) for rent in his 10-acre garden and orchard on the west bank, all tastefully decorated in Nubian style, but with cool marble floors, clean bathrooms and a sitting room. These houses are very peaceful, and, at night, dinner with garden produce is served on a terrace on the Nile.

✕ Eating

Aswan is a sleepy place and most tourists eat on board the cruise boats, but there are a few laid-back restaurants. Outside the hotels, few serve alcohol and few accept credit cards.

TOP CHOICE / **1902 Restaurant** FRENCH $$$
(Map p254; ☎231 6000; www.sofitel-legend.com; mains E£100-200, Sharia Abtal at-Tahrir; ☺7-11pm) The revamped Old Cataract Hotel has several top-end outlets, but none grander than the 1902. Under its Moorish-inspired dome, the chefs – trained here and in France – serve some of the finest food in the country. Duck from France, fish from the Red Sea, good oils and cheese from Italy, a serious wine list from around the world... The outcome is sophisticated, expensive and mostly *nouvelle cuisine*. Service is as attentive as the room is grand, and guests are invited to play their part by dressing for the occasion. As a dining experience, there is simply nothing like this south of Cairo.

Sunset PIZZERIA $$
(off Map p254; ☎233 0601, 012 166 1480; Sharia Abtal at-Tahrir, Nasr City; set menus E£45-60; ☺9am-3am) This great cafe terrace and restaurant is the place to be at sunset, with spectacular views over the First Cataract. Sit on the huge shady terrace for a mint tea, or enjoy the small selection of excellent grills

LOCAL CUISINE

Along Sharia as-Souq and Sharia Abtal at-Tahrir there are plenty of small restaurants and cafes, good for taking in the lively atmosphere of the souq and sampling the local flavours. **Haramein Foul & Ta'amiyya** (Map p256; Sharia Abtal at-Tahrir; E£3-10) is a tiny takeaway place hidden among the low-rise apartment blocks, where Aswanis go when they want good fuul (fava bean paste) and ta'amiyya (felafel). On the same street is **Koshary Aly Baba Restaurant** (Map p256; Sharia Abtal at-Tahrir), a good *kushari* place (*kushari* is a mix of noodles, rice, black lentils, fried onions and tomato sauce) that also sells takeaway shwarma and *kofta*.

Just off the souq in front of the train station is **El-Tahrer Pizza** (Map p256; Midan al-Mahatta; dishes E£14-25), a popular cafe that serves pizza and *fiteer* at rock-bottom prices. Tea and sheesha (E£5) are also served.

or pizzas (E£40 to E£50). Or take a taxi here after dark. Very popular with locals at night.

Nubian Beach EGYPTIAN **$$**
(Map p254; west bank; set menus per person E£55) Wonderful Nubian cafe-restaurant set in a quiet garden on the west bank of the Nile, against the backdrop of a towering sand dune. During the heat of the day or on cold winter nights, there is a beautifully painted room indoors. The food is simple but good, and alcohol is served – sometimes with live Nubian music.

Ad-Dukka EGYPTIAN **$$**
(Map p254; 231 8293; Essa island; mains E£35-50; 6.30-10pm) This Nubian restaurant, set on an island just beyond Elephantine, continues to serve excellent Nubian food, in large portions, and is wonderfully atmospheric. It comes recommended by our readers. To get here, there's a free ferry from the dock opposite the EgyptAir office.

Golden Pharaoh EGYPTIAN, INTERNATIONAL **$$**
(Map p254; 231 0361, 0100 229 2910; Sharia Abtal at-Tahrir; mains E£25-90; 9am-late;) A rather sophisticated eatery with an air-con dining room and a large terrace overlooking the Nile and the city. The menu includes Nu-

bian and international dishes, and the place is popular with better-off Aswanis.

Salah ad-Din INTERNATIONAL **$$**
(Map p256; 231 0361, 0100 229 2910; Corniche an-Nil; mains E£40-75; noon-late;) This is the best of the Nileside restaurants, with several terraces and a freezing air-conditioned dining room. The menu has Egyptian, Nubian and international dishes, a notch better than most restaurants in Aswan. The service is efficient and the beers are cool (E£18). There is also a terrace to smoke a sheesha.

Panorama EGYPTIAN **$**
(Map p254; 231 6169; Corniche an-Nil; dishes E£8-20) With its pleasant Nileside terrace, this is a great place to chill and sip a herbal tea or fresh juice. It also serves simple Egyptian stews cooked in clay pots, with salad, mezze (selection of starters) and rice or chips, or an all-day breakfast.

Al-Makka GRILL **$$**
(Map p256; 230 3232; Sharia Abtal at-Tahrir, opposite Ramses Hotel; mains E£35-50; noon-2am) Popular with meat-eating local families, this place is famous for its excellent fresh kebabs and *kofta* (mincemeat and spices grilled on a skewer), as well as pigeon and chicken, all served with bread, salad and tahini. There is a sister restaurant, **Al-Madina** (Map p256; 230 5696), with a similar menu, on Sharia as-Souq.

Aswan Moon Restaurant EGYPTIAN **$$**
(Map p256; 231 6108; Corniche an-Nil; meals E£15-35) This once-popular hang-out no longer serves alcohol, but it remains a pleasant place for dinner. The menu ranges from basic Egyptian and international dishes, including mezze (E£8), pizzas (E£25 to E£30) and grills (E£35).

Biti Pizza PIZZERIA **$$**
(Map p256; Midan al-Mahatta; dishes E£23-38; 10am-midnight;) Biti is a popular air-conditioned restaurant that serves good Western-style pizzas, but more recommended are the delicious sweet and savoury *fiteer* (flaky Egyptian pizza), including the excellent tuna *fiteer* (E£28) or the fruit-and-nut dessert version (E£25). Watch out for the more expensive English-language tourist menu with the offer of any topping for E£38. The main menu is cheaper.

Chef Khalil EGYPTIAN **$$**
(Map p256; 231 0142; Sharia as-Souq; meals E£25-60) Small but popular fish restaurant,

just along from the train station. It serves fish from Lake Nasser and the Red Sea, charged by weight and grilled, baked or fried to your choice and served with salad and rice or French fries.

☆ Entertainment

Between October and February/March, Aswan's folkloric dance troupe sporadically performs Nubian *tahtib* (dance performed with wooden staves) and songs depicting village life at the **Palace of Culture** (Map p256; ☑231 3390; Corniche an-Nil). Call to check about performances, as the venue was closed at the time of writing.

Nubian shows are also performed for tourists at the Mövenpick Resort Aswan and at some of the smaller hotels like Beit al-Kerem. If you're lucky, you may be invited to a Nubian wedding on a weekend night. Foreign guests are deemed auspicious additions to the ceremony, but don't be surprised if you're asked to pay some money, between E£30 to E£50, to help defray the huge costs of the band and the food.

Otherwise, strolling along the Corniche, watching the moon rise as you sit at a rooftop terrace or having a cool drink at one of the Nileside restaurants is about all that most travellers get up to in Aswan at night.

🔒 Shopping

Aswan's famous souq is a good place to pick up souvenirs and crafts. Handmade Nubian skullcaps (about E£10 to E£20), colourful scarves (E£25 to E£50), and traditional baskets and trays (E£80 to E£150) in varying sizes are popular. The spices and indigo powder prominently displayed are also good buys, and most of the spice shops sell the dried hibiscus used to make the refreshing drink *karkadai*. However, beware of the safflower that is sold as saffron. Aswan is also famous for the quality of its henna powder and its delicious roasted peanuts. The higher grade of the latter goes for E£30 per kilogram.

International newspapers and magazines are usually available from the newsstand near the Philae Hotel on the Corniche.

Hanafi Bazaar   HANDICRAFTS
(Map p254; Corniche an-Nil; ⏾8am-10pm) With its mock Pharaonic facade, this is the oldest, no doubt also the dustiest, and best bazaar in town, with genuine Nubian swords, baskets, amulets, silk kaftans and beads from all over Africa, run by the totally laid-back Hanafi brothers.

Nubia Tourist Book Centre   BOOKS
(Map p254; Sharia as-Souq; ⏾8am-10pm) Good, air-conditioned bookshop near the train station with loads of books on Aswan and Egypt. There's another branch in the tourist bazaar at the exit of the Unfinished Obelisk.

❶ Information

Emergency
Ambulance (☑123)
Police (Map p256; Corniche an-Nil) Near Thomas Cook.
Tourist police (Map p256; ☑230 3436, 231 4393; Corniche an-Nil) Contact the tourist office first to help with translation.

Internet Access
Internet prices range from E£10 to E£15 per hour.
Aswanet Internet Café (Map p256; 25 Sharia Keylany; ⏾9am-11pm) Next to Keylany Hotel.
Nuba Nile Internet (Map p256; Sharia Abtal at-Tahrir; ⏾24hr) Next to Nuba Nile Hotel.

Medical Services
Aswan Military Hospital (Map p254; ☑231 7985/4739; Sharia Sadat) The top hospital in town.
Ta'mim (Insurance) Hospital (off Map p254; ☑231 5112/6510; Sharia Sadat) Newest hospital, with a good reputation.

Money
Unless otherwise noted, banking hours are 8.30am to 2pm and 5pm to 8pm Sunday to Thursday. There are ATMs all along the Corniche and around Sharia as-Souq, as well as at the train station.
American Express (Map p254; ☑230 6983; Corniche an-Nil; ⏾9am-5pm Sun-Thu, to 2pm Fri & Sat)
Bank of Alexandria (Map p256; Corniche an-Nil)
Banque du Caire (Map p256; Corniche an-Nil) Branch & ATM.
Banque Misr (Map p256; Corniche an-Nil; ⏾8am-3pm & 5-8pm) ATM and foreign-exchange booth next to main building.
Thomas Cook (Map p256; ☑230 4011; www.thomascook.com.eg; Corniche an-Nil; ⏾8am-2pm & 5-9pm)

Post
Main post office (Map p256; Corniche an-Nil; ⏾8am-8pm Sat-Thu, 1-5pm Fri)

POLICE CONVOYS

Driving north to Luxor no longer needs to be done in convoy, but at the time of writing there is still a twice-daily (4.30am and 11am) convoy to go to Abu Simbel, compulsory for foreigners travelling there. Armed convoys congregate at the beginning of Sharia Sadat (Map p254), near the Coptic Cathedral. Be there at least 15 minutes in advance. It takes at least three hours to reach Abu Simbel.

Telephone

There are cardphones along the Corniche and at the train station.
Telephone centrale (Map p254; Corniche an-Nil; ⊕24hr)

Tourist Information

Tourist office (Map p256; ☑231 2811, 0100 576 7594; Midan al-Mahatta; ⊕8am-3pm & 7-9pm Sat-Thu, 9am-3pm & 6-8pm Fri) This tourist office has little material, and still no computer, but staff can advise on timetables, and give an idea of prices for taxis and feluccas.

ⓘ Getting There & Away

Air

Daily flights are available with **EgyptAir** (Map p254; ☑231 5000; Corniche an-Nil; ⊕8am-8pm) from Cairo to Aswan (one way E£320 to E£896, 1¼ hours). If tourist demand increases, the 30-minute flight to Luxor may be reinstated. Flights to Abu Simbel were also on hold at the time of writing.

Boat

For details about the five-star cruise boats and fishing safaris operating on Lake Nasser, see p35. For details on boat transport to Sudan, see p523.

Bus

The bus station is 3.5km north of the train station, but the tourist office advises against travelling by bus as it is too much of a hassle. At the time of writing, there were no buses to Luxor and travelling by bus to Abu Simbel was restricted to four foreigners per bus. Upper Egypt Bus Co has two daily buses to Abu Simbel (E£35, four hours, departing 8am and 5pm). A direct bus to Cairo (E£150, 14 hours) leaves at 6am and 3pm daily.

Servees

Servees and minibuses leave from the bus station, 3.5km north of the train station. A taxi there will cost E£15, or 50pt in a communal taxi. A seat in a *servees* or minibus to Luxor costs E£18, to Kom Ombo E£7 and to Edfu E£15.

Train

From **Aswan Train Station** (Map p256; ☑231 4754) a number of daily trains run north to Cairo from 5am to 9.10pm (E£175, 14 hours). Tickets should be bought in advance, but can be bought on the train for an additional E£6.

All trains heading north stop at Daraw (1st/2nd class E£22/15, 45 minutes), Kom Ombo (E£24/17, one hour), Edfu (E£28/19, two hours), Esna (E£38/23, 2½ hours) and Luxor (E£45/29, three hours). Student discounts are available on all of these trains.

Watania Egypt Sleeping Train (☑230 2124; www.wataniasleepingtrains.com) has two daily services to Cairo at 5pm and 7pm; per person/double cabin (fits two) including dinner and breakfast US$60/120.

ⓘ Getting Around

To/From the Airport

The airport is located 25km southwest of town. A taxi to/from the airport costs about E£50 to E£80.

Bicycle

Aswan is not a great town for cycling. However, there are a few places at the train-station end of Sharia as-Souq where you can hire bicycles for about E£15 a day. Bet al-Kerem (see p262) runs cycling trips in the countryside.

Ferry

Two public ferries (E£1) run to Elephantine Island; the one departing across from EgyptAir (Map p254) goes to the Aswan Museum, while the one across from Thomas Cook (Map p256) goes to Siou. A third public ferry (E£1) goes from the ferry landing across from the train station to West Aswan and the Tombs of the Nobles.

Taxi

A taxi tour that includes Philae, the High Dam and the Unfinished Obelisk near Fatimid Cemetery costs around E£150 to E£200 for five to six people. Taxis can also take you on day trips to Daraw and/or Kom Ombo for about E£250. A taxi anywhere within the town costs E£5 to E£10.

Servees (50pt) run along the major roads in Aswan.

AROUND ASWAN

Aswan Dam

At the end of the 19th century, Egypt's fast-growing population made it imperative to cultivate more agricultural land, which would only be possible by regulating the flow of the Nile. The British engineer Sir William Willcocks started construction of the old Aswan Dam in 1898 above the First Cataract. When completed in 1902, it was the largest dam in the world, measuring 2441m across, 50m tall and 30m wide, and was made almost entirely of Aswan granite.

It was raised twice to meet the demand, not only to increase the area of cultivable land but also to provide hydroelectric power. With the opening of the High Dam, it now only generates hydroelectricity for a nearby factory producing fertilisers, and otherwise serves as a tourist attraction on the way to the High Dam, 6km upstream. The road to the airport and all trips to Abu Simbel by road include a drive across the Aswan Dam.

Seheyl Island

The large island situated just north of the old Aswan Dam, **Seheyl** (adult/child E£25/15; ☺7am-4pm Oct-Apr, to 5pm May-Sep) was sacred to the goddess Anukis. Prior to the dam's construction, the Nile would rush noisily through the granite boulders that emerged from the riverbed just south of here, forming the First Cataract, called Shellal by the Egyptians. Herodotus reported that an Egyptian official had told him that this was the source of the Nile, which flowed north and south from there. Now the waters flow slowly and Seheyl makes an ideal destination for a slightly longer felucca trip. On the island's southern tip is a cliff with more than **200 inscriptions**, most dating to the 18th and 19th dynasties, of princes, generals and other officials who passed by on their journey to Nubia. The most famous is the so-called 'famine stele' from the 3rd dynasty that recounts a terrible seven-year famine during the reign of Zoser (2667–2648 BC), which the pharaoh tried to end by making offerings to the Temple of Khnum on Elephantine Island.

Next to the inscriptions is a friendly Nubian village with brightly coloured houses. Several houses now welcome visitors, selling

Around Aswan

tea and good Nubian lunches as well as local crafts. It's a pleasant place to stroll around.

Philae (Agilika Island)

TOP CHOICE **Temple of Isis**   TEMPLE

(adult/child E£50/25; ☺7am-4pm Oct-May, to 5pm Jun-Sep) Perched on the island of Philae (fee-*leh*), the Temple of Isis lured pilgrims for thousands of years and then became one of Egypt's most seductive sights. After the building of the old Aswan Dam, the temple was swamped for six months of every

Philae (Agilika Island)

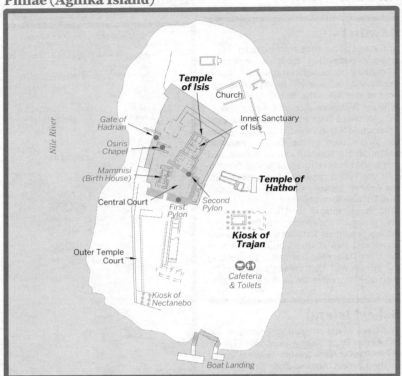

year by the high waters, allowing travellers to take rowing boats and glide among the partially submerged columns to peer down through the translucent green at the wondrous sanctuaries of the mighty gods below.

After the completion of the High Dam, the temple would have entirely disappeared had Unesco not intervened. Between 1972 and 1980, the massive temple complex was disassembled stone by stone. It was then reconstructed 20m higher on nearby Agilika Island, which was landscaped to resemble the original sacred isle of Isis.

Although the cult of Isis at Philae goes back at least to the 7th century BC, the earliest remains on the island date from the reign of the last native king of Egypt, Nectanebo I (380–362 BC). The most important ruins were begun by Ptolemy II Philadelphus (285–246 BC) and added to for the next 500 years until the reign of Diocletian (AD 284–305). By Roman times

Isis had become the greatest of all the Egyptian gods, worshipped right across the Roman Empire even as far as Britain. Indeed, as late as AD 550, well after Rome and its empire embraced Christianity, Isis was still being worshipped at Philae. Early Christians eventually transformed the main temple's hypostyle hall into a chapel and defaced the pagan reliefs, their inscriptions later vandalised by early Muslims.

Touring the Temple

The boat across to the temple leaves you at the base of the **Kiosk of Nectanebo**, the oldest part of the Philae complex. Heading north, you walk down the **outer temple court**, which has colonnades running along both sides; the western one is the most complete, with windows that originally overlooked the island of Bigga. At the end is the entrance of the Temple of Isis, marked by the 18m-high towers of the **first pylon** with reliefs of Ptolemy XII Neos Dionysos smiting enemies.

In the central court of the **Temple of Isis**, the *mammisi* is dedicated to Horus, son of Isis and Osiris. Successive pharaohs reinstated their legitimacy as the mortal descendants of Horus by taking part in rituals celebrating the Isis legend (see boxed text p186) and the birth of her son Horus in the marshes.

The **second pylon** leads to a hypostyle hall, with superb column capitals, and beyond lie three vestibules, leading into the **Inner Sanctuary of Isis**. Two granite shrines stood here, one containing a gold statue of Isis and another containing the barque in which the statue travelled, but those were long ago moved to Florence and Paris, and only the stone pedestal for the barque remains, inscribed with the names of Ptolemy III and his wife, Berenice. Take a side door west out of the hypostyle hall to the **Gate of Hadrian** where there is an image of the god Hapi, sitting in a cave at the First Cataract, representing the source of the river Nile.

East of the second pylon is the delightful **Temple of Hathor**, decorated with reliefs of musicians (including an ape playing the lute) and Bes, the god of childbirth. South of this is the elegant, unfinished pavilion by the water's edge, known as the **Kiosk of Trajan** (or 'Pharaoh's Bed'), perhaps the most famous of Philae's monuments and one that was frequently painted by Victorian artists.

Sound & Light Show

Each evening a **sound and light show** (www.soundandlight.com.eg; adult/child E£70/50; ⊙shows 6.30pm, 7.45pm & 9pm Oct-May, 7pm, 8.15pm & 9.30pm May-Sep) is shown at Philae. The commentary is cheesy, but wandering through the temple at night is quite delightful. Double-check the schedule at the tourist office.

DAY	SHOW 1	SHOW 2	SHOW 3
Monday	English	French	
Tuesday	French	English	
Wednesday	French	English	
Thursday	French	Spanish	English
Friday	English	French	Italian
Saturday	English	Arabic	
Sunday	German	English	

❶ Getting There & Away

The boat landing for the Philae complex is at Shellal, south of the old Aswan Dam. The only easy way to get there is by taxi or organised trip (which can be arranged by most travel agencies and major hotels in Aswan). The return taxi fare is about E£60. The return boat trip should not cost more than E£10 per person, plus baksheesh for the boatman, but often costs significantly more.

High Dam

Egypt's modern example of construction on a monumental scale, the controversial **Aswan High Dam** (As-Sadd al-Ali; adult/child E£20/10; ⊙8am-5pm) contains 18 times the amount of material used in the Great Pyramid of Khufu, and its construction created Lake Nasser, the world's largest artificial lake.

From the 1940s it was clear that the old Aswan Dam, which only regulated the flow of water, was not big enough to counter the unpredictable annual flooding of the Nile. In 1952, when Gamal Abdel Nasser came to power, plans were drawn up for a new dam, 6km south of the old one, but from the start there were political and engineering difficulties. In 1956, after the World Bank refused the promised loan for the project, Nasser ordered the nationalisation of the Suez Canal, which sparked the Suez Crisis in which France, the UK and Israel invaded the canal region. But Nasser got his way and also won additional funding and expertise from the Soviet Union. Work started in 1960 and was finally completed in 1971.

The dam has brought great benefits to Egypt's farmers, increasing cultivable land by at least 30%. At the same time, the country's power supply has doubled. But there are downsides. The dam has stopped the flow of silt essential to the fertility of the land, and the much higher use of artificial

---

HIGH DAM FACTS

» Length: 3600m

» Width at base: 980m

» Height at highest point: 111m

» Number of workers involved in construction: 35,000

» Number of workers who died during construction: 451

A GREAT IDEA

Fekra (Map p267; www.fekraculture. com; Gebal Shisha, Shellal) is located on 40,000 sq metres of land on the lake between the old and the High Dam, and overlooks Philae Island. The Fekra Cultural Centre – *fekra* means thought or idea in Arabic – is a fascinating project of artists from around the world, aiming to support Nubian and Upper Egyptian artists, and to promote an international cultural exchange through organising artistic events and workshops. It is a magical place for its energy and wonderful location: a Nubian-style mudbrick house right on the lake, perfectly peaceful and a great place for swimming. It has midrange accommodation for 12 people and a few extra Bedouin tents, with shared bathrooms.

fertilisers has led to increasing salinity of the agricultural areas. The groundwater tables have risen, too, and are damaging many monuments close to the Nile. The now perennially full irrigation canals have led to endemic infection with the bilharzia parasite, until recently a huge public health problem.

Most people visit the High Dam, 13km south of Aswan, as part of an organised trip to sights south of Aswan. There is a small pavilion with displays detailing the dimensions and the construction of the dam, and on the western side is a monument honouring Soviet-Egyptian friendship and cooperation. Video cameras and zoom lenses cannot be used, although nobody seems to police this.

ⓘ Getting There & Away

The quickest way to get to the High Dam is to take a taxi from Aswan (about E£25). Usually it is combined with a trip to the Temple of Kalabsha, which is about 3km from the western end of the dam and is visible from the dam on the western side of Lake Nasser.

LOWER NUBIA & LAKE NASSER

For thousands of years, the First Cataract marked the border between Egypt and Nubia, the land that stretched from Aswan to Khartoum. The Nile Valley on the Egyptian side was fertile and continuously cultivated, while the banks further south in Nubia were more rugged, with rocky desert cliffs and sand separating small pockets of agricultural land.

The building of the Aswan and High Dams irrevocably changed all that, and much of Nubia disappeared under the waters of Lake Nasser. The landscape now is dominated by the contrast of smooth desert and the calm green-brown water of the lake. Apart from the beauty and the peace of the lake itself, the main attraction of this region is the temples that were so painstakingly moved above the flood waters in the 1960s. See the boxed text p275 for more about this mammoth cultural rescue mission.

The area between the First and the Second Cataract is generally known as Lower Nubia (ancient Egyptian Wawat), and further south between the Second and Sixth Cataracts is Upper Nubia (Kush).

To the ancient Egyptians, Nubia was Ta-Sety, the Land of Bowmen, after the weapon for which the Nubians were famous. It was a crucial route for the trade with sub-Saharan Africa, and it was the source of much-needed raw materials, such as copper, ivory, ebony and gold. The modern name is thought to come from the ancient Egyptian word *nbw*, meaning 'gold'.

Egypt was always interested in Nubia and its riches, and the two peoples' histories were always connected: when Egypt was strong it dominated Nubia and aggressively exploited its natural resources; when Egypt was weak, the Nubians enjoyed periods of growth and development.

Evidence of 10,000-year-old settlements has been found in northern Nubia. At Nabta Playa, located some 100km west of Abu Simbel, archaeologists have recently discovered the remains of houses, sculpted monoliths and the world's oldest calendar, made of small standing stones, dating from around 6000 BC.

Until 3500 BC Nubia and Egypt both developed in roughly the same way, domesticating animals, growing crops and gradually adopting permanent settlements. Both people were ethnically linked, but the darker-skinned Nubians had more African features and spoke a Nilo-Saharan language, while the ancient Egyptian language is Afro-Asiatic.

With the unification of the land north of Aswan around 3100 BC, Egypt started to impose its authority on Nubia. From the beginning of the Old Kingdom, for nearly 5000 years, expeditions were sent to extract the region's considerable mineral wealth. During the First Intermediate Period (2160–2025 BC), central authority in Egypt collapsed, while Nubia became stronger, and Nubian soldiers played an important role in Egypt's civil war.

The reunification of Egypt, at the start of the Middle Kingdom, saw Lower Nubia again annexed and a chain of fortresses built at strategic points along the Nile to safeguard trade.

During the New Kingdom, instead of fortresses, the Egyptians built temples in Nubia, dividing the whole of the region into five nomes, ruled on the pharaoh's behalf by his viceroy, who took the title King's Son of Kush. Taking advantage of Egypt's political disunity during the Third Intermediate Period (1069–945 BC), the tables were turned and Nubians extended their authority far to the north, ruling Egypt for a century as the 25th Kushite dynasty (747–656 BC). The 25th dynasty ended with the Assyrian invasion of Egypt, after which Nubian action was guided by its own best interests, sometimes siding with foreign invaders, sometimes with their Egyptian neighbours.

Christianity gradually spread to Nubia after the 5th century AD and lasted long after Islam had spread along the Egyptian Nile. In AD 652 Egypt's new Muslim authorities made a peace treaty with the Christian king of Nubia. That treaty lasted more or less until the 13th century, when Egyptians moved south again: the last Christian king of Nubia was replaced by a Muslim in 1305 and most of the population converted to Islam. In the 19th century Nubia was again important to Egyptian ambitions as the route for its supply of slaves. The rise of the Mahdist state in Sudan at the end of the 19th century led to Nubia being divided for the last time: with the defeat of the Mahdi and his successor, and the establishment of the Anglo-Egyptian government in Sudan in 1899, a

FEAST, FAMINE OR WAR

Egypt's fate has always been closely intertwined with the amount of water in the Nile, and although the river flows through 10 countries, it is Egypt that has gained the most from its beneficence. Ancient Egyptians called their country Kemet (Black Land), after the fertile silt that the Nile's receding waters left in its wake. This annual dumping of a thick layer of dark, wet topsoil allowed ancient Egypt's agricultural system to develop and thrive, leading in turn to an accumulation of wealth and the flourishing of a sophisticated society and culture. When the floods failed and hunger turned to famine, the entire system broke down: consecutive years of inadequate flooding often coincided with the collapse of central authority or invasion by a foreign power.

Because of this dependence on the Nile, the Egyptians developed a highly organised irrigation system to help them deal with its unpredictability. Nilometers, a series of steps against which the rising water would be gauged, were used to measure the level of the flood, which was crucial for predicting soil fertility and crop yields. The Nilometer at Elephantine Island, on Egypt's southern frontier, was one of the first to show evidence of rising water in early June. Authorities also used the level of the flood to predict the size of the harvest and therefore to fix the level of taxes farmers should pay.

From the earliest times canals helped extend the reach of the floodplain, and devices were developed to help move water. These began as simple pots. Later, the *shadouf,* a long pole with a 'bucket' at one end and counterbalancing weight at the other, and the *saqia,* an animal-powered waterwheel, helped farmers to move greater amounts of water and extend the area of cultivable land.

Since the building of the High Dam, Egypt has been freed from the uncertainties of the Nile's annual flood, and yet the supply of water is still not entirely within its control. At present Egypt's use of Nile water is governed by a 1959 treaty with Sudan that essentially gives them control of some 90% of the flow of the river. The other countries around the Nile basin claimed – not without reason – that this is unfair and have pushed for a new agreement. Six of them signed a new Nile Basin Initiative in 2011 and have encouraged the other Nile-based states to reopen dialogue.

border between Egypt and Sudan was established 40km north of Wadi Halfa.

Modern Nubia

Following the completion of the old Aswan Dam in 1902, and again after its height was raised in 1912 and 1934, the water level of the Nile in Lower Nubia gradually rose from 87m to 121m, partially submerging many of the monuments in the area and, by the 1930s, totally flooding a large number of Nubian villages. With their homes flooded, some Nubians moved north where, with government help, they bought land and built villages based on their traditional architecture. Most of the Nubian villages close to Aswan, such as Elephantine, West Aswan and Seheyl, are made up of people who moved at this time. Those who decided to stay in their homeland built houses on higher land, assuming they would be safe, but they saw their date plantations, central to their economy, destroyed. This meant that many Nubian men were forced to search for work further north, leaving the women behind to run the communities.

Less than 30 years later, the building of the High Dam forced those who had stayed to move again. In the 1960s, 50,000 Egyptian Nubians were relocated to government-built villages around Kom Ombo, 50km north of Aswan.

Nubian Culture

The Nubians have paid the highest price for Egypt's greater good. They have lost their homes and their homeland, and with a new generation growing up far from the homeland, as Egyptians, or even Europeans and Americans, they are now also gradually losing their distinctive identity and traditions.

What is left of Nubian culture then seems all the more vibrant. Nubian music, famous for its unique sound (see boxed text below), was popularised in the West by musicians such as Hamza ad-Din, whose oud (lute) melodies are ethereally beautiful. As well as the oud, two basic instruments give the music its distinctive rhythm and harmony: the *douff,* a wide, shallow drum or tabla that musicians hold in their hands; and the *kisir,* a type of stringed instrument.

Less known abroad is Nubia's distinctive architecture, which was the main influence on Egyptian mud-brick architect Hassan Fathy. Traditional Lower Nubian houses are made with mud-bricks, but unlike the Upper Egyptian houses, they often have domed or vaulted ceilings, and further south the houses usually have a flat split-palm roof. They

NUBIAN MUSIC

It's one of those strange quirks, but it's almost easier to hear and buy Nubian music in the West than it is in Egypt, apart from in Aswan. Nubian music, very different to the more popular Egyptian music, is rarely heard on national TV and radio, and hard to find in music stores in Cairo. But Nubian artists sell CDs by the rackload in Europe and play to sell-out audiences.

The biggest name is Ali Hassan Kuban. A former tillerman from a village near Aswan, Kuban grew up playing at weddings and parties and made the leap to a global audience after performing at a Berlin festival in 1989. Before his death in 2001 he released several CDs on the German label Piranha (www.piranha.de), including *Walk Like a Nubian.*

The Nubian sound is easily accessible, particularly to a Western audience familiar with African music. It's rhythmic, warm and exotic, mixing simple melodies and soulful vocals. This can be heard at its best on a series of CDs by a loose grouping of musicians and vocalists recording under the name Salamat. Look out especially for *Mambo al-Soudani* (again on the Piranha label).

A slightly different facet of Nubian music is represented by Hamza ad-Din, a Sufi-inspired Nubian composer born in Wadi Halfa in 1929 and widely respected in the West for his semiclassical compositions written for the oud (lute). You can find ad-Din's *Escalay* (The Waterwheel) in a recording by the composer himself, or in an excellent version by the Kronos Quartet on their CD *Pieces of Africa.*

The best places to pick up CDs of Nubian music are from the music stores in the Aswan souq, where the sales assistants are happy to let you listen to different musicians. To hear authentic live Nubian music, try to get yourself invited to a Nubian wedding in Aswan. You can also head to Eskaleh in Abu Simbel (p277), where the renowned Nubian musician Fikry el Kashef plays with his friends.

are plastered or whitewashed and covered with decorations, including ceramic plates. The basic forms of these houses can be seen in the Nubian villages around Aswan and in Ballana, near Kom Ombo.

Nubians also have their own marriage customs. Traditionally, wedding festivities lasted for up to 15 days, although nowadays they are a three-day affair. On the first night of the festivities, the bride and groom celebrate separately with their respective friends and families. On the second night, the bride takes her party to the groom's home and both groups dance to traditional music until the wee hours. Then the bride returns home and her hands and feet are painted with beautiful designs in henna. The groom will also have his hands and feet covered in henna but without any design. On the third day, the groom and his party walk slowly to the bride's house in a *zaffer* (procession), singing and dancing the whole way. Traditionally the groom will stay at the bride's house for three days before seeing his family. The couple will then set up home.

❶ Getting There & Away

Although all the sights except Qasr Ibrim have roads leading to them, the only sites foreigners are currently allowed to drive to are Kalabsha, Beit al-Wali and Kertassi. The road to Abu Simbel is open, but foreigners are only allowed to travel in buses or microbuses in a police convoy. Abu Simbel can be reached by plane from Aswan, Luxor or Cairo. For more details on travelling to Abu Simbel, see p266.

For the moment, the rest of the sights can only be reached by boat, which is in any case the best way to see Lake Nasser's dramatic monuments. **African Angler** (www.african-angler.net) organises safaris on the lake, fishing safaris and safaris around the shore of the lake. See p35 for details.

Lake Nasser

Lake Nasser, the world's largest artificial lake, covers an area of 5250 sq km, and is 510km long and between 5km and 35km wide. On average it contains some 135 billion cu metres of water, of which an estimated six billion are lost each year to evaporation. Its maximum capacity is 157 billion cu metres of water, which was reached in 1996 after heavy rains in Ethiopia, forcing the opening of a special spillway at Toshka, about 30km north of Abu Simbel, the first time it had been opened since the dam was built. The Egyptian government has since embarked on a controversial project to build a new canal and irrigate thousands of acres in what is now the Nubian Desert between Toshka and the New Valley, a project ex-president Mubarak has likened to the Suez Canal and Aswan High Dam in its scale.

Numbers aside, the contrast between this enormous body of water and the remote desert stretching away on all sides makes Lake Nasser a place of austere beauty. Because the level of the lake fluctuates it has been difficult to build settlements around its edges. Instead the lake has become a place for migrating birds to rest on their long journeys north and south. Gazelles, foxes and several types of snake (including the deadly horned viper) live on its shores. Many species of fish live in its waters, including the enormous Nile perch. Crocodiles – some reportedly up to 5m long – and monitor lizards also live in the lake's shallows. The main human presence here, apart from the fast-growing population of Abu Simbel town and the few tourists who visit, is limited to the 5000 or so fishermen who spend up to six months at a time in small rowing boats, together catching about 50,000 tonnes of small fish each year.

Kalabsha, Beit al-Wali & Kertassi

As a result of a massive Unesco effort, the temples of **Kalabsha**, **Beit al-Wali** and **Kertassi** (adult/student E£30/15; ⊗8am-5pm) were transplanted from a now-submerged site about 50km south of Aswan. The new site is on the west bank of Lake Nasser just south of the High Dam.

The **Temple of Kalabsha**, started in the late Ptolemaic period and completed during the reign of Emperor Augustus (30 BC–AD 14), was dedicated to the Nubian solar god Merwel, known to the Greeks as Mandulis. Later it was used as a church.

An impressive stone causeway leads from the lake to the first pylon of the temple, beyond which are the colonnaded court and the eight-columned hypostyle hall. Inscriptions on the walls show various emperors or pharaohs in the presence of gods and goddesses. Just beyond the hall is the sanctuary, consisting of three chambers, with stairs leading from one up to the roof, where there are superb views of Lake Nasser and the High Dam, across the capitals of the hall and court. An inner passage, between the temple and the encircling wall, leads to a well-preserved Nilometer.

The nearby **Temple of Beit al-Wali**, mostly built by Ramses II, was cut into the rock and fronted by a brick pylon. On the walls of the forecourt, several fine reliefs detail the pharaoh's victory over the Nubians (on the south wall) and wars against the Libyans and Syrians (on the north wall). Ramses is gripping the hair of his enemies prior to smashing their brains while women plead for mercy. The finest scenes are those of Ramses on his throne, receiving the tribute paid by the defeated Nubians, including leopard skins, gold rings, elephant tusks, feathers and exotic animals.

Just north of the Temple of Kalabsha are the scant but picturesque remains of the **Temple of Kertassi**, with two Hathor columns, a massive architrave and four fine papyrus columns.

When the water level is low you can sometimes walk across to the site, otherwise you can find a motor boat on the western side of the High Dam (around E£30 for the return trip and an hour to visit).

Wadi as-Subua

The temples of **Wadi as-Subua** (adult/student E£35/20) were moved to this site, about 4km west of the original, now-submerged Wadi as-Subua, between 1961 and 1965.

Wadi as-Subua means 'Valley of Lions' in Arabic and refers to the avenue of sphinxes that leads to the **Temple of Ramses II**. Yet another monument built during the reign of the energetic pharaoh, the interior of the temple was hewn from the rock and fronted by a stone pylon and colossal statues. Behind the pylon is a court featuring 10 more statues of the pharaoh, beyond which lie a 12-pillared hall and the sanctuary. The central niche was once carved with relief scenes of Ramses making offerings to Amun-Ra and Ra-Horakhty. In Christian times this part was converted into a church, the pagan reliefs plastered over and painted with saints, so that now, with part of the plaster fallen away, Ramses II appears to be adoring St Peter!

About 1km to the north are the remains of the **Temple of Dakka**, begun by the Upper Nubian Pharaoh Arkamani (218–200 BC) us-

ing materials from much earlier structures and adapted by the Ptolemies and the Roman emperor Augustus. Originally situated 50km north of here, it is dedicated to the god of wisdom, Thoth, and is notable for its 12m-high pylon, which you can climb for great views of the lake and the surrounding temples.

The **Temple of Maharraqa**, the smallest of the three at this site, originally stood 40km north at the ancient site of Ofendina. Dedicated to Isis and Serapis, the Alexandrian god, its decorations were never finished and all that remains is a small hypostyle hall, where in the northeast corner an usual spiral staircase of masonry leads up to the roof.

Amada

Situated around 180km south of the High Dam there are two temples and a tomb at Amada (adult/student E£35/20).

The **Temple of Amada**, moved about 2.6km from its original location, is the oldest surviving monument on Lake Nasser. It was built jointly by 18th-dynasty pharaohs Tuthmosis III (1479–1425 BC) and his son Amenhotep II, with a hypostyle hall added by his successor, Tuthmosis IV (1400–1390 BC). Dedicated, like many temples in Nubia, to the gods Amun-Ra and Ra-Horakhty, it has some of the finest and best-preserved reliefs of any Nubian monument and contains two important historical inscriptions. The first, on a stele at the left (north) side of the entrance, describes the unsuccessful Libyan invasion of Egypt (1209 BC) during Pharaoh Merenptah's reign, and a second stele on the back wall of the sanctuary, describing Amenhotep II's military campaign (1424 BC) in Palestine, both no doubt designed to impress upon the Nubians that political opposition to the powerful Egyptians was useless.

The rock-cut **Temple of Derr**, built by Ramses II, stood on a curve of the Nile. The pylon and court have disappeared, but there are some well-preserved reliefs in the ruined pillared hall, illustrating the Nubian campaign of Ramses II, with the usual killing of his enemies, accompanied by his famous pet lion. Following cleaning, many of the scenes are once again brightly coloured.

Five minutes' walk away is the small rock-cut **Tomb of Pennut**, viceroy of Nubia under Ramses VI (1143–1136 BC), which was originally situated at Aniba, 40km south-

SAVING NUBIA'S MONUMENTS

When plans were finalised for the creation of the Aswan High Dam, worldwide attention focused on the many valuable and irreplaceable ancient monuments doomed by the waters of Lake Nasser. Between 1960 and 1980 the Unesco-sponsored Nubian Rescue Campaign gathered expertise and financing from more than 50 countries, and sent Egyptian and foreign archaeological teams to Nubia. Necropolises were excavated, many portable artefacts and relics were removed to museums and, while some temples disappeared beneath the lake, 14 were salvaged.

Ten of the temples, including the complexes of Philae, Kalabsha and Abu Simbel, were dismantled stone by stone and painstakingly rebuilt on higher ground. Four others were donated to the countries that contributed to the rescue effort, including the splendid Temple of Dendur, now reconstructed in the Metropolitan Museum of Art in New York.

Perhaps the greatest achievement of all was the preservation of the temples at Abu Simbel. Ancient magnificence and skill met with equally impressive modern technology as, at a cost of about US$40 million, Egyptian, Italian, Swedish, German and French archaeological teams cut the temples up into more than 2000 huge blocks, weighing from 10 to 40 tonnes each, and reconstructed them inside an artificially built mountain, 210m away from the water and 65m above the original site. The temples were carefully oriented to face the original direction, and the landscape of their original environment was recreated on and around the concrete, dome-shaped mountain.

The project took just over four years. The temples of Abu Simbel were officially reopened in 1968 while the sacred site they had occupied for more than 3000 years disappeared beneath Lake Nasser. A plaque to the right of the temple entrance eloquently describes this achievement: 'Through this restoration of the past, we have indeed helped to build the future of mankind.'

---

west of Amada. This well-preserved Nubian tomb consists of a small offering chapel and a niche at the rear, with reliefs depicting events and personalities from Pennut's life, including him being presented with a gift by Ramses VI.

Qasr Ibrim

The only Nubian monument visible on its original site, Qasr Ibrim once sat on top of a 70m-high cliff, about 60km north of Abu Simbel, but now has water lapping at its edges.

There is evidence that Ibrim was a garrison town from 1000 BC onward, and that around 680 BC the 25th-dynasty Pharaoh Taharka (690–664 BC), who was a Nubian by birth, built a mud-brick temple dedicated to Isis. During Roman times the town was one of the last bastions of paganism, its six temples converting to Christianity two centuries later than the rest of Egypt. It then became one of the main Christian centres in Lower Nubia and held out against the Muslims until the 16th century, when a group of Bosnian mercenaries, part of the Ottoman army, occupied the site. The mercenaries stayed on and eventually married into the local Nubian community, using part of the cathedral as a mosque.

Among the structural remains, the most impressive is an 8th-century sandstone cathedral built over Taharka's temple. The site is closed to visitors because of ongoing archaeological work.

Abu Simbel

☑097

Laid-back and quiet, the town of Abu Simbel lies 280km south of Aswan and only 40km north of the Sudanese border. Few tourists linger more than the few hours needed to visit the colossal temples for which it is famous. But anyone interested in the peace and tranquillity of the lake, in seeing the temples without the crowds, in wandering around a small non-touristy Nubian town without a police escort, or in listening to Nubian music might choose to hang around for a few days.

⊙ Sights & Activities

Temples of Abu Simbel   TEMPLES
(adult/student incl guide fee E£90/48.50; ☉6am-5pm Oct-Apr, to 6pm May-Sep) Overlooking Lake Nasser, the two temples of Abu Simbel are

reached by road or, if you are on a cruise boat, from one of the jetties leading directly into the fenced temple compound.

Great Temple of Ramses II

Carved out of the mountain on the west bank of the Nile between 1274 and 1244 BC, Ramses II's imposing temple was as much dedicated to the deified pharaoh himself as to Ra-Horakhty, Amun and Ptah. The four pharaoh's colossal statues fronting the temple are like gigantic sentinels watching over the incoming traffic from the south, undoubtedly designed as a warning of the strength of the pharaoh.

Over the centuries both the Nile and the desert sands shifted, and this temple was lost to the world until 1813, when it was rediscovered by chance by the Swiss explorer Jean-Louis Burckhardt. Only one of the heads was completely showing above the sand, the next head was broken off and, of the remaining two, only the crowns could be seen. Enough sand was cleared away in 1817 by Giovanni Belzoni for the temple to be entered.

From the temple's forecourt, a short flight of steps leads up to the terrace in front of the massive rock-cut facade, which is about 30m high and 35m wide. Guarding the entrance, three of the four famous colossal statues stare out across the water into eternity – the inner left statue collapsed in antiquity and its upper body still lies on the ground. The statues, more than 20m high, are accompanied by smaller statues of the pharaoh's mother, Queen Tuya, his wife Nefertari and some of his favourite children. Above the entrance, between the central throned colossi, is the figure of the falcon-headed sun god Ra-Horakhty.

The roof of the large hall is decorated with vultures, symbolising the protective goddess Nekhbet, and is supported by eight columns, each fronted by an Osiride statue of Ramses II. Reliefs on the walls depict the pharaoh's prowess in battle, trampling over his enemies and slaughtering them in front of the gods. On the north wall is a depiction of the famous Battle of Kadesh (c 1274 BC), in what is now Syria, where Ramses inspired his demoralised army, so that they won the battle against the Hittites. The scene is dominated by a famous relief of Ramses in his chariot, shooting arrows at his fleeing enemies. Also visible is the Egyptian camp, walled off by its soldiers' round-topped shields, and the fortified Hittite town, surrounded by the Orontes River.

The next hall, the four-columned vestibule where Ramses and Nefertari are shown in front of the gods and the solar barques, leads to the sacred sanctuary, where Ramses

Great Temple of Ramses II

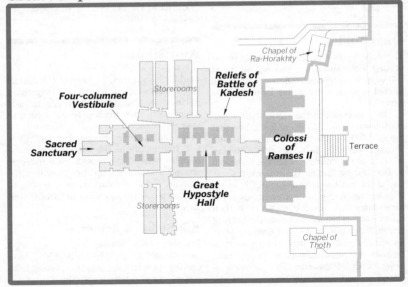

Chapel of Ra-Horakhty

Reliefs of Battle of Kadesh

Storerooms

Four-columned Vestibule

Sacred Sanctuary

Colossi of Ramses II

Terrace

Great Hypostyle Hall

Storerooms

Chapel of Thoth

and the triad of gods of the Great Temple sit on their thrones.

The original temple was aligned in such a way that each 21 February and 21 October, Ramses's birth- and coronation days, the first rays of the rising sun moved across the hypostyle hall, through the vestibule and into the sanctuary, where they illuminate the figures of Ra-Horakhty, Ramses II and Amun. Ptah, to the left, was never supposed to be illuminated. Since the temples were moved, this phenomenon happens one day later.

Temple of Hathor

Next to the Great Temple is the much smaller Temple of Hathor, with a rock-cut facade fronted by six 10m-high standing statues of Ramses and Nefertari, with some of their many children by their side. Nefertari here wears the costume of the goddess Hathor, and is, unusually, portrayed as the same height as her husband (instead of coming only up to his knees as most consorts were depicted).

Inside, the six pillars of the hypostyle hall are crowned with capitals in the bovine shape of Hathor. On the walls the queen appears in front of the gods very much equal to Ramses II, and she is seen honouring her husband. The vestibule and adjoining chambers, which have colourful scenes of the goddess and her sacred barque, lead to the sanctuary, with a weathered statue of Hathor as a cow emerging from the rock. The art here is softer and more graceful than in the Great Temple.

Sound-&-Light Show

(www.soundandlight.com.eg; adult/child E£80/45; ⊙shows 7pm, 8pm & 9pm Oct-Apr, 8pm, 9pm & 10pm May-Sep) A sound-and-light show is performed nightly. Headphones are provided, allowing visitors to listen to the commentary in various languages. While the text is flowery and forgettable, the laser show projected onto the temples is stunning and well worth the detour.

🛏 Sleeping & Eating

Few people stay the night in Abu Simbel, but there are a couple of places dedicated to package tours and a couple of others (listed here) for those looking for ultimate peace and quiet.

Along Abu Simbel's main road is a line-up of cheap cafes, with the Nubian Oasis and Wadi el-Nil among the most popular.

TOP CHOICE Eskaleh HOTEL **$$**
(☎0122 368 0521; www.eskaleh.net; d €60-70; ✳@) Part Nubian cultural centre with a library dedicated to Nubian history and culture, part ecolodge in a traditional Nubian mud-brick house, Eskaleh is known locally as the Nubian house (Beit an-Nubi). By far the most interesting place to stay in town, it's also a destination in its own right, if a bit pricey. The friendly owner, Fikry el Kashef, a Nubian musician, was educated in Switzerland but returned to his homeland after the Abu Simbel temples were moved. Having worked for years as a guide, Fikry created this wonderful enclave beside the lake with the idea of sharing the Nubian experience with interested foreigners. Comfy, simple rooms have local furniture, fans, air-con and good private bathrooms. Nubian kitchen staff prepare delicious home-cooked meals (three-course lunch or dinner E£70 to E£75) with organic produce from Fikry's garden and fish from the lake (beer is available). At night the quiet is absolute, a rare thing on the tourist trail along the Nile. Sometimes Fikry plays music with his friends, or he hosts performances of Nubian music and dance. A boat is available (E£200 per hour) to sail on the lake or to the temples.

Abu Simbel Village HOTEL **$**
(☎340 0092; s/d E£90/120; ✳) Abu Simbel's cheapest option, the faded Abu Simbel Village has basic vaulted rooms centred on a concrete courtyard.

Toya CAFE **$**
(☎012 357 7539; Tariq al-Mabad; breakfast E£8, mains E£15) A new place in town serving breakfast for early arrivals, or simple local cuisine in a lovely garden or madly painted rooms inside. It's a good place to stop for a drink or to smoke a sheesha.

ⓘ Information

Most things happen along the main road, including several banks with ATMs, **tourist police** (☎340 0277), post office, **hospital** (☎349 9237) and telephone centrale.

ⓘ Getting There & Away

Buses from Abu Simbel to Aswan (four hours, E£35) leave at 8am, 9.30am, 1pm and 4pm from Wadi el-Nil restaurant on the main road. There's no advance booking, and tickets are purchased on board. Micros make the same journey in three hours (E£30). EgyptAir flies to Abu Simbel from Cairo; if tourist demand increases, flights from Aswan may be restored; see p266 for flight details.

Siwa Oasis & the Western Desert

Why Go?

Older than the Pyramids, more sublime than any temple, Egypt's Western Desert stretches from the Nile and the Mediterranean to the Sudanese and Libyan borders, rolling far into Africa, oblivious to any lines drawn on the map. It's a place of elemental beauty as alluring as it is forbidding, where massive sand dunes ripple and swell, sunsets sear the sky, and wind sculpts rock into surreal works of art.

Amid this intense landscape, five major oases rise like islands of greenery, where flourishing palm plantations engulf crumbling medieval towns that were once important outposts along ancient caravan routes. Far from the hassle and hustle of the touristic Nile Valley, they're among the best spots in the country to glimpse rural Egyptian life – or just slow down, snack on locally grown dates and olives, and swim in natural hot and cold springs in the middle of a desert.

Best Places to Eat

» Kenooz Siwa (p313)

» Abdu's Restaurant (p313)

» Al-Babinshal Restaurant (p313)

Best Places to Stay

» Camping in the White Desert (p296)

» Shali Lodge (p311)

» Adrére Amellal (p312)

» Under The Moon Camp (p304)

» Al Tarfa Desert Sanctuary (p293)

When to Go

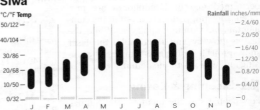

Siwa

Sep–Oct It's hot but not brutal, and dates are being harvested.	**Dec–Feb** Pleasant daytime temperatures give way to cold nights.	**Jun–Aug** Ridiculously hot; low seasons see fewer tourists and more discounts.

Siwa Oasis & the Western Desert Highlights

1 Exploring the geologic fantasyland of the **White Desert** (p296)

2 Soaking up the tranquil vibes and unique culture of breathtaking **Siwa Oasis** (p304)

3 Dipping into one of the numerous cool and hot **natural springs** (see boxed text p291) that lie scattered around the oases

4 Walking in wonder through the other-timely fortified mudbrick town of **Al-Qasr** (p292)

5 Taking a multiday safari among the endless dunes of the **Great Sand Sea** (p316)

6 Staying at one of the incredible **ecolodges** in Siwa or Dakhla Oasis (p313 & p293)

7 Scrambling around the old Roman fort at **Qasr el-Labakha** in Al-Kharga Oasis (p287)

History

As with the Sahara and other deserts that stretch across northern Africa, the Western Desert was once a savannah that supported all manner of wildlife. Giraffes, lions and elephants roamed here in Palaeolithic times, when the landscape is thought to have looked much like the African Sahel. All that you see in the desert – the huge tracts of sand, the vast gravel plains, the fossil beds and limestone rocks – were once the happy hunting grounds that supported nomadic tribes. Gradual climate change led to desertification and turned this vast area into the arid expanse seen today. Only depressions in the desert floor have enough water to support wildlife, agriculture and human settlement.

The ancient Egyptians understood the nature of the desert, which they saw as being synonymous with death and exile. Seth, the god of chaos who killed his brother Osiris, was said to rule here. It is believed the ancient Egyptians maintained links with the oases throughout the Pharaonic era, and with the accession of a Libyan dynasty (22nd dynasty, 945-715 BC), focus increased on the oases and the caravan routes linking the Nile Valley with lands to the west.

The oases enjoyed a period of great prosperity during Roman times, when new wells and improved irrigation led to the production of wheat and grapes for export to Rome. Garrisoned fortresses that protected the oases and trade routes can still be seen in the desert around Al-Kharga and Baharija, and Roman-era temples and tombs lie scattered across all the oases.

When the Romans withdrew from Egypt, the trade routes became a target for attacking nomadic tribes. Trade suffered, the oases went into gradual decline, and the population of settlements shrank. By medieval times, raids by nomads were severe enough to bring Mamluk garrisons to the oases. The fortified villages built to defend the population can still be seen in Dakhla (Al-Qasr, Balat) and Siwa (Shali).

The biggest change to the oases after the departure of the Romans occurred in 1958, when President Nasser created the so-called New Valley to relieve population pressure along the Nile. Roads were laid between the previously isolated oases, irrigation systems were modernised and an administration was established. The New Valley Governorate is the largest in Egypt and one of the least densely populated: there has never been enough work to draw significant numbers away from the Nile.

Long-Range Desert Safaris

Going on safari in the Western Desert can be one of the most rewarding experiences Egypt has to offer. It can also be one of the most frustrating. Each oasis has good local guides, but many of them operate on a shoestring and have neither the expertise nor the equipment to pull off a long-range expedition. This may not stop them from trying to persuade you they can do it. Included among the Western Desert's more challenging routes are the Great Sand Sea and remote Gilf Kebir (in Egypt's southwest corner), where you'll find the Cave of the Swimmers – made famous by *The English Patient* – and Gebel Uweinat, a 2000m-high peak trisected by the Egyptian, Libyan and Sudanese borders. These adventures require extensive organisation, quality equipment and plenty of experience to properly execute; the consequences of mishaps are severe, sometimes fatal. Military permits, which are available locally for short desert treks, must be procured in Cairo for longer trips.

The following operators have solid international reputations, are among the more reliable in Egypt, and will treat the desert with the respect it deserves. Multiday expeditions run only between October and April.

Al-Badawiya   DESERT TOUR
(☏02 2526 0994, 092 751 1163; www.badawiya.com) The three Ali brothers are Bedouin from Farafra, who have built up a significant business operating out of their Farafra-based hotel and an office in downtown Cairo. With considerable experience in the Western Desert, they can mount tailored camel or jeep safaris from three to 28 days in length. They have tents, cooking equipment and bedding.

Dabuka Expeditions   DESERT TOUR
(☏02-2525 7687; www.dabuka.de) Dabuka is a German-based company that specialises in North African desert travel, not only through Egypt but also through Libya, Sudan, Tunisia and Jordan. In Egypt it arranges multiday safaris into the Great Sand Sea, Gebel Uweinat and Gilf Kebir, as well as organising camel expeditions and running off-road driving courses.

Hisham Nessim   DESERT TOUR
(☏0100 667 8099; www.raid4x4egypt.com) Rally driver and owner of the Aquasun hotels in

Farafra and Sinai, Hisham Nessim has been driving in the desert for many years. With satellite phones, GPS and six 4WDs specially rigged for long-range desert travel, he is prepared to go to all corners of Egypt. He offers five programs (including self-drive) of seven to 14 days, or will tailor-make tours.

Khalifa Expedition   DESERT TOUR
(📞0122 321 5445; www.khalifaexpedition.com) Khaled and Rose-Maria Khalifa have been running camel and jeep tours throughout the Western Desert from their base in Bahariya Oasis for well over a decade. Rose-Maria is a qualified speech therapist and foot masseuse, which perhaps explains why they also offer meditation tours for people more interested in communing with nature than looking at antiquities.

Pan Arab Tours   DESERT TOUR
(📞02-2418 4409; www.panarabtours.com) With more than 30 years' experience, Pan Arab Tours has developed expertise in taking visitors into Egypt's deserts. Used by archaeologists as well as tourists, the company has a number of specially equipped vehicles and offers six itineraries throughout the country, from two to eight days.

Zarzora Expedition   DESERT TOUR
(📞0100 118 8221; www.zarzora.com) Captained by the experienced Ahmed Al-Mestekawi, a retired colonel who used to conduct military desert patrols, Zarzora does expeditions to Siwa, Gilf Kebir and the Great Sand Sea. Ahmed has in-depth knowledge of the area and moonlights as a lecturer on the desert's environment and history.

AL-KHARGA OASIS

📞092 / POP 100,000
As the closest of the oases to the Nile Valley, Al-Kharga used to have the unenviable role as a place of banishment for mischievous Nile Valley citizens. Its remote location, punishing summer heat and destructive winds meant that the oasis was synonymous with misery and exile. It may seem strange, then, that its chief town, Al-Kharga, was chosen as the capital of the New Valley Governorate in the 1950s. Life in the oasis has improved somewhat since then, and with a smattering of ancient sites it's not a bad stopover.

Lying in a 220km-long and 40km-wide depression, Al-Kharga Oasis was at the crossroads of vital desert trade routes, in-

DESERT NIGHTS

Most desert wildlife is nocturnal, and for good reason: daytime heat can be deadly. When visiting the Western Desert, it's smart – and fun – to think like an animal and experience it after sundown. When planning your desert adventures, consider the cycles of the moon. When it's full, the White Desert looks like it's been transplanted from Antarctica (long-exposure photographs will be surreal) and the Great Sand Sea slithers with shadow and light. On moonless nights, the star-filled sky dazzles with proof of the infinitude of the universe. Winter nights can be surprisingly cold, so be prepared; summer nights are deliciously cool.

cluding the famous **Darb al-Arba'een** (Forty Days Rd; see boxed text p283). This influential location brought it great prosperity, and with the arrival of the Romans, wells were dug, crops cultivated and fortresses built to protect caravan routes. Even as late as the 1890s, British forces were using lookout towers here to safeguard the 'back door' into Egypt. During the revolution of 2011, Al-Kharga was the only Western Desert oasis town to throw itself into the anti-Mubarak fray; after police fired into a crowd of protesters, the protesters set fire to the police station, a courthouse, and other buildings. Three demonstrators were reported killed, with about 100 injured.

Al-Kharga

The busy city of Al-Kharga is the largest town in the Western Desert and also the posterchild of the government's efforts to modernise the oases. Unfortunately, visitors are unlikely to see the town's drab housing blocks and wide, bare boulevards as a big improvement.

Still, the town makes a good base to explore some of the unique, gently crumbling sights found around this oasis valley floor. At the time of writing, police escorts for tourists in Al-Kharga were no longer common; if they start up again, you should be able to shake them by signing a paper at the tourist office refusing their 'protection.'

Al-Kharga Oasis

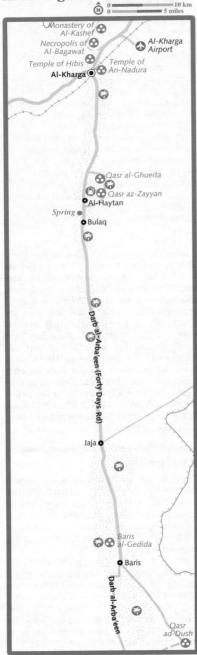

0 ————— 10 km
0 ————— 5 miles

Monastery of Al-Kashef

Necropolis of Al-Bagawat

Temple of Hibis

Al-Kharga

Al-Kharga Airport

Temple of An-Nadura

Qasr al-Ghueita

Qasr az-Zayyan

Al-Haytan

Spring

Bulaq

Darb al-Arba'een (Forty Days Rd)

Jaja

Baris al-Gedida

Baris

Darb al-Arba'een

Qasr ad-Dush

◉ Sights

Necropolis of Al-Bagawat ARCHAEOLOGICAL SITE
(Map p282; adult/student E£30/15; ⊘8am-5pm
Oct-Apr, to 6pm May-Sep) It may not look like
much from afar, but this necropolis is one
of the earliest surviving and best-preserved
Christian cemeteries in the world. About
1km north of the Temple of Hibis, it's built
on the site of an earlier Egyptian necropolis,
with most of the 263 mudbrick tombs appearing to date from the 4th to the 6th centuries AD. A few have vivid murals of biblical
scenes inside and some have ornate facades.
The **Chapel of Peace** has figures of the
Apostles on the squinches of the domes, just
visible through Greek graffiti. The **Chapel
of the Exodus**, one of the oldest tombs, has
the best-preserved paintings, including the
Old Testament story of Moses leading the
children of Israel out of Egypt, which is visible through some 9th-century graffiti. Another large family tomb (No 25) has a mural
of Abraham sacrificing Isaac, and the smaller **Chapel of the Grapes** (Anaeed al-Ainab)
is named after the images of grapevines that
cover the walls. A guardian will be anxious
to guide you to some of the more colourful
tombs; he'll expect a tip of about E£5.

Monastery of Al-Kashef RUIN
(Deir al-Kashef; Map p282) Dominating the cliffs
to the north of Al-Bagawat is the ruined
Monastery of Al-Kashef, strategically placed
to overlook what was one of the most important crossroads of the Western Desert – the
point where the Darb al-Ghabari from Dakhla crossed the Darb al-Arba'een. The magnificent mudbrick remains date back to the
early Christian era. Once five storeys high,
much of it has collapsed, but you can see the
tops of the arched corridors that criss-
crossed the building. To get here, walk or
drive on the left-hand track from the Necropolis of Al-Bagawat for about 2km. Admission
is included with the fee for Al-Bagawat.

Al-Kharga Museum of Antiquities MUSEUM
(Map p284; Sharia Gamal Abdel Nasser; adult/
student E£30/15; ⊘8am-5pm) Designed to resemble the architecture of nearby Bagawat,
this two-storey museum houses a small but
interesting selection of archaeological finds
from around Al-Kharga and Dakhla Oases.
The collection includes artefacts from prehistoric times through the Ottoman Era,
featuring tools, jewellery, textiles and other
objects that sketch out the cultural history
of the region.

THE WAY OF DUSTY DEATH

Al-Kharga Oasis sits atop what was once the only major African north–south trade route through Egypt's Western Desert: the notorious Darb al-Arba'een, or **Forty Days Rd**. A 1721km track linking Fasher in Sudan's Darfur province with Asyut in the Nile Valley, this was one of Africa's great caravan trails, bringing the riches of Sudan – gold, ivory, skins, ostrich feathers and especially slaves – north to the Nile Valley and beyond to the Mediterranean. It's thought to date back to the Old Kingdom, and the richness of the merchandise transported along this bleak track was such that protecting it was a priority. The Romans invested heavily here, building a series of fortresses – such as Qasr ad-Dush (p286), the Monastery of Al-Kashef (p282) and Qasr al-Ghueita (p286) – to tax the caravans and try to foil the frequent raids by desert tribesmen.

Despite the dangers, Darb al-Arba'een flourished until well into the Islamic era, by which time it was Egypt's main source of slaves. Untold numbers of tragic human cargo died of starvation and thirst on the journey north. According to 19th-century European travellers, slavers travelled in the intense summer heat, preferring to expose their merchandise to dehydration on what British geographer GW Murray (author of the 1967 *Dare Me to the Desert*) called 'the way of dusty death', rather than risk the possibility of bronchitis and pneumonia from the cold desert winter.

Despite repeated attempts by the British to suppress the trade, slaves were brought north until Darfur became part of Sudan at the beginning of the 20th century. The Darb al-Arba'een withered and today its route has been all but lost.

Temple of Hibis   TEMPLE
(Map p282) The town of Hebet ('the Plough', now corrupted into Hibis) was the capital of the oasis in antiquity, but all that remains today is the well-preserved limestone Temple of Hibis. Once sitting on the edge of a sacred lake, the temple was dedicated to Amun of Hibis (the local version of the god, who was sometimes given solar powers, becoming Amun-Ra), who appears with his usual companions, Mut and Khons. Construction of the temple began during the 25th dynasty, though the decorations and a **colonnade** were added over the next 300 years.

Look for reliefs in the **hypostyle hall** showing the god Seth battling with the evil serpent Apophis. There's also an **avenue of sphinxes**, a **court**, and an **inner sanctuary**.

The temple has been closed for a few years for restoration. It might be open by the time you read this – or not. It's 2km north of town, just to the left of the main road; pick-ups (50pt) heading to Al-Munira pass this way.

FREE Temple of An-Nadura   RUIN
(Map p282) Located on a hill to the right of the main road when heading north from town, just before the Temple of Hibis, the Temple of An-Nadura has strategic views of the area and once doubled as a fortified lookout. It was built during the reign of Roman emperor Antoninus Pius (AD 138-161) to protect the oasis. Now badly ruined, the superb vistas here are ideal for sunset adulation.

Tours
Al-Kharga has few private outfits offering desert trips, but **Mohsen Abd Al Moneam** (0100 180 6127) from the tourist office (see p285) is an experienced guide highly recommended by travellers. If you really dig archaeology, contact guide **Sameh Abdel Rihem** (0100 296 2192), an expert on Kharga's antiquities who has a palpable love for sights both popular and esoteric around the oasis. For information on longer desert safaris, see p280.

Sleeping
You'd better recalibrate your hotel expectations for Al-Kharga, where you can choose between dirty budget digs or pay a bunch for luxury. When we were there, there was nothing in between. Mohsen at the tourist office says that the **Kharga Oasis Hotel** (Map p284; Midan Nasser), once a good mid-range option that was closed at the time of research, should be re-opening soon under government management with rooms from about E£120 per night; call him for details.

Pioneers Hotel   HOTEL $$
(off Map p284; 792 9751; www.solymar.com; Sharia Gamal Abdel Nasser; s/d half board from €66/84; ✸@☲) While the salmon-pink, low-rise

Al-Kharga

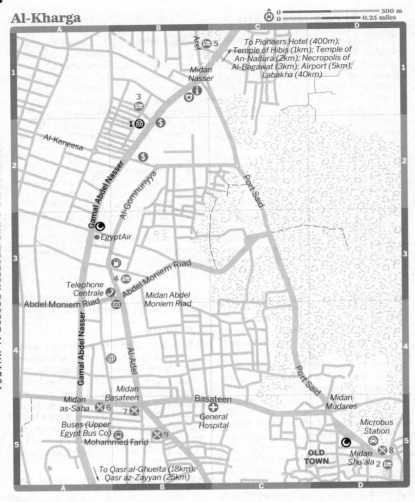

construction is reminiscent of a hollowed-out sponge cake, the hotel does offer the only clean rooms and by far the most comfort in Al-Kharga. There's a swimming pool, a fitness area, an outdoor cafe, billiards and a children's playground all connected by ridiculously lush grass. The restaurant is the only place in town where you can count on getting alcohol.

Hamadalla Hotel HOTEL **$**
(Map p284; ☎ 0122 831 3776; off Sharia Abdel Moniem Riad; s/d E£80/100, without air-con E£50/70; ✳) With torn carpeting, cracked plaster,

occasionally clean rooms and an obvious rodent issue, Hamadalla is one of the better budget choices in Al-Kharga. It's only a minute's walk from some good felafel and streetside cafes (around the *midan* by the main post office).

Dar al-Bida Hotel HOTEL **$**
(Map p284; ☎ 792 9393; Midan Sho'ala; s/d/tr E£65/85/125, without air-con E£50/60/80; ✳) Just off Midan Sho'ala, Dar al-Bida is convenient if you're arriving late or leaving early by minibus. Rooms are cramped but vie for cleanest budget digs in town – which isn't

Al-Kharga

saying much. Those with private and shared bathrooms are the same price. The family that runs this place is quite sweet.

El-Radwan Hotel HOTEL $
(Map p284; ☎792 1716; off Sharia Gamal Abdel Nasser; s/d E£70/90; ❄) Wow. Rarely have we seen a hotel fall so far so fast. What was once a solid budget place has become a filthy dive. And they've raised their prices! At least the air conditioning still works...

Waha Hotel HOTEL $
(Map p284; ☎792 0393; Sharia an-Nabawi; s/d with shared bathroom E£20/24) This gritty, tenement-like hotel is a great place to stay if you've lost your wallet, or want to use one of the shared toilets to re-enact the bathroom scene from the movie *Trainspotting*.

✕ Eating

There's a smattering of basic eateries around Midan Sho'ala, Sharia al-Adel and near Midan Basateen. Most are open for lunch and dinner. For breakfast, hit a felafel stand or a bakery.

Wembe EGYPTIAN $$
(Map p284; Midan Basateen; meals E£20-35; ☺lunch & dinner) This busy local eatery gets the thumbs up from people who are qualified to give such ratings, and serves the usual Egyptian comestibles: grilled meats, salads, rice and vegetables.

Pizza Ibn al-Balad EGYPTIAN FAST FOOD $$
(Map p284; Midan Sho'ala; pizzas E£20-40; ☺dinner) Strike us down if this place doesn't serve some of the best darned *fiteer* (Egyp-

tian pizza) in the oases. Deservedly, it's one of the most popular places to eat. Choose from cheese, veggie and tuna or beef toppings.

Al-Ahram GRILL $$
(Map p284; Sharia Basateen; mains E£7-35; ☺lunch & dinner) A small, friendly place serving roast chicken and *kofta* (minced meat and spices grilled on a skewer) accompanied by modest salads and vegetable dishes. The smell will lure you in.

Crepiano Cafe CREPERIE $
(Map p284; Midan Basateen; mains E£6-12; ☺dinner) If you're craving something different, head for this newcomer on the scene. They'll make you a crepe with virtually anything inside, from chocolate to sausage – or both together.

ℹ Information

Emergency
Ambulance (☎123)
Tourist police (Map p284; ☎792 1367; Sharia Gamal Abdel Nasser)

Internet Access
Internet cafe (Map p284; north of Midan Basateen; per hr E£2; ☺5pm-12am) Has wi-fi. May be open some mornings.

Medical Services
General hospital (Map p284; ☎792 0777; Sharia Basateen)

Money
Banque du Caire (Map p284; off Sharia Gamal Abdel Nasser) Has an ATM.
National Bank of Egypt (p284; Sharia Gamal Abdel Nasser) Across from the museum; has an ATM.

Post & Telephone
Private telephone shops are sprinkled all over Al-Kharga.
Main post office (Map p284; Sharia Abdel Moniem Riad; ☺8am-2.30pm Sat-Thu)
Telephone centrale (Map p284; Sharia Abdel Moniem Riad; ☺24hr)

Tourist Information
New Valley Tourist Office (Map p284; ☎792 1206; Midan Nasser; ☺9am-2pm Sat-Thu) Speak to Mohsen Abd Al Moneam, a motherlode of knowledge about Kharga and Dakhla Oases. He arranges private transport to sights around Al-Kharga and to Luxor. Call his mobile: ☎0100 180 6127.

ℹ Getting There & Away

Nope, there's no train to or from Luxor anymore.

Air

The airport is 5km north of town. The Petroleum Service Company (usually) has Sunday flights on a 15-seat plane, leaving Cairo at 8am and returning from Al-Kharga at 3pm (E£600 one way, 1½ hours). Contact the tourist office for schedules and bookings.

Bus

Upper Egypt Bus Co (Map p284; Sharia Mohammed Farid) operates buses to Cairo (E£65, eight to 10 hours) daily at 9pm and 10pm. There's one daily departure each to Asyut (E£15, three to four hours, 7pm), Baris (E£7, one hour, 6pm), and Dakhla Oasis (E£15, three hours, 2pm).

There's no direct bus service to Luxor. You can either catch a bus to Asyut and change there, or hire a private taxi.

Microbus

The most convenient way to get to Dakhla (E£15, three hours) or Asyut (E£15, three to four hours), minivans leave when full from the **microbus station** (Map p284; Midan Sho'ala).

Taxi

Special taxis can get you to Luxor (via Jaja) in three hours, but will set you back about E£400. Cairo (seven hours) costs E£1000 for the whole car (maximum seven people).

ℹ Getting Around

Al-Kharga is fairly spread out, with the bus station in the south-central part of town, the minibus stand in the southeast near the souq, and most hotels a fair hike away from both. Microbuses (50pt) run along the main streets of Al-Kharga, especially Sharia Gamal Abdel Nasser. Taxis between any two points in town cost E£2.

Around Al-Kharga

The most popular monuments near Al-Kharga lie along the good asphalt road that stretches south to Baris, but there are a few intriguing, harder-to-reach destinations north of town; though less visited, they are hands-down the best day or overnight trips you can make around the oasis.

QASR AL-GHUEITA & QASR AZ-ZAYYAN

It is easy to see why the Romans chose the site, some 18km south of Al-Kharga, for **Qasr al-Ghueita** (Map p282; adult/student E£25/15; ☺8am-5pm Oct-Apr). The imposing Roman mudbrick fortress has survived millennia and still dominates the road to Baris. Its name means 'Fortress of the Small Garden', which seems a misnomer for a place surrounded by desert. But in antiquity, Qasr al-Ghueita was the centre of a fertile agricultural community renowned for its grapes.

The garrison's massive outer walls enclose a 25th-dynasty sandstone temple, dedicated to the Theban triad Amun, Mut and Khons. In later centuries, the fortress served as the perimeter for a village, with some houses surviving along the outer wall. Within the hypostyle hall, a series of reliefs show Hapy, the potbellied Nile god, holding symbols of the nomes (provinces) of Upper Egypt. An asphalt road leads 2km to the temple from the main road.

About 7km further south are the remains of **Qasr az-Zayyan** (Map p282; adult/student E£25/15; ☺8am-5pm Oct-Apr), another fortress enclosing a temple, though less impressive than Qasr al-Ghueita and, frankly, not worth the admission price unless you're a die-hard archaeology fanatic.

If you don't have a vehicle you can get to the temples by taking a bus heading for Baris or a covered pick-up going to Bulaq (E£1.50). There is an asphalt road linking the two temples, but 7km is a long hike if you're on foot – be sure to take plenty of water.

BARIS

Baris, 90km south of Al-Kharga, was once one of the most important trading centres along the Darb al-Arba'een, but there is little left to remind you of that. Other than a few kiosks selling fuul (fava beans) and ta'amiyya (felafel), there is little of note apart from the mudbrick houses of **Baris al-Gedida**, about 2km north of the original town. Hassan Fathy, Egypt's most influential modern architect, designed the houses using traditional methods and materials and intended Baris al-Gedida to be a model for other new settlements. Work stopped at the outbreak of the Six Day War of 1967 and only two houses and some public spaces have ever been completed.

About 13km to the southeast of Baris is **Qasr ad-Dush** (Map p282; adult/student E£30/15; ☺8am-5pm Oct-Apr, to 6pm May-Sep), an imposing Roman temple-fortress completed around AD 177 on the site of the ancient town of Kysis. Dush was a border town strategically placed at the intersection of five desert tracks and one of the southern gateways to Egypt. It may also have been used to guard the Darb al-Dush, an east–west track to the Esna and Edfu temples in the Nile Valley. As a result it was solidly built and heavily garrisoned, with four or five more storeys lying underground. A 1st-century sandstone temple abutting the fortress was dedicated to Isis and Serapis. The gold decorations that once covered parts of the temple and earned it renown have long gone, but there is still some decoration on the inner stone walls.

ⓘ Getting There & Away

The frequent microbuses and pick-up trucks are the best public transport option between Al-Kharga and Baris, and cost about E£6. To cover the 15km between Qasr ad-Dush and Baris, negotiate a special ride with a covered pick-up, usually available for E£40, depending on waiting time. Hiring a private car for a day to see all the sights between Al-Kharga and Dush costs about E£300; this is best arranged through the tourist office in Al-Kharga.

QASR EL-LABAKHA

Set amid a desertscape of duney desolation, **Qasr el-Labakha** is a micro-oasis some 40km north of Al-Kharga. Scattered among sandy swells and rocky shelfs are the remains of a towering four-storey Roman fortress, two temples, and a vast necropolis where over 500 mummies have been unearthed (you can still see human remains in the tombs). A small camp, which is a perfect outpost for exploring the area, is run by the gentle-natured Sayed Taleb, who cleaned out the site's ancient aqueducts and uses them to water his garden. Day and overnight trips to Labakha can be arranged by the tourist office in Al-Kharga (see p285), with prices starting at around E£300 per vehicle.

About 20km west of Labakha lie the ruins at **Ain Umm el-Dabadib**, which has one of the most complex underground aqueduct systems built in this area by the Romans; keep going another 50km and you'll reach **Ain Amur** up on the Abu Tartur Plateau, the highest spring in the Western Desert (it's small so don't plan on swimming). Trips to these sites qualify as serious desert excursions that require 4WD and experienced drivers, who can be contacted through Al-Kharga's tourist office. Expect to pay around E£1600 per vehicle (which may include a back-up 4WD, for safety) to Ain Amur and back.

DAKHLA OASIS

📱 092 / POP 75,000

With more than a dozen fertile hamlets sprinkled along the Western Desert circuit road, Dakhla lives up to most visitors' romantic expectations of oasis life. Lush palm groves and orchards support traditional villages, where imposing, ancient mudbrick forts still stand guard over the townships and allude to their less tranquil past.

The region has been inhabited since prehistoric times, with fossilised bones hinting at human habitation dating back 150,000 years. In Neolithic times, Dakhla was the site of a vast lake, and rock paintings show that elephants, zebras and ostriches wandered its shores. As the area dried up, inhabitants migrated east to become the earliest settlers of the Nile Valley. In Pharaonic times, Dakhla retained several settlements and was a fertile land producing wine, fruit and grains. The Romans, and later Christians,

Dakhla Oasis

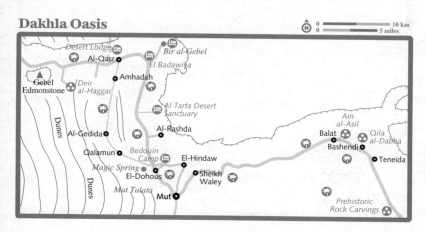

left their mark by building over older settlements, and during medieval times the towns were fortified to protect them from Bedouin and Arab raids. **Al-Qasr** (p292) is the best-preserved of these towns – and among the most enchanting places – anywhere in the Western Desert.

Mut

At the centre of the oasis lies the town of Mut, settled since Pharaonic times (Mut was the god Amun's consort). Although now a modern Egyptian town – it has the most facilities in the area and makes the most convenient base for travellers – you'll have a richer experience of Dakhla staying in or around Al-Qasr (see p292). Mut's wide boulevards and the proximity of the palm groves all help to give it a touch of charm – though only a touch.

◉ Sights

Ethnographic Museum MUSEUM
(Map p288; Sharia as-Salam; admission E£5; ☉by request) Dakhla's wonderful museum is only opened on request: ask at the tourist office (or call) and Omar Ahmad will arrange a time for your visit with the museum's

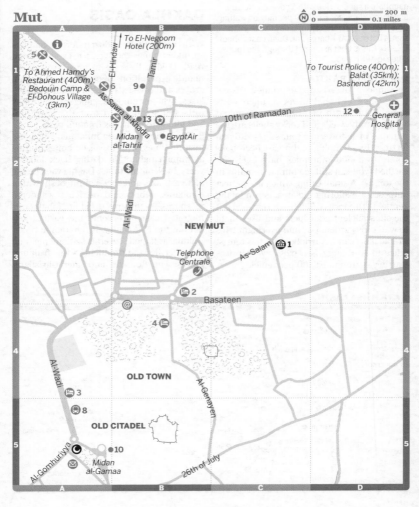

Mut

⊙ 0 —————— 200 m
0 —————— 0.1 miles

To El-Negoom Hotel (200m)

5 ⊗

ℹ

To Ahmed Hamdy's Restaurant (400m); Bedouin Camp & El-Dohous Village (3km)

⊗ 6   9 ●

● 11
⊗ ● 13 ✦
7 ⊗
Midan al-Tahrir   ● EgyptAir

El-Hindaw
Tamil
As-Sawra al-Khadra

$

To Tourist Police (400m); Balat (35km); Bashendi (42km)

10th of Ramadan   12 ●   ✚ General Hospital

Al-Wadi

NEW MUT

Telephone Centrale   As-Salam   🏛 1

🏤 2   Basateen

@

4 🏤

Al-Wadi

OLD TOWN

🏤 3

🏤 8

Al-Genayen

OLD CITADEL

Al-Gomhuriyya

✉   ● 10
Midan al-Gamaa

26th of July

manager, Ibrahim Kamel. The museum is laid out as a traditional home, with different areas for men, women and visitors. Displays of clothing, baskets, jewellery and other domestic items give an insight into oasis life.

Old Town of Mut

RUIN

For much of old Mut's existence, the villagers lived with the threat of raiding Bedouin. Most houses here have no outside windows, thus protecting against intruders and keeping out the heat and wind of the desert. The labyrinth of mudbrick houses and lanes that wind up the slopes of the hill is definitely worth exploring, even if you may sometimes stumble into a trash heap. From the top of the hill, at the old citadel (the original town centre), there are great views of the new town and the desert beyond.

☞ Tours

Most hotels and restaurants will also offer to take you on a trek around the area. A typical day trip includes visits to Al-Gedida (p293) and Qalamun (p292), a drive through the dunes, visits to a spring and a tour of Al-Qasr, with prices starting at around E£300 per car, which goes up to E£500 if you sleep in the desert (including dinner and breakfast). Alternatively, aspiring taxi drivers

---

Mut

◎ Sights
1 Ethnographic Museum..........................C3

🛏 Sleeping
2 Anwar Hotel...B3
3 El Forsan Hotel.......................................A4
4 Gardens Hotel B4

✕ Eating
5 Abu Mohamed Restaurant...................A1
   Anwar Restaurant.........................(see 2)
6 Fatri el-Wadi A1
7 Said Shihad..B2

ℹ Transport
8 Bus Station...A5
9 Microbuses & Servees B1
10 Microbuses to Farafra and
   Al-Kharga Oases A5
11 Pick-Ups to Al-Qasr B1
12 Pick-Ups to Balat & Bashendi.............D1
13 Upper Egypt Bus Co Booking
   Office B2
   Upper Egypt Bus Co Ticket
   Office ....(see 8)

---

can drive you to outlying sights for around E£300 for a full day or E£150 for a half day.

The owners of the Bedouin Camp (p289) are camel experts and can arrange long and short trips into the desert around Dakhla. You're looking at about E£60 for an hour, or up to E£250 to spend the night in the dunes, including food. If you want to go further afield, check with the tourist office to confirm whether the person taking you has the necessary permits – Dakhla is one of the closest oases to Gilf Kebir, but permits to go there are only issued from Cairo. For more information about desert safaris, see p280.

🛏 Sleeping

Mut has a decent selection of hotels, although most crowd the budget end of the spectrum.

You should be able to camp near the dunes west of Mut or by Al-Qasr (on a starlit plateau just north of town), but check first with the tourist office in Mut (see p290). If you need a room but are truly strapped for cash, there's always the grubby Gardens Hotel (Map p288; ☎782 1577; Sharia al-Genayen; s/d E£15/25)

El Forsan Hotel   HOTEL $
(Map p288; ☎782 1343; Sharia al-Wadi; s/d E£90/110, without air-con E£70/90; ✳@☎) While the main building is a typical concrete confabulation, the domed mudbrick bungalows out back are more stylish, if more worn, option. There's a garden cafe where movies or football matches are projected onto a screen every night. The manager, Zaqaria, has a wry sense of humour. Breakfast is huge.

El-Negoom Hotel   HOTEL $
(off Map p288; ☎782 0014; north of Sharia as-Sawra al-Khadra; s/d E£80/100, without air-con E£60/70; ✳@☎) On a quiet street behind the tourist office and near a selection of restaurants, this friendly hotel has a span of trim little abodes with bathrooms, some even with air-con and TV. This is one of the most dependable options, and the best value in town.

Bedouin Camp &
El-Dohous Village   HOTEL $$
(Map p287; ☎785 0480; www.dakhlabedouins.com; s/d half-board E£125/200; @☎) El-Dohous Village has a huge variety of domed and curvey rooms that give off good vibes, all decorated with local crafts. The hilltop restaurant has outstanding views and there are plenty of

cushioned chill-out areas strewn about the place. The friendliness of the staff is just one more reason to stay.

Anwar Hotel HOTEL **$**
(Map p288; ☑782 0070; Sharia Basateen; s/d/tr from E£50/75/100; ✳) The friendly and sociable Mr Anwar runs this family establishment with gusto and offers relatively clean rooms with flexible prices. Some have shared bathrooms, others private bathrooms, some with air-con, others without. Noise from the nearby mosque can be an issue, and the younger Anwars are a bit overeager to sell their tours.

✗ Eating & Drinking

There is no fancy dining in Mut, but there is some decent, fresh food (mostly of the chicken/kebab/rice variety) to be had. Most felafel/fuul takeaways usually close by noon.

Said Shihad GRILL **$$**
(Map p288; Sharia as-Sawra al-Khadra; meals E£20-35; ☺dinner) Owner Said is on to a good thing here: grilling up a meat-centric feast nightly to a dedicated following of hungry locals. The shish kebab is the thing to go for – perfectly succulent and served with potatoes in a tomato sauce, rice and beans.

Ahmed Hamdy's Restaurant EGYPTIAN **$$**
(Map p288; Sharia as-Sawra al-Khadra; meals E£20-30; ☺lunch & dinner) On the main road into town is Ahmed Hamdy's popular place serving delicious chicken, kebabs, vegetables and a few other small dishes inside or on the terrace. The freshly squeezed lime juice is excellent and you can request beer (E£12) and sheesha.

Abu Mohamed Restaurant EGYPTIAN **$$**
(Map p288; Sharia as-Sawra al-Khadra; meals E£20-40; ☺breakfast, lunch & dinner; @) Abu Mohamed touts, cooks and serves in this simple roadside restaurant. His set meal includes good vegetables with kebab or pigeon (order ahead) and ends with homemade *basbousa* (a sticky dessert). Cold beer, internet (E£10 per hour) and bike hire (E£20 per day) are available.

Fatri el-Wadi EGYPTIAN FAST FOOD **$$**
(Map p288; Sharia as-Sawra al-Khadra; mains E£20-60; ☺dinner) Fresh-from-the-oven *fiteers*, made to order by a friendly crew.

Anwar Restaurant EGYPTIAN **$**
(Map p288; Sharia Basateen; meals E£2-25; ☺breakfast, lunch & dinner) Below the hotel of the same name, Anwar serves up ta'amiyya and fuul, plus the usual chicken-and-rice combo.

Information

Emergency
Ambulance (☑123)
Tourist police (off Map p288; ☑782 1687; Sharia 10th of Ramadan)

Internet Access
Internet connections in Mut have been known to approach courier-pigeon speed. Some hotels now have internet terminals, though prices are much higher (E£10 per hour) than at the rare internet cafes.
Internet cafe (Map p288; Sharia Basateen; per hr E£2; ☺11am-midnight)

Medical Services
General hospital (Map p288; ☑782 1555; off Sharia 10th of Ramadan)

Money
Banque Misr (Map p288; Sharia al-Wadi; ☺8.30am-2pm Sun-Thu) Has an ATM, exchanges cash and makes cash advances on Visa and MasterCard.

Post & Telephone
Main post office (Map p288; Midan al-Gamaa; ☺8am-2pm Sat-Thu)
Telephone centrale (Map p288; Sharia as-Salam; ☺24hr)

Tourist Information
Tourist office (Map p288; ☑782 1685; Sharia as-Sawra al-Khadra; ☺8am-3pm & some evenings) Friendly tourist-office director Omar Ahmad is a mine of knowledge about the oases. He can be contacted anytime on his mobile: ☑0122 179 6467.

❶ Getting There & Away

Bus
Upper Egypt Bus Co (Map p288; ☑782 4366; Sharia al-Wadi) runs buses at 7pm and 8pm to Cairo (E£75, eight to 10 hours) via Al-Kharga Oasis (E£20, one to two hours) and Asyut (E£40, four to five hours). Additional buses head to Al-Kharga at 6am and 10pm. You can also go to Cairo via Farafra Oasis (E£25, four hours) and Bahariya Oasis (E£50, seven hours) at 6am and 5pm. There's a **ticket office** at Midan al-Tahrir, and buses stop to pick up passengers across the circle from the kiosk.

Servees & Microbus
Microbuses leave when full from the old part of Mut, near the mosque, and cost E£14 to Al-Kharga, E£20 to Farafra and E£80 to Cairo (night runs only).

ⓘ Getting Around

Abu Mohamed Restaurant (p290) rents out bicycles for E£20 per day.

Most places in Dakhla are linked by crowded pick-ups, Peugeots or microbuses, but working out where they all go requires a degree in astrophysics. Those heading to Al-Qasr (E£1.50) depart from Sharia as-Sawra al-Khadra. You can take pick-ups to Balat and Bashendi from in front of the hospital for E£1.50. Most others depart from the *servee* station on Sharia Tamir.

It may prove easier on occasion to bargain for a 'special' pick-up.

Around Mut
◉ Sights & Activities

Mut Talata   SPRING
(Map p287; admission E£10) There are several hot sulphur pools around the town of Mut, but the easiest to reach is Mut Talata. It's at the site of the small Mut Inn, so unless you are staying there, you've got to pay to take a dip. The pool's funny-coloured water is both warm and actually relaxing, though it may stain clothes.

Magic Spring   SPRING
(Map p287; admission E£10) Off the road to Qalamun is the so-called Magic Spring, a cool, rock-lined pool where you can relax with soft drinks (E£5-10) served at a small cafeteria under a couple of palm trees.

Bir al-Gebel   SPRING
(Map p287; admission E£10) Set among breathtaking desert scenery, Bir al-Gebel has been turned into a day-trip destination where blaring music and hundreds of schoolchildren easily overwhelm any ambience it might have had. It's best to come in the evening, when it's quieter and the stars blaze across the night sky. If you arrive during spring peak hour, there's a serene natural spring about 500m before Bir al-Gebel on the right, concealed behind a brick pump house. A sign marks the turn-off 20km north of Mut, from where it's about another 5km to the springs.

Sand Dunes & Camel Rides   DESERT TOURS
A few kilometres out past the southern or western end of town you can have a roll around in sand dunes which, while not the most spectacular in the desert, are easy to reach for people without their own transport (if on foot, count on at least an hour walk each way). Almost every hotel and restaurant in Mut offers day trips that include a sand-dune stop. Sunset camel rides out to the dunes can also be arranged (see Tours, p289).

THESE ARE A FEW OF OUR FAVOURITE SPRINGS...

There's nothing better after a hard day's rambling along the dusty roads of the desert than a soak or swim in one of the many springs that dot the Western Desert. The following are but a few of our best-loved waterholes.

Cleopatra's Bath (p306) One of the most famous, stunning and clear cool bubbling springs in the Western Desert.

Bir Wahed (p306) A hot, jacuzzi-like spring sitting among the dunes on the edge of the Great Sand Sea near a cold spring lake.

Ain Gomma (p302) A small, gushing, clear and cool isolated spring in a mini-oasis 45km south of Bawiti, surrounded on all sides by the vast desert expanse.

Bir al-Gebel (p291) Surrounded by breathtaking scenery, it's ideal in the evening, after rowdy crowds of kids are gone.

Spring Etiquette

When bathing in the public springs of the oases, it's important to be mindful of generally accepted spring etiquette:

» If local men are bathing, women should wait until they finish before entering the water.

» At springs within towns, women should wear a baggy T-shirt and shorts or, preferably, pants over their bathing suit. Use your best (conservative) judgement, and don't swim if the vibe is leery.

» Men should leave the Speedos at home.

Rock Carvings   ARCHAEOLOGICAL SITE

(Map p287) Carved into the weird rock formations 45km towards Al-Kharga, where two important caravan routes once met, are prehistoric petroglyphs of camels, giraffes and tribal symbols. The site has recently suffered from the attentions of less-scrupulous travellers who have all but ruined most of these curious images with their own graffiti. 4WD and a good driver are necessary to get here.

BALAT

For a captivating glance into life during medieval times, pay a visit to the Islamic village of Balat, 35km east of Mut. Built during the era of the Mamluks and Turks on a site that dates back to the Old Kingdom, charismatic winding lanes weave through low-slung corridors past Gaudí-like moulded benches. Palm fronds are still used for shelter as smoothly rounded walls ease into each other. The tiny doors here were designed to keep houses cool and confuse potential invaders. A guide will happily take you onto the roof of one of the three-storey mudbrick houses for commanding views (a small tip is expected). To get to Balat, a pick-up from near the general hospital in Mut will cost E£1.50.

A dirt track that meets the main road 200m east of Balat heads north about 2km to **Ain al-Asil**, or Spring of the Origin, the site of a ruined fortress that's much less interesting than its name suggests. Continue another 1.5km to find **Qila al-Dabba** (adult/student E£25/15; ⊘8am-5pm), Balat's ancient necropolis. The five mastabas (mudbrick structures above tombs that were the basis for later pyramids) here, the largest of which stands over 10m high, date back to the 6th dynasty. Four are ruined, but one has been restored and is now open to the public, though you may need to find a guardian in the nearby buildings to unlock it. You'll need a private vehicle – or plenty of endurance – to get here.

BASHENDI

This small village to the north of the main Dakhla–Al-Kharga road takes its name from Pasha Hindi, the medieval sheikh buried nearby. The **Tomb of Pasha Hindi** is covered by an Islamic-era dome, which sits over a Roman structure, clearly visible from inside the building. Locals make pilgrimages to pray for the saint's intercession. There's a **carpet-making cooperative** (admission E£3; ⊘9am-1pm Sun-Thu) in town, where you can

see rugs being woven and browse through the showroom. Nearby is the sandstone **Tomb of Kitines** (adult/student incl Tomb of Pasha Hindi E£25/15; ⊘8am-5pm), which was occupied by Senussi soldiers during WWI and by a village family after that. Nevertheless, some funerary reliefs have survived and show the 2nd-century AD notable meeting the gods Min, Seth and Shu.

AL-QASR

One of the must-see sights in the western oases is the extraordinary medieval/Ottoman town of Al-Qasr, which lies on the edge of lush vegetation at the foot of the pink limestone cliffs that mark the northern edge of the oasis. Portions of the old village have been thoughtfully restored to provide a glimpse of how other oasis towns looked before the New Valley development projects had their way with them; the effect is pure magic. Several hundred people still live in the town that not so long ago was home to several thousand.

Al-Qasr is also a prime spot to romp around in the desert without a guide. Just north of town the plateau is textured with shallow, sandy wadis (a valley or dry riverbed) that weave around rocky benches and weirdly hewn hills. The ground is littered with fossils, including sharks' teeth. Meander with ease, or, for what may be the most sweeping vistas in any of the oases, hike to the top of the high bluffs that rise from the plateau – just choose the massive ramp of sand that looks most promising, and trek on up! Running back down hundreds of feet of sand is an instant regression to childhood glee. From Al-Qasr, it takes about two hours to reach the top, and longer if you dawdle, so bring enough water and snacks for the round trip. If the moon is full, set out before sunset and return by moonlight.

◉ Sights

The Supreme Council for Antiquities has taken responsibility for the town, but doesn't charge an entrance fee. At some point while you meander around the mudbrick maze, it's helpful to hook up with one of the Antiquities guards (who will expect a 'donation' of E£10). They can lead you to the highlights listed below, which you'll have trouble finding on your own. A note to photographers: midday is actually a good time to take pictures here, since that's when the most light penetrates the canyonlike corridors.

The old town is built on the ancient foundations of a Roman city and is thought to be one of the oldest inhabited areas of the oases. The gateway of a temple to Thoth is now the front of a private house, and inscribed blocks from the temple have been used in other local buildings. Most of what you can see today, however, dates to the Ottoman period (1516–1798). During its heyday, this was probably the capital of the oasis, easily protected by barring the fort's quartered streets. The size of the houses and the surviving fragments of decoration suggest a puzzling level of wealth and importance given to this town by the Ottomans.

The architecture of the narrow covered streets harks back to its ancient origins. The winding lanes manage to remain cool in the scalding summer and also serve to protect their inhabitants from desert sandstorms. Entrances to old houses can be clearly seen and some are marked by beautiful lintels – acacia beams situated above the door. Carved with the names of the carpenter and the owner of the house, the date and a verse from the Quran, these decorative touches are wonderfully preserved.

There are 37 lintels in the village, the earliest of which dates to the early 16th century. One of the finest is above the **Tomb of Sheikh Nasr ad-Din** inside the old mosque, which is marked by a restored 12th-century mudbrick minaret. Adjoining it is **Nasr ad-Din Mosque**, with a 21m-high minaret. Several buildings have been renovated, including one that appears to have been a **madrassa**, a school where Islamic law was taught and which doubled as a town hall and courthouse: prisoners were tied to a stake near the entrance.

Also of interest is the restored **House of Abu Nafir**. A dramatic pointed arch at the entrance frames a huge studded wooden door. Built of mudbrick, and on a grander scale than the surrounding houses, it incorporates huge blocks from an earlier structure, possibly a Ptolemaic temple, decorated with hieroglyphic reliefs.

Other features of the town include the **pottery factory**, a **blacksmith's forge**, a **waterwheel**, an **olive press** and a huge old **corn mill** that has been fully restored to function with Flintstone-like efficiency when its shaft is rotated. Near the entrance is the **Ethnographic Museum** (admission E£3; ⊙9am–sunset). Occupying Sherif Ahmed's house, which itself dates back to 1785, the

museum's everyday objects try to give life to the empty buildings around them.

Heading back to Mut from Al-Qasr, take the secondary road for a change of scenery. You can visit several **tombs** near the ruined village of Amhadah, dating from the 2nd century. The road then passes through the villages of **Al-Gedida** and **Qalamun**, where there are Ottoman and modern houses built of mud.

🛏 Sleeping

TOP CHOICE Al Tarfa

Desert Sanctuary　　　BOUTIQUE HOTEL $$$
(Map p287; ☑910 5007; www.altarfa.net; r full board from €400; ❉@☰) Taking the high end to unheard-of heights in Dakhla, Al Tarfa is flat out desert-fabulous. The traditionally inspired decor is superbly tasteful and impeccably rendered, down to the smallest detail – from the embroidered bedspreads that look like museum-quality pieces to the mud-plastered walls that don't show a single crack. Even the golden dunes that flow behind the resort seem like they've been landscaped to undulating perfection. Each suite is unique, the pool is like a liquid sapphire, and the spa features massage therapists brought in from Thailand.

🏠 Desert Lodge

　　　　　　　　　　　　BOUTIQUE HOTEL $$$
(Map p287; ☑772 7061; www.desertlodge.net; s/d/tr half board €75/120/175; ❉@☰) This thoughtfully designed, ecofriendly mudbrick fortress of a lodge crowns a hilltop overlooking the old town of Al-Qasr. The restaurant is adequate, and there is also a bar, a private hot spring, a painting studio on the desert's edge, and many of the services you would expect for the price.

El Badawiya

　　　　　　　　　　　　BOUTIQUE HOTEL $$
(Map p287; ☑772 7451; www.badawiya.com; s/d €50/64; ❉@☰) Perched above the fork in the road to Bir al-Gebel, this luxurious hotel features comfortable domed rooms of stone, mud and tile, most with awesome balconies with mesmerising views of the oasis and desert. The sweet spot is the swimming pool. This is a great choice for families.

Al-Qasr Hotel

　　　　　　　　　　　　HOTEL $
(☑787 6013; r E£30) This old backpacker favourite sits above a cafe/restaurant near the old town. The simple rooms with shared bathroom are fine for the price, and some even boast views onto Al-Qasr. There's a breezy upstairs communal sitting area

where you can play games or relax, and for E£5 you can sleep on a mattress on the roof. Owner Mohamed has a long history of fine hospitality. Its located on the main highway that runs from Mut to Al Qasr and on to Farafra Oasis.

Bir Elgabal Camp HOTEL **$$**
(☑772 6600; elgabalcamp@hotmail.com; s/d E£90/160; ✆) Here you're definitely paying for location – an idyllic position at the base of the soaring desert mountains, next to Bir al-Gebel spring, with a guests-only spring of its own. Rooms are clean but very basic. Fairly isolated from any amenities, the hotel is 5km from the turn-off on the Mut road.

❶ Getting There & Away
Pick-ups to Al-Qasr leave from opposite Said Shihad restaurant in Mut and cost E£1.50, or take a minibus from Mut's minibus stand (E£1.50).

DEIR AL-HAGGAR
This restored **sandstone temple** (adult/ student E£25/15; ☻8am-sunset) is one of the most complete Roman monuments in Dakhla – which is saying something, but not that much. Dedicated to the Theban triad of Amun, Mut and Khons, as well as Horus (who can be seen with a falcon's head), it was built between the reigns of Nero (AD 54–68) and Domitian (AD 81–96). Some relief panels are quite well preserved, many are missing, and most of those in the inner sanctuary are covered in bird poop. If you look carefully in the adjacent Porch of Titus you can see the names of the entire team of Gerhard Rohlfs, the 19th-century desert explorer, carved into the wall. Also visible are the names of famous desert travellers Edmonstone, Drovetti and Houghton.

Deir al-Haggar is signposted about 7km west of Al-Qasr; from the turn-off it's another 5km to the temple.

FARAFRA OASIS

☑092 / POP 17,000
Blink and you might miss dusty Farafra, the least populated and most remote of the Western Desert's oases. Its exposed location made it prone to frequent attacks by Libyans and Bedouin tribes, many of whom eventually settled in the oasis and now make up much of the population.

In recent years, the government has been increasing its efforts to revitalise this region, and the production of olives, dates, apricots, guavas, figs, oranges, apples and sunflowers is slowly growing. Though light on tourist infrastructure or any real attractions, Farafra's proximity to the White Desert (only 20km away) and its torpid pace of life and extensive palm gardens manage to draw a small trickle of travellers each year.

Qasr al-Farafra

The only real town in Farafra Oasis, Qasr al-Farafra remains a barely developed speck on the Western Desert circuit, though it's in the process of getting a facelift. The town's tumbledown Roman fortress was originally built to guard this part of the desert caravan route, though these days all it has to show for it is a mound of rubble.

Some small, mudbrick houses still stand here, their doorways secured with medieval peg locks and their walls painted with verses of the Quran. The main reason for stopping is to visit the **White Desert** (p296). It's also a good place to buy camel hair socks, scarves and gloves, which are sold around town.

◉ Sights & Activities
If you've got time to kill before or after a safari trip, stroll through the palm gardens just west of 'downtown.' They're truly lovely,

Farafra Oasis

To Black Desert (40km); Bawiti (Bahariya Oasis; 90km)

Crystal Mountain

Naqb as-Sillim

Twin Peaks

Bahariya–Dakhla Rd

Bir Regwa

Abu Nuss Lake

Aquasun Farafra

Bir Sitta

Ain Bishay

Qasr al-Farafra

White Desert

Farafra Oasis

and full of activity during the date harvest (September/October).

Badr's Museum
MUSEUM

(Map p295; donation E£10; ☉8.30am-sunset) Badr Abdel Moghny is a self-taught artist whose gift to his town has become its only real sight. Badr's Museum features loads of his interesting work, much of which records traditional oasis life. His distinctive style of painting and sculpture in mud, stone and sand has won him foreign admirers; he exhibited successfully in Europe in the early 1990s and later in Cairo.

Bir Sitta
SPRING

(Well No 6; Map p294) A popular stop is Bir Sitta, a sulphurous hot spring 6km west of Qasr al-Farafra. Water gushes into a jacuzzi-sized concrete pool and then spills out into a larger tank. This is a good place for a night-time soak under the stars.

Ain Bishay
SPRING

(Map p294) The Roman spring of Ain Bishay bubbles forth from a hillock on the north-west edge of town. It has been developed into an irrigated grove of date palms together with citrus, olive, apricot and carob trees, and is a cool haven.

Abu Nuss Lake
LAKE

(Map p294) If you're hanging around in the summer, a plunge in cool Abu Nuss Lake offers instant relief from oppressive afternoons. You might see some interesting bird life, too.

☞ Tours

Farafra is nearer than Bahariya to the White Desert, yet there is a very limited choice of desert outfits. The sister hotels **Al-Waha** and **Sunrise** (p296) offer trips around Farafra and the White Desert, with prices starting at around E£400 per vehicle for an overnight stay. **Al-Badawiya** and **Aquasun** offer tours starting at about E£600. They're also well prepared for long-range desert travel; see also p280.

⌸ Sleeping

Al-Badawiya Safari & Hotel BOUTIQUE HOTEL $$
(Map p295; ☎751 0060; www.badawiya.com; s/d €20/25, ste with air-con €35/50; @☀) Al-Badawiya dominates Farafra tourism with their hotel and safari outfit. Immaculate, comfortable rooms have a Bedouin theme, there's a refreshing pool, and plenty of arches and domes. Reservations are recommended in

Qasr al-Farafra

◎ Sights
1 Badr's Museum A2

⌸ Sleeping
2 Al-Badawiya Safari & Hotel B1
3 Al-Waha Hotel A2
4 Sunrise Hotel & Safari B1

☒ Eating
5 Al-Abeyt A3
6 El-Aseil A3
7 Hussein's Restaurant A3
8 Samir Restaurant A3

⊙ Transport
9 Buses to Bahariya & Cairo B3
10 Microbuses to Dakhla and
      Bahariya B3

winter. Their White and Western Desert tours are thoroughly professional (see p280).

Aquasun Farafra BOUTIQUE HOTEL $$
(Map p294; ☎0122 780 7999; www.raid4x4egypt. com; Bir Sitta; s/d half board €35/50; ❄☀) Built beside Bir Sitta and nestled in its own idyllic oasis, Aquasun has 21 chalet-style rooms built around a peaceful garden. Each has its own porch, thatched with palm fronds.

Piping-hot water from Bir Sitta fills the hotel pool. Owner Hisham Nessim has had years of hotel-owning experience in Sinai and is also a long-time desert-safari operator (see p280).

Al-Waha Hotel   HOTEL $
(Map p295; ☏0122 720 0387; wahafarafra@ya-hoo.com; d with shared bathroom E£60, r E£75) A small, spartan hotel opposite Badr's Museum, Al-Waha is the only real budget choice in town. The location is convenient, and the rooms, with faux-oriental rugs, are well-worn but acceptably clean. In summer the cement walls throb with heat.

Sunrise Hotel & Safari   HOTEL $$
(Map p295; ☏0122 720 1387; wahafarafra@yahoo.com; r E£150) The newest hotel in Farafra is brought to you by the same family that owns Al-Waha Hotel. Here, they've gone for the Bedouin domed motif, and put refrigerators and televisions in brick bungalows that surround a rectangular courtyard. Some of the rooms have a strong septic stench, so check out a few.

✖ Eating

As with most other facilities, eating choices are limited in Farafra.

A trio of restaurants in the centre of town, **El-Aseil**, **Hussein's Restaurant** and **Samir Restaurant** (all Map p295) serve the typical Egyptian variety of grilled dishes for similar prices (about E£25 for a full meal, including rice, salad, beans, tahini and bread). Samir's is the most atmospheric of the three, but you'll pay a few pounds extra for the fancy tablecloths. For breakfast, hit **Al-Abeyt** (Map p295), a friendly felafel/fuul (from E£1) joint.

The Al-Badawiya and Aquasun hotels also have restaurants.

ⓘ Information

For tourist information, contact the tourist office in Mut (p290). For internet, you might be able to get online at either the computer shop or cellphone shop on the main drag.

Bank Misr (Map p295; main Bahariya–Dakhla rd) Being built at time of writing; *might* have an ATM. Or not.

Hospital (Map p295; ☏751 0047; main Bahariya–Dakhla rd) For dire emergencies only.

Post office (Map p295; Bir Sitta; ⊙8.30am-2.30pm Sat-Thu)

Telephone centrale (Map p295; Al Bosta)

Tourist police (Map p295; Sharia al-Mishtafa Nakhaz) No telephone.

ⓘ Getting There & Away

There are **Upper Egypt Bus Co** buses from Farafra to Cairo (E£45, eight to 10 hours) via Bahariya (E£25, three hours) at 10am and 10pm. Buses from Farafra to Dakhla (E£25, four hours) originate in Cairo and leave around 2pm to 3pm and around 2am. Tickets are bought from the conductor. Buses stop across from Al-Abeyt restaurant and at the petrol station.

Microbuses to Dakhla (E£20, three to four hours) and Bahariya (E£20, three hours) leave from the town's main intersection when full (not often), so you're better off going early in the morning. Rare *servees* to Dakhla cost E£20, to Al-Kharga E£30.

FARAFRA OASIS TO BAHARIYA OASIS

The stupefying desert formations between the Farafra and Bahariya Oases are responsible for attracting more travellers to this far-flung corner of Egypt than any other sight. No surprises there: this unearthly terrain varies from the bizarre and impossibly shaped rock formations of the White Desert to the eerie black-coned mountains of the nearby Black Desert, with a healthy dose of sand dunes interspersed for good measure. These regions are relatively easy to get to from either Farafra or Bahariya Oases and are immensely popular with one-day and overnight safari tours.

White Desert

Upon first glimpse of the White Desert (Sahra al-Beida) dreamscape, you'll feel like a modern Alice fallen through the desert looking glass. About 20km northeast of Farafra, on the east side of the highway, blinding-white spires of rock sprout almost supernaturally from the ground, each frost-coloured lollipop licked into an ever odder shape by the dry desert winds. As you get further into the 300-sq-km **White Desert National Park**, you'll notice that the surreal shapes start to take on familiar forms: chickens, ostriches, camels, hawks and other uncanny shapes abound. They are best viewed at sunrise or sunset, when the sun turns them hues of pink and orange, or under a full moon, which gives the landscape a ghostly arctic appearance. The sand around the outcroppings is littered with quartz and different varieties of deep-black iron pyrites, as well as small fossils.

On the west side of the highway, away from the wind-hewn sculptures, chalk towers called inselbergs burst from the desert floor like a smaller, more intimate (and, naturally, whiter) version of Arizona's Monument Valley. Between them run grand boulevards of sand, like geologic Champs-Élysées. No less beautiful than the east side of the road, the shade and privacy here makes it a great area to camp.

There's a US$5 entry fee to the national park, plus an extra fee of E£10 for each night you sleep in it. You can buy tickets at the entrance to the park, but don't worry about going in without one; you can just pay the rangers when they find you.

About 50km north are two flat-topped mountains known as the **Twin Peaks**, a key navigation point for travellers. A favourite destination of local tour operators, the view from the top of the surrounding symmetrical hills, all shaped like giant anthills, is spectacular. Just beyond here, the road climbs a steep escarpment known as **Naqb as-Sillim** (Pass of the Stairs); this is the main pass that leads into and out of the Farafra depression and marks the end of the White Desert.

A few kilometres further along, the desert floor changes again and becomes littered with quartz crystals. If you look at the rock formations in this area you'll see that they are also largely made of crystal. The most famous of the formations is the **Crystal Mountain**, actually a large rock made entirely of quartz. It sits right beside the main road some 24km north of Naqb as-Sillim, and is easily recognisable by the large hole through its middle.

Black Desert

The change in the desert floor from beige to black, 50km south of Bawiti, signals the beginning of the Black Desert (Sahra Suda). Formed by the erosion of the mountains, which have spread a layer of black powder and rubble over the peaks and plateaus, it looks like a landscape straight out of Hades. The Black Desert is a popular stop-off for tours running out of Bahariya, though few stay there overnight. Other sights in the region include **Gebel Gala Siwa**, a pyramid-shaped mountain that was formerly a lookout post for caravans coming from Siwa. **Gebel az-Zuqaq** is a mountain known for the red, yellow and orange streaks in its limestone base. There is an easily climbed path leading to the top.

KNOW YOUR DUNES

Classification of sand dune shapes was made in the 1970s, when scientists examined photographs of dune fields taken from space. Of the five typical shapes, four are found in Egypt.

Seif

Named for the Arabic word for sword, these long dunes form parallel to the prevailing wind. They are primarily found in the Great Sand Sea and the northern Western Desert. Usually on the move, they will even fall down an escarpment, reforming at its base.

Barchan

These are crescent-shaped dunes, with a slip face on one side. They are as wide as they are long and are usually found in straight lines with flat corridors between them. They can travel as far as 19 metres in one year. They are predominant in Al-Kharga and Dakhla Oases and also in the Great Sand Sea.

Star

Created by wind blowing in different directions, these dunes are usually found alone. Instead of moving, they tend to build up within a circle. They are rare in Egypt.

Crescent

These hill-like dunes, also called whaleback dunes, form when smaller dunes collide and piggyback on one another. With their sides pointing in different directions, these distinctive shapes can be seen between Al-Kharga and Dakhla Oases.

❶ Getting There & Away

Ordinary vehicles are able to drive the first kilometre or so off the road into the White or Black Deserts, but only 4WD vehicles can advance deeper into either area. Some travellers simply get off the bus and take themselves into the White Desert – but be sure you have adequate supplies, and remember that traffic between the neighbouring oases is rarely heavy. The megaliths west of the highway are easy to access by foot, as are the so-called mushrooms to the east; the weirdest wonderland of white hoodoos is quite far to the east, and walking there would be a real haul. **Bir Regwa** (Map p294), a small spring situated along the highway at one of the park entrances, usually has water; it's good to know where it is (just in case), though best not to rely on it.

There are plenty of safari outfits that can take you around these sights by jeep, camel, or on foot (camel and walking trips are vehicle-supported). If you're mainly interested in the White Desert, 4WD trips are significantly cheaper from Farafra than from Bahariya. See p295 and boxed text p303 for info.

BAHARIYA OASIS

📞 02 / POP 35,000

Bahariya is one of the more fetching of the desert circuit oases, and at just 365km from Cairo is also the most accessible. Surrounded on all sides by rocky, sandy mesas, much of the oasis floor is covered by forests of date palms and pockmarked with dozens of refreshing springs.

The conical hills that lie strewn around the valley floor may have once formed islands in the lake that covered the area during prehistoric times. During the Pharaonic era, the oasis was a centre of agriculture, producing wine sold in the Nile Valley and as far away as Rome. Its strategic location on the Libya–Nile Valley caravan routes ensured it prospered throughout later ages. In recent years, stunning archaeological finds, such as that of the Golden Mummies (see boxed text p302), and easy access to the White and Black Deserts have earned Bahariya a firm spot on the tourist map.

Bawiti

Take one look at Bawiti's dusty, unappealing main road, and you'll wonder why you came. You have to scratch beneath the surface of this town to find its charms. Stroll through its fertile palm groves, soak in one of the many hot springs or explore its quiet back streets, where you'll meet truly friendly, hospitable people.

Until recently, Bawiti was a quiet town dependent on agriculture, but it's become a tourist hub for trips to the White and Black Deserts, with the Golden Mummies an added draw. Be warned that upon arrival you may be accosted by overzealous safari guides before you even step off the bus (see boxed text p303).

◉ Sights & Activities

Oasis Heritage Museum   MUSEUM
(Map p299; 📞3847 3666; Bahariya–Cairo Rd; admission E£5-10; ⊘no set opening times) That giant sandcastle-looking-thing 3km east of town on the road to Cairo is Mahmoud Eed's Oasis Heritage Museum. Inspired by Badr's Museum in Farafra, its creator captures, in clay, scenes from traditional village life, among them men hunting, women weaving and a painful-looking barber/doctor encounter. There's also a display of old oasis dresses and jewellery.

**Golden Mummies Museum
(Al-Mathaf)**   MUSEUM
(Map p300; Sharia al-Mathaf; ⊘8am-2pm) Since the discovery of the Golden Mummies in the 1990s (see boxed text p302), growing interest in Bahariya's ancient past has led to the opening of this new museum. Yes, that building resembling a wartime bunker – complete with lookout turrets – is the museum (the ticket office is the hut situated outside the wall; see boxed text p301). Some of the 10 mummies on show are richly decorated and, while the motifs are formulaic and the work is second-rate, the painted faces show a move away from stylised Pharaonic mummy decoration towards Fayoum portraiture (see boxed text p161). Underneath the wrappings, the work of the embalmers appears to have been sloppy: in some cases the bodies decayed before the embalming process began, which suggests that these mummies mark the beginning of the end of mummification. Sadly, the exhibit embodies that spirit, and is entirely underwhelming.

Qarat Qasr Salim   ARCHAEOLOGICAL SITE
(Map p300) This small mound amid the houses of Bawiti is likely to have been built upon centuries of debris. There are two well-preserved 26th-dynasty tombs here that were robbed in antiquity and reused as collective

Bahariya Oasis

Gebel Dist

Bir al-Ghaba

Nature Camp

Gebel Maghrafa

Gebel Mandisha

Bir al-Mattar

Badr's Sahara Camp

Gebel al-Ingleez

Zabou

Bir al-Ramla

Qasr el-Bawity Hotel & Safari

Temple of Ain el-Muftella

Desert Safari Home

Mandisha

Qarat al-Hilwa

● Bawiti

Oasis Heritage Museum

El-Agouz

Temple of Alexander

Golden Mummies Site

To Black Desert (10km); / Under the Moon Camp & Ain Gomma (42km)

To Eden Garden Camp (1km); El Jaffara (1km)

burial sites in Roman times. The rock-cut **Tomb of Zed-Amun-ef-ankh** (☺8.30am-4pm) gives a glimpse of Bahariya in its heyday, the colourful tomb paintings hinting at the wealth of its former occupant. Next to it lies the **Tomb of Bannentiu** (☺8.30am-4pm), Zed-Amun-ef-ankh's son. Consisting of a four-columned burial chamber with an inner sanctuary, it is covered in fine reliefs depicting Bannentiu with the god Khons and goddesses Isis and Nephthys.

Hot & Cold Springs

The closest springs to central Bawiti are the so-called Roman springs, known as **El-Beshmo** (Map p300), beside El-Beshmo Lodge. The view over the oasis gardens and the desert beyond is wonderful, but unfortunately the spring is not suitable for swimming.

The hot sulphurous spring of **Bir al-Ramla** (Map p299), 3km north of town, is very hot (45°C) and suitable for a soak,

though you may feel a bit exposed to the donkey traffic passing to and fro. Women should stay well covered.

At **Bir al-Mattar** (Map p299), 7km north-east of Bawiti, cold springs pour into a viaduct, then down into a concrete pool, in which you can splash around during the hot summer months. As with all the springs, the mineral content is high and the water can stain clothing.

One of the most satisfying springs to visit is **Bir al-Ghaba** (Map p299), located about 15km northeast of Bawiti. It's quite a trek to get out here but there is nothing quite like a moonlit hot bath on the edge of the desert.

A few kilometres south of the Bahariya–Cairo road, about 7km from Bawiti, is the mini-oasis of **El Jaffara** (off Map p299), where two springs – one hot, one cold – make this a prime spot in winter or summer. Both are near **Eden Garden Camp** (p304).

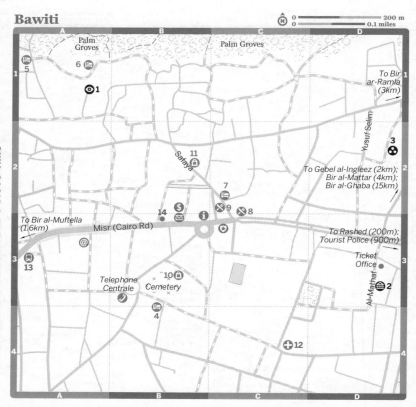

Bawiti

🛏 Sleeping

There is a decent selection of budget and mid-priced hotels in Bawiti, as well as elsewhere around Bahariya Oasis. If you want to catch the mellow oasis vibe, head for one of the camps outside of town; see p304.

It makes sense to sort out accommodation in Bawiti before you arrive, especially in high season, to avoid dealing with the frenzy of touts that swarm each bus arrival.

Old Oasis Hotel   HOTEL $$
(Map p300; ☎3847 3028; www.oldoasissafari.com; by El-Beshmo spring; s/d/tr E£120/180/220, without air-con E£90/120/180; ✺@🛜🏊) One of the most charming places to stay in Bawiti town sits among a pretty garden of palm and olive trees and has 13 simple but impeccable fan rooms, plus a few fancier stone-wall air-con rooms. A large pool receives steaming hot water from the nearby spring; the run-off waters the garden, where there's a shady restaurant/cafe.

Western Desert Hotel   HOTEL $$
(Map p300; ☎0122 301 2155; www.westernde serthotel.com; off Sharia Misr; s/d E£140/240; ✺@🛜) Right in the middle of town, the location is supremely convenient and the rooms are easily the best in Bawiti. They're well-kept, have a splash of style, and all have air-con. The ones in back have views of the gardens and desert in the distance – and the comfortable beds even have two sheets! If it's not busy, you'll get a discount if you ask.

New Oasis Hotel   HOTEL $
(Map p300; ☎0122 847 4171; max_rfs@hotmail.com; by El-Beshmo spring; s/d E£70/120, without air-con E£50/100; ✺) A study in curvaceous construction, this small homey hotel has several teardrop-shaped rooms, some with balconies overlooking the expansive palm groves nearby. Inside, the rooms are in good shape, though someone seems to have been a little

Bawiti

overzealous with the powder-blue paint. It's one of the nicer budget options in town.

Alpenblick Hotel   HOTEL $
(Map p300; ☏3847 2184; www.alpenblick-hotel-oasis.com; near Telephone Centrale; s/d E£70/140, without air-con E£60/120; ❄) This granddaddy of the Bahariya hotel scene keeps getting dragged out of retirement by its consecutive owners; the current ones give a warm welcome. The rooms are characterless but clean, and there's a large shaded courtyard where you can hang out and meet other travellers.

Desert Safari Home   HOTEL $
(Map p299; ☏0122 731 3908; www.desertsafarihome.com; s/d E£80/120, without air-con E£50/75; ❄@) Another decent budget option, which is inconveniently located 2km from the centre of town but has good rooms. Owner Badry Khozam willingly picks up from the bus station.

 Eating

The market area on Sharia Misr houses several good and cheap roasted chicken and kebab joints that fire up after dusk. Fresh veggies can be found along the street between Sharia Misr and Telephone centrale. As for restaurants, the scene is feeble.

Cleopatra Restaurant   EGYPTIAN FAST FOOD $
(Map p300; mains E£2-35; ⊙breakfast, lunch & dinner) Great for fuul, felafel and eggs. Confirm the price first, as the owner may try to impose a 'tourist tax.'

Popular Restaurant   EGYPTIAN $$
(Map p300; meals E£25; ⊙breakfast, lunch & dinner) The main option in town, with set multi-course meals. There's cold beer.

Rashed   EGYPTIAN $$
(off Map p300; meals E£25; ⊙lunch & dinner) Big and clean, serves set multi-course meals.

🛍 Shopping

There is a living craft tradition in the oases, though puzzlingly many handicraft stores sell crafts made elsewhere.

Girls Work Shop   HANDICRAFTS
(Map p300; south of Sharia Misr; ⊙10am-1pm Sat-Thu) This little store sells only crafts made in Bahariya Oasis, providing local women with skills and much-needed work. Unique items include hand-embroidered greeting cards.

Horass Handcraft   HANDICRAFTS
(Map p300; Sharia Safaya; ⊙8am-8pm) Sells some locally made crafts, including hand-decorated pouches cleverly marketed as 'mobile phone holders' or, our favourite, 'guidebook holders'. It also has standard adorned traditional Bedouin costumes and camel-hair socks. If the shop is closed, knock on the door directly across the street.

⊙ Information

Hospital (Map p300; ☏3847 2390) Head to Cairo except in dire emergency.

National Bank for Development (Map p300; ⊙9am-2pm Sun-Thu) Has an ATM and changes cash.

YOUR TICKET TO ANTIQUITIES

Bahariya's authorities issue a one-day ticket that gives entry to five of the oasis' ancient sites: the Golden Mummies Museum (Al-Mathaf), the tomb of Zed-Amun-ef-ankh, the tomb of Bannentiu, the Ain el-Muftella and the Temple of Alexander. Tickets are available at the **ticket office** (Map p300; adult/student E£45/25; ⊙8am-4pm) of the museum (Al-Mathaf; p298) so stop there first. Yup, you gotta pay for 'em all, even if you only visit one.

Sebt Internet (Map p300; off Sharia Misr; per hr E£5; ☺8am-3am) Go past the pool tables and behind the curtain into the darkened, air-con computer lair.

Telephone centrale (Map p300; off Sharia Misr; ☺11am-7pm Sat-Thu)

Tourist office (Map p300; ☎3847 3035/9; ☺8am-2pm Sat-Thu, plus 7-9pm Sat-Thu Nov-Apr) Run by helpful Mohamed Abd el-Kader, who can also be contacted on ☎0122 373 6567.

Tourist police (off Map p300; ☎3847 3900; Sharia Misr)

🛈 Getting There & Away

Bus

Upper Egypt Bus Co (Map p300; ☎3847 3610; Sharia Misr; ☺roughly 9am-1pm & 7-11pm) runs buses from Bawiti to Cairo (E£30, four to five hours) at 6.30am, 10am and 3pm from the kiosk near the post office. These are often full, so it's strongly advised to buy tickets the day before travelling. There are two more Cairo-bound buses that originate in Dakhla and pass through Bawiti around noon and midnight, stopping at the Hilal Coffeehouse at the western end of town. For those, buy your ticket on the bus, and hope there are seats!

If you're heading to Farafra (E£20, two hours) and Dakhla (E£40, four to five hours), you can hop on one of the buses headed that way from Cairo. They leave Bahariya around noon and 11.30pm from the Upper Egypt Bus Co kiosk and Hilal Coffeehouse.

Minibus

Whenever they're full, minibuses run from Bawiti to Cairo (E£25), ending near the Moneib metro station in Giza. Minibuses to Farafra (E£20) and Dakhla (E£45) are rare, best caught an hour or so before the night bus departs. All leave from Hilal Coffeehouse.

There is no public transport to Siwa, so you will have to hire a private 4WD for the journey (see p315). Expect to pay around E£1500 per car. If there's a 4WD from Siwa that's returning empty, you might be able to ride with it for half that amount. Permits (US$5 per person) are required and easy to get from the bank; drivers or the tourist office can help set that up.

Around Bawiti

While there are some antiquities outside Bawiti that are arguably worth seeing, the main attractions are the natural ones, including immense palm gardens, many fed by springs ideal for a night-time soak. Further afield lies wild desert scenery; the Black Desert, Gebel Dist and Gebel Maghrafa can be seen on a day trip or overnight safari.

👁 Sights

Temple of Ain el-Muftella TEMPLE
(Map p299) Slightly south of the spring of the same name are four 26th-dynasty chapels that together form the Temple of Ain el-Muftella. The bulk of the building was

---

BAHARIYA'S GOLDEN MUMMY CACHE

Put it down to the donkey: until 1996, no one had any idea of the extent of Bahariya's archaeological treasure trove. Then a donkey stumbled on a hole near the temple of Alexander the Great, and its rider saw the face of a golden mummy peering through the sand. (Or so the story goes. Some locals wink knowingly at what they assert is a much-popularised myth.) Since then Dr Zahi Hawass, head of the Supreme Council of Antiquities, and his team have done extensive research in a cemetery that stretches over 3 sq km (see Map p299). Radar has revealed more than 10,000 mummies, and excavation has revealed more than 250 of them in what has come to be called the Valley of the Golden Mummies.

These silent witnesses of a bygone age could shed new light on life in this part of Egypt during the Graeco-Roman period, a 600-year interlude marking the transition between the Pharaonic and Christian eras. Bahariya was then a thriving oasis and, with its rich, fertile land watered by natural springs, was a famous producer of wheat and wine. Greek and, later, Roman families set up home here and became a kind of expatriate elite.

Research has shown that after a brief decline when Ptolemies and Romans fought for control of the oasis, Roman administrators embarked on a major public works program, expanding irrigation systems, digging wells, restoring aqueducts and building roads. Thousands of mudbrick buildings sprang up throughout the oasis. Bahariya became a major source of grain for the empire and was home to a large garrison of troops; its wealth grew proportionately. Researchers are hoping that continued excavation of the necropolis will provide more answers about the region's early history and its inhabitants.

BAHARIYA TOURS

There is furious competition throughout the oases – and even in Cairo – for tour business, but it is particularly intense in Bahariya. Here, every hotel offers tours, as do a number of eager young men who have taken out bank loans to pay for their cars. The battle for customers is so fierce that buses arriving in Bahariya are sometimes greeted by a tourist-police officer, who escorts foreigners through the throng of aggressive touts to the safe haven of the tourist office. Here Mohamed Abd el-Kader can give you up-to-date information about local hotels and tour operators. If you're feeling overwhelmed, check with him first.

Many cheap Cairo hotels and hostels push their White Desert tours, but it's a much better idea to arrange things in Bawiti (or Farafra), where you can meet the people who will be responsible for your experience before forking over any cash. Well-established local safari outfits include **Eden Garden Tours** (0100 071 0707; www.edengardentours.com); **Helal Travel** (0122 423 6580; www.helaltravel.com); and **White Desert Tours** (0122 321 2179, www.whitedeserttours.com). Many freelance guides are also good, and slightly less expensive.

A typical itinerary will take you to the sights in and around Bahariya (**Temple of Alexander**, **Temple of Ain el-Muftella**, **Gebel Dist** and **Gebel Maghrafa**) then out through the **Black Desert**, with a stop at the **Crystal Mountain** and then into the **White Desert**.

A day trip to the local sights of Bawiti runs from E£150 to E£200; a half-day Black Desert trip is E£400; a one-night camping trip into the White Desert will cost E£800 to E£1200. If you're travelling into the remote corners of the desert on a multiday excursion, you'll be looking at E£1000 to E£1500 per day. One of the variables is how much of the distance is covered off-road. Remember, cheaper isn't always better. A reliable car and driver are well worth a few extra pounds.

Before signing up, check vehicles to make sure they're roadworthy, confirm how much food and drink is supplied (and what this will be), confirm start and end times (some operators start late in the afternoon and return early in the morning but charge for full days) and try to talk with travellers who have just returned from a trip to get their feedback.

If you're planning to explore remote parts of the desert such as Gilf Kebir, Gebel Uweinat or the Great Sand Sea, see p280.

ordered by 26th-dynasty high priest Zed-Khonsu-ef-ankh, whose tomb was recently discovered under houses in Bawiti (but is still closed to the public). Archaeologists suspect that the chapels could have been built during the New Kingdom and then significantly expanded during the Late Period and added to during Greek and Roman times. All have been extensively restored and have been given wooden roofs to protect them from the elements.

Other Sights

A number of other sights in Bahariya are included as part of a tour by the many safari operators in Bawiti. Most can also be done on foot if the weather is cool. Two of these are archaeological: the **Temple of Alexander**, southwest of Bawiti, which is the only place in Egypt where Alexander the Great's cartouche has been found; and **Qarat al-Hilwa**, an ancient necropolis that includes the 18th-dynasty Tomb of Amenhotep Huy. Neither will blow your mind, but the desert around Bawiti might.

Gebel Mandisha is a ridge capped with black dolomite and basalt that runs for 4km behind the village of the same name, just east of Bawiti.

Clearly visible from the road to Cairo, flat-topped **Gebel al-Ingleez**, also known as Black Mountain, takes its name from a WWI lookout post. From here Captain Williams, a British officer, monitored the movements of Libyan Senussi tribesmen.

Gebel Dist is an impressive pyramid-shaped mountain visible from most of the oasis. A local landmark, it is famous for its fossils; dinosaur bones were found here in the early 20th century, disproving the previously held theory that dinosaurs only lived in North America. In 2001 researchers from the University of Pennsylvania found the remains of a giant dinosaur, *Paralititan stromeri*. The discovery of this huge herbivore, which the team deduced was standing on the edge of a tidal channel when it died 94 million years ago, makes it likely that Bahariya was once a swamp similar to the Florida everglades. About 100m away is **Gebel Maghrafa** (Mountain of the Ladle).

One of the most magnificent springs around is **Ain Gomma** (off Map p299), 45km south of Bawiti. Cool, crystal-clear water gushes into this small pool surrounded by the vast desert expanse, and the funkiest cafe in all of the oases sits beside it. Situated near the town of El-Hayz, you can take a Dakhla-bound bus there, but it's difficult to get back without your own transport. Many safari trips to the White Desert will stop here en route. You can also stay at nearby **Under the Moon Camp** (p304).

Sleeping & Eating

TOP CHOICE **Under the Moon Camp** BUNGALOW **$$**
(off Map p299; ☑0122 423 6580; www.helaltravel.com; El-Hayz; huts half board E£150, bungalows s/d half board E£125/250) Isolated in the small oasis hamlet of El-Hayz, 45km south of Bawiti, this beautiful camp features several round, stone huts (no electricity) and some new mudbrick bungalows (with lights) scattered around a garden compound. The accommodation is as simple as it gets, but the hospitality and the setting can't be beat. The lovely **Ain Gomma spring** (p302) is nearby and there's a cold spring pool right in the camp, with powerful desert views. Helal, the Bedouin owner who once trained Egyptian military units in desert navigation, runs highly recommended safari trips and arranges free pickups from Bawiti.

Nature Camp BUNGALOW **$$**
(Map p299; ☑0122 337 5097; nature camps@hotmail.com; Bir al-Ghaba; r half board per person E£150) At the foot of Gebel Dist, Nature Camp sets new standards for environmentally focused budget accommodation. The peaceful cluster of candlelit and intricately designed thatch huts looks out onto the expansive desert beside Bir al-Ghaba. The food is very good (meals E£25) and the owner, Ashraf Lotfe, is a skilled desert hand. Staff will drive you the 17km to and from Bawiti if you arrive without transport.

Qasr el-Bawity Hotel & Safari BOUTIQUE HOTEL **$$**
(Map p299; ☑3847 1880; www.qasrelbawity.com; s/d/ste half board from €50/80/120; ❋❧) The relatively new Qasr el-Bawity offers some of the swankiest accommodation in Bahariya. With a finely trained eye for environmentally friendly design, this place has sumptuous rooms finished in cool stonework and sporting ornate domed roofs, fine furniture and arty, frilly touches. There are two pools (one natural and one chlorinated) and the restaurant here is suitably good.

Eden Garden Camp HUT **$**
(off Map p299; ☑0100 071 0707; www.edengardentours.com; huts with fan per person E£55, full board E£105) Located 7km east of Bawiti, in the small, serene oasis of El Jaffara, Eden Garden features simple huts, shaded lounge areas, fresh food and, best of all, two springs just outside its gates: one hot and one cold. Its desert safaris have a good reputation, and pick-ups from Bawiti are free.

Badr's Sahara Camp HUT **$**
(Map p299; ☑0122 792 2728; www.badrysaharacamp.com; huts per person E£50) A couple of kilometres from town, Badr's Sahara Camp has a handful of bucolic, African-influenced huts, each with two beds and small patios out front. Hot water and electricity can't always be counted on, but cool desert breezes and knockout views of the oasis valley can. Pick-ups are available.

International Hot Spring Hotel HOTEL **$$**
(Map p299; ☑02-3847 3014, 0122 321 2179; www.whitedeserttours.com; s/d half board per person US$50/40) About 3km outside Bawiti on the road to Cairo, this spa resort has 36 very comfortable rooms and eight chalets, built around a hot spring and set in a delightful garden. There's also a rooftop lounge and a good restaurant. German owner Peter Wirth is an old Western Desert hand and organises recommended trips in the area.

SIWA OASIS

☑046 / POP 23,000

Way out in the desert just 50km from the Libyan border, hundreds of thousands of olive and palm trees shade a fertile basin that sits about 25 metres below sea level. Mudbrick hamlets are set among the groves, connected by dirt lanes still mostly travelled by donkey carts. Crystal-clear coldwater springs bubble into deep pools that are irresistibly refreshing on hot days. From the edge of the gardens, the swells of the Great Sand Sea roll to the horizon. Siwa is the archetypal oasis.

Siwa's geographic isolation helped protect a unique society that stands distinctly apart from mainstream Egyptian culture. Originally settled by Berbers (roaming North African tribes), Siwa was still practically independent only a few hundred years ago. For centuries the oasis had contact with only the few caravan traders that passed along this way via Qara, Qattara and Kerdassa (near Cairo), and the occasional determined pilgrim seeking the famous Oracle of Amun. Today, local traditions and Siwi, the local Berber language, still dominate.

Well worth the long haul to get out here, Siwa casts a spell that's hard to resist.

History

Siwa has a long and ancient, ancient past: in late 2007, a human footprint was found that could date back three million years, making it the oldest known human print in the world. Flints discovered in the oasis show that it was inhabited in Palaeolithic and Neolithic times, but beyond that Siwa's early history remains a mystery.

The oldest monuments in the oasis, including the Temple of the Oracle, date from the 26th dynasty, when Egypt was invaded by the Assyrians. Siwa's **Oracle of Amun** (p307) was already famous then, and Egyptologists suspect it dates back to the earlier 21st dynasty, when the Amun priesthood became prominent throughout Egypt.

Such was the fame of Siwa's oracle that its prophecies threatened the Persians, who invaded Egypt in 525 BC and ended the 26th dynasty. One of the Western Desert's most persistent legends is of the lost army of Persian king Cambyses (see boxed text p308), which was sent to destroy the oracle but disappeared completely in the desert. This only helped increase the oracle's prestige, reinforcing the political power of the Amun priesthood.

The oracle's power – and with it, Siwa's fame – grew throughout the ancient world. The young conqueror Alexander the Great led a small party on a perilous eight-day journey across the desert in 331 BC. It is believed that the priests of Amun, who was the supreme god of the Egyptian pantheon and later associated with the Greek god Zeus, declared him to be a son of the god.

The end of Roman rule, the collapse of the trade route and the gradual decline in the influence of oracles in general all contributed to Siwa's gentle slide into obscurity. While Christianity spread through most of Egypt, there is no evidence that it ever reached Siwa, and priests continued to worship Amun here until the 6th century AD. The Muslim conquerors, who crossed the desert in AD 708, were defeated several times by the fierce Siwans. However, there was a cost to this isolation: it is said that by 1203 the population had declined to just 40 men, who moved from Aghurmi to found the new fortress-town of Shali. The oasis finally converted to Islam around the 12th century, and gradually built up wealth trading date and olive crops along the Nile Valley, and with Libyan Fezzan and the Bedouins.

European travellers arrived at the end of the 18th century – WG Browne in 1792 and Frederick Hornemann in 1798 – but most were met with a hostile reception and several narrowly escaped with their lives. Siwa was again visited in WWII, when the British and Italian/German forces chased each other in and out of Siwa and Jaghbub, 120km west in Libya. By then Siwa was politically incorporated into Egypt, but the oasis remained physically isolated until an asphalt road connected it to Marsa Matruh in the 1980s. As a result, Siwans still speak their own distinct Berber dialect and have a strong local culture, quite distinct from the rest of Egypt. The oasis is now home to some 21,000 Siwans and about 2000 Egyptians.

⊙ Sights & Activities

Even though there are some fascinating sights hidden in the dense palm greenery of this oasis, the main attraction in Siwa is its serene atmosphere. Strolling through the palm groves or riding a bike to a cool spring for a swim without being in a rush to get anywhere is really what it's all about here. Hang out with other travellers, have a picnic, ride a donkey cart, explore the dunes by 4WD and soak it all in.

One of Siwa's most impressive sights is the oasis itself, which boasts more than 300,000 palm trees, 70,000 olive trees and a great many fruit orchards. The vegetation is sustained by more than 300 freshwater springs and streams, and the area attracts an amazing variety of bird life, including quail and falcons.

Siwa Oasis

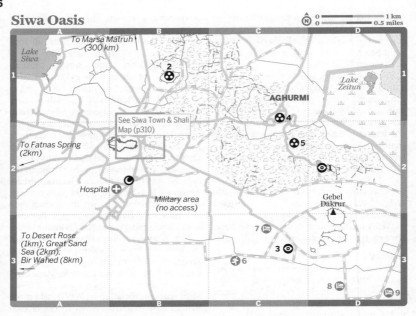

Siwa Oasis

⊙ Sights
1 Cleopatra's Bath	D2
2 Gebel al-Mawta	B1
3 Sherif Sand Bath	C3
4 Temple of the Oracle	C1
5 Temple of Umm Ubayd	C2

⊙ Activities, Courses & Tours
6 Am Agbenek Siwa Inn	C3
Tala Ranch	(see 9)

⊜ Sleeping
7 Alzaytuna	C3
8 Siwa Shali Resort	D3
9 Tala Ranch Hotel	D3

Hot & Cold Springs

Siwa has no shortage of active, bubbling springs hidden among its palm groves. At all of the springs in town, women should swim in pants and a shirt and use general good judgement concerning modesty.

TOP CHOICE **Cleopatra's Bath** SPRING

(Spring of the Sun; Map p306) Following the track that leads to the Temple of the Oracle and continuing past the Temple of Umm Ubayd will lead you to Siwa's most famous spring, Cleopatra's Bath. The crystal-clear

water gurgles up into a large stone pool, which is a popular bathing spot for locals as well as tourists. A couple of cafes beside the spring have comfortable shaded lounging areas and serve soft drinks; bring your own picnic if you want to hang out for a while.

TOP CHOICE **Bir Wahed** SPRING

(off Map p306) A favourite excursion from Siwa is the cold freshwater lake at Bir Wahed, 15km away on the edge of the Great Sand Sea. Once over the top of a high dune, you come to a hot spring, the size of a large jacuzzi, where sulphurous water bubbles in a pool and runs off to irrigate a garden. Cooling down in the lake, and then watching the sun setting over the dunes while soaking in a hot spring is a surreal experience. The thorns in this rose are the mosquitoes that bite at sunset. Because it's far from town, women can wear bathing suits here without offending locals. Bir Wahed can only be reached by 4WD, so if you don't have your own, you'll need to hire a guide and car. Permits are needed to visit Bir Wahed (see p315).

Fatnas Spring SPRING

(off Map p306) This fairly secluded pool is on a small island in the salty Birket Siwa (Lake Siwa) accessible across a narrow causeway.

Nicknamed 'Fantasy Island' for its idyllic setting, the pool is about 6km from Siwa Town, and surrounded by palm trees and lush greenery. There's a small cafe among the palms, which is good for a spot of tea or a puff of sheesha. This is an idyllic place to watch the sunset. A Ministry of Agriculture project to try to improve the lake's drainage has left the 'island' high and dry, so sometimes the cafe may look out over salty mudflats rather than water. A donkey cart round-trip from town will cost about E£25, with time to swim and hang out.

Ain al-Arais · SPRING
(Map p310) The closest spring to town is Ain al-Arais, a cool, inviting waterhole with a grotto-like bottom, just five minutes' walk from the central market. Beside the spring sits a casual cafe-restaurant.

SIWA TOWN
Siwa is a pleasant little town centred on a market square, where roads lead off into the palm groves in nearly every direction. Unfortunately, the recent proliferation of motorcycles zooming around the main square is killing the quiet rural ambience it once had.

Fortress of Shali · RUIN
(Map p310) The centre of the town is dominated by the spectacular organic shapes of the remains of this 13th-century mudbrick fortress. Built from a material known locally as kershef (large chunks of salt from the lake just outside town, mixed with rock and plastered in local clay), the labyrinth of huddled buildings was originally four or five storeys high and housed hundreds of people. For centuries, few outsiders were admitted inside – and even fewer came back out to tell the tale. But three days of rain in 1926 caused more damage than any invader had managed and, over the last decades, inhabitants moved to newer and more comfortable houses with running water and electricity. Now only a few buildings around the edges are occupied or used for storage, including the Old Mosque with its chimney-shaped minaret.

House of Siwa Museum · MUSEUM
(Map p310; adult/student E£10/5; ⊙9am-2.30pm Sun-Thu) A block northwest of the King Fuad Mosque is this small museum, which contains an interesting display of traditional clothing, jewellery and crafts typical of the oasis. It's worth the entry fee just to check out the wedding dresses.

RESPECTING LOCAL CUSTOMS
Take a look around, and when you see Siwan women, you probably won't glimpse more than an eye peeking out from behind a shawl. Modesty is serious business. When Western women wear shorts and tank tops here, it's about the same as walking naked around a stranger's home – in other words, you probably wouldn't do it. Perhaps even more than elsewhere in Egypt, women travellers should dress conscientiously in Siwa, covering legs, upper arms, and cleavage. Long pants are a good idea even for men, and displays of affection between couples should be saved for the hotel room. As with anywhere in the country, showing respect earns respect.

Gebel al-Mawta · ARCHAEOLOGICAL SITE
(Map p306; adult/student E£25/15; ⊙9am-5pm) A small hill at the northern end of Siwa Town, Gebel al-Mawta – whose name means Mountain of the Dead – is honeycombed with rock tombs, most dating back to the 26th dynasty, Ptolemaic and Roman times. Only 1km from the centre of town, the tombs were used by the Siwans as shelters when the Italians bombed the oasis during WWII.

The best paintings are in the Tomb of Si Amun, where beautifully coloured reliefs portray the dead man – thought to be a wealthy Greek landowner or merchant – making offerings and praying to Egyptian gods. Also interesting are the unfinished Tomb of Mesu-Isis, with a beautiful depiction of cobras in red and blue above the entrance; the Tomb of Niperpathot, with inscriptions and crude drawings in the same reddish ink you can see on modern Siwan pottery; and finally the Tomb of the Crocodile, whose badly deteriorating wall paintings include a yellow crocodile representing the god Sobek.

AGHURMI
Before Shali was founded in the 13th century, Siwa's main settlement was at Aghurmi, 4km east of the present town of Siwa. It was here that in 331 BC Alexander the Great consulted the oracle (see p303) at the 26th-dynasty Temple of the Oracle (Map p306; adult/student E£25/15; ⊙9am-5pm). Built

in the 6th century BC, probably on top of an earlier temple, it was dedicated to Amun (occasionally referred to as Zeus or Jupiter Ammon) and was a powerful symbol of the town's wealth. One of the most revered oracles in the ancient Mediterranean, its power was such that some rulers sought its advice while others sent armies to destroy it.

Today the Temple of the Oracle sits in the northwest corner of the ruins of Aghurmi village. Though treasure hunters have been at work here and the buttressed temple was poorly restored in the 1970s, it remains an evocative site, steeped in history. Surrounded by the ruins of Aghurmi, it has awesome views over the oasis palm-tops.

About 200m further along the track stands the remains of the almost totally ruined **Temple of Umm Ubayd** (Map p306), also dedicated to Amun. This was originally connected to the Temple of the Oracle by a causeway and was used during oracle rituals. Nineteenth-century travellers saw more of it than we can: a Siwan governor in need of building material blew up the temple in 1896 in order to construct the town's modern mosque and police building. Only part of a wall covered with inscriptions survives.

AROUND SIWA

There are a few villages and springs around Siwa that are worth a trip if you've got the time. To visit these sights you'll need your own vehicle. Mahdi Hweiti at the Siwa tourist office organises trips, as does almost every restaurant and hotel in town. None of these sights, with the exception of Shiatta, require permits.

Shiatta   SPRING

Sixty kilometres west of Siwa Town, this stunning salt lake on the edge of the Great Sand Sea is ringed by palm trees. It's a popular stopover for migratory birds – including flamingos – and gazelles may be seen here, too. The lake once reached all the way to Siwa Town, and an ancient boat is somewhere 7m below the surface. These days this area is mainly used by Bedouin tribes for grazing livestock and has first-rate desert views.

Ain Qurayshat   SPRING

(off Map p306) Ain Qurayshat, about 20km from Siwa Town, has the largest free-flowing spring in the oasis. The best way to reach the spring is via the causeway across salty Lake Zeitun, which has striking views.

Abu Shuruf   SPRING

(off Map p306) Abu Shuruf, a clean spring said by locals to have healing properties, is 7km east of Ain Qurayshat in the next palm thicket. The clear water here is deliciously cold, but the ambience is somewhat spoilt by the sight and noise of the nearby Hayat water-bottling plant.

Az-Zeitun   VILLAGE

(off Map p306) Five kilometres east of Abu Shuruf Qurayshat, this is an abandoned mudbrick village beaten by the sand and wind that sits alone on the sandy plain. Hundreds of Roman-era tombs have been discovered about 2km beyond Az-Zeitun and are currently under excavation, although little of interest has so far been found.

THE LOST ARMY OF CAMBYSES

Persian king Cambyses invaded Egypt in 525 BC, overthrowing Egyptian pharaoh Psamtek III and signalling the beginning of Persian rule for the next 193 years. This success, however, did not continue. In the years immediately following his conquest of Egypt, Cambyses mounted several disastrous offensives. In one, he sent a mercenary army down the Nile into Kush (now Sudan) that was so undersupplied it had to turn to cannibalism to survive, and the soldiers returned in disgrace without even encountering the enemy.

Cambyses' most famous failure remains his attempt to capture the Oracle of Amun in Siwa. Herodotus recounts how the oracle predicted a tragic end for Cambyses, and so the ruler dispatched an army of 50,000 men from Thebes, supported by a vast train of pack animals with supplies and weapons. The army is purported to have reached Farafra before turning west to cover the 325km of open desert to Siwa – a 30-day march without any shade or sources of water. Legend has it that after struggling through the Great Sand Sea, the men were engulfed by a fierce sandstorm, which buried the entire army.

Over the centuries, dozens of expeditions have searched in vain for a trace of the Cambyses' soldiers. Perhaps one day the shifting sands will reveal the remnants of this ancient army.

SAND BATHING

If you thought a soak in a hot spring was invigorating, wait until you try a dip in one of the scalding-hot sand baths of **Gebel Dakrur**, several kilometres southeast of Siwa Town. From July to September, people flock here from all over the world to take turns being immersed up to their necks in a bath of very hot sand for up to 20 minutes at a time. Local doctors claim that a treatment regime of three to five days can cure rheumatism and arthritis – and judging by the number of repeat customers they get they might just be on to something. There are several places around the western slope of the mountain where you can get therapeutically sand-dunked; **Sherif Sand Bath** (Map p306) has a good reputation. Expect to pay E£115 to E£160 for each treatment, which includes food and overnight lodging.

The mountain also supplies the oasis with the reddish-brown pigment used to decorate Siwan pottery. Siwans believe that the mountain is haunted and claim that *afrit* (spirits) can be heard singing in the gardens at night.

Ain Safi
VILLAGE

(off Map p306) Three kilometres east of Az-Zeitun, this is the last human vestige before the overwhelming wall of desert dunes that stretches for hundreds of kilometres, all the way south to Al-Kharga Oasis. Some 30 Bedouin remain here.

Kharmisah
VILLAGE

About 15km northwest of Siwa Town, this village has five natural springs and is renowned for the quality of its olive gardens.

Bilad ar-Rum
VILLAGE

Near Kharmisah, the City of the Romans has about 100 tombs cut into the rock of the nearby hills and the ruins of a stone temple, among the spots rumoured to be the final resting place of Alexander the Great. Nearby is **Maraqi**, where Liana Souvaltzi, a Greek archaeologist, claimed in 1995 to have found the tomb of Alexander the Great. Her findings proved controversial and the Egyptian authorities revoked her permit and closed the site.

☞ Tours

Almost all restaurants and hotels in Siwa offer tours, ranging from half a day in the desert around Siwa Town to a full five- or six-day safari. The **Palm Trees Hotel** (p312) and **Abdu's Restaurant** (p313) have established a good reputation for their trips. We highly recommend **Ghazal Safari** (☏0100 277 1234); driver/guide Abd El-Rahman Azmy has a kick-ass vehicle and a love for Siwa that's contagious. The tourist office can also help in organising tours.

All desert trips require permits, which cost US$5 plus E£11 (service charge) and are usually obtained by your guide from the tourist office. Prices and itineraries vary, but one of the most popular trips takes you to the cold lake and hot springs at Bir Wahed, on the edge of the Great Sand Sea. This half-day trip costs about E£120 per person including permission costs. Palm Trees offers this with an overnight option, but you'll sleep in a camp on the edge of town, not in the dunes.

Other popular half-day itineraries include a tour of the springs Ain Qurayshat, Abu Shuruf, Az-Zeitun and Ain Safi (E£50); and a tour of Siwa Town and its environs (Temple of the Oracle, Gebel al-Mawta, Cleopatra's Bath, Fortress of Shali and Fatnas; E£30). Overnight trips vary in length according to destination. Most trips are done by 4WD, so ensure that the vehicle is roadworthy before you set out and that you have enough water.

If you dream of riding camels, Sherif Fahmy of the **Tala Ranch** (Map p306; ☏0100 588 6003; talaranchsiwa@hotmail.com; Gebel Dakrur) can arrange it, at E£350 for a day trip, including lunch, or E£400 for an overnight in the desert (with a group of at least four people) including lunch, dinner, and breakfast in the morning. These are virtually impossible to arrange in summer, since daytime temperatures are too hot and guides won't travel by starlight.

You can also ride horses through the dunes or to various springs from the new stables at **Am Agbenek Siwa Inn Hotel** (Map p306; ☏0100 333 2042, 0128 245 0981; www.amagbeneksiwa.over-blog.com). Trip lengths range from one-hour jaunts (E£70) to three-day safaris.

Siwa Town & Shali

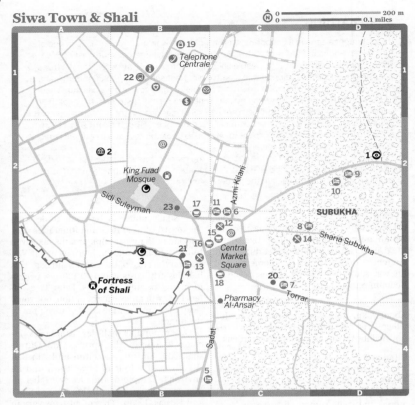

★ Festivals & Events

Gebel Dakrur is the scene of the annual **Si-yaha festival**. For three days around the October full moon, thousands of Siwans gather to celebrate the date harvest, renewing friendships and settling any quarrels that might have broken out over the previous year. All Siwans, no matter what their financial or social standing, eat together at a huge feast after the noon prayer each day during the festival. The festival is intertwined with Sufism, and each evening, hundreds of men form a circle and join together in a *zikr*, a long session of dancing, swaying and singing repetitive songs in praise of God. Siwan women do not attend the festivities, although girls up to about the age of 12 are present until sunset. Each year hundreds of non-Siwans – Egyptians and foreigners – attend the festival. Note that the festival was cancelled in 2011, ostensibly for security reasons following the revolution (despite Siwa

being entirely uninvolved in any protests), so confirm that it'll actually be happening if you're hoping to go.

Once a year, just after the corn harvest in late summer, the small tomb shrine of Sidi Suleiman, behind the King Fuad Mosque in the centre of Siwa Town, is the scene of a *moulid* (saints' festival), known in Siwi as the **Moulid at-Tagmigra**. Banners announce the *moulid,* and *zikr*s are performed outside the tomb.

Occasionally on Thursday nights, after the evening prayer, local Sufis of the Arusiya order gather near the tomb shrine for a *zikr* and they don't mind the odd foreigner watching.

🛏 Sleeping

Siwa town has a great collection of places to bed down in, with everything from competitively priced budget pads to dazzling top-end options. Many midrange and top-end

Siwa Town & Shali

sleeping options can also be found further afield in Siwa Oasis, around Gebel Dakrur and Sidi Jaafar.

The police here are jittery about people camping close to town. If you want to sleep in the desert, it's best to organise a tour with a local guide.

SIWA TOWN

Shali Lodge
BOUTIQUE HOTEL $$

(Map p310; 460 1299; www.siwa.com/accommodations.html; Sharia Subukha; s/d/tr E£285/365/450) This tiny, beautiful mud-brick hotel, owned by environmentalist Mounir Neamatallah, nestles in a lush palm grove about 100m from the main square. The large, extremely comfortable rooms have lots of curving mudbrick goodness, exposed palm beams, rock-walled bathrooms and cushioned sitting nooks. Tasteful and quiet, this is how small hotels should be (and should not be confused with Siwa Shali Resort).

Al-Babinshal
BOUTIQUE HOTEL $$

(Map p310; 460 1499; www.siwa.com/accommodations.html; s/d/tr E£275/375/450) Literally attached to the fortress of Shali, the cunning architects have seamlessly grafted this mud-brick hotel onto it. A maze of tunnels and stairways connects the spacious and cool cavelike rooms, making it impossible to tell where the hotel ends and the fort begins.

Entirely made from the same materials as the original fort, each intimate abode has wood-floor panelling, traditional wooden-shuttered windows and exposed palm-log supports.

Siwa Safari Gardens Hotel
BOUTIQUE HOTEL $$

(Map p310; 460 2801; www.siwagardens.com; s/d/tr half-board E£270/370/470; ❄❸❊) At this simple but tasteful hotel, ground-floor rooms are surprisingly plain; those on the 2nd floor have domed ceilings and much more character, but might cost E£50 extra per person during high season. The serene palm-shaded courtyard is set around a gleaming, tourmaline, spring-fed pool. The kindly manager, Sami, speaks fluent English and German. There's wi-fi in the lobby and parts of the garden.

Kelany Hotel
HOTEL $

(Map p310; 460 1052, 0122 403 9218; zaitsafari@yahoo.com; Azmi Kiliani; s/d E£120/150, without air-con E£70/100; ❄) A step above the other budget places, Kelany has decent rooms that are beginning to show their age. If you're looking for air-con, this is your best budget bet. The rooftop restaurant features views of Shali Fortress, Gebel Dakrur and everything in between.

Desert Rose
HOTEL $$

(off Map p306; 0122 440 8164; ali_siwa@hotmail.com; s/d/tr E£120/200/280, without bathroom

E£80/150/180; ☎) Overlooking the magnificent dunes that stretch out to the southeast of Siwa, this friendly, cosy hotel has creatively decorated, spotless rooms in a funky octagonal building. It has its own clear pool of natural spring water and a smattering of cushioned chill-out areas. There are no electric lights, but there is a small generator to charge camera and phone batteries. Head south from the main square, bear right at the mosque, and keep going, following the signs.

Siwa Safari Paradise
HOTEL $$

(Map p310; ☎460 1590; www.siwaparadise.com; s/d E£200/300, without air-con E£100/220; ✳☎) Laid out along a maze of garden paths, this resort-style hotel mainly attracts northern Europeans looking to sunbake by the natural spring pool. The decoration is a bit tacky and the place is showing its age, but the rooms are cool and comfortable, so it's not a bad option if other recommended hotels are full.

Palm Trees Hotel
HOTEL $

(Map p310; ☎460 1703, 0122 104 6652; m_s_siwa@ yahoo.com; Sharia Torrar; s/d E£35/50, without bathroom E£25/35, bungalows s/d E£50/70, r with air-con E£75; ✳) This deservedly popular budget hotel has sufficiently tidy rooms, all with screened windows, fans and balconies. The shady, tranquil garden with date-palm furniture is delightful (but mosquito-filled), and the few ground-level bungalows have porches spilling onto the greenery.

Yousef Hotel
HOTEL $

(Map p310; ☎460 0678; central market sq; s/d E£30/40, without bathroom E£20/30) With the cheapest beds in town, Yousef is perennially full with backpacking budgeters. The rooms are a bit tattered and hot in summer, but the four-storey rooftop has great views of the oasis. Noise can be an issue.

Cleopatra Hotel
HOTEL $

(Map p310; ☎460 0421; www.cleopatra-siwa.net; Sharia Sadat; s/d/tr main bldg E£20/30/40, new bldg E£35/45/65, ste with air-con E£130; ✳) Non-air-con rooms are simple get-what-you-pay-for crash pads. The air-con rooms are huge, with both a double and single bed, plus a separate sitting area with a couch and chairs – the perfect place to contemplate the question: 'If I saw eight dead cockroaches in the hallway, how many live ones are still running around?'

SIDI JAAFAR

TOP CHOICE Adrére Amellal
BOUTIQUE HOTEL $$$

(off Map p306; ☎02-736 7879; www.adrereamellal. net; Sidi Jaafar, White Mountain; s/d incl all meals, drinks & desert excursions US$460/605, ste from US$800; ☎) Backed by the dramatic White Mountain (called Adrére Amellal in Siwi), this impeccable desert retreat lies in its own oasis, with stunning views over the salt lake of Birket Siwa and the dunes of the Great Sand Sea beyond. It's a truly unique place, built by environmentalist Mounir Neamatallah out of *kershef,* and using revived traditional building techniques. Mobile phones are banned outside the rooms and there is no electricity, with the gardens lit by torches and the rooms by candlelight. It offers the ultimate in spartan chic, as gourmet dinners are eaten under the stars or in salt-encrusted chambers. The swimming pool is an ancient stone natural spring and the rooms and suites are palatial, yet simple and beautiful. This is one of the most innovative places to stay in all of Egypt.

GAY SIWA?

Much attention has been paid to Siwa's unique history of intimate male relations. Back when Siwa's citizens still lived in Shali fort, young men between the ages of 20 and 40 were expected to spend their nights outside the fortress to tend to the fields and protect the town from attack. These men of Siwa had a notorious reputation, not only for their bravery (they were known as *zaggalah,* or 'club bearers'), but for their love of palm wine, music and openly gay relations. Single-sex marriages were still practised in Siwa right up until WWII, although they had been outlawed in Egypt decades earlier.

Even though Siwa has been listed as a place to visit in several gay travel directories, the situation today is quite different. Residents of Siwa vehemently deny that local gay men exist in their town, and international travellers coming to Siwa in hope of 'hooking up' have been faced with increasingly homophobic sentiments. Siwan men are not amused at being propositioned by passing strangers – they are much more likely than foreigners to bear the brunt of antigay attitudes. Violent attacks on local men accused of homosexuality are not unheard of.

Taziry Ecolodge
BOUTIQUE HOTEL $$$

(off Map p306; ☎02-3337 0842, 0122 340 8492; www.taziry.com; Gaary; s/d/tr US$115/145/230, chalet from US$260; ☒) This lovely hotel was designed and built by its friendly owners, an artist and an engineer, both from Alexandria. The large natural-material rooms are decorated with local crafts and Bedouin rugs, and have their own bathroom. Tranquil and laid-back, with no electricity and a natural spring pool overlooking the lake, it is a great place to unwind and experience Siwa's magic. Families can choose their own adobe chalet.

GEBEL DAKRUR

Tala Ranch Hotel
BOUTIQUE HOTEL $$

(Map p306; ☎0100 588 6003; www.talaranch-hotel.com; s/d E£300/400) This low-key ecoresort offers a very different experience of Siwa, with six stylish and comfortable rooms on the edge of the desert. It promises generous helpings of hush and is as relaxing as things get, with the camels, the desert and the wind as the only distractions. Sherif can organise camel trips or safaris for guests, while his wife, Siham, prepares commendable Egyptian food served in a Bedouin tent (four-course dinner E£120).

Alzaytuna
HOTEL $$

(Map p306; ☎/fax 460 0037; www.alzaytuna.com; s/d E£180/250, without air-con E£140/180; ☒☒) Finely-kept bungalows surround a date palm garden with a spring fed pool and views of Gebel Dakrur. Rooms in the main building are comfortable, with balconies overlooking the garden. The important things are done right, like nice mattresses and modern bathrooms, and your host, Sammia, is as welcoming as could be.

Siwa Shali Resort
RESORT $$

(Map p306; ☎0100 630 1017; www.siwashaliresort.com; s/d/ste half board €35/54/100; ☒☒) One of the few places in Siwa that earns its 'resort' label, this self-contained village of traditionally-styled bungalows snakes its way along a 500m spring-fed pool. While the rooms are nothing special, suites have sitting rooms with two mattresses, perfect for young kids. It's popular with European tour groups on all-inclusive packages, as it's quite far from town.

✗ Eating

Many of the restaurants and cafes in Siwa cater to tourists. Most eateries are open from about 8am until late. There are a couple of falafel/fuul joints plus an *aysh* (flatbread) bakery about 50m off the main square past the Kelany Hotel.

Abdu's Restaurant
INTERNATIONAL $

(Map p310; central market sq; mains E£5-30; ☺8.30am-midnight) Before internet and mobile phones, there were places like this – a village hub where people gathered nightly to meet, catch up and swap stories. The longest-running restaurant in town remains the best eating option, with a huge menu of breakfast, pasta, traditional dishes, vegetable stews, couscous, roasted chickens and fantastic pizza whipped to your table by efficient service.

Kenooz Siwa
EGYPTIAN $$

(Map p310; Shali Lodge, Sharia Subukha; mains E£15-25) On the roof terrace of Shali Lodge (p311), this cafe-restaurant is a great place to hang out while enjoying a mint tea or a cold drink and conversation with the affable manager, Mohammed. Mains include some unique Siwan specialities, like baked lentils and eggplant with pomegranate sauce. The chicken with olive sauce and curry is uniquely delicious.

Al-Babinshal Restaurant
EGYPTIAN $$

(Map p310; Fortress of Shali; mains E£20-55) On the roof of the hotel of the same name, this might just be the most romantic dining spot in the oases. Moodily lit in the evenings, it's practically attached to the fortress of Shali and has sweeping views over all of Siwa. This is the place to try camel meat stew or to have a whole goat roasted for you and your friends (with 24-hour notice).

Abo Ayman Restaurant
GRILL $$

(Map p310; meals E£13-23) Roasted on a hand-turned spit over coals in an old oil drum, the chickens at Abo Ayman are the juiciest in Siwa. They're well seasoned, and served with salad, tahini and bread. You can sit inside at low tables, but we like the tables outside with street views.

Nour al-Waha
INTERNATIONAL $

(Map p310; Sharia Subukha; mains E£5-20) A popular hang-out in a palm grove opposite Shali Lodge, Nour al-Waha has shady tables and plenty of tea and games on hand for those who just want to while away the day in the shade. The food is a mixture of Egyptian and Western and is generally fresh and good.

There are several other cosy palm-garden restaurants around Siwa serving the usual combination of Egyptian and Western fare.

SIWA OASIS & THE WESTERN DESERT AROUND BAWITI

♟ Drinking

Many of the cafes around town are no-name places where Siwan men gather to watch TV and chat, but no alcohol is served. A couple of the most enjoyable cafes are found next to Cleopatra's Bath.

Shaqraza   CAFE
(Map p310; central market sq; ⊙24hr; 🛜) The newest, hippest cafe/restaurant in Siwa sits on a shaded rooftop overlooking the central square. Choose a regular table with chairs or lounge on cushions while browsing an extensive list of coffees, teas and juices, plus a full food menu (mains E£5-30). Throw in the wi-fi and this place seems like a sure hit.

Campione Cafe   CAFE
(Map p310; central market sq; ⊙sunrise-late) We can't argue with Campione's slogan: 'life is too short for bad coffee'. This cool streetside cafe serves imported Italian coffee made with an imported espresso machine and prepared any way you like it. The only drag is the growing number of motorcycles roaring past in the evening.

Taghaghien Touristic Island   OUTDOOR BAR
(off Map p306; ☎921 0060; www.taghaghien-island. com; admission E£25) If you're desperate for a beer, this small island 12km northwest of Siwa Town and connected by a causeway is one of the few places selling the amber nectar (for a whopping E£35 a bottle). There is some humble accommodation and a restaurant here, but its many shaded tables and chairs, paddleboat rentals and sweet sunset vistas make it better for a day trip or picnic. You'll need your own transport to get here. It's in the direction of Sidi Jaafar, northwest of town.

Right in town, **Zeytouna** (Map p310; central market sq) and **Abdu Coffeeshop** (Map p310; central market sq) face each other at opposite ends of the square and fill up with locals smoking *sheesha,* downing tea and slapping backgammon pieces with triumphant vigour.

🔒 Shopping

Siwa's rich culture is well represented by the abundance of traditional crafts that are still made for local use as well as for tourists. There are a ton of shops around Siwa Town selling very similar items, so browse around a bit before you buy. Happy haggling!

Siwan women love to adorn themselves with heavy silver jewellery and you should be able to find some interesting pieces around town. Local wedding dresses are famous for their red, orange, green and black embroidery, often embellished with shells and beads. Look for black silk *asherah nazitaf* and white cotton *asherah namilal* dresses.

A variety of baskets are woven from date-palm fronds. You can spot old baskets by their finer workmanship and the use of silk or leather instead of vinyl and polyester. The *tarkamt,* a woven plate that features a red leather centre, is traditionally used for serving sweets, the larger *tghara* is used for storing bread. Smaller baskets include the *aqarush* and the red-and-green silk-tasselled *nedibash.* You'll also find pottery coloured with pigment from Gebel Dakrur, used locally as water jugs, drinking cups and incense burners.

Siwa is also known for its dates and olives, found in every other shop around the main square. Ask to taste a few different varieties; you really can't go wrong.

Camera film, SD memory cards, and batteries can be bought at **Nada Studio Lab** (Map p310), just past the telephone centrale on the main road out of Siwa Town.

By the time you read this, a planned fairtrade handicrafts co-op may be open in the Bedouin village of **Bahy el-Din**, 30km west of Siwa; contact **Indigenous Collective** (☎0106 838 6484; www.indigenouscollective.org) for info.

ℹ Information

Emergency
Tourist police (Map p310; ☎460 2047; Siwa Town)

Internet Access
There's a sprinkling of computers around the centre of town, most for E£10 per hour.

Desert Net Cafe (Map p310; Siwa Town; per hr E£3; ⊙11am-3pm & 7pm-3am) The cheapest internet access in town, usually with decent connection speeds. It's on the street between King Fuad Mosque and the bank.

Al-Waha Internet (Map p310; Siwa Town) Pay E£10-15 per day for a wi-fi connection that works all around the centre of town, even into some of the hotels, giving you 24hr internet access from your laptop. Good speeds.

Medical Services
Hospital (Map p306; ☎460 0459; Sharia Sadat, Siwa Town) Only for emergencies.

Pharmacy Al-Ansar (Map p310; ☎460 1310; Sharia Sadat, Siwa Town; ⊙8am-2pm & 4pm-2am)

Money

Banque du Caire (Map p310; Siwa Town; ☺8.30am-2pm, plus 5-8pm Oct-Apr) Purported to be the only all-mudbrick bank in the world; the ATM usually works.

Permits

A permit is needed to venture off the beaten track from Siwa, but this is easily arranged by local guides. Mahdi Hweiti at the tourist office (p315) will arrange permissions quickly (but not on Friday) at the fixed rate of US$5, plus an extra E£11 for the local intelligence police. The same rate applies for the permit needed to travel from Siwa to Baharya. You'll need copies of your passport.

Post & Telephone

Main post office (Map p310; behind Arous al-Waha Hotel, Siwa Town; ☺8am-2pm Sat-Thu)

Telephone centrale (Map p310; Siwa Town; ☺24hr)

Tourist Information

Tourist office (Map p310; 460 1338; mahdi_hweiti@yahoo.com; Siwa Town; ☺9am-2pm Sat-Thu, plus 5-8pm Oct-Apr) Siwa's tourist officer, Mahdi Hweiti, is very knowledgeable and can help arrange trips to surrounding villages or the desert. His mobile number is ☏0100 546 1992.

Getting There & Away

Bus

West & Middle Delta Bus Co buses depart from the bus stop opposite the tourist police station, although when you arrive you'll be let off near the central market square. The ticket office is at the bus stop. It's sensible to buy your ticket ahead of time, as buses are often full.

There are three daily buses to Alexandria (E£37, eight hours), stopping at Marsa Matruh (E£17, four hours); these leave at 7am, 10am and 10pm. There's one daily departure to Cairo (E£70) at 8pm, except when there's not.

Microbus

Microbuses going to Marsa Matruh leave from the main square near the King Fuad Mosque. They are more frequent and *way* more comfortable than the West & Mid Delta bus; tickets cost the same.

4WD

A new road linking the oases of Siwa and Baharya began construction in 2005, and after many delays actually seems to be moving forward, though no one can guess when it'll be finished. About half the route is well asphalted, and the whole distance (about 400km) can be crossed in 5 hours. 4WD is still necessary (there are no buses or service taxis), and drivers and the required permits are easy to arrange at either end. You'll pay about E£1500 per car, so team up with others to share the cost. If you can afford it, it's totally worth it, both for the scenery and to avoid the buzzkill of going through Alexandria and Cairo just to travel from one oasis to the next. Ensure that the vehicle is a roadworthy 4WD and that you have food and water.

To/From Libya

Though Siwa is only about 50km from the Libyan border, it's currently illegal to leave or enter either country along this stretch of the frontier. The closest place to cross is up on the coast at Sallum (see p352).

❶ Getting Around

Bicycle

Bicycles are one of the best ways to get around and can be rented from several sources, including most hotels and a number of shops dotted around the town centre. Getting a bike from one of the **bicycle repair shops** (see Map p310) gives you a better chance of finding a bike in good condition. The going rate is E£15 to E£20 per day.

Donkey Cart

*Careta*s (donkey carts) are a much-used mode of transport for Siwans and can be a more amusing, if slower, way to get around than bicycles or cars. Some of the boys who drive the carts speak English and can be fierce hagglers. Expect to pay about E£30 for two to three hours, or E£10 for a short trip.

Motorcycle

Though not as enjoyable or tranquil as bicycles, motorbikes can also be rented. You can pick one up from the bike shop next to Al-Babinshal Hotel, or at Palm Trees Hotel. Expect to pay between E£100 and E£200 per day.

Servees

Pick-up trucks serve as communal taxis linking Siwa Town with the surrounding villages. To get to Bilad ar-Rum costs E£1 each way; closer destinations are 50pt. If you want to hire your own to get to more remote sites, Mahdi Hweiti at the tourist office will be able to help, or head for the petrol station and talk directly to drivers. One reliable, English-speaking driver with a good-quality vehicle is Anwar Mohammed (☏0122 687 3261). Prices are per truck, not per passenger, and depend on the duration of the trip, the distance to be covered and, of course, haggling skills.

BEYOND SIWA

Qara Oasis

About 120km northeast of Siwa as the crow flies, near the Qattara Depression, is another oasis, Qara (pronounced 'Ghara'). This remote oasis is home to 317 Berbers who, like the Siwans, built their fortresslike town on top of a mountain. There are a number of legends as to how the population here remained constant over the years: according to one, mystical forces kept things in balance, so for every birth or new arrival, someone living in the village would die. Needless to say, visitors to Qara were discouraged from spending the night! Nowadays this superstition is largely disregarded, but there aren't any hotels and most travellers visit on a day trip. The old clifftop fortress, no longer inhabited, is better preserved than the one in Siwa; there are springs to swim in; and the gardens are beautiful (but the mosquitoes are fierce!). A car and driver from Siwa should cost E£400 to E£500 for the round-trip. For more information, see p309. (A note: some locals in Siwa may suggest bringing candies for the local kids in Qara, but we strongly discourage this, both because it's bad for their teeth and because we've seen what's happened in places where kids learn to think every tourist is laden with sweets.)

Great Sand Sea

One of the world's largest dune fields, the Great Sand Sea straddles Egypt and Libya, stretching over 800km from its northern edge near the Mediterranean coast south to Gilf Kebir. Covering a colossal 72,000 sq km, it contains some of the largest recorded dunes in the world, including one that is 140km long. Crescent, *seif* (sword) and barchan dunes (see p297) are found here in abundance, and have challenged desert travellers and explorers for hundreds of years. The Persian king Cambyses is thought to have lost an army here, while the WWII British Long Range Desert Group spent months trying to find a way through the impenetrable sands to launch surprise attacks on the German army. Aerial surveys and expeditions have helped the charting of this vast expanse, but it remains one of the least-explored areas on the planet.

The Great Sand Sea is not a place to go wandering on a whim, and you will need military permits as well as good preparation. Guides will take you to the edges of the Great Sand Sea from Siwa, and many safari outfits will take you on expeditions that skirt the area (see p309). Remember that you don't need to penetrate far into the desert in order to feel the isolation, beauty and enormous scale of this amazing landscape.

Alexandria & the Mediterranean Coast

Includes »

Best Places to Eat

» Picnic at Agiba Beach (p349)

» Zephyrion (p343)

» Farag (p334)

» Mohammed Ahmed (p334)

Best Places to Stay

» Windsor Palace Hotel (p331)

» Sofitel Cecil Alexandria (p331)

» Almaza Bay (p350)

Why Go?

Egypt's northern coastline runs for 500km along dazzling Mediterranean shores. Think of it as an Egyptian Riviera, drawing swarms of summertime revellers who come to cool off in the sea air and splash in the water. Along its western stretches, the translucent shades of turquoise and lapis are so pure, so vibrant, you'll hardly believe your eyes.

The once-great port city of Alexandria is the region's hub, with ancient sights, terrific seafood restaurants, and a distinctly different urban pulse than that of Cairo. Further west, historic battlefields are reminders of the intense desert campaigns of WWII's North African front. During peak season, beach resort towns are as much a cultural experience as anything else, as you join throngs of vacationing families on the seashore. At other times, there's a good chance you'll have the irresistibly gorgeous waters all to yourself.

When to Go
Alexandria

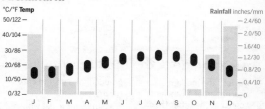

Jun–mid-Sep Best beach season; Alexandria and the coast are packed with Egyptians on holiday.

Apr–May & mid-Sep–Oct Beaches are virtually empty, but it's warm enough to enjoy them.

Nov–Mar Chilly for a beach break, great for hotel discounts.

ALEXANDRIA

🎵 03 / POP 4.1 MILLION

The city of Alexandria (Al-Iskendariyya) is the stuff that legends are made of: it was founded by none other than Alexander the Great; sassy queen Cleopatra made this the seat of her throne; the entrance to its harbour was marked by the towering Pharos lighthouse, one of the Seven Wonders of the Ancient World; and its Great Library was renowned as the ultimate archive of ancient knowledge. Alas, fate dealt the city a spate of cruel blows: today no sign remains of the great Alexander; the city of Cleopatra's day has been mostly swallowed up by the ocean; the Pharos lighthouse collapsed long ago; and the literary treasures of the Great Library were torched. To add insult to injury, Egypt's consequent Muslim rulers moved the capital to nearby Cairo, ignobly thrusting the once influential metropolis into near obscurity for centuries.

In the 19th century a cosmopolitan renaissance had Alexandria flirting with European-style decadence, but it was cut short in the 1950s by Nasser's nationalism. Today, Alexandria feels ready to forge a new identity. The daring new library of Alexandria is probably the most innovative modern building in the country; it may soon be surpassed if a cutting-edge underwater museum is built nearby in the bay, as planned, to showcase Alexandria's submerged archaeological treasures right where they lay. Meanwhile, the city is swooping in on the role of Egypt's culture vulture, as legions of young artists and writers are finding their voices here. Maybe this is why Alexandria feels like one of the most liberal cities in Egypt, where it's common to see women without headscarves and you may even spot Egyptian couples walking hand-in-hand.

Alexandria, the famed metropolis of the ages, is not always easy to find in the city that bears its name today. And for all its

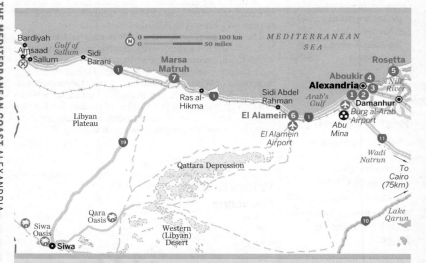

Alexandria & the Mediterranean Coast Highlights

❶ Tour the modern incarnation of an ancient wonder at the **Bibliotheca Alexandrina** (p327)

❷ Stroll the streets and souqs (markets) of soulful **Anfushi** at night (p325)

❸ Taste the last drops of Alexandria's 19th-century

grandeur at a **period cafe** (p337)

❹ Stuff your gullet with fresh seafood along the shore at **Aboukir** (p343)

❺ Wander the dusty, donkey-filled streets of **Rosetta** (Ar-Rashid; p343)

with its restored Ottoman architecture

❻ Remember the desert battles of WWII's North Africa campaign at **El Alamein** (p345)

❼ Splash in the stunning aqua waters at the beaches near **Marsa Matruh** (p348)

ALEXANDRIA IN...

Two Days

Start day one sipping coffee at one of the city's many time-warp **period cafes**, then get a taste of the past at the excellent **Alexandria National Museum**. Follow that up with lunch at the bustling **Mohammed Ahmed**, deservedly regarded as the king of fuul (fava beans) and felafel. Having gotten a sense of the city's history, explore the future at the iconic **Bibliotheca Alexandrina**, checking out several of its must-see museums and exhibits. When done, head across the street to **Selsela Cafe** for some tea or Turkish coffee, as the waves of the bay roll in alongside you. Hop into a microbus and ride the length of the Corniche, all the way down to **Fort Qaitbey**, a scenic spot for sunset, then walk back to the centre of town through the streets and souqs (markets) of **Anfushi**, stopping for a seafood dinner sooner – at **Kadoura** – or later – at **Farag**.

On day two, get an early start at the **Anfushi Fish Market**, one of the liveliest souqs in Egypt. Stop off for breakfast at the **Imperial Cafe**, then decide: if you're in the mood for ancient sights, head to the **Roman Amphitheatre**, **Villa of the Birds** and the underground **Catacombs of Kom ash-Shuqqafa**; but if you're up for the **beach** (and some great people-watching), head for one of the sandy strips along the shore to the east. For dinner, try something different at the casual grilled quail joint, **Malek es-Seman**. Finish off your day with an evening drink at the atmospheric **Cap d'Or**, or tea and a sheesha (water pipe) at **El Tugareya**.

Four Days

Follow the two-day itinerary, then add a day trip to **Rosetta** and the mouth of the Nile, and on the fourth day head to **El Alamein** and spend the afternoon on the beach in **Sidi Abdel Rahman**.

recent strivings, the city hardly feels entirely modern. Nevertheless, this is an ideal place to spend a few days sipping coffee in grand, old-world cafes at breakfast; pondering the city's glorious past at its many museums and monuments; and topping it all off with mouth-watering fish fare fresh from the sea.

History

Alexandria's history bridges the time of the pharaohs and the days of Islam. The city gave rise to the last great Pharaonic dynasty (the Ptolemies), provided the entry into Egypt for the Romans and nurtured early Christianity before rapidly fading into near obscurity when Islam's invading armies passed it by to set up camp on a site along the Nile that later became Cairo.

The city was conceived by Alexander the Great, who arrived from Sinai having had his right to rule Egypt confirmed by the priests of Memphis. Here, on the shores of his familiar sea, he chose a fishing village as the site for a new city that he hoped would link the old Pharaonic world and the new world of the Greeks. Foundations were laid in 331 BC, and almost immediately Alexander departed for Siwa in order to consult the famous oracle before then marching for

Persia. His conquering army went as far as India, and after his death at Babylon in 323 BC the rule of Egypt fell to the Macedonian general Ptolemy. Ptolemy won a struggle over Alexander's remains and buried them somewhere around Alexandria.

Ptolemy masterminded the development of the new city, filling it with architecture to rival Rome or Athens and establishing it as the cultural and political centre of his empire. To create a sense of continuity between his rule and that of the Pharaonic dynasties, Ptolemy made Alexandria look at least superficially Egyptian by adorning it with sphinxes, obelisks and statues scavenged from the old sites of Memphis and Heliopolis. The city developed into a major port and became an important halt on the trade routes between Europe and Asia. Its economic wealth was equally matched by its intellectual standing. Its famed library (p329) stimulated some of the great advances of the age: this was where Herophilus discovered that the head, not the heart, is the seat of thought; Euclid developed geometry; Aristarchus discovered that the earth revolves around the sun; and Eratosthenes calculated the earth's circumference. A grand tower, the Pharos (p328), one of the Seven

Alexandria

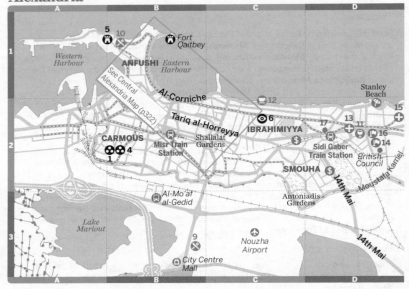

Alexandria

Wonders of the Ancient World, was built on an island just offshore and served as both a beacon to guide ships entering the booming harbour and an ostentatious symbol of the city's greatness.

During the reign of its most famous regent, Cleopatra, Alexandria rivalled Rome in everything but military power – a situation that Rome found intolerable and was eventually forced to act upon. Under Roman control, Alexandria remained the capital of Egypt, but during the 4th century AD, civil war, famine and disease ravaged the city's populace and it never regained its former glory. Alexandria's fall was sealed when the conquering Muslim armies swept into Egypt in the 7th century and bypassed Alexandria in favour of a new capital on the Nile.

Alexandria remained in decline through the Middle Ages and was even superseded in importance as a seaport by the nearby town of Rosetta. Over the centuries its monu-

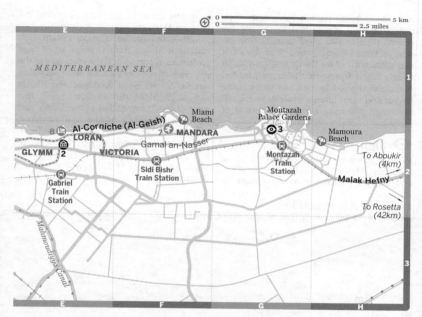

ments were destroyed by earthquakes and their ruins quarried for building materials, so much so that one of the greatest cities of the classical world was reduced to little more than a fishing village (now Anfushi), with a population of less than 10,000.

The turning point in Alexandria's fortunes came with Napoleon's invasion of 1798; recognising the city's strategic importance, he initiated its revival. During the subsequent reign of the Egyptian reformist Mohammed Ali, a new town was built on top of the old one. Alexandria once more became one of the Mediterranean's busiest ports and attracted a cosmopolitan mix of people, among them wealthy Turkish-Egyptian traders, Jews, Greeks, Italians and many others from around the Mediterranean. Multiculturally, sitting on the foundations of antiquity, perfectly placed on the overland route between Europe and the East, and growing wealthy from trade, Alexandria took on an almost mythical quality and served as the muse for a new string of poets, writers and intellectuals. But the wave of anticolonial, pro-Arab sentiment that swept Colonel Gamal Abdel Nasser to power in 1952 also spelt the end for Alexandria's cosmopolitan communities. Those foreigners who didn't stream out of the country in the wake of

King Farouk's yacht found themselves forced out a few years later following the Suez Crisis, when Nasser confiscated foreign properties and nationalised many foreign-owned businesses.

Since that time the character of the city has changed completely. In the 1940s some 40% of the city's population was made up of foreigners, while now most of its residents are native Egyptians. Where there were 300,000 residents in the 1940s, Alexandria is now home to more than four million.

Many people credit events that happened here with lighting the fuse that exploded into the revolution of 2011. In June 2010, a 28-year-old man named Khaled Said was beaten to death by police in Alexandria, apparently after he posted videos on the internet showing police pocketing drugs confiscated in a bust. Soon after the murder, a Facebook page called 'We are all Khaled Said' was created, showing photos of the young man's horribly smashed face and publicly exposing police accounts of his death as blatant fabrications. Outraged, tens of thousands of Egyptians 'friended' the page. A series of protests were held in Alexandria demanding justice. Khaled Said's killing, and the subsequent cover-up, became a symbol of everything that was wrong with the Mubarak regime. By January 2011, nearly 380,000 people had joined the Facebook page and its moderator, Google executive Wael Ghonim, used it as a virtual megaphone to call for the demonstrations in Cairo's Tahrir Square that ultimately ousted Mubarak. Alexandria itself saw some of the largest and most intense protests in the entire country, forcing a complete retreat of the police from the city's streets.

◉ Sights

Modern Alexandria lies protracted along a curving shoreline, stretching for 20km and rarely extending more than 3km inland. The centre of the city arcs around the Eastern Harbour, almost enclosed by two spindly promontories. The city's main tram station at Midan Ramla, where most lines terminate, is considered the epicentre of the city. Two of the city centre's main shopping streets, Sharia Saad Zaghloul and Sharia Safiyya Zaghloul, run off this square. Just west of the tram station is the larger and more formal square, Midan Saad Zaghloul, with a popular garden facing the seafront. Around these two *midan*s (city squares) are the central shopping areas, the tourist office, restaurants and the majority of the cheaper hotels.

Central Alexandria

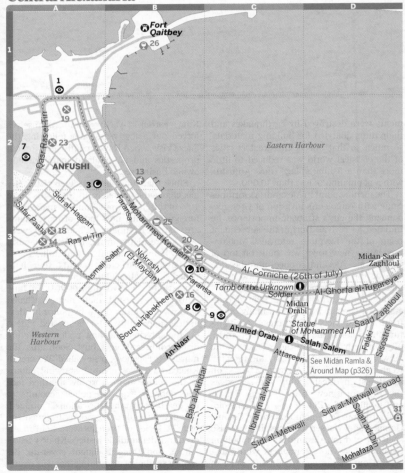

Northwest of this central area is the older, atmospheric neighbourhood of Anfushi; southwest is Carmous, with some notable Roman ruins. Heading east, a succession of newer districts stretches along the coast to the upmarket residential area of Rushdy, the trendy suburbs of San Stefano and further on to Montazah, with its palace and gardens, which marks the eastern limits of the city. The Corniche (Al-Corniche) is the long coastal road that connects nearly all parts of the city, though crossing it involves playing chicken with swarms of hurtling buses and taxis.

If you're spending significant time in the city, the street map produced by Mohandes Mostafa el Fadaly (see p340) is very useful.

CENTRAL ALEXANDRIA

'Like Cannes with acne' was Michael Palin's verdict on Alexandria's sweeping seafront **Corniche** (in his book *Around the World in 80 Days*). Right in the middle of the broad Corniche is the legendary **Cecil Hotel** (p331), now run by Sofitel, overlooking Midan Saad Zaghloul. Built in 1930, it's an Alexandrian institution and a memorial to the city's belle époque, when guests included

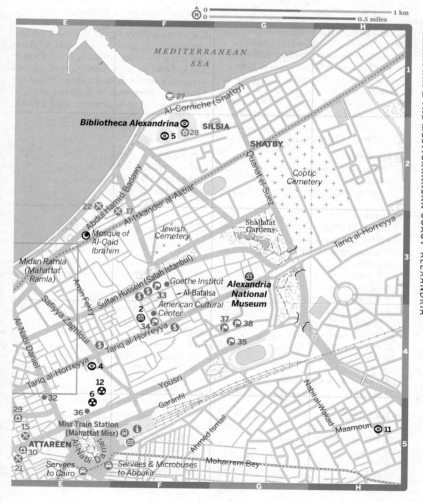

the likes of Somerset Maugham, Noël Coward and Winston Churchill, and the British Secret Service operated out of a suite on the 1st floor. The hotel was eternalised in Lawrence Durrell's *Alexandria Quartet*.

Interestingly, modern Alexandria is built directly on top of the ancient city and often follows the ancient street pattern. The street now known as Tariq al-Horreyya was the ancient Canopic Way, extending from the city's Gate of the Sun in the east to the Gate of the Moon in the west. The centre of town was where it crossed the Street of the Soma (now Sharia al-Nabi Daniel). In other words, if you stop into the Vinous cafe (p337), you can sip coffee right where the heart of the ancient city used to be.

Alexandria National Museum   MUSEUM
(Map p322; www.alexmuseum.org.eg; 110 Tariq al-Horreyya; adult/student E£35/20; ⊗9am-4.30pm)
The excellent Alexandria National Museum sets high benchmarks for summing up Alexandria's past. With a small, thoughtfully selected and well-labelled collection singled out from Alexandria's other museums, it does a sterling job of relating the city's history from antiquity until the modern period. Housed in a beautifully restored Italianate villa, it stocks several thousand years of Alexandrian history, arranged chronologically over three cryogenically air-conditioned floors.

The ground floor is dedicated to Graeco-Roman times, and highlights include a sphinx and other sculptures found during underwater excavations at Aboukir. Look for the small statue of the Greek god Harpocrates with a finger to his lips (representing silence), who was morphed from the original Egyptian god Horus. Also check out the beautiful statue of a Ptolemaic queen, with Egyptian looks and a Hellenistic body. The basement covers the Pharaonic period, with finds from all over Egypt. The top floor displays artefacts from Islamic and modern periods, with coins, Ottoman weapons and jewels. Don't miss the exquisite silver shield. Early coexistence of Alexandria's major religions is represented by a carved wooden cross encircled by a crescent. Well-written panels on the walls provide useful insights into the life, art and beliefs of the Alexandrians through the centuries.

Roman Amphitheatre (Kom al-Dikka)
ARCHAEOLOGICAL SITE

(Map p322; Sharia Yousri, off Midan Gomhuriyya; adult/student E£20/15; ⊙9am-4.30pm) While the 13 white-marble terraces of the only Roman amphitheatre in Egypt may not be impressive in scale, they remain a superbly preserved ode to the days of the centurion. This site was discovered when foundations were being laid for an apartment building on a site known unceremoniously as Kom al-Dikka (Mound of Rubble). Excavations continue to uncover more in the area; in early 2010 the ruins of a Ptolemaic-era temple were uncovered along with statues of gods and goddesses, including a number of the cat goddess Bastet.

In Ptolemaic times this area was known as the Park of Pan, a pleasure garden where citizens of Alexandria could indulge in various lazy pursuits.

Villa of the Birds

(Map p322; adult/student E£15/8) In the same complex, this wealthy urban dwelling dates to the time of Hadrian (AD 117–138). Despite being redecorated at least four times in antiquity before being destroyed by fire in the 3rd century AD, its floor mosaic of pigeons, peacocks, quails, parrots and water hens remains astonishingly well preserved. Additional mosaics feature a panther, and a stylised flower design known as a rosette. To see the villa, buy a separate ticket at the entrance to the amphitheatre.

Eliyahu Hanavi Synagogue
SYNAGOGUE

(Map p326; Sharia al-Nabi Daniel) Among the largest synagogues in the Middle East, this magnificent Italian-built structure served Alexandria's once thriving and cosmopolitan Jewish community. The interior features immense marble columns and space for over 700, with brass nameplates still affixed to the regular seats of male worshippers. Since the wars with Israel and the 1956 Suez Crisis, the community has dwindled and rarely musters the 10 men necessary to hold a service. Visits to this poignant and moving reminder of the city's multicultural past must be arranged through Ben Youssef Gaon, president of the local Jewish community and, aged in his 50s, among its youngest current members. Reach Ben Youssef on ☑0122 703 1031; if you can't make contact

this way, try asking at the front gate. A donation of E£10 to E£20 is appreciated but not required.

Graeco-Roman Museum
MUSEUM

(Map p322; 5 Al-Mathaf ar-Romani) As part of Alexandria's effort to spruce itself up, many of its prime tourist attractions are undergoing renovation. Unfortunately, this wonderful museum, normally home to one of the most extensive collections of Graeco-Roman art in the world, is one of them. There is no official completion date for the work, and the museum may be shuttered for the foreseeable future. Check with the tourist office for further information on opening dates.

ANFUSHI & FORT QAITBEY

Charismatic Anfushi, the old Turkish part of town, was once where stuffy Alexandria came to let down its hair. While Midan Ramla and the Midan Tahrir area were developed along the lines of a European model in the 19th century, Anfushi remained untouched, an indigenous quarter standing in counterpoint to the new cosmopolitan city. This is where writer Lawrence Durrell's characters came in search of prostitutes and a bit of rough trade. Today it remains one of the poorer parts of the city, where a huge number of people live squeezed into atmospheric but old and decaying buildings, many of which seem to be teetering on the verge of collapse.

Fort Qaitbey
FORT

(Map p322; Eastern Harbour; adult/student E£25/15; ⊙9am-4pm) The Eastern Harbour is dominated by the fairy-tale-perfect Fort Qaitbey. Built on a narrow peninsula by the Mamluk sultan Qaitbey in 1480, it sits on the remains of the legendary Pharos lighthouse (p328).

The lighthouse, which had been in use for some 17 centuries, was finally destroyed by an earthquake and was in ruins for more than 100 years when Qaitbey ordered the fortification of the city's harbour. Material from the fallen Pharos was reused, and if you get close to the outer walls you can pick out some great pillars of red granite, which in all likelihood came from the ancient lighthouse. Other parts of the ancient building are scattered around the nearby seabed.

The fort has been renovated and is now open to the public. It makes for a pleasant walk and the view back across the harbour is spectacular, with a foreground of colourful bobbing fishing boats and in the distance

Midan Ramla & Around

the sunlike disc of the new library. In the base of the fort there's a **museum** (E£5) with plenty of stuffed-and-mounted sea life; across the street is a small **aquarium** (E£5), which is just a hallway lined with fish tanks. Just west of the fort is the lively Anfushi Fish Market (p338).

From Midan Ramla, it's a 30- to 45-minute walk along the Corniche. Otherwise, take yellow tram 15 from Midan Ramla or flag down any of the microbuses barrelling along the Corniche. A taxi should cost E£5.

Terbana Mosque   MOSQUE
(Map p322) The beautiful little Terbana Mosque stands at the junction of Sharia Faransa and Wekalet al-Limon. This entire quarter, known as Gumruk, stands on land that was underwater in the Middle Ages. Late 17th-century builders managed to incorporate bits of ancient Alexandria in the mosque's structure, reusing two classical columns to support the minaret. The red-

and-black-painted brickwork on the facade is typical of the Delta-style architecture. The **Shorbagi Mosque** (Map p322; Sharia Nokrashi), nearby, is also built with salvaged remnants of antiquity.

Mosque of Abu Abbas al-Mursi   MOSQUE
(Map p322; Sharia Mohammed Koraiem) This stately mosque was originally the tomb of a 13th-century Sufi saint from Murcia in Spain. Today, it dominates a large midan that covers an entire city block, which is easily visible and accessible from the Corniche. Several successive mosques have been built and rebuilt on the site; though the current structure dates to the modern era, it's still an attractive octagonal building with a soaring central tower and an interior decorated with eye-catching Islamic mosaics, tiling and woodwork. Devotees still flock to al-Mursi's shrine under the main floor. Leave your shoes at the entrance and slip the attendant a little baksheesh (tip) when you collect

Midan Ramla & Around

them. On summer nights a carnival-like atmosphere surrounds the mosque, with everything from pony rides to bumper cars to merry-go-rounds.

Shipyards SHIPYARDS
(Map p322; Ras el-Tin) Where northern Anfushi hits the sea, you can wander among huge wooden vessels in various states of construction. In small workshops, craftsmen make accessories for the boats, such as intricately carved helms (steering wheels) and cabinets.

Further west along the shore, you'll spot **Ras el-Tin Palace** (Map p320). Originally built in the 1830s for Mohammed Ali, it's now part of a naval base and was an official presidential residence. It was here that King Farouk signed his abdication papers in 1952. Unfortunately it's not open to visitors.

EASTERN SUBURBS

TOP CHOICE **Bibliotheca Alexandrina** LIBRARY, MUSEUMS
(Map p322; www.bibalex.org; Al-Corniche, Shatby; adult/student E£10/5; ⊙9am-4pm Sat-Thu; 3-7pm Fri) Alexandria's ancient library was one of the greatest of all classical institutions (see p329), and while replacing it might seem a Herculean task, the new Bibliotheca Alexandrina manages it with aplomb. Opened in 2002, this impressive piece of modern architecture is a deliberate attempt to rekindle the brilliance of the original centre of learning and culture. The complex has become one of Egypt's major cultural venues and a stage for numerous international performers.

The building takes the form of a gigantic angled discus embedded in the ground, evoking a second sun rising out of the Mediterranean. The granite exterior walls are carved with letters, pictograms, hieroglyphs and symbols from more than 120 different human scripts. Inside, the jaw-dropping main reading room can accommodate eight million books and 2500 readers under its sloping roof, with windows specially designed to let sunlight flood in but keep out rays that might harm the collection.

In addition to the main reading room, the library boasts a huge array of diversions: three permanent museums, four specialised libraries, a planetarium, a conference centre, temporary and permanent exhibitions, and a full schedule of events. To fully explore this very worthy attraction, you should allot half a day, though to gape at the astounding main reading room and do a tour, you'll need an hour or so.

The **Manuscript Museum** (adult/student E£20/10) contains ancient texts, antiquarian books and maps, including a copy of the only surviving scroll from the ancient library. The **Antiquities Museum** (adult/student E£20/10) holds some overspill from the Graeco-Roman Museum, including a fine Roman mosaic of a dog that was discovered when the foundations of the library were dug. The **History of Science Museum** (admission 50pt; ⊙10am-3pm Sat-Thu, 4-6pm Fri) underneath the Planetarium is targeted at children of school age.

The four specialised libraries are a children's library for ages six to 11; a youth library for ages 11 to 17; a multimedia library; and a library for the blind.

Regular exhibitions include **Impressions of Alexandria**, which does a sterling job of tracing the city's long history through drawings, maps and early photographs. There's also a video program on Egyptian history called the Culturama, displayed on nine screens, and, most recently added, an exhibition on Anwar Sadat.

The **Planetarium** (admission E£25; ⊙11am-2pm Sat-Mon & Wed-Thu) is a futuristic neon-lit sphere looming on the plaza in front of the library, like a mini Death Star from *Star Wars*. It shows 3-D films hourly on a rotating schedule (see library website), and has an **Exploratorium** (E£4; ⊙9am-3.30pm Sat-Mon & Wed-Thu, 8.30am-12.30pm Tue, 3-5pm Fri) as well as the History of Science Museum, which are both great for kids.

Tickets to the library can be bought outside the main entrance, where all bags must be checked. The basic E£10 ticket includes free guided tours, entrance to the main reading room and any free exhibits or events. Hi-tech PDA (personal digital assistant) guides are also available in English, Arabic and French.

A combined ticket including the Antiquities and Manuscript Museums, but not the Planetarium, is E£45. You can also buy tickets to each of these individually at their respective ticket offices.

THE PHAROS

The Egyptian coast was a nightmare for ancient sailors, the flat featureless shoreline making it hard to steer away from hidden rocks and sandbanks. To encourage trade, Ptolemy I ordered a great tower to be built, one that could be seen by sailors long before they reached the coast. After 12 years of construction, the Pharos was inaugurated in 283 BC. The structure was added to until it acquired such massive and unique proportions that ancient scholars regarded it as one of the Seven Wonders of the Ancient World.

In its original form the Pharos was a simple marker, probably topped with a statue, as was common at the time. The tower became a lighthouse, so historians believe, in the 1st century AD, when the Romans added a beacon, probably an oil-fed flame reflected by sheets of polished bronze. According to descriptions from as late as the 12th century, the Pharos had a square base, an octagonal central section and a round top. Contemporary images of the Pharos still exist, most notably in a mosaic in St Mark's Basilica in Venice and another in a church in eastern Libya, and in two terracotta representations in Alexandria's Graeco-Roman Museum.

In all, the Pharos withstood winds, floods and the odd tidal wave for 17 centuries. However, in 1303 a violent earthquake rattled the entire eastern Mediterranean and the Pharos was finally toppled. More than a century later the sultan Qaitbey quarried the ruins for the fortress that still stands on the site.

THE GREAT LIBRARY OF ALEXANDRIA

The original Library of Alexandria was the greatest repository of books and documents in all of antiquity. Ptolemy I established the library in 283 BC as part of a larger research complex known as the Mouseion (Shrine of the Muses; the source of today's word 'museum'). This dedicated centre of learning housed more than 100 full-time scholars and boasted lecture areas, gardens, a zoo, shrines and the library itself. Uniquely, this was one of the first major 'public' libraries and was open to all persons with the proper scholarly qualifications.

Demetrius Phalereus, a disciple of Aristotle, was charged with governing the library and together with Ptolemy I and his successors established the lofty goal of collecting copies of all the books in the world. Manuscripts found on ships arriving at Alexandria's busy port were confiscated by law and copied, and merchants were sent to scour the markets of other Mediterranean cities looking for tomes of all descriptions. Most books back then consisted of papyrus scrolls, often translated into Greek and rolled and stored in the library's many labelled pigeonholes. At its height the library was said to contain more than 700,000 works, which indicated some duplication as this was believed to be more than the number of published works in existence. The library soon exceeded its capacity and a 'daughter library' was established in the Temple of Serapeum (p330) to stock the overflow. The vast collection established Alexandria's position as the pre-eminent centre of culture and civilisation in the world.

It is uncertain exactly who was responsible for the destruction of the ancient world's greatest archives of knowledge, though there are several suspects. Julius Caesar is the first. In his scrap with Pompey in 48 BC, Caesar set fire to Alexandria's harbour, which also engulfed the part of the city the library stood in. Then in AD 270, Zenobia, Queen of Palmyra (now Syria), had captured Egypt and clashed with Roman emperor Aurelian here, the resulting siege destroying more of the library. At this time, Alexandria's main centre of learning moved to the daughter library in the Serapeum. Early Christians are next in line for the blame: the daughter library was finally destroyed as part of an anti-pagan purge led by Christian Roman Emperor Theodosius in AD 391.

Note that while the library has a wide range of kid-friendly activities and diversions, little ones under the age of six are not admitted to the library complex. Helpfully, day care is available from 11am to 4pm daily except Friday and Saturday. The library is right on the Corniche, and you can easily get there by taxi or microbus.

Montazah Palace Gardens   GARDENS, BEACH
(Map p320; admission E£6) Khedive Abbas Hilmy (1892–1914) built Montazah as his summer palace, a refuge when Cairo became too hot. On a rocky bluff overlooking the sea, it's designed in a pseudo-Moorish style, which has been given a Florentine twist with the addition of a tower modelled on one at the Palazzo Vecchio. The palace itself is off-limits to the public but the surrounding lush groves and **gardens**, planted with pines and palms, are accessible. They're popular with courting couples and picnicking locals. There's also an attractive sandy cove here with a semiprivate **beach** (admission E£15) well suited to kids, although it's not particu-larly clean, and an eccentric Victorian-style bridge running out to a small island of pylons. In all, it's a pleasant escape from the city centre. A second royal residence, known as the Salamlek and built in an Austrian style, has been converted into a luxury hotel.

The simplest way to get here is to stand on the Corniche or on Tariq al-Horreyya and flag down a microbus; when it slows, shout 'Montazah' and if it's going that way (and most of them are), it'll stop and you can jump on. Or take the air-conditioned Red Bus (p343) – the upper level offers great views along the Corniche.

Mahmoud Said Museum   MUSEUM
(Map p320; 6 Sharia Mohammed Pasha Said, Gianaclis) He might be little known outside his home country, but Mahmoud Said (1897–1964) was one of Egypt's finest 20th-century artists. A judge by profession, he moonlighted as a painter and became a key member of a group of sophisticates devoted to forging an Egyptian artistic identity in the 1920s and '30s. This museum presents about

40 of his works in the beautiful Italianate villa in which he once lived. It was closed for renovation at the time of research, with no reopening date predicted.

From the San Stefano tram stop (on Line 2), cross the tracks and go up the steps to the raised road (opposite the huge mall). Go right and Sharia Mohammed Pasha Said is a short distance away on the left.

CARMOUS

Catacombs of Kom ash-Shuqqafa   ARCHAEOLOGICAL SITE

(Map p320; adult/student E£35/20; ⊙9am-5pm) A short walk from Pompey's Pillar is Kom ash-Shuqqafa. Discovered accidentally in 1900 when a donkey disappeared through the ground, these catacombs are the largest known Roman burial site in Egypt and one of the last major works of construction dedicated to the religion of ancient Egypt. Demonstrating Alexandria's hallmark fusion of Pharaonic and Greek styles, the architects used a Graeco-Roman approach. The catacombs consist of three tiers of tombs and chambers cut into bedrock to a depth of 35m (the bottom level is flooded and inaccessible).

As impressive as all this sounds, if you've been to the tombs on Luxor's west bank, Kom ash-Shuqqafa will surely leave you underwhelmed: most of the walls are unadorned, nearly all the paintings faded to invisibility.

Entry is through a spiral staircase; the bodies of the dead would have been lowered on ropes down the centre of this circular shaft. The staircase leads off to a **rotunda** with a central well piercing down into the gloom of the flooded lower level. When the catacombs were originally constructed in the 2nd century AD, probably as a family crypt, the rotunda would have led only to the triclinium (to your left) and principal tomb chamber (straight ahead). But over the 300 years that the tomb was in use, more chambers were hacked out until it had developed into a hive that could accommodate more than 300 corpses.

The **triclinium** was a banqueting hall where grieving relatives paid their last respects with a funeral feast. Mourners, who returned to feast after 40 days and again on each anniversary, reclined on the raised benches at the centre of the room around a low table. Tableware and wine jars were found when the chamber was excavated.

Back in the rotunda, head down the stairs to the **principal tomb**, the centrepiece of the catacombs. Here, an antechamber with columns and pediment leads through to an inner sanctum. The typical Alexandrian-style decoration shows a weird synthesis of ancient Egyptian, Greek and Roman funerary iconography. The doorway to the inner chamber is flanked by figures representing Anubis, the Egyptian god of the dead, but dressed as a Roman legionary and with a serpent's tail representative of Agathos Daimon, a Greek divinity.

From the antechamber a couple of short passages lead to a large U-shaped chamber lined with **loculi** – the holes in which the bodies were placed. After the body (or bodies, as many of the loculi held more than one) had been placed inside, the small chamber was sealed with a plaster slab.

Back up in the rotunda, four other passageways lead off to small clusters of tombs. One of these gives access to an entirely different complex, known as the **Hall of Caracalla**. This had its own staircase access (long-since caved in) and has been joined to Kom ash-Shuqqafa, which it pre-dates, by industrious tomb robbers who hacked a new passageway. Beside the hole in the wall, a painting shows the mummification of Osiris and the kidnapping of Persephone by Hades, illustrating ancient Egyptian and Greek funerary myths.

To get to the catacombs, you can take a cab or walk from Pompey's Pillar. If walking from the pillar, start from in front of the ticket office. With your back to the entrance, take the small street to the right, slightly uphill and away from the tram tracks. Follow this street for several hundred metres past a small mosque on the left, and the entrance to the catacombs will be on your left. No cameras are allowed inside the site, so you'll have to check yours at the entrance.

Pompey's Pillar & the Temple of Serapeum   ARCHAEOLOGICAL SITE

(Map p320; adult/student E£20/15; ⊙9am-4.30pm) The massive 30m column that looms over the debris of the glorious ancient settlement of Rhakotis, the original township from which Alexandria grew, is known as **Pompey's Pillar**. For centuries the column, hewn from red Aswan granite, has been one of the city's prime sights: a single, tapered shaft, 2.7m at its base and capped by a fine Corinthian capital. The column was named by travellers who remembered the murder of the Roman general Pompey by Cleopatra's brother, but an inscription on the base (presumably once covered with rubble) announces that it was erected in AD 291 to support a statue of the emperor Diocletian.

The column rises out of the disappointing ruins of the **Temple of Serapeum**, a magnificent structure that stood here in ancient times. It had 100 steps leading past the living quarters of the priests to the great temple of Serapis, the man-made god of Alexandria. Also here was the 'daughter library' of the Great Library of Alexandria (p329), which was said to have contained copies and overflow of texts. These scrolls could be consulted by anyone using the temple, making it one of the most important intellectual and religious centres in the Mediterranean. In AD 391, Christians launched a final assault on pagan intellectuals and destroyed the Serapeum and its library, leaving just the lonely pillar standing. The site is now little more than rubble pocked by trenches and holes with a few sphinxes (originally from Heliopolis), a surviving Nilometer (a structure used to measure and record the level of the Nile in ancient times) and the pillar – the only ancient monument remaining whole and standing today in Alexandria.

When taking a taxi here, ask for it by the Arabic name, *amoud el sawari*. The fare should be E£5 to E£7 from Midan Saad Zaghloul.

☞ Tours

Tamer Zakaria　　　　　　GUIDED TOUR
(☏0122 370 8210; tamerzakaria@yahoo.com) A highly recommended English-speaking guide and Egyptologist, friendly and knowledgeable, available for day guiding. He can also organise trips.

Ann & Medhat Hashem　　　DRIVING TOUR
(☏0122 035 4711; www.muzhela.com) This English expat and her Egyptian husband organise car and driver services starting at around E£200 per day. They also do short- and long-term apartment rental.

Mena Tours　　　　　　　　　TOUR
(Map p326; ☏480 9676; menatoursalx@yahoo.com; ◷9am-5pm Sat-Thu) Reliable standard tour agency.

🛏 Sleeping

As Alexandria has had an overhaul, the accommodation scene is also slowly getting better. While several five-star hotel chains

are setting up shop, hotels in the midrange category are still few and far between. Budget places run the whole gamut from downright seedy to pretty darn comfortable, but the selection from here mostly shoots straight into the US$100 a night top-end category.

The summer months of June to September are the high season in Alexandria, when half of Cairo seems to decamp here to escape the heat of the capital. At the peak of the season, in August, you may have difficulty finding a room at some of the more popular hotels.

Quite a few of the budget hotels front at least partly onto the Corniche. One of the pleasures of staying in Alexandria is pushing open the shutters in the morning to get a face full of fresh air off the Mediterranean, but the unrelenting din of traffic on the Corniche can make it seem like you're trying to snooze next to an airport runway. Light sleepers may want to consider a room off the Corniche. At any of Alexandria's budget hotels, it's wise to bring along your own soap, towel and toilet paper, as supplies can be erratic.

TOP CHOICE **Windsor Palace Hotel**　　　　HISTORIC HOTEL $$$
(Map p326; ☏480 8123; www.paradiseinnegypt.com; 17 Sharia el-Shohada; r with sea view US$150; ✳@🛜) This bejewelled Edwardian gem is an institution unto itself, towering over the Corniche and keeping a watchful eye on the Med since 1907. In the 1990s the Windsor was bought by Paradise Inn, after its success with the Metropole, and was given a much-needed nip and tuck. Thankfully the wonderful old elevators and grand lobby have been retained, and the rooms boast the sort of old-world, green- and gold-flavoured pizazz that wouldn't be out of place on the *Orient Express*. The pricier rooms have splendid sea views.

TOP CHOICE **Sofitel Cecil Alexandria**　　　HISTORIC HOTEL $$$
(Cecil Hotel; Map p326; ☏487 7173; www.sofitel.com; 16 Midan Saad Zaghloul; s with/without sea view US$145/130, d with/without sea view US$185/165; ✳@🛜) The historic Cecil Hotel, an Alexandria legend, has been refitted several times over the last couple of decades, sometimes for the better. The rooms are fully equipped, though a little sombre, while the grand lobby and famous bar (now

ALEXANDRIA & THE MEDITERRANEAN COAST ALEXANDRIA

relocated to the 1st floor) have retained only a fraction of the lustre they had when Durrell and Churchill came to visit. To that extent the Cecil very much reflects the city in which it stands, where the past has to be imagined. The big consolation is the sweeping view over the Eastern Harbour, and the excellent top-floor China House restaurant.

Metropole Hotel　HISTORIC HOTEL **$$$**
(Map p326; ☑486 1467; www.paradiseinnegypt.com; 52 Sharia Saad Zaghloul; s/d US$100/150; ✸@☏) Location, location, location! The Metropole sits right in the thick of things, with most rooms overlooking Midan Saad Zaghloul and the sea. It was entirely renovated in the 1990s, but don't be too put off by the magnificently tacky lobby with

LITERARY ALEXANDRIA

Many a traveller arrives at Misr Train Station with a copy of Lawrence Durrell's *Alexandria Quartet* in hand, for Alexandria is better known for its literature and writers than for any bricks-and-mortar monuments. Unlike the Alexandria of ancient days past, the Alexandria evoked by Durrell, EM Forster and the Alexandrian-Greek poet Constantine Cavafy can still be seen draped over the buildings of the city's central area.

Born of Greek parents, Cavafy (1863–1933) lived all but a few of his 70 years in Alexandria. In some poems he resurrects figures from the Ptolemaic era and classical Greece, in others he captures fragments of the city through its routines or chance encounters. He was born into one of the city's wealthiest families, but a reversal of fortune forced him to spend most of his life working as a clerk for the Ministry of Public Works, in an office above the Trianon cafe (see boxed text p337).

Cavafy spent the last 25 years of his life in a 2nd-floor apartment, above a ground-floor brothel, on the former rue Lepsius (now Sharia Sharm el-Sheikh). With a Greek church (St Saba Church) around the corner and a hospital opposite, Cavafy thought this was the ideal place to live; somewhere that could cater for the flesh and provide forgiveness for sins and a place in which to die. The flat is now preserved as the **Cavafy Museum** (Map p326; ☑486 1598; 4 Sharia Sharm el-Sheikh; adult/child E£15/free; ☉10am-4pm Tue-Sun), with two of the six rooms arranged as Cavafy kept them. Editions of the poet's publications and photocopies of his manuscripts, notebooks and correspondence lie spread out on tables throughout the rooms. Note there are no elevators.

Cavafy was first introduced to the English-speaking world by EM Forster (1879–1970), the celebrated English novelist who'd already published *A Room with a View* and *Howards End* when he arrived in Alexandria in 1916. Working for the Red Cross, Forster spent three years in the city and, although it failed to find a place in his subsequent novels, he compiled what he referred to as an 'antiguide'. His *Alexandria: A History & Guide* was intended, he explained, as a guide to things not there, based on the premise that 'the sights of Alexandria are in themselves not interesting, but they fascinate when we approach them from the past'.

The guide provided an introduction to the city for Lawrence Durrell (1912–90), who arrived in Egypt 22 years after Forster's departure. Durrell had been evacuated from Greece and resented Alexandria, which he called a 'smashed up broken down shabby Neapolitan town'. But as visitors discover today, first impressions are misleading and between 1941 and 1945 Durrell found great distraction in the slightly unreal air of decadence and promiscuity engendered by the uncertainties of the ongoing desert war.

Committed fans of the *Alexandria Quartet* might like to search out **Villa Ambron** (Map p322), where Durrell lived and wrote during the last two years of the war. Gilda Ambron, whose name appeared in the *Quartet*'s 'Balthazar', painted with her mother in a studio in the garden which they shared with their neighbour Clea Badaro, who provided inspiration for the character of Clea in the *Quartet*. Durrell's room was on top of an octagonal tower in the garden, though sadly the place has deteriorated badly over the past couple of decades. If you're in for a pilgrimage anyway, from Misr Train Station walk southeast down Sharia Moharrem Bey, then at the little square at the end turn left onto Sharia Nabil al-Wakad. Sharia Maamoun is about 200m along on the right. Villa Ambron is at No 19.

its fake Parthenon-style friezes – once past here, the lushly carpeted hallways lead to tastefully decorated rooms with gigantic gilded doors and walls panelled like a St Petersburg palace.

Four Seasons Hotel   LUXURY HOTEL $$$
(Map p320; ☑581 8000; www.fourseasons.com/ alexandria; 399 Corniche, San Stefano; r from US$470, ste US$900-12,000; ❋@🖵🏊) The much-loved old Casino San Stefano made way for this grand edifice, certainly the most luxurious place to stay in town. No expense has been spared: the marble lobby gleams, the army of staff is eager to please, and the rooms sport all modern conveniences while reflecting Alexandria's Egyptian, Greek and French heritage. An infinity pool overlooks the sea, and a tunnel under the Corniche leads to a private beach and partially constructed marina. Kids will be happy, too, with their own pool, babysitting services and entertainment.

Egypt Hotel   HOTEL $$
(Map p326; ☑481 4483; 1 Sharia Degla; s US$50-60, d US$60-70; ❋🖵) The Egypt single-handedly fills a desperate need for decent midrange digs. A noticeable step up from the budget choices, it's set in a renovated 100-year-old Italian building right on the Corniche. The lobby is tiled floor to ceiling in a turgid cream and brown, but the rooms have lush beds, wood floors, clean en suite bathrooms, powerful air-con and small balconies with sea or street views. Wi-fi is in the lobby only.

Hotel Union   HOTEL $
(Map p326; ☑480 7312; 5th fl, Al-Cornich; s E£80-140, d E£120-160; ❋🖵) One of the best budget choices in the city centre, this is a busy place that caters equally to foreign travellers and Egyptians. The relatively well maintained rooms are simple and almost charming, and come in a bewildering mix of bathroom/ view/air-con options and rates. Our rates quoted include a Byzantine mix of taxes, but no breakfast.

Hotel Crillon   HOTEL $
(Map p326; ☑480 0330; 3rd fl, 5 Sharia Adib Ishaq; s E£110-120, d E£150-180) Smack-dab on the Corniche, this place has oodles of character but is a little rough around the edges. It boasts high ceilings plus balconies with cane furniture and divine vistas from the slightly more expensive (and worth it) front-facing rooms. That said, the furnishings are a bit worse for wear, the shared bathroom could

be cleaner, and there's no fan or air-con. You can have breakfast served on your balcony – ask for the traditional Egyptian spread of fuul (fava beans cooked with garlic and garnished with olive oil and spices) and eat it while admiring the view of the graceful sweep of the harbour.

Swiss Canal Hotel   HOTEL $
(Map p326; ☑480 8373; 14 Sharia al-Bursa al-Qadima; s with/without air-con E£100/80, d with/ without air-con E£120/100; ❋) The walls here are an iridescent shade of pink that really has to be seen to be believed, but if you look past that the rooms are generally clean, with towering ceilings, mammoth wooden doors, spongy, soft beds, en suite bathrooms, and windows overlooking a reasonably quiet souq area. In summer, the rooms with *takeef* (air-con) are better value.

Triomphe Hotel   HOTEL $
(Map p326; ☑480 7585; 3rd fl, Sharia Gamal ad-Din Yassin; s/d E£90/140, without bathroom E£70/120) This quiet and good value old-timer sits half a block off the Corniche, and features a reassuringly sturdy-looking lift opening onto a tiled, leafy lobby. The rooms cling to shreds of former elegance, with high ceilings, timber floors and handy washbasins, though some are aging more gracefully than others. Doubles have balconies with side sea view; singles have no view.

Nile Excelsior Hotel   HOTEL $
(Map p326; ☑480 0799; nile _hotel@yahoo.com; 16 Sharia al-Bursa al-Qadima; s with/without air-con E£120/90, d with/without air-con E£170/120; ❋) A very central hotel with smallish rooms that are pretty well-worn but not bad; it's not as good value as its neighbour, the Swiss Canal. You'll find your morning ahwa (coffee) right outside the hotel's front door.

✖ Eating

Sure, the old and once-grand restaurants such as Pastroudis and the Union have long closed, but one of the pleasures of Alexandria is eating the freshest catch from the Mediterranean in one of the seafood restaurants overlooking the Eastern Harbour. Equally enjoyable is to sit in one of the many cafes around the city centre and watch Alexandrians at play. Many restaurants don't serve alcohol. Western-style cooking can be found in upmarket hotels and noisy shopping malls where Alexandrians love to hang out.

CENTRAL ALEXANDRIA

TOP CHOICE Mohammed Ahmed
FELAFEL $

(Map p326; 17 Sharia Shakor Pasha; mains E£2-5; ☺24hr; ⚏) Under no circumstances should you miss this classic, the undisputed king and still champion of fuul and felafel, filled day and night with locals downing small plates of spectacularly good and cheap Egyptian standards. From the English menu, select your type of fuul (iskandarani is good), add some felafel, and choose a few accompanying salads, such as tahini, banga (beetroot) or pickles – then, sit back and wait for the magic to happen. Note that the street sign on the corner of Saad Zaghloul calls this Abdel Fattah El Hadary St.

Malek es-Seman
GRILL $$

(Map p322; 48 Midan el-Soriyin Masguid el-Attarine; two birds E£25; ☺8pm-3am) Off Sharia Attareen, just south of the junction with Sharia Mohafaza, by day this is a small courtyard clothes market, by night it's an open-air restaurant doing one thing and doing it very, very well: quail. Birds are served grilled or stuffed; both ways are delicious, but we especially like the slightly charred and crispy flavour of the grilled. Orders come with bread and six different salads. It's a bit hard to find, but look for a painted sign with a small bird. Serves beer.

China House
ASIAN $$

(Map p326; 16 Midan Saad Zaghloul; mains E£30-50; ☺lunch & dinner) Atop the Sofitel Cecil Alexandria (Cecil Hotel), this highly recommended restaurant serves scrumptious Asian food beneath a tent with dangling lanterns and stunning views over the harbour. The ambience is breezy, the chicken dumplings and grilled beef with garlic first-rate, and the banana fritters unmissable. Beer and Egyptian wine are served.

Abu Nasr
EGYPTIAN FAST FOOD $

(Map p326; cnr Sharia Ibn el-Roumi & Sharia al-Ghorfa al-Tugareya; mains E£5; ☺lunch & dinner) This unusually tidy place serves good, filling kushari. If you find it lacks mojo, throw in a dash of the vinegar and spicy red sauce it's served with. If it's still a bit plain for your taste, order sides of tahini and banga and chuck them in too. There's no sign in English, so look for the gleaming gold bowls.

Taverna
EGYPTIAN FAST FOOD $$

(Map p326; Mahattat Ramla; mains E£9-30; ☺breakfast, lunch & dinner) This deservedly popular establishment serves excellent hand-thrown sweet or savoury fiteer (Egyptian pancakes), pizza, and some of the best shwarma in town. Eat in or takeaway.

Awalad Abdou
SANDWICHES $

(Map p322; Sharia Mohafaza; sandwiches E£2-3; ☺24hr) With only minor concessions made to hygiene, this uberbudget place is nonetheless a smashing find. In two shakes of a lamb's tail, these guys will whip up micro sandwiches with a scrumptious, meaty filling of your choice. Just point to what looks good and quaff it down while standing at the counter. It can be a challenge to find – there's no sign, so look for a small shop with hanging cured meats, near Sharia Attareen.

Gad
EGYPTIAN FAST FOOD $

(Map p326; Sharia Saad Zaghloul; snacks E£1-9; ☺24hr) Egypt's answer to (although a vast improvement on) McDonald's, this chain of absurdly popular takeaway joints has people flocking (think gadflies) day and night. It serves a huge range of filled sandwiches, kebabs, ta'amiyya (Egyptian felafel) and mouth-watering shwarma. There's another branch on Sharia Mohammed Azmy Tossoun.

ANFUSHI

For some authentic Alexandrian flavour and atmosphere, head for the simple, good-value streetside restaurants in Anfushi's baladi (working class; 'of the land') district. Sharia Safar Pasha is lined with a dozen places where the fires are crackling and flaming under the grills barbecuing meat and fish. You could chance a table at any of them and probably come away satisfied, but those listed here deserve a special mention. Don't hesitate to bring the kids to any of the places we list here; most are filled with families. All are open well past midnight.

TOP CHOICE Farag
SEAFOOD $$

(Map p322; 7 Souq al-Tabakheen, Manshey; mains E£35-75; ☺lunch & dinner) Deep in the heart of the souq, sit outdoors under an awning or inside in an air-conditioned dining room feasting on perfectly cooked and seasoned seafood. This spot is very local and a bit hard to spot – the sign is high above street level, so look up to be sure you don't miss it. If you do, just ask around; everyone knows it.

Samakmak
SEAFOOD $$

(Map p322; 42 Qasr Ras at-Tin; mains E£50-120; ☺lunch & dinner) Owned by Zizi Salem, the

NAUTICAL ARCHAEOLOGY

Alexandria has sunk 6m to 8m since antiquity, so most of what remains of the ancient city lies hidden beneath the modern city or the waters of the Mediterranean. On land, much has been destroyed as the city has grown. Rescue archaeologists are allowed to excavate before a new building, tunnel or road project goes ahead, but they are rarely given enough time – usually only a few weeks, or months at most.

But underwater the story is different and each year reveals more finds from the Ptolemaic period. So far, exploration has been concentrated around the fortress of Qaitbey, where the Pharos (p328) is believed to have stood; the southeastern part of the Eastern Harbour, where parts of the submerged Ptolemaic royal quarter were found; and Aboukir, where remains of the two sunken cities of Herakleion (Thonis) and Menouthis were found.

The Qaitbey dive has recorded hundreds of objects, including sphinx bodies, columns and capitals, and fragments of obelisks. Divers also discovered giant granite blocks broken as if by a fall from a great height, and, more recently, pieces of stone believed to have formed the frame of a massive gateway – all more circumstantial evidence for the likely end of the Pharos.

In the royal-quarter area, a French-Egyptian diving team has discovered platforms, pavements and red-granite columns that they speculate were part of a former palace ('Cleopatra's Palace', as it is being called), as well as a remarkably complete shipwreck carbon dated to between 90 BC and AD 130. In 1998 archaeologists raised a beautiful black-granite statue of a priest of Isis, followed by a diorite sphinx adorned with the face of what's thought to be Ptolemy XII, father of Cleopatra. And in December 2009 they raised a large temple pylon, which is believed to be part of the palace complex.

The most recent excavations in Aboukir have revealed *L'Orient* (Napoleon's flagship that sank in 1798); the city of Menouthis with a harbour, houses, temples, statues and gold jewellery; and another city believed to be Herakleion, a port that guarded the Canopic branch of the Nile.

Some recovered treasures can be seen in the city's museums, and there are tentative plans for a major underwater museum. For now, it's possible to explore the submerged harbour sites through **Alexandra Dive** (Map p322; ☑483 2045; Corniche, Anfushi), where a two-dive package costs €60, with equipment rental an extra €20. Several divers have reported that poor visibility in the bay (as little as 1m depending on the time of year) affected their enjoyment of the harbour dives.

retired queen of the Alexandrian belly-dancing scene, Samakmak is definitely one step up from the other fish eateries in the neighbourhood. The fish is as fresh as elsewhere, but customers flock to this place for its specials, including crayfish, marvellous crab *tagen* (stew cooked in a deep clay pot) and a great spaghetti with clams.

Kadoura
SEAFOOD $$

(Map p322; 33 Sharia Bairam at-Tonsi; mains E£35-80; ☉lunch & dinner) Pronounced 'Adora', this is one of Alexandria's most authentic fish restaurants, where food is served at tables in the narrow street. Pick your fish from a huge ice-packed selection, which usually includes sea bass, red and grey mullet, bluefish, sole, squid, crab and prawns, and often a lot more. A selection of mezze is served with all orders (don't hope for a menu). Most fish is E£40 to E£80 per kilo, prawns E£180 per kilo. It has a second, air-conditioned (though less atmospheric) branch along the Corniche.

Abu Ashraf
SEAFOOD $$

(Map p322; 28 Sharia Safar Pasha, Bahari; mains E£35-60; ☉lunch & dinner) One of this street's fish specialists. Make your selection from the day's catch then take a seat under the green awning and watch it being cooked. Sea bass stuffed with garlic and herbs is a speciality, as is the creamy prawn *kishk* (casserole). Price is determined by weight and type of fish, ranging from grey mullet at E£45 per kilo to jumbo prawns at E£200 per kilo.

Hosny Grill
GRILL $$

(Map p322; Sharia Safar Pasha, Bahari; mains E£30-50; ☉lunch & dinner) If you're a little fished out in Anfushi, Hosny Grill, opposite Abu

Ashraf, is a semi-outdoor restaurant specialising in tasty grilled chicken, kebabs and other meats, served with the usual triumvirate of vegetables, salad and rice.

El-Sheikh Wafik
DESSERTS $

(Map p320; Qasr Ras at-Tin; desserts E£3-9; ⊙breakfast, lunch & dinner) This unassuming and breezy corner cafe has a secret – the best dessert in town. You can get the usual ice cream in several flavours, but the real treats are Egyptian classics such as *couscousy* (E£8) – a yummy mix of couscous, shredded coconut, nuts, raisins and sugar, topped with hot milk.

Hassan Fouad
SELF-CATERING $

(Map p326; cnr Sharia Abdul Hamid Badawy & Moursi Gamil Aziz; ⊙9.30am-4am) This tiny and incredibly tidy market offers beautifully displayed produce, like grapes from Lebanon and tasty Egyptian mangoes, and a good selection of imported staples such as digestive biscuits. There's no sign in English, so look for the place with artfully stacked fruits and a bright-red sign.

Patisserie Assad
BAKERY $

(Map p326; 14 Sharia Abdul Hamid Badawy; ⊙9.30am-4am) Just east of Midan Saad Zaghloul, this hole-in-the-wall bakery does good sweets, *fiteer* and croissants, sold by weight. It also offers a selection of hard-to-find local honey and olive oil. There's no sign, so look for the honey stacked in the window.

OUTSIDE THE CITY
Abo Faris
EGYPTIAN $

(Map p320; mains E£10-20; ⊙lunch & dinner) An excellent eatery specialising in Syrian shwarma, a mouth-watering concoction of spicy grilled lamb or chicken slathered in garlicky mayonnaise and pickles, rolled up inside roasted flatbread. A full menu is available, and seating is indoors or in a garden patio (you can also do takeaway). It's about 500m before the City Centre Mall, on the left as you're coming from the city. Most taxi drivers will know it.

🍷 Drinking
Juice Bars
Freshat Juice Bar
JUICE BAR

(Map p326; 18 Sharia Amin Fekry) This sparkling little find has a cornucopia of different juices on offer, including all the standards plus some interesting and hard-to-find traditional drinks. If you're keen to try some-

thing new, ask the friendly owner, Ayman, to show you. All juices can be made without sugar on request.

El Qobesi
JUICE BAR

(Map p322; 51 Corniche; ⊙24hr) El Qobesi has crowned itself the 'king of mango' but take one sip and you will bow down a loyal peon. Slivers of several ripe mangoes are cajoled nearly whole into a tall, chilled glass to make some of the best mango juice we've ever tried. Open around the clock, it's always bustling, often with locals parked outside for a quick in-car slurp (we've even seen full microbuses stop by).

Cafes & Ahwas
During summer the 20km length of the Corniche from Ras at-Tin to Montazah seems to become one great strung-out ahwa (coffeehouse). With a few exceptions, these are not the greatest places – they're catering for a passing holiday trade and tend to overcharge. Nevertheless, Alexandria is a great place to get some quality sheesha (water pipe) time in. While many ahwas remain the exclusive domain of backgammon-playing men, families are welcome at these places, unless otherwise mentioned.

⌐TOP⌐CHOICE Selsela Cafe
CAFE

(Map p322; Chatby Beach) This fantastic ahwa across from the Bibliotheca Alexandrina is practically unique in Alexandria – you can sip tea and sheesha to the sound of waves rolling in, smelling sea air instead of petrol fumes. Directly on the water, it has rustic open-air tables and palm trees with cheerful coloured lights, set around a small curving beach where you can hardly hear the traffic. It's a great place to relax in the sultry breeze, enjoying the Mediterranean vibe. To find it, look for the modern sculpture with three white needles, directly across the Corniche from the library. Walk past the sculpture towards the sea; the entrance is down the steps to the right.

Imperial Cafe & Restaurant
CAFE

(Map p326; Midan Saad Zaghloul; 🛜) This recently renovated classic cafe is now Alexandria's most modern, a chic yet comfortable air-conditioned space with wi-fi and a list of espresso-based coffees. There's a full menu (E£15 to E£40), too, with everything from tasty snacks to pizza to steak. You can also sit out on the sidewalk at an umbrella-covered table. It's a great place to take a break.

El Tugareya COFFEEHOUSE

(Map p326; Corniche) Although it may not look like much to the uninitiated (it doesn't even sport a sign), this 90-year-old institution is one of the most important ahwas in town. It's an informal centre of business and trade (the name roughly translates to 'commerce'), where deals are brokered in time-honoured tradition – over a glass of tea. The cafe is separated into multiple rooms, covering a whole block. The southern side is a male-dominated area dedicated to games and informal socialising, while along the Corniche you're likely to be part of a rambunctious mix of writers, film-makers, students, expats and courting couples filling the hall with a cacophony of animated conversation. You'll even see women smoking sheesha.

El Rehany COFFEEHOUSE

(Map p320; cnr Corniche & Sharia Ismail Fangary, Camp Chesar) This expansive and breezy Alexandrian classic is reputed to have the best sheesha in town, served with a flourish by attentive boys in smart two-toned waistcoats while waiters in black-and-white bring tea in silver urns. The decor is eclectically elegant, with lofty ceilings etched with elaborate floral patterns, tables and chairs in Islamic designs, and burgundy tablecloths. Check out the bizarre assortment of knick-knacks in the glass displays in back, too. There's no sign in English, so look for the place with green awnings, next to the Premiere Wellness and Fitness Centre.

> **DON'T MISS**

CAFE CULTURE

In case you hadn't noticed, Alexandria is a cafe town – and we're not talking Starbucks double-decaf-soy-low-fat-vanilla-grande lattes here. Ever since the first half of the 20th century, Alexandria's culture has revolved around these venues, where the city's diverse population congregated to live out life's dramas over pastries and a cup of tea or coffee. Famous literary figures met here, chattering and pondering the city they could not quite grasp. Many of these old haunts remain and are definitely worth a visit as living relics of times past and for a glimpse of their grand decor, but not always for the food or drink. Here's a rundown of classic java joints where you can get a sip of the old days. Most open early and close late.

Athineos (Map p326; 21 Midan Saad Zaghloul) Opposite Midan Ramla, this place lives and breathes nostalgia. The cafe part still has its original 1940s fittings, and pastries that taste like they've been sitting around since then. Come for the period character, skip the food.

Trianon (Map p326; 56 Midan Saad Zaghloul) A favourite haunt of the Greek poet Constantine Cavafy (see boxed text p332), who worked in offices on the floor above. Stop here to admire the 1930s grandeur of its sensational ornate ceiling and grab one of its decent but expensive continental-style breakfasts.

Delices (Map p326; 46 Sharia Saad Zaghloul; 🛜) This enormous old tearoom drips with atmosphere, has the best food of any place in this list and is attached to a bakery. You also can sit outside under the awning and people-watch.

Vinous (Map p326; cnr Sharia al-Nabi Daniel & Tariq al-Horreyya) An old-school patisserie with more grand art deco styling than you can poke a puff pastry at. You can sense some of its old glory in the decorative (if worn) details.

Sofianopoulos Coffee Store (Map p326; 21 Sharia Saad Zaghloul) A gorgeous coffee retailer that would be in a museum anywhere else in the world. Dominated by huge silver coffee grinders, stacks of glossy beans and the wonderful, faintly herbal aroma of roasted java, it serves Turkish coffee fit for a king.

If you're possessed by literary nostalgia, you can make a historical detour to the place where the famous **Pastroudis** (Map p326; Tariq al-Horreyya) once stood. Though now closed, this was a frequent meeting point for the characters of Lawrence Durrell's *Alexandria Quartet*.

Farouk Cafe COFFEEHOUSE

(Map p322; Sharia Ismail Sabry, Anfushi) This venerable sheesha joint doesn't look like it's changed an iota since it opened in 1928. It's a charmingly ramshackle old place, with dusty bronze lanterns outside, and charmingly fusty old men arguing and playing board games at the tables under huge photos of the former king.

Ahwa Sayed Darwish COFFEEHOUSE

(Map p326; Sharia Abu Shusha) Named for the composer of Egypt's national anthem, this tiny and highly enjoyable local coffeeshop, near Sharia al-Nabi Daniel, is set on a quiet and leafy side street around the corner from the Cavafy Museum. The chairs are comfortably padded, and the sheesha is clean. The clientele is exclusively men.

Bars

Sixty years ago Alexandria was so famous for its Greek tavernas and divey little watering holes that the 1958 movie *Ice Cold in Alex* was entirely based around a stranded WWII ambulance crew struggling through the desert, dreaming of making it back to Alexandria to sip a beer. Times have changed and Alex isn't much of a drinking town any more; there are few places worth crossing the desert for.

TOP Cap d'Or BAR

(Map p326; 4 Sharia Adbi Bek Ishak; ⊙10am-3am) The Cap d'Or, just off Sharia Saad Zaghloul, is a top spot to relax, and one of the only surviving typical Alexandrian bars. With beer flowing generously, stained-glass windows, a long marble-topped bar, plenty of ancient memorabilia decorating the walls and crackling tapes of old French *chanson* (a type of traditional folk music) or Egyptian hits, it feels very much like an Andalusian tapas bar. Bohemian crowds come to drink cold Stella beer, snack on great seafood, and just hang out at the bar talking or playing guitar with fellow drinkers. Thursday and Friday nights are more 'open-minded' than most nights in Alexandria.

Greek Club COCKTAIL BAR

(Club Nautique Hellenique; Map p322; Corniche, Anfushi; ⊙noon-11pm) The Greek Club is a great place for a sunset drink, inside its

TOP SOUQS

Although you won't find the sort of antediluvian bazaars here that you do in Cairo, Alexandria has several busy souqs (markets) that are ideal spots to immerse in some lively market action.

Anfushi Fish Market (Map p322; Qasr Ras at-Tin) For a city that devours more fish than a hungry seal, you'd expect to find a pretty impressive fish market – and Alexandria delivers. The fish market at the northern tip of Anfushi bustles daily with flapping seafood that's literally just been thrown off the boat. Vendors belt out the prices of their wares, while ever-sceptical buyers prod the merchandise and ponder the quality of the catch of the day. Be sure to get here early, when the market is at its best, as things die down by midmorning.

Souq District (Map p322) At the western end of Midan Tahrir, the battered, grand architecture switches scale to something more intimate as you enter the city's main souq district. Sharia Faransa begins with cloth, clothes and dressmaking accessories. The tight weave of covered alleys running off to the west are known as Zinqat as-Sittat ('the alley of the women'). Here you'll find buttons, braid, baubles, bangles, beads and much more, from junk jewellery to frighteningly large padded bras. Beyond the haberdashery you will find the gold and silver dealers, then herbalists and spice vendors. A couple of blocks west of Sharia Faransa, Sharia Nokrashi (also known as El-Maydan) starts at Midan Nasr and runs for about a kilometre through the heart of Anfushi. It's one long, heaving bustle of produce, fish and meat stalls, bakeries, cafes and sundry shops selling every imaginable household item. This is a great area to check out at night.

Souq Ibrahimiyya (Map p320; Sharia Omar Lofty) This is one of our favourite little markets in town for peeking into daily Egyptian life as it goes about its business. Down several tiny, covered side streets near the Sporting Club, it's packed to the brim with bright fruits and vegetables, piles of still-wet seafood, and stalls selling all kinds of clucking poultry and meats, both before and after they've seen the butcher's block. It's best in the morning, when the vendors are at their most vocal and enthusiastic.

large newly restored rooms or, even better, on the wide terrace catching the afternoon breeze or watching the lights on this legendary bay. The menu has a selection of fresh fish cooked any way you like it (grilled with olive oil, oregano and lemon, baked or Egyptian style), as well as Greek classics such as moussaka (E£16) and souvlaki (E£34). Minimum charge in the cafe is E£25; in the upstairs restaurant it's E£75.

Spitfire   BAR
(Map p326; 7 Sharia L'Ancienne Bourse; ⏰2pm-1.30am Mon-Sat) Just north of Sharia Saad Zaghloul, Spitfire feels almost like a Bangkok bar – sans go-go girls. It has a reputation as a sailors' hang-out and the walls are plastered with shipping-line stickers, rock-and-roll memorabilia and photos of drunk regulars. It's a great place for an evening out on one of the world's finest harbours, listening to American rock and roll from the 1970s.

Centro de Portugal   BAR
(Map p320; ☎0122 336 5608; 42 Sharia Abd al-Kader, off Sharia Kafr Abdou; admission E£25; ⏰3pm-1am) This hard-to-find expat haven is fully equipped for fun: a garden bar in a leafy patio, darts, foosball and pool, plus a tiny disco complete with mirrored ball. Best of all, the beverages are very cold. Drinks are purchased via an unusual card system: E£75 gets you enough credits for five beers, three glasses of wine, two cocktails or 10 soft drinks. The food menu (mains E£35 to E£70) sports Western standards, and there's a small playground for kids (who get free admission). It's a great place to unwind and meet local expats while sucking down an icy gin and tonic.

Drinkies   LIQUOR STORE
(Map p326; ☎delivery 480 6309; Sharia al-Ghorfa al-Tugareya; ⏰noon-midnight) Takeaway beer is available in the city centre at this aptly named place. It also delivers.

☆ Entertainment

Alexandria's cultural life has never really recovered from the exodus of Europeans and Jews in the 1940s and '50s, but in recent years things have started to change for the better. Since the opening of the Bibliotheca Alexandrina, the town is once again trying to compete with Cairo as the proprietor of Egyptian arts. The **Alexandria International Film Festival** takes place every September or October, offering Alexandrians

a rare opportunity to see uncensored films from around the globe. Films are screened at several cinemas around town – ask at the tourist office for more information.

The free monthly booklet *Alex Agenda,* available at some hotels, is extremely useful for its extensive list of concerts, theatre events and live gigs throughout Alexandria; its Facebook page also has links about some events. Also, check the French Cultural Centre (p341) and Alexandria Centre of Arts (p341), as both organise occasional performances.

Bibliotheca Alexandrina   PERFORMING ARTS
(Map p322; ☎483 9999; www.bibalex.org; Corniche al-Bahr, Shatby) The Bibliotheca Alexandrina is the most important cultural venue in town, hosting major music festivals, international concerts and performances.

Alexandria Opera House   OPERA
(Map p326; ☎486 5106; www.cairoopera.org/sayed_darwish.aspx; 22 Tariq al-Horreyya) The former Sayed Darwish Theatre has been refurbished and now houses the city's modestly proportioned but splendid opera house. Most performances of opera and classical music are staged in this gorgeous auditorium.

Alexandria Centre of Arts   PERFORMING ARTS
(Map p326; ☎495 6633; info@aca.org.eg; 1 Tariq al-Horreyya; ⏰9am-9pm Sat-Thu) This active cultural centre, housed in a whitewashed villa, hosts contemporary arts exhibitions, poetry readings and occasional free concerts in its theatre. There is also an art studio, library and cinema on the 1st floor.

🔒 Shopping

The city's main souq district (see boxed text, p338) is just west of Midan Tahrir, and Sharia Safiyya Zaghloul and Sharia Saad Zaghloul are lined with an assortment of old-fashioned and more trendy clothes and shoe shops.

Attareen Antique Market   ANTIQUES
(Map p322) Antique collectors will have a blast diving through the confusion of backstreets and alleys of this antique market; many items found their way here after the European upper class was forced en masse to make a hasty departure from Egypt following the 1952 revolution.

Sayed el-Safty   ANTIQUES
(Map p322; 63 Sharia Attareen) Probably the most interesting antique shop in the city. Well worth a browse.

Mohammed Abdo SMOKING
(Map p322; cnr Attareen & Mohafaza) Build-your-own sheesha like the locals do.

Al-Maaref Bookshop BOOKS
(Map p326; 32 Midan Saad Zaghloul) Has a decent English-language section, including many titles on Egypt and Alexandria.

ⓘ Information

Emergency
Tourist police (Map p326; ☎485 0507; Midan Saad Zaghloul) Upstairs from the main tourist office.

Internet Access
Farous Net Café (Map p326; Tariq al-Horreyya; per hr E£3; ⊙10am-midnight)

Hightop Internet Café (Map p326; 71 Sharia al-Nabi Daniel; per hr E£3; ⊙10am-midnight)

MG@Net (Map p326; 10 Sharia el-Shohada; per hr E£3; ⊙7am-2am)

Maps
Mohandes Mostafa el Fadaly (Map p326; 2nd fl, 49 Sharia Safiyya Zaghloul; ⊙9am-4pm

Sat-Thu) An engineer (mohandes) who created and sells a street map (E£30) of Alexandria, indispensable if you're spending any significant time in the city. Find Mostafa above the Mr Sanyo clothes store.

Medical Services
HOSPITALS
Al-Madina at-Tibiya (Map p320; ☎543 2150/7402; Sharia Ahmed Shawky, Rushdy; ⊙24hr) Well-equipped private hospital, also called Alexandria Medical City Hospital.

German Hospital (Map p320; ☎584 0757; 56 Sharia Abdel Salaam Aarafa, Glymm; ⊙8am-10pm) Near Saba Basha tram stop (line 2) and next to Al-Obeedi Hospital. Staffed by highly qualified doctors, with a day clinic for non-emergency patients.

PHARMACIES
There's no shortage of pharmacies around Midan Ramla, all with at least one English-speaking staff member.

Central Pharmacy (Map p326; 19 Sharia Ahmed Orabi; ⊙9am-10pm) This 100-year-old establishment is worth visiting just for the soaring ceilings and beautiful display cabinets.

ALEXANDRIA'S BEACHES

If you want to get in the water, there are plenty of public and private beaches along Alexandria's waterfront. But the shoreline between the Eastern Harbour and Montazah can be grubby and packed sardine-full in summer, and most locals head for beaches on the North Coast for the high season. If you're seeking an unspoilt beach experience, you're better off heading to El Alamein, Sidi Abdel Rahman or Marsa Matruh.

Women should note that at everywhere but the beaches owned by Western hotels, modesty prevails and covering up when swimming is strongly recommended – wear a baggy T-shirt and shorts over your swimsuit. At these and any city beaches, expect to pay an entrance fee and more for umbrellas and chairs, if desired.

Mamoura Beach (Map p320) About 1km east of Montazah, Mamoura is the 'beachiest' of Alexandria's beaches. There's a cobblestone boardwalk with a few ice-cream shops, food stalls and souvenir stands, but what really makes this feel different from other beaches is the half-mile between it and the main road, meaning there's no noisy speedway behind you. Local authorities are trying to keep this suburb exclusive by charging everyone who enters the area E£3.25 (though you might not have to pay if you walk in), plus another E£8 to get onto the sand. It's still jammed during high season. There's a much less crowded private beach next to the main beach, with nice frond-type umbrellas and an E£40 per person entry fee. To get there, flag down an Aboukir-bound microbus along the Corniche and let the driver know you want Mamoura.

Miami Beach (Map p320) Miami Beach (pronounced me-ami) has a sheltered cove with a waterslide and jungle gym set up in the sea for kids to frolic on, but note that these get almost comically crowded during peak season. It's 12.5km east of Midan Saad Zaghloul along the Corniche.

Stanley Beach (Map p320) This spectacular beach, on a tiny bay with Stanley Bridge soaring above it, has a modest patch of sand for bathing backed by three levels of beach cabins. The sight of the sea crashing against the bridge's concrete supports is dramatic, but this beach is less suitable for kids due to the wave action.

CULTURAL CENTRES

Many of the city's cultural centres operate libraries and organise occasional films, lectures, exhibitions and performances. Take along your passport as you may have to show it before entering.

» **American Cultural Center** (Map p322; ☑486 1009; www.usembassy.egnet.net; 3 Sharia al-Pharaana, Azarita; ⊙10am-4pm Sun-Thu; @)

» **British Council** (Map p320; ☑545 6512; www.britishcouncil.org.eg; 11 Sharia Mahmoud Abu al-Ela, Kafr Abdu, Rushdy; ⊙11am-7pm Sat-Thu; @)

» **French Cultural Centre** (Map p326; ☑391 8952; 30 Sharia al-Nabi Daniel; ⊙9am-9pm Mon-Sat; @) Has a bookstore with extensive French and some English-language titles.

» **Goethe Institut** (Map p322; ☑487 9870; www.goethe.de/kairo; 10 Sharia al-Batalsa, Azarita; ⊙9am-1pm Mon-Thu, to 2pm Sun; @)

Khalil Pharmacy (Map p326; Midan Ramla; ⊙8am-2am) Across the street from the tram station.

Money

For changing cash or cashing travellers cheques it's simplest to use one of the many exchange bureaus on the side streets between Midan Ramla and the Corniche. Otherwise, try the following.

American Express (Amex; Map p320; ☑420 2288; www.americanexpress.com.eg; Elsaladya Bldg, Sharia 14th Mai, Smouha; ⊙9am-4pm Sun-Thu) This office is also a travel agency.

Thomas Cook (Map p326; www.thomascook egypt.com; 15 Midan Saad Zaghloul; ⊙8am-5pm)

ATMS

There are dozens of ATMs in central Alexandria, particularly on Sharia Salah Salem and Talaat Harb, the city's banking district. You can also find one at the following branch offices.

Banque du Caire Salah Salem (Map p326; 5 Sharia Salah Salem); Talaat Harb (Map p326; cnr Sharia Sisostris & Talaat Harb)

Barclays (Map p322; 11 Sharikat Misr, off Sharia Sultan Hussein, Azarita)

Credit Agricole (Map p326; 14 Sharia Salah Salem)

HSBC (Map p322; 47 Sharia Sultan Hussein; ⊙8.30am-5pm Sun-Thu)

MIBank (Map p322; 45 Sharia Safiyya Zaghloul)

TRANSFERS

For receiving money from overseas or wiring money abroad, Western Union has two offices in town.

Western Union Central Tariq al-Horreyya (Map p322; ☑420 1148; 281 Tariq al-Horreyya); Eastern Tariq al-Horreyya (Map p320; ☑492 0900; 73 Tariq al-Horreyya)

Photography & Electronics

Radio Shack (Map p326; 68 Sharia Safiyya Zaghloul; ⊙11am-midnight) Stocks standard electronic and digital accessories and camera memory cards, and has a Vodafone desk.

Post

DHL (Map p326; 9 Sharia Salah Salem; ⊙9am-5pm Sat-Thu)

Main post office (Map p326; Sharia al-Bursa al-Qadima; ⊙9am-9pm Sat-Thu) Just east of Midan Orabi; several other branches are dotted around the city.

Telephone

Menatel cardphones can be found all over the city, although the policy of placing them on street corners can make it hard to hear and be heard. Private call centres are a more convenient option. You can also buy an inexpensive prepaid SIM card for your unlocked mobile phone.

Telephone centrale (Map p326; Sharia Saad Zaghloul; ⊙8.30am-10pm)

Vodafone main office (Map p326; 13 Sharia Salah Salem; ⊙9am-11pm Sat-Thu, 1.30-11pm Fri); Radio Shack (Map p326; 68 Sharia Safiyya Zaghloul; ⊙11am-midnight) Vodafone's main office and the desk at Radio Shack sell cash (prepaid) SIM cards for E£20.

Tourist Information

Mahattat Misr tourist office (Map p322; ☑392 5985; Platform 1, Misr Train Station; ⊙8.30am-6pm) Closed for renovation at time of research.

Main tourist office (Map p326; ☑485 1556; Midan Saad Zaghloul; ⊙8.30am-6pm, reduced hours during Ramadan) Closed for renovation at time of research.

❶ Getting There & Away

Air

All flights to Alexandria arrive at the newly refurbished Burg al-Arab airport, about 45km southwest of the city. Smaller Nouzha airport, 7km southeast, was being renovated at the time of research, scheduled to reopen at the end of 2013; domestic flights will likely be routed here then.

Bus

All long-distance buses leave from **Al-Mo'af al-Gedid** (New Garage; Map p320). It's several kilometres south of Midan Saad Zaghloul; to get there either catch a microbus from Misr Train Station (50pt) or grab a taxi from the city centre (E£15). The main companies operating from here are West & Mid Delta Bus Co and Super Jet.

Super Jet (Map p320; ☑543 5222; ⊗8am-10pm) More expensive but considerably nicer buses. A less convenient booking office, however, opposite Sidi Gaber Train Station, next to the large fountain.

West & Mid Delta Bus Co (Map p326; ☑480 9685; Midan Saad Zaghloul; ⊗9am-9pm) A convenient city-centre booking office.

CAIRO Super Jet has hourly buses to Cairo (E£30, 2½ hours), also stopping at Cairo airport (E£35), from early morning. Services stop in the late evening, though there may be a single late service. West & Mid Delta also has hourly departures (E£30).

NORTH COAST & SIWA West & Mid Delta has hourly departures to Marsa Matruh (E£25 to E£35, four hours); a few of these buses continue on to Sallum (E£35 to E£45, nine hours) on the border with Libya. Three services daily go to Siwa (E£38, nine hours) at 8.30am, 11am and 10pm. Otherwise just take any Marsa Matruh bus and change to a microbus there. Super Jet runs five buses to Marsa Matruh (E£35) daily during summer (June to September), the last one generally leaving in the late afternoon. Most Marsa Matruh buses stop in El Alamein (one hour), and will stop at Sidi Abdel Rahman if you want to get off, though you will have to pay the full Marsa Matruh fare.

SINAI West & Mid Delta has one daily service to Sharm el-Sheikh (E£110, eight to 10 hours) at 9pm.

SUEZ CANAL & RED SEA COAST Super Jet has a daily evening service to Hurghada (E£100, nine hours). West & Mid Delta has several services a day to Port Said (E£30, four to five hours), two to Ismailia (E£35, five hours) and four to Suez (E£35, five hours). It also has two buses a day to Hurghada and Port Safaga (E£90). The Upper Egypt Bus Co has three daily Hurghada buses (E£90) that continue on down to Port Safaga.

Servees & Microbus

Servees (service taxis) and microbuses for Aboukir, and *servees* for Cairo, depart from outside Misr Train Station (Map p322); all others go from the Al-Mo'af al-Gedid (New Garage; Map p320) bus station out at Moharrem Bey. Fares cost around E£25 to Cairo or Marsa Matruh. To more local destinations, some sample fares are Zagazig E£10, Tanta E£10, Mansura E£12, Rosetta E£4 and Aboukir E£1.50.

Train

There are two train stations in Alexandria. The main terminal is **Mahattat Misr** (Misr Train Station; Map p322; ☑426 3207), about 1km south of Midan Ramla. **Mahattat Sidi Gaber** (Sidi Gaber Train Station; Map p320; ☑426 3953) serves the eastern suburbs. Trains from Cairo stop at Sidi Gaber first, and most locals get off here, but if you're going to the city centre around Midan Saad Zaghloul, make sure you stay on until Misr Train Station.

There are more than 15 trains daily between Cairo and Alexandria, from 6am to 10pm. There are two train types: Spanish *(esbani)* and French *(faransawi)*. Spanish trains (1st/2nd class E£50/35, 2½ hours) are much better, as they make fewer stops. The French train (1st/2nd class E£35/19, 3½ to four hours) makes multiple stops. There are two daily trains to Luxor at 5pm and 10pm (1st/2nd class E£129/69), with the 5pm train continuing to Aswan (1st/2nd class E£148/77).

At Misr Train Station, 1st- and 2nd-class tickets to Cairo are sold at the ticket office along Platform 1; 3rd- and 2nd-class ordinary tickets are purchased in the front hall. If you're getting a taxi from the station, it's advisable to bypass the drivers lurking outside the entrance – just walk out onto the street and flag one down there.

❶ Getting Around

As a visitor to Alexandria, you'll rarely use the buses, and while the tram is fun it's painfully slow. Taxis and microbuses are generally the best options for getting around.

To/From the Airport

Transport to Burg al-Arab is via the air-conditioned airport bus (one-way E£6 plus E£1 per bag, one hour), leaving from in front of the Sofitel Cecil Alexandria (Cecil Hotel; Map p326) three hours before all departures; confirm the exact bus departure time at the Cecil. A taxi to/from the airport should cost between E£100 and E£150. You can also catch bus 475 (one hour) from Misr Train Station.

If you do need to get to/from Nouzha, a taxi should cost no more than E£20. There are also minibuses from Midan Orabi and Midan Ramla.

Car

Driving in Alexandria is not necessarily the suicide mission it might appear, as city traffic tends to move slowly. **Avis** (Map p326; ☎485 7400; Sofitel Cecil Alexandria, Midan Saad Zaghloul; ⏲8am-6pm) hires cars from US$40 per day (including 100km), with drivers available for an additional US$20 per day. If you do rent, ensure that you're especially scrupulous with the initial and return inspections, to avoid any compensation claims for very minor vehicle damage.

The price of using a car and driver service (see p331) can be comparable, and saves the headache of negotiating traffic yourself.

Microbus

Want to travel like the locals? Hop on a microbus. The most useful are the ones zooming along the Corniche. There are no set departure points or stops, so when one passes, wave and shout your destination; if it's heading that way it will stop to pick you up. It costs anywhere from 50pt for a short trip to E£1.50 to go all the way to Montazah.

Red Bus

The new air-conditioned red double-decker bus (E£3) plies the Corniche every 15 to 30 minutes between Ras at-Tin and the Sheraton in Montazah. You can flag it down anywhere along the route, but go to a major intersection like Midan Saad Zaghloul to be sure to catch it. Let the driver know when you want to get off. The fare is the same regardless of how far you travel. It's worth riding the length of the Corniche on the upper deck, just for the views.

Taxi

There are no working taxi meters in Alexandria. Locals simply pay the correct amount as they get out of the taxi, but since fares are both unpublished and subjective, this can be a challenge for a visitor to pull off (especially considering many drivers expect visitors to pay higher fares and won't hesitate to aggressively argue the point). Negotiate a price before you get in and try to give the driver the exact amount.

Some sample fares are: Midan Ramla to Misr Train Station E£5; Midan Saad Zaghloul to Fort Qaitbey E£5; Midan Saad Zaghloul to the Bibliotheca Alexandrina E£5; Sofitel Cecil Alexandria (Hotel Cecil) to Montazah or Mamoura E£25.

Tram

Alexandria's rumbling, clackety old trams are fun to ride, but they can be almost unbearably slow and hence not the best option for getting around.

The central tram station is Mahattat Ramla; from here lime-yellow-coloured trams go west and blue-coloured ones travel east. Check the easy-to-read route maps at the stations to find the line you're looking for. The line numbers on each tramcar are in Arabic, but you can tell which line it is by the colour of the sign in front and matching that to the colour of the line number on the route map. Some trams have two or three carriages, in which case one of them is reserved for women. The standard fare is 25pt.

Tram 14 goes to Misr Train Station; tram 15 goes through Anfushi; trams 1 and 25 go to Sidi Gaber Train Station.

AROUND ALEXANDRIA

Aboukir

Aboukir (pronounced abu-eer), a small coastal town 24km east of Alexandria, was slingshot into fame in 1798 when the Battle of the Nile saw the British admiral Horatio Nelson administer a crushing defeat over Napoleon's French fleet.

Recent underwater excavation (see p335) has revealed two sunken cities believed to be the legendary Herakleion (Thonis) and Menouthis, with several rescued treasures now on display at the Alexandria National Museum. The beach here isn't the cleanest, so the main reason to head in this direction is for lunch at one of the excellent fish restaurants, particularly at the seafront **Zephyrion** (☎03-562 1319; fish per kg E£40-160; ⏲lunch & dinner). This old Greek fish taverna (the name is Greek for 'sea breeze') was founded in 1929 and serves first-class fish and seafood on the sweeping blue-and-white terrace that overlooks the bay. Beer is available.

The easiest way to get to Aboukir is by flagging down an eastbound microbus along the Corniche (E£1.50). It will drop you at a roundabout; the sea is to your left as you face the large mosque beyond the roundabout.

Alternatively, a taxi from Alexandria's city centre should cost around E£50, each way.

Rosetta (Ar-Rashid)

☎045 / POP 69,000

It's hard to believe that this dusty town, squatting on the western branch of the Nile 65km northeast of Alexandria, was once Egypt's most significant port. Locally known as Ar-Rashid, Rosetta was founded in the 9th century and outgrew Alexandria in importance during that town's 18th- and 19th-century decline. Alas, as Alexandria got back on its feet and regained power in the late

19th century, Rosetta was thrust once again into near irrelevance.

Today Rosetta is most famous as the discovery place of the stone stele that provided the key to deciphering hieroglyphics (see p345). It strikes a contrast with the modern turmoil of nearby Alexandria – the streets are packed with donkeys pulling overloaded carts, basket-weavers artfully working fronds and blacksmiths hammering away in medieval-looking shop fronts.

Rosetta's main draw is its striking Islamic architecture, in the form of beautifully crafted Ottoman-era merchants' houses. There are at least 22 of them tucked away along the streets but unfortunately most are undergoing renovation and are not open to visitors.

The Beit Killi museum on the main square is also closed, and at present there's no official reopening date.

At the time of writing, the sights open to the public were the House of Amasyali, House of Abu Shaheen and Hammam Azouz.

◉ Sights

Ottoman Houses
HISTORIC BUILDINGS

Built in the traditional Delta style using small, flat bricks painted alternately red and black, Rosetta's Ottoman houses are generally three-storey structures with the upper floor slightly overhanging the lower. Together with their jutting and ornate *mashrabiyyas* (intricately assembled wooden screens that serve for windows), the buildings are reminiscent of an upside-down chocolate wedding cake.

Tickets (adult/student E£15/10; ⊘8am-4pm) good for all of the open monuments in the town centre can be bought at the House of Abu Shaheen.

House of Amasyali

One of the most impressive of all Rosetta's fine buildings is the House of Amasyali, one of two restored houses on Sharia al-Anira Feriel. The facade has beautiful small lantern lights and vast expanses of *mashrabiyyas,* which circulate cool breezes around the house. One of the rooms here is a reception room, where guests would have been entertained by groups of musicians, and is overlooked by a screened wooden gallery behind which the women would sit, obscured from view. The stairs to the gallery are hidden behind a false cupboard and there are some

fine examples of mother-of-pearl inlay work in wooden panels along the same wall.

House of Abu Shaheen

Next door to the House of Amasyali is the House of Abu Shaheen (Mill House), with a reconstructed mill on the ground floor, featuring enormous wooden beams and planks. You can actually see the gears and teeth rotate, which 200 years ago would have been pushed in an endless circle by a bored draught animal.

Hammam Azouz

One of the most extraordinary buildings in Rosetta has to be the Hammam Azouz, a 400-year-old bathhouse still in operation as late as 1980 using water plumbed in from the Nile. It features a fine marble interior with elaborately carved wooden ceilings. Several bathing rooms encircle the main, fountain-centred bathing room, and tall domed ceilings crown each chamber. It's located south of the main market area, a few blocks in from the Corniche.

Fort of Qaitbey
FORT

(adult/student E£15/8; ⊘8am-5pm) About 5km north of Rosetta along the Nile, this fort was built in 1479 to guard the mouth of the Nile 6km further on. It was on this spot that the famous Rosetta Stone was found; we'll wager that this is now the site of the lamest historical exhibit in the world, especially in relation to the importance of the discovery that was made here. A round-trip by taxi should cost E£15.

🛏 Sleeping & Eating

Rosetta sees few travellers and has limited tourist facilities, with only a handful of hotels and restaurants.

Rasheed International Hotel
HOTEL $$

(☎293 4399; www.rosettahotel.jeeran.com; Museum Garden Sq; s/d E£100/130; ❋) This skinny 11-storey place has plainly decorated but spotless rooms, all with satellite TV, minibar and balconies with top views – on a clear day you can see the Mediterranean from the higher floors.

Abaza Restaurant
GRILL $$

(mains E£5-45) Just down the street from the museum, this hole-in-the-wall serves straight-ahead *kofta* (mincemeat and spices grilled on a skewer) and other grilled meats in a little upstairs room with a red carpet and single table. There's no sign in English,

THE ROSETTA STONE

Now a crowd-pulling exhibit at the British Museum in London, the Rosetta Stone is the most significant find in the history of Egyptology. Unearthed in 1799 by a French soldier doing his duty improving the defences of Fort St Julien near Rosetta, the stone is the lower half of a large, dark granitic stele. It records a decree issued in 196 BC by the priests of Memphis, establishing the religious cult of Ptolemy V and granting the 13-year-old pharaoh status as a deity – in exchange for tax exemptions and other priestly perks. In order to be understood by Egyptians, Greeks and others then living in the country, the decree was written in the three scripts current at the time – hieroglyphic, demotic (a cursive form of hieroglyphs) and Greek, a language that European scholars would have read fluently. The trilingual inscription was set up in a temple beside a statue of the pharaoh. At the time of its discovery, much was known about ancient Egypt, but scholars had still not managed to decipher hieroglyphs. It was quickly realised that these three scripts would make it possible to compare identical texts and therefore to crack the code and recover the lost world of the ancient Egyptians.

When the British defeated Napoleon's army in 1801, they wrote a clause in the surrender document insisting that antiquities be handed to the victors, the Rosetta Stone being foremost among them. The French made a cast and the original was shipped to London, where Englishman Thomas Young established the direction in which the hieroglyphs should be read, and recognised that hieroglyphs enclosed within oval rings (cartouches) were the names of royalty.

But in 1822, before Young devised a system for reading the mysterious script, Frenchman Jean François Champollion recognised that signs could be alphabetic, syllabic or determinative, and established that the hieroglyphs inscribed on the Rosetta Stone were actually a translation from the Greek, and not the other way around. This allowed him to establish a complete list of signs with their Greek equivalents. His obsessive work not only solved the mystery of Pharaonic script but also contributed significantly to a modern understanding of ancient Egypt.

so look out for the chickens spit-roasting in a metal grill at the front.

ⓘ Getting There & Away

The easiest way to get to Rosetta from Alexandria is to organise a private car and driver (see p331) or hire a taxi, which should cost you around E£150 return, including waiting time. Taking a microbus (E£4, one hour) from the Al-Mo'af al-Gedid bus station in Alexandria is also pretty simple, and much cheaper.

MEDITERRANEAN COAST

Almost the entire stretch of coastline between Alexandria and Sidi Abdel Rahman is jam-packed with resorts paying homage to the modern gods of concrete construction. This is where well-to-do Cairenes and the top brass of Egypt's military establishment come to escape the oppressive city heat of the summer. While some of these getaways border on the truly luxurious, there's little for the independent traveller – virtually all of these developments are private residential resorts owned or rented by Egyptian families. Halfway down the coast to Libya, El Alamein is home to several poignant memorials to the WWII battles that ensued here. Past here, and all the way to the Libyan border, the striking coast lies deserted until you reach Marsa Matruh, sitting on a brilliant, sandy bay. Marsa Matruh is either heaving with Egyptian holidaymakers in summer or completely deserted in the winter months.

El Alamein
♪046

This small coastal outpost is famed for the decisive victory doled out here by the Allies during WWII (see boxed text p347). More than 80,000 soldiers were killed or wounded in the series of desert battles fought nearby which helped cement Allied control of North Africa. The thousands of graves in the Commonwealth, German and Italian war cemeteries in the vicinity of the town are a bleak reminder of the losses.

Much cheerier are the fine sands and heavenly water of the nearby beaches. Finding a place to access the sea is easier if you're staying at one of the local resorts, but there are also a few places where independent visitors can get in the water.

It's possible to stay overnight here and in nearby Sidi Abdel Rahman, but El Alamein is best visited as a day trip from Alexandria. Beaches aside, there really isn't much that would detain any but the most enthusiastic of military historians for more than a few hours.

◉ Sights

War Museum   MUSEUM
(adult/student E£20/10; ⊙9am-4pm) This museum is a great introduction to the North African campaigns of WWII, including the Battle of El Alamein. There's a collection of memorabilia, uniforms, photos and maps, with explanations in Arabic, English, German and Italian. A range of tanks, artillery and hardware from the fields of battle is displayed outside the museum. The turn-off to the museum is along the main highway; just look for the large tank in the middle of the road.

Commonwealth War Cemetery   CEMETERY
(⊙7am-2.30pm) About 1km east of the War Museum is the Commonwealth War Cemetery. It's a haunting place where more than 7000 tombstones stand in regimented rows. Soldiers from the UK, Australia, New Zealand, France, Greece, South Africa, East and West Africa, Malaysia and India who fought for the Allied cause lie here. As you enter, a separate memorial commemorating the Australian contingent is to your right; look here for a small plaque with a relief map giving an insightful overview of the key battlefield locations. The memorial is supposedly visitable outside of regular hours via a key left outside the gate, but this may not be reliable.

The cemetery itself was a rear area during the fighting; the front line ran from nearby the Italian memorial and wound its way 65km south to the Qattara Depression. If you spend time in town, you may field offers of desert excursions to visit key battle sites, such as Ruweisat ridge or Alam el Halfa. Aside from the fact that millions of landmines were planted during the fighting and no one seems to know how many remain, officially you must obtain approval from the Egyptian military to access the battlefield. It's a controlled area and if you're caught without permission you risk serious trouble; what's more, if anything goes wrong

in the desert you will not be able to rely on authorities for assistance.

German War Memorial   MEMORIAL
About 7km west of El Alamein, what looks like a hermetically sealed sandstone fortress overlooking the sea is actually the German War Memorial. Inside this silent but unmistakable reminder of war lie the tombs of approximately 4000 German servicemen and, in the centre, a memorial obelisk. To reach the memorial, take the marked turn-off from the main highway; the entrance to the memorial is locked, but if you wait for a moment the friendly Bedouin keeper will let you in – he'll even let you sleep there (bring your own sleeping kit).

From the memorial, there's a panoramic view of the undeveloped stretch of shore in this area. Across roughly 2km of desert directly in front of the memorial is the tiny and glorious German Memorial Beach, which is relatively rubbish-free. The sea here is superb, in multiple shades of blue, and you'll feel miles away from Alexandria's teeming beaches. To get there, you can drive or ask the Bedouin keeper at the memorial to open the gate leading to the sand tracks across the desert – but he'll urge you to first get permission from the Coast Guard post (visible from the memorial, but well out of the way if on foot). He may offer to accompany you.

There's also a road direct to the beach from the Alexandria–Matruh highway. It's an unmarked sand track, leading over some low hills to the beach. The turn-off is 150m east of the road to the German memorial.

Italian Memorial   MEMORIAL
About 4km further on, the Italian Memorial has a tall, slender tower as its focal point. This was roughly where the front line between the opposing armies ran.

Before reaching the German memorial, you'll notice on the left (south) side of the road what appears to be a large rock milestone. Inscribed on it is the Italian summary of the battle: 'Mancò la fortuna, non il valore' ('We were short on luck, not on bravery').

🛏 Sleeping & Eating

The store opposite the War Museum has a small cafeteria where you can get a good spread of fuul, ta'amiyya and salads. Rooms are available at the ridiculously overpriced **Max 24** (☏0122 310 0006; s/d US$60/80; ﷯), just east of the War Museum. It also may be

TURNING POINT AT EL ALAMEIN

For a brief period in 1942, the tiny railway station at El Alamein commanded the attention of the entire world. Since 1940, the British had battled the Italians and Germans for control of North Africa; fighting raged back and forth from Tunisia to Egypt as first one side and then the other seized the advantage.

By 1942, Axis units under Field Marshal Erwin Rommel, the celebrated 'Desert Fox', had pushed the Allies back to the last defensible position before Cairo – a line running from El Alamein 65km south to the impassable Qattara Depression. The situation appeared hopeless. British staffers burnt their papers to prevent them from falling into enemy hands, the Germans were expected in Alexandria any day, and Mussolini flew to Egypt to prepare for his triumphal entry into Cairo.

However, in desperate fighting the Allies repulsed the next German thrust by late July. In early September, galvanised by the little-known General Bernard Law Montgomery, the Allies parried a second attack focused on the famous Alam al-Halfa ridge.

Monty husbanded his strength for an all-out counteroffensive, which he launched on 23 October 1942. Intense fighting raged for 13 days, with each side suffering appalling losses, until the Axis line at last crumbled. Rommel's routed legions retreated westward, never to return to Egypt. The Desert Fox was recalled to Germany to spare him the disgrace of defeat, but 230,000 of his soldiers eventually surrendered in Tunisia.

Monty was knighted, and became the most famous British general of the war. In 1946 he was made the First Viscount Montgomery of Alamein, a title he used for the rest of his life. About the battle, Winston Churchill famously said, 'Before Alamein we never had a victory. After Alamein we never had a defeat.'

possible to camp on the beaches nearby but you'll have to hunt around for the police and attempt to get a *tasreeh* (camping permit).

If you want to stay on the beach – and who wouldn't with water like this? – the closest viable place is the Ghazala Regency (p347) at Sidi Abdel Rahman, west of El Alamein town.

❶ Getting There & Away

The easiest option is to organise your own car and driver (see p331). A taxi will charge around E£300 to E£400 to take you to the War Museum, ferry you between the cemeteries, make a stop at a beach, and bring you back to Alexandria.

Alternatively, catch any of the Marsa Matruh buses from the Al-Mo'af al-Gedid long-distance bus station in Alexandria (see p342). You'll be dropped on the main road about 200m down the hill from the War Museum.

Sidi Abdel Rahman
☑046

The gorgeous beaches of Sidi Abdel Rahman are the raison d'être for this growing resort hamlet, and with charter flights between Europe and nearby El Alamein (23km east), development is likely to continue. Several resorts take prime position on the sparkling

waters and white sands of the Mediterranean and are the major draw – though there is little else to see or do here.

◉ Sights

Shaat al-Hanna BEACH
This uncrowded beach is a real find, with irresistible milky-blue water that's great for swimming. There are a few tents set up, and camping should be possible, but you'll need to ask around. Even out here, conservative dress for women applies. The main, free beach is, unfortunately, more trashy than it used to be, so if that turns you off, pay E£50 per person for the clean, private part of the beach, with umbrellas and comfy lounge chairs. There's no sign in English; heading west along the Alexandria–Marsa Matruh road, the turn-off for the beach is marked by three rusting yellow signs 1.9km after the 155km to Marsa Matruh milestone, or 4.9km after the checkpoint and turn-off for the Marassi Hotel. The road is part paved and part sand, but fine for regular cars.

🛏 Sleeping & Eating

Ghazala Regency RESORT $$
(☑419 0060; www.ghazalaregencyalamein.com; km140 on Alexandria–Marsa Matruh rd, Ghazala Bay; s/d €93/107; ❄@🛇🏊) The Ghazala

Regency caters to European families on package tours. The granite-floored rooms are large, but the decor uninspired, the housekeeping variable and the buffet meals bland. The beach, however, is out of this world, with azure water as clear as a pool, and empty stretches of sand perfect for walking. Youngsters are well catered for, with a kids' pool and artificial cove, plus jet-ski and kayak rental. If you're looking to lie about on a gorgeous beach checking out tanned Italians in skimpy swimwear (and we're not talking about the ladies), this fits the bill.

🛈 Getting There & Away

The same buses that can drop you at El Alamein en route to or from Marsa Matruh (see p342) can also drop you here, but it's quite a trek to the resort from the road. It's better to arrive by private car or taxi.

Marsa Matruh

🗐046 / POP 120,600

Your experience of the brilliant-white sand and turquoise-lined bays of Marsa Matruh will depend on what time of year you arrive. In the summer months of June to Septem-

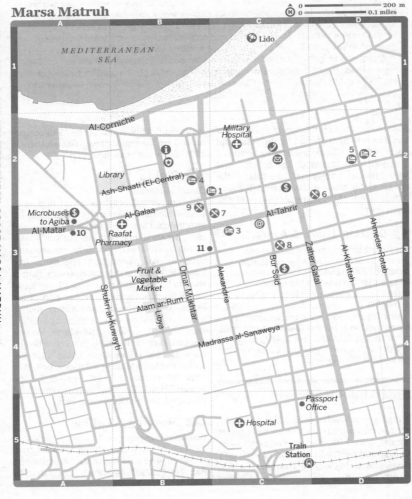

Marsa Matruh

ber, half of the lower Nile Valley descends on this sleepy Mediterranean town for their holiday spell. During this time the streets buzz with people late into the night, throngs of street stalls sell hot food and souvenirs, and impromptu street musicians bang out rhythmic tunes. The beaches are sardine-packed full of picnicking families, hotels raise their rates to astronomical heights, and buses to and from town overflow. The rest of the year, Marsa Matruh returns to its usual near-comatose state. Many hotels shut their doors at this time, the city's beautiful bay of white, sandy beaches lies empty, and the only visitors are Bedouins and Libyans stocking up on goods. Whatever the time of year, few foreign tourists make the trip out here, except to break the journey to Siwa.

The two key streets in Marsa Matruh are the Corniche (Al-Corniche), which winds its way around the waterfront, and Sharia Alexandria, which runs perpendicular to the Corniche. The pricier hotels are along the Corniche, while most others, as well as most of the restaurants and shops, are along Sharia Alexandria.

◉ Sights & Activities

The luminescence of the water along this stretch of the coast is only marred by the town's overflowing hotel scene. Further away, the water is just as nice and you can still find a few places where the developers have yet to start pouring cement. During the hot sum-

mer months women cannot bathe in swim-suits, unless they can handle being the object of intense harassment and ogling. The exceptions are the private beaches at Hotel Beau Site and San Giovanni Cleopatra (Map p352), although even here most Egyptian women remain fully dressed and in the shade.

Lido
BEACH

(Map p348) The Lido, the main beach in town, has decent sand and clear water, but is jam-packed in summer. The beaches on the east side of town, near the bridge over to Rommel's Beach, have calm, shallow water great for small kids, plus palm-frond shade cubicles. At any of the town beaches expect to pay from E£5 to E£10 for a chair and umbrella.

Cleopatra's Beach
BEACH

(Map p352) Possibly the most beautiful piece of coastline in the area is Cleopatra's Beach, about 14km west of town around the bay's thin tentacle of land. The sea here is an exquisite hue, and the rock formations are worth a look. You can wade to Cleopatra's Bath, a natural pool where legend has imagined the great queen and Mark Antony enjoying a dip, but there's actually no swimming due to the waves and rocks just offshore.

Shaati al-Gharam
BEACH

(Map p352) Three kilometres beyond Cleopatra's Beach, at the tip of the tentacle of land, is Shaati al-Gharam (Lovers' Beach). Unsurprisingly, the water here is sublime but the sand is only marginally less busy than at the main city beaches. In summer, boats (E£3) shuttle back and forth from near Hotel Beau Site across the bay. Taxis will charge about E£20 each way, and more if you want the driver to wait while you enjoy the beach.

Agiba Beach
BEACH

(off Map p352) Agiba means 'miracle' in Arabic and Agiba Beach, about 24km west of Marsa Matruh, is just that. It is a small but spectacular cove, accessible only via a path leading down from the clifftop. The water here is a dazzlingly clear turquoise, though it isn't ideal for toddlers, as the waves roll in strongly. It's absolutely packed in summer and near empty the rest of the year. There is a cafe nearby (open in summer only) where you can get light refreshments. Microbuses (E£2) to Agiba leave from in front of the National Bank of Egypt (known locally as Ahly Bank).

About 1km to 2km east of the hilltop above Agiba is a long expanse of accessible beach, with fine sand and deep blue water,

---

Marsa Matruh

🛏 **Sleeping**

1	El-Lido	C2
2	Hotel des Roses	D2
3	Hotel Hamada	C3
4	Riviera Palace Hotel	B2
5	Rommel House Hotel	D2

🍴 **Eating**

6	Abdu Kofta	D2
7	Abou Aby Pizza	C3
8	Felfela	C3
9	Kamana Restaurant	B3

ℹ️ **Information**

| | SpeedNet | (see 7) |

ℹ️ **Transport**

| 10 | EgyptAir | A3 |
| 11 | West & Mid Delta Bus Co | B3 |

and far less crowded than the cove. Confusingly, this stretch of shore is also known as Agiba Beach. To get here, take the turn-off marked by a blue, white and yellow sign (in Arabic) 3km west of Carol's Beau Rivage resort. This paved road leads to the beachfront; the entrance is gated, but at the time of writing there was no fee.

Along the highway to Agiba, there are multiple **roadside stands** selling excellent produce from Siwa, such as green and black olives, olive oil, spices, and lots of dates, which are considered the best in Egypt.

🛌 Sleeping

The accommodation situation in Marsa Matruh leaves a lot to be desired. With a few exceptions, hotels generally specialise in mediocrity at unreasonable rates, but demand for rooms over summer is such that hoteliers really don't need to try very hard. We list a few of the better, more central options.

Prices fluctuate wildly from winter to summer. From June to September, you're advised to book well ahead. Note that many hotels will make you pay for a double room even if you are travelling solo.

TOP CHOICE Almaza Bay　　　RESORT $$$
(off Map p348; ☏436 0000; www.jaz.travel; r from E£840; ❉@🛜🏊) On a remote stretch of seafront 37km east of town, this resort includes five luxury hotels; see the website for info specific to each one. All share a beachfront, and guests can use facilities at any of them, including sampling the tasty buffets. There are kids clubs for the little ones and the beach is something out of a dream. Golf courses and an artificial marina are in the works, for better or for worse.

Carol's Beau Rivage　　　RESORT $$$
(off Map p352; s/d US$350/400; ❉@🛜🏊) Set around a delightful bay with glowing aquamarine water, 15km west of Marsa Matruh on Sallum highway, this recently opened resort has comfortable rooms in a weird safari theme, with elephant paintings, dark-wood furnishings and cane chairs on the balconies. The overall feel is a bit institutional, but the beach is certainly one of the nicest in the area.

Negresco Hotel　　　HOTEL $$$
(Map p352; ☏493 4491/2; Al-Corniche; r high season E£800, s/d low season E£400/600; ❉@🛜) The Negresco adds a much-needed dollop of Mediterranean charm to Marsa Matruh's hotel scene, with whitewashed walls and pretty

blue balconies. The rooms are overpriced and surprisingly sparse but immaculate, with big bathrooms, good beds and flat-screen TVs.

Hotel des Roses　　　INN $
(Map p348; ☏0464932755; Sharia al-Galaa; per person E£85; ⊘mid-Jul–mid-Sep) This charming old hotel feels almost like a country inn, with more character than any other place in town. Oil paintings cover the walls downstairs, bed frames look like hospital surplus, and the pipe-smoking owner has a true bohemian air. Not the most modern, and no air-conditioning, but we like it anyway.

Reem Hotel　　　HOTEL $$
(Map p352; ☏493 3605; Al-Corniche; s with/without air-con E£400/250, d with/without air-con E£500/400; ❉) The Reem has rooms with balconies facing the ocean – great for views, not great for street noise. Some have couches, some are more faded, others more modern, but all are well kept.

Riviera Palace Hotel　　　HOTEL $$
(Map p348; ☏01746 5666; Sharia Alexandria; s/d E£200/300; ❉🛜) With big singles, smallish doubles, and beds with satin headboards covered in clear plastic, Riviera Palace is a solid choice. The schizophrenic lobby decor blends a chandelier-clad nautical theme to a stuffed-tiger motif – soak it up while you check your email on your laptop.

El-Lido　　　HOTEL $$
(Map p348; ☏493 2248; Sharia Alexandria; s/d E£100/150; ❉) The air-con rooms in this centrally located tower block see less daylight than Dracula – on the plus side, they're quiet. Rooms with fan have balconies over the street. It's well run and clean; overall a good value.

Rommel House Hotel　　　HOTEL $$
(Map p348; ☏493 5466; Sharia al-Galaa; s/d E£150/250; ❉) Well away from the hubbub of the Corniche and Sharia Alexandria, rooms at this dependable, long-standing and cavernous hotel come with TV and refrigerator, and some have posters of kittens. Prices are significantly lower off-season.

Hotel Hamada　　　HOTEL $
(Map p348; ☏493 3300; Sharia al-Tahrir; s/d without bathroom E£50/70) Located right in the centre of town, the Hamada is a rudimentary budget option with sort-of-cleanish rooms and overly friendly staff. Note that in summer the riotous party noise from Sharia Alexandria below can be deafening.

✕ Eating

Marsa Matruh is a great town for self-catering, as it's centred on the outdoor food market; pick up bread, cheese and fruit along
with dates and olives from Siwa Oasis for a
perfect beach picnic.

Abdu Kofta   GRILL $$
(Map p348; Sharia al-Tahrir; dishes E£7-60; ⊙lunch
& dinner) Locals will swear black and blue
that this is the best restaurant in town. In
the clean and cool 1st-floor room, it serves
kofta or grilled meat by the weight served
with good mezze and salads.

Kamana Restaurant   GRILL $
(Map p348; Sharia al-Galaa; meals E£8-20; ⊙lunch
& dinner) This simple restaurant does a roaring trade in grilled meats (ie just chicken and
kebabs). Follow your nose at the intersection
with Sharia Alexandria and you can't miss it.

Felfela   FELAFEL $
(Map p348; Sharia Port Said; meals E£1-3; ⊙break-
fast, lunch & dinner; ✍) The best fuul and felafel
joint in town, this is the spot vegetarians – or
anyone looking to fill up cheaply – should
seek out.

Abou Aby Pizza   PIZZA $$
(Map p348; Sharia Alexandria; mains from E£15;
⊙lunch & dinner; ✍) This popular place serves
up tasty Western-style pizza. Upstairs seating
offers good views onto the street action below.

🛍 Shopping

It's easy to find everything you need for the
beach, from towels to float toys to sun hats,
at plenty of stores in town.

For locally made crafts, head to the **rug
shop** (Map p348) on Sharia Gamel Abdel
Nasser, across from Abdu Rahman Mosque.
Here you'll find Bedouin carpets, handmade
in the traditional style, from shearing to spin-
ning to weaving. There are also rugs handwoven on standing looms by Bedouin women
who work in a small-scale factory, creating
their own designs based on traditional motifs.

ℹ Information

There are several exchange bureaus on Sharia
al-Galaa.

Banque Misr (Map p348; Sharia al-Galaa;
⊙9am-2.30pm Sun-Thu) Has an ATM.

CIB Bank (Map p348; Sharia Port Said; ⊙8am-
3pm Sun-Thu) Has 24-hour ATM.

Fr3on (Map p348; 14 Sharia al-Tahrir; per hr
E£3; ⊙24hr; ✳🛜) Internet cafe.

Main post office (Map p348; Sharia ash-
Shaati; ⊙9am-9pm Sat-Thu)

Military Hospital (Map p348; ☎493 5286;
Sharia ash-Shaati)

National Bank of Egypt (Map p348; off Sharia
al-Matar; ⊙9am-2pm & 6-9pm Sun-Thu)

Passport office (Map p348; ☎493 5351; off
Sharia Alexandria; ⊙8am-3pm Sat-Thu) No
sign, so look for the yellow/brown building with
a line in front, or ask for the *gawezaat*.

Raafat Pharmacy (Map p348; 1 Sharia al-
Galaa; ⊙9am-3am)

SpeedNet (Map p348; 7 Sharia Alexandria; per
hr E£2) Internet cafe with hot and soft drinks.

Telephone centrale (Map p348; Sharia ash-
Shaati; ⊙8am-10pm)

Tourist office (Map p348; ☎493 1841; Sharia
Omar Mukhta; ⊙8.30am-7pm Jun-Sep, to 5pm
Oct-May) One block off the Corniche, the office
was closed for renovation at time of research.

Tourist police (Map p348; ☎493 5575; cnr
Sharia Omar Mukhtar & Al-Corniche)

ℹ Getting There & Away

Air
EgyptAir (Map p348; ☎493 6573; Sharia al-
Matar) has twice-weekly flights between Cairo
and Marsa Matruh from June to September,
leaving Cairo at 3.15pm and returning at 5pm.
Tickets are about E£700 one way. Get to or from
the airport in one of the EgyptAir minibuses.

Bus
Marsa Matruh's bus station (Map p352) is 2km
south of town on the main coastal highway.
Expect to pay about E£5 for a taxi to the town
centre. Microbuses (50pt) cruise Sharia
Madrassa al-Sanaweya around where the fruit
and vegetable market dead-ends.

West & Mid Delta Bus Co (☎490 5079) Hourly
services to Alexandria from 7am to 2am (E£20 to
E£35, four hours). In summer, plenty of departures daily serve Cairo (E£65, five hours), leaving
between 7.30am and 2am, with special VIP buses
at 8.30am and 3.30pm. In winter, buses go Cairo
at noon and 3.30pm. There are buses daily to
Sallum (E£15, three hours) at 7am, 1.30pm,
4.30pm and 8pm. Buses head to Siwa (E£17, four
hours) at 1.30pm, 4pm and 2am. Note that the
West & Mid Delta buses running between Alexandria and Marsa Matruh and on to Siwa seem like
the oldest fleet in the country and break down
often. In summer there's a West & Mid Delta office open in the centre on Sharia Alexandria.

Super Jet (☎490 4787) Daily service to Alexandria and Cairo from June to September only.

Microbuses
The microbus lot is beside the bus station. Minivans to Siwa, if there are enough passengers,

ALEXANDRIA & THE MEDITERRANEAN COAST MARSA MATRUH

cost E£13; they are much more comfortable and efficient than the West & Mid Delta buses. Other fares include El Alamein E£20, Alexandria E£20, Cairo E£40 and Sallum E£20.

Train

From 15 June to 15 September three **sleeper trains** (www.wataniasleepingtrains.com) run weekly (per person single/double cabin US$60/43, seven hours) between Cairo and Marsa Matruh. Trains depart Cairo Monday, Wednesday and Saturday, and make the return journey Sunday, Tuesday and Thursday. In both directions, trains depart at 11pm and arrive at 6am. Make reservations in Cairo (📞02-3748 9488) or buy your ticket on the train.

Air-conditioned 1st-/2nd-class express trains run daily between Cairo and Marsa Matruh (1st/2nd class E£58/34, seven hours) from June to September only.

Ordinary 2nd-/3rd-class trains without air-con run year-round between Marsa Matruh and Alexandria (6½ hours), but these are not recommended – even those working at the station have described the trains as 'horrible'.

ℹ Getting Around

Private taxis or pick-ups can be hired for the day, but you must bargain aggressively, especially in summer. Expect to pay E£80 to E£150, depending on the distance. Bikes can be rented from makeshift rental places along Sharia Alexandria during the high season for E£10 to E£20 per day.

Sallum

📞046

Look up 'middle of nowhere' in the dictionary and you might find the town of Sallum, a mere 12km from the Libyan frontier. Nestled at the foot of Gebel as-Sallum and lying on the Gulf of Sallum, the town was once the ancient port of Baranis. While a few Roman wells testify to its history, it is now mostly a Bedouin trading post that still sees few international visitors – though this may change, as Libya's border is now easier than ever to cross.

The sea here, as along the rest of this stretch of coast, is crystal clear and aquamarine in colour, but don't think about frolicking in the water – dumped rubbish lines the sand, government property surrounds the town, permits are needed to be on the beach after 5pm, and the whole town reeks like stale garbage.

On the eastern entrance to the town there is a modest WWII Commonwealth War Cemetery, commemorating the destruction of hundreds of British tanks by the Germans at nearby 'Hell Fire' pass.

Around Marsa Matruh

Sallum has a **National Bank of Egypt** (📞480 0590; ⊙9am-2pm Sun-Thu) branch, where you pick up your Libyan visa (US$15) before heading to the border. An ATM accepts international currency into Egyptian pounds but not Libyan dinars. If you're heading into Libya and want cash before crossing the border, you'll have to deal with the moneychangers on the street by the bus stand. They'll find you.

🛏 Sleeping & Eating

You will want to avoid staying in Sallum, but if you have no choice, your best bets are the insanely overpriced **Sirt Hotel** (📞480 1113; s/d E£150/250) about 700m east of the bus stand, or the merely overpriced **El-Gezira Hotel** (📞480 0616; s/d E£100/150) right behind the bus stand. Both are clean; El-Gezira has TV. For something cheaper and waaaay grungier, there's **Hotel al-Ahram** (📞480 0148; r without bathroom from E£30); women would probably feel uncomfortable here.

There are a few simple food stands around.

ℹ Getting There & Away

There are buses and the odd *servees* heading to Sallum from Alexandria and Marsa Matruh.

From Sallum, buses for Marsa Matruh (E£15, three hours) depart at 6am, 10am, noon, 7pm and 9pm. A 10pm bus goes to Alexandria (E£35, eight hours) and Cairo (E£70, eleven hours). A *servees* or minibus to Marsa Matruh will cost E£20 to E£30.

For Libya, a E£5 ride in a *servees* (or E£35 for a whole car) takes you to the border crossing at Amsaad. For visa details, see p523

Suez Canal

Best Places to Eat

» El Borg (p357)

» Nefertiti (p360)

» Pizza Pino (p357)

» Abou Essam (p357)

Best Places to Stay

» New Palace Hotel (p359)

» Hotel de la Poste (p356)

» Mercure Forsan Island (p360)

Why Go?

The Suez Canal, Egypt's glorious triumph of engineering over nature, dominates this region, slicing through the sands of the Isthmus of Suez for 163km, not only severing mainland Egypt from Sinai but also Africa from Asia. The canal was the remarkable achievement of Egypt's belle époque, an era buoyed by grand aspirations and finished by bankruptcy and broken dreams. This period also gave birth to the canalside cities of Port Said and Ismailia. Today their streets remain haunted by this fleeting age of grandeur, their distinctive architecture teetering into picturesque disrepair.

Although it's a region often bypassed by all but the most rampant supertanker-spotters, anyone with an interest in Egypt's modern history will enjoy the crumbs of former finery on display. And while the Canal Zone may have no vast ruins or mammoth temples, there's a slower pace to life here that those with travelling time up their sleeve will appreciate.

When to Go
Port Said

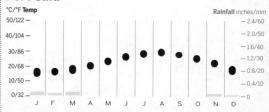

Apr Witness the riotous effigy-burning spectacle at the annual El-Limbo Festival.

Aug Escape the frazzling summer heat with cooling canalside breezes in Port Said.

Sep Spot flocks of storks as they head south, swooping over the skies across the Canal Zone.

Suez Canal Highlights

1 Commute from Africa to Asia in 15 minutes flat by jumping on the **ferry** (p355) from Port Said to Port Fuad and sampling life on the canal

2 Take a break from Egypt's usual hectic pace among the colonial-era villas of slumberous **Ismailia** (p358)

3 Explore the dreamy faded grandeur of **Port Said's waterfront quarter** (p355)

4 Admire more than 4000 objects from Pharaonic and Graeco-Roman times at the rarely visited **Ismailia Museum** (p358)

5 Feast on super-fresh seafood along **Port Said's Corniche** (p357)

6 Stroll down Port Said's **canalside boardwalk** (p355) for supertanker-spotting heaven

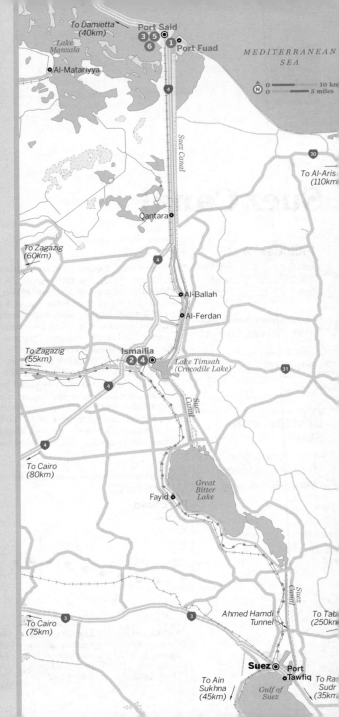

Port Said

☑066 / POP 570,600

In its late 19th-century raffish heyday, Port Said was Egypt's city of vice and sin. This louche past of boozing seafarers and packjard brothels may have long since been scrubbed away but the period is still evoked in the waterfront's muddle of once grand architecture today slowly going to seed. The yesteryear allure of the centre is enough of a reason to visit but the main attraction, and the reason for the town's establishment, is the Suez Canal. The raised pedestrian-only boardwalk running along the waterfront provides up-close views over the canal's northern entry point, and the free ferry that crosses the canal to the languid suburb of Port Fuad is the only opportunity for casual visitors to ride the waters of this manmade marvel themselves. Although heavily damaged in the 1967 and 1973 wars with Israel, Port Said was swiftly rebuilt and today is a fascinating blend of bustling modern port and colonial-era charm, which seems a world apart from Egypt's other cities.

⊙ Sights

Waterfront Quarter   HISTORIC BUILDINGS
The heart of Port Said is located along the edge of the canal, on and around Sharia Palestine. Here, the waterfront neighbourhood seems infused with a 'back in the good old days' atmosphere, the streets lined with late 19th-century and early 20th-century buildings complete with rickety wooden balconies, louvred doors and high verandahs. The raised **boardwalk** all the way along Sharia Palestine affords sweeping views over the canal.

Take a stroll down Sharia Memphis, with its old **Woolworth's building**, Sharia al-Gomhuriyya, and around the streets just north of the Commercial Basin. There are wonderfully odd colonial remnants, such as the **old canal shipping agency building**, the once highly fashionable **Simon Arzt department store** and the archway entrances still announcing the **Bible Society building**.

Northeast of here, on Sharia 23rd of July, is the **Italian consulate building**, erected in the 1930s and adorned with an engraved piece of the propaganda of Fascist dictator Benito Mussolini: 'Rome – once again at the heart of an empire'.

Several blocks inland, on and around Sharia Salah Salem, is an impressive collection of churches, including the **Coptic**

DON'T MISS

CROSSING THE CANAL

Don't have your own yacht? Not best buddies with the captain of a super-tanker? Stroll down to the boat terminal at the southwestern end of Sharia Palestine and hop aboard the ferry to Port Fuad to travel upon the waters of the Suez Canal for free. Ferries leave about every 10 minutes throughout the day and the quick journey offers panoramic views of all the canal action. Once deposited in Port Fuad, founded in 1925, head south from the quayside mosque to explore boulevards lined with sprawling French-inspired residences. Although the streets are now mired by litter and many of the villas teeter on the brink of decay, their sloping tiled roofs, lush gardens and wooden balconies hung with colourful washing still invoke the genteel splendour of a bygone era.

Orthodox Church of St Bishoi of the Virgin and the **Franciscan compound**.

At the very northern end of Sharia Palestine is a large **stone plinth** that once held a statue of Ferdinand de Lesseps, until it was torn down in 1956 with the nationalisation of the Suez Canal.

Suez Canal House   HISTORIC BUILDING
(Commercial Basin) If you've ever seen a picture of Port Said, it was probably of the striking green domes of the Suez Canal House, which was built in time for the inauguration of the canal in 1869. As it's currently fenced off (it's not open to the public), the best way to get a good look at the building's famous facade is by hopping on the free ferry to Port Fuad.

Military Museum   MUSEUM
(☑322 4657; Sharia 23rd of July; admission E£5; ⊙10am-3pm Sat-Thu) This little museum is worth a peek for its information on the canal and also some rather curious exhibits (complete with toy soldiers) documenting the 1956 Suez Crisis and the 1967 and 1973 wars with Israel. In the museum gardens you can view a few captured US tanks with the Star of David painted on them, as well as an odd collection of UXOs (unexploded ordnance).

Port Said & Port Fuad

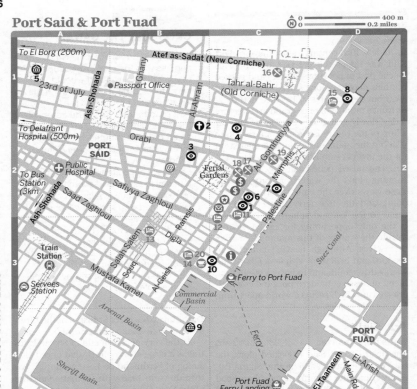

✨ Festivals & Events

El-Limbo Festival CULTURAL FESTIVAL
Despite authorities dampening the all-out fire havoc of the old days, the effigy-burning El-Limbo Festival still takes place annually along the Corniche. El-Limbo began in the 19th-century when townspeople took to the streets protesting against their hated governor Limbo Bey by burning effigies of him. These days the festival still stays true to its roots and the dolls burnt usually represent a villain from recent current affairs. It's usually held in April; festivities run over two nights beginning the night before the Egyptian holiday Sham el-Nessim.

🛌 Sleeping

TOP CHOICE Hotel de la Poste HISTORIC HOTEL $
(☎322 4048; 42 Sharia al-Gomhuriyya; s/d E£75/95; ▣) Port Said's best budget option, this faded classic still manages to maintain

a hint of its original charm. That said, it will definitely take a bit of imagination (and perhaps some hazy vision) to evoke the colonial yesteryear, but clean and comfortable rooms (balconies cost an extra E£15) and a decent on-site restaurant are good perks if your imagination starts to fail you.

New Continental HOTEL $$
(☎322 5024; 30 Sharia al-Gomhuriyya; s/d E£110/183; ▣) Efficient and friendly management makes this typical Egyptian midrange hotel stand out from the crowd. Light-filled rooms lead out onto teensy balconies and come in a range of sizes so ask to see a few. All come with TV and an astounding overclutter of furniture.

Mereland Hotel HOTEL $
(☎322 7020; Sharia Digla; s/d E£67/79, without bathroom E£30/42) This shabby old place has seen better days but the fan-only rooms have

Port Said & Port Fuad

clean linen and friendly manager Ahmed tries hard to help. Do yourself a favour and shell out the extra for the en suite rooms as the shared facilities leave a lot to be desired. Rooms at the back are quieter and come with a balcony (of sorts).

Resta Port Said Hotel   HOTEL **$$$**
(☏332 5511; www.restahotels.com; off Sharia Palestine; s/d US$160/295; ❋☏☲) Nicely appointed with modern, business-style furnishings, the rooms at the Resta are about as snazzy as Port Said gets. The pool area and some of the other communal areas have excellent views out to the canal. Management intends to renovate in 2012 which will hopefully bring the bathrooms up to the standard they are charging for.

Holiday Hotel   HOTEL **$$**
(☏322 0711; Sharia al-Gomhuriyya; s/d E£325/375; ❋☏) The clean rooms at the Holiday Hotel are on the small side and they come with TV and interiors that are best described as tangerine-dream overload.

✖ Eating & Drinking

Self-caterers will find all the groceries they need at Metro Supermarket on Sharia al-Geish. For fruit and vegetables, try the lively market on Sharia Souq, three blocks north of Sharia al-Gomhuriyya. There are a couple of good juice stands near the ferry terminal on Sharia Saad Zaghloul which are perfect for quenching your thirst.

Seafood is a real highlight of Port Said's dining scene. The best fish restaurants are located between Sharia Atef as-Sadat and the Corniche (the pedestrian promenade which runs directly opposite to the beach).

TOP CHOICE El Borg   SEAFOOD **$$**
(Beach Plaza, just off Sharia Atef as-Sadat; mains E£20-50) This massive Port Said institution is always buzzing with families on a night out. There's a small menu of grills if you don't feel like fish, but the good-value fresh seafood is really what the crowds flock here for. Eat on the shorefront terrace in the evening for superb people-watching on the beach promenade.

Pizza Pino   ITALIAN **$$**
(Sharia al-Gomhuriyya; mains E£20-50) An art-deco style bistro with cosy appeal, Pizza Pino is a local favourite for its hearty portions of pasta, good pizzas and decently priced grills. It's a lovely place with attentive staff; if only the background music didn't make you feel like you were stuck in an elevator with Kenny G.

Abou Essam   SEAFOOD **$$**
(Sharia Atef as-Sadat; mains E£30-60) This flashy glass-fronted place does a great selection of fish, pasta and grilled meat and has a popular serve-yourself salad bar.

Galal   EGYPTIAN **$$**
(60 Sharia al-Gomhuriyya; mains E£20-50) Good for a lunch stop between gazing at the crumbling relics of Port Said's architecture, the friendly Galal has shaded streetside seating and a menu covering all the usual Egyptian favourites from *shish tawooq* (marinated chicken grilled on skewers) to pigeon.

ℹ Information

Port Said was declared a duty-free port in 1976. In theory, everyone must pass through customs when entering and leaving the city, though in practice this is seldom enforced. Regardless, be sure to have your passport with

LADY LIBERTY ON THE CANAL

New York's famous Statue of Liberty has its origins in Egypt. The empty plinth at the end of Port Said's Sharia Palestine was originally meant to host a colossal lighthouse in statue form to celebrate the incredible achievement of completing the Suez Canal. Inspired by the massive statues at Abu Simbel (p275), French sculptor Frédéric-Auguste Bartholdi designed a torch-bearing Egyptian woman who would tower over the canal's entrance to symbolise 'Egypt carrying the light of Asia'. Sketches were drawn and models were made but the statue was ultimately abandoned due to costs. Instead Bartholdi's grandiose vision found new life on a completely different continent. With some tweaking, the 'Light of Asia' statue design eventually morphed into New York's Lady Liberty.

you. Most banks and important services are on Sharia al-Gomhuriyya, two blocks inland from the canal.

Bank of Alexandria (Sharia al-Gomhuriyya)

Delafrant Hospital (322 2663; Sharia Orabi)

Main post office (Sharia al-Geish)

Mody Net (324 4202; Sharia Salah Salem; per hr E£3; 9am-midnight) Internet access.

National Bank of Egypt (Sharia al-Gomhuriyya)

Public Hospital (322 0694; Sharia Safiyya Zaghloul)

Tourist office (323 5289; 8 Sharia Palestine; 10am-7pm Sat-Thu) Enthusiastic staff and good maps of town.

Tourist police (322 8570; post office bldg, Sharia al-geish)

ⓘ Getting There & Away

BOAT Ferries and cruise ships running between Port Said and Limassol (Cyprus) and Lattakia (Syria) were suspended in 2011 due to political instability. The service may be restored as the situation settles; see p523 for contact information.

BUS The bus station is about 3km from the town centre at the beginning of the road to Cairo (about E£5 in a taxi).

Super Jet (372 1779) Has bi-hourly buses to Cairo (E£25, four hours) and a bus to Alexandria (E£30, four hours) at 4.30pm daily. Bookings are advisable.

East Delta Travel Co (372 9883) Also has hourly buses to Cairo (E£23, four hours) from 5am to 9pm daily. Buses to Alexandria (E£25, four to five hours) leave at 7am, 11am, 2pm, 4pm, 6pm and 8pm. Buses to Ismailia (E£6, one to 1½ hours) depart hourly between 6am and 6pm. Buses to Suez (E£11, 2½ to three hours) depart at 6am, 10am, 2pm and 4pm.

SERVEES The *servees* (service taxi) station is next door to the train station. Sample fares: Cairo (E£20), Ismailia (E£10) and Suez (E£12).

TRAIN Services to Cairo (2nd-/1st-class, E£11/21, five hours), via Ismailia (E£4/11, two hours), run at 5.30am, 1pm and 5.30pm. There's also a 2nd-class only service at 7.30pm. Delays are common and buses are, in general, quicker and more comfortable.

ⓘ Getting Around

MICROBUS Microbuses run along main arteries such as Sharia Orabi and Sharia ash-Shohada, and cost 50pt for a short ride.

TAXI There are plenty of blue-and-white taxis around Port Said. Fares for short trips within the town centre average E£3.

Ismailia

064 / POP 285,000

Ismailia was founded by and named after Pasha Ismail, who was khedive of Egypt in the 1860s while the Suez Canal was being built. The city was also the temporary home of Ferdinand de Lesseps, the director of the Suez Canal Company, who lived here until the canal was completed. Not surprisingly, Ismailia grew in the image of the French masters who had ensconced themselves in Egypt during the colonial era. Today, Ismailia's historic town centre, with its elegant colonial streets, expansive lawns and late 19th-century villas, is one of the most peaceful and picturesque neighbourhoods in the country. The heart of Ismailia and the area most worth exploring is the old European quarter around Sharia Thawra and the central square, Midan al-Gomhuriyya.

⊙ Sights & Activities

Ismailia Museum   MUSEUM
(391 2749; Mohammed Ali Quay; adult/child E£15/5; 8am-4pm, closed for Fri noon prayers) More than 4000 objects from Pharaonic and Graeco-Roman times are housed at this small but interesting museum on the eastern edge of town. The collection includes statues, scarabs, stelae and records of the first canal, built between the Bitter Lakes and

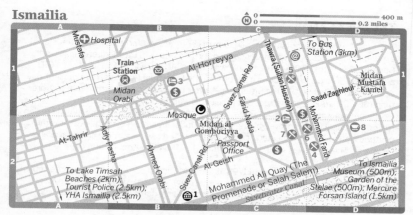

Bubastis by the Persian ruler Darius. The highlight of the museum is a 4th-century-AD mosaic depicting characters from Greek and Roman mythology. At the top Phaedra is sending a love letter to her stepson Hippolytus, while below Dionysus is riding a chariot driven by Eros. The bottom section recounts the virtues of Hercules.

Garden of the Stelae   MONUMENT
(Mohammed Ali Quay) Just southwest of the Ismailia Museum is a garden containing a rather forlorn little sphinx from the time of Ramses II (1279–1213 BC). You need permission from the museum to visit the garden but you are able to see the unremarkable statue from the street. The attractive grounds of the majestic residence between the garden and the museum belong to the head of the Suez Canal Authority and are off limits to the public.

De Lesseps' House   HISTORIC BUILDING
(Mohammed Ali Quay) The residence of the one-time French consul to Egypt used to be open to the public. These days you can see the interior only if you're a VIP of some sort, as the building currently serves as a private guesthouse for visitors of the Suez Canal Authority.

If you're not a privileged guest, you might be interested to know that de Lesseps' bedroom looks as if it has hardly been touched in over a century – old photos, books and various utensils are scattered around the desk and on the floor. Inside the grounds is also de Lesseps' private carriage, which has been encased in glass and remains in impeccable condition. The house is located near the corner of Sharia Ahmed Orabi.

Lake Timsah   BEACHES
There are several beaches around Lake Timsah, on the southeastern edge of town. The better ones are owned by the various clubs dotting the shore and you'll need to pay to use them (on average about E£20); the public beaches charge between E£3 and E£5. For a taxi between town and the beaches expect to pay E£5.

🛌 Sleeping

New Palace Hotel   HISTORIC HOTEL **$$**
(391 7761; Midan Orabi; s/d E£100/170; ✱) This old-timer hotel has bundles of character and evokes a decent measure of colonial flair. Good-sized, front-facing rooms are home to comfortable beds and charming yesteryear touches such as dinky balconies and old fashioned barrel chairs. Interior-facing rooms are far plainer and pokier but will save you E£20.

THE SUEZ CANAL

The Suez Canal represents the culmination of centuries of effort to enhance trade and expand the empires of Egypt by connecting the Red Sea with the Mediterranean Sea. Construction of the first recorded canal was begun by Pharaoh Nekau II between 610 and 595 BC. The canal stretched from the Nile Delta town of Bubastis, near present-day Zagazig, to the Red Sea via the Bitter Lakes. After reputedly causing the death of more than 100,000 workers, construction of the canal was quickly abandoned.

The project was completed about a century later under Darius, one of Egypt's Persian rulers. The canal was improved by the Romans under Trajan but over the next several centuries it was either neglected or dredged for limited use depending on the available resources. The canal was again briefly restored in AD 649 by Amr ibn al-As, the Arab conqueror of Egypt.

Following the French invasion in 1798, the importance of some sort of sea route south to Asia was again recognised. For the first time, digging a canal directly from the Mediterranean Sea to the Red Sea, across the comparatively narrow Isthmus of Suez, was considered. The idea was abandoned, however, when Napoleon's engineers mistakenly calculated that there was a 10m difference between the two sea levels.

British reports detected that mistake several years later but it was Ferdinand de Lesseps, the French consul to Egypt, who pursued the Suez Canal idea through to its conclusion. In 1854, de Lesseps presented his proposal to the Egyptian khedive Said Pasha, who authorised him to excavate the canal; work began in 1859.

A decade later the canal was completed amid much fanfare and celebration. When two small fleets, one originating in Port Said and the other in Suez, met at the new town of Ismailia on 16 November 1869, the Suez Canal was declared open and Africa was officially severed from Asia.

Ownership of the canal remained in French and British hands for the next 86 years until, in the wake of Egyptian independence, President Gamal Abdel Nasser nationalised the Suez in 1956. The two European powers, in conjunction with Israel, invaded Egypt in an attempt to retake the waterway by force. In what came to be known as the 'Suez Crisis', they were forced to retreat in the face of widespread international condemnation.

Today, the Suez Canal remains one of the world's most heavily used shipping lanes and toll revenues represent one of the largest contributors to the Egyptian state coffers with more than 50 ships passing through the Suez each day.

Mercure Forsan Island RESORT $$$
(☎391 6316; www.mercure.com; Gezirat Forsan; s/d from €93/103; ❄☁☏⊠) Occupying its own island 1.6km southeast of the centre of town, the Mercure's private beach and gardens make it a tranquil haven. The snazzy rooms outfitted with modern bathrooms and brightened by colourful textiles are worth splashing out for. Even if you're not staying here, stop by for a refreshing dip (day passes are available for E£160) or a gourmet dinner by the water.

YHA Ismailia HOSTEL $
(☎392 2850; Lake Timsah Rd; s/d E£47/52; ❄) This cement block out of town on the shore of the lake doesn't look like much, but its sparkling clean, if institutional, rooms are decent-sized and all come with their own bathrooms so are a budget steal. It's a E£5 taxi ride from the centre; ask the driver for Beit Shebab.

Crocodile Inn HOTEL $$
(☎391 2555; cnr Sharia Thawra & Sharia Saad Zaghloul; s/d E£200/250; ❄) The rather dark and characterless rooms here are clean but well past their sell-by date with tired and drab furnishings. It's a good fall-back if the New Palace is full.

🍴 Eating & Drinking

Takeaway and budget places are concentrated on and around Sharia Thawra and around Midan Orabi. There's a large Metro Supermarket on the corner of Sharia Thawra and Sharia at-Tahrir.

TOP CHOICE **Nefertiti** SEAFOOD $$
(Sharia Thawra; mains E£20-45) This dinky place, with walls covered in quirky decorations (everything from Chinese posters to papyrus) has a tasty menu serving up fresh

seafood, grills and a bit of pasta. The grilled shrimp is delicious.

George's
SEAFOOD $$
(Sharia Thawra; mains E£30-65) An Ismailia classic, George's has been around since 1950 and serves up seafood dishes amid a cosy British-pub-style ambience.

Thebes Patisserie
DESSERTS $
(Sharia Thawra; pastries E£3-10) Nearly always packed with local families, Thebes dishes out the best desserts in town and is a great ice-cream stop on a hot day.

El-Mestkawu
COFFEEHOUSE
(Sharia Al-Geish) A fabulous shady verandah cafe where the old-timers of town go to gossip, drink coffee and watch the world go by while smoking a sheesha (water pipe).

ℹ Information

Anash Net (Sharia Mohammed Farid; per hr E£2; ⏰10am-12am) Internet access.
Bank of Alexandria (Midan Orabi) Has an ATM.
Banque du Caire (Sharia al-Geish) Has an ATM.
Banque Misr (Sharia Thawra) Has an ATM.
Hospital (☎337 3902/3; Sharia Mustafa)
Main post office (Sharia al-Horreyya)
Tourist office (☎332 1078; 1st fl, New Governorate Bldg, Sharia Tugary, Sheikh Zayeed area; ⏰8.30am-3pm Sat-Thu) About 1.5km north of Midan Orabi.
Tourist police (☎333 2910) About 2.5km south of Midan Orabi, the Tourist Police is situated in the Lake Timsah beach area.

ℹ Getting There & Away

BUS Ismailia's bus station is about 3km northwest of the old quarter; taxis to the town centre cost around E£5.

East Delta Travel Co (☎332 1513) has buses to Cairo (E£15 to E£20, four hours) every half-hour between 6am and 8pm. Buses to Alexandria (E£30, five hours) leave at 7am and 2.30pm. Buses to Port Said (E£6, one to two hours) depart every hour between 7am and 5pm; and to Suez (E£6, 1½ hours) every hour between 6.30am and 11.30am, and 1.30pm and 6.30pm.

There are also hourly buses to Al-Arish (E£12, three to four hours) between 8.30am and 6.30pm. Buses to Sharm el-Sheikh (E£40, six hours) leave at 6.30am, 11.30am, 2pm, 4pm and 10.30pm. This last service also heads on to Dahab (E£55, seven to eight hours).

TRAIN Services to Cairo (2nd-/1st-class E£8/15, four to five hours) run at 11am, 2.20pm, 4.15pm and 5.20pm. The 5.20pm service is 2nd-class only. To Port Said (2nd-/1st-class, E£4/10)

there are three trains daily at 9.45am, 11.15am and 2.15pm. There are also six 2nd-class only trains daily to Suez (E£1.50) at 7am, 8.10am, 10.30am, 1.15pm, 3.15pm and 6pm.

ℹ Getting Around

MICROBUS Microbuses ply the main arteries of the city. Fares average 50pt.
TAXI There are plenty of orange taxis around town. Short trips cost about E£3.

Suez
☎062 / POP 500,000

Poor old Suez; the heavy thumping delivered during the 1967 and 1973 wars with Israel wiped out most of its colonial relics and so it has none of the nostalgic appeal of Port Said and Ismailia. Instead, a sprawl of grim and gritty concrete blocks overwhelms much of the city, with the additional piles of festering rubbish sprouting along most of the streets simply enhancing the down-and-out air. There are a few old remnants hanging on along a couple of streets in Port Tawfiq which managed to escape the bombing, but nothing of note to deserve a stopover. If you do get stuck here, note that over-zealous security measures have made canal-viewing here a no-go with plenty of barbed wire and bored guards to stop any wannabe sightseers from snapping photos.

Suez is divided between Suez proper and Port Tawfiq – the latter at the mouth of the canal. Joining Port Tawfiq with Suez is Sharia al-Geish, a wide thoroughfare that cuts through an industrial area before leading through the heart of Suez.

🛏 Sleeping

Hotel Green House
HOTEL $$$
(☎319 1553/4; greenhouse-suez@hotmail.com; Sharia al-Geish; s/d from E£500/628; ❄@✻) Although ridiculously overpriced, Hotel Green House is still the nicest place to bed down in Suez (there's not much competition). Rooms are large but desperately dated. Grab one with a balcony so at least you can benefit from the sweeping views over Suez Bay.

Red Sea Hotel
HOTEL $$
(☎319 0190; 13 Sharia Riad, Port Tawfiq; s/d E£405/500; ❄✺) In a quiet location near the yacht basin, the decent-sized rooms here are home to a range of rough-around-the-edges furniture and ugly brown carpets. The top-floor restaurant, with great views and decent seafood, is the hotel's highlight.

Suez

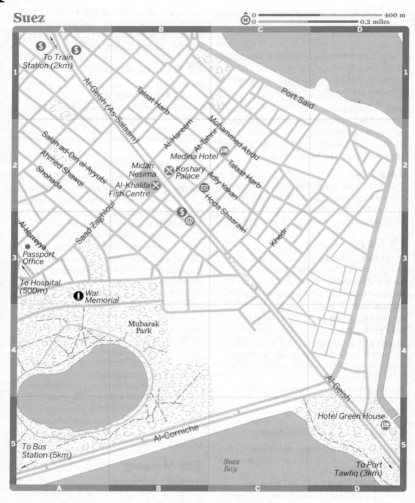

Medina Hotel HOTEL **$**
(☑322 4056; Sharia Talaat Harb; s/d E£75/125; ☒)
If you don't mind candy-cane painted walls
and lack of windows, the Medina is probably Suez' top budget choice. It's kept clean
and well cared for, and the location, just off
the main drag, can't be beaten.

Arafat Hotel HOTEL **$**
(☑333 8355; Sharia Arafat, Port Tawfiq; r E£30,
without bathroom E£25) Seriously down on
your luck? Love a bit of bawdy port action?
Then the Arafat could be the place to crash
for a night. Single female travellers should
probably look elsewhere.

✗ Eating

For inexpensive favourites like ta'amiyya
(mashed, deep-fried fava beans; Egyptian
variant of felafel) and shwarma, take a
wander around the Sharia Talaat Harb
area.

Al-Khalifa Fish Centre SEAFOOD **$$**
(Midan Nesima; mains E£20-50) Tucked away
on the edge of Midan Nesima in the congested town centre, this no-frills place sells
the day's ocean catch by weight; you can
pick out your fish, then wait for it to be
grilled.

Koshary Palace EGYPTIAN FAST FOOD **$**
(Sharia al-Geish; meals E£3-5) Clean and friendly, with lots of local flavour and good *kushari* in your choice of sizes.

❶ Information

Banque Misr (Sharia al-Geish) Has an ATM.
CACE (Sharia al-Geish; per hr E£4; ☺9am-8pm) Internet access.
General Hospital (☏333 1190; Sharia al-Baladiya)
Main post office (Sharia Hoda Shaarawi)
Union National Bank (Sharia al-Geish) Has an ATM.

❶ Getting There & Away

BUS The bus station is 5km out of town along the road to Cairo.
East Delta Travel Co (☏356 4853) Has buses to Cairo (E£15 to E£20, two hours) every 30 minutes from 6am to 9pm. Buses to Sharm el-Sheikh (E£35 to E£40, six hours) depart at 8.30am, 11am, 1.30pm, 3pm, 4.30pm, 5.15pm and 6pm. Most stop in Al-Tor (E£25 to E£30, 4½ hours) and the 11am service goes on to Dahab (E£40, seven hours). There is one bus daily at 2pm to St Katherine Protectorate (E£25, four hours). Buses to Taba and Nuweiba (both E£45 to E£50) leave at 3pm and 5pm. Buses to Ismailia (E£6, 1½ hours) depart every half-hour from 6am to 4pm. Departures to Port Said (E£14, 2½ hours) are at 7am, 9am, 11am, 12.15pm and 3.30pm.

Upper Egypt Bus Co (☏356 4258) Buses to Hurghada (E£35 to E£40, four hours) leave almost hourly between 5am and 11pm. There are buses to Luxor (E£60 to E£70, nine to 10 hours) via Qena (E£45 to E£50, five to six hours) at 8am, 2pm and 8pm.

SERVEES The *servees* station is beside the bus station and prices are similar to the buses. The only place in the Sinai they serve is Al-Tor (E£15).

TRAIN Six uncomfortable 2nd-class Cairo-bound trains depart Suez daily (E£15 to E£18, three hours) going only as far as Ain Shams, 10km northeast of central Cairo; the first Cairo-bound train leaves at 5.30am. There are also eight slow trains to Ismailia.

❶ Getting Around

MICROBUS There are regular microbus services along Sharia al-Geish to Port Tawfiq. They will pick up or drop off anywhere along the route and cost 50pt.

TAXI Taxis (painted blue) are easy to find almost everywhere. Expect to pay E£10 between the bus station and town, E£15 between the bus station and Port Tawfiq, and E£5 between Suez and Port Tawfiq.

SUEZ CANAL SUEZ

Red Sea Coast

Includes »

Best Places to Eat

» Kastan (p375)

» Shade Bar & Grill (p375)

» Restaurant Marianne (p381)

» Dolce & Salato (p383)

Best Places to Stay

» Wadi Lahami Village (p382)

» Al-Quseir Hotel (p381)

» Oberoi Sahl Hasheesh (p375)

» 4 Seasons Hotel (p373)

Why Go?

Egypt's Red Sea coast has never loomed large on any independent traveller's itinerary, yet some of the most important sites in Christianity's early evolution lay tucked away amid the barren mountains of the north. Venture south of brashly loud and proud Hurghada and you'll not only find some of Egypt's best diving but also the epically wild expanse of the Eastern Desert. Criss-crossed by trade routes dating back to the far reaches of prehistory, and scattered with ancient rock art and lonely ruins, this little visited area is a desert adventurer's dream.

Back on the 'Red Sea Riviera', famous (or infamous, depending on your view) for being a bargain bonanza of cheap package holidays, overdevelopment has pockmarked the coastline deeply, leaving a trail of mega-resorts and half-finished hotels in its wake. Dig a little deeper into this region though, and the Red Sea may just surprise you.

When to Go
Hurghada

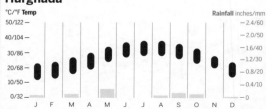

Feb A good time to bargain hunt as generally produces the cheapest resort deals.

Mar–Apr While temperatures stay mild dust off your explorer hat and head to the Eastern Desert.

Sep Migratory birds arrive en masse in the deep south.

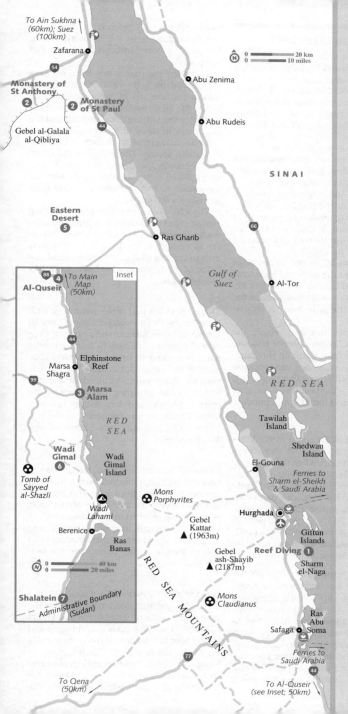

Red Sea Highlights

1 Make a diving date with the **world class reefs** off Hurghada and discover why the Red Sea was catapulted onto the tourism stage in the first place.

2 Reflect on monasticism's centuries-old roots at **St Anthony's** and **St Paul's**.

3 Plunge into the lesser-known kaleidoscope-hued **reefs of the deep south** from one of the beach camps around Marsa Alam.

4 Wander the **old town of Al-Quseir**, where the streets are imbued with an evocative yesteryear haze.

5 Trek through wadis, mountains and endless expanses of sand in the **Eastern Desert**.

6 Explore remnants of Rome's mighty emerald mines from **Wadi Gimal**.

7 Head to **Shalatein's camel market** and village souq, with its ramshackle frontier vibe and meld of cultures coming to sell, haggle and buy.

Red Sea Monasteries

The Coptic monasteries of St Anthony and St Paul are Egypt's and Christianity's oldest monasteries, and are among the holiest sites in the Coptic faith. In fact, the establishment of the religious community of St Anthony's, hidden in the barren cliffs of the Eastern Desert, marks the beginning of the Christian monastic tradition.

If you're at all interested in Egypt's lengthy Christian history, both monasteries make for fascinating and inspiring visits, and the surrounding desert scenery is simply breathtaking. And, depending on where you're coming from, the Red Sea monasteries are a refreshing change of scene from the hassles and noise of Cairo and the Nile Valley, or the package tourism and rampant commercialism of the coastline.

The two monasteries are only about 25km apart but thanks to the cliffs and plateau of Gebel al-Galala al-Qibliya (which lies between 900m and 1300m above sea level), the distance between them by road is around 85km.

If you don't have your own vehicle, the easiest way to visit the monasteries is to join an organised tour from Cairo or Hurghada (any hotel or travel agency can organise these). It's also possible to join a pilgrimage group from Cairo – the best way to arrange this is by enquiring at local Coptic churches.

⊙ Sights

Both St Paul's and St Anthony's monasteries are open daily throughout the year except during Advent and Lent, when they can only be visited on Friday, Saturday and Sunday. During Holy Week they are closed completely to visitors. For enquiries or to confirm visiting times, contact the monasteries' headquarters: **St Paul's** (☑02-2590 0218; 26 Al-Keneesa al-Morcosia) or **St Anthony's** (☑02-2590 6025; 26 Al-Keneesa al-Morcosia), located off Clot Bey, south of Midan Ramses in Cairo.

Monastery of St Anthony   MONASTERY
(admission free, donation appreciated for guided tour; ⊙4am to 5pm) This historic monastery traces its origins to the 4th century AD when monks began to settle at the foot of Gebel al-Galala al-Qibliya, where their spiritual leader, Anthony (see boxed text p368), lived. Over the next few centuries, the community moved from being a loosely organised grouping of hermits to a somewhat more communal existence in which the monks continued to live anchoritic lives, but in cells grouped together inside a walled compound.

Today the monastery is a large complex surrounded by high walls (it's possible to walk along the top of some sections and to see the large basket and wooden winch that were the only means of getting into the monastery in times of attack), with several churches and chapels, a bakery, a lush garden and a spring. The source of the latter, deep beneath the desert mountains, produces 100 cu metres of water daily, allowing the monks to cultivate olive and date trees as well as a few crops.

The 120 monks who live here, following centuries-old traditions and the examples set by St Anthony, St Paul and their followers 16 centuries ago, have dedicated their lives to seeking God in the stillness and isolation of the desert, in a life built completely around prayer.

Church of St Anthony

This is the oldest part of the monastery, built over the saint's tomb and containing one of Egypt's most significant collections of Coptic wall paintings. Painted in secco (whereby paint is applied to dry plaster), most date back to the early 13th century, with a few possibly much older. Stripped of the dirt and grime of centuries, the paintings are clear and bright, and demonstrate how medieval Coptic art was connected to the arts of the wider Byzantine and Islamic eastern Mediterranean.

Citadel

In the 8th and 9th centuries, the monastery suffered Bedouin raids, followed in the 11th century by attacks from irate Muslims and, in the 15th century, a revolt by bloodthirsty servants that resulted in the massacre of the monks. The small mud-brick citadel into which they would retreat during attacks can still be seen, although visitors are not usually admitted.

Cave of St Anthony

Perched about 300m – 1158 wooden steps – above the monastery on a nearby cliff is the cave where Anthony spent the final 40 years of his life. The climb up is hot and steep and takes about half an hour if you're reasonably fit. At the top is a small clearing (now littered with the graffiti of countless pilgrims) with wide vistas over the hills and valley below. In the cave itself, which is for the svelte

COPTIC ART 101

Before you set foot into the Coptic monasteries of the Eastern Desert, here is a quick introduction to the history and tradition of Egyptian Coptic art.

Coptic art refers to the distinct Christian art of Egypt. Although it originated from the ancient Egyptian and Greek heritages, it has also been influenced by the Persians, Byzantines and Syrians. In fact, due to its myriad influences, the exact nature of Coptic art can be difficult to define, though it is fortunately easy to identify. Since early Christian artisans were extremely utilitarian in their aims, Coptic art typically manifests itself in daily items such as textiles and religious illustrations. Furthermore, Coptic art has a strong tradition of painting, particularly portraits and wall paintings.

Textiles

The Coptic Church inherited a strong tradition of textile-making from the ancient Egyptians, particularly loom and tapestry weaving. For the most part, Coptic textiles are made from linen, though there is some evidence of sophisticated silk-weaving. In regards to design, Coptic textiles borrow heavily from Greek-Egyptian themes, and include traditional pattern motifs such as cupids, dancing maidens and animals. However, these are typically incorporated with specific Christian motifs such as fish, grapes and biblical scenes, especially the Immaculate Conception.

Religious Illustrations

Religious illustration originated in ancient Egypt when pharaohs started adorning papyrus texts with liturgies and prayers. Coptic Christians retained this tradition, and early papyrus texts maintained the original Egyptian design of protective illustrations surrounded by elaborate borders and text. Like the Egyptians, Coptic artisans used bright colours for vignettes, and striking black ink for all texts. Later on, however, Coptic illustrations began to take on greater complexity as they started to incorporate religious imagery, landscapes and intricate geometric designs.

Portraits

In comparison to other early Christian movements, the Coptic Church is unique in regard to their abundance of martyrs, saints and ascetics. Since the actions and deeds of these individuals helped to form the foundation of the church, their images were immortalised in portraits, and hung in every chapel and church throughout the land. In these paintings, the human figure is usually depicted in the front position, with placid, almond-shaped eyes and idealised expressions. Coptic portraits of Jesus Christ are unique in that they usually depict him enthroned by saints and angels as opposed to suffering on the cross.

Wall Paintings

Early Coptic wall paintings were unsophisticated in comparison to later endeavours, primarily because ancient Egyptian temples were being converted into churches. In order to complete the transformation, Pharaonic reliefs were covered with layers of plaster, and Christian themes were painted on top. However, as Coptic art developed and prospered, wall painting became increasingly complex, particularly following the mastery of dye mixing and gold stencilling. Some of the finest Coptic wall paintings depict spiritual scenes that are awash with vibrant colours and accented with gold.

Coptic Art Today

Long overshadowed by both ancient Egyptian and Islamic themes, Coptic art does not receive much attention in Egypt despite its lengthy history and established tradition. Fortunately, this cultural heritage has been preserved in museums, churches and monasteries throughout Egypt and the world, and the artistic traditions continue to flourish among communities of modern-day Coptics.

and nonclaustrophobic only (you need to squeeze through a narrow tunnel to get inside), there is a small chapel with an altar as well as a tiny recessed area where Anthony lived – bring a torch (flashlight) along to illuminate the interior.

Monastery of St Paul MONASTERY
(admission free, donation appreciated for guided tour; ☺6am-6pm) Dating to the 4th century, the Monastery of St Paul began as a grouping of hermitages in the cliffs of Gebel al-Galala al-Qibliya around the site where St Paul had his hermitage. Paul, who was born into a wealthy family in Alexandria in the mid-3rd century, originally fled to the Eastern Desert to escape Roman persecution. He lived alone in a cave here for over 90 years, finding bodily sustenance in a nearby spring and palm tree. According to tradition, in AD 343 the then 90-year-old St Anthony had a vision of Paul. After making a difficult trek through the mountains to visit him, Paul died, and was buried by Anthony's hands.

The heart of the monastery complex is the **Church of St Paul**, which was built in and around the cave where Paul lived. It's cluttered with altars, candles, ostrich eggs (the symbol of the Resurrection) and murals representing saints and biblical stories. The **fortress** above the church was where the monks retreated during Bedouin raids.

St Paul's monastery is quieter and much more low-key than St Anthony's, and is often bypassed in favour of its larger neighbour. But a visit is well worthwhile, and gives a glimpse into the life of silence, prayer and asceticism that has flowered here in the Eastern Desert for almost two millennia. Visitors are welcome and can wander freely around the monastery but taking a guided tour with an English-speaking monk will allow you to access many of the locked areas.

🏃 Activities

Monastery Trail HIKING
It is possible to hike between the two monasteries along a 30km trail (approximately) across the top of the plateau, taking one to two days to do so. However, hiking this rugged area, commonly known as 'Devil's Country', is only for the fit and experienced and should under no circumstances be attempted without a local guide. In 2001, a lone tourist attempting the walk died of thirst after losing his way. Those who have made the hike recommend starting from St Paul's.

🛏 Sleeping & Eating

There is no official accommodation for the general public at either monastery, although male pilgrims are allowed to spend the night in a dormitory at the Monastery of St Anthony with written consent from

THE FATHER OF MONASTICISM

Although St Paul is honoured as the earliest Christian hermit, it is St Anthony who is considered to be the Father of Monasticism. Anthony was born around AD 251, the son of a provincial landowner from a small Upper Egyptian town near Beni Suef. Orphaned with his sister at the age of 18, he was already more interested in the spiritual than the temporal, and soon gave away his share of the inheritance to the poor. After studying with a local holy man, Anthony went into the Eastern Desert, living in a cave and seeking solitude and spiritual salvation. Word of his holiness soon spread and flocks of disciples arrived, seeking to imitate his ascetic existence.

After a brief spell in Alexandria ministering to Christians imprisoned under Emperor Maximinus Daia in the early 4th century, Anthony returned to the desert. Once again, he was pursued by eager followers, though he managed to flee even further into the desert in search of solitude. After establishing himself in a cave on a remote mountain, his disciples formed a loose community at its base and thus was born the first Christian monastery.

The number of Anthony's followers grew rapidly, and within decades of his death, nearly every town in Egypt was surrounded by hermitages. Soon after, the whole Byzantine Empire was alive with monastic fervour, which by the next century had spread throughout Italy and France.

It is ironic that, for all his influence, Anthony spent his life seeking to escape others. When he died at the advanced age of 105, his sole wish for solitude was finally respected and the location of his grave became a closely guarded secret.

the monastery's Cairo headquarters. Since this is a major destination for Coptic Christians on religious pilgrimages, guests are expected to attend prayer sessions, respect the atmosphere of the grounds and leave a donation at the time of departure.

Both monasteries have canteens that sell snacks, drinks and simple meals.

Sahara Inn Motel   MOTEL **$$**
(s/d from E£140/165; ❋) If you haven't made reservations in advance, or your double X-chromosome prevents you from bedding down in the monastery, consider spending the night in the nearby junction town of Zafarana. Here you'll find the Sahara Inn Motel, which offers up some bare-bones concrete cubicles and a basic roadside restaurant.

ℹ Getting There & Away

Zafarana is located 62km south of Ain Sukhna and 150km east of Beni Suef on the Nile. Buses running between Cairo or Suez and Hurghada will drop you at Zafarana, but direct access to the monasteries is limited to private vehicles and tour buses from Cairo or Hurghada.

To get to St Anthony's, start from the main Zafarana junction and follow the road west towards Beni Suef for 37km where you'll reach the monastery turn-off. From here, it's 17km further south along a good road through the desert to St Anthony's.

The turn-off for St Paul's is about 27km south of the Zafarana lighthouse along the road to Hurghada (watch for a small signpost). Once at the turn-off, it's then 10km further along a good tarmac road to the main gate of the monastery, and about 3km further to the monastery itself.

Buses running between Suez and Hurghada will drop you along the main road at the turn-off, from where the only options are walking or hitching. If you do decide to hike in from the main road (which isn't the best idea), don't go alone, and be sure you're properly equipped, especially with water, as it's a long, hot, dry and isolated stretch.

El-Gouna

✆065 / POP 10,000
The brainchild of Egyptian multibillionaire Onsi Sawiris, El-Gouna was largely built from the ground up during the 1990s. Today, this self-contained resort town is largely frequented by Egypt's rich and famous, and increasingly by Westerners on package tours. Boasting more than a dozen hotels, several golf courses, countless shopping malls and the odd casino, El-Gouna serves up heaps of family fun, albeit of the homogenised,

vacation-community variety. But if you're looking for a place to laze on a beach, cushioned from the chaos of Egyptian life, you'll most definitely enjoy your time here.

Most of the action in El-Gouna takes place within the resorts and there is little reason to leave if you're on an all-inclusive package. Of course, if you do feel the need to venture out, you can take one of the shuttle buses that connect the various hotels to the central 'downtown' area, where you'll find a cluster of banks, several dive centres, supermarkets, shops and restaurants.

🏃 Activities

El-Gouna is a veritable paradise for water sports. The various activity centres inside the resorts offer a laundry list of activities including sailing, ocean kayaking, boogieboarding, parasailing, jet-skiing, windsurfing, kitesurfing, water-skiing and many, many others. Offshore, you'll find a good number of snorkelling and diving sites. For an overview of diving in the Red Sea see p36, where you'll find a rundown of some of the best dive sites in the area, in the Hurghada section.

🛏 Sleeping

Unlike Hurghada, its brasher and less refined neighbour to the south, El-Gouna is solely an upmarket destination. Although you will have to pay to play, splurging on a resort hotel will ensure a memorable vacation, especially if the kiddies are in tow.

Be advised that advanced reservations are necessary and all-inclusive packages are the norm. Booking through a travel agent or online can score you great deals and as such, rates given here should only be taken as guides.

Also check out www.elgouna.com for more accommodation listings.

Mövenpick   RESORT **$$$**
(✆354 4501; www.moevenpick-hotels.com; El-Gouna; s/d half board from US$120/150; ❋@≋) All streamlined decor in soothing neutrals and white, Mövenpick offers all of the luxury amenities you'd expect in this price bracket. Drawing its inspiration from a desert oasis, the manicured grounds are lined with soaring palm trees, which shed ample shade on the swimming pools and lagoons.

Sheraton Miramar   RESORT **$$$**
(✆354 5845; www.starwoodhotels.com/sheraton; El-Gouna; s/d from €120/135; ❋@≋) A five-star,

pastel-coloured, postmodern desert fantasy, the Sheraton was designed by well-known architect Michael Graves, and is one of the signature properties of El-Gouna. The entire complex is strung along a series of beach-fringed private islands, which seek to maximise intimacy despite being a large resort hotel.

Dawar el-Omda　　　　　RESORT $$

(📞358 0063; www.dawarelomda-elgouna.com; Kafr El-Gouna; s/d from €50/66; ❄❅) In the heart of downtown El-Gouna, this tastefully decorated four-star eschews European design in favour of classic Egyptian lines and arches and has cosy, well-appointed rooms and a convenient lagoon-side location. There's no beach but shuttles are at the ready to whisk you away to the sands.

ⓘ Getting There & Away

Air

Several domestic charter companies serve El-Gouna, though most international flights touch down in Hurghada, about 20km south along the main coastal highway. For the vast majority of package travellers, flight arrangements are booked in conjunction with hotel packages.

Bus

El-Gouna Transport buses travel three times daily between the Hilton Ramses in Cairo, El-Gouna and Hurghada (E£85 to E£95, five hours), best booked a day in advance. The ticket office and bus stop in El-Gouna is on the main plaza downtown, opposite the tourist information centre.

Taxi

Taxis run frequently between El-Gouna and Hurghada, with fares ranging from E£60 to E£75, depending on your destination.

ⓘ Getting Around

The El-Gouna sprawl is readily accessible by a fairly comprehensive network of local buses – a daily bus pass will only cost you E£5. *Tuk-tuks* also scan the streets for potential fares; prices for these are highly variable, around E£3 to E£10.

Hurghada

📞065 / POP 160,900

Plucked from obscurity and thrust into the limelight during the early days of the Red Sea's tourism drive, the tiny fishing village of Hurghada has long since morphed into today's dense band of concrete which marches relentlessly along the coastline for

Hurghada Coast

over 20km. Rampant construction has left the town blighted by half-finished shells of pleasure palaces that were never to be. The coral reefs closest to the shore – which put Hurghada on the international hot-spot map originally – have been degraded by

Hurghada Coast

illegal landfill operations and irresponsible reef use. In recent years Hurghada's star has largely lost its lustre with many travellers migrating to the newer, glossier resorts of El-Gouna and Sharm el-Sheikh (p395).

There is hope on the horizon though. Further offshore there is still superb diving aplenty and local NGOs are now playing a leading role in getting the town to clean up its act while new construction projects are attempting to bring back some of Hurghada's resort sheen. If you want to combine a diving holiday with the Nile Valley sites, Hurghada is a convenient destination. However, independent travellers might prefer to press on to Dahab in Sinai (p405).

Sights

Hurghada is split into three main areas. To the north is Ad-Dahar, the most 'Egyptian' part of the city, with lively backstreet neighbourhoods and a bustling souq. Separated from Ad-Dahar by a sandy mountain called Gebel al-Afish is the fast-growing and congested Sigala area, where resort hotels jostle for sea frontage. South of Sigala, lining the coastal road, is the resort strip. Here you'll find an increasingly lengthening row of mostly upmarket resorts, Western-style shopping malls and half-finished shells of hotels.

Although many of Hurghada's beaches are bare and stark, developers have snapped up almost every available spot. Apart from the not-so-appealing **public beach** (Map

p376; Sigala; admission E£2; ⊙8am-sunset), the main option for enjoying sand and sea is to go to one of the resorts, most of which charge nonguests between E£25 and E£75 for beach access.

Aquarium AQUARIUM
(Map p374; ☑354 8557; Corniche, Ad-Dahar; admission E£5; ⊙9am-10pm) If you don't want to put your head under the water in the ocean, the aquarium, just north of the public hospital, has a reasonable, if somewhat neglected, selection of fish and other marine creatures.

Activities
Snorkelling & Diving

In recent years, the reefs close to Hurghada and El-Gouna have suffered heavy damage due to unfettered tourism development. Thanks to tireless campaigns by local NGOs, conservation measures have now been implemented and the situation around both towns is beginning to improve. However, most experienced divers head to sites further afield and the only way to see them is to join a snorkelling or diving boat excursion. For all excursions, shop around a bit. Relying on your hotel may not be the best way to do things as travellers often complain about not getting everything they expected. For any boat trip, take your passport as you'll need to show it at the port.

The following are just a small selection of some of the most popular dive sites in the Hurghada area listed from north to south. All of the sites listed here are only accessible by boat. For an overview of diving in the Red Sea see p36.

Siyul Kebira DIVING
(Map p38; Southern Straits of Gubal) While the reef's upper section is home to bannerfish, angelfish and snappers, if the current is strong you can drift along the wall skirting the edges of huge coral outcroppings. Depth: 10m to 30m; rating: intermediate.

Sha'ab al-Erg DIVING
(Map p38; off El-Gouna) Ease of access means this is an excellent dive site for beginners, though veteran divers will still enjoy the towering brain corals and fan-encrusted rock formations. Depth: 5m to 15m; rating: novice.

Umm Qamar DIVING
(Map p38; 9km north of the Giftun Islands) Umm Qamar is highlighted by three coral towers that are swathed in beautiful purple, soft

coral and surrounded by glassfish. Depth: 10m to 27m; rating: intermediate.

Giftun Islands
DIVING

(Map p38; off Hurghada) These islands are surrounded by a number of spectacular reefs teeming with marine life, including Hamda, Banana Reef, Sha'ab Sabrina, Erg Somaya and Sha'ab Torfa. Depth: 5m to 30m; rating: intermediate.

Gota Abu Ramada
DIVING

(Map p38; 5km south of the Giftun Islands) A mind-boggling abundance of marine life is on display here making Gota Abu Ramada a popular spot for underwater photographers, snorkellers and night divers. Depth: 3m to 15m; rating: novice.

DIVE OPERATORS

 Jasmin Diving Centre
DIVING

(Map p370; ☑346 0334; www.jasmin-diving. com; Grand Seas Resort Hostmark, resort strip, Hurghada) This centre has an excellent reputation and was a founding member of HEPCA (see p372).

Subex
DIVING

(Map p374; ☑354 7593; www.subex.org; Ad-Dahar) A branch of the well-known Swiss outfit.

Emperor Divers
DIVING

(Map p370; ☑0122 234 0995; www.emperordivers. com; Hilton Plaza Hotel, resort strip, Hurghada) A highly reputable dive centre.

Easy Divers
DIVING

(Map p374; ☑0122 230 5202; www.easydivers-redsea.com; Triton Beach Resort, Corniche, Ad-Dahar) This British-managed club has a long history of first-class service.

Aquanaut Blue Heaven
DIVING

(Map p376; ☑344 0892; www.aquanaut.net; Royal Regina Resort, off Sharia Sheraton, Sigala) Long-standing Hurghada dive centre.

Submarine Rides

Sindbad Submarine
TOUR

(Map p370; ☑344 4688; www.sindbad-group.com; Sindbad Beach Resort, resort strip, Hurghada; adult/child US$50/25) This is one way to plumb the depths of the Red Sea while staying dry. The submarine takes up to 46 people to a depth of 22m. Bookings can be made at any hotel or travel agency.

☞ Tours

Tours to almost anywhere in Egypt can be organised from Hurghada. The most popular option is a desert jeep safari (from

---

RESCUING THE RED SEA

Conservationists estimate that more than 1000 pleasure boats and almost as many fishing boats ply the waters between Hurghada and the many reefs situated within an hour of the town. Fifteen years ago, there was nothing to stop captains from anchoring to the coral, or snorkellers and divers breaking off a colourful chunk to take home. However, due largely to the efforts of the Hurghada Environmental Protection & Conservation Association (HEPCA) and the Egyptian National Parks Office in Hurghada, the Red Sea's reefs are at last being protected.

Set up in 1992 by 12 of the town's larger, more reputable dive companies, HEPCA's program to conserve the Red Sea's reefs includes public-awareness campaigns, direct community action and lobbying of the Egyptian government to introduce appropriate laws. Thanks to these efforts, the whole coast south of Suez Governorate is now known as the Red Sea Protectorate. One of their earliest successes was to establish a system of over 570 mooring buoys at popular dive sites in the region to prevent boat captains dropping anchor on the coral.

While continuing in their efforts to ensure the Red Sea's diving sites are protected, in recent years HEPCA has branched out into even more ambitious conservation projects. In 2009 the NGO took over responsibility for waste management in the southern Red Sea, a service which had been sporadic and unregulated until then. Now Marsa Alam and its environs have a regular door-to-door rubbish collection service and a recycling plant. The service has been judged such a success that in 2010 it was expanded to include Hurghada as well and is seen as a model for solid waste management in Egypt.

For more information on safe diving practices or about how you can help **HEPCA** (Map p376; ☑344 6674; www.hepca.com; off Corniche, Sigala) in its efforts to protect the Red Sea, check the organisation's website or call in between 9am and 5pm Saturday to Thursday.

E£200), which usually includes visits to either Mons Porphyrites (p384) or Mons Claudianus (p384). Other possibilities include a full-day excursion to the monasteries of St Paul and St Anthony (p366), camel treks and sunset desert excursions.

To arrange any of these tours, enquire at either your hotel or a travel agency in town – there are dozens and dozens, so you shouldn't have a problem finding one. Note that a minimum number of people are needed for most trips, so it's best to enquire several days in advance.

🛏 Sleeping

Hurghada has the greatest selection of accommodation outside Cairo, though virtually everything in town is midrange to top-end resorts. Travel agencies in Europe and the UK can offer significant reductions if you book in advance, especially since prices fluctuate according to the season and state of the tourism industry. If you haven't booked a package deal in advance, you can still show up and request a room, though accommodation can get expensive. Fortunately, supply outstrips demand, so there is always room for negotiation – be patient and shop around.

Accommodation in Hurghada is split into three principal areas: Ad-Dahar, Sigala and the resort strip. Most budget accommodation is located within Ad-Dahar not far from the sea, though the water is rarely within sight. Sigala is a convenient base but it is extremely congested and noisy, while the resort strip, which extends south of Hurghada along the coast, is home to the majority of the city's four- and five-star resorts.

AD-DAHAR

TOP CHOICE **4 Seasons Hotel** HOSTEL $
(Map p374; ☎0122 704 3917; fourseasonshurghada@hotmail.com; off Sharia Sayyed al-Qorayem; s/d E£60/80; ❄) This should be every budgeteer's first port of call in Hurghada. Manager Mohammed runs a real old-school style hostel with bags of character. Hang out in the cheerfully decorated common area to meet other travellers and find Mohammad, who is always on hand to dish out advice and help. The rooms, though nothing special, are clean and great value. Guests can pay E£20 for beach day use at the nearby Sandbeach Hotel.

Luxor Hotel HOTEL $$
(Map p374; ☎354 2877; www.luxorhotel-eg.com; off Sharia Sayyed al-Qorayem; s/d €20/30; ❄🛜) Some of the rooms may be on the small side and the furnishings are a bit bland but the Luxor is still a solid midrange choice. Management are eager to help, there's a pleasant terrace and it's surprisingly quiet for the central location.

El-Arosa Hotel HOTEL $$
(Map p374; ☎354 8434; elarosahotel@yahoo.com; off Corniche; s/d E£125/180; ❄❄) El-Arosa overlooks the sea in the distance from the inland side of the Corniche. Few of the cosy rooms actually have ocean views but they boast decent amenities and there's even a pool (albeit located in the dining room).

Geisum Village RESORT $$
(Map p374; ☎354 6692; Corniche; s/d E£180/300; ❄@❄) The gloomy, peeling-paint corridors don't inspire confidence but the rooms (decked out in a cream and green combo) are surprisingly tidy and bright. The centre of the action here is the large swimming pool surrounded by a grassy lawn, and you can always take a dip in the ocean or lie on the beach (er, spot of sand).

Happy Land HOTEL $
(Map p374; ☎354 7373; Sharia Sheikh Sabak; s/d from E£45/75) The name is a bit optimistic given the indifferent management, however the Happy Land's dingy and noisy rooms will suffice if the 4 Seasons is full.

SIGALA
Bella Vista Resort RESORT $$
(Map p376; ☎344 6012; www.bellavista-hurghada.com; Sharia Sheraton; s/d €55/70; ❄@❄) This large midrange option may be a little dated but pleasant management, well-cared for grounds and a wee patch of private beach more than make up for it. The rooms here are well-cared for, light, airy and decorated in soothing neutrals.

White Albatross HOTEL $$
(Map p376; ☎344 2519; walbatros53@hotmail.com; Sharia Sheraton; s/d/tr US$25/30/35; ❄) Well-run, with spick-and-span comfortable rooms complete with small homely touches, the White Albatross is a good choice if you want to be slap in the centre of the Sigala action. There's no beach access but you can drop into any of the nearby resorts for a small fee.

Roma HOTEL $$
(Map p376; ☎344 8141; www.minasegypt.com; Sharia Al-Hadaba; s/d/tr from US$37/47/52; ❄❄) The Roma is functional rather than fun; this business-style hotel has a glitzy

Ad-Dahar

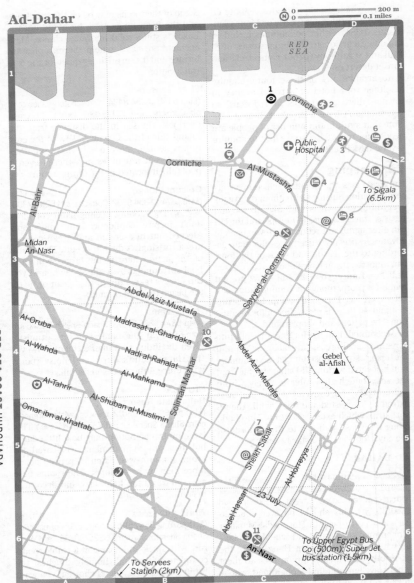

RED SEA

Corniche

1

2

Corniche

12

Public Hospital

3

6

Al-Mustashfa

5

4

To Sigala (6.5km)

Midan An-Nasr

@

8

9

Sayyed al-Qorayem

Abdel Aziz Mustafa

Madrasat al-Ghardaka

Abdel Aziz Mustafa

Gebel al-Afish

Nadi al-Rahalat

Al-Mahkama

Al-Tahrir

Al-Shuban al-Muslimin

Soliman Mazhar

Omar ibn al-Khattab

Al-Oruba

Al-Wahda

Al-Bahr

7

Sheikh Sabak

@

Al-Hofreyya

23 July

11

An-Nasr

To Upper Egypt Bus Co (500m); Super Jet bus station (1.5km)

To Servees Station (2km)

lobby that promises much more than the simple rooms deliver, but for these prices we can't really complain. The hotel's swimming pool and private beach are extra bonuses.

Sea Garden   HOTEL $$
(Map p376; ☎344 7493; www.seagarden.com.eg; off Sharia Sheraton; s/d/tr US$55/70/90; ❄@☀) This high-rise block is tucked down a quiet side street and is a discernible step up in quality from budget options. You can expect

Ad-Dahar

◎ Sights

1 Aquarium C1

✪ Activities, Courses & Tours

2 Easy Divers D1
3 Subex.. D2

◻ Sleeping

4 4 Seasons Hotel D2
5 El-Arosa Hotel D2
6 Geisum Village............................ D2
7 Happy Land C5
8 Luxor Hotel D3

✗ Eating

9 Chez Pascal C3
10 El-Taybeen B4
11 Red Sea I C6

◎ Drinking

12 Memories C2

---

well-cared-for rooms and a reasonably professional level of service.

Le Pacha Resort   RESORT $$
(Map p376; ☏344 4150; www.lepacharesort.com; Sharia Sheraton; s/d incl all meals from US$75/115; ❄@☰) If you're looking for a comparatively cheap all-inclusive, this long-standing relic offers a wide range of amenities including private beach and is right in the heart of the Sigala hustle.

RESORT STRIP

TOP CHOICE **Oberoi Sahl Hasheesh**   RESORT $$$
(☏344 0777; www.oberoihotels.com; Sahl Hasheesh; ste from €200; ❄@☰) Peaceful, exclusive and opulent beyond your imagination, the Oberoi features palatial suites decorated in minimalist Moorish style. Each individually decorated accommodation comes complete with sunken marble baths, walled private courtyards – some with private pools – and panoramic sea views. Justifiably advertised as the most luxurious destination on the Red Sea, the Oberoi is world-class, and guests here are pampered to their hearts' content.

Kempinski Soma Bay   RESORT $$$
(☏356 1500; www.kempinski.com/somabay; Soma Bay; s/d from €135/165; ❄@☰) Kempinski don't do understated and this massive complex is no exception. From the palatial arabesque lobby to the immense beach and huge pool area, this is luxury firing on all five cylinders.

Hurghada Marriott
Beach Resort   RESORT $$
(Map p370; ☏344 6950; www.marriott.com; resort strip; s/d US$95/105; ❄@☰) Within walking distance of the resort strip's nightlife and restaurants, the well-kept rooms here exude a modern, beachy feel. Some may be disappointed by the small beach area, but if you want the freedom to pick and choose where to eat it's a good choice.

Dana Beach Resort   RESORT $$
(Map p370; ☏346 0401; www.pickalbatros.com; resort strip; s/d full board €60/80; ❄@☰) This megaresort serves up masses of amenities at cheap prices making it a winner for families on a budget. If you're just here for the beach, and don't mind business-style bland rooms, this is a decent choice.

Jasmine Village   RESORT $$$
(Map p370; ☏346 0460; www.jasminevillage.com; resort strip; s/d full board E£640/800; ❄@☰) A great beach with a stunning coral reef is what keeps the punters coming to this old stalwart of the Hurghada scene. Be aware though that this is an aging resort and your chalet comes complete with a bit of wear and tear.

✗ Eating

With its diverse expat population and large pool of tourists, Hurghada has a good variety of restaurants. If you're travelling on a budget, Ad-Dahar and Sigala have dozens of inexpensive local-style restaurants while the resort strip eating scene tends to be dominated by the hotels with restaurants open to hotel guests and nonguests alike.

Kastan   SEAFOOD $$
(Map p376; inside Arena Mall, Sharia Sheraton, Sigala; meals E£40-100) For affordable, fresh seafood with an Egyptian twist Kastan is one of Hurghada's top choices. We love their hearty and filling seafood soup and cheap shrimp curry. It may not have the slick location of the restaurants along New Marina Rd but the quality and service here make it stick out from the crowd.

Shade Bar & Grill   INTERNATIONAL $$$
(Map p376; Marina Rd; Sigala; mains E£50-95) If you're pining for a steak look no further. Sprawl out on the terrace beanbags and order your red meat fix. For those too lazy to bar-hop, Shade conveniently turns into a popular bar late at night.

Sigala

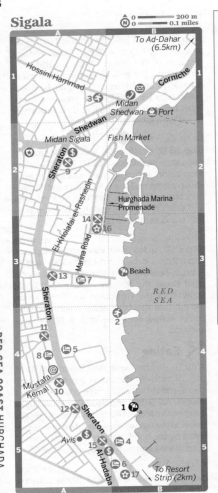

To Ad-Dahar (6.5km)

Hurghada Marina Promenade

RED SEA

To Resort Strip (2km)

or a snack of *baba ghanoog* (eggplant dip) Al-Araby is a decent bet.

Abu Khadigah   EGYPTIAN $
(Map p376; Sharia Sheraton, Sigala; meals E£10-20) This no-frills place is known for its *kofta* (mincemeat and spices grilled on a skewer), stuffed cabbage leaves and other Egyptian staples.

La Casa del Mar   EUROPEAN $$$
(Map p376; just off Sharia Sheraton, Sigala; meals E£70-100) Whether tucking into Swedish meatballs or a steak, this casual dining spot, just off the main drag, hits all the right buttons if you're craving European cuisine.

Tokyo Joe's   ASIAN $$$
(Map p376; Sharia al-Hadaba, Sigala; meals E£60-150) Great sushi deals and curry nights make this American diner-style restaurant a top choice for anyone craving Japanese or Thai-inspired dining.

Chez Pascal   INTERNATIONAL $$$
(Map p374; Sharia Sayyed al-Qorayem, Ad-Dahar; mains E£65-150; ✿) A charming European-style bistro that's a good spot for eclectic cuisine served amid bright and clean surroundings.

Red Sea I   SEAFOOD $$
(Map p374; ☎354 9630; off Sharia an-Nasr, Ad-Dahar; mains E£30-70; ✿) Slap in the souq, Red Sea I has a wide selection of seafood, plus Egyptian and international dishes, all at decent prices. Choose from fairy-light-strewn rooftop seating or pavement dining, for those who want to people-watch.

Al-Araby   EGYPTIAN $$
(Map p376; Sharia Sheraton, Sigala; mains E£25-50) This popular place, with street-side seating in the heart of downtown, serves up a satisfying menu of Egyptian classics. If you're hankering for *shish tawooq* (grilled chicken)

El Taybeen
GRILL $$

(Map p374; Sharia Soliman Mazhar, Ad-Dahar; meals E£30-50; ✦) All the usual kebab favourites are dished up at this no-nonsense restaurant. Service can be a bit slow but meals are tasty and filling.

Gad
EGYPTIAN FAST FOOD $$

(Map p376; Sharia Sheraton, Sigala; dishes E£15-45) With a menu that covers all the bases you simply can't go wrong at Egypt's favourite fast-food restaurant. Come here for Egyptian comfort-food such as *fiteer* (Egyptian-style pizza) and macaroni al-forn.

☆ Drinking & Entertainment

Thanks to its large community of resident dive instructors, tour guides, hotel employees and other foreigners, Hurghada has some of Egypt's liveliest nightlife. Almost all of the three- to five-star hotels and tourist villages have one or several bars, and there are many independent places as well.

Retro
LIVE MUSIC

(Map p376; Sharia Sheraton, Sigala) This relaxed pub dishes up live music every Sunday and Wednesday and on other days plays an eclectic mash of rock, blues and soul. An easy-going vibe, decent bar menu and pool table make it an all-round winner.

Papas Bar
CLUB

(Map p376; www.papasbar.com; New Marina Rd, Sigala) The centre of Hurghada nightlife is this popular Dutch-run bar. Filled with diving instructors and other foreign residents, it's lively and has a great atmosphere most nights.

Memories
BAR

(Map p374; Corniche, Ad-Dahar) Good for early-evening drinks on the outside terrace, this casual, friendly place has a dark wooden interior, cold beer and regular live music.

Little Buddha
CLUB

(Map p370; www.littlebuddha-hurghada.com; Village Rd, resort strip) Cocktails at the ready for Hurghada's top bling-fest. Little Buddha has been the centre of resort strip nightlife for years now. Anyone fancy a bottle of Moet for E£1950?

❶ Information

Dangers & Annoyances

Although Hurghada is a resort town, this is still Egypt and both men and women will garner more respect, and receive less hassle, if they save their swimwear for the hotel beaches. Women should dress modestly when walking around town, especially in the souq area of Ad-Dahar. Likewise men should refrain from wandering around shirtless once off the beach.

Emergency

Air ambulance (☎0100 154 1978)
Ambulance (☎354 9982, 123)
Police (Map p376; ☎354 6303, 122; Sharia Shedwan, Sigala)
Tourist police Ad-Dahar (Map p374; ☎344 4774; Sharia Al-Tahrir); resort strip (Map p370; ☎344 4773/4) Next to the tourist office.

Internet Access

There are internet cafes all over the city and in many hotels, most charging between E£5 and E£10 per hour.
Estenv Internet (Map p374; Sharia Sheikh Sabak, Ad-Dahar; ☺24hr; ✦)
Internet Café (Map p374; off Sharia Sayyed al-Qorayem, Ad-Dahar; ☺10am-midnight; ✦)
O2 Internet (Map p376; Sharia Sheraton, Sigala; ☺10.15am-11.15pm; ✦)

Medical Services

As-Salam Hospital (Map p370; ☎354 8785/6/7; Corniche) Just north of Iberotel Arabella.
Naval Hyperbaric & Emergency Medical Center (Map p370; ☎344 9150, 354 8450; Corniche) Has hyperbaric Chamber. Near Iberotel Arabella.
Public Hospital (Map p374; ☎354 6740; Sharia al-Mustashfa, Ad-Dahar)

Money

ATMs are all over the city, including the following locations.
Banque Misr (Map p374; Corniche, Ad-Dahar)
HSBC Sigala (Map p376; Sharia Sheraton); Resort Strip (Map p370; Village Rd)
National Bank of Egypt (Map p374; Sharia an-Nasr, Ad-Dahar)
Other money outlets:
Thomas Cook Ad-Dahar (Map p374; ☎354 1870/1; Sharia an-Nasr; ☺9am-2pm & 6-10pm); Sigala (Map p376; ☎344 3338; Sharia Sheraton; ☺9am-3pm & 4-10pm); resort strip (Map p370; ☎344 6830; ☺9am-5pm)
Western Union (Map p376; ☎344 2771, 19190; Sharia Sheraton, Sigala; ☺8.30am-10pm Sat-Thu, 3-10pm Fri)

Post

Post office (Map p374; Sharia al-Mustashfa, Ad-Dahar)

Telephone

Telephone centrale Ad-Dahar (Map p374; Sharia an-Nasr; ☺24hr); Port area (Map p376;

Midan Shedwan; ⊙24hr); Sigala (Sharia Sheraton; ⊙24hr)

Tourist Information

Tourist office (Map p370; ☑344 4420; resort strip; ⊙9am-8pm Sat-Thu, 2-10pm Fri)

❶ Getting There & Away

Air

EgyptAir (Map p370; ☑344 3592/3; www. egyptair.com; resort strip) has daily flights to Cairo and Sharm el-Sheikh, though prices tend to fluctuate greatly depending on the season and availability. If you book in advance, it is sometimes possible to snag a ticket for as little as US$90, though prices can climb much higher during the busy summer and winter holiday seasons.

If you book a package holiday in either the UK or Europe, it is likely that your travel agent will arrange a charter flight directly to Hurghada for you. Even if you're an independent traveller, it's worth visiting a few travel agents before booking your ticket to Egypt as charter flights to Hurghada are often significantly cheaper than round-trip airfares to Cairo.

Boat

The ferry service between Hurghada and Sharm el-Sheikh stopped operating in 2010. During the course of research for this book a new ferry schedule was announced but had yet to begin operation. The proposed schedule has departures for Sharm el-Sheikh at 9am every Tuesday, Thursday and Saturday (adult/child E£250/150, two hours). Enquire at any of the hotels and travel agencies in Hurghada for up-to-date information. If you're staying in Ad-Dahar, the 4 Seasons Hotel is a good contact point.

For information on the ferries to Duba and Jeddah in Saudi Arabia, see p523.

Bus

Schedules for the two companies listed here seem to change randomly. Confirm departure times at the bus station and try to book ahead for long-distance trips such as to Luxor and Cairo.

Super Jet (☑354 4722; Sharia an-Nasr, Ad-Dahar) Has daily buses to Cairo (E£65, six hours) departing at 9.30am, noon, 2.30pm, 5pm, 12.30am and 2.30am. The 2.30pm service also goes to Alexandria (E£95, nine hours). There's a service to Luxor (E£45, four hours) at 8.30am.

Upper Egypt Bus Co (☑354 7582; off Sharia an-Nasr, Ad-Dahar) Has buses to Cairo (E£45 to E£60, six to seven hours) at 10.30am, 3pm, 5.30pm and 1am. For Suez (E£50, four to five hours) services leave at 7am, 11am, 12.30pm, 3pm, 4pm, 5.30pm and 11.30pm. Departures to

Luxor (E£30, five hours) are at 8pm, 10.30pm, 12.30am, 1.30am, 2am, 3am and 3.30am. Only the 10.30pm and 12.30am buses go on to Aswan (E£45 to E£50, seven hours). Finally, four buses per day head south to Al-Quseir (E£20, 1½ hours) at 5.30am, 4pm, 8pm and 1.30am. The last three services go on to Marsa Alam (E£35, four hours) and Shalatein.

Servees

Servees station (off Sharia an-Nasr, Ad-Dahar) Has cars to Cairo (E£55 to E£60, six hours), Safaga (E£10, one hour) and Al-Quseir (E£10, 1½ hours). It is also possible to take a *servees* to Luxor (E£25, five hours).

❶ Getting Around

To/From the Airport

The airport is close to the resort strip. A taxi to downtown Ad-Dahar will cost between E£25 and E£30.

Car

There are numerous car rental agencies along Sharia Sheraton in Sigala, including **Avis** (Map p376; ☑344 7400).

Microbus

Microbuses run throughout the day from central Ad-Dahar south along the resort strip (E£1), and along Sharia an-Nasr and other major routes. Short rides cost 50pt.

El-Gouna Transport operates a more comfortable route (E£5 to E£10) between El-Gouna, Ad-Dahar and the end of Sharia Sheraton in Sigala about every half-hour, beginning at 9am. You can flag the bus down at any point along the way and pay on board.

Taxi

Taxis from Ad-Dahar to the start of the resort strip (around the Marriott hotel) charge about E£15. Travelling from the bus station to the centre of Ad-Dahar, expect to pay between E£5 and E£10.

Safaga

☑065 / POP 33,715

Safaga is a rough-and-ready port town that keeps itself in existence through the export of phosphates from local mines. It's also a major local terminal for the ferry to Saudi Arabia, and during the hajj thousands of pilgrims from the Nile Valley embark here on their voyages to Mecca. Despite the turquoise waters and the reefs that lie offshore, the town itself is an unattractive grid of flyblown, litter-strewn streets. Unless you're into windsurfing (which is top notch here) or diving and are staying at one of the beach hotels along the resort strip at the northern end of the bay, it's not worth a stopover.

It's a long town based around Sharia al-Gomhuriyya, the main road running parallel to the waterfront. At the far-northern end of town, near the roundabout with the large dolphin sculptures, a road branches northeast off Sharia al-Gomhuriyya leading to the northern resort strip.

🏃 Activities

Most people come to Safaga for the diving but it's also a famously windy place, with a fairly steady stream blowing in from the north, and most of the resort hotels have windsurfing centres, plus kitesurfing and other aquatic sports.

For an overview of diving in the Red Sea see p36.

Panorama Reef   DIVING
(Map p38; outer Safaga Bay) Panorama Reef is famous for its schooling barracuda, as well as numerous dolphins, eagle rays, grey reef sharks and silvertips. Depth: 3m to 40m; rating: intermediate; access by boat.

Salem Express   DIVING
(Map p38; south Safaga Bay) The *Salem Express* is a stunning yet mournful sight. In 1991 this passenger ferry sank along with hundreds of pilgrims returning from the hajj – while diving, take a moment to reflect on this watery graveyard. Depth: 15m to 30m; rating: intermediate; access by boat.

Dive Operators

Mena Dive   DIVING
(☑326 0060; www.menadive.com; resort strip, Safaga) The centre of the scuba scene in Safaga is this diver-centric resort hotel.

Orca Dive Club   DIVING
(☑326 0111; www.orca-diveclub-safaga.com; resort strip, Safaga) One of the Red Sea's leading technical diving centres.

🛏 Sleeping & Eating

At the northern end of town, just south of the dolphin roundabout, are several inexpensive restaurants, though nothing is particularly noteworthy. Most travellers prefer to eat in their hotels, and all-inclusive plans are generally available at upmarket properties.

Intercontinental Abu Soma   RESORT $$$
(☑326 0700; www.abusomaredsea.com; resort strip; r from US$180; ❄@☃) Featuring una-

bashedly over-the-top decoration at every turn, this large complex is great for families with a myriad of seaside activities on offer. The rooms themselves are much more generic but suitably comfortable and the massive swath of beach is the main drawcard.

Menaville Resort   RESORT $$
(☑326 0600; www.meanville-resort.com; resort strip; s/d half board from US$60/90; ❄@☃) This low-key, four-star resort has a reputable scuba centre and is very popular with European divers. Accommodation is in whitewashed two-storey villas that are looking rather worn and tired these days but remain spacious, bright and airy.

ℹ Information

Post office (◷8.30am-2.30pm Sat-Thu)

ℹ Getting There & Away

The bus station is near the southern end of town. About 1.5km north of the bus station is the service taxi station, followed by the port entrance (for ferries to Saudi Arabia).

Boat

There are regular passenger boats from Safaga to Duba (Saudi Arabia), and services to Jeddah (Saudi Arabia) during the hajj. For more information, see p523.

Bus

Safaga is located along the main coastal highway, 53km south of Hurghada. There are seven daily buses to Cairo (E£65 to E£75, seven to eight hours) and regular daily departures to Suez (E£40 to E£45, five to six hours), which also stop in Hurghada (E£10, one hour). There are also a few daily departures to Al-Quseir (E£10, one hour), Marsa Alam (E£25 to E£30, three hours) and Shalatein (E£50, seven hours).

Service Taxi

Service taxis run to Cairo (E£55 to E£60 per person, seven hours), Hurghada (E£10, one hour), Al-Quseir (E£10, one hour) and Marsa Alam (E£15 to £20, two to three hours).

Al-Quseir

☑065 / POP 35,045

Far removed from the resort clamour of the rest of the Red Sea coast, the historic city of Al-Quseir is a muddle of colourful and creaky coral-block architecture dating from the Ottoman era that is sadly bypassed by most tourists. This charmingly sleepy seaside town has a history stretching back to Pharaonic times

Al-Quseir

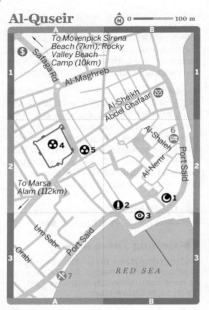

Within the map:
- To Mövenpick Sirena Beach (7km); Rocky Valley Beach Camp (10km)
- Safaga Rd
- Al-Maghreb
- Al-Sheikh Abdel Ghaffaar
- Al-Shaleh
- Al-Nemr
- Port Said
- 4
- 5
- 6
- To Marsa Alam (112km)
- Um Sabr
- Port Said
- Orabi
- 2
- 1
- 3
- RED SEA
- 7
- N 0 — 100 m

Al-Quseir

⊙ Sights
1 Faran Mosque B2
2 Granary B2
3 Old Police Station B3
4 Ottoman Fortress A2
5 Shrine of Abdel Ghaffaar
  al-Yemeni A2

🛏 Sleeping
6 Al-Quseir Hotel B2

🍴 Eating
7 Restaurant Marianne A3

when it was the main port for boats heading south to the fabled East African kingdom of Punt. Although nothing remains from this earliest era, strolling through Al-Quseir's photogenic old streets – backed by the battered ramparts of the Ottoman fortress and speckled with the domed tombs of various holy men who died en route to or from Mecca – provides a fascinating glimpse into this region before tourism took over.

History

Prior to the 10th century, Al-Quseir was one of the most important ports on the Red Sea and a major departure point for pilgrims travelling to Mecca for the hajj. It also served as a thriving centre of trade and export between the Nile Valley and the Red Sea and beyond. Even during its period of decline, the city remained a major settlement and was sufficiently important for the Ottomans to fortify it during the 16th century. Later the British beat the French for control of Al-Quseir and for some time it was the main import channel for the spice trade from India to Britain. However, the opening of the Suez Canal in 1869 put an end to all this and the town's decline accelerated, with only a brief burst of prosperity as a phosphate-processing centre in the early decades of the 20th century.

⊙ Sights

Ottoman Fortress   HISTORIC BUILDING
(Map p380; admission E£15; ⊙9am-5pm) Much of the original exterior wall of this small fortress remains intact, although it was modified several times by the French, as well as the British, who permanently altered the fortress by firing some 6000 cannonballs upon it during a heated battle in the 19th century. Inside some of the rooms are interesting information boards documenting the history of Al-Quseir.

Shrine of Abdel Ghaffaar al-Yemeni SHRINE
(Map p380) Just across from the fortress is the 19th-century shrine of a Yemeni sheikh, Abdel Ghaffaar al-Yemeni, which is marked by an old gravestone in a niche in the wall.

🏃 Activities

Al-Quseir is a lesser-known dive destination and most dive operators are affiliated with the hotels. For an overview of diving in the Red Sea see p36.

El Qadim   DIVING
(Map p38; 7km north of Al-Quseir) Located in a small bay abutted by the Mövenpick Resort, this dive site boasts a complex network of interconnecting caves and canyons. Depth: 5m to 30m; rating: intermediate; access from the shore.

El Kaf   DIVING
(Map p38; 10km south of Al-Quseir) An easy plunge that appeals to divers of all skill levels, El Kaf is a canyon pitted with small caves and passages, and accented by massive coral boulders and sandy ravines. Depth: 18m to 25m; rating: novice; access from the shore.

🛏️ Sleeping & Eating

TOP CHOICE Al-Quseir Hotel HISTORIC HOTEL **$$**
(Map p380; ☎333 2301; www.alquseirhotel.com; Sharia Port Said; s/d without bathroom E£150/180) If you're looking for atmosphere rather than amenities this renovated 1920s merchant's house is a delightful place to stay. Sitting right on the seafront Al-Quseir Hotel has just six simple but spacious rooms and is brimming full of character with its original narrow wooden staircase, high wooden ceilings and latticework on the windows. Grab a seafront room for views. If you order ahead they can provide meals.

Rocky Valley Beach Camp BEACH CAMP **$$**
(☎333 5247; www.rockyvalleydiverscamp.com) About 10km north of town, this camp is a veritable paradise for shoestringing scuba aficionados. Rocky Valley lures in divers by offering a variety of cheap all-inclusive packages (4/8 days €200/350), which include Bedouin-style tents, beachside barbecues, late-night beach parties and some incredible reefs right off shore. It's a fun place where management work hard to foster a communal atmosphere.

Mövenpick Sirena Beach RESORT **$$$**
(☎333 2100; www.moevenpick-quseir.com; s/d US$125/175; ❀@❀) This low-set, domed ensemble 7km north of the town centre is top of the line in Al-Quseir, and one of the most laidback resorts along the coast. Its amenities include excellent food and the usual five-star facilities, diving centre, quiet evenings and a refreshing absence of glitz. The management is known for its environmentally conscious approach.

Restaurant Marianne EGYPTIAN **$$**
(Map p380; Sharia Port Said; mains E£20-40) One of the best places in town to sample the bounty of the Red Sea, this local favourite has super-friendly service, a great menu featuring all the usual Egyptian favourites as well as seafood and seating right on the waterfront.

ℹ️ Information

Main post office (Safaga Rd)
National Bank of Egypt (Safaga Rd) ATM.
Tourist police (☎335 0024; Safaga Rd)

ℹ️ Getting There & Away

The bus and *servees* stations are next to each other about 3km northwest of the Safaga Rd.

DON'T MISS

STROLLING AROUND THE OLD TOWN

Ringed in between Sharia Al-Gomhuriyya and the waterfront is Al-Quseir's old town; a twisting labyrinth of alleyways where progress seems happy to hit the snooze button and local life is snail-paced. The once grand **old police station** (Map p380) on the waterfront, originally an Ottoman diwan (council chamber), is now a picturesque but dilapidated shell. Just behind, the fortresslike facade of the **granary** (Map p380) dates to the early 19th century and was used to store wheat before being shipped to Mecca. Just next to this is the **Faran Mosque** (Map p380) with its minaret built in 1704. The real highlight here though is the lanes themselves. Wind your way past pretty pastel-washed houses, many still boasting original *mashrabiyya* (latticework) window screens and in various states of photogenic decay, while looking out for hand-painted hajj decorations and quirkily coloured doors.

Bus

Buses run to Cairo (E£60 to E£80, 10 hours) via Hurghada (E£20 to E£25, 1½ to two hours), departing at 8.30am, 1pm, 3.30pm and 10pm. Buses to Marsa Alam (E£15, two hours) are at 4am, 6pm, and 10pm but the schedule changes frequently so check beforehand.

Servees

Sample fares (with a little haggling): Hurghada (E£10, 1½ hours) and Marsa Alam (E£10, two hours).

ℹ️ Getting Around

Microbuses go along Sharia al-Gomhuriyya, with some also going to the bus and *servees* stations. Fares are between 50pt and E£1, depending on the distance travelled. A taxi from the bus station to the waterfront costs E£5.

Marsa Alam & Around
☎065

In-the-know divers have been heading to Marsa Alam for years, attracted to the seas just off the rugged coastline offering up some of Egypt's best diving. Despite this, for a long time this far-flung destination stayed well off the tourism-radar. The secret though is now out. Heavily touted as the Red Sea Riviera's new tourist drawcard by the Egyptian government, the last few years have seen a construction boom along the coastline. While the town of Marsa Alam itself is a rather nondescript place which most of the development has passed by, the strip of coast to its north and south has been snapped up by eager developers and is now home to a plethora of resorts and half-built hotels.

Despite the construction, Marsa Alam's coastline is still a diving aficionado's dream and there are some long-standing beach camps here specifically for those who want to spend most of their time underwater. This is also the best base from which to venture into the southern reaches of Egypt's vast Eastern Desert where gold and emeralds were once mined by the Romans in the barren, mineral-rich mountains just inland.

🏃 Activities

Diving and desert excursions are the main activities around Marsa Alam. For more on desert excursions, see p385.

A small selection of the area's boat-accessed dive sites are listed north to south below. For more general information on diving in the Red Sea, see p36.

Elphinstone   DIVING
(Map p38; 125km north of Marsa Alam) Elphinstone has steep reef walls covered with soft corals, and washed by strong currents that are ideal for sharks – seven species reportedly frequent its waters. Depth: 20m to 40m; rating: advanced.

Sha'ab Samadai   DIVING
(Map p38; 18km southeast of Marsa Alam) This popular diving and snorkelling lagoon is home to a school of spinner dolphins and a daily cap on visitor numbers is in place to protect them. Depth: 10m to 15m; rating: novice to intermediate.

Sha'ab Sharm   DIVING
(Map p38; 30km northeast of Wadi Gimal) Impressive topography and excellent marine life (hammerheads, barracuda, groper and yellowmouth moray eels) mark this large, kidney-shaped offshore reef. Depth: 15m to over 40m; rating: advanced.

Hamada   DIVING
(Map p38; 60km north of Berenice) Atop an inshore reef lies the wreck of this 65m-long cargo ship. Lying on her side in just 14m of water, *Hamada* is a fairly easy, extremely picturesque dive site. Depth: 6m to 14m; rating: novice.

Sataya (Dolphin Reef)   DIVING
(Map p38; 50km north of Berenice) The horseshoe-shaped Dolphin is the main reef of the Fury Shoals, and has steep walls leading down to a sandy slope scattered with a great variety of coral heads. Depth: 4m to over 40m; rating: intermediate.

Red Sea Diving Safari   DIVING
(📞02-337 1833, 02-337 9942; www.redsea-diving safari.com; Marsa Shagra) PADI. Run by environmentalist and long-time diver Hossam Hassan, who pioneered diving in the Red Sea's deep south.

🛌 Sleeping

There are few places to stay in Marsa Alam village itself but north and south along the coast there's an ever-growing number of all-inclusive resorts, plus a handful of simpler, diver-oriented camps, many of which focus on sustainable tourism practices.

TOP CHOICE Wadi Lahami Village   BEACH CAMP $$
(📞023-337 1833; www.redsea-divingsafari.com; Wadi Lahami; tent/royal tent/chalet full board per person €40/45/55) Tucked into a remote mangrove bay 120km south along the main road from Marsa Alam, just north of Ras Banas, this simple place is worth the extra effort it takes to get here. Diving is the main activity, with the famed pristine reefs of the Fury Shoals easily accessed by boat, but the lonely location, and nearby mangrove forests, are a perfect setting for nature lovers and bird watchers as well. Wadi Lahami has a thorough environmental policy and recycles waste and water as well as supporting and promoting sustainable diving practices. It offers simple but spotless and comfortable accommodation in a choice of two-bed tents sharing bathroom facilities or stone chalets with en suite. A superb choice for those seeking beautiful vistas and lashings of tranquillity.

🏅 Marsa Shagra Village   BEACH CAMP $$
(📞023-337 1833; www.redsea-divingsafari.com; tent/royal tent/chalet full board per person €40/45/55) The big sister camp to Wadi Lahami, Shagra was one of the first eco-minded places to open up on the Red Sea and, despite the development that has gone

RED SEA COAST EASTERN DESERT

on around it, has stayed true to its sustainable tourism credentials. It's a similar setup as Lahami (with the same environmental policy in place) but on a larger scale and offers excellent snorkelling just offshore as well as diving – which is the real attraction here. It's 24km north of Marsa Alam along the main road.

Oasis Resort   RESORT $$$
(☏0100 505 2855; www.oasis-marsaalam.de; s/d half board €68/112) 24km north of Marsa Alam along the main road, and smaller than many of the mega-resorts along this stretch of sand, Oasis is unique for utilising local materials and traditional architecture rather than the usual concrete-splurge. Rooms here are spacious, airy and comfortable with great sea views.

Um Tondoba   BEACH CAMP $$
(☏0100 191 1414; www.ecolodge-redsea.com; hut/chalet full board per person €25/35) Stripping it right back to the basics of sun, sea and sand, Um Tondoba offers basic palm-thatch beach huts (located across the road from the beach rather than on the shore), good diving packages and an exceptionally mellow atmosphere. It's 14km south of Marsa Alam along the main road.

Kahramana Beach Resort   RESORT $$$
(☏022-748 0883; www.kahramanaresort.com/k_marsa/home.htm; s/d full board from US$120/135; ✿@☀) Built over two hills that surround an attractive beach, the Kahramana, 26km north of Marsa Alam along the main road, is one of the more sympathetically designed large complexes along the coastline. Although not luxurious, chalets are bright, generously-sized and well-appointed. Booking a deal through a travel agent will give you a much cheaper deal than the rates quoted above.

✗ Eating

In Marsa Alam there are a couple of cafes at the junction where you can find basic fare as well as a small supermarket with a modest selection. However, all of the resorts and lodges have restaurants as well as full-board packages.

Dolce & Salato   ITALIAN $$
(68 St, Marsa Alam; mains E£18-35) This little gem of a place in the centre of town dishes up surprisingly authentic pizza and pasta. It is one block down from the mosque.

❶ Information

Air ambulance (☏0100 154 1978)
Hyperbaric chamber (☏0122 218 7550, 0109 510 0262, emergency VHF code16; Marsa Shagra) Located 24km north of Marsa Alam.
Tourist police (☏375 0000; Quaraya Hotel, coastal road)

❶ Getting There & Away

Air
The Marsa Alam International Airport is 67km north of Marsa Alam along the Al-Quseir road. There is no public transport, so you'll need to arrange a transfer in advance with your hotel.

EgyptAir (www.egyptair.com) has flights to Cairo five days per week. Prices tend to fluctuate wildly depending on the season and availability. The airport is also served by charter flights originating in either the UK or Europe.

Bus
Marsa Alam bus station is just past the T-junction along the Edfu road. Buses to Cairo (E£85 to E£90, 10 to 11 hours) via Al-Quseir (E£10 to E£15, two hours) and Hurghada (E£25 to E£35, 3½ to four hours) depart at 1.30pm and 8.30pm but check beforehand as timetables change frequently. There are also a couple of services per day to Shalatein (E£20 to E£25, four hours).

Servees
The *servees* station is beside the bus station and has pretty regular services to Al-Quseir (E£10, two hours).

Eastern Desert

The Eastern Desert – a vast, desolate area rimmed by the Red Sea Mountains to the east and the Nile Valley in the west – was once criss-crossed by ancient trade routes and dotted with settlements that played vital roles in the development of many of the region's greatest civilisations. Today the desert's rugged expanses are filled with fascinating footprints of this history, including rock inscriptions, ancient gold and mineral mines, wells and watchtowers, and religious shrines and buildings. Indeed, it is one of the highlights of any visit to the Red Sea coast, and a world apart from the commercialised coastline.

None of the roads crossing the desert can be freely travelled – some are completely closed to foreigners – and all the sites require a guide. As a result, it is strongly advised (in fact necessary) that you explore the Eastern Desert with the aid of an experienced tour operator. See p385 for more information.

◎ Sights

Mons Porphyrites   RUIN

This is the site of ancient porphyry quarries worked by the Romans. The precious white-and-purple crystalline stone was mined and then transported across the desert along the Via Porphyrites to the Nile for use in sarcophagi, columns and other decorative work elsewhere in the Roman world. The quarries were under the direct control of the imperial family in Rome, which had encampments, workshops and even temples built for the workers and engineers here. Evidence of this quarry town can still be seen, although not much of it is standing.

To get here, you will travel about 40km northwest of Hurghada; a road leading to the site branches off the main road about 20km north of Hurghada. Tours can be easily arranged in Hurghada.

Mons Claudianus   RUIN

This old Roman granite quarry/fortress complex is one of the largest of the Roman settlements dotting the Eastern Desert. A stark and remote place, this was the end of the line for Roman prisoners brought to hack the granite out of the barren mountains, and was a hardship post for the soldiers sent to guard them. It was more a concentration camp than a quarry – you can still see the remains of the tiny cells that these unfortunates inhabited. There is also an immense cracked pillar, left where it fell 2000 years ago, a small temple and some other ruins.

Once the granite was mined, it was carved and transported more than 200km across the desert to the Nile, from where it then was taken to the Mediterranean and the heart of the empire.

There's a signposted turn-off about 40km along the Safaga–Qena rd; from there it's another 25km northwest along a track of deteriorated tarmac. Tours can be easily arranged in Hurghada

Rock Inscriptions

This region is also home to incredible collections of rock inscriptions, many of which date to prehistoric times. One of the most

NOMADS OF THE EASTERN DESERT

Although the desert of the southern Red Sea may seem empty and inhospitable, the area has been home to nomadic Ababda and Besharin tribes for millennia. Members of the Beja, a nomadic tribe of African origin, they are thought to be descendants of the Blemmyes, the fierce tribesmen mentioned by classical geographers. Until well into the 20th century, the extent of the territory in which they roamed was almost exactly as described by the Romans, with whom they were constantly at war some 2000 years earlier.

Expert camel herders, the Ababda and Besharin lived a nomadic lifestyle that hardly changed until the waters of Lake Nasser rose and destroyed their traditional grazing lands. While most Besharin, many of whom do not speak Arabic, live in Sudan, most of the Arabic-speaking Ababda are settled in communities in the Nile Valley between Aswan and Luxor. A small number continue to live in their ancestral territory, concentrated in the area from Marsa Alam to Wadi Gimal, as well as on the eastern shores of Lake Nasser.

If you spend time in the region, you'll still likely see the traditional Ababda hut, lined inside with thick, hand-woven blankets, or hear Ababda music, with its rhythmic clapping and drumming and heavy use of the five-stringed lyre-like *tamboura*. At the centre of Ababda social life is *jibena* – heavily sweetened coffee prepared from fresh-roasted beans in a small earthenware flask heated directly in the coals.

With the rapid expansion of tourism along the southern Red Sea, long-standing Ababda lifestyles have become increasingly threatened. Tourism has begun to replace livestock and camels as the main source of livelihood, and many Ababda men now work as guards or labourers on the resorts springing up around Marsa Alam, while others have started working with travel companies, offering camel safaris to tourists.

There are differing views on the impact of tourism in this region. On one hand, revenue from tourism can play a vital role in the development of the region, particularly through the sale of locally produced crafts or payment for services of a local guide. However, indigenous tourism sometimes becomes exploitative and visits can take on an unfortunate 'human zoo' quality. If you are considering a visit, ask questions about the nature of your trip and consider the potential positive and negative impact that it may have on the community.

impressive collections is at **Barrameya**, which fringes the Marsa Alam–Edfu road. Here, in the smooth, grey rock are hunting scenes with dogs chasing ostriches, depictions of giraffes and cattle and hieroglyphic accounts of trade expeditions.

Another good collection is found along the high, smooth walls of **Wadi Hammamat**, about halfway along the road connecting Al-Quseir to the town of Qift. This remarkable graffiti dates from Pharaonic times down to Egypt's 20th-century King Farouk. The road through the wadi runs along an ancient trade route, and remains of old wells as well as other evidence of the area's long history can be seen along the way. In Graeco-Roman times, watchtowers were built along the trail at short enough intervals for signals to be visible, and many of them are still intact on the barren hilltops on either side of the road.

Tombs & Shrines
In addition to the many traces of Pharaonic and other ancient civilisations, the Eastern Desert is also home to numerous Islamic tombs and shrines. One of the best known is the **tomb of Sayyed al-Shazli**, a 13th-century sheikh who is revered as one of the more important Sufi leaders. His followers believe that he wanted to die in a place where nobody had ever sinned. Evidently such a place was difficult to find, as the site was a journey of several days from either the Nile Valley or the coast. Al-Shazli's tomb – which lies about 145km southwest of Marsa Alam at Wadi Humaysara – was restored under the orders of King Farouk in 1947, and there is now an asphalt road leading to it. His *moulid* (saints' festival), on the 15th of the Muslim month of Shawal, is attended by thousands of Sufis.

Tours
Although second-rate travel agencies occupy every corner of the tourist hub of Hurghada, it is recommended that you book a tour through **Red Sea Desert Adventures** (0122 399 3860; www.redseadesertadventures.com; Marsa Shagra). This extremely professional safari outfit is run by Dutch geologist Karin van Opstal and Austrian Thomas Krakhofer, and offers tailor-made walking, camel and jeep safaris throughout the area. Both have lived in Marsa Alam for over a decade and are authorities on the geography, culture and history of this area and work closely with local Ababda tribesmen.

Tours start at approximately €60 per person, though they vary depending on the specifications of your uniquely catered tour, the size of your party and the time of year. In order for the necessary permits to be organised for multiday desert safaris, try to book at least one month in advance.

Alternatively, you can arrange your trip through Fustat Wadi El Gimal (see p385).

Sleeping
If you've booked a tour through Red Sea Desert Adventures they'll organise a combination of desert camping and Bedouin village stays depending on the length and depth of your tour.

Fustat Wadi El Gimal LODGE $$
(240 5132; prices vary) Another option is to bed down at Fustat Wadi El Gimal, a permanent tented camp and project aimed at generating a sustainable revenue for the Bedouin community. Fustat Wadi El Gimal serves as a base for all manner of excursions into the Eastern Desert, which shouldn't set you back more than US$50 to US$100 per person per day. The camp itself is a highly memorable affair modelled on a traditional nomadic camp, albeit with a healthy amount of artistic flourishes. Advance reservations recommended.

Getting There & Away
Trips to Mons Claudianus and Mons Porphyrites are easily arranged in Hurghada. For the more southern Eastern Desert sites, Red Sea Desert Adventures can organise all your travel and permissions. The only viable option for accessing this area is to make transport arrangements with a local operator such as this.

Berenice
The military centre and small port of Berenice, 150km south of Marsa Alam, was founded in 275 BC by Ptolemy II Philadelphus. From about the 3rd to the 5th century AD, it was one of the most important harbours and trading posts on the Red Sea coast, and is mentioned in the 1st-century AD mariner's chronicle *Periplus of the Erythraean Sea*.

The ruins of the ancient town, including ruins of the **Temple of Serapis**, are located just south of the present-day village, and have been the subject of ongoing archaeological investigations. At the time of research these ruins had been covered up to aid preservation

ON THE EMERALD TRAIL

Source of Egypt's famed emerald mines, the southern region of the Eastern Desert is a wild place of white sand wadis and craggy peaks which are rarely visited. Starkly beautiful **Wadi Gimal Protectorate** extends inland for about 85km from its coastal opening south of Marsa Alam, and is home to a rich variety of bird life, gazelles and stands of mangrove. Throughout the interior are scattered the tumbled remains of emerald and gold mines dating from the Pharaonic and Roman eras. This area provided emeralds that were used throughout the ancient world and was the exclusive source of the gem for the Roman Empire.

Thought to be the miner's main settlement, **Sikait**, about 80km southwest of Marsa Alam, has a small Temple of Isis still standing while the remnants of buildings lie strewn across the hillside. The ruins of the mines themselves can be seen among the slopes of **Nugrus** where the ground is littered with pottery fragments. The smaller ruins of **Geili** and **Appalonia** (both trading points) are nearby. A little further is the mysterious ruin of **Karba Matthba** where the remains of what must have once been a substantial villa or complex sit on top of an isolated desert ridge. From here there are incredible panoramas over the sprawling desert tracts.

meaning there was nothing to see. Today the main activity is at Ras Banas peninsula – jutting into the sea just northeast of Berenice – which is an important military base. Because of this, and because of the region's proximity to the Sudanese border, independent visits are not allowed – you can expect to be questioned by the tourist police, and to be accompanied by an escort even if you succeed in getting to Berenice.

There is no official accommodation, and camping needs to be cleared with the police.

Buses (E£50, nine hours) departing from Hurghada, bound for Shalatein, stop in Berenice. You will need to arrange your own transport in order to get out to the ruins.

Shalatein

This dusty outpost 90km south of Berenice marks the administrative boundary between Egypt and Sudan. With that said, Egypt considers the political boundary to be another 175km southeast, beyond the town of Halaib, a once-important Red Sea port that has long since fallen into obscurity. Sudan strongly disagrees, resulting in a large swath of disputed territory that is probably worth avoiding in the interest of personal safety.

Shalatein's colourful camel market is a major stop on the camel-trading route from Sudan, which for many of the camels finishes in the Birqash camel market outside Cairo (p165). Amid the dust and the vendors, Rashaida tribesmen in their lavender *galabeyas* (full-length robes) mix with Ababda, Besharin and other peoples from southern Egypt and northern Sudan.

The old souq is also worth a ramble for its intriguing world-apart atmosphere to the rest of Egypt, with a tangle of haphazard wooden-plank shacks selling everything from the latest digital photo frame (we kid you not) to the traditional earthenware jugs used for making *jibena*.

As with Berenice, independent visitors are discouraged, and the area is sporadically closed to foreigners completely. You can expect to be questioned by the tourist police, and to be accompanied by an escort even if you succeed in getting to Shalatein. In contrast to the suspicion cast on sole travellers here, Shalatein has become a popular daytrip option for large groups bussed in from Marsa Alam's resort area. However, a more sensitive approach to visiting this fascinating area is by organising an excursion to the camel market through Red Sea Desert Adventures (p385).

There is no official accommodation and camping needs to be cleared with the police.

Buses (E£55, nine to 10 hours) departing from Hurghada via Berenice terminate in Shalatein.

Sinai

Best Places to Eat

» Wadi Itlah garden lunch (p434)

» Seabride Restaurant (p412)

» Fairuz (p401)

» Kitchen (p412)

» Blue House (p412)

Best Places to Stay

» Sawa Camp (p426)

» Al-Karm Ecolodge (p434)

» Alaska Camp & Hotel (p410)

» Nakhil Inn (p419)

» Sinai Old Spices (p399)

Why Go?

Rugged and starkly beautiful, the Sinai Peninsula's vast and empty desert heart has managed to capture imaginations throughout the centuries. It's coveted for both its deep religious significance and strategic position as a crossroads of empires. Prophets and pilgrims, conquerors and exiles have all left their footprints on the sands here.

A springboard to the underwater wonders of the Red Sea, Sinai's seaside resorts serve travellers with a medley of sundrenched holiday fun that's a world apart from the rest of Egypt. Step away from the buzz of the coast, however, and you'll find Sinai's true soul. Here amid the red-tinged, ragged peaks and endless never-never of sand, the Bedouin continue to preserve their proud traditions while dealing with the endless march of progress. On a star-studded night, surrounded by the monstrous silhouettes of mountains, you'll realise why Sinai continues to cast a spell over all who visit.

When to Go

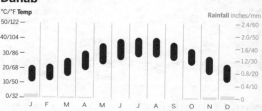

Dahab

Mar In the desert spring's colourful flurry of life carpets the sands.

Apr–May Celebrate all things Sinai at the Dahab Festival.

Oct Sneak in some autumn sun along the coast.

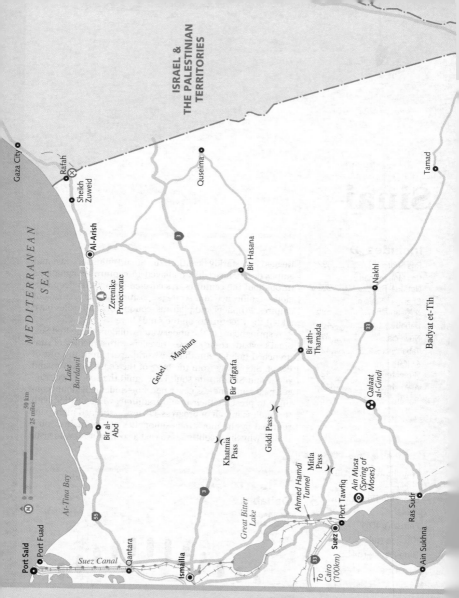

Sinai Highlights

1 Dive into **Ras Mohammed** (p393), an underwater fantasia of coral mountains and ghostly shipwrecks

2 Follow in the footsteps of prophets and pilgrims on the time-worn rock stairs of **Mt Sinai's Steps of Repentance** (p432)

3 View one of the world's most important collections of early religious art and manuscripts at **St Katherine's Monastery** (p428)

4 Snorkel the **Lighthouse Reef** (p408) then relax with a beer, sheesha and new friends at a waterfront restaurant

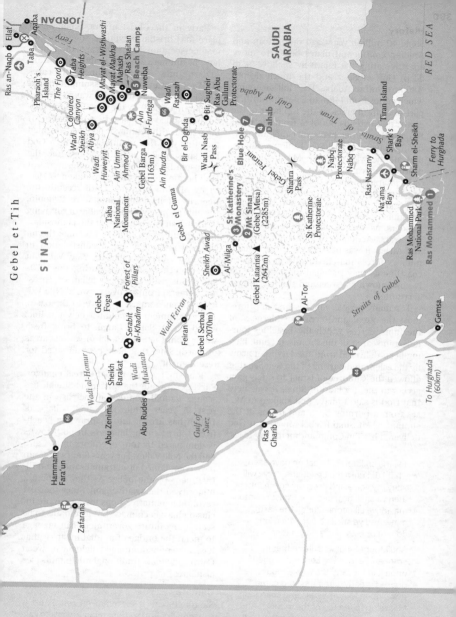

in the backpacker vortex of Dahab

5 Escape the crowds to laze on a beach, with a blissful to-do list of nothing, at one of

the **beach camps north of Nuweiba** (p426)

6 Discover the majestic beauty of Sinai's vast desert interior on a **trek or camel safari** (p409 and p432) into

the craggy mountains with a Bedouin guide

7 Explore the plunging chasm of South Sinai's **Blue Hole** (p410)

History

Some 40 million years ago the African and Arabian continental plates began to move apart, creating the relatively shallow (95m deep) Gulf of Suez and the much deeper (1800m) Gulf of Aqaba. The Gulf of Aqaba, which varies from 14km to 25km in width, is part of a rift (a crack in the top layer of the earth) that extends 6000km from the Dead Sea, on the border between Israel and Jordan, through the Red Sea, Ethiopia, Kenya, and all the way down to Mozambique in southern Africa.

In Pharaonic times the quarries of Sinai provided great quantities of turquoise, gold and copper. The importance of this 'Land of Turquoise' also made it the goal of empire builders, as well as the setting for countless wars. Acting as a link between Asia and Africa, it was of strategic value – many military forces marched along its northern coastline as they travelled to or from what is now known as Israel and the Palestinian Territories.

For many people, Sinai is first and foremost the 'great and terrible wilderness' of the Bible, across which the Israelites journeyed in search of the Promised Land, having been delivered from the Egyptian army by the celebrated parting of the Red Sea that allowed the 'Children of Israel' to safely gain access to the dry land of Sinai. It was here that God is said to have first spoken to Moses from a burning bush and it was at the summit of Mt Sinai (Gebel Musa) that God delivered his Ten Commandments to Moses:

Tell the children of Israel; Ye have seen what I did unto the Egyptians... If ye will obey my voice and keep my covenant, then ye shall be a peculiar treasure unto me above all people: for all the earth is mine. And ye shall be unto me a kingdom of priests, and a holy nation.

And Mount Sinai was altogether in smoke, because the Lord descended upon it in fire; and the whole mount quaked greatly... And the Lord came down upon Mount Sinai...and called Moses up to the top of the mount... And God spoke all these words, saying, I am the Lord thy God, which have brought thee out of the land of Egypt, out of the house of bondage. Thou shalt have no other gods before me.

Exodus 19:4-6; 19:18-20:3

Early in the Christian era, Sinai was a place for Christian Egyptians to escape Roman persecution. Monasticism is thought to have begun here as early as the 3rd century AD, with most hermits settling in the caves of Wadi Feiran, on the assumption that Gebel Serbal, located nearby, was in fact the 'Mountain of God'. By the time Emperor Justinian founded a monastery at the foot of Mt Sinai in the 6th century, it had been decided that this was the mountain on which God had spoken. For centuries thereafter, the peninsula became a place of pilgrimage. It later became one of the routes taken to Mecca by Muslim pilgrims. Until recently the majority of its inhabitants were Bedouin, the only people who are capable of surviving in the harsh environment of the peninsula.

In recent years Sinai has become the focus of development and 'reconstruction' in much the same way that the New Valley in the Western Desert was during the 1970s and 1980s, when landless fellaheen (peasant farmers) from an overcrowded Nile Valley were encouraged to move to the oases. The government has built a new pipeline, called the Al-Salam Canal, to bring fresh water from the Suez Canal to various areas of North Sinai that have been targeted for resettlement.

Tourism, too, has brought great changes. Surveys estimate that Sharm el-Sheikh has seen a tenfold population increase in the past 15 years, while the small village of Dahab has grown into a sprawling beachfront tourist town; business in both towns is dominated by tour operators from Cairo and the Nile Valley. For years Sinai's Bedouin have complained of marginalisation and ill-treatment by the police as they become a minority in their native land. Since the 2011 revolution, tentative steps towards more inclusion have been made but it remains to be seen if any future government can manage to mend the bridge of mutual mistrust that has, up to now, dominated dialogue between Cairo and Sinai's traditional inhabitants (see also boxed text p433).

Climate

Sinai's climate is extreme: on one hand it can get very hot, so remember always to carry water, use copious amounts of sunblock and wear sensible clothes to avoid sunburn (wearing a T-shirt while snorkelling is advisable). On the other hand, while summer temperatures can climb to 50°C, it gets very cold at night, and the mountains can

PROTECTING SINAI'S FRAGILE ECOSYSTEMS

Although much of Sinai is made up of hot, dry desert, it is full of life. Craggy mountains are sliced by dry gravel wadis in which sprout the odd acacia tree or clump of gnarled tamarisk, while a surprisingly rich variety of plants tenuously cling to the loose, sandy flanks of coastal dunes. Once every few years, when storm clouds gather over the mountains and dump buckets of water onto this parched landscape, the entire scene is transformed into a sea of greenery as seeds that have lain dormant for months burst into life. For Sinai's wildlife, such as the gazelle and rock hyrax (as well as for the goats herded by local Bedouin people), these rare occasions are times of plenty.

Yet these fragile ecosystems have come under increasing threat from the rapid onslaught of tourism. Until relatively recently, the only people to wander through this region were Bedouin on camels. Now adventure seekers in ever-multiplying numbers are ploughing their way through in 4WDs and on quad bikes (four-wheeled motorcycles) in search of pristine spots and, in so doing, churning up the soil, uprooting plants and contributing to erosion.

In order to minimise the environmental damage, the government has banned vehicles from going off-road in certain areas, including Ras Mohammed National Park and the protected areas of Nabq, Ras Abu Gallum and Taba. Yet enforcement in Sinai's vast wilderness areas is difficult, and while rangers do patrol protectorates, a large part of the responsibility is left with visitors to follow the rules. To do your part, try not to be persuaded by overeager guides wanting to show you something that's off the beaten track. If you really want to explore the region in depth, do it in the age-old fashion – go on foot or by camel, with the necessary provisions. Also be aware of rubbish, which has become an increasingly serious threat to Sinai's ecosystems. Dive clubs located in Dahab and Sharm el-Sheikh organise regular rubbish dives, and always find far more than they can collect. You should carry out all your litter with you, and dispose of it thoughtfully. And wherever you visit, treat Sinai's ecosystems – both those above and below the sea – with care.

be freezing during the day. Come prepared with warm clothing, especially if you'll be trekking or climbing Mt Sinai.

Dangers & Annoyances

Because of the peninsula's unique position between cultures and continents, plus its mountainous terrain and – in more recent times – its tourist masses, Sinai has traditionally had a higher security profile than other parts of the country.

In recent years, the region of Sinai has been thrust into the international spotlight following a string of high-profile bombings. On 7 October 2004, three bomb attacks in Taba killed 34 people and injured more than 150. On 23 July 2005, a series of coordinated bombings in the tourist market of Sharm el-Sheikh killed 88 people and injured close to 200, becoming the deadliest terrorist action in the country's history. In 2006 Dahab became the latest victim of terrorist activity when on 24 April three bombs exploded, killing 23 people and injuring more than 75.

Security concerns have again been highlighted in the region since the revolution of 2011, although much of the activity has occurred far from any tourist centre. Between

February and November 2011 a gas line in the far north of Sinai (which supplies Israel and Jordan with Egyptian natural gas) was blown up eight times by unidentified gunmen. On 30 July 2011, members of local Islamist group Takfir-wal Hijra attacked the police station in the northern city of Al-Arish, leaving seven dead and dozens injured.

Tensions along the border Egypt shares with Israel and the Palestinian territory of Gaza also hit a new high on 18 August 2011 when militants (claimed by Israeli authorities to have crossed into Israel from Gaza through Sinai) carried out a series of deadly attacks near the Israeli border town of Eilat. During the ensuing gun battle, when Israeli forces chased militants along the border close to Taba, two Egyptian border guards were killed mistakenly by Israeli troops and four others injured (who all later died in hospital). The incursion caused widespread outrage in Egypt and led to Israel allowing Egypt to move more troops into Sinai to help maintain security.

In a separate issue, in February 2012 two kidnapping incidents involving tourists occurred on the road between St Katherine and

Sharm el-Sheikh. The hostages were taken by Bedouin tribesmen in a high-profile attempt to pressurise the Egyptian government to release jailed Bedouin. In both instances, the hostages were released unharmed after a short period of negotiation.

It is impossible to offer anything other than blind speculation regarding the possibility of a future terrorist attack in Sinai. With that said, it's worth checking your embassy's travel advisory to get an update on the situation before making any plans. However, it's important to remember that the overwhelming majority of travellers to Sinai enjoy their visits without incident.

On a different note, travellers should be aware that while bikinis are fine for the beach, Egypt is a conservative country and walking around town in your swimwear is likely to offend a great number of local people (and attract a lot of unwanted attention). Likewise it should be noted that although topless sunbathing seems to be de rigueur for some tourist groups in Sharm el-Sheikh, you should keep in mind that it is illegal here, as in the rest of Egypt.

ⓘ Getting There & Away

Sinai's international air hub is at Sharm el-Sheikh, which receives regular flights from Europe in addition to local flights. There is also an international airport in Taba, though it receives only occasional charter flights. For overland travel, the peninsula is linked to the mainland by the Ahmed Hamdi Tunnel, and by the Mubarak Peace Suspension Bridge, both of which connect to main arteries to Cairo. There are regular buses connecting Cairo and other destinations with the major towns on the Sinai Peninsula.

ⓘ Getting Around

Because of Sinai's rugged landscape, paved roads link only the permanent settlements, and public transport is not quite as regular as elsewhere in Egypt. The bus network between the main South Sinai coastal towns is decent, but to other destinations there are only a couple of connections each day – and sometimes fewer. *Servees* cars are also in short supply and are only a popular means of transport in northern Sinai (primarily along the route connecting Rafah and Al-Arish with Suez and Cairo).

If you are driving, you will need to exercise caution at all times. Stick to tracks when going off the road, as there are still mines left over from the wars with Israel. When at the wheel in winter, remember that it rains with some frequency in Sinai, and flash floods often wash out paved roads, particularly around Wadi Feiran.

SINAI COAST

A barren coastline of extraordinary beauty, the Sinai coast is the meeting spot of choice for the world's political leaders, a booming package-tourism destination, and nirvana for the members of the international diving fraternity. Over the past several millennia some of human history's most significant events have played out against these isolated shores, and today the region remains sacred to all the world's major monotheistic religions. Of course, this doesn't alter the simple fact that the majority of international travellers make regular pilgrimages to the coast for its isolated beaches, superb coral reefs and unique Bedouin culture.

Ras Sudr
🎵069

Ras Sudr (or simply Sudr) was originally developed as the base town for one of Egypt's largest oil refineries, though its coastline and proximity to Cairo have spurred its transition into a resort area for wealthy Cairene families. With near constant winds, blowing at mostly force five or six, Sudr also enjoys a fine reputation among windsurfers. The town centre lies just off the main highway while to the south and north lay a handful of ageing resorts interspersed with holiday villas.

This is also a good base from which to explore the local hot springs. To the north of Ras Sudr is **Ain Musa** (Spring of Moses), said to be where Moses – on discovering that the water was too bitter to drink – took the advice of God and threw a special tree into the springs, miraculously sweetening the water. Unfortunately, however, only one of the 12 original springs still exists, and is now sadly filled with litter. The waters of **Hammam Fara'un** (Pharaoh's Bath), 50km south of Ras Sudr, are used by local Bedouin as a cure for various ailments. Women who want to take a dip here should do so clothed.

One of the most famous places for wind- and kitesurfing, **Moon Beach** (☎340 1500; www.moonbeachretreat.com; 7-/14-night half-board package per person UK£310/460, 7-/14-day kit hire UK£150/240, 7-day windsurfing course incl kit hire UK£120; ❄@) has beachfront bungalows with all the trimmings. Additionally, there's a professionally staffed and stocked wind- and kitesurfing centre and school.

Nightly rates and shorter-stay packages are available.

East Delta has a bus station along the main road about 500m south of the main junction. Buses to Cairo (E£25 to E£30, two to three hours) depart at 7.30am, 2pm and 4pm. A taxi from the bus station in Ras Sudr to Moon Beach costs about E£30.

Al-Tor

📞 069 / POP 19,826

Al-Tor, also known as Tur Sinai, has been a significant port since ancient times, though today it primarily serves as the administrative capital of the South Sinai Governorate. With stiff and constant breezes, Al-Tor has been trying in recent years to establish itself as a wind- and kitesurfing destination.

National Bank of Egypt has a branch with an ATM; it's in the town centre near the post office. If you've overstayed your welcome in Egypt, you can extend your visa at the Mogamma, the large administrative building on the main road in the town centre.

About 5km from town are some hot springs known as **Hammam Musa** (admission E£25), which tradition holds to have been one of the possible stopping points used by Moses and the Israelites on their journey through Sinai.

The focal point of wind- and kitesurfing in Al-Tor is the **Moses Bay Hotel** (📞377 4343; www.oceansource.net/hotel; 7-/14-night half-board package, incl equipment rental, per person €435/756; ❄❅), located approximately 3km from town. Moses Bay has its own private stretch of sand, pleasant rooms, a restaurant, and a wind- and kitesurfing centre.

The East Delta bus station is along the main road at the northern edge of town opposite the hospital. Buses depart from 7am onward throughout the day to Sharm el-Sheikh (E£15 to E£20, two hours). From the bus station, you can hire a pickup for E£10 to take you to Moses Bay Hotel.

Ras Mohammed National Park

About 20km west of Sharm el-Sheikh on the road from Al-Tor lies the headland of **Ras Mohammed National Park** (admission per person €5, plus per vehicle €5; ☺8am-5pm), named by local fishermen for a cliff that resembles a man's profile. The waters surrounding the peninsula are considered the jewel in the crown of the Red Sea. The park is visited by more than 50,000 visitors annually, enticed by the prospect of marvelling at some of the world's most spectacular coral-reef ecosystems, including a profusion of coral species and teeming marine life. Most, if not all, of the Red Sea's 1000 species of fish can be seen in the park's waters, including sought-after pelagics, such as hammerheads, manta rays and whale sharks.

Ras Mohammed occupies a total of 480 sq km of land and sea, including the desert in and around the *ras* (headland), Tiran Island, and the shoreline between Sharm el-Sheikh harbour and Nabq Protectorate.

Activities

If you're planning to dive in Ras Mohammed, you will need to arrive via a boat tour or a live-aboard, both of which typically depart from Sharm el-Sheikh or Dahab. For more information on dive operators in the area see p398 for Sharm el-Sheikh and p408 for Dahab.

If you arrive at the national park by private car, it's possible to hike to a variety of wilderness beaches and go snorkelling on offshore reefs – you will need to bring your own equipment.

At the park's visitors centre, a pink trail leads to **Khashaba Beach** and a camping area. Yellow arrows lead to the sandy beaches and calm waters of **Marsa Bareika**, excellent for snorkelling and safe for children. Blue arrows take you to **Main Beach**, which gets crowded with day visitors but remains one of the best places to see vertical coral walls. Brown arrows lead to **Aqaba Beaches**, which border the **Eel Garden**, named after a colony of garden eels 20m down. Just beyond here, orange arrows lead to the **Shark Observatory**, a clifftop area where you can sometimes see sharks as they feed on Ras Mohammed's rich offerings. The red arrows lead to **Jolanda Bay**, another beach with good snorkelling, and green arrows lead to the **Mangrove Channel** and **Hidden Bay** and to **Old Quay**, a spectacular vertical reef teeming with fish and accessible to snorkellers.

⛺ Sleeping

Camping is permitted in designated areas, with permits (€5 per person) available from the entrance gate. You'll need to bring all supplies with you; the nearest shops are in Sharm el-Sheikh. If you camp, respect the

Ras Mohammed National Park

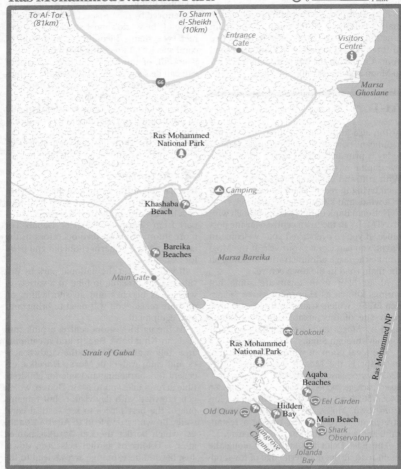

environment and clean up. In particular, don't bury toilet paper or rubbish, as the relentless winds here mean that nothing stays under the sand for long. Camp rules are strictly enforced by rangers, and if you're caught violating them, you will be fined and possibly even prosecuted.

ℹ️ Information

You'll need your passport to enter the park. Visitors on Sinai-only permits cannot go to Ras Mohammed overland as it is beyond the Sharm el-Sheikh boundary, but should not have any

problem on dive-boat trips – check with the dive clubs if you have any doubts.

The entrance to the park is about 20km from the reefs. A **visitors centre** (⏰10am-sunset Sat-Thu) with a restaurant is clearly marked to the left of the main access road in an area known as Marsa Ghoslane.

ℹ️ Getting There & Around

If you don't have a car, you can hire a taxi from Sharm el-Sheikh to bring you here, but expect to pay at least E£150 for the day. If you don't mind company, the easiest option is to join one of the many day tours by jeep or bus from Sharm el-Sheikh, most of which will drop you at the

HISTORY'S FOOTPRINTS

Sinai's rugged expanses are dotted with traces of early settlements and pilgrimage routes. One of the most impressive sites is Serabit al-Khadim, a ruined Pharaonic temple surrounded by ancient turquoise mines and starkly beautiful landscapes. Despite the remoteness of the location, turquoise was mined here as far back as the Old Kingdom. The temple itself dates back to the 12th dynasty and is dedicated to the goddess Hathor. Beside it is a New Kingdom shrine to Sopdu, god of the Eastern Desert. Throughout the temple's many courts, inscriptions list the temple's benefactors, including Hatshepsut (1473–1458 BC) and Tuthmosis III (1479–1425 BC). It is thought to have been abandoned during the reign of Ramses VII (1136–1129 BC).

Serabit al-Khadim can be reached via an unsignposted track just south of the coastal settlement of Abu Zenima or, more interestingly, from a track branching north off the road running east through Wadi Feiran via Wadi Mukattab (Valley of Inscriptions), which itself is well worth a visit. Here Sinai's largest collection of rock inscriptions and stelae, some dating back to the 3rd dynasty, give further evidence of ancient turquoise-mining activities. Unfortunately, many of the workings and stelae were damaged when the British unsuccessfully tried to revive the mines in 1901.

Heading inland from Serabit al-Khadim, another track takes you through the colourful wadis of Gebel Foga to the cliffs that edge Gebel et-Tih and the Forest of Pillars, a naturally occurring phenomenon accessible with 4WD and camel via a long track.

All of these destinations require guides and a 4WD. The most straightforward way to visit is to arrange a jeep trip with any of the tour agencies in Dahab or Moon Beach resort in Ras Sudr.

If you're travelling in your own vehicle, you can head into the village of Sheikh Barakat and get a guide: coming from Ras Sudr, follow the marked track that leads off into the desert, just south of Abu Zenima, for about 39km. When you see a white dome on your right, take the track to your left. After about 3km you'll come to Sheikh Barakat, where you can camp and organise a guide to take you the remaining 7km to the trail leading up to Serabit al-Khadim. At the end of this you'll need to park your vehicle and climb for about an hour. The track up the mountain is steep at times and involves a bit of scrambling but can be handled by anyone who is reasonably fit. Coming from Wadi Feiran, you can negotiate for a guide in the village of Feiran.

---

beaches and snorkelling sites. Alternatively, divers are often brought in by boat from tourist centres on the Red Sea.

To move around the park you'll need a vehicle. For conservation reasons, it's forbidden to leave the official tracks.

Sharm el-Sheikh & Na'ama Bay

069 / POP 38,478

The southern coast of the Gulf of Aqaba, between Tiran Island and Ras Mohammed National Park, features some of the world's most amazing underwater scenery. The crystal-clear waters, rare and lovely reefs and an incredible variety of exotic fish darting in and out of the colourful coral have made this a snorkelling and scuba-diving paradise. Unfortunately, the proudly brash resort destination of Sharm el-Sheikh, which comprises the two adjacent bays of Na'ama Bay and Sharm al-Maya, does not always reflect this serene underwater beauty.

Commonly described as Egypt's answer to Las Vegas, Sharm draws in legions of European holidaymakers every year on all-inclusive sun-and-sea tour packages. Over the past decade the march of concrete sprawl along the coastline to cater for these crowds has been relentless.

Sharm has both adoring fans and harsh critics, and opinions tend to fall solely in either camp. Defenders of the town, particularly resident expats and package travellers, claim that Sharm simply is what it is, namely a pleasure-seeking European enclave on the edge of Sinai. It is also touted as being a great destination for families who want to bring the little ones to Egypt for a beach holiday.

On the other hand, critics accuse Sharm of being sterile, and claim that its airbrushed facade covers up some serious environmental

Sharm el-Sheikh & Na'ama Bay

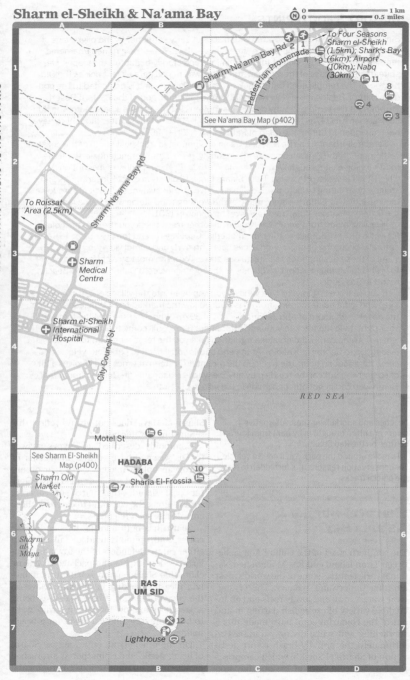

SINAI SHARM EL-SHEIKH &NA'AMA BAY

RED SEA

To Four Seasons
Sharm el-Sheikh
(1.5km); Shark's Bay
(6km); Airport
(10km); Nabq
(30km)

To Roissat
Area (2.5km)

Sharm Medical
Centre

Sharm el-Sheikh
International
Hospital

See Na'ama Bay Map (p402)

See Sharm El-Sheikh
Map (p400)

Sharm Old
Market

Motel St

HADABA

Sharia El-Frossia

Sharm
al-
Maya

RAS
UM SID

Lighthouse

Sharm el-Sheikh & Na'ama Bay

degradation which has led to pressing issues of sustainability. Independent travellers who are turned off by gated resorts would be wise to skip Sharm, passing through only en route to the more low-key and backpacker-friendly town of Dahab.

Activities

Snorkelling & Diving

It's something of a tragedy that Sharm's truly exquisite diving has been overshadowed by unfettered tourist development. However, offshore dive sites in both Sharm and the adjacent Ras Mohammed National Park are easily accessible by live-aboards, or even from boat trips departing from Dahab. For more information on diving in the Red Sea, see p36.

Snorkelling in the waters around Sharm is excellent. While there are some easily accessed reefs in central Na'ama Bay, it's better to make your way to the more impressive Near Garden and Middle Garden, even more beautiful Far Garden, or Ras Um Sid reef, near the lighthouse at Sharm el-Sheikh, which is known for its fan corals and plethora of fish, although the small beach is parcelled up between several resorts and can get quite crowded. Many of the dive sites further afield are also suitable for snorkellers and access can be arranged by joining a dive boat at most local dive clubs.

A small selection of Sharm's most popular dive sites are given below, listed from north to south.

Jackson Reef
DIVE SITE

(Map p38; location: Straits of Tiran) Home to sharks and large pelagic fish, Jackson Reef is crowned with the remains of a Cypriot freighter, the *Lara*, which ran aground here in 1985. Depth: surface to over 40m; rating: intermediate to advanced; access: boat.

Thomas Reef
DIVE SITE

(Map p38; location: Straits of Tiran) The smallest, but easily the most spectacular of the Tiran reefs, Thomas is home to steeply plunging walls that are lined with soft coral, schooling fish and patrolling sharks. Depth: surface to over 40m; rating: advanced; access: boat.

Gardens
DIVE SITE

(Map p396; location: btwn Shark's & Na'ama Bays) At the perennially popular Gardens there are actually three sites in one. **Near Garden** is home to a lovely chain of pinnacles, **Middle Garden** features a sandy path leading to a scenic overlook, and **Far Garden** is home to 'The Cathedral', a colourful overhang in deep water. Depth: surface to over 40m; rating: intermediate; access: shore or boat.

Ras Um Sid
DIVE SITE

(Map p396; location: opposite Hotel Royal Paradise) One of the best dive sites in the area, Ras Um Sid features a spectacular gorgonian forest along a dramatic drop-off that hosts a great variety of reef fish. Depth: 15m to 40m; rating: intermediate; access: shore or boat.

Ras Za'atir
DIVE SITE

(Map p38; location: south lip of the mouth of Marsa Bareika) Marking the start of the Ras Mohammed wall, Ras Za'atir has a series of small caves and overhangs where black coral trees flourish. Depth: surface to over 40m; rating: intermediate; access: boat.

Jackfish Alley
DIVE SITE

(Map p38; location: just south of Ras Za'atir) A comparatively shallow site that is good for a second or third dive, Jackfish Alley has two enormous caves filled with shoaling glassfish. Depth: 6m to 20m; rating: intermediate; access: boat.

Shark & Jolanda Reefs
DIVE SITE

(Map p38; location: southern tip of Ras Mohammed) This two-for-one special is among the most famous dives in the Red Sea, and rated one of the top five dives in the world – strong currents take divers on a thrilling ride along sheer coral walls, through vast schools of fish and eventually to the remains of the *Jolanda,* a Cypriot freighter that sank in 1980. Depth: surface to over 40m; rating: advanced; access: boat.

Dunraven
DIVE SITE

(Map p38; location: southeast tip of Sha'ab Mahmud) The *Dunraven* sunk in 1876 on her way from Bombay to Newcastle. Today the wreck is encrusted in coral and home to various knick-knacks including china plates, metal steins and jars of gooseberries and rhubarb among the detritus. Depth: 15m to 28m; rating: intermediate; access: boat

DIVE OPERATORS

Sinai Divers
DIVING

(Map p402; ☑360 0697; www.sinaidivers.com; Na'ama Bay) Based at the Ghazala Beach Hotel, this is one of Sharm el-Sheikh's most established dive centres.

Camel Dive Club
DIVING

(Map p402; ☑360 0700; www.cameldive.com; Camel Hotel, King of Bahrain St, Na'ama Bay) A respected club owned by Sinai diver Hisham Gabr.

Shark's Bay Diving Club
DIVING

(off Map p396; ☑360 0942; www.sharksbay. com; Shark's Bay Umbi Diving Village, Shark's Bay) Shark's Bay is a Bedouin-run centre with years of experience and its own house reef.

Emperor Divers
DIVING

(Map p402; ☑360 1734; www.emperordivers.com; Sharm–Na'ama Bay rd, Na'ama Bay) A branch of the five-star outfit offers courses aimed at families of all ages.

Oonas Dive Centre
DIVING

(Map p396; ☑360 0581; www.oonasdiveclub.com; Na'ama Bay) A popular centre at the northeastern end of Na'ama Bay.

Water Sports

Most major hotels offer a range of water sports, including sailing lessons, windsurfing, parasailing, pedalos, banana boats and glass-bottom boats. Most hotels also have beach access – either their own stretch of waterfront, or by agreement with another resort. Check when booking, as the beaches of some hotels are fairly distant (up to 10km) from the hotel itself and can only be accessed via shuttle. There is a narrow stretch of public beach diagonally opposite Hilton Fayrouz Resort on Na'ama Bay, but it is so crowded with rental chairs that it is difficult to see the sand. The other stretch of public beach is in Sharm al-Maya but note that women swimming here in bikinis or other skimpy attire are likely to feel uncomfortable.

Camel Rides

Camel rides to 'traditional Bedouin villages' can be easily arranged with most hotels.

SHARM EL-SHEIKH: THE LAY OF THE LAND

Most resorts are clustered along or just inland from the beach at Na'ama Bay. If you enjoy being in the centre of the action and don't mind the nightclub noise, central Na'ama Bay – consisting of a beachfront promenade and a pedestrians-only area lined with hotels, restaurants and shops – is the most convenient base. The further away from this central strip you go, the quieter things become: most of the resorts lining the coast north of Na'ama Bay are comparatively tranquil upmarket retreats with their own patch of sand and easy taxi access to the central area.

Sharm al-Maya, about 6km southwest of Na'ama Bay, centres on a large, walled market area known as Sharm Old Market, with a selection of inexpensive eateries. A large section of the Old Market area was badly damaged in the bombings of July 2005 and has been heavily rebuilt.

Spread out on a clifftop above Sharm al-Maya is the administrative area of Hadaba, which is rimmed by a barren network of long, treeless avenues lined with primarily mid-range resorts. To the southeast of the administrative area is Ras Um Sid, with an agreeable stretch of coastline, a lighthouse and a row of upmarket hotels.

Expect to pay US$40 to US$60 and to find yourself in the midst of a large group.

Horse Riding

Several top-end hotels, including **Sofitel Sharm el-Sheikh** (Map p396; ☑360 0081; www.sofitel.com; Na'ama Bay), offer horse riding from about US$30 to US$60 per hour.

Tours

Almost all travel agencies and large hotels organise jeep or bus trips to St Katherine's Monastery (p428), and to desert attractions such as the Coloured Canyon (p409). However, most of the guides are Nile Valley dwellers, not Bedouin, and the groups are often large. Better, more sensitive trips can be arranged from Dahab.

Black Jack Bike   CYCLING
(☑0122 370 3116; www.blackjackbike.com) This small company organises highly recommended half-day (five-hour) mountain-bike tours (bikes are European standard) into the Nabq Protectorate. Tours cost €50 and include pickup from hotel, helmet, water and a support van. It also offers tailor-made tours for people interested in full-day or multiday trips. Call or book online.

Sleeping

Sharm el-Sheikh and the surrounding area have one of the greatest concentrations of hotels in Egypt, but budget accommodation places are few and far between, with the all-inclusive resort being the standard rather than the exception. For anyone who is serious about pinching their pennies, it's probably wise to continue on to Dahab.

Be advised that the hotel scene in Sharm is changing rapidly and prices tend to be subject to wild fluctuations depending on the number of tourists in town. Despite the high rack rates, most of the resorts sell their rooms at much cheaper prices as part of all-inclusive packages. Cheaper rates for most are always available if you book in advance.

 Sinai Old Spices   B&B $$
(off Map p396; ☑0122 680 3130; www.sinaioldspices.com; Roissat area; s/d E£150/240; ❄) Hidden behind a terracotta wall, this charmingly dinky B&B serves up bundles of quirky style using locally inspired architecture. The individually decorated rooms all come with kitchenette and fabulous modern bathrooms. It's a E£30 taxi ride from Sharm itself so won't suit everyone, but for those seeking a peaceful retreat from the bright lights of Na'ama Bay it's a perfect choice. Phone beforehand to arrange a pickup, or get directions, as it's tricky to find.

Camel Hotel   HOTEL $$
(Map p402; ☑360 0700; www.cameldive.com; King of Bahrain St; r from €40; ❄🛜🏊) Attached to the dive centre of the same name, Camel Hotel is one of the best places to stay if diving is your main Sharm agenda. Despite being in the heart of Na'ama Bay, the spacious, modern rooms are gloriously quiet (thanks to soundproof windows) so you're guaranteed a good night's sleep.

Sofitel Sharm el-Sheikh   RESORT $$$
(Map p396; ☑360 0081; www.sofitel.com; s/d €98/128; ❄@🏊) This whitewashed hotel terraces majestically down towards the sea like a sultan's palace from a children's fairy tale. The distinctly Middle Eastern–style rooms are decked out in exotic wooden furniture, and boast stunning views over the bay. True to its name, the Sofitel offers an incredibly sophisticated resort experience to the guests privileged enough to be staying here.

**Shark's Bay Umbi
Diving Village**   BEACH CAMP $$
(off Map p396; ☑360 0942; www.sharksbay.com; s/d huts without bathroom €17/20; s/d beach cabins €24/35, s/d room €35/45; ❄🛜) This long-standing Bedouin-owned place is a tumble of cute chalets that flow down to the sea. Pine beach cabins are spick and span, if a bit of a squeeze, and there are larger rooms built into the cliff above. If you're really strapped for cash, spartan huts (with just mattress and mosquito net) are up on the clifftop. To reach the camp, just tell the taxi driver 'Shark's Bay Umbi'; expect to pay about E£25 from Na'ama Bay and E£35 to E£45 from the bus station.

**Four Seasons
Sharm el-Sheikh**   RESORT $$$
(off Map p396; ☑360 3555; www.fourseasons.com/sharmelsheikh; r from US$325; ❄@🏊) Dripping elegance at every turn, this palatial resort is the height of secluded luxury built around palm-fringed courtyards and manicured gardens overlooking the Straits of Tiran. Huge rooms blend modern design seamlessly with Arabesque accents boasting intricate lattice woodwork and ornate bronze fixtures. Of course, you're going to need a small fortune to spend some time here, but it's difficult to put a price on over-the-top indulgence.

Sharm el-Sheikh

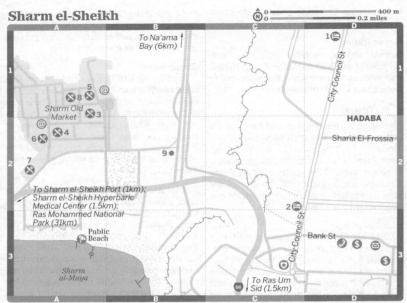

SINAI SHARM EL-SHEIKH &NA'AMA BAY

Sharm el-Sheikh

🛌 Sleeping

🍴 Eating

ℹ Transport

Ritz Carlton Sharm el-Sheikh　　RESORT **$$$**
(Map p396; ☏366 1919; www.ritzcarlton.com; Ras Um Sid; r from US$170; ❄@☀) Towering Egyptian-temple columns, lashings of glass and grand Louis XV furniture welcome you into the sweeping foyer. Unfortunately, after this onslaught of uncompromising luxury, the rather bland (though supremely comfortable) rooms are a bit of a let-down.

Tropicana Tivoli　　HOTEL **$$**
(Map p400; ☏366 1384; www.tropicanahotels.com; Hadaba; s/d from US$70/80; ❄☀) A well-maintained midrange winner with tidy rooms (including kitchenette) set around a large pool, plus helpful staff. A good option for families on a strict budget.

Oonas Hotel　　HOTEL **$$**
(Map p402; ☏360 0581; www.oonasdiveclub.com; Na'ama Bay; s/d €45/60; ❄@☀) This combo dive centre and hotel has bland but well-equipped rooms on a prime spot along the promenade. Accommodation is a bargain if booked in conjunction with a dive package.

Hyatt Regency Sharm el-Sheikh RESORT **$$$**
(Map p396; ☏360 1234; www.sharm.hyatt.com; r/ ste from US$185/350; ❄@☀) With grand villa styling, superior service and vast landscaped gardens, the Hyatt is a serene retreat. Standard rooms are classically decorated and many have sweeping sea views.

Ghazala Gardens　　HOTEL **$$**
(Map p402; ☏360 0150; http://redseahotels.com; Sharm–Na'ama Bay rd; r from US$100; ❄@☀) All glitzy water features and Moroccan styling, the friendly Ghazala has weathered the storm of terrorism (it was the target of the massive truck bomb that claimed 45 lives in 2005) and is as popular as ever. Although it's not actually on the beach, guests can simply cross the road and access the hotel's sister property, the Ghazala Beach.

Hilton Sharm el-Sheikh
Fayrouz Resort
RESORT $$

(Map p402; ☑360 0137; www.hiltonworldresorts.com; Sharm–Na'ama Bay rd; s/d US$80/100; ✽@☲) This family-friendly resort is in prime position along the promenade. The bungalows are large and light-filled though pale in comparison to the shows of wealth found at competing hotels.

Amar Sina
HOTEL $$

(Map p396; ☑366 2222/9; www.minasegypt.com; Hadaba; r E£300; ✽@☲) Decked out like an Egyptian village, this midranger offers brick-domed rooms complete with plenty of kitsch styling, furniture sourced from the 1970s and dinky balconies.

Coral Hills Resort
HOTEL $$

(Map p396; ☑366 5807; www.coralhillsresorts.com; Hadaba; s/d US$35/50; ✽@☲) The rooms may be characterless and full of tired, dated furniture but for this price who's complaining. The large pool area is a highlight.

Youth Hostel
HOSTEL $

(Map p400; ☑366 0317; City Council St, Hadaba; dm E£65; ✽) The only attraction of this shabby affair is that it's the cheapest place to stay in the area and the management is extremely sweet.

✖ Eating

It's a shame most tourists on all-inclusive packages never stray from their resort, as Sharm dishes up a glutton's paradise of enticing restaurants spanning the culinary globe. You should prepare for a wallet-bashing, however, as eating out here is by no means cheap (and be aware that most high-end restaurants add a service tax of 10% and a government tax of 12% on top of your bill) – still, the foodie manna of multiple cuisines on offer here makes splurging on a slap-up meal well worth the extra expense.

⌂TOP CHOICE Fairuz
LEBANESE $$$

(Map p402; King of Bahrain St; mezze dishes E£18; mains E£80-100; ✽) Lebanese is flavour of the month in Sharm and this Levantine restaurant will lead you on a mouth-watering journey through the subtle flavours of the Middle East. Forgo the main-course menu completely and concentrate on the mezze (starter-sized dishes), which are the heart of any Lebanese dining experience. Choose a bundle of mezze such as *batingan bi laban* (aubergine in garlicky yoghurt), *makinek*

(spicy sausages) and *loubieh* (a green-bean stew) to share with delicious fresh-from-the-oven bread. The great-value mezze set menu (E£105 per person, minimum two people) is the best way to sample a full array of flavours.

Abou El Sid
EGYPTIAN $$

(Map p402; Sultan Qabos St; dishes E£30-100; ✽) This branch of the famous Zamalek restaurant now flies the flag for Egyptian cuisine in Sharm, and is one of the few places in town where you can experience the full gamut of Egypt's national dishes. Specialities such as *molokhiyya* (stewed leaf soup), stuffed pigeon and *kirsha* (spicy lentil stew) are menu highlights. Don't skip the mezze selection as it's full of delightfully tasty and tangy surprises.

El-Masrien
EGYPTIAN $$

(Map p400; dishes E£25-40) El-Masrien's continued success is due to the fact it delivers succulent kebabs and *kofta* (mincemeat and spices grilled on a skewer) that perfectly hit the spot, without hiking its prices to try and compete with fancier Sharm restaurants. It's an old-fashioned neighbourhood place with tables pouring out onto the pavement, perfect for Sharm Old Market people-watching.

Safsafa Restaurant
SEAFOOD $$

(Map p400; mains E£20-50; ✽) This tiny, cheerful restaurant manages to serve up fresh seafood platters, *tagen* (stews cooked in a deep clay pot) and pasta at budget-friendly prices.

Pomodoro
ITALIAN $$

(Map p402; King of Bahrain St; dishes E£40-80; ◷from 6.30pm) Hearty portions of Italian classics keep this place full of customers most evenings. Risottos, pasta and a fair whack of seafood are all featured on the menu, as well as favourites like pepper steak.

Tandoori
INDIAN $$$

(Map p402; Camel Hotel, King of Bahrain St; dishes E£40-125; ◷from 6.30pm) The courtyard of the Camel Hotel is home to what many consider Sharm's best Indian food, including a selection of tandoori dishes and an excellent *dhal makhani* (dish of black lentils and red kidney beans).

Tam Tam
EGYPTIAN $$

(Map p402; Na'ama Bay promenade; dishes E£20-60) Great for those who want to sample a range of Egyptian fare. This laid-back waterfront restaurant is the place to while away a

Na'ama Bay

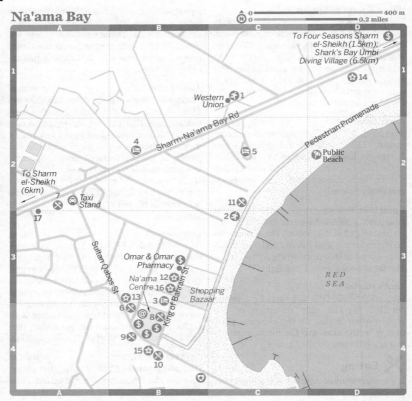

few hours while relaxing on cushions overlooking the beach and puffing on a sheesha.

Little Buddha
ASIAN $$$
(Map p402; Sultan Qabos St; mains E£45-115; ✳) One of the most popular Asian restaurants in Sharm, Little Buddha serves excellent Asian fusion cuisine alongside a fresh and varied sushi bar. Later in the night it turns into a loungey bar.

Sala Thai
ASIAN $$$
(Map p396; Hyatt Regency Sharm el-Sheikh; dishes E£40-120; ✳) Delicious Thai food (fiery curries and delicately spiced noodle dishes) and pleasing aesthetics (teak decor and an outdoor terrace) are yours to enjoy at this comfortable spot overlooking the sea.

Al-Fanar
ITALIAN $$$
(Map p396; Ras Um Sid; dishes E£40-150; ⊙10am-10.30pm; ✳) All nooks and crannies of scattered Bedouin-style seating, seafront vistas

and decent Italian (vast pasta and pizza menu) dining. Al-Fanar (named after its lighthouse location) is a well-deserved upmarket Sharm dining favourite.

Koshary El-Sheikh
EGYPTIAN FAST FOOD $
(Map p400; meals E£5-10) Egypt's favourite carbohydrate-fuelled feast, *kushari* (a blend of pasta, rice, lentils and fried onion smothered in a tomato sauce) is dished up here.

Self-Catering
There are several small but well-stocked supermarkets in Sharm Old Market, including **Supermarket El-Baraka** (Map p400) and the large **Sharm Express** (Map p400). Beer and wine can be bought at **Al-Ahram Beverages** (Map p400). There are also numerous supermarkets in central Na'ama Bay, including the large and well-stocked **Carrefour Supermarket** (Map p402; ⊙9am-1am) and **Panorama Supermarket** (Map p402; ⊙9am-2am).

Na'ama Bay

☆ Entertainment

Considering Egypt is a fairly conservative country that typically shuns alcohol and excess pleasures of the flesh, Sharm el-Sheikh can either be a shock to the senses or a welcome relief – depending on your own vices, of course. The entire charade may be wholly un-Egyptian, but after a few beers and a couple of uninhibited dancing sessions, fun is usually had by all.

Camel Roof Bar   BAR
(Map p402; Camel Hotel, King of Bahrain St, Na'ama Bay; ☻3pm-2.30am) Camel is a favourite among dive instructors for its relaxed, casual vibe. This is the optimal place to start off the evening, especially if you've been diving all day and are looking to swap stories from down under.

Bus Stop Lounge   CLUB
(Map p402; King of Bahrain St, Na'ama Bay; ☻4pm-3am) This popular disco-bar is known for its good music and up-for-it, fun-loving crowd. There's a pool table for those who don't feel like getting on the dance floor, and happy hour from 8pm to 9pm gets you two-for-one beers and half-price cocktails.

Little Buddha   CLUB
(Map p402; Sultan Qabos St, Na'ama Bay; ☻11pm-3am) With dim lights, big cushiony chairs and a mellow ambience, the bar at this Asian fusion restaurant gets going after the kitchen closes.

Pacha   CLUB
(Map p402; www.pachasharm.com; King of Bahrain St, Na'ama Bay) The hub of Sharm's nightlife, Pacha goes wild pretty much every night of the week. Watch for Pacha's advertising around town to see what's playing.

Pirates' Bar   BAR
(Map p402; Hilton Fayrouz Reort, Na'ama Bay) A cosy pub where divers congregate for an early-evening drink or bar meal. Happy hour is from 5.30pm to 7.30pm.

Hard Rock Café   BAR
(Map p402; Sultan Qabos St, Na'ama Bay) A late-night disco-bar with dancing, and one of Sharm's most popular nightspots. Dancing starts at midnight and goes until the wee hours of the morn'.

Harry's Pub   PUB
(Map p402; Marriott Beach Resort, Na'ama Bay) This English pub has a large selection of beers on tap and occasional special nights with unlimited draught beer at a very reasonable price.

La Folie Bar   BAR
(Map p396; Iberotel Lido, Na'ama Bay; ☻2pm-2am) For a more sedate start to your evening, head to this quiet, pleasant bar on the water overlooking the bright lights of Na'ama Bay.

Mexicana Bar   BAR
(Map p402; Na'ama Bay Hotel, Na'ama Bay) A small and sometimes happening bar close to the promenade, this is a great place to down a few bowls of nachos followed by a decent margarita.

ℹ Information

Dangers & Annoyances

In July 2005, three terrorist bombs exploded in Sharm el-Sheikh, killing 88 people and injuring over 200. The worst damage was in the Sharm Old Market area and near Ghazala Gardens hotel in Na'ama Bay. Security in Sharm was beefed up considerably in the aftermath and the town has not been targeted since.

Sharm is generally considered to be a safe destination, and – barring another major attack – it is a relaxed and hassle-free destination, even if you're travelling with young children.

For an overview of the history of terrorism in Sinai, see p391.

Emergency

Ambulance (☑123)

Tourist police Hadaba (Map p400; ☑366 0311); Na'ama Bay (Map p402; ☑360 0554, 366 0675; booth next to Marina Sharm Hotel)

Internet Access

Many hotels have internet access and there are internet cafes dotted around town, each charging between E£5 and E£10 per hour depending on your length of use. Many of the restaurants and hotels offer wi-fi (the luxury hotels usually charge for this service).

Tiba Net (Map p400; Sharm Old Market; ⊙24hr)

Speed Net (Map p400; Sharm Old Market; ⊙24hr)

Naama Internet (Map p402; Na'ama Centre, Na'ama Bay; ⊙noon-3am)

Medical Services

Omar & Omar Pharmacy (Map p402; ☑360 0960; King of Bahrain St, Na'ama Bay; ⊙9am-1am)

Sharm el-Sheikh Hyberbaric Medical Center (off Map p396; ☑366 0922/3, 0122 212 4292; hyper_med _center@sinainet.com.eg; Sharm el-Sheikh; ⊙24hr)

Sharm el-Sheikh International Hospital (Map p396; ☑366 0893/4/5; Sharm–Na'ama Bay rd, Sharm el-Sheikh; ⊙24hr)

Sharm Medical Center (Map p396; ☑366 1744; Sharm–Na'ama Bay rd, Sharm el-Sheikh; ⊙24hr) Next to the bus station.

Money

You will find ATMs every few metres in Na'ama Bay, including several in the **Na'ama Centre** (Map p402), as well as ATMs in the lobbies of all the larger hotels. Otherwise, all the major banks have branches in Hadaba.

Banque du Caire (Map p400; Hadaba) Has an ATM.

Commercial International Bank (Map p402; Na'ama Centre, Na'ama Bay; ⊙9am-1pm & 6-10pm Sat-Thu, 10-11am Fri) Has an ATM.

HSBC (Map p402; ☑360 0614; Na'ama Centre, Na'ama Bay) Has an ATM.

National Bank of Egypt Hadaba (Map p400; Bank St; ⊙8.30am-2pm & 6-9pm Sat-Thu, 9am-1pm & 6-9pm Fri); Na'ama Bay (Map p402) Both have an ATM.

Thomas Cook (Map p402; ☑360 1808; Gafy Mall, Sharm–Na'ama Bay rd, Na'ama Bay; ⊙9am-2pm & 6-10pm) Just west of Sinai Star Hotel.

Western Union (Map p402; ☑364 0466; Rosetta Hotel, Na'ama Bay; ⊙8.30am-2pm & 6-10pm Sat-Thu, 3-10pm Fri)

Post

Main post office (Map p400; Bank St, Hadaba)

Telephone

Most internet cafes allow you to dial internationally for E£4 to E£7 per minute.

Telephone centrale (Map p400; Bank St, Hadaba; ⊙24hr).

ℹ Getting There & Away

Air

Sharm el-Sheikh Airport (☑360 1140, www. sharm-el-sheikh.airport-authority.com) is Sinai's major travel hub. For domestic destinations **EgyptAir** (Map p400; ☑366 1056; www. egyptair.com; Sharm al-Maya; ⊙9am-9pm) has several flights per day to Cairo and five per week direct to Luxor. For all other domestic destinations you usually have to change in Cairo. Prices fluctuate wildly depending on season. If you book in advance it's sometimes possible to snag a ticket for less than US$100.

EasyJet (www.easyjet.com) operates daily flights to the UK and, if booked in advance, can be one of the cheapest ways to fly in or out of Egypt. BMI also offer flights (via Cairo) and Royal Jordanian has daily flights to Amman. There are also plenty of charter flights in and out of Sharm, which usually offer significantly cheaper fares. Even if you're an independent traveller, it's worthwhile seeing if you can book a seat on one of them.

Boat

The ferry service between Sharm el-Sheikh and Hurghada stopped operating in 2010. During the course of research for this book a new ferry schedule was announced but had yet to begin operation. The proposed schedule has departures for Hurghada at 5pm every Tuesday, Thursday and Saturday (adult/child E£250/150, two hours). Enquire at any of the hotels and travel agencies in Sharm el-Sheikh for up-to-date information. You could also contact the

Sharm el-Sheikh **Port Office** (off Map p400; ☏366 0217; Sharm el-Sheikh Port).

Bus

The bus station (Map p396) is along the Sharm–Na'ama Bay road behind the Mobil petrol station. Seats on the buses to Cairo should be reserved in advance. Buy tickets from the following bus companies at the bus station.

Super Jet (☏366 1622, in Cairo 02-2290 9017) runs buses to Cairo (E£85, six to seven hours) at 11am, 1pm, 3pm and 11.30pm. The 3pm service continues on to Alexandria (E£110, eight to nine hours).

East Delta Travel Co (☏366 0660) also has buses to Cairo (E£60 to E£80) at 7.30am, 9.30am, 11am, 12.30pm, 2.30pm, 3.30pm, 8pm, 9.30pm, 11pm, midnight and 1am. All except the 11am, 2.30pm, 11pm and midnight services stop in Al-Tor (E£11, one to two hours). There are daily buses to Suez (E£80, six to seven hours) at 7am and 10am. Heading north there are buses to Dahab (E£15 to E£20, one to two hours) at 6am, 7am, 9am, 3pm, 5pm and 9pm; to Nuweiba (E£25 to E£30, two to three hours) at 9am and 5pm; and to Taba (E£30 to E£35, three to four hours) at 9am.

❶ Getting Around

To/From the Airport

Sharm el-Sheikh International Airport is about 10km north of Na'ama Bay at Ras Nasrany; taxis generally charge from E£20 to E£25 from the airport to Sharm or Na'ama Bay. Prepare to bargain hard.

Bicycle

Standard and cross-country bicycles can be rented from many hotels. **Black Jack Bike** (☏0122 370 3116; www.blackjackbike.com) rents out European-standard mountain bikes for €22 per day (including helmet) and will deliver to your hotel door.

Car

Car-rental agencies in Na'ama Bay include **Avis** (Map p402; ☏360 2400/0979; Sharm–Na'ama Bay rd, Na'ama Bay), just west of Carrefour Supermarket; **Hertz** (Map p396; ☏366 2299; Bank St, Hadaba) and **Sixt Car Rental** (Map p402; ☏360 0137; Hilton Fayrouz Resort). All charge about US$80 per day for a basic saloon, and US$120 and up for a roomier 4WD. Unlimited-kilometre arrangements generally require a minimum three- to four-day rental.

Microbus & Taxi

Blue-and-white microbuses regularly ply the stretch between central Na'ama Bay and Sharm el-Sheikh. The fare is E£2, though foreigners are often charged E£5. Taxis charge a minimum of E£10 between the two centres, and between Hadaba and Na'ama Bay, and from E£5 within Na'ama Bay. Many of the hotels above Ras Um Sid have their own shuttles to Na'ama Bay.

Nabq Protectorate

Thirty-five kilometres north of Sharm el-Sheikh is **Nabq**, the largest coastal protectorate on the Gulf of Aqaba. Named after an oasis that lies within its boundaries, Nabq straddles 600 sq km of land and sea between the Straits of Tiran and Dahab. Because it is less frequently visited than Ras Mohammed, Nabq is a good place to see Sinai as it was before the arrival of mass tourism.

There is a **visitors centre** (admission €5; ⊙8am-5pm) located off the road leading from Sharm el-Sheikh past the airport and Ras Nasrany. Within the park itself, you'll find several hiking trails, clearly marked snorkelling spots and designated camping areas.

Nabq's main attraction is its **mangrove forest**, which runs along the shoreline at the mouth of Wadi Kid and is the most northerly mangrove stand in the world. Mangrove root systems filter most of the salt from seawater and help to stabilise shorelines, while also providing an important habitat for birds and fish. Just inland from the mangrove forest are the dunes of Wadi Kid, which are home to one of the Middle East's largest stands of **arak bushes** (arak twigs were traditionally used by Bedouin to clean teeth). Gazelles, rock hyraxes and Nubian ibexes can be seen in the protectorate, as well as two villages of Bedouin from the Mizena tribe. Offshore there are rich reefs with easy access, although visibility can be poor because of sediment from the mangroves.

To visit Nabq, you'll need a vehicle or will have to join an organised tour. Most hotels and resorts in Sharm el-Sheikh and Dahab offer safaris, both on the land and in the water. If you drive, remember that vehicles are strictly forbidden to leave the tracks.

Dahab
☏069

Low-key, laid-back and low-rise, Dahab continues its ongoing evolution into the Middle East's prime beach resort for independent travellers. The startling transformation from dusty Bedouin outpost to spruced-up

Dahab

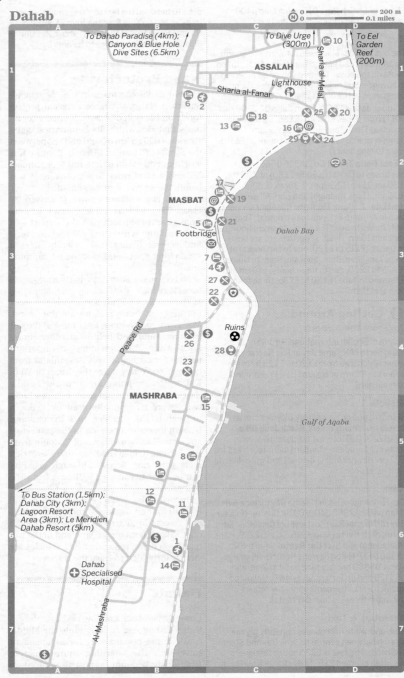

N 0 ———————— 200 m
0 ———————— 0.1 miles

To Dahab Paradise (4km);
Canyon & Blue Hole
Dive Sites (6.5km)

To Dive Urge
(300m)

10

To Eel
Garden
Reef
(200m)

ASSALAH

Lighthouse

Sharia al-Fanar

Sharia al-Melai

6 2

18

13

25   20

16 @

29   24

3

$

17

MASBAT @

19

$

5 21

Footbridge

Dahab Bay

7

4

27

22

26 $

Ruins

23

28

MASHRABA

15

Gulf of Aqaba

8

9

To Bus Station (1.5km);
Dahab City (3km);
Lagoon Resort
Area (3km); Le Meridien
Dahab Resort (5km)

12

11

$ 1

*Dahab
Specialised
Hospital*

14

Al-Mashraba

$

Dahab

tourist village is not without its detractors, who reminisce fondly of the days when you dossed in basic huts by the shore. But for all the starry-eyed memories of 'the good old days', there are plenty of plusses that have come with prosperity. Diving is now a much safer and more organised activity thanks to better regulation of operators; the shoreside restaurants have calmed down their touting to become more friendly 'hello' than sales barrage; and it's cleaner and much more family-friendly, offering accommodation choices for everyone rather than just hardened backpackers.

Meaning 'gold' in Arabic – a reference to the area's sandy coastline (despite the main tourist area having no golden sands to speak of) – Dahab is the perfect base from which to explore some of Egypt's most spectacular diving and snorkelling. A short walk or jeep ride will bring you to plenty of the Red Sea's most memorable dive sites, and a boat can bring you within easy striking distance of the world-class reefs in nearby Ras Mohammed National Park. Predominantly a Bedouin enclave at its heart, Dahab is also the preferred base for organising guided trekking and camel excursions into the interior deserts, as well as to the lofty heights of Mt Sinai.

This is the one town on the south Sinai Peninsula where independent travellers are the rule rather than the exception and Dahab's growth has not destroyed its budget-traveller roots. Reeled in by a fusion of hippy mellowness and resort chic (where good cappuccino and sushi are as much a part of the action as cheap rooms and herds of goats fossicking in the back alleys), many travellers plan a few nights here and instead stay for weeks. If Dahab is in your sights, be forewarned – after a few days of crystal-clear diving, desert trekking, oceanside dinners and countless sheesha sessions, you're probably going to want to cancel the rest of your itinerary.

🏃 Activities

Snorkelling & Diving
Other than just lounging around, snorkelling and diving are the most popular activities in Dahab. The best reefs for snorkelling are **Lighthouse Reef** and **Eel Garden**, both in Assalah. You can hire snorkelling gear from all the dive centres and many other places in Masbat for about E£25 to E£40 per day. Keep in mind that some of the reefs have unexpected currents – drownings have occurred in Dahab – so keep your wits about you.

ONE TOKE OVER THE LINE

Dahab's hippy roots and backpacker-friendly atmosphere often go hand in hand with drug use. At some point here, you will likely be offered marijuana or hashish (and possibly harder stuff), and you may see people around you openly using drugs. Some misinformed travellers have the attitude that toking is legal – it's not at all, and the penalty for being caught with drugs is harsh.

Dahab veterans may fondly recall smoking on the beach in broad daylight, but these days police patrol with drug-sniffing dogs and are quick to make a bust. Please heed our advice – if you're going to indulge, do it discreetly, either under cover of night or hidden away from prying eyes and sensitive nostrils. Of course, given the state of Egyptian prisons, it's probably better to just hold off on the herb until you get home.

An overview of some of the most popular diving sites – from north to south – is given below. Note that despite the intimidating reputation of the Canyon and Blue Hole dive sites as danger zones for careless divers, the tops of the reefs are teeming with life, making them fine snorkelling destinations too when the sea is calm. It's easy to find half-day tours to both sites but watch for hidden 'extras', such as overpriced drinks and gear-minding fees at some of the cafes around the Blue Hole. Many dive centres also organise snorkelling and dive safaris to the nearby **Ras Abu Gallum** and **Nabq** protectorates, as well as overnights to **Ras Mohammed National Park**.

For an overview of diving in the Red Sea, see p36.

Canyon   DIVE SITE
(Map p38; location: north side of Dahab) One of the area's most popular dives, the Canyon is a long, narrow trench that runs perpendicular to the reef shelf, and is home to prolific hard and soft corals. Depth: 5m to 33m; rating: intermediate; access: shore.

Eel Garden   DIVE SITE
(off Map p406; location: north side of Dahab) Eel Garden takes its name from the countless garden eels that carpet the sea floor. Other highlights include huge coral boulders and dense congregations of barracudas. Depth: 5m to 20m; rating: intermediate; access: shore.

Lighthouse   DIVE SITE
(Map p406; location: Masbat) This sloping reef is home to a bounty of fish life and is Dahab's main night-diving site. More experienced divers can descend to the sandy bottom where there's a profusion of coral towers. Depth: 5m to 30m; rating: novice; access: shore.

Islands   DIVE SITE
(Map p38; location: south side of Dahab) This underwater *Alice in Wonderland*-esque site offers an outstanding topography of coral alleyways, amphitheatres, valleys and gulleys. Depth: 5m to 18m; rating: novice; access: shore.

Umm Sid   DIVE SITE
(Map p38; location: 15km south of Dahab) An impressive entrance through a wide corridor carved into a steeply sloping reef is a highlight of this dive. Further down you'll find table corals and two enormous gorgonians. Depth: 5m to 35m; rating: intermediate to advanced; access: shore.

Gabr el-Bint   DIVE SITE
(Map p38; location: 25km south of Dahab) This dive features a dramatic seascape highlighted by a 60m wall cut by numerous chasms, faults and sandy ravines. If you access the site by land the journey combines a 4WD trip and a Bedouin-led camel convoy. Depth: 10m to 30m; rating: intermediate; access: boat/camel.

DIVE OPERATORS

Red Sea Relax Dive Centre   DIVING
(☑364 1309; www.red-sea-relax.com; Red Sea Relax, Masbat) Long-standing five-star PADI centre with excellent reputation.

Poseidon Divers   DIVING
(☑364 0091; www.poseidondivers.com; Crazy Camel Camp, Mashraba) Award-winning PADI centre that consistently gets recommended by travellers.

Big Blue Dive Centre   DIVING
(☑364 0045; www.bigbluedahab; Mashraba) Popular and friendly five-star PADI centre with a good reputation.

Dive Urge   DIVING
(☑364 0957; www.dive-urge.com; Sharia al-Melal, Assalah) Five-star PADI centre with commendable environmental credentials.

Nesima Dive Centre DIVING
(☎364 0320; www.nesima-resort.com; Nesima Resort, Mashraba) A reputable club owned by local environmental activist and veteran diver Sherif Ebeid.

Camel & Jeep Safaris

Dahab is one of the best places in Sinai to arrange camel safaris into the dramatic mountains lining the coast, especially the spectacular Ras Abu Gallum Protectorate. When choosing who to go with, make sure that the tour operator works with the Bedouin. Unfortunately, local communities have been excluded from the tourist industry, which tends to be dominated by migrants from the Nile Valley. Make sure that your camel driver registers with the police before beginning the safari. Itineraries – and as a result, prices – are generally custom-designed, but expect to pay around E£200 per person for an evening trip into the mountains with dinner at a Bedouin camp, and from about E£300 to E£400 per person per day for a safari including all food and water.

One of the most popular jeep safaris is a trip to **Coloured Canyon**, northwest of Nuweiba. The canyon derives its name from the layers of bright, multicoloured stones that resemble paintings on its steep, narrow walls, and is magnificently beautiful. As the canyon is sheltered from the wind, the silence – assuming you aren't there with a crowd – is one of its most impressive features. Unfortunately, the canyon has become overtouristed in recent years, and many operators have also begun offering trips to other sites where the rock formations are equally impressive and the sense of wilderness more intact. All of the hotels, dive centres and travel agencies offer jeep safaris, though prices vary considerably depending on the time of year, your destination and the

size of your party – don't be afraid to shop around and bargain hard.

Water Sports

There's no beach to speak of in Assalah itself – instead the rocky coastline leads straight out onto the reef. For the golden sands after which Dahab was named, you'll need to head down to the lagoon where the resorts are clustered. Most resorts offer beach-use day access starting from E£50.

Kayaks can be rented through **Red Sea Relax** in Masbat. At the resorts around the lagoon you can hire pedalos and kayaks as well as take windsurfing and kitesurfing courses. The main windsurfing centre is **Club Mistral** (☎364 1577; www.club-mistral.com), which operates out of its office at the Hilton Dahab Resort. **Happy Kite** (☎0109 224 4822; www.happy-kite.com) offers kitesurfing courses (from beginner to advanced) from its base nearby.

☞ Tours

All the tour operators in Dahab offer tours to Mt Sinai and St Katherine's Monastery (usually leaving late at night to climb the mountain for sunrise, and returning midday). Nearly all also offer one-day, whirlwind trips to either Petra in Jordan or Jerusalem in Israel. Unless you are really strapped for time it's usually best to make your own independent arrangements for Jordan and Israel. If you do decide to take one of these international tours, be aware that most of your time will be spent travelling there and back with very little time at the actual sights. For more information on how to get to Petra see p421.

Desert Riders QUAD BIKING
(☎0111 515 4411; Sharia al-Fanar, Masbat) Most tours do a loop circuit from town taking in one of either Wadi al-Rayan or Wadi Con-

DAHAB: THE LAY OF THE LAND

There are two parts to Dahab: the small and newer area of Dahab City to the south, with a smattering of resort hotels at the lagoon, the bus station, post and phone offices, and a bank; and Assalah, which runs along the beach and is the major tourist stretch. Assalah is further divided into three areas. The most northern point, and the main local residential area, is still known as Assalah. From the lighthouse the Masbat area begins, made up of a stretch of 'camps', hotels and laid-back restaurants that curve along the bay. To the south, starting roughly at the ruins (no entry) is the slightly more staid Mashraba, named after the freshwater springs that apparently exist around the beach. In the centre of Masbat is a small pedestrian bridge, which makes a convenient landmark and is a good place to find taxis.

DON'T MISS

BELLS & BLUE HOLE

Carved into a reef just offshore from Dahab is Egypt's most infamous dive site. The **Blue Hole** (Map p38; location: 8km north of Dahab) is a gaping sinkhole that drops straight down – some say to as deep as 130m. Unfortunately, the site has claimed several lives, mainly thrill-seekers venturing well below the sport-diving limit.

The trap is an archway at approximately 65m, which connects the sinkhole to the open ocean. Underprepared solo divers attempting to find this archway have succumbed to narcosis, missed the archway entirely, lost all sense of direction or simply run out of air. If you leave the depths to the experienced technical divers, you'll find the outer lip of the Blue Hole is full of marine life, and a reasonable plunge into the hole itself is somewhat akin to skydiving.

The entry point is at the Bells, a narrow breach in the reef table that forms a pool close to shore. From here, you descend through a chimney, exiting at 27m on a ledge that opens to the sea. If you swim south along the wall, a saddle in the reef at 7m allows you to enter the Blue Hole. As long as you monitor your depth carefully, you can finish up the dive by swimming across the sinkhole towards shore. Depth: 7m to 27m; rating: intermediate; access: shore

nexion and the lagoon. A two-hour tour, including helmet, costs E£120.

Blue Beach Club　　　　　　HORSE RIDING
(☑364 0411; www.bluebeachclub.com; Assalah) This professional-standard stable runs highly recommended hacks and treks (of up to three days) as well as riding lessons for beginners. Rates start at about E£100 per hour.

★☆ Festivals

The **Dahab Festival** (www.dahabfestival.info) takes place every April for one week, combining water-sport competitions, Bedouin cultural activities, live bands and beach parties.

🛏 Sleeping

Increased competition has raised the bar in town and there are some excellent rooms to be had for the price of a decent meal back home. Assalah boasts bedding-down options ranging from cell-like cement huts to attractive backpacker palaces with cushioned seating shaded by palm groves, as well as a good mix of more midrange resorts that are still small enough for guests to catch the mellow Dahab vibe. Luxury accommodation is available at the lagoon area. The following is only a small sampling of what is available. New places are going up all the time while older establishments are being knocked down. Budget and many midrange hotel rates in Dahab do not include breakfast.

TOP CHOICE **Alaska Camp & Hotel**　　HOSTEL $
(☑364 1004; www.dahabescape.com; Masbat; r with/without air-con E£200/100; ❉⊜) Easy on the wallet without sacrificing the small comforts, Alaska has a variety of spacious, bright and sparkling clean rooms with super comfortable beds. The attractive courtyard garden is a welcoming shady spot to relax and meet other travellers and the central location means you're just a couple of steps from the promenade bustle.

TOP CHOICE **Sunrise Lodge**　　GUESTHOUSE $
(☑0109 057 4242; www.sunrisedahab.com; Masbat; r E£120; ❉⊜) Tucked down a sandy alley just off the promenade, this welcoming home-from-home has just five large, spotless rooms (one fan-only room is a cheaper E£80) set around a sandy courtyard shaded by palm trees. There's free tea and coffee, hammocks and a cushion area to lounge in, a small play area for children, and management provides a highly personalised service and can help with any query.

Dahab Paradise　　　　　　RESORT $$
(☑0100 700 4133; www.dahabparadise.com; s/d US$58/68; ❉⊜⊠) This low-key resort, on a secluded sweep of bay on the main road to the Blue Hole, is the perfect get-away-from-it-all. Decorated in warm earthy tones with accents of antique wood, the charming rooms are a touch of understated beach-chic elegance. If all the peace and serenity gets too much, the bright lights of Masbat are a 10-minute taxi-ride away.

Red Sea Relax
HOTEL **$$**

(☏364 1309; www.red-sea-relax.com; Masbat; dm/s/d €8/37/46; ✳@🏊) With rooms wrapped around a glistening pool, Red Sea Relax dishes up a winning formula of resort-like facilities for bargain prices. Large rooms come with nice added extras such as tea- and coffee-making facilities and TV. It's a well-organised set-up with free water fill-ups, a beckoning rooftop bar and an excellent dive centre. Cheap dormitory accommodation means you get all the resort facilities for backpacker costs.

Seven Heaven
HOSTEL **$**

(☏364 0080; www.7heavenhotel.com; Masbat; dm E£20, r with/without air-con E£80/60, without bathroom E£30; ✳🛜) An all-in-one stalwart of the Dahab scene that still offers one of the best-value shoestringer deals in town. There's a huge range of rooms, which go up in price as you add in extras; the six-bed dorms, which come with air-con and bathroom, are a bargain. You'll find a good range of amenities here including a dive shop and tour booking centre and staff are very helpful.

Alf Leila
B&B **$$**

(☏364 0595; www.alfleila.com; cnr of Peace Rd & Sharia al-Fanar, Masbat; s/d €30/36; ✳🛜) With a nod towards its namesake '1001 Arabian Nights', Alf Leila's seven rooms are a day-dream of gorgeous tile-work and traditional textiles decorated using lashings of muted earthy colours, stone and wood. Unfortunately the location (on the main road) isn't the best but if you don't mind a walk to the beach, and a bit of traffic noise, for its sheer uniqueness this place is still worth it.

Le Meridien Dahab Resort
RESORT **$$$**

(☏364 0425; www.lemeridien.com/dahab; lagoon resort area, Dahab City; s/d/ste from US$125/150/175; ✳🛜🏊) By far the best of the lagoon's resorts, Le Meridien spills over a series of terraces that flow down to a sweep of white sand. The rooms are the height of contemporary chic, decorated in a palette of burnt orange and stone. This is where to come if you want your Dahab experience served up with oodles of five-star service and comfort.

Dahab Coach House
GUESTHOUSE **$$**

(☏364 1027; www.dahabcoachhouse.dk; Masbat; s/d €38/40; ✳🛜) What this place lacks in midrange resort facilities, it more than makes up for with hugely helpful management and a genuine welcoming feel. The rooms are simple but comfortable and the courtyard is the perfect place to chill out after a long day's diving.

Nesima Resort
RESORT **$$**

(☏364 0320; www.nesima-resort.com; Mashraba; s/d/ste €47/61/84; ✳🛜🏊) A lovely compromise if you want resort living without being isolated from town. Set amid a mature garden of blooming bougainvillea, Nesima's cosy cottages have pleasing stone and wood overtones, domed ceilings and dinky terraces.

Ghazala Hotel
HOTEL **$$**

(☏364 2414; www.ghazaladahab.com; Mashraba; s/d E£100/140; ✳🛜) Ghazala's cute white-domed rooms surround a narrow courtyard set with colourful mosaic tiles. Some rooms are larger than others so ask to see a few

---

LOCAL KNOWLEDGE

DIVING INTO DAHAB

Mohamed Ali is the manager of Big Blue Dive Centre in Dahab.

What makes Dahab so special for novice divers? We're really lucky here as our shallow, shore-access reefs host an incredible array of marine life. Lighthouse is where a lot of the open water training happens and is also one of the best reefs for spotting fish.

What are some great dives for newly qualified divers? Banner Fish Bay is home to lots of seagrass, seahorses, octopuses and fog fish and Eel Garden as well is fantastic because it's a very virginal area where the coral is still alive. Islands Reef and Canyon Garden are also home to lots of different coral and fish.

Top tips for experienced divers? If you want to dive the Blue Hole, start early in the morning to escape the crowds. Visibility is at its best at this time and the fish will be just waking up. Later in the day, when there are too many divers, the fish tend to hide. For a great drift dive, Eel Garden to Lighthouse Reef is excellent for experienced divers.

before you decide. There are a couple of cheaper fan-only rooms as well.

Christina Beach Palace & Christina Pool HOTEL $$
(☎364 0390; www.christinahotels.com; Mashraba; s/d with air-con US$62/83, without air-con US$55/76; ❄📶≈) This small Swiss-run hotel offers a degree of efficiency unmatched in town. Depending on your preference, Beach Palace rooms have lovely sea views, while the recently renovated Pool-side ones are more luxurious.

Christina Residence HOTEL $$
(☎364 0390; www.christinahotels.com; Mashraba; s/d with air-con US$32/40, without air-con US$25/33; ❄📶≈) The large, airy rooms here come with surprisingly modern bathrooms, good beds, and surround a leafy, quiet garden. Guests get to use all the facilities of Christina Beach Palace across the road.

Bishbishi Garden Village HOSTEL $
(☎364 0727; www.bishbishi.com; Sharia al-Mashraba; s/d without bathroom €5/8; 📶) A classic of the Dahab camp scene, Bishbishi continues to offer a winning mix of easy-on-the-wallet rooms and lots of shaded communal areas for socialising.

Blue Beach Club RESORT $$
(☎364 0411; www.bluebeachclub.com; Assalah; s/d/ste €28/36/44; ❄📶≈) Blue Beach's recently renovated annex rooms (across the road from the main resort) are bright, comfortably outfitted and boast the snazziest modern bathrooms in Dahab.

Bamboo House Hotel GUESTHOUSE $$
(☎364 0263; www.bamboohouse-dahab.com; Masbat; s/d E£120/150, seaview E£130/180; ❄📶) This central hotel has seven spacious rooms styled in a fresh jazzy palette of olive green and white.

Bedouin Lodge GUESTHOUSE $
(☎364 1125; www.bedouin-lodge-dahab.com; Mashraba; s/d with air-con €17/25, without air-con €14/20) A local Bedouin family runs this simple but highly friendly hotel.

Eating

The waterfront is lined with Bedouin-style restaurants where you can relax on cushions while gazing out over the sparkling waters of the Gulf of Aqaba. Unfortunately, places serving up quality Egyptian cuisine are thin on the ground but seafood is on almost all menus, together with a good selection of international dishes.

If you're after a cheap, filling lunch, look out for **Ali's Kushari Cart**, which makes the rounds up and down the promenade, with Ali shouting out his sales pitch of '*kushari, kushari*' roughly between noon and 4pm. Not only does he ladle out Egypt's finest carbohydrate extravaganza, but also a delicious *ruz bi laban* (rice pudding). Either will set you back E£5. For self-caterers, there are numerous supermarkets dotted around Assalah, including the **Ghazala Supermarket** (Masbat; ⌚8am-2am), near the main junction at the southern end of Masbat.

TOP CHOICE **Seabride Restaurant** SEAFOOD $$
(Mashraba; meals E£40-60) Away from the shorefront, this is the local's favourite haunt for seafood, serving up startling good value. All meals come loaded down with fish soup, rice, salad, *baba ghanoog* (purée of grilled aubergines), a delectably tangy tahini and bread. Either chose your fish fresh from the display or from the menu. Order the spicy Bedouin calamari to sample seafood Dahab-style.

Kitchen INTERNATIONAL $$$
(Masbat; mains E£60-95) With a menu offering a choice of Indian, Chinese, Thai and Japanese plus superb service, this is as close as Dahab gets to fine dining. The Indian is the real stand-out here with delicious madras and biryani dishes, while the sushi plates are as good as any you'll get in Egypt. If you've got a sweet tooth you won't be able to resist the fried pineapple and ice-cream dessert.

Blue House THAI $$
(Masbat; mains E£35-60) An inspiring selection of authentic Thai cuisine keeps this breezy upstairs terrace packed with diners. Tuck into its flavour-filled curries or the zingy papaya salad and you'll understand why this place has so many fans.

Ali Baba INTERNATIONAL $$
(Masbat; mains E£30-80) One of the most popular restaurants along the waterfront strip for good reason: this place adds flair to its seafood selection with some inspired menu choices. Great service, comfy sofas to lounge on, stylish lanterns and twinkly fairy lights add to the relaxed seaside ambience.

Fighting Kangaroo
EGYPTIAN $

(Masbat; meals E£15-20) Despite the unfortunate name this narrow waterfront restaurant should be commended for serving up Egyptian-style feasts at bargain-basement prices. Simple and hearty meals (pick from fish, *kofta,* chicken or vegetarian) all come with soup, salad and tahini.

Ralph's German Bakery
BAKERY $

(Sharia al-Fanar, Masbat; Ghazala Supermarket courtyard, Masbat; sandwiches E£18-25, pastries E£4-15; ⊘7am-6pm) Singlehandedly raising the bar for coffee in Dahab, this place is caffeine heaven and also serves up a range of particularly tempting calorific pastries and excellent sandwiches. The Sharia al-Fanar branch has the best selection and also does some original breakfast dishes.

Nirvana
INDIAN $$

(Masbat; dishes E£45-75) A slice of the subcontinent complete with direct beach access and sun-loungers. Although not particularly authentic, the meals are tasty all the same and the ice cream, with homemade waffle cone, is perfect for a promenade stroll after dinner.

Athanor
ITALIAN $$

(Sharia al-Melal; pizzas E£18-40, Assalah) Dahab's best thin-crust pizzas are served up here on the shady garden terrace.

King Chicken
EGYPTIAN $

(Sharia al-Mashraba; dishes E£15-25) Always crowded with locals, this cheap and cheerful little place hits the spot for budget chicken-dinner heaven.

🍷 Drinking

In comparison with Sharm el-Sheikh, Dahab is fairly quiet at night, but there is a good selection of lively bars, some of which turn into discos if the atmosphere is right. Of course, after a long day of diving and desert exploration, most travellers are content with sprawling out in any of Dahab's waterfront restaurants and nursing a few cold Stellas.

Lavazza Cafe
CAFE

(Masbat; coffee E£10-15) Excellent cappuccino and decent espresso make this cafe a good stop for your morning caffeine fix.

Tree Bar
BAR

(Mashraba; ⊘10pm-late) Two-for-one cocktail deals and a thumping soundtrack of urban, house and R&B make this open-air beach-front bar Dahab's top late-night party venue.

Churchill's
BAR

(Red Sea Relax, Masbat; beer E£10-14) Dahab's sports bar has a big-screen TV so you won't miss your favourite team play, plus a breezy rooftop terrace perfect for sunset drinks.

Yalla Bar
BAR

(Masbat; beer E£10-12) This popular waterfront bar-restaurant has a winning formula of friendly staff and excellent happy-hour beer prices from 5pm to 9pm.

ℹ Information

Dangers & Annoyances

Dahab remains one of Egypt's most relaxed destinations but solo female travellers should still exercise common sense after dark. Buddy-up late at night, to avoid negotiating unlit alleyways alone.

Since the Dahab suicide bombing of April 2006 (which killed 23 people and injured dozens) the government has cracked down on the seeds of Islamic fundamentalism in South Sinai and although the potential for a future terrorist attack can never be wholly ruled out, it is important to emphasise that the overwhelming majority of visitors to Dahab and the greater Sinai region enjoy their time immensely, and never experience any sort of problem.

For an overview of the history of terrorism in Sinai, see p413.

Emergency

Police (☑364 0213/5; Mashraba; main junction near Ghazala Supermarket)

Tourist police (☑364 0188; Dahab City)

Internet Access

Wi-fi is widely available free at most hotels and many of the restaurants.

Aladdin Bookstore & Internet (Masbat; per hr E£5)

Net Internet Cafe (Sharia al-Mashraba; per hr E£5; ⊘24hr)

Seven Heaven Internet Cafe (Seven Heaven, Masbat; per hr E£5; ⊘24hr)

Medical Services

Dahab Specialised Hospital (☑364 2714; Mashraba) An excellent private hospital with full hyperbaric chamber facilities.

Dr Haikal (☑0100 143 3325; lagoon, Dahab City) Local doctor whose surgery also has a hyperbaric chamber.

Money

There are plenty of ATMs scattered along the waterfront throughout Masbat.

Banque du Caire (Sharia al-Mashraba & Masbat, near the bridge) Has an ATM.

1. Na'ama Bay (p395)
Sharm el-Sheikh's beachfront promenade is lined with restaurants and shops.

2. Coloured Canyon (p409)
Northwest of Nuweiba, this canyon is named for the multicoloured stones in its walls.

3. Snorkelling & Diving (p36)
The waters around Ras Mohammed National Park are the jewel in the crown of the Red Sea.

4. Sharm el-Sheikh (p395)
The resort town sits between the region's beautiful waters and its jagged mountains.

National Bank of Egypt (Sharia al-Mashraba & Masbat) Has an ATM.

Post

As well as the main post office, there is a handy post office/bookshop on the waterfront in Masbat next to Bamboo House Hotel.

Main post office (Dahab City)

Telephone

International call services are available at the post office/bookshop in Masbat. You can also place calls at Bamboo House Hotel and at Seven Heaven. All cost E£7 per minute.

Telephone centrale (Dahab City; ⊘24hr)

❶ Getting There & Away

Bus

From the bus station in Dahab City, well southwest of the centre of the action, **East Delta Travel Co** (📞364 1808) has one bus a day heading north at 10.30am to Nuweiba (E£15, one hour) before continuing on to Taba (E£35, two hours). There is a 5.30pm bus to Sharm el-Sheikh (E£15 to E£20, two hours) but all the following buses also stop there. Buses to Cairo (E£90, nine hours) leave at 9am, 12.30pm, 3pm and 10pm. There is also a non-air-con service at 7.30pm (E£65). Buses to Al-Tor (E£25 to E£30, four hours) and Ismailia (E£60, seven hours) leave at 10am, 8.30pm, 9.30pm and 10.30pm. At 8am there is a bus to Suez (E£45, seven hours) also via Al-Tor. For Hurghada (E£105, 10 hours) and Luxor (E£130, 18 hours) there is one bus daily at 4pm. Be sure to check departure times with hotel staff as they're subject to change without notice.

There are no public buses to St Katherine but during research of this book a fantastic local transport initiative called **Bedouin Bus** (📞0101 668 4274; www.bedouinbus.com) began running transport between Dahab and St Katherine every Tuesday and Friday (E£50, two hours). Check the website for up-to-date details.

Taxi drivers at the bus station (and around town) charge E£100 to Sharm el-Sheikh and E£250 to St Katherine.

❶ Getting Around

Pickups go up and down the Peace Rd in Assalah and, less frequently, around the resort strip. The usual fare is E£3 to E£5 for trips around town, and E£10 if you find one doing the entire stretch between Assalah and Dahab City. The standard taxi fare to/from the bus station is E£10. To get to the Blue Hole independently you can negotiate with any of the pickup drivers in town. Don't forget to arrange a return time (E£60 to E£80 return).

Bicycles are a great way to get around Dahab and you can hire them from many hotels and travel agencies in town. Ghazala Hotel in Mashraba has hire rates of E£30 for one day.

Ras Abu Gallum Protectorate

The starkly beautiful Ras Abu Gallum Protectorate covers 400 sq km of coastline between Dahab and Nuweiba, mixing coastal mountains, narrow valleys, sand dunes and fine-gravel beaches with several excellent diving and snorkelling sites. Scientists describe the area as a 'floristic frontier', in which Mediterranean conditions are influenced by a tropical climate. This, together with its 165 plant species (including 44 that are found nowhere else in Sinai) and wealth of mammals and reptiles, gives it great environmental importance and makes it a fascinating place to visit.

As in nearby Nabq, Bedouin of the Mizena tribe live within the protectorate confines, fishing here as they have done for centuries (although this is now regulated by the protectorate).

Travel agencies in Nuweiba and Dahab offer camel, jeep and walking excursions to Ras Abu Gallum. Hiking into the reserve by following the path from the Blue Hole is also popular. The track takes you along the shoreline to Ras Abu Gallum village and El-Omeyid village (one hour), one where you can camp overnight in a hut. Most tour agencies in Dahab offer this trip for around E£200 or E£350 for overnight (including return transport to Blue Hole, lunch and snorkelling gear) or you can easily do this yourself.

There are several walking trails in the reserve, and you can hire Bedouin guides and camels either at Ras Abu Gallum village or, if coming from the Nuweiba side, through the ranger house at the edge of **Wadi Rasasah**. Popular destinations within the protectorate include **Bir el-Oghda**, a now-deserted Bedouin village, and **Bir Sugheir**, a water source at the edge of the protectorate.

Nuweiba

📄069

Stretched randomly over about 15km, Nuweiba lacks a defined centre and a cohesive ambience, and functions primarily as a port town rather than a travellers' retreat. For a brief period, following the Egypt–Israel peace treaty of 1979, a thriving Israeli tourism trade here meant Nuweiba could claim rivalry to Dahab as Sinai's hippy beach paradise. However, due to the vagaries of the regional political situation over recent decades, Israeli travellers have for the most part shunned Nuweiba – and much of Sinai for that matter. While Sharm has boomed under waves of foreign and domestic investment, and Dahab has grown steadily into a low-key resort town, Nuweiba has been left to go to seed. As a result, most travellers pass through Nuweiba either on their way to the scenic beach camps further north, or to catch the Aqaba-bound ferry en route to Petra in Jordan.

Although it's perhaps not a tourist destination in itself, some fine sandy beaches, a number of laid-back resorts and backpacker-friendly camps make Nuweiba a pleasant enough place to spend a few days. All the camps and hotels here can organise jeep and camel safaris into the interior, and the modest diving scene means that its offshore reefs are comparatively uncrowded.

🏃 Activities

Snorkelling & Diving

Underwater delights are the feature attraction of Nuweiba, and while not as dramatic as at other resorts on the Gulf of Aqaba, the dive sites tend to be less busy, with an impressive variety of marine life. There are shallow reefs offshore that are reasonable places to snorkel, but the best snorkelling is the **Stone House Reef** just south of town.

For an overview of diving in the Red Sea, see p36.

Ras Shaitan   DIVE SITE

(Map p38; location: 15km north of Nuweiba) The highlight of this dive is undoubtedly the contoured topography, including narrow valleys, sand-filled depressions and deep chasms. Depth: 10m to 30m; rating: intermediate; access: shore.

Sinker   DIVE SITE

(Map p38; location: Nuweiba) The Sinker is a massive submerged mooring buoy designed for cargo ships, which was sunk by mistake in the mid-1990s. Since then, it has developed into a fantastic artificial reef, attracting a host of small, colourful species. Depth: 6m to 35m; rating: intermediate; access: shore.

🛈 NUWEIBA: THE LAY OF THE LAND

Nuweiba is divided into three parts: to the south is the port, with a bus station, banks and a couple of scruffy hotels; about 8km further north is Nuweiba City, a small but spread-out settlement with a variety of accommodation options, a small bazaar and several cheap places to eat; and about a 10-minute walk north along the beach is Tarabin, Nuweiba's equivalent of Dahab's Assalah area.

Ras Mumlach   DIVE SITE

(Map p38; location: about 30km south of Nuweiba) A sloping reef interspersed with enormous boulders and excellent table corals. Depth: 10m to 25m; rating: intermediate; access: shore.

DIVE OPERATORS

Emperor Divers   DIVING

(☑352 0321; www.emperordivers.com; Nuweiba Hilton)

Sinai Dolphin Divers   DIVING

(☑350 0879, www.sinaidolphindivers.com; Nakhil Inn, Tarabin)

Camel & Jeep Safaris

With the exception of Dahab, Nuweiba is the best place along the coast to arrange camel or jeep safaris into the interior. Almost every camp in Tarabin offers these trips, but take care that whoever you pick is a local Bedouin – not only are they marginalised by tour operators from the Nile Valley and therefore need the work, but there have been some instances of travellers lost in the desert without water because their so-called guides didn't know the routes.

Register with the police before beginning the safari, and don't pay the camel driver until you return to the village. Itineraries – and as a result, prices – are generally custom-designed, but expect to pay from E£75 to E£100 per person for an evening camel trip into the mountains with dinner at a Bedouin camp, and from about E£300 to E£400 per person per day for a safari including all food and water.

In addition to trips to the popular **Coloured Canyon** (see p409 for more information), other popular destinations are **Ain al-Furtega**, a palm-filled oasis 16km northwest of Nuweiba; and **Mayat el-Wishwashi**, a

Nuweiba

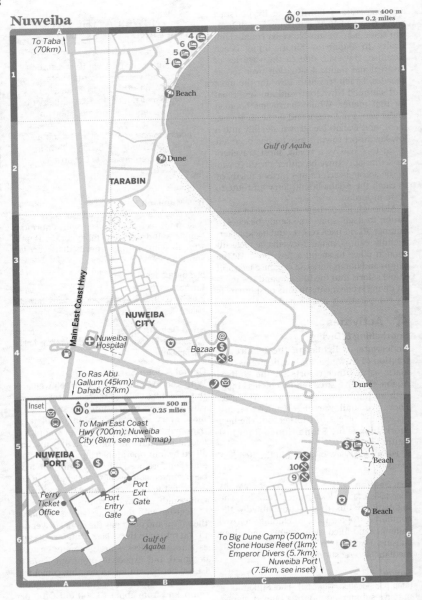

To Taba (70km)

4

6

5

1

Beach

Gulf of Aqaba

Dune

TARABIN

NUWEIBA CITY

Nuweiba Hospital

Bazaar

@

5

8

To Ras Abu Gallum (45km); Dahab (87km)

Dune

Inset

500 m
0.25 miles

To Main East Coast Hwy (700m); Nuweiba City (8km, see main map)

NUWEIBA PORT

$ $

Ferry Ticket Office

Port Entry Gate

Port Exit Gate

Gulf of Aqaba

3

$

Beach

7

10

9

Beach

To Big Dune Camp (500m); Stone House Reef (1km); Emperor Divers (5.7km); Nuweiba Port (7.5km, see inset)

2

large cistern hidden between two boulders in a canyon – it used to be the largest cistern in Sinai but now has only a trickle of water, except after floods. Nearby is **Mayat Malkha**, a palm grove fed by the waters of Mayat el-Wishwashi and set amid colourful sandstone.

Wadi Huweiyit is an impressive sandstone canyon with lookouts giving panoramic views over to Saudi Arabia. **Ain Khudra** (Green Spring) is where Miriam was sup-

Nuweiba

posed to have been struck by leprosy for criticising Moses. The picturesque **Ain Umm Ahmed** is the largest oasis in eastern Sinai, with lots of palms, Bedouin houses and a famous stream that becomes an icy river in the winter months.

Further afield, **Wadi Sheikh Atiya** is named after the father of the Tarabin tribe – the largest tribe in the area – who lies buried here under a white dome. There is an oasis here and Bedouin frequently come on pilgrimage. **Gebel Barga** is a mountain that is difficult to climb, yet affords stunning views over the mountains of eastern Sinai.

🛏 Sleeping

On the northern edge of town is Tarabin, essentially a pedestrian-only boardwalk that stretches along the waterfront for 1.5km. Unfortunately the lack of business in recent years has contributed to a lackadaisical attitude in both beach cleaning and camp repairs; a shame because if Tarabin was spruced up a little it could easily be the mellow beach-camp paradise that Dahab was a decade ago.

The camps and hotels listed below all keep their patch of sand clean and are good choices for those seeking a more serene scene than Dahab. If you're looking for a complete beach escape with traditional Egyptian palm-thatch huts on the beach, you're probably better off looking further north along the coast (see boxed text p426).

TOP CHOICE Nakhil Inn INN $$
(☑350 0879; www.nakhil-inn.com; Tarabin; s/d US$46/56; ❋❡) The friendly Nakhil is a cosy compromise for those who want hotel comforts without the crowds. Local textiles and stained wood have been used in abundance throughout the communal areas while the charming studio-style wooden cabins exude simple beach chic. Guests can snorkel the reef just a few metres from the shore, go kayaking or diving, or simply unwind while lazing about in one of the hammocks or shaded seating spots strewn across the private beach.

Petra Camp BEACH CAMP $
(☑350 0855; www.petra-camp.com; Tarabin; s/d hut E£40/80; ❋) One of the nicest camps in Tarabin. The centrepiece here is an atmospheric open-air restaurant that was constructed from recycled wood salvaged from a defunct Cairo theatre. Huts are simple but well cared for and most come with air-con. The communal bathrooms are clean, and the restaurant serves up a decent selection of Egyptian and international favourites.

Big Dune BEACH CAMP $
(☑0100 610 8731; Nuweiba City; hut E£25) Chilled out to the max and reminiscent of the hippy beach camps of old, this is one of the few Nuweiba camps that still use traditional *hoosha* (palm-thatch) huts. It's bare-bones basic – the setting is the drawcard here, with the huts scattered across a wide sweep of golden sand.

Habiba Village INN $$
(☑0122 217 6624; habiba@sinai4you.com; Nuweiba City; s/d US$20/30; ❋) The rooms are a little rough around the edges, but are set around a quiet courtyard a hop-skip-and-jump from a nice beach with a good snorkelling reef. Management is engaged in a local permaculture project and has set up an organic farm where interested long-stayers can volunteer.

Saraya Beach BEACH CAMP $
(☑0109 198 7803; Tarabin; hut/r E£30/80) This well-looked-after Tarabin camp has a wide variety of accommodation ranging from rustic wooden huts with fan through to more expensive air-con rooms (E£100).

Al-Badawi BEACH CAMP $
(☑0122 731 1455; Tarabin; s/d E£60/130, without bathroom E£40/80; ❋) Spartan but spotless rooms in a well-cared-for garden slap in the middle of the Tarabin scene. Management really endeavours to keep everything spick and span and is a friendly bunch.

LONELY PLANET JORDAN (ABRIDGED)

Planning a brief excursion to Jordan? Wishing you had a bit of info on the ancient city of Petra? Here's a quick guide to one of the 'New Seven Wonders of the World'. For the full story on Jordan, pick up a copy of the guidebook, or buy and download individual chapters from the Lonely Planet website, lonelyplanet.com.

Petra

Hewn from rock walls of multicoloured sandstone, the imposing facades of Petra's great temples and tombs are an enduring testament to the vision of the desert tribes who sculpted them. The Nabataeans – Arabs who dominated the region in pre-Roman times – chose as their capital a place concealed from the outside world, and fashioned it into one of the Middle East's most remarkable cities. Almost as spectacular as the monuments are the countless shades and swirls in the rock. Petra is often called the 'Rose-Red City', but this hardly does justice to the extraordinary range of colours that blend as the sun makes its daily passage over the site.

SIGHTS & ACTIVITIES

The ancient city is approached via the **Siq**, a canyon-like passage that is actually a single block that has been rent apart by tectonic forces – at various points you can see where the grain of the rock on one side matches the other. The Siq can seem to continue forever, and the sense of anticipation builds as you look around each corner for your first glimpse of the Treasury, Petra's most famous monument.

Al-Khazneh, or the Treasury, is where most visitors fall in love with Petra. The Hellenistic exterior is an astonishing piece of craftsmanship; the sophistication, symmetry, scale and grandeur of the carving enough to take away the breath of first-time visitors. Standing here is a magical introduction to the ancient city, especially since it's the precise location of the Holy Grail – at least according to the Hollywood classic *Indiana Jones and the Last Crusade*.

Heading towards the ancient city centre are over 40 tombs and houses built by the Nabataeans and known as the **Street of Facades**. Continuing along you'll reach a Roman-style **theatre**, which was built over 2000 years ago and has a capacity of about 3000 in 45 rows of seats, with three horizontal sections separated by two corridors. The Wadi Musa riverbed widens out after here – to the right (or north), carved into the cliff, are the burial places known as the **Royal Tombs**. There are more tombs around Petra than any other type of structure, and for years archaeologists assumed the city was just one vast necropolis. The reason why so few dwellings have been discovered is that the Nabataeans lived in tents, much as some Bedouin do today.

One of Petra's most magnificent sights is **Al-Deir**, or the Monastery, which is reached via a one-hour uphill slog from the **Colonnaded Street** (Cardo Maximus). Similar in design to the Treasury, the imposing Monastery – 50m wide and 45m high – is just as impressive. Built in the 3rd century BC as a Nabataean tomb, the Monastery gets its name from the crosses carved on its inside walls, suggesting that the building was used as a church in Byzantine times. The building has towering columns and a large urn flanked by two half-pediments, and like the Treasury has heavy Hellenistic influences.

Petra by Night (admission JD12; ⊗8.30-10.30pm Mon, Wed & Thu) is a magical way to see the old city, taking you along the Siq (lined with hundreds of candles) in silence as far as the Treasury, where traditional Bedouin music is played and mint tea is served.

SLEEPING

Amra Palace Hotel   HOTEL $$

(☏3-215 7070; www.amrapalace.com; s/d JD46/54; ❄@☀) This lovely hotel has a magnificent lobby, marble pillars, giant brass coffeepots and Damascene-style furniture. The brothers who have run this hotel for more than a decade take a personal interest in the details, and each room has spotless linen, in addition to wooden headboards, upholstered furniture and satellite TV.

Cleopatra Hotel   HOSTEL $

(☏3-215 7090; s/d/tr JD12/16/21; @) Located in the centre of Wadi Musa, this popular backpacker spot offers the obligatory nightly screening of *Indiana Jones and the Last Crusade*. The rooms here, all with private bathroom and hot water, are on the small side, but there's a cosy communal sitting area that feels like your aunt's sitting room. You can sleep on the roof for JD5 with breakfast.

Mövenpick Hotel

HOTEL $$$

(☎3-215 7111; www.moevenpick-petra.com; r JD155; ❀🛜🏊) This beautifully crafted Arabian-style hotel, 100m from the entrance to Petra, is worth a visit simply to admire the inlaid furniture, marble fountains, wooden screens and brass salvers. Petals are floated daily in the fountains, a roaring fire welcomes residents to the lounge, and pleasant views are afforded from the roof garden. As the hotel is in the bottom of the valley, there are not sweeping views, but the large and super-luxurious rooms all have huge picture windows regardless.

EATING & DRINKING

Petra Kitchen

JORDANIAN $$$

(cooking course incl meal JD35) On the main street to the site entrance, this is one of the few places where you can sample Jordanian home cooking. Guests help prepare the three-course meal in the kitchen before tucking into the results.

Al-Wadi Restaurant

INTERNATIONAL $$

(mains JD4-5; ⏲7am-late) Right on Shaheed roundabout, this lively local spot offers pasta and pizza, as well as a range of vegetarian dishes and local Bedouin specialities.

Cave Bar

BAR

(drinks from JD6) If you've never been to a bar in a 2000-year-old Nabataean rock tomb (and we're guessing you haven't!), then this memorable spot near the visitors centre is an absolute must.

INFORMATION

The base town for exploring Petra is Wadi Musa (Valley of Moses), a patchy mass of hotels, restaurants and shops located about 3km from the **visitors centre** (☎3-215 6020; ⏲6am-5.30pm May-Sep, to 5pm Oct-Apr). Entry fees are JD50/55/60 for one-/two-/three-day passes. Note that at the time of publication, one Jordanian dinar (JD) was approximately equal to US$1.40 and €1. The country code for calling Jordan is ☎962.

GETTING THERE & AWAY

Ferries depart from Nuweiba, Egypt, and arrive in Aqaba, Jordan. For more information on the crossing, see p424. From the ferry terminal in Aqaba, taxis meet arriving ships in order to shuttle tourists to Wadi Musa. When dealing with taxi drivers, it helps to be a good negotiator – and to have a lot of friends with you to bring down the price. Generally speaking, a taxi costs about JD35 to Wadi Musa. Microbuses depart when full for Wadi Musa (JD2, two hours) from Aqaba's bus station on Sharia King Talal between 8am and 2pm.

Given that the ferry crossing to Jordan isn't always smooth sailing, a good alternative is to travel by bus via Israel. From Taba, you can cross the Egypt–Israel border, and then catch a quick taxi (US$15 to US$20) to the Wadi Araba border crossing between Israel and Jordan. Note that you can still cross into Jordan and return to Egypt with an Israeli stamp, though you will not be allowed to enter Lebanon, Syria and a whole slew of other Middle Eastern countries. Although Israeli border guards are usually happy to not stamp your passport, the Egyptian and Jordanian border guards generally won't comply. If you're carrying on to Syria it's best to take the ferry.

GETTING AROUND

In Wadi Musa, most hotels offer a free shuttle service to and from the visitors centre, though a taxi ride from anywhere in Wadi Musa to Petra shouldn't cost you more than JD1 or JD2. Although hikers have little difficulty exploring Petra's sights, donkeys and camels accompanied by guides are available all around Petra for negotiable prices.

Petra

WALKING TOUR

Splendid though it is, the Treasury is not the full stop of a visit to Petra that many people may imagine. In some ways, it's just the semicolon – a place to pause after the exertions of the Siq, before exploring the other remarkable sights and wonders just around the corner.

Even if you're on a tight schedule or worried the bus won't wait, try to find another two hours in your itinerary to complete this walking tour. Our illustration shows the key highlights of the route, as you wind through Wadi Musa from the **Siq** 1, pause at the **Treasury** 2 and pass the tombs of the broader **Outer Siq** 3. With energy and a stout pair of shoes, climb to the **High Place of Sacrifice** 4 for a magnificent eagle's-eye view of Petra. Return to the **Street of Facades** 5 and the **Theatre** 6. Climb the steps opposite to the **Urn Tomb** 7 and neighbouring **Silk Tomb** 8: these Royal Tombs are particularly magnificent in the golden light of sunset.

Is the thought of all that walking putting you off? Don't let it! There are donkeys to help you with the steep ascents and Bedouin stalls for a reviving herb tea. If you run out of steam, camels are on standby for a ride back to the Treasury.

Treasury
As you watch the sun cut across the facade, notice how it lights up the ladders on either side of Petra's most iconic building. These stone indents were most probably used for scaffolding.

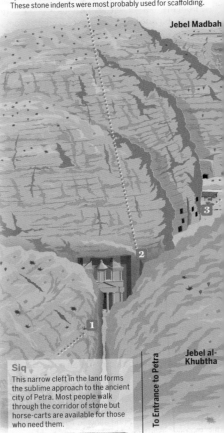

Jebel Madbah

Jebel al-Khubtha

To Entrance to Petra

Siq
This narrow cleft in the land forms the sublime approach to the ancient city of Petra. Most people walk through the corridor of stone but horse-carts are available for those who need them.

TOP TIPS

» **Morning Glory** From around 7am in summer and 8am in winter, watch the early morning sun slide down the Treasury facade.

» **Pink City** Stand opposite the Royal Tombs at sunset (around 4pm in winter and 5pm in summer) to learn how Petra earned its nickname.

» **Floral Tribute** Petra's oleanders flower in May.

Down Differently

A superb walk leads from the High Place of Sacrifice, past the Garden Tomb to Petra City Centre.

igh Place of acrifice

agine the ancients eading the stone eps and it'll take ur mind off the steep cent. The hilltop atform was used for cense-burning and ation-pouring in nour of forgotten ds.

Outer Siq

Take time to inspect the tombs just past the Treasury. Some appear to have a basement but, in fact, they show how the floor of the wadi has risen over the centuries.

Street of Facades

Cast an eye at the upper storeys of some of these tombs and you'll see a small aperture. Burying the dead in attics was meant to deter robbers – the plan didn't work.

5

6

**Souvenir shops,
teashops & toilets**

Wadi Musa

Wadi Musa

**To Petra City
Centre →**

7

8

**Jebel Umm al'Amr
(1066m)**

Royal Tombs

Royal Tombs

Head for Heights

For a regal view of Petra, head for the heights above the Royal Tombs, via the staircase.

rn Tomb

arning its name om the urn-shaped nial crowning the ediment, this grand lifice with supporting ched vaults was erhaps built for the an represented by e toga-wearing bust the central aperture.

Silk Tomb

Perhaps Nabataean builders were attracted to Wadi Musa because of the colourful beauty of the raw materials. Nowhere is this more apparent than in the weather-eroded, striated sandstone of the Silk Tomb.

Theatre

Most stone amphitheatres are freestanding, but this one is carved almost entirely from the solid rock. Above the back row are the remains of earlier tombs, their facades sacrificed in the name of entertainment.

Helnan Nuweiba RESORT $$$

(📞350 0401; www.helnan.com; Nuweiba City; s/d US$125/160; ❄❄) Although lacking in character, the newly renovated cottages here are comfortable and modern, and the private beach and pool area is attractive.

Eating

At the port there is a cluster of places selling *fuul* (fava bean paste) and *ta'amiyya* (felafel) in the area behind the National Bank of Egypt and before the ticket office for Aqaba ferries. If you'd prefer a bit more than a quick bite, however, the selection is a little better in and around Nuweiba City. If you're out in Tarabin, you'll probably take meals at your camp or hotel. For general groceries, **Swiss Market** (Nuweiba City) has a good selection of basic supplies.

Cleopatra Restaurant SEAFOOD $$

(Nuweiba City; dishes E£20-50) One of the more popular tourist restaurants in Nuweiba City, Cleopatra offers up the bounty of the sea along with a few Western fast-food favourites.

Han Kang ASIAN $$

(Nuweiba City; dishes E£20-40) This surprisingly good Chinese restaurant hits the spot, especially if you've been on the road for a while and can't bear to look at another felafel sandwich.

Dr Shishkebab GRILL $$

(Bazaar, Nuweiba City; dishes E£10-30) The place to head to for filling and tasty kebab meals.

ℹ Information

Emergency

Tourist police Nuweiba City (📞350 0231; near Helnan Nuweiba; ☺24hr); Nuweiba Port (📞350 0401)

Internet Access

Al-Mostakbal Internet Café (Nuweiba City; per hr E£4; ☺9am-3am)

Medical Services

Nuweiba Hospital (📞350 0302; Nuweiba City; ☺24hr) Just off the Main East Coast Hwy to Dahab.

Money

None of the banks will handle Jordanian dinars.
Banque du Caire (Nuweiba Port) Has an ATM.
Banque Misr (Nuweiba Port) Has an ATM.
National Bank of Egypt (Helnan Nuweiba) Has an ATM.

National Bank of Egypt (Nuweiba City; ☺24hr) ATM only.

Post

Branch post office (Nuweiba Port)
Main post office (Nuweiba City)

Telephone

Telephone centrale (Nuweiba City; ☺24hr)

ℹ Getting There & Away

Boat

There are two public ferries run by **ABMaritime** (www.abmaritime.com.jo). The so-called 'fast-ferry' service between Nuweiba in Egypt and Aqaba in Jordan leaves Nuweiba Sunday to Friday (supposedly) at 3.30pm and takes roughly two hours assuming normal sea conditions. Heading back to Nuweiba, fast ferries depart from Aqaba at noon. One-way tickets cost US$75 for economy and US$95 for first class. You must be at the port two hours before to get through the shambolic departure formalities in the main ferry terminal building.

A word of caution: we have received numerous letters from readers detailing the aggravating specifics of interminable delays along this sea route. A small sampling of horror stories includes a monumental 20-hour delay due to heavy thunderstorms and rough seas, as well as a truly epic three-day delay due to severe power outages. While the majority of travellers experience a delay of no more than an hour or two, you might want to leave some flexibility in your travel schedule if you're planning on taking the ferry to Jordan.

There's also a 'slow-ferry' service, leaving Nuweiba at 2pm daily and arriving in Aqaba on average about five hours later. Heading back to Nuweiba, slow ferries depart from Aqaba at midnight. One-way tickets cost US$65 for economy and US$70 for first class. As previously mentioned, while the fast ferry isn't always fast – or even on time – we can't stress how much more comfortable it is than the slow ferry.

Tickets can be paid in either US dollars or Egyptian pounds and you must also pay your Egyptian departure tax (US$10/E£50) when you purchase them. Tickets must be purchased on the day of departure only at the **ferry ticket office** (📞352 0427; ☺9am-3pm), in a small building near the port. Note that the only exception to this rule is during the hajj, when boats are booked weeks prior to departure. During this period, it's necessary to buy your ticket as far in advance as possible.

To find the ticket office, turn right when you exit the bus station, walking towards the water, and turn right again after the National Bank of Egypt. Continue along one block, and you'll see the sand-coloured ticket office building ahead to your left.

Most nationalities are entitled to receive a free Jordanian visa upon arrival in Aqaba. You hand in your passport to the immigration officials once onboard the ferry and collect it once you've arrived in the immigration building in Aqaba.

TOURISTIC FERRY

As well as the two public ferries stated above, during research for this book, AB Maritime began running a new tourist ferry (named the 'Babel Ferry') on the Nuweiba to Aqaba route. Operated by **Meenagate Marine** (☑in Aqaba 3-201 3100; info@meenagate.com), this daily fast-ferry service leaves Nuweiba Port at 6.30am and has a sailing time of 1½ hours. You must be at the port one hour earlier. Heading back to Nuweiba the ferry leaves from Aqaba's Royal Yacht Club port (rather than the public port) at 7pm. Tickets cost US$85 one way or US$125 return and include Egyptian departure tax.

As this service is newly opened to independent travellers, tickets are best booked by emailing Meenagate directly 48 hours prior to sailing. You will then receive your ticket and pay for it on arrival at the port. Note that you cannot buy tickets for this ferry at the Nuweiba ferry ticket office. Meenagate is planning to open a ticket office in Nuweiba in the near future and it will most likely be possible to also buy tickets for this ferry through any of the tour operators in Dahab or Sharm el-Sheikh soon.

Bus

East Delta Travel Co (☑352 0371; Nuweiba Port) has buses at 9am and 3pm to Cairo (E£60 to E£100, seven to eight hours) which go via Taba (E£15); there is also a noon service to Taba only. Buses to Sharm el-Sheikh (E£25, three to four hours) via Dahab (E£15, one hour) leave at 6.30am and 4pm. There are no public bus services to St Katherine but local transport initiative **Bedouin Bus** (☑0101 668 4274; www.bedouin bus.com) began running transport between Nuweiba and St Katherine every Wednesday and Sunday (E£50) in late 2011. Check the website for up-to-date details.

Servees

Taxis and a couple of *servees* hang out by the port. Unless you get there when the ferry has arrived from Aqaba, you'll have to wait a long time for a *servees* to fill up. A taxi to Dahab costs about E£150 and roughly E£100 to the beach camps on the Nuweiba–Taba road.

① Getting Around

Expect to pay E£10 to E£20 for a taxi from the port/bus station to Nuweiba City, depending on your destination and negotiating powers, and from E£5 for the few kilometres between Tarabin and Nuweiba City.

Taba

☑069

Taba holds the dubious distinction of being the last portion of Sinai to be returned to Egypt under the terms of the 1979 Egypt–Israel peace treaty. It had been a minor point of contention between the two countries for nearly a decade. Egypt argued that Taba was on the Egyptian side of the armistice line agreed to in 1949, while Israel contended that it was on the Ottoman side of a border agreed between the Ottomans and British Egypt in 1906, and therefore the lines drawn in 1949 and 1979 were in error. In 1988 the issue was submitted to an international commission, which ruled in Egypt's favour – Israel returned Taba to Egypt later that year.

As part of this agreement, Israeli travellers were permitted to visit Taba visa-free for up to 48 hours, which sparked tourism development throughout the town. However, following a series of deadly bomb attacks in 2004 that killed and injured a large number of Israeli travellers, tourism virtually ceased in Taba. Today the town primarily serves as a border crossing for overlanders heading between Egypt and Israel and the Palestinian Territories. However, the flashy Taba Heights project just to the south, aimed almost exclusively at high-rolling overseas tourists, is the latest attempt by the Egyptian government to reinvigorate the stagnant local economy.

◉ Sights

Taba Heights   RESORT COMPLEX
(www.tabaheights.com) About 20km south of Taba is Taba Heights, one of the lynchpins in Egyptian efforts to create a 'Red Sea Riviera'. After years of construction, it now houses five luxury hotels, a casino, upmarket shops, bars and restaurants, a private medical clinic and extensive water-sports facilities.

Pharaoh's Island   FORTRESS
(Gezirat Fara'un; adult/child E£20/10; ☉9am-5pm) About 7km south of Taba and 250m off the Egyptian coast, this tiny islet in turquoise waters is dominated by the much-restored Castle of Salah ad-Din. The castle is actually a fortress built by the Crusaders in 1115, but captured and expanded by Saladin in 1170 as a bulwark against feared Crusader penetration south from Palestine.

GO EXPLORE THE OTHER SINAI SHORE

If you're seeking a sandy shore that hasn't succumbed to restaurant touts and rowdy bar music – where lazing in a hammock is the de rigueur activity – the stunning coastline between Nuweiba and Taba, speckled by simple beach camps, may be for you. This region's business for years came from Israelis looking for a close-to-home-Goa. Unfortunately political turmoil in recent years has kept many of them away and other travellers have yet to venture north and discover this tranquil beach-bum haven. For those who want to seriously veg out this is Egypt's last bastion of the traditional beach camp.

Here are some places to get you started but there are plenty more camps along this stretch if you want to explore. All the camps listed here have restaurants and can help organise desert treks for those who tire of slothing out on the sand. If you don't have your own transport and don't want to hire a taxi the East Delta buses running between Dahab and Taba or Cairo and Nuweiba can drop you anywhere along this shore.

Sawa Camp
BEACH CAMP $

(☑0111 322 7554; www.sawacamp.com; Mahash area; s/d hut E£50/60) A strip of perfect white beach, hammocks on your hut porch, solar-powered showers and a restaurant dishing up delicious meals – Sawa is our idea of heaven. Bedouin owner Salama has got all the little touches right. Huts have electricity at night, the communal bathrooms win our award for most spotlessly clean toilets in Egypt, and the service and welcome make you instantly feel at home. Laid-back, family-friendly and the perfect de-stress travel stop.

Basata
BEACH CAMP $$

(☑350 0480; www.basata.com; Ras Burgaa area; camping per person €14, s/d hut €23/42, 3-person chalets €80) Basata ('simplicity' in Arabic) is an ecologically minded settlement that lives by its name – using organically grown produce and recycling its rubbish. There are simple huts sharing facilities, or traditionally designed mud-brick chalets. Self-catering is the norm here with a communal kitchen and cooking ingredients available to buy, though if you're feeling lazy there's a bakery here too. The ambience is very laid-back and family-friendly with a New Age twist.

Ayyash Camp
BEACH CAMP $

(☑0122 760 4668; Ras Shaitan area; s/d hut E£30/60) Located on the rocky point of the frighteningly named Ras Shaitan (Satan's Head), Ayyash's stretch of sand is a bit stony and the facilities really are basic. Still, that doesn't dissuade its fans, who come here to flop out on its hippy vibes and cheap, chilled-out beach-bum living.

Castle Beach
BEACH CAMP $$

(☑0122 739 8495; http://castlebeachsinai.net/home.html; Ras Shaitan area; s/d hut incl half-board E£150/300; ❄) Just north of Ayyash Camp, Castle Beach has more-upmarket huts made of palm-thatch and stone on a wide strip of beach.

The only boat to the island runs from the Salah ad-Din Hotel, on the coast just opposite. Unfortunately the service is unreliable, though if the boat is running, a return ticket costs only US$4. Boat tickets are available from the hotel reception, and tickets for the fortress are available on landing.

🛏 Sleeping & Eating

Most of the tourism in Taba these days is focused on package holiday deals in the Taba Heights project. This is also where you'll find a good range of upmarket restaurants and bars.

TOP CHOICE **Tobya Boutique Hotel**
RESORT $$

(☑353 0275; www.tobyaboutiquehotel.com; Taba; s/d/ste half-board US$90/110/140; ❄❄) A resort with a difference, Tobya is a beautifully designed, intimate resort incorporating traditional Egyptian architecture and huge amounts of quirky interior details. With spacious, light-filled rooms decked out in local textiles, friendly staff and its own patch of private beach (which you access through a tunnel under the road), Tobya is the perfect compromise for those who want resort comforts without being dished up a homogenised experience.

Hyatt Regency Taba Heights   RESORT $$$
(☎358 0234; www.taba.regency.hyatt.com; s/d US$160/175; ❋@▨) The showpiece of the Taba Heights project, this elegant desert-pastel hotel captures the essence of beach luxury with its fabulously modern and breezy design by American architect Michael Graves. Nestled beside the mountains close to the beach, it has excellent facilities, including several pools, a large health centre, extensive water sports and a rapidly expanding list of gourmet restaurants.

Castle Zaman   EGYPTIAN $$$
(☎350 1234; www.castlezaman.com; meals from E£100; ⊙from 10am; ▨) This atmospheric stone castle on a cliff with views over the gulf has the best cuisine along this stretch of coast, specialising in slow food and featuring huge portions of items such as a full rack of grilled lamb. There's also a bar and a pool to lounge by while waiting for your meal. Phone beforehand as the castle is sometimes booked for weddings or other events.

❶ Information

The town centre is home to a couple of banks, a small hospital and various shops. Just inside the border are an ATM and several foreign-exchange booths. Cash and travellers cheques can also be exchanged at the Taba Hilton.

Dangers & Annoyances
On 7 October 2004, three bomb attacks in the Taba area killed 34 people and injured more than 150 people – the worst of these attacks occurred when a truck bomb brought down several floors of the Taba Hilton. Although another attack in Taba can never be completely ruled out, tourism in the town has since then slowed dramatically, which means that there are perhaps more likely targets in other parts of the country.

Despite the 18 August 2011 attack that occurred near Eilat (on the Israeli side of the border), the Egypt–Israel border remains perfectly safe and relatively hassle-free to cross. It's also worth mentioning that this 2011 attack was not aimed at tourists. Still, if you are planning to cross the border here, it's worth paying attention to warnings.

For an overview of the history of terrorism in Sinai, see p413.

❶ Getting There & Away
The Taba–Eilat border, which is open 24 hours daily, is the only safe and reliable crossing between Egypt and Israel. Egyptian departure tax is E£75. For more information, see p522.

Air
At the time of research, the Taba International Airport was only being used by European charter flights.

Bus
East Delta Travel Co (☎353 0250) has its bus station along the main road about 800m south of the border. Buses to Nuweiba (E£11, one hour) leave at 3pm and 4pm. The 3pm bus carries on to Dahab (E£25, 2½ hours) and Sharm el-Sheikh (E£30, four hours). To Cairo (E£60 to £80, six to seven hours) there are two buses every day at 10.30am and 4.30pm.

Car
Car rental is available at **Max Car Rental** (☎353 0333; tabareservation@max.com.eg; ⊙6am-8pm), situated just before the border post, opposite the Taba Hilton.

Servees
Taxis and minibuses wait by the border for passengers. If business is slack, you may have a long wait for the vehicle to fill up – or you can pay the equivalent of all seven fares and leave immediately. Per-person fares are about E£15 to Nuweiba, E£30 to Dahab, E£45 to Sharm el-Sheikh and E£55 to Cairo. Your bargaining power increases when the bus departure times are approaching.

SINAI INTERIOR

Sinai's rugged interior is populated by barren mountains, wind-sculpted canyons and wadis that burst into life with even the briefest rains. The rocks and desert landscapes turn shades of pink, ochre and velvet black as the sun rises and falls, and what little vegetation there is appears to grow magically out of the rock. Bedouin still wander through the wilderness, and camels are the best way to travel, with much of the terrain too rocky even for a 4WD. Against this desolate backdrop some of the most sacred events in recorded human history are said to have taken place, which has consequently immortalised Sinai in the annals of Judaism, Christianity and Islam.

St Katherine Protectorate

♪069

The 4350-sq-km St Katherine Protectorate was created in 1996 to counteract the detrimental effects of rapidly increasing tourism on St Katherine's Monastery and the adjacent Mt Sinai. In addition to the area's unique high-altitude desert ecosystem, it protects a wealth of historical sites sacred to the world's three main monotheistic religions, and the core part around the monastery has been declared a Unesco World Heritage site. Although at times it can be difficult to pry yourself away from Sinai's beaches, a visit to the St Katherine Protectorate is not to be missed.

Rising up out of the desert and jutting above the other peaks surrounding the monastery is the towering 2285m Mt Sinai (Gebel Musa). Tucked into a barren valley at the foot of Mt Sinai is the ancient St Katherine's Monastery. Approximately 3.5km from here is the small town of Al-Milga, which is also called Katreen and is known as the 'Meeting Place' by local Jabaliyya Bedouin.

◉ Sights

St Katherine's Monastery MONASTERY
(admission free; ⊙9am-noon Mon-Thu & Sat, except religious holidays) This ancient monastery traces its founding to about AD 330, when the Roman empress Helena had a small chapel and a fortified refuge for local hermits built beside what was believed to be the burning bush from which God spoke to Moses. In the 6th century Emperor Justinian ordered a fortress to be constructed around the original chapel, together with a basilica and a monastery, to provide a secure home for the monastic community that had grown here, and as a refuge for the Christians of southern Sinai. Since then the monastery has been visited by pilgrims from throughout the world, many of whom braved extraordinarily difficult and dangerous journeys to reach the remote and isolated site. Today St Katherine's is considered one of the oldest continually functioning monastic communities in the world, and its chapel is one of early Christianity's only surviving churches.

The monastery – which, together with the surrounding area, has been declared a Unesco World Heritage site – is named after St Katherine, the legendary martyr of Alexandria, who was tortured on a spiked wheel and then beheaded for her faith. Tradition holds that her body was transported by angels away from the torture device (which spun out of control and killed the pagan onlookers) and onto the slopes of Egypt's highest mountain peak. The peak, which lies about 6km south of Mt Sinai, subsequently became known as Gebel Katarina. Katherine's body was subsequently 'found' about 300 years later by monks from the monastery in a state of perfect preservation.

Today a paved access road has removed the hazards that used to accompany a trip to the monastery, and both the monastery and the mountain are routinely packed with tour buses and people. It is especially full early in the morning, although somehow the monastery's interior tranquillity manages to make itself felt despite the crowds. When you visit, remember that this is still a functioning monastery, which necessitates conservative dress – no one with shorts is permitted to enter, and women must cover their shoulders.

Church of the Transfiguration
This ornately decorated 6th-century church has a nave flanked by massive marble columns and walls covered in richly gilded icons and paintings. At the church's eastern end, a gilded 17th-century iconostasis separates the nave from the sanctuary and the apse, where St Katherine's remains are interred (off limits to most visitors). High in the apse above the altar is one of the monastery's most stunning artistic treasures, the 6th-century mosaic of the transfiguration, although it can be difficult to see past the chandeliers and the iconostasis. To the left of and below the altar is the monastery's holiest area, the **Chapel of the Burning Bush**, which is off limits to the public.

The Burning Bush
It's possible to see what is thought to be a descendant of the original burning bush in the monastery compound. However, due to visitors snipping cuttings of the bush to take home as blessings, the area surrounding the bush is now fenced off. Near the burning bush is the **Well of Moses**, a natural spring that is supposed to give marital happiness to those who drink from it.

Sacred Sacristy
(Monastery Museum; adult/student E£25/10) Above the Well of Moses is the superb monastery museum, which has been magnificently restored. It has displays (labelled in

Arabic and English) of many of the monastery's artistic treasures, including some of the spectacular Byzantine-era icons from its world-famous collection, numerous precious chalices, and gold and silver crosses.

Although it contains a priceless collection of ancient manuscripts and illuminated bibles, the monastery's **library** is unfortunately closed to the general public.

Outside the monastery walls is a gift shop selling replicas of icons and other religious items (there's also a branch inside the monastery compound just near the entrance), and a cafe with an array of cold drinks and snacks. The least-crowded days for visiting the monastery are generally Tuesday and Wednesday, while Saturday and Monday tend to be the most crowded.

Mt Sinai
MOUNTAIN

(guide E£125; camel ride one way E£125) Known locally as Gebel Musa, Mt Sinai is revered by Christians, Muslims and Jews, all of whom believe that God delivered his Ten Commandments to Moses at its summit. The mountain is easy and beautiful to climb, and although you'll invariably be overwhelmed with crowds of other visitors, it offers a taste of the magnificence of southern Sinai's high mountain region. For those visiting as part of a pilgrimage, it also offers a moving glimpse into biblical times. All hikers must be accompanied by a guide (hired from the monastery car park), which helps provide work for the local Bedouin.

There are two well-defined routes up to the summit – the camel trail and the Steps of Repentance – which meet about 300m below the summit at a plateau known as Elijah's Basin. Here, everyone must take a steep series of 750 rocky and uneven steps to the top, where there is a small chapel and mosque (although these are kept locked).

Both the climb and the summit offer spectacular views of nearby plunging valleys and of jagged mountain chains rolling off into the distance, and it's usually possible to see the even-higher summit of Gebel Katarina in the distance. Most people make the climb in the pre-dawn hours to see the magnificence of the sun rising over the surrounding peaks, and then arrive back at the base before 9am, when the monastery opens for visitors. As late as mid-May, be prepared to share the summit with up to several hundred other visitors, some carrying stereos, others bibles and hymn books. With the music and singing, and people nudging each

TREAD LIGHTLY IN THE PROTECTORATE

To limit tourism impact on this special place, the following code is in force:

» Respect the area's religious and historical importance and the local Bedouin culture and traditions.

» Carry your litter out, bury your bodily waste and burn your toilet paper.

» Do not contaminate or overuse water sources.

The following acts are illegal:

» Removing any object, including rocks, plants and animals.

» Disturbing or harming animals or birds.

» Cutting or uprooting plants.

» Writing, painting or carving graffiti.

other for space, it can be difficult to actually sleep, especially in the small hours before sunrise.

A more serene alternative is to walk up for sunset, when you'll rarely have more than 40 other people sharing the summit with you. If you decide on this option you must be comfortable making the descent down the camel trail in the dark and make sure you have sturdy shoes and a good torch (flashlight).

Due to the sanctity of the area, and the tremendous pressure that large groups place on the environment, the Egyptian National Parks Office has instituted various regulations. If you spend the night on the mountain, you are asked to sleep below the summit at the small Elijah's Basin plateau. Here you'll find several composting toilets and a 500-year-old cypress tree, marking the spot where the prophet Elijah is said to have heard the voice of God. Bring sufficient food and water, warm clothes and a sleeping bag. It gets cold and windy, even in summer, and in winter light snows are common.

Camel Trail

The start of the camel trail is reached by walking along the northern wall of the monastery past the end of the compound. This is the easier route, and takes about two hours to ascend, moving at a steady pace. The trail is wide, clear and gently sloping as it moves

St Katherine's Monastery

A HISTORY OF THE MONASTERY

4th Century With hermetic communities congregating in the area, a chapel is established around the site of Moses' miraculous **Burning Bush** `1`.

6th Century In a show of might, Emperor Justinian adds the monastery **fortifications** `2` and orders the building of the basilica, which is graced by Byzantine art, including the **Mosaic of the Transfiguration** `3`.

7th Century The prophet Mohammed signs the **Ahtiname** `4`, a declaration of his protection of the monastery. When the Arab armies conquer Egypt in AD 641, the monastery is left untouched. Despite the era's tumultuous times, monastery abbot St John Klimakos writes his famed **Ladder of Divine Ascent** `5` treatise, depicted in the Sacred Sacristy.

9th Century Extraordinary happenings surround the monastery when, according to tradition, a monk discovers the body of St Katherine on a nearby mountain summit.

11th Century To escape the wrath of Fatimid caliph Al-Hakim, wily monks build a mosque within the monastery grounds.

15th Century Frequent raids and attacks on the monastery lead the monks to build the **Ancient Gate** `6` to prevent the ransacking of church treasures and to keep the monastic community safe.

19th Century In 1859 biblical scholar Constantin von Tischendorf borrows 347 pages of the **Codex Sinaiticus** `7` from the monastery, but fails to get his library books back on time. Greek artisans travel from the island of Tinos in 1871 to help construct the **bell tower** `8`.

20th Century Renovations inside the monastery reveal 18 more missing parchment leaves from the Codex Sinaiticus, proving that all the secrets hidden within these ancient walls may not yet be revealed.

Fortifications

The formidable walls are 2m thick and 11m high. Justinian sent a Balkan garrison to watch over the newly fortified monastery, and today's local Jabaleyya tribe are said to be their descendents.

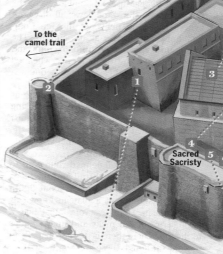

To the camel trail ←

Sacred Sacristy

The Burning Bush

This flourishing bramble (the endemic Sinai shrub *Rubus Sanctus*) was transplanted in the 10th century to its present location. Tradition states that cuttings of the plant refuse to grow outside the monastery walls.

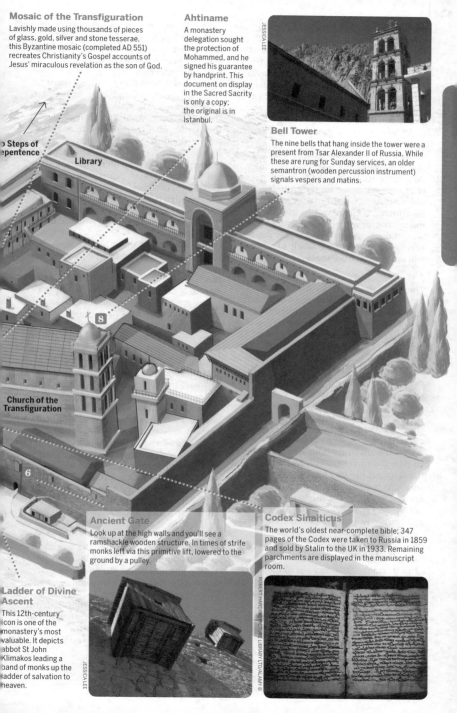

Mosaic of the Transfiguration

Lavishly made using thousands of pieces of glass, gold, silver and stone tesserae, this Byzantine mosaic (completed AD 551) recreates Christianity's Gospel accounts of Jesus' miraculous revelation as the son of God.

Ahtiname

A monastery delegation sought the protection of Mohammed, and he signed his guarantee by handprint. This document on display in the Sacred Sacrity is only a copy; the original is in Istanbul.

Bell Tower

The nine bells that hang inside the tower were a present from Tsar Alexander II of Russia. While these are rung for Sunday services, an older semantron (wooden percussion instrument) signals vespers and matins.

Steps of Repentence

Library

Church of the Transfiguration

Ancient Gate

Look up at the high walls and you'll see a ramshackle wooden structure. In times of strife monks left via this primitive lift, lowered to the ground by a pulley.

Codex Sinaiticus

The world's oldest near-complete bible; 347 pages of the Codex were taken to Russia in 1859 and sold by Stalin to the UK in 1933. Remaining parchments are displayed in the manuscript room.

Ladder of Divine Ascent

This 12th-century icon is one of the monastery's most valuable. It depicts abbot St John Klimakos leading a band of monks up the ladder of salvation to heaven.

JESSICA LEE

ROBERT HARDING PICTURE LIBRARY LTD/ALAMY ©

up a series of switchbacks, with the only potential difficulty – apart from sometimes fierce winds – being gravelly patches that can be slippery on the descent. Most people walk up, but it's also possible to hire a camel at the base, just behind the monastery, to take you to where the camel trail ends at El-ijah's Basin. If you decide to try a camel, it's easier on the anatomy (especially if you're male) to ride up the mountain, rather than down.

En route are several kiosks selling tea and soft drinks, and near the summit vendors rent out blankets (E£5) and mattresses (E£10) to help ward off the chill. If you are ascending in the night to wait for sunrise at the summit, both the mattresses will provide a layer of protection from the ice-cold rocks, and the blankets (even though they smell like camels) will protect you from the howling winds.

Steps of Repentance
The alternative path to the summit comprises the taxing 3750 Steps of Repentance, which begin outside the southeastern corner of the monastery compound. They were laid by one monk as a form of penance. The steps – 3000 up to Elijah's Basin and then the final 750 to the summit – are made of roughly hewn rock, and are steep and uneven in many places, requiring strong knees and concentration in placing your feet. The stunning mountain scenery along the way, though, makes this path well worth the extra effort and the lower reaches of the trail afford impressive views of the monastery.

If you want to try both routes, it's easier to take the camel trail on the way up and the steps on the way back down. This trail shouldn't be attempted in the dark, so if you are heading to the summit for sunset and not staying overnight, go up via the steps and come down the easier camel trail.

🏃 **Activities**

Trekking
St Katherine's Monastery lies in the heart of South Sinai's high mountain region, and the surrounding area is an ideal trekking destination for anyone with a rugged and adventurous bent. Treks range from half a day to a week or more, and can be done either on camel or on foot. Even if you decide to walk, you'll need at least one camel for your food and luggage. For detailed information on trekking in this area check out www.discov ersinai.net and www.st-katherine.net.

One of the most common circuits goes to the **Galt al-Azraq** (Blue Pools) and takes four to five days. The trail leaves Al-Milga via the man-made **Abu Giffa Pass** and goes through **Wadi Tubug**, taking a detour around **Wadi Shagg**, where there are springs, waterholes and lush, walled gardens *(bustans)*. The walk then goes through the picturesque **Wadi Zuweitin** (Valley of the Olives), with ancient olive trees said by local Bedouin to have been planted by the founder of the Jabaliyya tribe. The first night is often spent here, and there is a small stone hut in which hikers can sometimes sleep. The hike continues through **Wadi Gibal**, through high passes and along the valleys of **Farsh Asara** and **Farsh Arnab**. Many hikers then climb either **Ras Abu Alda** or **Gebel Abu Gasba** before heading to the spring of **Ain Nagila** and the ruins of a Byzantine monastery at **Bab ad-Dunya** (Gate of the World). On the third day the trail leads to the crystal-clear, icy waters of the **Galt al-Azraq**, a deep, dramatic pool in the rock, before continuing on the fourth day through more dramatic wadis to a camel pass on **Gebel Abbas Basha**. A one-hour hike up a fairly easy but steep path leads to a ruined palace built by the 19th-century viceroy Abbas Hilmi I, with stunning views from the summit (2304m). The trail then goes back to Wadi Zuweitin and retraces its way to Al-Milga.

Other destinations include **Sheikh Awad**, with a sheikh's tomb and Bedouin settlement; the **Nugra Waterfall**, a difficult-to-reach, rain-fed cascade about 20m high, which is reached through a winding canyon called **Wadi Nugra**; and **Naqb al-Faria**, a camel path with rock inscriptions. A shorter trip is the hike to the top of **Gebel Katarina**, Egypt's highest peak at 2642m. It takes about five hours to reach the summit along a straightforward but taxing trail. The views from the top are breathtaking, and the panorama can even include the mountains of Saudi Arabia on a clear day. The **Blue Valley**, given its name after a Belgian artist painted the rocks here blue some years ago, is another popular day trip.

All treks must be done with a Bedouin guide, which can be easily arranged in St Katherine using either of the tour companies listed under Tours or through any of the camps and hotels listed.

Tours

The majority of visitors arrive at the St Katherine Protectorate on organised tours departing from either Sharm el-Sheikh or Dahab. However, it's easy to sleep within the confines of the protectorate, and to organise everything independently. Guided treks typically start at around €50 per day including food and equipment. You should also buy firewood here in order to discourage destruction of the few trees in the mountains.

Whoever you go with, be sure to register with the police prior to leaving.

Make sure you bring water-purification tablets, unless you want to rely on the mountain springs. You'll also need comfortable walking boots, a hat and sunglasses, sunblock, a warm jacket, a good sleeping bag and toilet paper. Keep in mind that it can get very cold at night – frost, and even snow, are common in winter.

THE BEDOUIN OF SINAI

Sinai's rugged tracts are home to desert dwellers, most of whom live in the north of the peninsula. The Bedouin – whose numbers are variously estimated to be between 80,000 and 300,000 – belong to 14 distinct tribes, most with ties to Bedouin in the Negev, Jordan and northern Saudi Arabia, and each with their own customs and culture. The Sukwarka, who live along the northern coast near Al-Arish, are the largest tribe. Others include the Tarabin, who have territory in both northern and southern Sinai; the Tyaha in the centre of the peninsula who, together with the Tarabin, trace their roots to Palestine; and the Haweitat, centred in an area southeast of Suez, and originally from the Hejaz in Saudi Arabia.

The seven Bedouin tribes in southern Sinai are known collectively as the Towara or 'Arabs of Al-Tor', the provincial capital. Of these, the first to settle in Sinai were the Aleiqat and the Suwalha, who arrived soon after the Muslim conquest of Egypt. The largest southern tribe is the Mizena, who are concentrated along the coast between Sharm el-Sheikh and Nuweiba. Some members of the tiny Jabaliyya tribe, centred in the mountains around St Katherine, are said to be descendants of Macedonians sent by Emperor Justinian to build and protect the monastery in the 6th century.

Thanks to centuries of living in the harsh conditions of Sinai, the Bedouin have developed a sophisticated understanding of their environment. Strict laws and traditions govern the use of precious resources. Water use is closely regulated and vegetation carefully conserved, as revealed in the Bedouin adage 'killing a tree is like killing a soul'. Local life centres on clans and their sheikhs (leaders), and loyalty and hospitality – essential for surviving in the desert – are paramount. Tea is traditionally taken in rounds of three, and traditional dwellings are tents made of woven goat hair, sometimes mixed with sheep wool. Women's black veils and robes are often elaborately embroidered, with red signifying that they are married, and blue unmarried.

Sinai's original inhabitants are often left behind in the race to build up the coast, and they are sometimes viewed with distrust because of their ties to tribes in neighbouring countries, and allegations of criminal activity and links to terrorist cells throughout Sinai. Bedouin traditions also tend to come second to the significant economical benefits brought by development in the peninsula – benefits that, according to Bedouin activists, Bedouins are yet to fully experience. Egyptian human rights organisations have also reported ongoing persecution of Bedouin people, including imprisonment without charges, and there have been regular demonstrations by Bedouin claiming mistreatment by the police. These concerns, as well as loss of traditional lands, pollution of fishing areas, and insensitive tourism, have contributed to the sense of marginalisation and unrest.

Fortunately, the news isn't all bad – indeed, the Bedouin are arguably more organised and unified than they have ever been and there is hope that Egypt's revolution will, in the end, bring more autonomy for Sinai's tribes.

Throughout the world – and especially in Egypt – tourism has the power to shape the destinies of communities. Travellers can limit any negative effects by seeking out Bedouin-owned businesses, buying locally, staying informed of prevalent issues and never being afraid to ask questions.

Mountain Tours Office
HIKING

(☑347 0457; www.sheikmousa.com; El-Malga Bedouin Camp) The main hub for trekking activities in the St Katherine region, this office can organise anything from a short afternoon stroll to a multiday itinerary. It can also arrange yoga and meditation retreats, rock climbing and 4WD tours.

Wilderness Ventures Egypt
HIKING

(☑0128 282 7182; www.wilderness-ventures-egypt.com) Working closely with local Jabaliyya Bedouin, this highly recommended company organises a variety of treks, walks and activities inside the St Katherine Protectorate, with a strong focus on Bedouin culture and the history of the area. Of particular note, it runs Sinai's only proper camel-riding school (where you'll be taught how to properly handle your trusty steed before setting out on a trek), arranges fascinating evening astronomy sessions where you can learn about Bedouin star-lore, and organises walks in the nearby Wadi Itlah gardens where you'll learn about local flora and medicinal plants before a slap-up lunch in one of the gardens.

🛏 Sleeping

Most hotels and guesthouses are based in the village of Al-Milga (Katreen), approximately 3.5km from the monastery.

TOP CHOICE Al-Karm Ecolodge
LODGE $

(☑0100 132 4693; Sheikh Awaad; r without bathroom incl half/full board per person E£100/120) Surrounded by lush walled gardens in a remote wadi, this Bedouin-owned ecolodge is the perfect spot to sample the tranquillity and rugged beauty of southern Sinai. It deserves kudos for its environmental efforts with solar-powered showers, composting toilets, and beautifully designed, simple stone and palm-trunk rooms, decorated with local textiles, that blend into the scenery. Lit only by the flicker of candlelight by night, this is a truly unique spot that is worth the effort to get here. There is plenty of good trekking which can be arranged by the lodge.

Transport here and lodge booking is easiest done through the **Mountain Tours Office** (above) at Al-Milga in St Katherine, as only minimal English is spoken at the lodge itself. The lodge is only accessible by 4WD. The turn-off is signposted 'Garaba Valley' about 20km from St Katherine on the Wadi Feiran road.

El-Malga Bedouin Camp
HOSTEL $

(☑0100 641 3575; www.sheikmousa.com; dm E£25, s/d E£100/150, without bathroom E£55/85; 🛜) Also the base of the Mountain Tours Office, this popular and friendly camp run by the affable Sheikh Mousa is a backpacker favourite and offers excellent quality for the price. The new-built en suite rooms are large and comfortable while the cheaper rooms all share excellent bathroom facilities with hot water. It's an easy 500m walk from the bus station.

Monastery Guesthouse
GUESTHOUSE $$

(☑347 0353; St Katherine's Monastery; s/d US$35/60) A favourite of pilgrims the world over, this guesthouse right next to St Katherine's Monastery offers well-kept rooms with heaters and blankets to keep out the mountain chill, and a pleasant patio area with views towards the mountains. Meals at the on-site cafeteria are filling and tasty, and lunches can be arranged for a few extra dollars per person. Make sure to ask for a mountain-view rather than a courtyard-view room.

Daniela Village
HOTEL $$

(☑347 0379; www.daniela-hotels.com; s/d half-board US$65/95; ❄) One of the nicest mid-range hotels in Al-Milga, this reasonably priced three-star affair comprises stone-clad chalets that are scattered around attractive grounds. The on-site bar-restaurant is a popular tourist hang-out, and is especially good if you're in need of a Stella after an all-night trek. It's diagonally opposite the hospital and about 1.5km from the bus station.

Desert Fox Camp
HOSTEL $

(☑347 0344; www.desertfoxcamp.com; s/d without bathroom E£30/60) This ultra-friendly and laid-back camp offers a variety of bare-bones basic and battered rooms amid a quiet garden setting. It's on the way out of Al-Milga on the main road (about 1.5km from the bus station) near the turn-off to the monastery.

Catherine Plaza
HOTEL $$

(☑347 0288; www.catherineplaza.com; s/d half-board US$65/90; ❄🛜) Al-Milga's fanciest accommodation option offers decent-sized rooms with rather festive green and red decor and teensy balconies. It's looking a little rough around the edges these days but the pleasant gardens and friendly service are a bonus.

Eating

In Al-Milga, there's a bakery opposite the mosque, a couple of simple restaurants and several well-stocked supermarkets – perfect for stocking up on supplies before hitting the trails. Most tourists take their meals at their camp or hotel, or in the monastery's cafeteria.

If you are spending a little time in St Katherine, don't miss the opportunity of having lunch, surrounded by shady fruit trees, in the gardens of Wadi Itlah. Local tour company **Wilderness Ventures Egypt** (p434) can arrange this for you.

Shopping

Fansina

HANDICRAFTS

(☑347 0155; Al-Milga; ☺10am-3pm Sat-Thu) This Bedouin women's cooperative works with over 300 local women and displays a huge range of their textiles and local handicrafts. It's signposted on the first left-hand turn coming into town from Desert Fox Camp.

Information

The **St Katherine Protectorate Office** (☑347 0032), located near the entrance to Al-Milga, sometimes has informative booklets to four 'interpretive trails' established in the area, including one for Mt Sinai. These booklets take you through each trail, explaining flora and fauna as well as sites of historical and religious significance.

The following listings are in the town of Al-Milga.

Banque Misr (beside petrol station) Has an ATM. Also changes US dollars and euro.

Nahda Internet (beside El-Malga Bedouin Camp)

Police (☑347 0046; beside the St Katherine Protectorate Office)

Post office (beside the bakery)

St Katherine Hospital (☑347 0263) Provides very basic care only.

Telephone centrale (beside the bakery; ☺24hr)

Getting There & Away

In addition to the transport options listed here, many hotels and camps in Sinai, as well as travel agencies in Cairo, organise trips to the protectorate.

Bus

East Delta Travel Co (☑347 0250) has its bus station and ticket office just off the main road in Al-Milga, behind the mosque. There is a daily bus to Cairo (E£50, seven hours) at 6am, via Wadi Feiran and Suez (E£40, five hours).

There hasn't been a public bus service between St Katherine and the Sinai coast for well over a year, but during the course of research for this book a local transport initiative, **Bedouin Bus** (☑0101 668 4274; www.bedouinbus. com), began operating twice weekly between Al-Milga and Dahab and Nuweiba. To Dahab the bus departs every Tuesday and Friday at 11am, and to Nuweiba at 8am every Wednesday and Sunday. Both cost E£50 and take two hours. The bus leaves from next to the bakery (opposite the mosque).

Servees

Taxis and pickups usually wait at the monastery car park for people coming down from Mt Sinai in the morning, and then again around noon when the monastery's visiting hours end. A lift to the village costs E£10 to E£15. The rate per car to either Dahab or Sharm el-Sheikh is E£250.

Wadi Feiran

This long valley serves as the main drainage route for the entire high mountain region into the Gulf of Suez. Sinai's largest oasis, it is lush and very beautiful, containing more than 12,000 date palms, as well as Bedouin communities representing all of Sinai's tribes. Stone walls surround the palms, and the rocky mountains on each side of the wadi have subtly different colours that stand out at sunrise and sunset, making the landscape even more dramatic.

Feiran also has biblical significance – it is believed to be the Rephidim mentioned in the Old Testament where the Israelites defeated their enemies. Because of this it later became the first Christian stronghold in Sinai. An extensively rebuilt early Christian convent remains from this time, although you need permission from St Katherine's Monastery if you want to visit.

The valley is also an ideal spot from which to trek into the surrounding mountains. To the south, the 2070m **Gebel Serbal** (believed by early Christians to have been the real Mt Sinai) is a challenging six-hour hike to the summit along a track also known as **Sikket ar-Reshshah**. Those who persevere are rewarded with fantastic panoramic views. You must be accompanied by a Bedouin guide for all hikes, which can be arranged either in Al-Milga (at St Katherine) or at the Bedouin Flower Garden Restaurant in Wadi Feiran itself.

Qalaat al-Gindi & Nakhl

In the centre of Sinai, about 80km southeast of the Ahmed Hamdi Tunnel, is Qalaat al-Gindi, which features the 800-year-old **Fortress of Saladin** (Salah ad-Din). In the 12th century, Muslims from Africa and the Mediterranean streamed across Sinai on their way to Mecca. The three caravan routes they followed all converged at Qalaat al-Gindi, prompting Saladin to build a fortress here to protect the pilgrims making their hajj. He also planned to use the fort, which today is still largely intact, as a base from which to launch attacks on the Crusaders, who had advanced as far as Jerusalem. As it turned out, Saladin managed to evict the Crusaders from the Holy City even before the completion of his fortress. At the time of research, visiting this area is severely restricted and foreigners need to acquire special permission from the military (which is rarely granted).

NORTHERN SINAI

Rarely visited by tourists, northern Sinai has a barren desert interior, much of which is off limits to foreigners, and a palm-fringed Mediterranean coast backed by soft white sands sculpted into low dunes. As a crossroad between Asia and Africa, the coastal highway follows what must be one of history's oldest march routes. Known in ancient times as the Way of Horus, it was used by the Egyptians, Persians, Greeks, Crusaders and Arab Muslims. In fact, the Copts believe that the infant Jesus also passed along this route with his parents during their flight into Egypt.

Al-Arish

📞 068 / POP 140,000

Much of the north coast of Sinai between Port Fuad and Al-Arish is dominated by the swampy lagoon of Lake Bardawil, separated from the Mediterranean by a limestone ridge. As a result of this inhospitable geography, Al-Arish is the only major city in the region, and by default the capital of North Sinai Governorate. The town's sprawl of ugly low-rise cement blocks wouldn't win any design awards but the long palm-fringed (though litter-strewn) coastline is a popular weekend getaway for holidaying Cairenes in summer. The weekly market draws in thousands of Bedouin traders from around the peninsula, making for a vibrant and completely chaotic experience.

The main coastal road, Sharia Fuad Zikry (which changes its name to Sharia al-Geish as it heads north), forms a T-junction with Sharia 23rd of July, which runs a couple of kilometres south – changing name to Sharia Tahrir on the way – to the main market area.

◉ Sights & Activities

Zerenike Protectorate　　　　PARK

Stretched along the Mediterranean coast from the eastern edge of Lake Bardawil until about 25km east of Al-Arish is this 220-sq-km **protectorate** (📞0100 544 2641; per son/car US$5/5; ◷sunrise-sunset), a haven for migrating birds and a good destination for nature lovers. There are more than 250 avian species here and for most of the year it's possible to spot flamingos. The entrance to

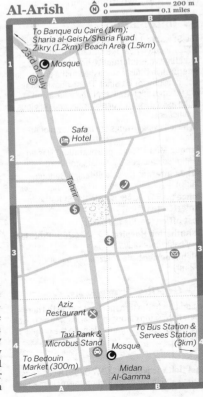

the protectorate, which was established by the Egyptian National Parks Office in 1985, is about 35km east of Al-Arish.

Inside the gates there is a small but highly informative **visitors centre** (◐9am-5pm Sat-Thu), with a cafeteria and information about some of the species of birds that stop here as they migrate between Europe and Africa. If you call in advance, you can book simple **rooms** (per person US$25) and **camping** (per person US$10). For both options, you'll need to bring all food and drink with you as there is no restaurant. Basic cooking facilities are available on-site.

If you don't have your own transport, it's best to take a taxi from Al-Arish to the park entrance – a one-way trip should cost around E£30.

Al-Arish Museum MUSEUM
(Coast rd; adult/student E£20/10, camera E£20; ◐9.30am-2pm Sat-Thu) This massive, fortress-like building sits on the outskirts of Al-Arish along the coastal road to Rafah. The exhibits span the full breadth of Egypt's history, from Pharaonic right through to the Islamic era, and are thoughtfully displayed. Unfortunately, due to the lack of visitor numbers, opening hours are haphazard at best.

Bedouin Market MARKET
(◐9am-2pm Thu) Held at the southern edge of town near the main market (note that it's signposted in Arabic and in English as the Souq al-Hamis), this fascinating market is a kaleidoscope of colour, smell and sound. Squeezing between the bleating goats, chicken cages and huge mounds of onions, while trying to manoeuvre through the crowds, is an experience itself. Bedouin arrive en masse for the occasion with veiled women trading silver, beadwork and embroidered dresses.

🛏 Sleeping & Eating

Macca Hotel HOTEL $$
(☏335 2632; Sharia As-Salam; s/d E£105/155; ❄) The Macca staff members take their 'welcome to Al-Arish' commitments seriously and the no-nonsense, spotless rooms help to make this hotel an affordable and comfortable place to bed down. There's a decent restaurant on-site as well. It's on a side street off Sharia al-Geish.

Swiss Inn RESORT $$
(☏335 1321; www.swissinn.net; Sharia Fuad Zikry; s/d US$90/110; ❄❄) It may be a tad faded but

the cheerful, tidy rooms all have sea views and balconies and if you come outside of summer you're likely to have the beach all to yourself.

Safa Hotel HOTEL $
(☏335 3798; Sharia Tahrir; s/d E£30/40) This bare-bones hotel is at least friendly and safe. Run-down rooms come with peeling paintwork, a bed and a symphony of street noise rising up from the main road below.

Aziz Restaurant EGYPTIAN $
(Sharia Tahrir; dishes E£5-25) An affordable restaurant offering filling meals of *fuul* and *ta'amiyya*, as well as grilled chicken, *kofta*, rice and spaghetti.

ℹ Information

Emergency
Ambulance (☏123)
Tourist police (☏336 1016; Sharia Fuad Zikry; ◐24hr)

Internet Access
Tornado Net (per hr E£3; ◐11am-3am)

Medical Services
Military Hospital (☏332 4018; near Governorate Bldg, Coast rd; ◐24hr)
Public Hospital (☏336 0010; Sharia Fuad Zikry; ◐24hr) To be avoided except in the direst emergencies.

Money
Banque du Caire (Sharia 23rd of July) Has an ATM.
Banque Misr (off Sharia Tahrir) Has an ATM.
National Bank of Egypt (Sharia Tahrir; Sharia 23rd of July) Has an ATM.

Post
Main post office (off Sharia Tahrir)

Telephone
Telephone centrale (Sharia Tahrir; ◐24hr)

Tourist Information
Tourist office (☏336 3743; Sharia Fuad Zikry; ◐9am-2pm Sat-Thu)

ℹ Getting There & Away

The main bus and *servees* stations are next to each other, about 3km southeast of the town centre (about E£5 in a taxi).

Bus
East Delta Travel Co (☏332 5931) has buses to Cairo (E£30, five hours) departing at 8am and 4pm. Departures to Ismailia (E£15 to E£20, three to four hours) leave at 7am, 10.30am,

11.30am, 1pm, 2pm, 3pm and 4pm. For Suez, change in Ismailia.

Servees

A *servees* from Al-Arish to Cairo costs around E£20 to E£25 per person. To Ismailia costs about E£15; to Rafah E£10.

❶ Getting Around

The main taxi rank and microbus stand is at Midan al-Gamma, near the market at the southern end of town. Microbuses shuttle regularly between here and the beach (50pt).

Rafah

 068 / POP 31,500

This coastal town, 48km northeast of Al-Arish, marks the border with the Gaza Strip, an area that is a world away from the relative peace and calm of Sinai. On 28 May 2011 the border between Egypt and Gaza was opened for the first time since Hamas took control of Gaza in 2007. The atmosphere remains tense and the border has been closed without warning several times since then due to security fears.

Crossing the border as a foreigner here requires obtaining permission beforehand. For details on permission, border crossing and warnings, see p522. If you have a pressing reason to head to the border, and have acquired the correct paperwork, you can take the daily *servees* between Al-Arish and the Rafah border crossing for about E£10.

For border-crossing details and warnings, see p522.

Understand
Egypt

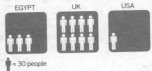
Egypt Today

You say you want a Revolution...

It's all change in Egypt at the moment. After three decades of President Hosni Mubarak's regime, and almost another three before that under Presidents Nasser and Sadat, Egyptians decided to break the mould. The extent of change is still not known at the time of writing, but two things are clear now as they have been for many years: Egyptians demand their right to vote and many of them will use it to support the Muslim Brotherhood and more extreme Islamist parties, banned under Mubarak.

This state of revolution clashes with the idea that Egypt is a place where time stands still. This is, after all, where Menes united the two states of Upper and Lower Egypt, and set the stage for one of the greatest civilisations the world has ever known. It is a land of magnificent World Heritage Sites built by the many pharaohs. But it has seen more than its share of upheavals. This was where Alexander conquered, Mark Antony flirted and the Holy Family sheltered. Napoleon stopped long enough to print propaganda and pilfer antiquities, while the British stayed around to get the train system running, ensure the safety of their passage to India, and at the same time take enough items to furnish every spare nook of the British Museum.

Lingering over coffee in one of Alexandria's cosmopolitan cafes or sipping a calming glass of *shai* (tea) after a frenzied shopping episode in Cairo's Khan al-Khalili are activities as popular today as they were back when 19th-century tourists started to arrive en masse. Magnificent monuments are everywhere – the pointed perfection of the Pyramids, soaring minarets of Cairo's skyline and the majestic tombs and temples of Luxor are just a few of the wonders that generations of visitors have admired during their city sojourns, jaunts up and down the Nile and expeditions through spectacularly stark desert landscapes.

» Population: 83 million

» Annual population growth rate: 1.8%

» Average male life expectancy: 71 years

» Average female life expectancy: 75 years

» Male literacy rate: 83%

» Female literacy rate: 59%

Key Words

» **Insha' Allah**, God willing – as in 'The flight to Luxor takes one hour, insha' Allah'

» **Bukra**, tomorrow – often used in conjunction with the above

» **Mumkin**, maybe – best used as 'everything is mumkin' or, 'mish mumkin', no way!

Mosque Etiquette

» Remove your shoes at the entrance to a mosque

» Dress respectfully – Egyptians wouldn't enter a mosque in shorts or with women showing their shoulders or legs

» Avoid visiting during prayer times

Take time to...

» Say hello – Egyptians are usually extremely courteous, however busy they might be

» Sit in a cafe and watch the world go by

» Learn a few words in Arabic – the effort will be hugely appreciated

belief systems
(% of population)

90 Muslim

9 Coptic

• 1

Other

if Egypt were 100 people

63 would be 15-64 years old
33 would be under 14 years old
4 would be over 64 years old

Pressing Problems

But modern Egypt is bursting at the seams. More than half a century on from the great Nasser-led revolution, Egypt is again in flux following the overthrow of President Mubarak in February 2011. Although the dictator has gone, the problems he allowed to grow remain: a booming population, notably high unemployment and a basket-case economy. Once home to the all-powerful pharaohs, the country has largely been reduced to a dependent state of the USA, having received more than US$30 billion dollars in military aid and economic assistance over the past three decades.

The list of woes continues, exacerbated by a state of emergency that has been in place for decades: torture and ill-treatment of prisoners in detention, described by Amnesty International as 'systematic'; the issue of child labour, particularly within the lucrative national cotton industry (UNICEF reports over one million children are believed to work in this industry alone); regularly reported cases of 'administrative detention' of individuals without trial, which has brought criticism from both local media and international human-rights organisations; continuing restrictions on women under personal-status laws, which, for example, deny the freedom to travel without permission; rampant inflation, leading to food shortages within the poorest communities; and constant environmental threats, with polluted waterways, overpopulation, unregulated emissions, a looming water crisis and soil salinity being of serious concern.

» GDP: US$219 billion

» Revenue from tourism in 2010: US$12.5 billion

» Inflation: 9.1%

» Main exports: Petroleum, petroleum products, cotton

» Unemployment: 9%

» Average annual income: US$4200

After Mubarak

Against the backdrop of America's 'War on Terror' and in the aftermath of the 'Arab Spring', Egypt has weathered a storm of internal strife, and struggled to define its identity as a moderate Islamic country. On one hand, protesters in Midan Tahrir managed to overthrow Mubarak and

Top Songs

» Alf Layla wa Layla, Om Kalthoum's masterpiece, almost an hour of unbridled passion

» Nour al Ain, Amr Diab's triple-Platinum selling album

» Leave, Ramy Essam's 2011 protest song that became the tune of the revolution

Top Reads

» Naguib Mahfouz, *The Cairo Trilogy* – by the Nobel prizewinner

» Alaa Al Aswany, *The Yacoubian Building* – best-selling exposé of contemporary Egyptian society

» Mansoura Ez-Eldin, *Maryam's Maze* – one of the brightest new talents to come out of Egypt

Top Websites

» Arabist (www.arabist.net) Independent website about Arab politics and culture

» Egyptology News (http://egyptology.blogspot.com) The latest news in Egyptology

» Daily News (www.dailystaregypt.com) Independent newspaper

his ruling National Democratic Party without too much bloodshed. On the other hand, the Muslim Brotherhood and the more extreme Salafi groups scored very high in the assembly elections.

Whatever might come in the following years, it is hard to overstate the significance of the fall of Mubarak. But however longed for, Mubarak's demise has raised serious questions about the future political and economic stability of Egypt. Whoever eventually holds the reins of power will have to address some very real issues, including sectarian conflict, the Israeli–Palestinian deadlock and the worsening economic outlook. All are to some degree interconnected and none of them can be resolved in the short term.

The role of the armed forces, one of the taboo subjects under Mubarak, has become one of the main bones of contention in post-revolution Egypt. The riots and return to Tahrir that occurred in late 2011 were in part due to outrage at the continuing presence and growing power of the Supreme Council of the Armed Forces (SCAF).

Messages from Tahrir, by Karima Khalil, is a wonderful and moving collection of images taken in the square during the anti-Mubarak protests, many of them wry or poignant, most of them extremely witty.

Eternally Egypt

One thing that can be said with certainty is this: the Egypt that emerges from this tumultuous time will be as fascinating as ever. The monuments that tell the story of the country's glorious past remain as does the special talent that has always singled out the Egyptians: their ability to laugh. Whether in the suffocating density of Cairo's city streets or the harsh elements of the open desert, they remain an incredibly resilient people who find humour and optimism in the most unlikely of circumstances. While your travels in Egypt won't always be easygoing, nor hassle-free, they'll certainly be eye-opening, to say the least.

Water

» Tap water should generally be avoided, though it's not deadly in Cairo

» There isn't enough in the tap so use it sparingly

» Only swim in fast-flowing water in the Nile

Food

» If eating with your hands, only use your right

» Egyptians regard hospitality as a pleasure and a duty, but it isn't always one they can afford

» During Ramadan, the fasting population will appreciate you eating discreetly

Things to avoid

» Don't touch walls of tombs or temples. Ancient paint and plaster is in danger of disappearing

» Showing the soles of your feet is considered very disrespectful

» Avoid touching members of the opposite sex in public

History

The history of Egypt is as rich as the land, as varied as the landscape and as long as the Nile, longer than most in the world. As recent events have shown, it can also be as lively as the character of its people. While much of Europe was still wrapped in animal skins and wielding clubs, ancient Egyptians enjoyed a sophisticated life, dedicated to maintaining order in the universe and to making the most of their one great commodity, the Nile.

The Nile

The Nation's Gift

The Greek historian Herodotus observed that Egypt was the gift of the Nile and although it might now be a cliché, it also happens to be true. The ancient Egyptians called it simply *iteru,* the river. Without the Nile, Egypt as we know it would not exist.

The exact history is obscure, but many thousands of years ago the climate of North Africa changed dramatically. Patterns of rainfall also changed and Egypt, formerly a rich savannah, became increasingly dry. The social consequences were dramatic. People in this part of Africa lived as nomads, hunting, gathering and moving across the region with the seasons. But when their pastures turned to desert, there was only one place for them to go: the Nile.

Rainfall in east and central Africa ensured that the Nile in Egypt rose each summer; this happened some time towards the end of June in Aswan. The waters would reach their height around the Cairo area in September. In most years, this surge of water flooded the valley and left the countryside hidden. As the rains eased, the river level started to drop and water drained off the land, leaving behind a layer of rich silt washed down from the hills of Africa.

The Penguin Guide to Ancient Egypt by William J Murnane is one of the best overall books on the lifestyle and monuments of the Pharaonic period, with illustrations and descriptions of major temples and tombs.

TIMELINE	c 250,000 BC	c. 13,000 BC	c 3100 BC
	Earliest human traces in Egypt. The valley savannah provides ample food for hunter-gatherers until climate change turns lush countryside to desert and forces settlement along the fertile Nile.	The rock carvings at Qurta, near Kom Ombo, the oldest rock art in North Africa, had already been created.	Legend credits a pharaoh named Narmer with uniting the people between the Mediterranean and the First Cataract at Aswan. Memphis becomes capital of a united Upper Egypt and Lower Egypt.

Ramses: The
Son of Light by
Christian Jacq is
the first of a five-
volume popular
hagiography
of the famous
pharaoh. The
prose is simplis-
tic, but Jacq is
an Egyptologist,
so the basics are
accurate.

Egyptians learned that if they planted seed on this fertile land, they could grow a good crop. As more people settled along the valley, it became more important to make the best use of the annual floodwater, or there would not be enough food for the following year. A social order evolved to organise the workforce to make the most of this 'gift', an order that had farmers at the bottom, bureaucrats and governors in the middle and, at the top of this pyramid, the pharaoh.

Egyptian legend credited all this social development to the good king Osiris, who, so the story went, taught Egyptians how to farm, how to make the best use of the Nile and how to live a good, civil life. The myth harks back to an idealised past, but also ties in with what we know of the emergence of kingship: one of the earliest attributions of kingship, the predynastic Scorpion Macehead, found in Hierakonpolis around 3000 BC, shows an irrigation ritual. This suggests that even right back in early times, making use of the river's gift was a key part of the role of the leader.

Source Stories

The rise of the Nile was a matter of continual wonder for ancient Egyptians, as it was right up to the 19th century, when European explorers settled the question of the source. There is no evidence that ancient Egyptians knew where this lifeline came from. In the absence of facts, they made up stories.

One of the least convincing of all Egyptian myths concerning the rise of the Nile places the river's source in Aswan, beneath the First Cataract. From here, they believed, the river flowed north to the Mediterranean and south into Africa.

The Complete
Pyramids: Solving
the Ancient
Mysteries by
Mark Lehner and
Richard H Wilkin-
son is a readable
reference to the
famous three-
some of Giza and
the other 70-plus
triangular-sided
funerary monu-
ments besides.

The river's life-giving force was revered as a god, Hapy. He was an unusual deity in that, contrary to the slim outline of most gods, Hapy was most often portrayed as a pot-bellied man with hanging breasts and a headdress of papyrus. Hapy was celebrated at a feast each year when the Nile rose. In later images, he was often shown tying papyrus and lotus plants together, a reminder that the Nile bound people together.

But the most enduring and endearing of all Egyptian myths concerning the river is devoted to the figure of Isis, the mourning wife. Wherever the river originated, the annual rising of the Nile was explained as being tears shed by the mother goddess at the loss of the good king Osiris.

Matters of Fact

Wherever it came from, the Nile was the beginning and end for most Egyptians. They were born beside it and had their first postnatal bath in its waters. It sustained them throughout their lives, made possible the vegetables in the fields, the chickens, cows, ducks and fish on their plates,

2650–2323 BC	2125–1650 BC	1650–1550 BC	1550–1186 BC
This period of great pyramid building at Giza and Saqqara suggests that for at least part of each year, presumably when the Nile flooded, a substantial workforce was available for civic projects.	Thebes emerges as capital of Upper Egypt and as the pre-eminent seat of religious power. When the Theban ruler Montuhotep II establishes the Middle Kingdom, Thebes becomes its capital.	The Hyksos – western Asian tribes who settled in northern Egypt – control the valley, ushering in the Second Intermediate Period, a time of great technological and social innovation.	Ahmose, prince of Thebes, defeats the Hyksos c 1532 BC and begins a period of expansion into Nubia and Palestine. Over the next two centuries, his successors expand the empire.

and filled their drinking vessels when they were thirsty. When it was very hot or at the end of a day's work, it was the Nile that provided relief, a place to bathe. Later, when they died, if they had the funds, their body would be taken along the river to the cult centre at Abydos. And it was water from the Nile that the embalmers used when they prepared the body for burial. But burial was a moment of total separation from this life source for, if you were lucky, you were buried away from the damp, where the dry sands and rocks of the desert would preserve your remains throughout eternity.

Not everything about the river was generous – it also brought dangers in many forms: the crocodile, the sudden flood that washed away help-less children and brought the house down on your head, the diseases that thrived in water, and the creatures (among them the mosquito) that carried them. The river also brought the taxman, for it was on the level of flood that the level of tax was set. The formula was simple. Bureaucrats watched the rise of the river on Elephantine Island, where a gauge had been cut along the side of the rock. Each year's flood was recorded at its height. If the water rose to the level of 14 cubits, there would be enough food to go around. If it rose to 16, there would be an abundance – and abundance meant good taxation. And if there were, say, only eight cubits, then it was time to prepare for the worst because famine would come and many would follow Osiris to the land of spirits beyond the valley.

The river also dictated the rhythm of life and everything started with the beginning of the inundation: New Year fell as the waters rose. This was a time of celebration and also, for some, of relaxation. As the land was covered with water and a boat was needed to travel from one village to the next, farmers found time to catch up on long-neglected chores, fixing tools and working on their houses. This was also the period of the corvée, the labour system by which it is thought many civic projects were built, among them the pyramids, the canal cut through from the Nile to the Red Sea and, in the 19th century, the Suez Canal.

The Rise and Fall of Ancient Egypt by Toby Wilkinson gives an authoritative overview of ancient Egypt.

Old Habits

Even when the old gods were long dead, and roads and railways ran alongside the river, the Nile exerted its magic and its power. In the 18th and 19th centuries it was the way in which foreigners uncovered the mysteries of the past, sailing upriver when the winds blew from the north, and finding themselves face to face with unimaginable splendour. Even then, Egyptians clung to their habits and their dependence on the river. In the 1830s, the British Orientalist Edward Lane recorded that 17 June was still called the Night of the Drop. 'It is believed,' he wrote, 'that a miraculous drop then falls into the Nile; and causes it to rise.' Lane also recorded the custom of creating a figure of a girl, the 'Bride of the Nile',

1352– 1336 BC	1294– 1279 BC	1279– 1213 BC	1184– 1153 BC
Akhenaten establishes monotheism at his new capital, Akhetaten. But by the death of his heir, Tutankhamun, in 1327 BC, Thebes is again the capital and power is restored to the priests of Amun.	Seti I restores the empire and initiates a period of neoconservatism: his temple at Abydos copies Old Kingdom styles. He then constructs the finest tomb in the Valley of the Kings.	Seti's son, Ramses II, constructs more buildings than any other pharaoh. He makes Avaris, his home town, the centre of Egyptian trade, but adds to the glory of Thebes.	Ramses III provides a stable moment in an unstable century, controlling the Libyans, defeating the 'Sea People' and suppressing internal dissent. After his death, power slips from the throne.

ST ANTHONY: CREATOR OF MONASTICISM

St Anthony was the son of wealthy landowners, but found himself orphaned at an early age. As an adult, he sold his inheritance, gave the proceeds to the poor and retreated to the desert near St Paul. Other Christians soon followed, inspired by his example and perhaps also to escape persecution. The hermit moved further up into the hills, hiding alone in a cave, while leaving his followers to a life of collective retreat – the first monastery – in the valley below.

There may have been earlier religious communities in the desert, especially one in Palestine, but St Anthony is credited with creating this new way of living, one that sought salvation through retreat. It was left to St Pachomius, born around AD 285, to order the life of these hermits into what we would now recognise as monasteries, which has proved to be one of the most important movements in Christianity.

out of mud, which was then washed away as the river rose, an echo of an ancient ceremony in which effigies – and perhaps also young women – were sacrificed to the rising river.

Some 100 years later, in 1934, the Egyptologist Margaret Murray spent a mid-September night in a Coptic village, celebrating the night of the high Nile, giving thanks 'to the Ruler of the river, no longer Osiris, but Christ; and as of old they pray for a blessing upon their children and their homes'.

This kind of spiritual bond with the river was broken when dams and barrages stopped the annual flood. But Egyptians, whether they live along the river or in one of the new satellite cities in the desert, remain as dependent on the Nile as ever. Now, instead of praying to the 'Ruler of the river', they put their faith in engineers, who, like kings of old, help them make the most of the water; and in politicians, who are currently renegotiating water-sharing agreements with Nile-basin neighbours. Wherever they pin their hopes, they know that, as ever, their happiness, their very existence, depends on water flowing past Aswan on its way to the Mediterranean.

Christian Egypt

In the beginning...

Coptic tradition states that Christianity arrived in Egypt in AD 45 in the form of St Mark. According to this tradition, St Mark, originally from Cyrene in modern-day Libya, was in Alexandria when his sandal broke. He took it to a cobbler, Ananias, who hurt his hand while working on the sandal and shouted 'O One God', at which St Mark recognised his

1070 BC	945–715 BC	663 BC	610–595 BC
By the time of his death, Ramses XI has lost control of much of southern Egypt, the palace and many Theban tombs have been robbed, and central authority has disappeared. The New Kingdom grown old.	Libyan settlers become increasingly powerful in the Delta, eventually taking power as the 22nd and 23rd dynasties, but the Egyptian Nile is divided among a series of princes.	Ashurbanipal, King of the Assyrians, attacks Egypt, sacks Thebes and loots the Temple of Amun. Devastated Egypt is ruled by Libyan princes from Sais in the Delta.	Late Period pharaoh Necho encourages foreign trade by strengthening ties (and his navy) in the Mediterranean, cutting a canal to the Red Sea and sending an expedition to sail around Africa.

first convert to the new religion. While there is no way to prove the story, there is no denying the basic truth that Christianity arrived early in Egypt, direct from Palestine.

The country had long been open to foreign religious influences and nowhere more so than Alexandria. At the height of their power, ancient Egyptians had exported their religions – Amun of Thebes was known and feared throughout the Mediterranean. And even in times of weakness, the cult of the goddess Isis spread throughout the Roman Empire. But Egyptians were also open to foreign religious ideas. The Persians did little to impose their gods on the country when they sacked Thebes in the 6th century BC and made Egypt part of their empire. Two centuries later, Alexander the Great viewed things differently, at least in the north of the country: while he built shrines to Amun at Karnak and was happy to be welcomed as pharaoh by the priests at Memphis, he also encouraged Greeks and Jews to bring their gods to his new city. Alexandria, under the Macedonian's successors, the Ptolemies, became a centre for multiculturalism, where people of many different beliefs and religions lived and worshipped side by side.

The best source for accurate plans of the Theban tombs can be found in Nicholas Reeves and Richard H Wilkinson's *The Complete Valley of the Kings*, supplemented by Alberto Siliotti's *Guide to the Valley of the Kings*.

HISTORY CHRISTIAN EGYPT

The Early Church

Egypt's Coptic Christians absorbed much from both the form and the content of the ancient pagan religion. It is impossible to make direct parallels, but the rise of the cult of Mary appears to have been influenced by the popularity of Isis: both were said to have conceived through divine intervention. According to the late Coptic musicologist Dr Ragheb Moftah, the way in which the Coptic liturgy was performed seems to have evolved from ancient rites and in it, even today, we can hear an echo of ancient Egypt's rituals. Even the physical structure of Coptic churches echoes the layout of earlier pagan temples in the use of three different sacred spaces, the innermost one containing the altar reserved for priests. This is hidden from the rest of the congregation by the iconostasis, with its images of saints, just as ancient priests were hidden behind walls decorated with gods and pharaohs.

The early need to hold hidden prayer, the desire to follow Jesus' example of retreat from the world, the increasing difficulty of reconciling spiritual values with the demands and temptations of urban life, and perhaps also the memory of pagan hermits, led some Christians to leave the Nile Valley and seek spiritual purity in the desert. The man credited with being the first is St Paul, born in Alexandria in AD228. He fled to the Eastern Desert to escape the persecutions around AD250. The desert life obviously suited him for he is said to have survived there for over a century, dying around AD343. Although there are 5th-century accounts

Coptic Egypt by Christian Cannuyer tells the story from the earliest preachings by Mark the Evangelist in 1st-century AD Alexandria to 21st-century Christianity in Egypt.

525 BC	521–486BC	c 450BC	331 BC
The Persian king Cambyses makes Egypt part of his empire and rules as pharaoh, launching an attack against Nubia and then on Siwa, in which his army disappears into the desert.	Persian king Darius I appeases Egyptians by building temples and promoting trade, completing Necho's canal to the Red Sea.	The Greek historian Herodotus visited Egypt and called it 'the gift of the Nile'.	Alexander invades Egypt and visits the capital, Memphis, and the oracle at Siwa. He lays out a city, Alexandria, that will become the pivot of Hellenic culture in the Mediterranean.

of the man, there is still some controversy as to whether St Paul existed. There is no such problem with the man he is said to have inspired.

Egypt's Christians played a decisive role in the evolution of the young religion. In a series of meetings with Christians from across the empire, Copts argued over the nature of divinity, the duties of a Christian, the correct way to pray and many other aspects of religious life. In one matter in particular, Copts found themselves isolated. Many Christians argued that, as Jesus was born, there must have been a time when he was not divine and part of God. The Coptic clergy, particularly one Athanasius, argued that this idea of a dual nature was a throwback to polytheism. The crunch came in 325 at a council in Nicea, organised by the emperor, at which the Alexandrians triumphed: the Nicene Creed stated unequivocally that Father and Son are one. With this success, Alexandria confirmed its status as the centre of Mediterranean culture.

The site of Luxor Temple has been a place of worship for the last 3500 years and remains one today: the Mosque of Abu al-Haggag is situated high above the great court.

Death of the Old Gods

In 391 AD, Emperor Theodosius issued an edict that banned people from visiting pagan temples, but also even looking at pagan statues. While the edict was ignored in some places, it was taken seriously in Alexandria, where the Temple of Serapis still stood in the city centre. The golden statue of the god remained in his sanctuary, adored by the faithful, until the Christian patriarch of Alexandria stirred a crowd and led them in an attack on the temple: the god was toppled from his plinth – proving false the prophets who foresaw doom should he be damaged – and then dragged through the streets and burned. The crowd is also believed to have set fire to the temple library, which had contained one of the largest collections of scrolls in the world since the Alexandrian 'mother library'

MARTYRS AND HEROES

Alexandria's history is scarred by fights between devotees of different religions, as St Mark discovered to his cost: the man who brought Christianity to Egypt was executed for speaking out against the worship of the city's pagan god Serapis. Many decrees came from Rome that litigated against Christians, the worst coming from Emperor Diocletian. The persecution was so extreme and cost so many lives (some Coptic historians have estimated 144,000) that the Coptic Church calendar, the Era of Martyrs, begins with the year of Diocletian's accession, AD 284. But change was not far away.

In AD 293, Diocletian found himself sharing power with Constantine. In 312, just as Constantine went into battle against his opponents, he had a vision of a cross blazing in the sky, on which was written, *In This Conquer*. When he emerged victorious, becoming ruler of the empire, Constantine converted to Christianity and, in 324, made Christianity the imperial religion.

323 BC	c 310–250 BC	246–221 BC	170–116 BC
On Alexander's death in Babylon, his general Ptolemy is given control of Egypt. Alexander's body is buried in Alexandria, where Ptolemy builds the Museion and Library and perhaps also the Pharos.	Under Ptolemaic patronage and with access to a library of 700,000 written works, scholars in Alexandria calculate the earth's circumference, discover it circles the sun and compile the definitive edition of Homer's poems.	Ptolemy III Euergetes I begins a building program that includes the Serapeum in Alexandria and the Temple of Horus at Edfu. His successor continues his work.	Ptolemy VIII Euergetes II's reign is characterised by violence and brutality, but also by the opening of the Edfu Temple and by building at Philae and Kom Ombo.

had been burned during an attack by Julius Caesar. The patriarch then built a church over the ruins.

Constantine had moved his capital to the city of Byzantium, renamed Constantinople (now Istanbul), in 330 and from that moment power seeped from Alexandria. More than a century later, in 451, the Egyptians were officially sidelined at the Council of Chalcedon. Refusing to accept that Jesus had one person but two natures, which again seemed a revival of polytheism, the Egyptians split with the rest of Christianity, their patriarch was excommunicated and soon after Alexandria was sacked.

Yet in spite of the religious split, Egypt was still part of the Byzantine Empire, ruled by a foreign governor, and its fortunes were tied to the empire. This caused ever-greater tension, which peaked in the reign of Emperor Justinian (528–565). Alexandrians stoned the emperor's governor, who retaliated by sending his army to punish the people. In 629, a messenger travelled to the emperor in Byzantium from Arabia. He had been sent by a man named Mohammed to reveal a new religion, Islam. The messenger was murdered on the way. Ten years later, Arab armies invaded Egypt.

After Byzantium

Under their brilliant general Amr ibn al-As, the Arabs swept through a badly defended and ill-prepared Egypt, defeated the Byzantine army near Babylon (see p72) and found the gates of Alexandria opened to them without a fight.

Amr didn't force Egyptians to convert to the new religion, but did levy a tax on nonbelievers and showed preference to those who did convert. Slowly, inevitably, the population turned, although how fast is open to dispute. Eventually, however, some monasteries emptied and Coptic writing and language, the last version of the language of the pharaohs, stopped being spoken in public. Christian communities remained strongest in the new capital, Cairo, and in the valley south as far as the ancient capital, Thebes (Luxor). Increasingly Christians also fell back on the monasteries. In places such as Wadi Natrun and studded along the Nile Valley, monastic communities hid behind their high walls, preserving the old language, the old traditions and, in their libraries, some of the old wisdom.

By the middle of the 19th century, even the monasteries were under threat and European travellers sailing up the Nile were shocked to discover monks swimming naked up to their boats to beg for food and money. The decline continued until the 20th century. By then, only around 10% of Egyptians were Christians and the great monasteries were at their lowest ebb. Ironically Christianity has responded to threats by enjoying something of a revival. Modernising influences in the early 20th cen-

Ancient Egypt: The Great Discoveries by Nicholas Reeves is a chronology of 200 years of marvellous finds, from the Rosetta Stone (1799) to the Valley of the Golden Mummies (1999).

48BC	30 BC	AD 45
The fire that Julius Caesar lit to destroy the fleet in Alexandria harbour spreads through the city and burns down the Great Library.	After Antony and Cleopatra are defeated at Actium, Ptolemaic rule ends and Roman rule starts, with Egypt initially the personal property of the Octarian (the future emperor Augustus Caesar).	According to Coptic tradition, St Mark arrive in Alexandria this year and convert an Alexandria cobbler. Christianity is certainly established in Egypt by the end of the century.

» Coptic cathedral interior

tury sparked a cultural renewal that breathed new life into, among other things, the long-defunct tradition of icon painting. Islamist violence aimed at Copts in the 1980s and 1990s had the effect of significantly increasing the number of monks. At St Anthony's Monastery numbers rose from 24 in 1960 to 69 in 1986, and in St Bishoi from 12 to 115. But the majority of Christians in Egypt still live in towns and cities along the Nile, still coping with continual threat from Muslim extremists, still cut off from the rest of the world's Christians and still, as ever, proud of their claim to be the true heirs of ancient Egypt.

The sixth Fatimid caliph, El Hakim, was notorious for his unusual behaviour: convinced that a woman's place was in the home, he banned the manufacture of women's shoes.

The Coming Of The Arabs

Around 628 AD a man called Mohammed, the leader of a newly united Arab force, wrote to some of the most powerful men in the world, including the Byzantine Emperor Heraclius, inviting them to convert to Islam. The emperor, who had never heard of this religion and who regarded the people of Arabia as a mild irritant on the edge of his empire, declined. By the time of Heraclius's death in 641, Arab armies had conquered much of the Byzantine Empire, including Syria and most of Egypt, and were camped outside the walls of the Egyptian capital, Alexandria.

The Victorious

Egyptians were used to foreign invaders but had never before experienced any like the Arabs, who came with religious as well as political intentions. After Alexandria fell, the Arab general Amr wrote to his leader, the Caliph Omar, to say that he had captured a city of 4000 palaces, 4000 baths, 400 theatres and 12,000 sellers of green vegetables. Omar, perhaps sensing danger in such sophistication, ordered his army to create a new Muslim capital. The site chosen was beside the Roman fort of Babylon, at the place where the Nile fanned out into the delta. Initially a tented camp known as al-Fustat, Arabic for 'the tents', it soon grew into one of the region's key cities, until it was eclipsed by newer neighbouring settlements – the 8th-century Abbassid city al-Askar, the 9th-century Tulunid city al-Katai and, finally, the 10th-century Fatimid city al-Qahira, Arabic for 'victorious' and the origin of the word Cairo.

Many of the tales recounted each night by Sheherazade in The Thousand and One Nights are set in Mamluk-era Egypt, particularly in Cairo, referred to as 'Mother of the World'.

Arabs and Egyptians

The majority of Egyptians were Christian at the time of the Arab conquest, none of whom Amr forcibly converted. The new religion was prepared to cohabit with the older ones. In order to uphold their beliefs, Copts and other non-Muslims were obliged to pay a tax, but this was initially less than they had had to pay to the Byzantine emperor. Yet there was a gradual move towards conversion and by the 10th century, the majority of people in Egypt were Muslims.

130-131	c 271	391	451
The Roman Emperor Hadrian spends eight to 10 months touring in Egypt, a journey that turns sour when his favourite, Antinoos, drowns in the Nile. The youth is deified and a temple is dedicated to him at Antinoopolis.	St Anthony begins his retreat from the world, living in a cave in the Eastern Desert. He soon attracts others, whom he organises into a loose community, Christianity's first monks.	Fifty years after the Byzantine emperor Constantine spoke against the religion of the pharaohs, his successor Theodosius makes paganism a treasonable offence and Alexandria's Temple of Serapis burns.	At the Council of Chalcedon, Egyptian Christians refuse to accept that Jesus Christ had two natures, human and divine, and the Coptic Church separates from the rest of Christianity.

Sunni or Shia?

The shift of Egypt's capitals reflected the instability in the Arab empire as the capital moved from Mecca to Damascus and then Baghdad. This also reflects the shifting nature of the caliphate, the leadership of Islam, divided between the Sunni and the Shiite factions. The earlier Arab dynasties were Sunni. The Fatimids, who conquered Egypt in the 10th century and created the city of al-Qahira, were Shiite. At the centre of their new city was a mosque, Al-Azhar, which became the country's main authority on religious matters. But Saladin (Salah ad-Din), who took power in Egypt in 1171 and created the Ayyubid dynasty, was a Sunni. From then on, and ever since, the sheikhs of Al-Azhar have taught Sunni orthodoxy. The majority of Egyptians today are Sunni.

The Mamluks

One of the last rulers of Saladin's Ayyubid dynasty, a man named Sultan as-Salih, brought the innovation of a permanent Turkic slave-soldier class. Most sultans relied on friends and relatives to provide a measure of security. As-Salih was so despised by all that he thought it wise to provide his own protection and did so by purchasing a large number of slaves from the land between the Urals and the Caspian. These men were freed on arrival in Egypt – their name, Mamluks, means 'owned' or 'slave' – and formed into a warrior class, which came to rule Egypt.

Mamluks owed their allegiance not to a blood line but to their original owner, the emir. New purchases maintained the groups. There was no system of hereditary lineage; instead it was rule by the strongest. Rare was the sultan who died of old age. Natural-born soldiers, Mamluks fought a series of successful campaigns that gave Egypt control of all of Palestine and Syria, the Hejaz and much of North Africa, the largest Islamic empire of the late Middle Ages. Because they were forbidden to bequeath their wealth, Mamluks built on a grand scale, endowing Cairo with the most exquisite mosques, schools and tombs. During their 267-year reign (1250–1517), the city was the intellectual and cultural centre of the Islamic world.

The contradictions in the Mamluk constitution are typified in the figure of Sultan Qaitbey, who was bought as a slave-boy by one sultan and witnessed the brief reigns of nine more before clawing his way to power. As sultan he rapaciously taxed all his subjects and dealt out vicious punishments with his own hands, once tearing out the eyes and tongue of a court chemist who had failed to transform lead into gold. Yet Qaitbey marked his ruthless sultanship with some of Cairo's most beautiful monuments, notably his mosque, which stands in the Northern Cemetery (p88).

Zayni Barakat by Gamal al-Ghitani is full of intrigue, backstabbing and general Machiavellian goings-on in the twilight of Mamluk-era Cairo.

Favoured punishments employed by the Mamluks included *al-tawsit*, in which the victim was cut in half at the belly, and *al-khazuq* (impaling).

640	832	868	969
An Arab army under Amr ibn al-As sweeps through Egypt and establishes a base at the Roman fort of Babylon (now part of Cairo). The following year, Amr captures the Byzantine capital, Alexandria.	The caliph Al-Mamun, son of Haroun ar-Rashid, arrives to suppress a Coptic uprising. He also forces a way into the Pyramid of Cheops, although no treasure is recorded as being found.	Ahmed ibn Tulun, the son of a Turkish Mamluk, took control of Egypt, creating a new dynasty (Tulunid) and a new capital, al-Qatai, in Cairo of which only his mosque survives.	The Shiite general Jawhar lays the foundations for a new palace-city, Al-Qahira (Cairo), and founds a new university-mosque, Al-Azhar. Two years later the Fatimid caliph, Al-Muizz, settles here from Tunis.

The funding for the Mamluks' great buildings came from trade. A canal existed that connected the Red Sea with the Nile at Cairo, and thus the Mediterranean, forming a vital link in the busy commercial route between Europe and India and east Asia. In the 14th and 15th centuries, the Mamluks worked with the Venetians to control east–west trade and both grew fabulously rich from it.

The end of these fabled days came about for two reasons at the beginning of the 16th century: Vasco da Gama's discovery of the sea route around the Cape of Good Hope freed European merchants from the heavy taxes charged by Cairo; and the Ottoman Turks emerged as a mighty new force, looking to unify the Muslim world. In 1516 the Mamluks, under the command of their penultimate sultan Al-Ghouri, were obliged to meet the Turkish threat. The battle, which took place at Aleppo in Syria, resulted in complete defeat for the Mamluks. In January of the following year the Turkish sultan Selim I entered Cairo and although the Mamluks remained in power in Egypt, they never again enjoyed their former prominence or autonomy.

> The Great Pyramid of Khufu (built in 2570 BC) remained the tallest artificial structure in the world until the building of the Eiffel Tower in 1889.

Modern Times

Napoleon & Description de l'Egypte

When Napoleon and his musket-armed forces blew apart the scimitar-wielding Mamluk cavalry at the Battle of the Pyramids in 1798, which he claimed he was doing with the approval of the Ottoman sultan, he dragged Egypt into the age of geopolitics. Napoleon professed a desire to revive Egypt's glory, free it from the yoke of tyranny and educate its masses, but there was also the significant matter of striking a blow at Britain. Napoleon found a way to strike at British interests by capturing Egypt and in the process taking control of the quickest route between Europe and Britain's fast-growing empire in the East.

> At the Battle of the Pyramids, Napoleon's forces took just 45 minutes to rout the Mamluk army, killing 1000 for the loss of 29 of their own men.

Napoleon's forces weren't always successful. In 1798, a British fleet under Admiral Nelson had been criss-crossing the Mediterranean trying to find the French force and, on 1 August, they found them at anchor in Aboukir Bay, off the coast of Alexandria. Only three French warships survived the ensuing Battle of the Nile. Encouraged by the British, the Ottoman sultan sent an army that was trounced by the French, which put paid to any pretence that the French were in Egypt with the complicity of Constantinople. Despite these setbacks, the French still maintained rule.

During Napoleon's time in the newly conquered Egypt, he established a French-style government, revamped the tax system, brought in Africa's first printing press, implemented public-works projects and introduced new crops and a new system of weights and measures. He also brought 167 scholars and artists, whom he commissioned to make a complete

996	1171	1249	1250
Fatimid caliph al-Hakim ushers in one of the least tolerant of all regimes, forbidding women to leave their houses, discriminating against Christians and Jews, banning the sale of grapes and having all dogs in Cairo killed.	Saladin, a Kurdish Sunni, seizes power and establishes the Ayyubid dynasty. In 1176 he begins work on a citadel in Cairo, home to the city's rulers for the next seven centuries.	The start of the Fifth Crusade, directed against Egypt and led by Louis IX. The following year, the French king was taken captive by the Egyptians and ransomed for a huge sum.	On the death of her husband, Sultan al-Salih Ayyub, his wife Shagar ad-Durr becomes sultana. She has her second husband killed in the bath, only to be killed herself a few days later.

study of Egypt's monuments, crafts, arts, flora and fauna, and of its society and people. The resulting work was published as the 24-volume *Description de l'Egypte,* which did much to stimulate the study of Egyptian antiquities.

However, relations between the occupied and occupier deteriorated rapidly and there were regular uprisings against the French in Cairo. When the British landed an army, also at Aboukir, in 1801, the French agreed to an armistice and departed.

The Albanian Kings

The French and then British departure left Egypt politically unstable, a situation that was soon exploited by a lieutenant in an Albanian contingent of the Ottoman army, named Mohammed Ali. Within five years of the French evacuation, he had fought and conspired his way to become pasha (governor) of Egypt. Although he was nominally the vassal of Constantinople, like so many governors before him, he soon realised that the country could be his own.

The sultan in Constantinople was too weak to resist this challenge to his power. And once he had defeated a British force of 5000 men, the only threat to Mohammed Ali could come from the Mamluk beys (leaders). Any danger here was swiftly and viciously dealt with. On 1 March 1811, Mohammed Ali invited some 470 Mamluk beys to the Citadel to feast his son's imminent departure for Mecca. When the feasting was over the Mamluks mounted their lavishly decorated horses and were led in procession down the narrow, high-sided defile below what is now the Police Museum. As they approached the Bab al-Azab, the great gates were swung closed and gunfire rained down from above. After the fusil-

Famed as an American icon, the monument now known as the Statue of Liberty was originally intended to stand at the mouth of the Suez Canal.

As a young Egyptian officer during WWII, Anwar Sadat was imprisoned by the British for conspiring with German spies.

HISTORY MODERN TIMES

FOREIGN INVADERS

The story of ancient Egypt is the story of Egypt's relationships with its neighbours, for its wealth attracted some and its strategic location on the Mediterranean and Red Seas, and on the trade routes between Africa and Asia, attracted others. When it was strong, it controlled the gold of Nubia and the trade route across the Levant – not for nothing was the image of Ramses II crushing the Hittites at Kadesh splashed across so many temple walls. When it was weak, it caught the attention of the power of the moment. In 663 BC, the Assyrian leader Ashurbanipal sacked Thebes. A century later the Persians were in control of the Nile. In 331 BC, Alexander the Great moved against the Egyptians and incorporated them into his Hellenic empire. In 30 BC, Octavian, the future emperor Augustus Caesar, annexed the country as his own property. Arab armies stormed through in the 7th century AD just as Ottoman ones did in the 16th century and Egypt remained officially a part of the Ottoman Empire until 1919.

1250	**1260**	**1468**	**1517**
Mamluk slave warriors, most of Turkish or Kurdish origin, seize control of Egypt. Although their rule is often harsh and anarchic, they build some of Cairo's most impressive and beautiful monuments.	The mamluk Baybars becomes sultan. Having created a strong alliance at home, he moves against the last Crusaders in the Holy Land, capturing their Syrian stronghold of Krak des Chevaliers in 1271.	Mamluk sultan Qaitbey begins a 27-year reign that brings stability and wealth to the country. Qaitbey constructs a tomb complex in Cairo and a fort over the Pharos in Alexandria.	Turkish sultan Selim I takes Cairo, executes the last Mamluk sultan and makes Egypt a Turkish province. For almost 300 years, it will be ruled, however weakly, from Istanbul.

lades, Mohammed Ali's soldiers waded in with swords and axes to finish the job. Legend relates that only one Mamluk escaped alive, leaping over the wall on his horse.

Mohammed Ali's reign is pivotal in the history of Egypt. Having watched the old Mamluk army flounder against modern European weapons and tactics, he recognised the need to modernise his new army, as well as his new country. Under his uncompromising rule, Egypt abandoned its medieval-style feudalism and looked to Europe for innovation. In his long reign (he died in 1848), Mohammed Ali modernised the army, built a navy, built roads, cut a new canal linking Alexandria with the Nile, introduced public education, improved irrigation, built a barrage across the Nile and began planting Egypt's fields with the valuable cash crop, cotton. His heirs continued the work, implementing reforms and social projects, foremost of which were the building of Africa's first railway, opening factories and starting a telegraph and postal system. Egypt's fledgling cotton industry boomed as production in the USA was disrupted by civil war, and revenues were directed into ever-grander schemes. Grandest of all was the Suez Canal, which opened in 1869 to great fanfare and an audience that included European royalty, including Empress Eugenie of France.

Khedive Ismail had taken on more debt than even Egypt's booming economy could handle and European politicians and banks were quick to exploit his growing weakness. Six years after opening the canal, Ismail was forced to sell his controlling share to the British government and soon after that, bankruptcy and British pressure forced him to abdicate. This sort of foreign involvement in Egyptian affairs created great resentment, especially among a group of officers in the Egyptian army, who moved against the new khedive. In 1882, under the pretext of restoring order, the British fleet bombarded Alexandria, and British soldiers defeated a nationalist Egyptian army.

The opera *Aida* was originally commissioned for the opening ceremony of the Suez Canal, but Verdi was late delivering. *Rigoletto* was performed in 1869 and *Aida* first performed on Christmas Eve, 1871, two years after the opening.

PACKAGING TOURISM

In 1869, with the opening of the Suez Canal, the Khedive (Viceroy) Ismail announced that Egypt was now part of Europe, not Africa. Wherever it was, the massive amounts the khedive spent on developing and promoting his country boosted the number of people who wanted to see the treasures along the Nile. So at the same time as the British Prince and Princess of Wales were sailing the royal dahabiyya (houseboat), Thomas Cook took the first organised package tour up the Nile by steamer. It was the start of an industry that has since become one of Egypt's core businesses – mass tourism.

1768	1798	1805	1827
Scottish laird James Bruce arrives in Cairo on his way in search of the source of the Nile; later he returns to Britain having secured permission for European ships to sail up the Red Sea to Suez.	Napoleon invades, bringing a group of scholars, who produce the first full description of Egypt's antiquities. The British force the French but the French – and European – fascination with ancient Egypt, lives on.	An Albanian mercenary, Mohammed Ali, exploits the power vacuum left by the French to seize power and establish a new 'Egyptian' dynasty; his modernisation program transforms the country.	Muhammed Ali's reformed Egyptian fleet sails to support the Ottoman sultan in a struggle with Greece, but is destroyed by a combined British, French and Russian fleet at the Battle of Navarino.

The Veiled Protectorate

The British had no desire to make Egypt a colony: their main reason for involvement was to ensure the safety of the Suez Canal. So they allowed the heirs of Mohammed Ali to remain on the throne, while real power was concentrated in the hands of the British agent, Sir Evelyn Baring. By appointing British 'advisors' to Egyptian ministries and himself advising the khedive, Baring operated what became known as the veiled protectorate, colonisation by another name.

British desire to ensure the safety of their passage to India coloured Egyptian policy for the next few decades. For instance, it became increasingly obvious that controlling Egypt meant controlling the Nile and therefore an Egyptian force was sent to protect that interest in Sudan. When they came up against the Islamist uprising of the Mahdi, and following the death of General Charles Gordon in Khartoum in 1885, British troops became involved on the middle Nile.

The protectorate did much to achieve its ends. The canal was secure, Egypt's finances were bolstered, the bureaucracy and infrastructure improved, and there were some social advances. But it remained that Egypt and its resources were being used to further British foreign policy. This situation became even more frustrating for Egyptians with the outbreak of WWI. When Turkey, still officially sovereign of Egypt, sided with Germany and against Britain, the British felt the need to make Egypt an official protectorate.

The Egyptians' desire for self-determination was strengthened by the Allies' use of the country as a barracks during a war that most Egyptians regarded as having nothing to do with them. Popular national sentiments were articulated by riots in 1919 and, more eloquently, by the likes of Saad Zaghloul, the most brilliant of an emerging breed of young Egyptian politicians, who said of the British, 'I have no quarrel with them personally but I want to see an independent Egypt'. The British allowed the formation of a nationalist political party, called the Wafd (Delegation), and granted Egypt its sovereignty, but this was seen as an empty gesture. King Fuad enjoyed little popularity among his people and the British still kept a tight rein on the administration.

The British and their Allies came to Egypt in greater numbers following the outbreak of WWII. The war wasn't all bad news for the Egyptians – certainly not for shopkeepers and businessmen who saw thousands of Allied soldiers pouring into the towns and cities with money to burn on 48-hour leave from the desert. But there was a vocal element who saw the Germans as potential liberators. Students held rallies in support of Rommel, and a small cabal of Egyptian officers, including

Cairo: The City Victorious by Max Rodenbeck is the most authoritative and entertaining read on the convoluted and picturesque 1000-year history of the Egyptian capital.

Both Egypt and Israel were able to claim victory in the October 1973 war. The Egyptians boast of having broken the Israeli hold on Sinai while the Israelis were fighting their way towards Cairo when the UN imposed a ceasefire. This sense of victory helped make the Camp David peace talks possible.

1833	1856	1859	1869
Muhammaed Ali's new army moves through the Levant and crushes the Ottoman army at Konya. Constantinople is exposed, but the European powers force the Egyptians to withdraw.	Africa's first railway, between Tanta and Cairo, is built by British engineer Robert Stephenson. The line, extended to Suez in 1858, carries Europeans heading East until the opening of the Suez Canal.	Ferdinand de Lesseps, a French engineer, sees work begin on his project to build a canal between the Mediterranean and Red seas, making it the quickest way from Europe to the East. The canal takes 10 years to complete.	Khedive Ismail, Mohammed Ali's grandson, opens the Suez Canal. The British, who had preferred a railway, soon take control of the waterway as the quickest route to their Eastern empire.

future presidents Nasser and Sadat, plotted to aid the German general's advance on their city.

Rommel pushed the Allied forces back almost to Alexandria, which had the British hurriedly burning documents in such quantities that the skies over Cairo turned dark with the ash, but the Germans did not break through. Instead, the British maintained a military and political presence in Egypt until a day of flames almost seven years after the war.

Independent Egypt

Emerging from the Ashes

After years of demonstrations, strikes and riots against foreign rule, an Anglo-Egyptian showdown over a police station in the Suez Canal zone provided the spark that ignited the capital. Shops and businesses owned or frequented by foreigners were torched by mobs and many landmarks of 70 years of British rule were reduced to charred ruins within a day.

On 26 January 1952, a day that came to be known as Black Saturday, Cairo was set on fire.

While the smoke cleared, the sense of agitation remained, not just against the British but also against the monarchy that most Egyptians regarded as too easily influenced by the British. King Farouk assumed the monarchy would survive the turmoil because it could count on the support of the Egyptian army. But a faction within the officer corps, known as the Free Officers, had long been planning a coup. On 20 July 1952, the leader of the Free Officers, Colonel Gamal Abdel Nasser, heard that a new minister of war knew of the group and had planned their arrest. Two nights later, army units loyal to the Free Officers moved on key posts in the capital and by the following morning the monarchy had fallen. King Farouk, descendant of the Albanian Mohammed Ali, departed from Alexandria harbour on the royal yacht on 26 July 1952, leaving Egypt to be ruled by Egyptians for the first time since the pharaohs.

Colonel Nasser became president in elections held in 1956. With the aim of returning some of Egypt's wealth to its much-exploited peasantry, but also in an echo of the events of Russia in 1917, the country's landowners were dispossessed and many of their assets nationalised. Nasser also moved against the country's huge foreign community and, although he did not force them to emigrate, his new measures persuaded many to sell up and ship out.

In the year of his inauguration, Nasser successfully faced down Britain and France in a confrontation over the Suez Canal, which was mostly owned by British and French investors. On 26 July, the fourth anniversary of King Farouk's departure, Nasser announced that he had nationalised the Suez Canal to finance the building of a great dam that would

1879	1882	1902	1914
Having bankrupted the country, running up debts of more than £100m, Khedive Ismail is forced to abdicate but not before selling his shares in the Suez Canal to Britain.	British troops invade to suppress nationalist elements in the army. Although they officially restore power to the khedive, Britain effectively rules Egypt in what becomes the 'veiled protectorate'.	Inauguration of the Aswan Dam and the Asyut Barrage, which help control the Nile flood. The Egyptian Museum is also opened on what is now Cairo's Midan Tahrir.	When Turkey sides with Germany in the war, Britain moves to make Egypt an official British protectorate. A new ruler, Hussein Kamel, takes the title of Sultan of Egypt.

control the flooding of the Nile and boost Egyptian agriculture. A combined British, French and Israeli invasion force, intended to take possession of the canal, resulted in diplomatic embarrassment and undignified retreat after the UN and US applied pressure. Nasser emerged from the conflict a hero of the developing world, a sort of Robin Hood and Ramses rolled into one, and the man who had finally and publicly shaken off the colonial yoke.

Neighbours & Friends

Nasser's show of strength in 1956 led to many years of drum-beating and antagonism between Egypt and its Arab friends on one side, and their unwelcome neighbour Israel on the other. On June 1967 Israel launched a surprise attack and destroyed Egypt's air force before it even got into the air. With it went the confidence and credibility of Nasser and his nation.

Relations with Israel had been hostile ever since its founding in 1948. Egypt had sent soldiers to fight alongside Palestinians against the newly proclaimed Jewish state and ended up on the losing side. Although privately Nasser acknowledged that the Arabs would probably lose another war against Israel, for public consumption he gave rabble-rousing speeches about liberating Palestine. But he was a skilled orator and by early 1967 the mood engendered throughout the Arab world by these speeches was beginning to catch up with him. Soon other Arab leaders started to accuse him of cowardice and of hiding behind the UN troops stationed in Sinai since the Suez Crisis. Nasser responded by ordering the peacekeepers out and blockading the Straits of Tiran, effectively closing the southern Israeli port of Eilat. He gave Israel reassurances that he wasn't going to attack but meanwhile massed his forces east of Suez. Israel struck first.

When the shooting stopped six days later, Israel controlled all of the Sinai Peninsula and had closed the Suez Canal (which didn't reopen for another eight years). A humiliated Nasser offered to resign, but in a spontaneous outpouring of support, the Egyptian people wouldn't accept this move and he remained in office. However, it was to be for only another three years; abruptly in November 1970, the president died of a heart attack.

Anwar Sadat, another of the Free Officers and Egypt's next president, instigated a reversal of foreign policy. Nasser had looked to the Soviet Union for inspiration, but Sadat looked to the US, swapping socialist principles for capitalist opportunism. Having kept a low profile for a decade and a half, the wealthy resurfaced and were joined by a large, new, moneyed middle class who grew rich on the back of Sadat's much-

The Modern History of Egypt by PJ Vatiokis is the best one-volume history of the 19th and 20th centuries. Jason Thompson's A History of Egypt is the latest attempt to tell the whole 5000 year story.

1922

Britain grants Egypt independence, but reserves the right to defend Egypt, its interests in Sudan and, most importantly, the Suez Canal, where Britain continues to maintain a large military presence.

1922

Howard Carter discovers the tomb of Tutankhamun. The first great Egyptological discovery in the age of mass media, the tomb contains more than 3000 objects and takes 10 years to excavate.

1936

The Anglo-Egyptian treaty committed British troops to confining themselves to the Suez Canal and to leaving Egypt within 20 years.

DONALD C. & PRISCILLA EASTMAN/LONELY PLANET IMAGES©

» A shrine from the tomb

touted *al-infitah* (open-door policy). Sadat also believed that to revitalise Egypt's economy he would have to deal with Israel.

In November 1977, a time when Arab leaders still refused to talk publicly to Israel, Sadat travelled to Jerusalem to negotiate a peace treaty with Israel. The following year, he and the Israeli premier signed the Camp David Agreement, in which Israel agreed to withdraw from Sinai in return for Egyptian recognition of Israel's right to exist. There was shock in the Arab world, where Sadat's rejection of Nasser's pan-Arabist principles was seen as a betrayal. As a result, Egypt lost much prestige among the Arabs, who moved the HQ of the Arab League out of Cairo, and Sadat lost his life. On 6 October 1981, at a parade commemorating the 1973 war, one of his soldiers, a member of an Islamist group, broke from the marching ranks and sprayed the presidential stand with gunfire. Sadat was killed instantly.

Mubarak & the Rise of the Islamist Movement

Sadat was succeeded by Hosni Mubarak, a former air force chief of staff and vice president. Less flamboyant than Sadat and less charismatic than Nasser, Mubarak was regarded as unimaginative and indecisive, but managed to carry out a balancing act on several fronts, abroad and at home. To the irritation of more hard-line states such as Syria and Libya, Mubarak rehabilitated Egypt in the eyes of the Arab world without abandoning the treaty with Israel. At the same time, he managed to keep the lid on the Islamist extremists at home. In the early 1990s the lid blew off.

The trilogy of *The Mummy* (1999), *The Mummy Returns* (2001) and *The Scorpion King* (2002) was written by Stephen Sommers. The films feature fabulous art direction and far-fetched plots set in ancient and early 20th-century Egypt.

Theories abound regarding the rise of fundamentalist Islamist groups in Egypt. Some believe it had more to do with harsh socio-economic conditions, despite the use of religion by Islamist groups. More than 30 years after the revolution, government promises had failed to keep up with the population explosion and a generation of youths was living in squalid, overcrowded housing, without jobs and many feeling little or no hope for the future. With a political system that allowed little chance to voice legitimate opposition, many felt the only hope lay with Islamist parties such as the Muslim Brotherhood and their calls for change. Denied recognition by the state as a legal political entity, in the 1980s and 1990s the Islamists turned to force. There were frequent attempts on the life of the president and his ministers, and clashes with the security forces. The matter escalated from a domestic issue to a matter of international concern when Islamists began to target one of the state's most vulnerable and valuable sources of income: tourists.

Several groups of foreign tourists were shot at, bombed or otherwise assaulted throughout the 1990s, including the 1997 fire-bomb attack on a tour bus outside the Egyptian Museum in Cairo, followed a few weeks

1942	1952	1956	1967
The German Field Marshal Rommel pushes his tanks corps across the Libyan coast and into Egypt, causing panic in Cairo. His adversary, British General Montgomery pushes him back from El Alamein to Tunisia.	Anti-British sentiment leads to many foreign buildings in Cairo being burned. By the summer, Nasser and his fellow Free Officers have overthrown King Farouk and established the Republic of Egypt.	After President Nasser nationalises the Suez Canal, British, French and Israeli forces attack the canal zone, but are forced to retreat.	Egypt, Syria and Jordan are defeated by Israel in the Six Day War. Egypt loses control of the Sinai Peninsula and Nasser resigns, but is returned to power by popular demand.

later by the killing of holidaymakers at the Temple of Hatshepsut in Luxor by members of the Gama'a al-Islamiyya (Islamic Group), a Muslim Brotherhood splinter group.

The brutality of the massacre and its success at deterring foreign visitors destroyed grassroots support for militants, and the Muslim Brotherhood declared a ceasefire the following year. Things were relatively quiet until October 2004, when bombs at Taba, on the border with Israel, and the nearby Ras Shaytan camp, killed 34 and signalled the start of an unsettled 12 months.

First Elections

In 2005 President Mubarak bowed to growing international pressure to bring the country's political system in line with Western-style democracy, and proposed a constitutional amendment (subsequently approved by parliament and ratified at a national referendum) that aimed to introduce direct and competitive presidential elections. While some pundits saw this as a step in the right direction, others suspected it was a sham, particularly as popular opposition groups such as the Muslim Brotherhood were still banned and other independent candidates were required to have the backing of at least 65 members of the lower house of parliament. As the lower house was dominated by the National Democratic Party (NDP), the possibility of real change was slight. When the Kifaya! (Enough!) coalition of opposition groups protested at these restrictions, security forces cracked down. Ayman Nour, the leader of the popular Ghad (Tomorrow) party, was jailed on forgery charges. Local human rights organisations questioned the validity of the charges and expressed concern for Nour's safety, while the US released a statement declaring it was 'deeply troubled' by the conviction.

At this stage the banned Muslim Brotherhood began holding its own rallies and there were two isolated terrorist incidents in Cairo aimed at foreign tourists, both carried out by members of the same pro-Islamist family. Soon afterwards, three bombs at the popular beach resort of Sharm el-Sheikh claimed the lives of 88 people, most of them Egyptian. Various groups claimed responsibility, tourism took an immediate hit and Egyptians braced themselves for the possibility of further terrorist incursions and domestic unrest.

In 2005 Mubarak won the country's first multicandidate presidential election with 89% of the vote, after a turnout of just 23% of the 32 million registered voters. There were many reports from observers, such as the Egyptian Organization for Human Rights (EOHR), of disorganisation, intimidation and abusive security forces at the polls, and opposition parties and candidates (including Ayman Nour) alleged the vote was unfair

The past and present are described and ruminated over by the archaeologists leading the ongoing harbour explorations in Alexandria Rediscovered by Jean-Yves Empreur.

1970	1971	1973	1981
Fifty-two-year-old Gamal Abdel Nasser, Egyptian president since 1956, dies of a heart attack and is replaced by his fellow revolutionary, Anwar Sadat.	The Aswan High Dam is completed. Eleven years in the making, it extends Lake Nasser to some 510km and Egypt's farmland by 30%. Around 50,000 Nubians and many monuments are relocated.	In October, Egyptian forces attack and cross Israeli defences along the Suez Canal. Although the Egyptians are repulsed and Israel threatens Cairo, the war is seen as an Egyptian success.	President Sadat is assassinated, an event precipitated by his having signed the Camp David peace accord with Israel in 1978. He is replaced by Vice President Hosni Mubarak.

and the result invalid. Still, other observers noted the process was a great improvement on previous elections.

In subsequent parliamentary elections in November 2005, the Muslim Brotherhood independents won 88 seats in the 444-seat national parliament (six times the number they had previously held), making the Brotherhood a major player on the national political scene despite its officially illegal status.

Egypt Today

On 11 February 2011, President Mubarak resigned as president. The most obvious reason for his departure, 30 years into his presidency, was the hundreds of thousands of people who had been demonstrating for months, most notably in an 18-day occupation of Cairo's Midan Tahrir. Mubarak's loss of support among the Egyptian military and the US may have been equally significant.

The euphoria that followed Mubarak's departure was heightened by the fact that security forces had not fired on protestors. The army was seen as the protector of the revolution and people in Tahrir chanted 'the people, the army, one hand'. This made it possible for Mubarak's old generals, including his former minister for defence and head of armed forces, Field Marshal Tantawi, to take power in the form of a ruling council.

The Supreme Council of the Armed Forces (SCAF) presented itself as an honest broker to usher the country towards democracy, but before elections were held, ensured that the autonomy of the armed forces would be guaranteed, whoever wins the vote. The SCAF has ruled that future presidents or governments will not be able to select the head of the armed forces or intervene in the military's internal or economic affairs. The new government, dominated by the Muslim Brotherhood and Salafist parties, seem to have accepted that ruling.

The success of the Islamist government will rest on its ability to deal with the issue that brought so many people onto the streets: the continuing Egypt economic crisis. President Mubarak failed to do so. Egypt's future stability depends on the ability of the country's new rulers to meet the aspirations of an increasingly young population.

1988	1997	2011	2012
Naguib Mahfouz becomes the first Arab to win the Nobel Prize for Literature. His nomination is the cause of great national pride.	62 foreign tourists and Egyptians are gunned down at the Temple of Hatshepsut in Luxor, an event that sparks a security crackdown and a tourism crisis.	Mubarak resigns as president after mass protests against his regime throughout the country, most notably in Cairo's Midan Tahrir. He is replaced by a ruling council of his former generals.	The Muslim Brotherhood emerges from Egypt's first democratic parliamentary elections with 235 of the 508 seats. The biggest surprise is the 121 seats won by the extreme Islamist Salafi party, Nour.

Pharaonic Egypt

Dr Joann Fletcher
Dr Joann Fletcher of the University of York is an Egyptologist,
a writer and a consultant to museums and the media.

Despite its rather clichéd image, there is so much more to ancient Egypt than temples, tombs and Tutankhamun. As the world's first nation-state, predating the civilisations of Greece and Rome by several millennia, Egypt was responsible for some of the most important achievements in human history – it was where writing was invented, the first stone monuments were erected and an entire culture set in place, which remained largely unchanged for thousands of years.

All this was made possible by the Nile River, which brought life to this virtually rainless land. In contrast to the vast barren 'red land' of desert that the Egyptians called *deshret,* the narrow river banks were known as *kemet* (black land), named after the rich silt deposited by the river's annual floods. The abundant harvests grown in this rich earth were then gathered as taxes by a highly organised bureaucracy working on behalf of the king pharaoh. They redirected this wealth to run the administration and to fund ambitious building projects designed to enhance royal status. Although such structures have come to symbolise ancient Egypt, the survival of so many pyramids, temples and tombs have created a misleading impression of the Egyptians as a morbid bunch obsessed with religion and death, when in fact they simply loved life so much that they went to enormous lengths to ensure it continued for eternity.

The depth of this conviction suffused almost every aspect of the ancient Egyptians' lives and gave the culture its incredible coherence and conservatism. They believed they had their gods to take care of them, and each pharaoh was regarded as the gods' representative on earth, ruling by divine approval. Absolute monarchy was integral to Egyptian culture and the country's history was shaped around the lengths of each pharaoh's reign. Thirty royal dynasties ruled over a 3000-year period, now divided into the Old, Middle and New Kingdoms separated by intermittent periods of unrest (Intermediate periods) when the country split into north (Lower Egypt) and south (Upper Egypt).

When this split finally became permanent at the end of the New Kingdom (around 1069 BC), foreign powers were gradually able to take control of the government. Yet even then Egyptian culture was so deeply rooted that the successive invaders could not escape its influence, and Libyans, Nubians and Persians all came to adopt traditional Egyptian ways. It was only at the end of the 4th century AD, when the Roman Empire adopted Christianity, that ancient Egypt finally died; their gods were taken from them, their temples were closed down and all knowledge of the 'pagan' hieroglyphs that transmitted their culture was lost for some 1400 years.

> The Greeks were so impressed with the ancient culture that they regarded Egypt as the 'cradle of civilisation', and even the occupying Romans adopted the country's ancient gods and traditions.

Pharaonic Who's Who

Egypt's Pharaonic history is based on the regnal years of each pharaoh, a word derived from *per-aa,* meaning palace. Among the many hundreds of pharaohs who ruled Egypt over a 3000-year period, the following are some of the names found most frequently around the ancient sites.

Narmer (Menes) c 3100 BC First king of a united Egypt after he conquered the north (Lower) Egypt, Narmer from south (Upper) Egypt is portrayed as victorious on the famous Narmer Palette (p137) in the Egyptian Museum. He is perhaps to be identified with the semimythical King Menes, founder of Egypt's ancient capital city Memphis (p148).

Zoser (Djoser) c 2667–2648 BC As second king of the 3rd dynasty, Zoser was buried in Egypt's first pyramid, the world's oldest monumental stone building, designed by the architect Imhotep. Zoser's statue (p137) in the foyer of the Egyptian Museum shows a long-haired king with a slight moustache, dressed in a tight-fitting robe and striped *nemes* (royal headcloth). See also p149.

Sneferu c 2613–2589 BC The first king of the 4th dynasty, and held in the highest esteem by later generations, Sneferu was Egypt's greatest pyramid builder. He was responsible for four such structures, and his final resting place, the Red (Northern) Pyramid at Dahshur (p154), was Egypt's first true pyramid and a model for the more famous pyramids at Giza. See also Pyramid of Meidum (p160).

Khufu (Cheops) c 2589–2566 BC As Sneferu's son and successor, Khufu was the second king of the 4th dynasty. Best known for Egypt's largest pyramid, the Great Pyramid at Giza, his only surviving likeness is Egypt's smallest royal sculpture, a 7.5cm-high figurine in the Egyptian Museum (p138). The gold furniture of his mother, Hetepheres, is also in the museum. See also p125.

Khafre (Khephren, Chephren) c 2558–2532 BC Khafre was a younger son of Khufu who succeeded his half-brother to become fourth king of the 4th dynasty. He built the second of Giza's famous pyramids (p125) and although he is best known as the model for the face of the Great Sphinx, his diorite statue (p138) in the Egyptian Museum is equally stunning.

Menkaure (Mycerinus) c 2532–2503 BC As the son of Khafre and fifth king of the 4th dynasty, Menkaure built the smallest of Giza's three huge pyramids (p127). He is also well represented by a series of superb sculptures (p137) in the Egyptian Museum, which show him with the goddess Hathor and deities representing various administrative divisions (nomes) of Egypt.

Pepi II c 2278–2184 BC As fifth king of the 6th dynasty, Pepi II was a child at his accession; his delight with a dancing pygmy was recorded in the Aswan tomb of his official Harkhuf. As one of the world's longest-reigning monarchs (96 years), Pepi contributed to the decline of the Pyramid Age. See p153 and p259.

Montuhotep II c 2055–2004 BC As overlord of Thebes, Montuhotep II reunited Egypt and his reign began the Middle Kingdom. He was the first king to build a funerary temple at Deir al-Bahri (p219), in which he was buried with five of his wives and a daughter, with further wives and courtiers buried in the surrounding area. See also p140.

Sesostris III (Senwosret, Senusret) c 1874–1855 BC The fifth king of the 12th dynasty, Sesostris III reorganised the administration by taking power from the provincial governors (nomarchs). He strengthened Egypt's frontiers and occupied Nubia with a chain of fortresses, and is recognisable by the stern, 'careworn' faces of his statues. His female relatives were buried with spectacular jewellery. See also p155.

Amenhotep I c 1525–1504 BC As second king of the 18th dynasty, Amenhotep I ruled for a time with his mother Ahmose-Nofretari. They founded the village of Deir el-Medina for the workers who built the tombs in the Valley of the Kings, and Amenhotep I may have been the first king to be buried there. See also p142, and p199.

Hatshepsut c 1473–1458 BC As the most famous of Egypt's female pharaohs, Hatshepsut took power at the death of her brother-husband Tuthmosis

II and initially ruled jointly with her nephew-stepson Tuthmosis III. After taking complete control, she undertook ambitious building schemes, including obelisks at Karnak Temple and her own spectacular funerary temple at Deir al-Bahri (p219). See also p140.

Tuthmosis III c 1479–1425 BC As sixth king of the 18th dynasty, Tuthmosis III (the Napoleon of ancient Egypt) expanded Egypt's empire with a series of foreign campaigns into Syria. He built extensively at Karnak, added a chapel at Deir al-Bahri and his tomb was the first in the Valley of the Kings to be decorated. See p140, p140 and p216.

Amenhotep III c 1390–1352 BC As ninth king of the 18th dynasty, Amenhotep III's reign marks the zenith of Egypt's culture and power. He is the creator of Luxor Temple and the largest ever funerary temple marked by the Colossi of Memnon (p223), and his many innovations, including Aten worship, are usually credited to his son and successor Amenhotep IV (later 'Akhenaten'). See also p203.

Akhenaten (Amenhotep IV) c 1352–1336 BC Changing his name from Amenhotep to distance himself from the state god Amun, Akhenaten relocated the royal capital to Amarna with his wife Nefertiti. While many still regard him as a monotheist and benign revolutionary, the evidence suggests he was a dictator whose reforms were political rather than religious. See p140, p176 and p203.

Nefertiti c 1338–1336 BC (?) Famous for her painted bust in Berlin, Nefertiti ruled with her husband Akhenaten, and while the identity of his successor remains controversial, this may have been Nefertiti herself, using the throne name 'Smenkhkare'. Equally controversial is the suggested identification of her mummy in tomb KV 35 in the Valley of the Kings. See p140, p176; and p203.

Tutankhamun c 1336–1327 BC As the 11th king of the 18th dynasty, Tutankhamun's fame is based on the great quantities of treasure discovered in his tomb in 1922. The son of Akhenaten by one of Akhenaten's sisters, Tutankhamun reopened the traditional temples and restored Egypt's fortunes after the disastrous reign of his father. See p203 and p211.

Horemheb c 1323–1295 BC As a military general, Horemheb restored Egypt's empire under Tutankhamun and after the brief reign of Ay, eventually became king himself, marrying Nefertiti's sister Mutnodjmet. His tomb at Saqqara was abandoned in favour of a royal burial in a superbly decorated tomb in the Valley of the Kings (p215).

Seti I c 1294–1279 BC The second king of the 19th dynasty, Seti I continued to consolidate Egypt's empire with foreign campaigns. Best known for building Karnak's Hypostyle Hall (p195), a superb temple at Abydos (p185) and a huge tomb in the Valley of the Kings (p217), his mummy (p142) in the Egyptian Museum is one of the best preserved examples.

Ramses II c 1279–1213 BC As son and successor of Seti I, Ramses II fought the Hittites at the Battle of Kadesh and built temples including Abu Simbel (p276) and the Ramesseum, once adorned with the statue that inspired poet PB Shelley's 'Ozymandias'. The vast tomb of his children was rediscovered in the Valley of the Kings in 1995. See also p141, p142, p148, p186, p211, p214 and p274.

Ramses III c 1184–1153 BC As second king of the 20th dynasty, Ramses III was the last of the warrior kings, repelling several attempted invasions portrayed in scenes at his funerary temple Medinat Habu (p221). Buried in a finely decorated tomb in the Valley of the Kings, his mummy was the inspiration for Boris Karloff's *The Mummy*.

Taharka 690–664 BC As fourth king of the 25th dynasty, Taharka was one of Egypt's Nubian pharaohs and his daughter Amenirdis II was high priestess at Karnak, where Taharka undertook building work. A fine sculpted head of the king is in Aswan's Nubian Museum, and he was buried in a pyramid at Nuri in southern Nubia. See p195.

Alexander the Great 331–323 BC During his conquest of the Persian Empire, the Macedonian king Alexander invaded Egypt in 331 BC. Crowned pharaoh at Memphis, he founded Alexandria, visited Amun's temple at Siwa Oasis to confirm his divinity and after his untimely death in Babylon in 323 BC, his mummy was eventually buried in Alexandria. See p303 and p319.

Ptolemy I 323–283 BC As Alexander's general and rumoured half-brother, Ptolemy seized Egypt at Alexander's death and established the Ptolemaic line of pharaohs. Ruling in traditional style for 300 years, they made Alexandria the greatest capital of the ancient world and built many of the temples standing today, including Edfu, Philae and Dendera. See also p319.

Cleopatra VII 51–30 BC As the 19th ruler of the Ptolemaic dynasty, Cleopatra VII ruled with her brothers Ptolemy XIII, then Ptolemy XIV before taking power herself. A brilliant politician who restored Egypt's former glories, she married Julius Caesar then Mark Antony, whose defeat at Actium in 31 BC led to the couple's suicide. See also p319 and p325.

Everyday Life

With ancient Egypt's history focused on its royals, the part played by the rest of the ancient population is frequently ignored. The great emphasis on written history also excludes the 99% of the ancient population who were unable to write, and it can often seem as if the only people who lived in ancient Egypt were pharaohs, priests and scribes.

The silent majority are often dismissed as little more than illiterate peasants, although these were the very people who built the monuments and produced the wealth on which the culture was based.

Fortunately Egypt's climate, at least, is democratic, and has preserved the remains of people throughout society, from the mummies of the wealthy in their grand tombs to the remains of the poorest individuals buried in hollows in the sand. The worldly goods buried with them for use in the afterlife give valuable details about everyday life and how it was lived, be it in the bustling, cosmopolitan capital Memphis or in the small rural settlements scattered along the banks of the Nile.

Domestic Life

In Egypt's dry climate, houses were traditionally built of mudbrick, whether they were the back-to-back homes of workers or the sprawling palaces of the royals. The main differences were the number of rooms and the quality of fixtures and fittings. The villas of the wealthy often incorporated walled gardens with stone drainage systems for small pools, and some even had en-suite bathroom facilities – look out for the limestone toilet seat found at Amarna and now hanging in the Egyptian Museum in Cairo.

Just like the mudbrick houses in rural Egypt today, ancient homes were warm in winter and cool in summer. Small, high-set windows reduced the sun's heat but allowed breezes to blow through, and stairs gave access to the flat roof where the family could relax or sleep.

Often whitewashed on the outside to deflect the heat, interiors were usually painted in bright colours, the walls and floors of wealthier homes further enhanced with gilding and inlaid tiles. Although the furniture of most homes would have been quite sparse – little more than a mudbrick bench, a couple of stools and a few sleeping mats – the wealthy could afford beautiful furniture, including inlaid chairs and footstools, storage chests, beds with linen sheets and feather-stuffed cushions. Most homes also had small shrines for household deities and busts of family ancestors, and a small raised area seems to have been reserved for women in childbirth.

The home was very much a female domain. The most common title for women of all social classes was *nebet per* (lady of the house), emphasising their control over most aspects of domestic life. Although there is little evidence of marriage ceremonies, monogamy was standard practice for the majority, with divorce and remarriage relatively common and initiated by either sex. With the same legal rights as men, women were responsible for running the home and although there were male launderers, cleaners and cooks, it was mainly women who cared for the children, cleaned the house, made clothing and prepared food in small open-air kitchens adjoining the home.

The staple food was bread, produced in many varieties, including the dense calorie-laden loaves mass-produced for those working on government building schemes. Onions, leeks, garlic and pulses were eaten in great quantities along with dates, figs, pomegranates and grapes. Grapes were also used, along with honey, as sweeteners. Spices, herbs, nuts and seeds were also added to food, along with oil extracted from native plants and imported almonds and olives. Although cows provided milk for drinking and making butter and cheese, meat was only eaten regularly by the wealthy and by priests allowed to eat temple offerings once the gods had been satisfied. This was mostly beef, although sheep, goats and pigs were also eaten, as were game and wild fowl. Fish was generally dried and salted and, because of its importance in workers' diets, a fish-processing plant existed at the pyramid builders' settlement at Giza.

Although the wealthy enjoyed wine (with the best produced in the vineyards of the Delta and western oases, or imported from Syria), the standard beverage was a rather soupy barley beer, which was drunk throughout society by everyone, including children. The ancient Egyptians' secret to a contented life is summed up by the words of one of their poems: 'it is good to drink beer with happy hearts, when one is clothed in clean robes'.

Public Life/At Work

The majority of ancient Egyptians were farmers, whose lives were based around the annual cycle of the Nile. This formed the basis of their calendar with its three seasons – *akhet* (inundation), *peret* (spring planting) and *shemu* (summer harvest). As the flood waters covering the valley floor receded by October, farmers planted their crops in the silt left behind, using irrigation canals to distribute the flood waters where needed and to water their crops until harvest time in April.

Agriculture was so fundamental to life in both this world and the next that it was one of the main themes in tomb scenes. The standard repertoire of ploughing, sowing and reaping is often interspersed with officials checking field boundaries or calculating the grain to be paid as tax in this pre-coinage economy. The officials are often accompanied by scribes busily recording all transactions, with hieroglyphs now known to have been first developed c 3250 BC as a means of recording produce.

A huge civil service of scribes worked on the pharaoh's behalf to record taxes and organise workers and, taught to read and write in the schools attached to temples where written texts were stored and studied, the great majority of scribes were male. However, some women are also shown with documents and literacy would have been necessary to undertake roles they are known to have held, including overseer, steward, teacher, doctor, high priestess, vizier and even pharaoh on at least six occasions.

In a society where less than 1% were literate, scribes were regarded as wise and were much admired.

Closely related to the scribe's profession were the artists and sculptors who produced the stunning artefacts synonymous with ancient Egypt. From colossal statues to delicate jewellery, all were fashioned using simple tools and natural materials.

Building stone was hewn by teams of labourers supplemented by prisoners, with granite obtained from Aswan, sandstone from Gebel Silsila, alabaster from Hatnub near Amarna and limestone from Tura near

CHRONOLOGY OF THE PHARAOHS

This includes the most significant rulers mentioned throughout this book.

EARLY DYNASTIC PERIOD	
1st Dynasty	**3100–2890 BC**
including:	
Narmer (Menes)	c 3100 BC
2nd Dynasty	**2890–2686 BC**
OLD KINGDOM	
3rd Dynasty	**2686–2613 BC**
including:	
Zoser	2667–2648 BC
Sekhemket	2648–2640 BC
4th Dynasty	**2613–2494 BC**
including:	
Sneferu	2613–2589 BC
Khufu (Cheops)	2589–2566 BC
Djedefra	2566–2558 BC
Khafre (Chephren)	2558–2532 BC
Menkaure (Mycerinus)	2532–2503 BC
Shepseskaf	2503–2498 BC
5th Dynasty	**2494–2345 BC**
including:	
Userkaf	2494–2487 BC
Sahure	2487–2475 BC
Neferirkare	2475–2455 BC
Shepseskare	2455–2448 BC
Raneferef	2448–2445 BC
Nyuserra	2445–2421 BC
Unas	2375–2345 BC
6th Dynasty	**2345–2181 BC**
including:	
Teti	2345–2323 BC
Pepi I	2321–2287 BC
Pepi II	2278–2184 BC
7th–8th Dynasties	**2181–2125 BC**
FIRST INTERMEDIATE PERIOD	
9th–10th Dynasties	**2160–2025 BC**
MIDDLE KINGDOM	
11th Dynasty	**2055–1985 BC**
including:	
Montuhotep II	2055–2004 BC
Montuhotep III	2004–1992 BC
12th Dynasty	**1985–1795 BC**
including:	
Amenemhat I	1985–1955 BC
Sesostris I	1965–1920 BC
Amenemhat II	1922–1878 BC
Sesostris II	1880–1874 BC
Sesostris III	1874–1855 BC
Amenemhat III	1855–1808 BC
Amenemhat IV	1808–1799 BC
13th–14th Dynasties	**1795–1650 BC**

SECOND INTERMEDIATE PERIOD	
15th–17th Dynasties	**1650–1550 BC**
NEW KINGDOM	
18th Dynasty	**1550–1290 BC**
including:	
Ahmose	1550–1525 BC
Amenhotep I	1525–1504 BC
Tuthmosis I	1504–1492 BC
Tuthmosis II	1492–1479 BC
Tuthmosis III	1479–1425 BC
Hatshepsut	1473–1458 BC
Amenhotep II	1427–1400 BC
Tuthmosis IV	1400–1390 BC
Amenhotep III	1390–1352 BC
Akhenaten	1352–1336 BC
Tutankhamun	1336–1327 BC
Horemheb	1323–1295 BC
19th Dynasty	**1295–1186 BC**
including:	
Ramses I	1295–1294 BC
Seti I	1294–1279 BC
Ramses II	1279–1213 BC
Seti II	1200–1194 BC
20th Dynasty	**1186–1069 BC**
including:	
Ramses III	1184–1153 BC
THIRD INTERMEDIATE PERIOD	
21st Dynasty	**1069–945 BC**
including:	
Psusennes I	1039–991 BC
22nd–23rd Dynasties	**945–712 BC**
24th–26th Dynasties	**727–525 BC**
LATE PERIOD	
27th Dynasty	**525–404 BC**
including:	
Cambyses	525–522
Darius	521–486
28th–31st Dynasties	**404–332 BC**
GRAECO-ROMAN PERIOD	
Macedonian and Ptolemaic	**332–30 BC**
including:	
Alexander the Great	332–323 BC
Ptolemy I	305–282 BC
Ptolemy III	246–222 BC
Ptolemy VIII	170–163 and 145–116 BC
Cleopatra VII	51–30 BC
Roman	**30–313 BC**
including:	
Augustus	30 BC – 14 AD
Hadrian	117–138
Diocletian	284–305

modern Cairo. Gold came from mines in the Eastern Desert and Nubia, and both copper and turquoise were mined in the Sinai. With such precious commodities being transported large distances, trade routes and border areas were patrolled by guards, police (known as *medjay*) and the army, when not out on campaign.

Men also plied their trade as potters, carpenters, builders, metalworkers, jewellers, weavers, fishermen and butchers, with many of these professions handed down from father to son. (This is especially well portrayed in the tomb scenes of Rekhmire, see p209). There were also itinerant workers such as barbers, dancers and midwives, and those employed for their skills as magicians. Men worked alongside women as servants in wealthy homes, performing standard household duties, and thousands of people were employed in the temples, which formed the heart of every settlement as a combination of town hall, college, library and medical centre. As well as a hierarchy of priests and priestesses, temples employed their own scribes, butchers, gardeners, florists, perfume makers, musicians and dancers, many of whom worked on a part-time basis.

Clothing, Hairstyles & Jewellery

Personal appearance was clearly important to the Egyptians, with wigs, jewellery, cosmetics and perfumes worn by men and women alike. Garments were generally linen, made from the flax plant before the introduction of cotton in Ptolemaic times. Status was reflected in the fineness and quantity of the linen, but as it was expensive, surviving clothes show frequent patching and darning. Laundry marks are also found; male launderers were employed by the wealthy, and even a few ancient laundry lists have survived, listing the types of garments they had to wash in the course of their work.

The most common garment was the loincloth, worn like underpants beneath other clothes. Men also wore a linen kilt, sometimes pleated, and both men and women wore the bag-tunic made from a rectangle of linen folded in half and sewn up each side. The most common female garments were dresses, most wrapped sari-like around the body, although there were also V-neck designs cut to shape, and detachable sleeves for easy cleaning.

Royal footwear featured gold sequins, embroidery and beading, with enemies painted on the soles to be crushed underfoot

Linen leggings have also been found, as well as socks with a gap between the toes for wearing with sandals made of vegetable fibre or leather. Plain headscarves were worn to protect the head from the sun or during messy work; the striped *nemes* (headcloth) was only worn by the pharaoh, who also had numerous crowns and diadems for ceremonial occasions.

Jewellery was worn by men and women throughout society for both aesthetic and magical purposes. It was made of various materials, from gold to glazed pottery, and included collars, necklaces, hair ornaments, bracelets, anklets, belts, earrings and finger rings.

Wigs and hair extensions were also popular and date back to c 3400 BC, as does the use of the hair dye henna *(Lawsonia inermis)*. Many people shaved or cropped their hair for cleanliness and to prevent head lice (which have even been found in the hair of pharaohs). The clergy had to shave their heads for ritual purity and children's heads were partially shaved to leave only a side lock of hair as a symbol of their youth.

Gods & Goddesses

Initially representing aspects of the natural world, Egypt's gods and goddesses grew more complex through time. As they began to blend together and adopt each other's characteristics, they started to become difficult to identify, although their distinctive headgear and clothing can provide clues as to who they are. The following brief descriptions should help travellers spot at least a few of the many hundreds who appear on monuments and in museums.

Amun The local god of Thebes (Luxor) who absorbed the war god Montu and fertility god Min and combined with the sun god to create Amun-Ra, king of the gods. He is generally portrayed as a man with a double-plumed crown and sometimes the horns of his sacred ram.

Anubis God of mummification, patron of embalmers and guardian of cemeteries, Anubis is generally depicted as a black jackal or a jackal-headed man.

Apophis The huge snake embodying darkness and chaos was the enemy of the sun god Ra and tried to destroy him every night and prevent him reaching the dawn.

Aten The solar disc whose rays end in outstretched hands, first appearing in texts c 1900 BC and becoming chief deity during the Amarna Period c 1360–1335 BC.

Atum Creator god of Heliopolis who rose from the primeval waters and ejaculated (or sneezed depending on the myth) to create gods and humans. Generally depicted as a man wearing the double crown, Atum represented the setting sun.

Bastet Cat goddess whose cult centre was Bubastis; ferocious when defending her father Ra the sun god, she was often shown as a friendly deity, personified by the domestic cat.

Bes Grotesque yet benign dwarf god fond of music and dancing; he kept evil from the home and protected women in childbirth by waving his knives and sticking out his tongue.

Geb God of the earth generally depicted as a green man lying beneath his sister-wife Nut, the sky goddess, supported by their father Shu, god of air.

Hapy God of the Nile flood and the plump embodiment of fertility shown as an androgynous figure with a headdress of aquatic plants.

Hathor Goddess of love and pleasure represented as a cow or a woman with a crown of horns and sun's disc in her guise as the sun god's daughter. Patron of music and dancing whose cult centre was Dendara, she was known as 'she of the beautiful hair' and 'lady of drunkenness'.

Horus Falcon god of the sky and son of Isis and Osiris, he avenged his father to rule on earth and was personified by the ruling pharaoh. He can appear as a falcon or a man with a falcon's head, and his eye *(wedjat)* was a powerful amulet.

Isis Goddess of magic and protector of her brother-husband Osiris and their son Horus, she and her sister Nephthys also protected the dead. As symbolic mother of the pharaoh she appears as a woman with a throne-shaped crown, or sometimes has Hathor's cow horns.

Khepri God of the rising sun represented by the scarab beetle, whose habit of rolling balls of dirt was likened to the sun's journey across the sky.

Khnum Ram-headed god who created life on a potter's wheel; he also controlled the waters of the Nile flood from his cave at Elephantine and his cult centre was Esna.

Khons Young god of the moon and son of Amun and Mut. He is generally depicted in human form wearing a crescent moon crown and the 'sidelock of youth' hairstyle.

Maat Goddess of cosmic order, truth and justice, depicted as a woman wearing an ostrich feather on her head, or sometimes by the feather alone.

Mut Amun's consort and one of the symbolic mothers of the king; her name means both 'mother' and 'vulture' and she is generally shown as a woman with a vulture headdress.

Nekhbet Vulture goddess of Upper Egypt worshipped at el-Kab; she often appears with her sister-goddess Wadjet the cobra, protecting the pharaoh.

Nut Sky goddess usually portrayed as a woman whose star-spangled body arches across tomb and temple ceilings. She swallows the sun each evening to give birth to it each morning.

Osiris God of regeneration portrayed in human form whose main cult centre was at Abydos. As the first mummy created, he was magically revived by Isis to produce their son Horus, who took over the earthly kingship, while Osiris became ruler of the underworld and symbol of eternal life.

Ptah Creator god of Memphis who thought the world into being. He is patron of craftsmen, wears a skullcap and usually clutches a tall sceptre (resembling a 1950s microphone).

Ra Supreme sun god generally shown as a man with a falcon's head topped by a sun disc, although he can take many forms (eg Aten, Khepri) and other gods merge with him to enhance their powers (eg Amun-Ra, Ra-Atum). Ra travelled through the skies in a boat, sinking down into the underworld each night before re-emerging at dawn to bring light.

Sekhmet Lioness goddess of Memphis whose name means 'the powerful one'. As a daughter of sun god Ra she was capable of great destruction and was the bringer of pestilence; her priests functioned as doctors.

Seth God of chaos personified by a mythological, composite animal. After murdering his brother Osiris he was defeated by Horus, and his great physical strength was harnessed to defend Ra in the underworld.

Sobek Crocodile god representing Pharaonic might, he was worshipped at Kom Ombo and the Fayuum.

Taweret Hippopotamus goddess who often appears upright to scare evil from the home and protect women in childbirth.

Thoth God of wisdom and writing, and patron of scribes. He is portrayed as an ibis or baboon and his cult centre was Hermopolis.

Temples

Although many gods had their own cult centres, they were also worshipped at temples throughout Egypt. Built on sites considered sacred, existing temples were added to by successive pharaohs to demonstrate their piety. This is best seen at the enormous complex of Karnak (p194), the culmination of 2000 years of reconstruction.

Surrounded by huge enclosure walls of mudbrick, the stone temples within were regarded as houses of the gods where daily rituals were performed on behalf of the pharaoh. As the intermediary between gods and humans, the pharaoh was high priest of every temple, although in practice these powers were delegated to each temple's high priest.

As well as the temples housing the gods (cult temples), there were also funerary (mortuary) temples where each pharaoh was worshipped after death. Eventually sited away from their tombs for security reasons, the best examples are on Luxor's West Bank, where pharaohs buried in the Valley of the Kings had huge funerary temples built closer to the river. These include Ramses III's temple at Medinat Habu (p221), Amenhotep III's once-vast temple marked by the Colossi of Memnon (p223) and the best known example built by Hatshepsut into the cliffs of Deir al-Bahri (p219).

Tombs & Mummification

Tombs

Initially, tombs were created to differentiate the burials of the elite from the majority, whose bodies continued to be placed directly into the desert sand. By around 3100 BC the mound of sand heaped over a grave was replaced by a more permanent structure of mudbrick, whose characteristic bench-shape is known as a mastaba, after the Arabic word for bench.

As stone replaced mudbrick, the addition of further levels to increase height created the pyramid, the first built at Saqqara (p149) for King Zoser. Its stepped sides soon evolved into the familiar smooth-sided structure, with the Pyramids of Giza (p125) the most famous examples.

Pyramids are generally surrounded by the mastaba tombs of officials wanting burial close to their pharaoh in order to share in an afterlife, which was still the prerogative of royalty; see Cemeteries (p131), Tomb of Akhethotep & Ptahhotep (p152) and Mastaba of Ti (p153.

It was only when the power of the monarchy broke down at the end of the Old Kingdom that the afterlife became increasingly accessible to those outside the royal family, and as officials became more independent they began to opt for burial in their home towns. With little room for grand superstructures along many of the narrow stretches beside the Nile, an alternative type of tomb developed, cut tunnel-fashion into the cliffs that border the river. Most were built on the west bank, the traditional place of burial where the sun was seen to sink down into the underworld each evening. These simple rock-cut tombs consisting of a single chamber gradually developed into more elaborate structures complete with an open courtyard, offering a chapel and entrance facade carved out of the rock, with a shaft leading down into a burial chamber; see Tomb of Kheti (p175), Tomb of Baqet (p175), Tomb of Khnumhotep (p175) and Tombs of the Nobles (p259).

The most impressive rock-cut tombs were those built for the kings of the New Kingdom (1550–1069 BC), who relocated the royal burial ground south to the religious capital Thebes (modern Luxor) to a remote desert valley on the west bank, now known as the Valley of the Kings. There is evidence suggesting the first tomb (KV 39) here may have been built by Amenhotep I. The tomb of his successor Tuthmosis I was built by royal architect Ineni, whose biographical inscription states that he supervised its construction alone, 'with no one seeing, no one hearing'. In a radical departure from tradition, the offering chapels that were once part of the tomb's layout were now replaced by funerary (mortuary) temples built some distance away to preserve the tomb's secret location.

The tombs themselves were designed with a long corridor descending to a network of chambers decorated with scenes to help the deceased reach the next world. Many of these were extracts from the Book of the Dead, the modern term for ancient funerary works including the Book of Amduat (literally, 'that which is in the underworld'), the Book of Gates and the Litany of Ra. These describe the sun god's nightly journey through the darkness of the underworld, the realm of Osiris, with each hour of the night regarded as a separate region guarded by demigods. In order for Ra and the dead souls who accompanied him to pass through on their way to rebirth at dawn, it was essential that they knew the demigods' names in order to get past them. Since knowledge was power in the Egyptian afterlife, the funerary texts give 'Knowledge of the power of those in the underworld, knowledge of the hidden forces, knowing each hour and each god, knowing the gates where the great god must pass and knowing how the powerful can be destroyed'.

Mummification

Although mummification was used by many ancient cultures across the world, the Egyptians were the ultimate practitioners of this highly complex procedure, which they refined over 4000 years.

Their preservation of the dead can be traced back to the very earliest times, when bodies were simply buried in the desert away from the limited areas of cultivation. In direct contact with the sand, the hot, dry conditions allowed body fluids to drain away while preserving the skin, hair and nails intact. Accidentally uncovering such bodies must have had a profound effect upon those able to recognise people who had died years before.

As society developed, those who would once have been buried in a hole in the ground demanded tombs befitting their status. But as the bodies were no longer in direct contact with the sand, they rapidly decomposed. An alternative means of preservation was therefore required. After a long process of experimentation, and a good deal of trial and error, the Egyptians seem to have finally cracked it around 2600 BC when they started to remove the internal organs, where putrefaction begins.

As the process became increasingly elaborate, all the organs were removed except the kidneys, which were hard to reach, and the heart, considered to be the source of intelligence. The brain was generally removed by inserting a metal probe up the nose and whisking until it had liquefied sufficiently to be drained down the nose. All the rest – lungs, liver, stomach and intestines – were removed through an opening cut in the left flank. Then the body and its separate organs were covered with natron salt (a combination of sodium carbonate and sodium bicarbonate) and left to dry out for 40 days, after which they were washed, purified and anointed with a range of oils, spices and resins. All were then wrapped in layers of linen, with the appropriate amulets set in place over the various parts of the body as priests recited the necessary incantations.

'a thousand of every good and pure thing for your soul and all kinds of offerings'.

With each of the internal organs placed inside its own burial container (one of four Canopic jars), the wrapped body with its funerary mask was placed inside its coffin. It was then ready for the funeral procession to the tomb, where the vital Opening of the Mouth ceremony (p472) reanimated the soul and restored its senses. Offerings could then be given and the deceased wished

The Egyptians also used their mummification skills to preserve animals, both much-loved pets and creatures presented in huge numbers as votive offerings to the gods with which they were associated. Everything from huge bulls to tiny shrews were mummified, with cats, hawks and ibis preserved in their millions by Graeco-Roman times.

Art In Life & Death

Ancient Egyptian art is instantly recognisable and its distinctive style remained largely unchanged for more than three millennia. With its basic characteristics already in place at the beginning of the Pharaonic Period c 3100 BC, the motif of the king smiting his enemies on the Narmer Palette (p137) was still used in Roman times.

Despite being described in modern terms as 'works of art', the reasons for the production of art in ancient Egypt are still very much misunderstood. Whereas most cultures create art for purely decorative purposes, Egyptian art was primarily functional. This idea is best understood when gazing at the most famous and perhaps most beautiful of all Egyptian images, Tutankhamun's death mask (p144), which was quite literally made to be buried in a hole in the ground.

The majority of artefacts were produced for religious and funerary purposes and, despite their breathtaking beauty, would have been hidden away from public gaze, either within a temple's dark interior or, like Tut's mask, buried in a tomb with the dead. This only makes the objects – and those who made them – even more remarkable. Artists regarded the things they made as pieces of equipment to do a job rather than works of art to be displayed and admired, and only very occasionally in 3000 years did an artist actually sign their work.

This concept also explains the appearance of carved and painted wall scenes, whose deceptively simple appearance and lack of perspective reinforces their functional purpose. The Egyptians believed it was essential that the things they portrayed had every relevant feature shown as clearly as possible. Then when they were magically reanimated through the correct rituals they would be able to function as effectively as possible, protecting and sustaining the unseen spirits of both the gods and the dead.

Figures needed a clear outline, with a profile of nose and mouth to let them breathe, and the eye shown whole as if seen from the front, to allow the figure to see. This explains why eyes were often painted on the sides of coffins to allow the dead to see out and why hieroglyphs such as snakes or enemy figures were sometimes shown in two halves to prevent them causing damage when re-activated.

The vast quantities of food and drink offered in temples and tombs were duplicated on surrounding walls to ensure a constant supply for eternity. The offerings are shown piled up in layers, sometimes appearing to float in the air if the artist took this practice too far. In the same way, objects otherwise hidden from view if portrayed realistically appear to balance on top of the boxes that actually contained them.

While working within such restrictive conventions, the ancient artists still managed to capture a feeling of vitality. Inspired by the natural world around them, they selected images to reflect the concept of life and rebirth, as embodied by the scarab beetles and tilapia fish thought capable of self-generation. Since images were also believed to be able to transmit the life force they contained, fluttering birds, gambolling cattle and the speeding quarry of huntsmen were all favourite motifs. The life-giving properties of plants are also much in evidence, with wheat, grapes, onions and figs stacked side by side with the flowers the Egyptians loved so much. Particularly common are the lotus (water lily) and papyrus, the heraldic symbols of Upper and Lower Egypt often shown entwined to symbolise a kingdom united.

Colour was also used as a means of reinforcing an object's function, with bright primary shades achieved with natural pigments selected for their specific qualities. Egypt was represented politically by the White Crown of Upper Egypt and the Red Crown of Lower Egypt, fitted together in the dual crown to represent the two lands brought together. The country could also be represented in environmental terms by the colours red and black, the red desert wastes of *deshret* contrasting with the fertile black land of *kemet*. For the Egyptians, black was the colour of life, which also explains the choice of black in representations of Osiris, god of fertility and resurrection, in contrast to the redness associated with his brother Seth, god of chaos. Colour does not indicate ethnic origins, however, since Osiris is also shown with green skin, the colour of vegetation and new life. Some of his fellow gods are blue to echo the ethereal blue of the sky, and the golden yellow of the sun is regularly employed for its protective qualities. Even human figures were initially represented with different coloured skin tones, the red-brown of men contrasting with the paler, yellowed tones of women, and although this has been interpreted as indicating that men spent most of the time working outdoors whereas women led a more sheltered existence, changes in artistic convention meant everyone was eventually shown with the same red-brown skin tone.

The choice of material was also an important way of enhancing an object's purpose. Sculptors worked in a variety of different mediums, with stone often chosen for its colour – white limestone and alabaster (calcite), golden sandstone, green schist (slate), brown quartzite and both black and red granite. Smaller items could be made of red or yellow jasper; orange carnelian or blue lapis lazuli; metals such as copper, gold or silver; or less costly materials such as wood or highly glazed blue faïence pottery.

All these materials were used to produce a wide range of statuary for temples and tombs, from 20m-high stone colossi to gold figurines a few centimetres tall. Amulets and jewellery were another means of ensuring the security of the dead. While their beauty would enhance the appearance of the living, each piece was also carefully designed as a protective talisman or a means of communicating status. Even when creating such small-scale masterpieces, the same principles employed in larger-scale works of art applied, and little of the work that the ancient craftsmen produced was either accidental or frivolous.

Regardless of their dimensions, each figure was thought capable of containing the spirit of the individual they represented – useful insurance should anything happen to the mummy.

There was also a standard repertoire of funerary scenes, from the colourful images that adorn the walls of tombs to the highly detailed vignettes illuminating funerary texts. Every single image, whether carved on stone or painted on papyrus, was designed to serve and protect the deceased on their journey into the afterlife.

Initially the afterlife was restricted to royalty and the texts meant to guide the pharaohs towards eternity were inscribed on the walls of their burial chambers. Since the rulers of the Old Kingdom were buried in pyramids, the accompanying funerary writings are known as the Pyramid Texts – see Pyramid & Causeway of Unas (p150) and Pyramid of Teti (p153).

In the hope of sharing in the royal afterlife, Old Kingdom officials built their tombs close to the pyramids until the pharaohs lost power at the end of the Old Kingdom. No longer reliant on the pharaoh's favour, the officials began to use the royal funerary texts for themselves. Inscribed on their coffins, they are known as Coffin Texts – a Middle Kingdom version of the earlier Pyramid Texts, adapted for nonroyal use.

This 'democratisation' of the afterlife evolved even further when the Coffin Texts were literally brought out in paperback, inscribed on papyrus and made available to the masses during the New Kingdom. Referred to by the modern term the Book of the Dead, the Egyptians knew this as the Book of Coming Forth by Day, with sections entitled 'Spell for not dying a second time', 'Spell not to rot and not to do work in the land of the dead' and 'Spell for not having your magic taken away'. The texts also give various visions of paradise, from joining the sun god Ra in his journey across the sky, joining Osiris in the underworld or rising up to become one of the Imperishable Stars, the variety of final destinations reflecting the ancient Egyptians' multifaceted belief system. These spells and instructions acted as a kind of guidebook to the afterlife, with some of the texts accompanied by maps, and images of some of the gods and demons that would be encountered en route together with the correct way to address them.

The same scenes were also portrayed on tomb walls; the New Kingdom royal tombs in the Valley of the Kings are decorated with highly formal scenes showing the pharaoh in the company of the gods and all the forces of darkness defeated. Since the pharaoh was always pharaoh, even in death, there was no room for the informality and scenes of daily life that can be found in the tombs of lesser mortals (see Tombs of the Nobles, p207).

This explains the big difference between the formal scenes in royal tombs and the much more relaxed, almost eclectic nature of nonroyal tomb scenes, which feature everything from eating and drinking to dancing and hairdressing. Yet even here these apparently random scenes of daily life carry the same message found throughout Egyptian art – the eternal continuity of life and the triumph of order over chaos. As the pharaoh is shown smiting the enemy and restoring peace to the land, his subjects contribute to this continual battle of opposites in which order must always triumph for life to continue.

In one of the most common nonroyal tomb scenes, the tomb owner hunts on the river (see Tombs of Menna & Nakht, p208). Although generally interpreted on a simplistic level as the deceased enjoying a day out boating with his family, the scene is far more complex than it first appears. The tomb owner, shown in a central position in the prime of life, strikes a formal pose as he restores order amid the chaos of nature all around him. In his task he is supported by the female members of his family, from his small daughter to the wife standing serenely beside him. Dressed far too impractically for a hunting trip on the river, his wife wears an outfit more in keeping with a priestess of Hathor, goddess of love and sensual pleasure. Yet Hathor is also the protector of the dead and capable of great violence as defender of her father, the sun god Ra, in his eternal struggle against the chaotic forces of darkness.

Some versions of this riverside hunting scene also feature a cat. Often described as a kind of 'retriever' (whoever heard of a retriever cat?), the cat is one of the creatures who was believed to defend the sun god on his nightly journey through the underworld. Similarly, the river's teeming fish were regarded as pilots for the sun god's boat and were themselves potent symbols of rebirth. Even the abundant lotus flowers are significant since the lotus, whose petals open each morning, is the flower that symbolised rebirth. Once the coded meaning of ancient Egyptian art is understood, such previously silent images almost scream out the idea of 'life'.

Another common tomb scene is the banquet at which guests enjoy generous quantities of food and drink – see Tombs of Menna & Nakht (p208) and Tombs of Sennofer & Rekhmire (p209). Although no doubt reflecting some of the pleasures the deceased had enjoyed in life, the food portrayed was also meant to sustain their souls, as would the accompanying scenes of bountiful harvests which would ensure supplies never ran out. Even the music and dance performed at these banquets indicate much more than a party in full swing – the lively proceedings were another way of reviving the deceased by awakening their senses.

The culmination of this idea can be found in the all-important **Opening of the Mouth ceremony**, performed by the deceased's heir (either the next king or the eldest son). The ceremony was designed to reanimate the soul (ka), which could then go on to enjoy eternal life once all its senses had been restored. Noise and movement were believed to reactivate hearing and sight, while the sense of smell was restored with incense and flowers. The essential offerings of food and drink then sustained the soul that resided within the mummy as it was finally laid to rest inside the tomb.

Hieroglyphs

Hieroglyphs, meaning 'sacred carvings' in Greek, are the pictorial script used by the ancient Egyptians. The script was developed as a means of recording produce, and recent discoveries at Abydos dating to around 3250 BC make this the earliest form of writing yet found, even predating that of Mesopotamia.

The impact of hieroglyphs on Egyptian culture cannot be overestimated, as they provided the means by which the state took shape. They were used by a civil service of scribes working on the king's behalf to collect taxes and organise vast workforces.

Within a few centuries, day-to-day transactions were undertaken in a shorthand version of hieroglyphs known as hieratic, whereas hieroglyphs remained the perfect medium for monumental inscriptions. They were in constant use for more than 3500 years until the last example was carved at Philae temple on 24 August AD 394. Covering every available tomb and temple surface, hieroglyphs were regarded as 'the words of the Thoth', the ibis-headed god of writing and patron deity of scribes, who, like the scribes, is often shown holding a reed pen and ink palette.

The small figures of humans, animals, birds and symbols that populate the script were believed to infuse each scene with divine power. In fact certain signs were considered so potent they were shown in two halves to prevent them causing havoc should they magically reanimate. Yet the ancient Egyptians also liked a joke, and their language was often onomatopoeic – for example, the word for cat was *miw* after the noise it makes, and the word for wine was *irp,* after the noise made by those who drank it.

Evolving from a handful of basic signs, more than 6000 hieroglyphs have been identified, although less than 1000 were in general use.

Although they may at first appear deceptively simple, the signs themselves operate on several different levels and can best be understood if divided into three categories – logograms (ideograms), determinatives and phonograms. While logograms represent the thing they depict (eg the sun sign meaning 'sun'), and determinatives are simply placed at the ends of words to reinforce their meaning (eg the sun sign in the verb 'to shine'), phonograms are less straightforward and are the signs that represent either one, two or three consonants. The 26 signs usually described in simple terms as 'the hieroglyphic alphabet' are the single consonant signs (eg the owl pronounced 'm', the zig-zag water sign 'n'). Another 100 or so signs are biconsonantal (eg the bowl sign read as 'nb'), and a further 50 are triconsonantal signs (eg 'nfr' meaning good, perfect or beautiful).

Unfortunately there are no actual vowels as such, and the absence of any punctuation can also prove tricky, especially since the signs can be arranged either vertically to be read down or horizontally to be read left to right or right to left, depending which way the symbols face.

Although they can seem incredibly complex, the majority of hieroglyphic inscriptions are simply endless repetitions of the names and titles of the pharaohs and gods, surrounded by protective symbols. Names were of tremendous importance to the Egyptians and as vital to an individual's existence as their soul (ka), and it was sincerely believed that 'to speak the name of the dead is to make them live'.

The loss of one's name meant permanent obliteration from history, and those unfortunate enough to incur official censure included commoners and pharaohs alike. At times it even happened to the gods themselves, a fate which befell the state god Amun during the reign of the 'heretic' pharaoh Akhenaten, who in turn suffered the same fate together with his god Aten when Amun was later restored.

In order to prevent this kind of obliteration, names were sometimes carved so deeply into the rock it is possible to place an outstretched hand right inside each hieroglyph, as is the case of Ramses III's name and titles at his funerary temple of Medinat Habu (p221).

Royal names were also followed by epithets such as 'life, prosperity, health', comparable to the way in which the name of the Prophet Mohammed is always followed by the phrase 'peace be upon him'. For further protection, royal names were written inside a rectangular fortress wall known as a *serekh,* which later developed into the more familiar oval-shaped cartouche (the French word for cartridge).

Although each pharaoh had five names, cartouches were used to enclose the two most important ones: the 'prenomen' or 'King of Upper and

Lower Egypt' name assumed at the coronation and written with a bee and a sedge plant; and the 'nomen' or 'Son of Ra' name, which was given at birth and written with a goose and a sun sign.

As an example, Amenhotep III is known by his nomen or Son of Ra name 'Amun-hotep' (meaning Amun is content), although his prenomen or King of Upper and Lower Egypt name was Neb-maat-Re (meaning Ra, lord of truth). His grandson had the most famous of all Egyptian names, Tut-ankh-amun, which literally translates as 'the living image of Amun', yet he had originally been named Tut-ankh-aten, meaning 'the living image of the Aten' – a change in name that reflects the shifting politics of the time.

Gods were also incorporated into the names of ordinary people and as well as Amunhotep there was Rahotep (the sun god Ra is content) and Ptahhotep (the creator god Ptah is content). By changing 'hotep' (meaning 'content') to 'mose' (meaning 'born of'), the names Amenmose, Ramose and Ptahmose meant that these men were 'born of' these gods.

In similar fashion, goddesses featured in women's names. Hathor, goddess of love, beauty and pleasure, was a particular favourite, with names such as Sithathor (daughter of Hathor). Standard male names could also be feminised by the simple addition of 't', so Nefer (good, beautiful or perfect) becomes Nefert, which could be further embellished with the addition of a verb, as in the case of the famous name Nefertiti (goodness/beauty/perfection has come).

Others were known by their place of origin, such as Panehesy (the Nubian), or could be named after flora and fauna – Miwt (cat), Debet (hippopotamus) and Seshen (lotus), which is still in use today as the name Susan.

Pharaonic Glossary

Akh Usually translated as 'transfigured spirit', produced when the ka (soul) and ba (spirit) united after the deceased was judged worthy enough to enter the afterlife.

Ammut Composite monster of the underworld who was part crocodile, part lion, part hippo and ate the hearts of the unworthy dead; her name means 'The Devourer'.

Ba Usually translated as 'spirit', which appeared after death as a human-headed bird, able to fly to and from the tomb and into the afterlife.

Book of the Dead Modern term for the collection of ancient funerary texts designed to guide the dead through the afterlife, developed at the beginning of the New Kingdom and partly based on the earlier Pyramid Texts and Coffin Texts.

Canopic jars Containers usually made of limestone or calcite to store the preserved entrails (stomach, liver, lungs and intestines) of mummified individuals.

Cartouche The protective oval shape (the name derived from the French word for cartridge), which surrounded the names of kings and queens and occasionally gods.

cenotaph A memorial structure set up in memory of a deceased king or queen, separate from their tomb or funerary temple.

Coffin Texts Funerary texts developed from the earlier Pyramid Texts, which were then written on coffins during the Middle Kingdom.

Coregency A period of joint rule by two pharaohs, usually father and son.

cult temple The standard religious building(s) designed to house the spirits of the gods and accessible only to the priesthood, usually located on the Nile's east bank.

deshret 'Red land', referring to barren desert.

djed pillar The symbolic backbone of Osiris, bestowing strength and stability and often worn as an amulet.

false door The means by which the soul of the deceased could enter and leave the world of the living to accept funerary offerings brought to their tomb.

funerary (mortuary) temple The religious structures where the souls of dead pharaohs were commemorated and sustained with offerings, usually built on the Nile's west bank.

Heb-Sed festival The jubilee ceremony of royal renewal and rejuvenation, which pharaohs usually celebrated after 30 years' rule.

Heb-Sed race Part of the Heb-Sed festival when pharaohs undertook physical feats such as running to demonstrate their prowess and fitness to rule.

Hieratic Ancient shorthand version of hieroglyphs used for day-to-day transactions by scribes.

hieroglyphs Greek for 'sacred carvings', referring to ancient Egypt's formal picture writing used mainly for tomb and temple walls.

hypostyle hall Imposing section of temple characterised by densely packed monumental columns.

ka Usually translated as 'soul', this was a person's 'double', which was created with them at birth and which lived on after death, sustained by offerings left by the living.

kemet 'Black land', referring to the fertile areas along the Nile's banks.

king lists Chronological lists of each king's names kept as a means of recording history.

lotus (water lily) The heraldic plant of Upper (southern) Egypt.

mammisi The Birth House attached to certain Late Period and Graeco-Roman temples and associated with the goddesses Isis and Hathor.

mastaba Arabic word for bench, used to describe the mudbrick tomb structures built over subterranean burial chambers and from which pyramids developed.

name An essential part of each individual given at birth, and spoken after their death to allow them to live again in the afterlife.

naos Sanctuary containing the god's statue, generally located in the centre of ancient temples.

natron Mixture of sodium carbonate and sodium bicarbonate used to dry out the body during mummification and used by the living to clean linen, teeth and skin.

nemes The yellow-and-blue striped headcloth worn by pharaohs, the most famous example found on Tutankhamun's golden death mask.

nomarch Local governor of each of Egypt's 42 nomes.

nome Greek term for Egypt's 42 provinces – 22 in Upper Egypt and later 20 added in Lower Egypt.

obelisk Monolithic stone pillar tapering to a pyramidal top that was often gilded to reflect sunlight around temples and usually set in pairs.

Opening of the Mouth ceremony The culmination of the funeral, performed on the mummy of the deceased by their heir or funerary priest using spells and implements to restore their senses.

Opet festival Annual celebration held at Luxor Temple to restore the powers of the pharaoh at a secret meeting with the god Amun.

Papyrus The heraldic plant of Lower (northern) Egypt whose reedlike stem was sliced and layered to create paperlike sheets for writing.

Pharaoh Term for an Egyptian king derived from the ancient Egyptian word for palace, *per-aa*.

pylon Monumental gateway with sloping sides forming the entrance to temples.

Pyramid Texts Funerary texts inscribed on the walls of late Old Kingdom pyramids and restricted to royalty.

sacred animals Living creatures thought to represent certain gods – eg the crocodile (identified with Sobek), the cat (identified with Bastet) – and often mummified at death.

sarcophagus Derived from the Greek for 'flesh eating' and referring to the large stone coffins used to house the mummy and its wooden coffin(s).

scarab The sacred dung beetle believed to propel the sun's disc through the sky in the same way the beetle pushes a ball of dung across the floor.

Serapeum Vast network of underground catacombs at Saqqara in which the Apis bulls were buried, later associated with the Ptolemaic god Serapis.

Serdab From the Arabic word for cellar, a small room in a mastaba tomb containing a statue of the deceased to which offerings were presented.

shabti (or ushabti) Small servant figurines placed in burials designed to undertake any manual work in the afterlife on behalf of the deceased.

shadow An essential part of each individual, the shadow was believed to offer protection, based on the importance of shade in an extremely hot climate.

sidelock of youth Characteristic hairstyle of children and certain priests in which the head is shaved and a single lock of hair allowed to grow.

solar barque The boat in which the sun god Ra sailed through the heavens, with actual examples buried close to certain pyramids for use by the spirits of the pharaohs.

Uraeus An image of the cobra goddess Wadjet worn at the brow of royalty to symbolically protect them by spitting fire into the eyes of their enemies.

Weighing of the Heart (The Judgement of Osiris) The heart of the deceased was weighed against the feather of Maat with Osiris as judge; if light and free of sin they were allowed to spend eternity as an *akh,* but if their heart was heavy with sin it was eaten by Ammut and they were damned forever.

The Egyptians

A sign held up by a protester in Midan Tahrir in February 2011 read, 'I used to be afraid.... Then I became Egyptian.' A badge worn by a Cairene woman soon after President Mubarak stepped down read, 'Egyptian and proud.' Understanding what it means to be Egyptian has never been easier, nor more difficult – there are so many possibilities. But one characteristic that still links the majority of Egyptians, from the university professor in Alexandria to the shoeshine boy in Luxor, is an immense pride in simply being Egyptian.

It's hard sometimes for outsiders to see where that pride could come from, given the pervasive poverty, low literacy levels, high unemployment, housing shortages, infrastructure failings and myriad other pitfalls that face the country. But aiding each Egyptian in the daily struggle is every other Egyptian, and indeed there is a real sense that everybody's in it together. Large extended families and close-knit neighbourhoods act as social support groups, strangers fall easily into conversation with each other, and whatever goes wrong somebody always knows someone somewhere who can help fix it.

The official site of the Egyptian Tourist Authority (www.egypt.travel) has magazine-type features, news and a huge range of resources and links, while the State Information Service (www.sis.gov.eg) provides information on everything from geography to the economy.

Comforters

Religion also cushions life's blows. Religion permeates Egyptian life. Islam is manifested not in a strictly authoritarian manner – Egyptians love enjoying themselves too much for that – but it's there in the background. Ask after someone's health and the answer, from a Christian or a Muslim, is *Alhamdulallah* (Fine. Praise to God). Arrange to meet tomorrow and it's *Inshallah* (God willing). Then, if your appointee fails to turn up, God obviously didn't mean it to be.

And when all else fails – and it so often fails – there's humour. Egyptians are renowned for it. Jokes and wisecracks are the parlance of life. Comedy is the staple of the local cinema industry and the backbone of TV scheduling. The stock character is the little guy who through wit and a sharp tongue always manages to prick pomposity and triumph over the odds. Laughter lubricates the wheels of social exchange and one of the most enjoyable aspects of travelling in Egypt is how much can be negotiated with a smile.

Lifestyle

There's no simple definition of Egyptian society. There are obviously differences between someone living off their land in the Nile Delta and someone working in Cairo. But even among the latter, there are extremes of experience. On the one hand there's religious conservatism, where women wear the long, black, all-concealing *abeyya* and men wear the gownlike *galabeya*. In traditional circles, cousins marry cousins; going to Alexandria constitutes the trip of a lifetime; and all is 'God's will'. On the other hand, there are sections of society whose members order out from McDonald's; whose daughters wear slinky black numbers and flirt

SILENT COMMUNICATION IN EGYPT

Egyptians have an array of nonverbal ways of getting a point across – and if you know some of them, you'll be much less likely to get offended, run over or neglected in a restaurant.

First, 'no' is often communicated with a simple upward nod or a brusque *tsk* sound – which can seem a bit rude if you're not expecting it. But if you use it casually to touts on the street, they're more likely to leave you alone.

Another signal that's often misinterpreted by foreigners is a loud hissing sound. No, that guy isn't commenting on your hot bod (well, OK, sometimes he might be) – he's trying to get your attention so you don't get trampled by his donkey cart coming down the narrow lane. Translate a hiss as 'Heads up – comin' through'.

But the most essential gesture to learn is the one for asking for the bill at a restaurant. Make eye contact with your waiter, hold out your hand palm up, then make a quick chopping motion across it with the side of your other hand, as if to say 'Cut me off'. Works like a charm.

outrageously; who think nothing of regular trips to the USA; and who never set foot in a mosque until the day they're laid out in one.

A City Story

The bulk of the Egyptian populace falls somewhere between these two extremes. The typical urban family lives in an overcrowded suburb in a six-floor breeze-block apartment building with cracking walls and dodgy plumbing. If they're lucky they may own a small car. Otherwise the husband will take the metro to work or, more likely, fight for a handhold on one of the city's sardine-can buses. He may well be a university graduate (about 40,000 people graduate each year), although a degree is no longer any guarantee of a job – graduate unemployment has shot up in the past decade. He may also be one of the million-plus paper-pushing civil servants, earning a pittance to while away each day in an undemanding job. This at least allows him to slip away from work early each afternoon to borrow his cousin's taxi for a few hours to bring in some much-needed supplementary income. His wife remains at home cooking, looking after the three or more children, and swapping visits with his mother, her mother and various other family members.

The Country Scene

Meanwhile life in rural Egypt is undergoing a transformation. Just over half the country's population lives there, creating some of the most densely populated agricultural land in the world. What little land remains is divided into small plots (averaging just 0.6 hectares), which don't even support a medium-sized family. Just under one third of Egyptians make their living off the land. Returns are small – agriculture accounts for just 14% of Egypt's GDP. The small size of plots prevents mechanisation and improved yields. As a result, farmers increasingly rely on animal husbandry or look for other ways of surviving. The farmer you see working his field may spend his afternoons working as a labourer or selling cigarettes from a homemade kiosk to make ends meet.

The countryside remains the repository of traditional culture and values. Large families are still the norm, particularly in Upper Egypt, and extended families still live together. High rates of female illiteracy are standard. Whether all this will change with the steady diet of urban Cairene values and Western soap operas, or with the prospect of an Islamist government, remains to be seen.

BACKHAND ECONOMY

Baksheesh means tip, but it's more than just a reward for services rendered. Salaries and wages in Egypt are much lower than in Western countries, so baksheesh is an essential means of supplementing income. Even Egyptians have to constantly dole out the baksheesh – to park their cars, receive mail and ensure they get fresh produce at the grocers.

For travellers not used to tipping, demands for baksheesh for pointing out the obvious in museums can be quite irritating. But services such as opening a door, delivering room service or carrying your bags warrant baksheesh. This may only be a few Egyptian pounds, but will always be welcome. For suggested tip amounts, see p514.

We suggest carrying lots of small change with you (trust us – you'll need it!) and also to keep it separate from bigger bills. And remember, there is only one immutable rule and that is that you can never give too much.

Sport

Egypt is football obsessed. The country hosts the Egyptian Premier League, which is regarded as one of the top 20 most competitive leagues in the world. The two most popular clubs are Ahly and Zamalek, both of which are located in Cairo, and inspire fervent loyalty in their fans. The Egyptian national team hasn't qualified for the FIFA World Cup since 1990 (and its 2009 loss to Algeria in a qualifier match sparked passionate protests and riots in Egypt and abroad). But it has won the African Nations Cup six times, including in 2008.

Multiple Identities

Egypt also has a strong national team of swimmers and tennis players, the latter being ex-president Mubarak's favourite sport.

Most Egyptians will proudly tell you that they are descendants of the ancient Egyptians, and while there is a strand of truth in this, any Pharaonic blood still flowing in modern veins has been seriously diluted. The country has weathered invasions of Libyans, Persians, Greeks, Romans and, most significantly, the 4000 Arab horsemen who invaded in AD 640. In the centuries following the Arab conquest, there was significant Arab migration and intermarriage with the indigenous population. The Mamluks, rulers of Egypt between the 13th and 16th centuries, were of Turkish and Circassian origins, and then there were the Ottoman Turks, rulers and occupiers from 1517 until the latter years of the 18th century.

Desert Tribes

Beside the Egyptians of the Nile Valley, there is a handful of separate indigenous groups with ancient roots. The ancestors of Egypt's Bedouins are believed to have migrated from the Arabian Peninsula, before settling the Western and Eastern Deserts and Sinai. But their nomadic way of life is under threat as the interests of the rest of the country increasingly intrude on their once-isolated domains

In the Western Desert, particularly in and around Siwa Oasis, are a small number of Berbers who have retained much of their own identity. They are quite easily distinguished from other Egyptians by the dress of the women, who usually don the *meliyya* (head-to-toe garment with slits for the eyes). Although many speak Arabic, they have preserved their own native tongues.

People of the South

In the south, the tall, dark-skinned Nubians originate from Nubia, the region between Aswan in southern Egypt and Khartoum in Sudan. Their homeland almost completely disappeared in the 1970s when the High Dam created Lake Nasser. Some of Egypt's Nubians emigrated to Cairo, but the majority were resettled in towns and villages between Edfu and Aswan. Their cultural identity has survived, however, and whether in the way they decorate their homes or play their music, Nubians are recognisably distinct from other Egyptians.

Religion

Some 90% of Egypt's population is Muslim. Islam prevails in Egyptian life at a low-key, almost unconscious level, and yet almost all men heed the amplified call of the muezzin (mosque official) each Friday noon, when the crowds from the mosques block streets and footpaths. The vast majority of the 10% of Egypt that isn't Muslim is Coptic Christian. The two communities have a mixed history, with periodic flare-ups, most recently the burning of a church near Aswan in October 2011, which led to protests and deaths in Cairo. But one of the most inspiring images of the 2011 Tahrir protests was the sight of Muslims protecting Christians while they prayed, and vice versa.

Islam

Islam, the predominant religion of Egypt, shares its roots with Judaism and Christianity. Adam, Abraham (Ibrahim), Noah and Moses are all prophets in Islam; Jesus is recognised as a prophet, but not the son of God. Muslim teachings correspond closely to the Torah (the foundation book of Judaism) and the Christian Gospels. The essence of Islam is the Quran, which Muslims believe is the last and truest message from God, delivered by the Archangel Gabriel to the Prophet Mohammed.

The Life of Mohammed

Islam was founded in the early 7th century by Mohammed, who was born around AD 570 in Mecca. Mohammed is said to have received his first divine message at about the age of 40. The revelations continued for the rest of his life and were transcribed to become the holy Quran. To this day not one dot of the Quran has been changed, making it, Muslims believe, the direct word of God.

Mohammed started preaching in 613, three years after the first revelation, but could only attract a few dozen followers. Having attacked the ways of Meccan life, especially the worship of a wealth of idols, he made many enemies. In 622 he and his followers retreated to Medina, an oasis town some 360km from Mecca. This Hejira, or migration, marks the start of the Muslim calendar.

Mohammed died in 632 but the new religion continued its rapid spread, reaching all of Arabia by 634 and Egypt in 642.

Pillars of Islam

Islam means 'submission' and this principle is visible in the daily life of Muslims. The faith is expressed by observance of the five 'pillars of Islam', which oblige Muslims to:

» Publicly declare that 'there is no god but God, and Mohammed is His Prophet'.

» Pray five times a day: at sunrise, noon, mid-afternoon, sunset and night.

» Give *zakat* (alms) for the propagation of Islam and to help the needy.

» Fast during daylight hours during the month of Ramadan.

» Complete the hajj (the pilgrimage to Mecca).

The first pillar is accomplished through prayer, which is the second pillar and an essential part of the daily life of a believer. Five times a day the muezzins sing out the call to prayer through speakers on top of the minarets. It is perfectly permissible to pray at home or elsewhere; only the

THE EGYPTIANS RELIGION

The people of the south - anywhere south of Minya and down as far as Aswan - are known as Saidis (pronounced sai-eed-ees). They tend to be the subject of the sort of jokes that Irish and Polish will find familiar.

One of the most influential Islamic authorities in Egypt is the Grand Sheikh of Al-Azhar, a position appointed by the Egyptian president and currently held by Sheikh Ahmed al-Tayeb. It is his role to define the official Egyptian Islamic line on any particular matter from organ donations to heavy-metal music.

THE MOULID

A cross between a funfair and a religious festival, a *moulid* celebrates the birthday of a local saint or holy person – typically Muslim, but in Egypt, there are Coptic *moulid*s too. They are often a colourful riot of celebrations attended by hundreds of thousands of people. Visitors from out of town set up camp in the streets, close to the saint's tomb, where children's rides, sideshows and food stalls are erected. In the midst of the chaos, barbers perform mass circumcisions; snake charmers induce cobras out of baskets; and children are presented at the shrine to be blessed and the sick to be cured.

Tartours (cone-shaped hats) and *fanous* (lanterns) are made and sold to passers-by and in the evenings local Sufi orders usually hold hypnotic *zikr*s (literally 'remembrance') in colourful tents. In a *zikr* the *mugzzabin* (Sufi followers who participate in *zikr*s) stand in straight lines and sway from side to side to rhythmic clapping that gradually increases in intensity over a period of hours. Other *zikr*s are formidable endurance tests where troupes of musicians perform for hours in the company of ecstatic dancers.

Most *moulid*s last for about a week, with one night, the *leila kebira* (big night), being the rowdiest. Much of the infrastructure is provided by 'professional' *mawladiyya*, or *moulid* people, who spend their lives going from one *moulid* to another.

For visitors, the hardest part about attending a *moulid* is ascertaining dates. Events are tied to either the Islamic or Gregorian calendars and dates can be different each year. The country's biggest *moulid*, for al-Sayyed al-Badawi, in Tanta, does have a fixed date, in the last week of October. Cairo hosts several *moulid*s, and there are a number of smaller *moulid*s in the area around Luxor.

If you do attend the festivities, be prepared for immense crowds (hold on to your valuables) and incredible noise. These are typically family events, so crowds are usually mixed, but women should always be escorted by a male.

noon prayer on Friday is meant to be conducted in the mosque. Women typically pray at home; when they go to the mosque, there is a separate section for them.

The fourth pillar, *sawm* (fasting), is done during the ninth month of the Muslim calendar, Ramadan, when all believers fast during the day. Pious Muslims do not allow anything to pass their lips in daylight hours. Although many Muslims do not follow the injunctions to the letter, most conform to some extent. The impact of the fasting is often lessened by a shift in waking hours (aided by the cancellation of daylight saving time in Egypt when necessary), and people tend to sleep late if they can, or nap in the afternoon. They then live much of their social life until sunrise.

Far from being a month of austerity, Ramadan is a joyous time, with great camaraderie among fellow fasters. The evening meal during Ramadan, called *iftar* (breaking the fast), is always a celebration. In some parts of town, tables are laid out in the street as charitable acts by the wealthy to provide food for the less fortunate. Evenings are imbued with a party atmosphere and there's plenty of street entertainment, often through until sunrise.

For information on how Ramadan affects travel plans, see p516. For information on other Islamic holidays, see p515.

> The Coptic church was influential in shaping the rituals of the early Christian church. Some, including the hidden altar and use of incense, were adapted from existing pagan practices.

Christianity

The majority of Egyptian Christians are known as Copts. The term is the Western form of the Arabic *qibt*, derived from the Greek *aegyptios* (Egyptian), which in turn comes from the ancient Egyptian language.

Although Christianity did not become the official religion of Egypt until the 4th century, Egypt was one of the first countries to embrace the new faith. St Mark, companion of the apostles Paul and Peter, is said to have begun preaching Christianity in Egypt around AD 45. From the closure of the pagan temples to the arrival of Islam, Christianity was the predominant religion in Egypt.

The Monophysite Controversy

Egyptian Christians split from the Orthodox Church of the Eastern (or Byzantine) Empire, of which Egypt was then a part, after the main body of the church described Christ as both human and divine. Dioscurus, the patriarch of Alexandria, refused to accept this description, and embraced the theory that Christ is totally absorbed by his divinity and that it is blasphemous to consider him human.

The Coptic Church is ruled by a patriarch (presently Pope Shenouda III), other members of the religious hierarchy and an ecclesiastical council of laypeople. It has a long history of monasticism and in fact the first Christian monks, St Anthony and St Pachomius, were Copts.

The Coptic language, which has its origins in Egyptian hieroglyphs and ancient Greek, is still used in religious ceremonies, sometimes in conjunction with Arabic for the benefit of the congregation. Today the Coptic language is based on the Greek alphabet with an additional seven characters taken from hieroglyphs.

The Copts

The Copts have long provided something of an educated elite in Egypt, filling many important government and bureaucratic posts. They're perceived as being an economically powerful minority, and a good number of Copts are wealthy and influential.

With that said, there are also a lot of Copts at the very bottom of the heap: the *zabbalin,* the garbage-pickers of Cairo, who sort through much of the city's rubbish, have always been Copts.

The Copts have suffered as a result of recent upheavals, most notably when a bomb went off outside a church in Alexandria on January 1, 2011, killing at least 23 people, and in Cairo in October 2011, when some 26 people were killed by security forces.

Other Denominations

Other Christian denominations are represented in Egypt, each by a few thousand adherents. In total, there are about one million members of other Christian groups. Among Catholics, apart from Roman Catholics of the Latin rite, the whole gamut of the fragmented Middle Eastern rites is represented, including the Armenian, Syrian, Chaldean, Maronite and Melkite rites. The Anglican communion comes under the Episcopal Church in Jerusalem. The Armenian Apostolic Church has around 10,000 members, and the Greek Orthodox Church is based in Alexandria.

Women in Egypt

Some of the biggest misunderstandings between Egyptians and Westerners occur over the issue of women. Half-truths and stereotypes exist on both sides: many Westerners assume all Egyptian women are repressed victims, while many Egyptians see Western women as sex-obsessed and immoral.

For many Egyptians of both genders, the role of a woman is specifically defined: she is the mother and the matron of the household. The man is the provider. But there are thousands of middle- and upper-middle-class professional women in Egypt who, like their counterparts in the West, juggle work and family responsibilities. Among the working classes, where adherence to tradition is theoretically strongest, it's certainly the ideal for women to concentrate on home and family, but

THE EGYPTIANS WOMEN IN EGYPT

Women in Egypt received the vote in 1956. Six years later, Hakmet abu Zeid became the first woman in the Egyptian cabinet.

WOMEN

economic reality means that millions of women are forced to work (and are still responsible for all the domestic chores).

The issue of sex is big, naturally. Premarital sex (or any sex outside marriage) is taboo in Egypt. But marriage is an expensive business, so men must often put it off until well into their 30s. This leads to a frustration that can often seem palpable in the streets. For women the issue is potentially far more serious. Women are typically expected to be virgins when they marry and a family's reputation can rest on this point. Thus the social restrictions placed on young women are meant to protect her for marriage.

This has long had the effect of dampening discussions of sexual abuse and harassment, as the social costs of a woman being perceived in a sexual way are quite high. But in 2008, a woman for the first time sued a man who had attacked her in the street, and the perpetrator was sentenced to jail. And the 2011 revolution has since shifted gender dynamics a bit, as young urban women were very visible in the street. As with so many aspects of Egyptian culture after the revolution, the role of women is in flux as well.

On their return from a women's suffrage conference in Rome in 1923, pioneer Arab feminists Huda Sharawi and Saiza Nabarawi threw away their *abeyyas* at Ramses Station in Cairo. Many in the crowd of women who had come to welcome them home followed suit.

The Arts

To the Arab world, Egypt (or more specifically Cairo) is a powerhouse of film, TV, music and theatre. While little of this culture has had much impact in the West, a great many Egyptian actors and singers are revered cultural icons to Arabic-speakers around the world. In more recent years, many visual artists have been successful and popular in the global art market. The 2011 revolution has spawned a cultural energy like never before, evident in music, theatre and visual arts.

Literature

20th-Century Writing

Awarded the Nobel Prize for Literature in 1988, Naguib Mahfouz was one of the first and most important contemporary writers of Arabic literature. Born in 1911 in Cairo's Islamic quarter, Mahfouz began writing when he was 17 and published over 50 novels and 350 short stories, as well as movie scripts and plays. His first efforts were influenced by the European greats, but over the course of his career he developed a voice that was uniquely Arab, and drew its inspiration from the talk in the coffeehouses and the dialect of Cairo's streets. In 1994 he was the victim of a knife attack that left him partially paralysed. The attack was a response to a book Mahfouz had written, which was a thinly disguised allegory of the life of the great religious leaders including Prophet Mohammed. In 2006 Mahfouz died after falling and sustaining a head injury.

Beyond Mahfouz

On the strength of what's available in English, it's easy to view Egyptian literature as beginning and ending with Mahfouz, but other respected writers include Taha Hussein, a blind author and intellectual who spent much of his life in trouble with whichever establishment happened to be in power; the Alexandrian playwright Tawfiq al-Hakim; and Yousef Idris, a writer of powerful short stories.

Egypt's women writers are also enjoying international success. Feminist and activist Nawal al-Saadawi's fictional work *Woman at Point Zero* has been published, at last count, in 28 languages. An outspoken critic on behalf of women, she is marginalised at home – her nonfiction book *The Hidden Face of Eve,* which criticises the role of women in the Arab world, is banned in Egypt. For many years following its publication, Saadawi was forced to stay out of the country after reportedly receiving death threats from Islamist groups. Those interested in learning more about her fascinating and inspirational life should read her autobiography *Walking Through Fire,* which was published in 2002.

Though Egyptian, born and brought up in Cairo, Ahdaf Soueif writes in English as well as Arabic, but most of her work has yet to appear in Arabic. Her wonderful novel *The Map of Love*, set in Egypt, was shortlisted for the Booker prize, and her other novels are *Aisha, Sandpiper*

Author Alaa Al-Aswany (*The Yacoubian Building*) is a professional dentist whose first office was located in the real-life Yacoubian Building, at 34 Sharia Talaat Harb in Downtown Cairo.

CONTEMPORARY EGYPTIAN ARTISTS

» Chant Avedissian (www.chantavedissian.com) – Armenian-Egyptian artist whose stencils of iconic celebrities from the past have become very much in demand from Middle Eastern art collectors.

» Youssef Nabil (www.youssefnabil.com) – Egyptian artist living in New York who does hand-coloured gelatin silver prints of photographs of Egyptian and international celebrities.

» Ghada Amer (www.ghadaamer.com) – Egyptian artist who embroiders on abstract canvases that deal with female sexuality and eroticism.

» Lara Baladi – Egyptian-Lebanese multimedia artist who works with personal and collective memory.

» Mohamed Abla (www.ablamuseum.com) – His work on social injustice was not exhibited in Egypt during the Mubarak years.

and *In the Eye of the Sun*. In early 2012 she published her memoir: *Cairo: My City, Our Revolution*.

Egyptian Classics

Beer at the Snooker Club by Waguih Ghali is a fantastic novel of youthful angst set against a backdrop of 1950s revolutionary Egypt and literary London. It's the Egyptian *Catcher in the Rye*.

The Cairo Trilogy by Naguib Mahfouz is usually considered Mahfouz' masterpiece; this generational saga of family life is rich in colour and detail, and has earned comparisons with Dickens and Zola.

Love in Exile and *Sunset Oasis* by Bahaa Taher have both won awards, with Taher being one of the most respected living writers in the Arab world.

The Harafish by Naguib Mahfouz would be our desert-island choice if we were allowed only one work by Mahfouz. This is written in an episodic, almost folkloric style that owes much to the tradition of *The Thousand and One Nights*.

Proud Beggars, *The Colours of Infamy* and *The Jokers* by Albert Cossery were all recently translated and published following the author's death in 2008. His novels were written in French, and have a bit of a cult following among Egyptophiles.

Zayni Barakat by Gamal al-Ghitani is a drama set in Cairo during the waning years of the Mamluk era. It was made into an extremely successful local TV drama in the early 1990s.

Egyptian Contemporary Novels

As well-known globally as Naguib Mahfouz, contemporary dentist-turned-writer Alaa Al-Aswany writes about Egyptians, poverty and class differences. His 2002 blockbuster *The Yacoubian Building* is a bleak but compelling snapshot of contemporary Cairo seen through the stories of the occupants of a Downtown building. The world's biggest-selling novel in Arabic, it is reminiscent (though not at all derivative) of the novels of Rohinton Mistry. If you read only one contemporary Egyptian novel before or during your visit, make it this one.

The story is really just an elaborate soap opera, though it's remarkable in that it depicts Egypt in a particular time and introduces archetypes that hadn't previously been captured in Arabic literature. Al-Aswany's subsequent writing – *Chicago*, a novella, and *Friendly Fire*, a collection of short stories – both have a strong focus on contemporary Egypt. His most recent book, published after the 2011 revolution, is *On the State of Egypt: A Novelist's Provocative Reflections.*

Salwa Bakr tackles taboo subjects such as sexual prejudice and social inequality. Her work includes the novels *The Golden Chariot* and the excellent *The Man from Bashmour*. One of the most promising of a very vibrant new generation of writers is Mansoura Ez-Eldin, whose novel *Maryam's Maze* is the wonderfully written story of a woman trying to find her way in the confusion all around her.

Egypt in Western Novels

The Alexandria Quartet by Lawrence Durrell is essential reading perhaps, but to visit Alexandria looking for the city of the *Quartet* is a bit like heading to London hoping to run into Mary Poppins.

Baby Love by Louisa Young is a smart, hip novel that shimmies between Shepherd's Bush in London and the West Bank of Luxor, as a former belly dancer, now single mother, skirts romance and a violent past.

City of Gold by Len Deighton is a thriller set in wartime Cairo, elevated by solid research. The period detail is fantastic and brings the city to life.

Death on the Nile by Agatha Christie draws on Christie's experiences of a winter in Upper Egypt. An absolute must if you're booked on a cruise.

Although the well-known film of the same name bears little resemblance to the novel, Michael Ondaatje's *The English Patient* – a story of love, desert and destiny in WWII – remains a beautifully written, poetic novel.

Egypt during the war serves as the setting for the trials and traumas of a despicable bunch of expats in *The Levant Trilogy* by Olivia Manning. It has some fabulous descriptions of life in Cairo during WWII, and was filmed by the BBC as *Fortunes of War* starring Kenneth Branagh and Emma Thompson.

A NEW GENERATION

» Youssef Ziedan – Not strictly new generation after more than fifty books, but in the months before the 2011 revolution, this controversial novelist dominated the bestseller lists with a nonfiction work *Arab Theology and the Roots of Religious Violence* (2010).

» Mansoura Ez-Eldin – This journalist, activist and writer was a voice of the 2011 revolution and her novel, *Maryam's Maze*, is considered a masterpiece of imagination and literary form.

» Khaled Al-Khamissi (www.khaledalkhamissi.com) – His wonderful novel *Taxi* consists of essays of the novelist's conversations with Cairene taxi drivers, highlighting the Egyptian passion and sense of humor. His second novel is *Noah's Ark*.

» Muhammad Aladdin (http://alaaeldin.blogspot.com) – This young novelist and activist is very much part of the new literary scene in Cairo, and his second novel, *The Gospel According to Adam,* set in Midan Tahrir, illustrates a society that has lost all certainties.

» Ahmed Alaidy – The author of *Being Abbas El Abd* is part of the same generation, writing with cynicism and humour about the despair of Egypt's youth.

» Ibrahim Abdel Meguid – *No One Sleeps in Alexandria* is an antidote to the mythical Alexandria of Lawrence Durrell. It portrays the city in the same period as the *Quartet* but as viewed by two poor Egyptians.

» Miral al-Tahawy – *The Tent* is a bleak but beautiful tale of the slow descent into madness of a crippled Bedouin girl.

Moon Tiger by Penelope Lively is an award-winning romance, very moving in parts, with events that occurred in Cairo during WWII at its heart.

The Photographer's Wife by Robert Sole is one of three historical romances by this French journalist set in late-19th-century Egypt. They're slow-going but worth it for the fine period detail and emotive stories.

The father-and-son team of screenwriter Wahis Hamed and director Marwan Hamed adapted Alaa Al-Aswany's bestselling *The Yacoubian Building* into a feature film. The budget of over US$3 million was the largest ever seen in Egypt.

Cinema

In the halcyon years of the 1940s and 1950s, Cairo's film studios turned out more than 100 movies annually, filling cinemas throughout the Arab world with charming musicals that are still classics of regional cinema. These days, Cairo is still a major player in the film industry, but only about 20 films are made each year. The chief reason for the decline, according to the producers, is excessive government taxation and restrictive censorship. Asked what sort of things are censored, one film industry figure replied, 'Sex, politics, religion – that's all'. However, at least one Cairo film critic has suggested that another reason for the demise of local film is that so much of what is made is of poor quality. The ingredients of the typical Egyptian film are shallow plot lines, farcical slapstick humour, over-the-top acting and perhaps a little belly dancing.

One Egyptian director who consistently stood apart from the mainstream was Youssef Chahine. Born in 1926, he directed over 35 films and was accorded messiah-like status by critics in Egypt. He has been called Egypt's Fellini and was honoured at Cannes in 1997 with a lifetime achievement award. Chahine's films are also some of the very few Egyptian productions that are subtitled in English or French. Chahine passed away at his home in Cairo in 2008.

His later and more well-known works are 1999's *Al-Akhar* (The Other), 1997's *Al-Masir* (Destiny) and 1994's *Al-Muhagir* (The Emigrant),

EGYPT IN WESTERN CINEMA

With the exception of *Transformers 2: Revenge of the Fallen*, Egypt hasn't been seen much at the cinema in recent years. A large part of the Oscar-sweeping *The English Patient* (1996) was set in the Western Desert and Cairo, but this was silver-screen trickery, achieved with scenic doubles – the Egyptian locations were filmed in Tunisia, and the building interiors were filmed in Venice. The same goes for several other movies such as *The Mummy* (1999) and *The Scorpion King* (2002), all filmed in Morocco. Filmmakers don't head for photogenic Egypt because extortionate taxes are levied on foreign film companies. It wasn't always so, and the 1970s and 1980s in particular resulted in a number of films shot on location in Egypt, most of which you should still be able to find.

» *Ice Cold in Alex* (1958) – Classic wartime thriller about Brits fleeing Rommel's forces across the Western Desert while dreaming of an ice-cold beer in a little bar in Alexandria.

» *The Spy Who Loved Me* (1977) – The Pyramids, Islamic Cairo and Karnak provide glamorous backdrops for the campy, smirking antics of Roger Moore as James Bond.

» *Death on the Nile* (1978) – Agatha Christie's whodunit has Poirot investigating the murder of an heiress on board a Nile cruiser. There's gorgeous scenery but the real mystery is how the boat manages to sail from Aswan down to Karnak in Luxor and back up to Abu Simbel all in the same day.

» *Sphinx* (1980) – adapted from a bestselling novel by Robin Cook *(Coma)*, this is a tale about antiquities smuggling shot entirely in Cairo and Luxor, but from which no one emerges with any credit, except the location scout.

» *Ruby Cairo* (1992) – A wife tracks down her missing-presumed-dead husband to a hideaway in Egypt, but the real star of the film is Cairo, where no cliché is left unturned, including camels, pyramids and feluccas.

SOUNDTRACK OF THE REVOLUTION

The following songs and bands are the soundtrack of the 2011 revolution. Some of these are available internationally; all are on YouTube.

» *Irhal* (Leave) by Ramy Essam – This song made Ramy Essam one of the stars of the revolution; he sang it on stage on February 11, when it was announced that Mubarak had gone.

» *Eid Fi Eid* (Hand in Hand) by The Arabian Knightz – One of the first Egyptian rap bands to release music about the revolution, they filmed a video for their track in Midan Tahrir.

» *Rebel* by The Arabian Knightz, featuring Lauryn Hill – This track was recorded during the first days of the revolution.

» *Thawra* by Rayess Bek – Lebanese band sings about and for the revolution with a background of the slogan 'as-shab yurid thawra' ('the people want revolution') chanted in Midan Tahrir.

» *Sout el Hurriya (Voice of Freedom)* by Amir Eid, Hany Adel, Hawary and Sherif – The YouTube clip shows the song sung by people in Midan Tahrir.

effectively banned in Egypt because of Islamist claims that it portrays scenes from the life of the Prophet. Others to look out for are *Al-Widaa Bonaparte* (Adieu Bonaparte), a historical drama about the French occupation, and *Iskandariyya Ley?* (Alexandria Why?), an autobiographical meditation on the city of Chahine's birth. Chahine also contributed to *11'09"01 September 11,* a short film of 11 minutes, nine seconds, and one frame about the World Trade Center bombing.

Music

Classical

Classical Arabic music peaked in the 1940s and '50s. These were the golden days of a rushing tide of nationalism and then, later, of Nasser's rule when Cairo was the virile heart of the Arab-speaking world. Its singers were icons, and through radio their impassioned words captured and inflamed the spirits of listeners from Algiers to Baghdad.

Chief icon of all was Umm Kolthum, the most famous Arab singer of the 20th century. Her protracted love songs and *qasa'id* (long poems) were the very expression of the Arab world's collective identity. Egypt's love affair with Umm Kolthum was such that on the afternoon of the first Thursday of each month, streets would become deserted as the whole country sat beside a radio to listen to her regular live-broadcast performances. She had her male counterparts in Abdel Halim Hafez and Farid al-Attrache, but they never attracted anything like the devotion accorded 'As-Sitt' (the Lady). She retired after a concert in 1972, and when she died in 1975, her death caused havoc, with millions of grieving Egyptians pouring onto the streets of Cairo.

The Umm Kolthum Museum (p70) opened in Cairo in 2002.

Popular

Ahmed Adawiyya did for Arabic music what punk did to popular music in the West. Throwing out traditional melodies and melodramas, his backstreet, streetwise and, to some, politically subversive songs captured the spirit of the times and dominated popular culture throughout the 1970s. He set the blueprint for a new kind of music known as *al-jeel* (the generation), characterised by a clattering, hand-clapping rhythm overlaid with synthesised twirling and a catchy, repetitive vocal. This evolved

SISTERS ARE DANCIN' IT FOR THEMSELVES *LOUISA YOUNG*

It's easy to forget, when you're being dragged up onto a tiny nightclub stage by a strapping Ukrainian lass in a sequinned bikini, that belly dancing is older than the hills, deeply private and an icon of postfeminism. Men and foreigners tend to see it as a sexual show but for many Arab women – and an increasing number of Western women – it is a personal activity incorporating identity, history and community alongside fun, exercise and girl-bonding.

The Babylonian goddess Ishtar, when she went down to the underworld to get her dead husband Tammuz back, danced with her seven veils at each of the seven entrances. Ancient Egyptian wall paintings, the Bible, Greek legend and *The Thousand and One Nights* are full of women dancing by and for themselves and each other. Salome's dance for Herod – the seven veils again – was so powerful because she was bringing into public what normally only happened in the women's quarters.

Arab domestic dancing nowadays tends to involve tea, cakes, female friends and relations, little girls and old ladies, a scarf around the hips and a lot of laughter and gossip. Western versions, particularly in the US and Germany, are the bastard children of aerobics classes, women's groups, new-age-goddess awareness, and for some, a female weakness for fancy underwear and showing off in it. Belly dancing is extremely good exercise – for the back, the figure, stamina, sex life. It's also good for the soul – it's an art, and requires the distilled concentration, self-respect and 'heart' necessary to art.

Louisa Young is an author whose work includes the novels Baby Love, Desiring Cairo and Tree of Pearls.

into a more Western-style pop, helmed by Amr Diab, who is often described as the Arab world's Ricky Martin.

Adawiyya's legacy also spawned something called *shaabi* (from the word for popular), much cruder than *al-jeel,* and often with satirical or politically provocative lyrics. The acceptable face of *shaabi* is TV-friendly Hakim, whose albums regularly sell around the million mark. In 2010 *shaabi* singer Mohamed Mounir brought out a song *Ezay?* (How?), that was banned for being too political; he brought it out again with the backdrop of the people in Midan Tahrir during the 2011 revolution.

During the revolution popular pop stars such as Amr Diab bolted for London in his private jet while some others came out in support of Mubarak. But after Mubarak was ousted, they changed their tune and pop became more political, some of it called 'Martyr Pop'.

Anyone interested in contemporary art should visit the Mashrabia or Townhouse galleries (p70) in Cairo.

The uprisings of the revolutionary youth in Cairo and elsewhere was fuelled by rap and hip-hop music, the so-called *shebabi* (youth) music. Egyptian and Arab MCs, living in the Arab world and in the diaspora, such as US rapper Freeway, Syrian-American rapper Omar Offendum, and Iraqi journalist and MC Narcicyst in Canada, among others, brought out songs about the Egyptian revolution.

Visual Arts

Visual artists have been documenting the people's uprising, first in Midan Tahrir, and then across galleries in Cairo. The artist and musician Ahmed Bassiouny, killed on the third day of the revolution, had his work shown posthumously at the 2011 Venice Biennale. The art scene in Egypt is energetic and is enjoying a chaotic freedom following the 2011 revolution. But like so much else in the country, no one is entirely sure of where it's going.

Since the revolution graffiti artists have made the streets their canvas. As an Egyptian graffiti artist said in an interview: 'Creating graffiti involves taking ownership of the streets, just like we did during the uprising. And so of course it's political, and illegal.' Check the Facebook page Graffiti of Cairo.

Belly Dancing

Tomb paintings in Egypt prove that the tradition of formalised dancing goes back as far as the pharaohs. During medieval times the *ghawazee*, a cast of dancers, travelled with storytellers and poets and performed publicly. In the 19th century the Muslim authorities were outraged that Muslim women were performing for 'infidel' men on their Grand Tour, and dancers were banished from Cairo to Esna. Belly dancing began to gain credibility and popularity in Egypt with the advent of cinema, which imbued belly dancing with glamour and made household names of a handful of dancers.

Since the early 1990s Islamist conservatives have patrolled weddings in poor areas of Cairo and forcibly prevented women from dancing or singing, cutting off a vital source of income for lower-echelon performers. At the same time, a number of high-profile entertainers donned the veil and retired, denouncing their former profession as sinful. Now few Egyptian belly dancers perform in public, and their place has been taken by foreigners mainly dancing for tourists. The future for Egyptian belly dancing looks pretty bleak.

One of Egypt's most famous belly dancers, Soheir el-Babli, renounced show business and adopted the Islamic veil in 1993, setting off a wave of religiously motivated resignations among the country's belly-dance artists.

Egyptian Cuisine: Bi-l Hana wa-Shifa!

Bon appétit, or more literally 'with health and gratification'! Compared with the fabulous regional cuisines of Lebanon, Turkey and Iran, Egyptian food might seem to lack refinement and diversity, but the food here is good, honest peasant fare that packs an occasional sensational punch.

True to their Middle Eastern roots, Egyptian meals typically centre on lightly spiced lamb or chicken, though there's enough coastline to reel in the fruits of the sea. Of course, even meat lovers will wait in line for hot and crispy ta'amiyya, as Cairenes call felafel, the ubiquitous Middle Eastern vegetarian staple.

There is always room for dessert in Egypt, accompanied by a glass of equally sweet tea or a cup of thick, knock-your-socks-off-strong coffee. Just when your stomach is about to explode, signal your waiter to bring an apple-scented sheesha (water pipe) – regular smokers swear a few long puffs can not only settle the stomach but also relax the mind and calm the nerves.

Staples & Specialities

Mezze

Largely vegetable based and always bursting with colour and flavour, mezze (a selection of hot and cold starters) aren't strictly Egyptian, as many standards hail from the Levant or Turkey. But they have been customised here in a more limited and economical form. They're the perfect start to any meal, and it's usually perfectly acceptable for diners to order an entire meal from the mezze list and forego the mains.

Bread

'A'aish' (bread) is the most important staple of the national diet. 'A'aish baladi', the traditional bread, is made from a combination of plain and wholemeal flour with sufficient leavening to form a pocket and soft crust, and is cooked over an open flame. Locals use it in lieu of cutlery to scoop up dips, and rip it into pieces to wrap around morsels of meat. 'A'aish shammy', a bigger version made with plain white flour only, is the usual wrapping for ta'amiyya. In the countryside, the women bake a round leavened bread with three handles – the same shape in which the ancient Egyptians made bread. Bakeries also sell a sweetish white Western-style roll, called kaiser, often served in restaurants or hotels for breakfast.

A TABLE OF MEZZE

» Hummus – A paste of mashed chickpeas with lemon, garlic and tahini.

» Tahini – A paste of sesame seeds with oil, garlic and lemon, served with pita bread or grilled fish.

» *Baba ghanoog* – A puree of grilled aubergines with garlic and oil.

» *Wara ainab* – Vine leaves stuffed with rice, herbs and meat, cooked in a broth.

» *Makhallal* – Pickled vegetables, spiked with red chilli – try the eggplant.

» *Bessara* – Cold broad-bean puree.

» *Kibbeh* – Fried patty of bulgur wheat stuffed with minced lamb and pine nuts.

» *Sambusas* – Cheese- or meat-filled mini pies.

» *Torshi* – Crunchy pickled cucumbers, carrots and turnips.

Salads

Simplicity is the key to Egyptian salads, which are eaten as a mezze or as an accompaniment to a meat or fish main. The standard *salata baladi* of chopped tomatoes, cucumber, onion and pepper sometimes gets a kick from peppery arugula. The Middle East's delicious and healthy signature salad, tabbouleh (bulgur wheat, parsley and tomato, with a sprinkling of sesame seeds, lemon and garlic), is also common. Seasonal vegetables, such as beetroot or carrots, are often boiled and served cold with a tangy oil-and-lemon dressing.

Vegetables & Soups

In Egypt there's none of the Western practice of preparing vegetables that are out of season – here tomatoes are eaten when they're almost bursting out of their skins with sweet juices, eggplant is picked when it's heavy and firm, and cucumbers are munched when they're crisp and sweet.

The archetypal Egyptian veg is *molokhiyya,* a leafy green that was known to be part of the pharaohs' diet. It has a similar sticky texture to okra, and Egyptians prepare it as a slimy and surprisingly sexy soup with a bright, nourishing flavour. Traditionally served as an accompaniment to rabbit, it inspires an almost religious devotion among locals.

A big meal isn't complete without a soup. The most popular is *shurbat ads* (lentil soup), made with red split lentils and served with cumin and wedges of lemon. *Fuul nabed* (broad-bean soup) is also common.

Meats

Kofta and kebab are two of the most popular meat dishes in Egypt. *Kofta,* spiced minced lamb or beef peppered with spices and shaped into balls, is skewered and grilled. It is the signature element of the Egyptian favourite *daood basha,* meatballs cooked with pine nuts and tomato sauce in a *tagen* (clay pot). Kebab is skewered and flame-grilled chunks of meat, normally lamb (the chicken equivalent is called *shish tawooq*). The meat usually comes on a bed of *baqdounis* (parsley), and may be served in upmarket restaurants with grilled tomatoes and onions; otherwise you eat it with bread, salad and tahini.

Firekh (chicken) roasted on a spit is common, and in restaurants is typically ordered by the half. *Hamam* (pigeon) is also extremely popular, and is eaten stuffed and roasted, grilled or as a *tagen* with onions, tomatoes and rice.

TRAVEL YOUR TASTEBUDS

» *Fatta* – A dish involving rice and bread soaked in a garlicky-vinegary sauce with lamb or chicken, which is then oven cooked in a *tagen* (clay pot). It's very heavy; after eating retire to a chaise longue.

» *Mahshi kurumb* – These rice- and meat-stuffed cabbage leaves are decadently delightful when correctly cooked with plenty of dill and lots of sinful *samna* (clarified butter).

» *Molokhiyya* – A slightly slippery soup made from a green mallow. When properly prepared with rabbit and plenty of garlic, it's quite delicious.

» *Hamam mahshi* – Roast pigeon stuffed with *fireek* (green wheat) and rice. This dish is served at all traditional restaurants and can be fiddly to eat; beware the plentiful little bones.

Fish & Seafood

DIY Food

» www.egyptian food.org: dozens of recipes for tasty Egyptian dishes

» www.foodby country.com: a basic overview of Egyptian food and recipes

» www.food timeline.org: the history of food from Mesopotamia through the Middle Ages

When in Alexandria, along the Red Sea and in Sinai, you'll undoubtedly join the locals in falling hook, line and sinker for the marvellous array of fresh seafood on offer. Local favourites are *kalamaari* (squid), *balti (*fish that are about 15cm long, flattish and grey with a light belly), and the larger, tastier *bouri* (mullet). You'll also commonly find sea bass, seabream, red mullet, bluefish, sole and *subeit* or *gambari* (shrimp) on restaurant menus. The Red Sea is famous for its spiny lobsters, while the tilapia from Lake Nasser is a delight. The most popular ways to cook fish are to grill them over coals or fry them in olive oil.

Quite rare on the menu, but popular at home, is *betarekh,* dried salted cod roe, served with bread and olive oil. Copts are very fond of *fesikh,* traditionally eaten during the Sham an-Nessim festival, a spring celebration that goes back to ancient times. *Fesikh* is a traditional Egyptian dish of sun-dried, salted and fermented grey mullet, from the Mediterranean or from the Red Sea. The shops selling *fesikh* are recognisable by the smell; the recipe for the preparation is given from father to son, and the flavour is an acquired taste.

Desserts & Sweets

Omm Ali

Omm ali is said to have been introduced into Egypt by Miss O'Malley, an Irish mistress of Khedive Ismail; another tradition has it that it was prepared to mark the murder of Omm Ali (Mother of Ali), the wife of a 13th-century sultan of Egypt, by her rival.

If you have a sweet tooth, be prepared to flex it on your travels in Egypt. The prince of local puds is *mahallabiye,* a concoction like blancmange, made using rice flour, milk, sugar and rose or orange water, topped with chopped pistachios and almonds. Almost as popular are *ruz bi laban* (rice pudding) and *omm ali* (layers of *fiteer* pastry with nuts and raisins, soaked in cream and milk, and baked in the oven).

Best of all are the pastries, including *kunafa,* a vermicelli-like pastry soaked in syrup, or rolled and stuffed with nuts, that is often associated with feasts and is always eaten in Ramadan. The most famous of all pastries is baklava, made from delicate filo drenched in syrup. Variations on baklava are flavoured with fresh nuts or stuffed with wickedly rich clotted cream *(ishta).*

Drinks

Tea & Coffee

Drinking *shai* (tea) is the signature pastime of the country, and it is seen as strange and decidedly antisocial not to sip the tannin-laden beverage at regular intervals throughout the day. *Shai* usually comes as a strong brew of local leaves, ground fine and left in the bottom of the glass, or served 'English'-style, as a teabag plonked in a cup or glass of hot water (Lipton is the usual brand). It is usually served sweet; to moderate this, order it *sukar khafif* – with 'a little sugar'. If you don't want any sugar, ask for *min ghayr sukar*. Far more refreshing is *shai* served with mint leaves: ask for *shai bi-na'na*. In winter locals love to drink sweet *shai bi-haleeb* (tea with milk).

Arabic coffee (ahwa), traditionally served in coffeehouses, is a thick and powerful Turkish-style brew that's served in small cups and drunk in a couple of short sips. As with tea, you have to specify how much sugar you want: *ahwa mazboot* is a moderate amount of sugar, *ahwa saada* is without sugar, and *ahwa ziyada* (extra sweet) will likely make your teeth fall out on contact. Traditionally you can tell your future from the coffee mud left at the bottom. In hotels and Western-style restaurants you are more likely to be served instant coffee (always called *neskafe*), although upmarket places increasingly serve Italian-style espressos and cappuccinos.

Before There Was Starbucks

The coffeehouse, known as ahwa (the Arabic word for coffee is now synonymous with the place in which it's drunk), is one of the great Egyptian social institutions. Traditionally ahwas have been all-male preserves, but it's now common to see young, mixed-sex groups of Egyptians in ahwas, especially in Cairo and Alexandria. The ahwa is a relaxed and unfussy place where regulars go every day to sip a glass of tea, meet friends, talk about politics or wind down for the night. The hubbub of conversation is usually accompanied by the incessant slamming of *domina* (dominoes) and *towla* (backgammon) pieces, and the burbling of smokers drawing on their sheeshas.

A feature of coffeehouses from Alexandria to Aswan, sheesha is a pastime that's as addictive as it is magical. Most people opt for tobacco soaked in apple juice *(tuffah)* but in trendier places it's also possible to order strawberry, melon, cherry or mixed-fruit flavours. A decorated glass pipe filled with water will be brought, hot coals will be placed in it to get it started and you will be given a disposable plastic mouthpiece to slip over the pipe's stem. The only secret to a good smoke is to take a puff every now and again to keep the coals hot. Bliss!

Of course, it's worth mentioning that even though the smoke from sheesha is filtered through water and tastes nothing like the tobacco from cigarettes, it's smoke nevertheless, and the nicotine hit you'll get is far more intense.

Fish Love Power

Ancient Egyptians believed that fish was an aphrodisiac, but they didn't eat catfish. The story went that when the body of the good king Osiris was chopped into pieces by his evil brother Seth, his wife, the goddess Isis, found the pieces strewn all over Egypt. She found all but one, because his penis had been swallowed by a catfish. Even today some Egyptians are reluctant to eat catfish.

FAST FOOD, EGYPTIAN STYLE

Once you've sampled the joys of the traditional Egyptian fast food you'll be hooked. These are the staples:

» *Fuul* – The national dish is an unassuming peasant dish of slow-cooked fava beans with garlic, parsley, olive oil, lemon, salt, black pepper and cumin.

» *Ta'amiyya* (also known as felafel) – Ground broad beans and spices rolled into patties and deep fried, often stuffed in *shammy* bread as a sandwich.

» *Shwarma* – Strips of lamb or chicken sliced from a vertical spit, sizzled on a hot plate with chopped tomatoes and garnish, and then stuffed into *shammy* bread.

» *Kushari* – A vegetarian's best friend: noodles, rice, black lentils, chickpeas and fried onions, with a tangy tomato sauce. Many *kushari* shops also sell *makaroneh bi-lahm*, a baked pasta-and-lamb casserole.

» *Fiteer* – The Egyptian pizza has a thin, flaky pastry base, and is topped with salty haloumi cheese and olives, or comes sweet with jam, coconut and raisins.

WATER FROM THE NILE

Egyptians say that once you drink water from the Nile, you will always come back. Once you drink water from the tap, however, you might not feel like going anywhere – the stuff can be toxic. The exception is in Cairo, where, if you have a hardier constitution, you can drink it without injury – most locals do, even if it tastes heavily of chlorine. Bottled water is cheap and readily available in even the smallest towns, though we encourage the use of iodine or other sterilizing agents, to cut down on waste.

Beer & Wine

For beer in Egypt just say 'Stella'. Not to be confused with the Belgian lager, it's been brewed and bottled in Cairo now for more than 100 years. Light and perfectly drinkable, the beer shook off its dodgy reputation when it was privatized in 1997, then bought by Heineken in 2002. It now has sister brews in crisp, lower-alcohol Sakara Gold and the dangerous Sakara King (10%). Most locals just stick to the unfussy basic brew – it's the cheapest (around E£15 in restaurants) and, as long as it's cold, it tastes fine.

> The delicious drink *karkadai* is famous for 'strengthening the blood' (lowering blood pressure).

Over the past decade, Egyptian wine has improved significantly, though this still puts it on the lower end of drinkable. For the better wines, such as the Château des Rêves cabernet sauvignon, the grapes are imported from Lebanon. The Gianaclis whites are serviceable. These wines average between E£100 and E£150 per bottle in restaurants throughout the country. Imported wines are both hard to find and prohibitively expensive.

Other Drinks

Over the hot summer months many ahwa-goers opt for cooler drinks such as chilled, crimson-hued *karkadai*, a wonderfully refreshing drink boiled up from hibiscus leaves (it's also served hot in winter). Another refresher is fresh *limoon* (lemon juice), sometimes blended with mint (*bi-nana*). In winter many prefer *sahlab*, a thick warm drink made with the starch from the orchid bulb, milk and chopped nuts; *helba*, a fenugreek tea; or *yansoon*, a digestive aniseed drink.

> **Books for Cooks**
>
> *Egyptian Cooking: A Practical Guide* by Samia Abdennour is published by Hippocrene and is readily available in Egypt.
>
> *The Complete Middle East Cookbook* by Tess Mallos is full of easy-to-follow recipes and devotes an entire chapter to the cuisine of Egypt.

Juice stands are recognisable by the hanging bags of netted fruit (and carrots) that adorn their facades and are an absolute godsend on a hot summer's day. Standard juices (*asiir*) include *moz* (banana), *guafa* (guava), *limoon*, *manga* (mango), *bortuaan* (orange), *rumman* (pomegranate); say *min ghayr sukar* to avoid sugar overload), *farawla* (strawberry) and *qasab* (sugar cane). A glass costs between E£3 and E£10 depending on the fruit used.

Where & When To Eat & Drink

Unfortunately for visitors, the best food in Egypt is invariably in private homes. If you are lucky enough to be invited to share a home-cooked meal, take up the offer (bring a box of sweets for the hostess). But you will most likely be stuffed to the point of bursting – the minute you look close to cleaning your plate, you will be showered with more food, which no amount of protesting can stop.

In restaurants, stick with Egyptian standards and you'll be well fed, if not dazzled by variety. The only place we'd recommend trying other regional cuisines is Cairo, as well as the tourist zones of Luxor, Sharm el-Sheikh and Dahab. In Alexandria, follow locals' lead and dine out in the seafood restaurants – they're some of the best in the region.

DOS & DON'TS

» Remember to always remove your shoes before sitting down on a rug or carpet to eat or drink tea.

» Avoid putting your left hand into a communal dish if you're eating Egyptian style – your left hand is used for, well, wiping yourself in the absence of toilet paper.

» If you need to blow your nose in a restaurant, leave the dining area and go outside or to the toilet.

» Make sure you refrain from eating, drinking or smoking in public during the day-time in the holy month of Ramadan (international hotels are an exception to this rule).

» Always sit at the dinner table next to a person of the same sex unless your host or hostess suggests otherwise.

Egyptians usually dine at a later hour than in the West; it's usual to see diners arrive at a restaurant at 10pm or even later in the cities, particularly in summer. They also dine in large family groups, smoke like chimneys and linger over their meals.

Unless it's a special occasion, the main meal of the day is usually lunch – see p510 for standard restaurant and cafe business hours. At night, Egyptians typically eat lighter or grab snacks. Portion sizes can be enormous at any time, so order with restraint – wasting food is not appreciated.

The New Book of Middle Eastern Food (1968) by Egyptian-born Claudia Roden brought the cuisines of the region to the attention of Western cooks. It's still an essential reference, now updated and expanded, as fascinating for its cultural insights as for its great recipes.

Vegetarians & Vegans

Though it's usual for Egyptians to eat lots of vegetables, the concept of voluntary vegetarianism is quite foreign. Observant Copts follow a vegan diet much of the year (hence the popularity of *kushari*), but more standard Egyptian logic is, 'why would you not eat meat if you can afford it?'

Fortunately, it's not difficult to order vegetable-based dishes. You can eat loads of mezze and salads, fuul, ta'amiyya, the occasional omelette, or oven-baked vegetable *tagen*s with okra and eggplant. When in doubt, you can always order a stack of pita bread and a bowl of hummus. If you do eat fish, note that fresh seafood is nearly always available in tourist towns and along the coasts.

The main cause of inadvertent meat eating is meat stock, which is often used to make otherwise vegetarian *tagen*s and soups. Your hosts or waiter may not even consider such stock to be meat, so they will reassure you that the dish is vegetarian. See the Language chapter (p530) for some useful phrases.

For younger readers, www. historyforkids. org has a great overview of food in ancient Egypt.

Habits & Customs

Egyptians eat a standard three meals a day. For most people breakfast consists of bread and cheese, maybe olives or a fried egg at home, or a fuul sandwich on the run to work. Lunch is the day's main meal, taken

RAMADAN NIGHTS

Ramadan is the Muslim holy month of fasting from sunrise to dusk, but it is also a month of feasting and eating well at night. *Iftar*, the evening meal prepared to break the fast, is a special feast calling for substantial soups, chicken and meat dishes, and other delicacies. It's often enjoyed communally in the street or in large, specially erected tents. Like other celebrations it is also accompanied by a flurry of baking of sweet pastries.

TOP PICKS

» **Kadoura** (p335; Alexandria) The best seafood in the country, especially when the sea has been bountiful.

» **Farahat** (p105; Cairo) Legendary stuffed, roasted pigeon joint, wedged in an alley.

» **Sofra** (p233; Luxor) Original Egyptian decor and a cool roof terrace complement the wonderful Egyptian food and good choice of fresh juices at this charming house restaurant.

» **1902 Restaurant** (p263; Aswan) The grand dining experience of the newly refurbished Old Cataract Hotel has old-world charm, style and some very fine French- and Italian-inspired cuisine. Somewhere to dress up for.

» **Citadel View** (p105; Cairo) Grand setting overlooking the city, with an eclectic menu featuring rarely seen Egyptian dishes.

from 2pm onwards, but more likely around 3pm or 4pm when dad's home from work and the kids are back from school. Whatever's served, the women of the house (usually the mother) will probably have spent most of the morning in the kitchen preparing it, it'll be hot and there'll probably be plenty to go around. Whatever's left over is usually served up again later in the evening as supper.

Environment

The Land

The Nile Valley is home to most Egyptians, with some 90% of the population confined to the narrow carpet of fertile land bordering the great river. To the south the river is hemmed in by mountains and the agricultural plain is narrow, but as the river flows north the land becomes flatter and the valley widens to between 20km and 30km.

To the east of the valley is the Eastern Desert (this is also known as the Arabian Desert), a barren plateau bounded on its eastern edge by a high ridge of mountains that rises to more than 2000m and extends for about 800km. To the west is the Western Desert (also known as the Libyan Desert), which officially comprises two-thirds of the land surface of Egypt. If you ignore the political boundaries on the map, it stretches right across the top of North Africa under its better-known and highly evocative name, the Sahara.

Cairo also demarcates Egyptian geography as it lies roughly at the point where the Nile splits into several tributaries and the valley becomes a 200km-wide delta. Burdened with the task of providing for the entire country, this Delta region ranks among the world's most intensely cultivated lands.

To the east, across the Suez Canal, is the triangular wedge of Sinai. It's a geological extension of the Eastern Desert; the terrain here slopes from the high mountain ridges, which include Mt Sinai and Gebel Katarina (the highest mountain in Egypt at 2642m) in the south, to desert coastal plains and lagoons in the north.

Wildlife

Egypt is about 94% desert – such a figure conjures up images of vast, barren wastelands where nothing can live. However, there are plenty of desert regions where fragile ecosystems have adapted over millennia to extremely hostile conditions. For more information on desert flora, see the boxed text, p391.

> Egypt has four of the world's five officially identified types of sand dunes, including the *seif* (sword) dunes, so named because they resemble the blades of curved Arab swords.

Animals

Egypt is home to about 100 species of mammals, though you'd be lucky to see anything other than camels, donkeys, horses and buffalo. Although Egypt's deserts were once sanctuaries for an amazing variety of larger mammals, such as the leopard, cheetah, oryx, aardwolf, striped hyena and caracal, all of these have been brought to the brink of extinction through hunting. Creatures such as the sand cat, the fennec fox and the Nubian ibex are rarely sighted, and Egyptian cheetahs and leopards have most likely already been wiped out.

There were three types of gazelle in Egypt: the Arabian, dorcas and white. Unfortunately, Arabian gazelles are thought to be extinct, and there are only individual sightings of dorcas and white gazelles, though herds were common features of the desert landscape only 35 years ago.

The zorilla, a kind of weasel, lives in the Gebel Elba region. In Sinai you may see the rock hyrax, a small creature about the size of a large rabbit, which lives in large groups and is extremely sociable.

Less loveable are the 34 species of snake in Egypt. The best known is the cobra, which featured prominently on the headdress of the ancient pharaohs. Another well-known species is the horned viper, a thickset snake that has horns over its eyes. There are also plenty of scorpions, although they're largely nocturnal and rarely seen. Be careful if you're lifting up stones as they like to burrow into cool spots.

Birds

About 430 bird species have been sighted in Egypt, of which about one-third actually breed in Egypt, while most of the others are passage migrants or winter visitors. Each year an estimated one to two million large birds migrate via certain routes from Europe to Africa through Egypt. Most large birds, including flamingos, storks, cranes, herons and all large birds of prey, are protected under Egyptian law.

The most ubiquitous birds are the house sparrow and the hooded crow, while the most distinctive is the hoopoe. This cinnamon-toned bird has a head shaped like a hammer and extends its crest in a dramatic fashion when it's excited. Hoopoes are often seen hunting for insects in gardens in central Cairo, though they're more common in the countryside.

Birding Egypt (www.birdingin egypt.com) serves the Egyptian birding community by listing top birding sites, rarities and travel tips.

Marine Life

For details on Egypt's marine life, see p41.

Plants

The lotus that symbolises ancient Egypt can be found, albeit rarely, in the Delta area, but the papyrus reed, depicted in ancient art in vast swamps where the pharaohs hunted hippos, has disappeared from its natural habitats. Except for one clump found in 1968 in Wadi Natrun, papyrus is now found only in botanical gardens.

NOTABLE NATIONAL PARKS

Egypt has a number of notable national parks:

» **Lake Qarun Protectorate** (p158) Scenic lake important for wintering water birds.

» **Nabq Protectorate** (p405) Southern Sinai coastal strip with the most northerly mangrove swamp in the world.

» **Ras Mohammed National Park** (p393) Spectacular reefs with sheer cliffs of coral; a haven for migrating white storks in autumn.

» **Siwa Reserve** (p304) Three separate areas of natural springs, palm groves, salt lakes and endangered dorcas gazelles.

» **St Katherine Protectorate** (p428) Mountains rich in plant and animal life including Nubian ibex and rock hyrax.

» **Wadi Rayyan Protected Area** (p158) Uninhabited Saharan lake with endangered wildlife.

» **White Desert** (p296) White chalk monoliths, fossils and rock formations.

» **Zerenike Protectorate** (p436) A lagoon on Lake Bardawil that harbours migrating water birds.

RESPONSIBLE TRAVEL

Tourism is vital to the Egyptian economy and the country would be a mess without it. At the same time, millions of visitors a year can't help but add to the ecological and environmental overload. As long as outsiders have been stumbling upon or searching for the wonders of ancient Egypt, they have also been crawling all over them, chipping bits off or leaving their own contributions engraved in the stones. Needless to say, this is not sustainable.

Mass tourism threatens to destroy the very monuments that visitors come to see. At sites such as the Valley of the Kings, thousands of visitors a day mill about in cramped tombs designed for one occupant. The deterioration of the painted wall reliefs alarms archaeologists, whose calls for limits on the number of visitors have largely fallen on deaf ears.

Even the Pyramids, which have so far survived 4500 years, are suffering. Cracks have begun to appear in inner chambers and, in cases such as these, authorities have been forced to limit visitors and to close the great structures periodically to give them some rest and recuperation. It is likely only a matter of time before similar measures are enforced elsewhere.

In the meantime it's up to the traveller to be aware of these serious concerns. Don't be tempted to baksheesh guards so you can use your flash in tombs. Don't clamber over toppled pillars and statues. Don't touch painted reliefs. It's all just common sense.

More than 100 varieties of grass thrive in areas where there is water, and the date palm can be seen in virtually every cultivable area. Along with tamarisk and acacia, the imported jacaranda and Poinciana (red and orange flowers) have come to mark Egyptian summers with their vivid colours.

Environmental Issues

Under A Black Cloud

The Egyptian tortoise, native to the Mediterranean coastal desert, is one of the world's smallest tortoises; most males are less than 9cm long.

Cairo is close to claiming the dubious title of the world's most polluted city. Airborne smoke, soot, dust and liquid droplets from fuel combustion constantly well exceed World Health Organisation (WHO) standards, leading to skyrocketing instances of emphysema, asthma and cancer among the city's population. A startling feature article by Ursula Lindsey published in *Cairo* magazine asserted that as many as 20,000 Cairenes die each year of pollution-related disease and that close to half a million contract pollution-related respiratory diseases.

The government blames the city's pollution on its dry, sandy climate, which leads, it says, to a thick dust rarely cleared by rain. It hasn't commented on other contributing factors such as the increase in 'dirty' industry and Cairo's ever-burgeoning population, a result of people moving to the city from rural areas in search of work.

Cars are, of course, major offenders. Some estimates place over two million cars in the greater Cairo area, and it's clear that this number is increasing every year. Very few run on unleaded petrol; most are poorly maintained diesel-run Fiats and Peugeots that spew out dangerous fumes.

Though factories are officially required to undertake environmental impact assessments and the government lays out a system of incentives and penalties designed to encourage industrial polluters to clean up their acts, few have done so and little is being done to prosecute offenders. Laws designed to have emission levels of vehicles tested don't appear to be regularly enforced. Organisations such as the US Agency for International Development (USAID) are trying to turn the situation around, funding initiatives such as the Cairo Air Improvement project, costing several hundreds of millions of US dollars.

The seriousness of the situation is particularly apparent each October and November, when the infamous 'black cloud' appears over the city. A dense layer of smog that is variously blamed on thermal inversion, rice-straw burning in the Delta, automobile exhaust, burning rubbish and industrial pollution, it is a vivid reminder of an increasingly serious environmental problem.

Impact of Tourism

Ill-planned tourism development remains one of the biggest threats to Egypt's environment, particularly along the Red Sea coast and in Sinai. Following decades of frenzied development along the Red Sea coast, damaged coral reefs now run along most of its length. In Sinai, the coastline near Sharm el-Sheikh has been the site of a building boom for many years, and half-finished resorts are competing for every speck of seafront. Whether the businesspeople investing here will make good on their promises to protect the reefs around the area remains to be seen.

Since the opening of the Nile bridge in Luxor (previously there was only a ferry) many more visitors visit the west bank monuments, causing much damage in the fragile tombs. Several villages built over the tombs have been bulldozed as part of the project to make Luxor the largest open-air museum in the world. Large residential areas in Luxor are also being demolished to clear areas around historical sites, despite protests from some locals and organisations.

Fortunately, there have been some positive developments. A National Parks office (see boxed text p372) has opened in Hurghada and is hoping to rein in some of the more grandiose development plans in the Marsa Alam area. And new 'green' guidelines for running hotels are being trialled under a joint US–Egyptian Red Sea Sustainable Tourism Initiative (RSSTI). Recommendations focus on energy use, water conservation, and the handling and disposal of waste, including simple measures such as installing foot-pedal taps at sinks, which make it harder to leave water running.

Finally, Egypt has an increasing number of high-profile eco-lodges. It started with the fabulous Basata (p426) in Sinai and Adrére Amellal (p312) at Siwa and they appear to have inspired a few others towards environmentally responsible tourism.

National Parks

Egypt currently has 29 'protected areas' in a bid to protect the incredible range of biodiversity in the country, which ranges from river islands and underwater coral reefs to desert ecosystems. However, just what 'protected area' means varies wildly. Take, for instance, the Nile Islands Protected Area, which runs all the way from Cairo to Aswan: nobody is clear which islands are included and most are inhabited and cultivated without restriction. Other sites are closed to the public while some, such as Egypt's oldest national park, Ras Mohammed National Park (p393) in the Red Sea, are popular tourist destinations that have received international plaudits for their eco smarts. Even hunting is allowed in some of the protectorates if you have the right permit from Egyptian environmental authorities.

The problem, as always, is a lack of funding. The Egyptian Environmental Affairs Agency (EEAA) has neither the high-level support nor the resources needed to provide effective management of the protectorates. Some help has arrived through foreign donors and assistance: the

At www.hepca.com you can learn about the efforts of HEPCA (Hurghada Environmental Protection and Conservation Association) to conserve the Red Sea's reefs through public awareness campaigns, direct community action and lobbying efforts.

Natural Selections: A Year of Egypt's Wildlife, written and illustrated by Richard Hoath and published locally by the American University in Cairo Press, is a passionate account of the birds, mammals, insects and marine creatures that make Egypt their home.

ALTERNATIVE ENERGY: EGYPT'S WAVE OF THE FUTURE *HASSAN ANSAH*

One of Egypt's most acclaimed achievements is the High Dam in Aswan, which gave the country the opportunity to generate a large portion of its electricity cleanly and freely. For a country that still relies heavily on thermal power plants, increased reliance on hydropower was definitely a step in the right direction. Hydropower projects are under way in towns like Qanater and Nag Hammadi, and this will hopefully set a precedent for further investment in this industry.

Another form of alternative energy that has huge potential in Egypt is wind power; more precisely, large-scale wind farms. One of the largest wind farms in all of Africa and the Middle East is located in the town of Zafarana, approximately halfway between Cairo and Hurghada. Here, along the windswept Red Sea coast, the average wind speed is 9m/s, which allows a production capability of over 150MW.

There is also a growing business sector in Egypt for diverse forms of solar-power usage, particularly in remote areas that are unable to access the unified power grid. A good example of this is the use of photovoltaics, which are high-powered reflectors that can produce voltage when exposed to sunlight. Photovoltaics are extremely advantageous in that they can be easily utilised for anything from illuminating roads to strengthening scattered mobile-phone signals. Considering that Egypt basks in sunshine virtually year-round, there is an incredible amount of potential in this field.

Of course, despite the progress that has been made so far in the renewable-energy industry within Egypt, significant problems and obstacles for its development remain. There are still heavy government regulations within the energy industry that protect existing large companies and hinder entrepreneurial innovation. As more and more countries start to take drastic steps to reach sustainability in a time of depleting resources, there's reason to be optimistic that Egypt will follow suit. Furthermore, as an influential player in both Africa and the Middle East, Egypt is in a unique position to be able to induce a change in attitude beyond its borders.

Hassan Ansah is a freelance writer and journalist who has taught at the Western International University in Phoenix, Arizona, and at the American University in Cairo (AUC).

Italians at Wadi Rayyan; the EU at St Katherine; and USAID at the Red Sea coast and islands.

High Dam Effect

The Aswan High Dam (p267) and its sibling, Lake Nasser, have been a mixed blessing. They allowed more irrigation for farming, but stopped the rich deposits of silt that were left after the annual flood and fertilised the land. This has led to a serious degradation of Egypt's soil and has made agriculture in Egypt entirely dependent on fertilisers. The annual inundations also used to flush away the salts from the soil. But now that there is no annual flood, the biggest problem facing farmers is the high salinity of the soil.

Soil erosion has also become a major problem, particularly in the Delta region. The Nile has so little outflow and deposits so little silt that the Mediterranean is now gradually eating away the coastline. This also threatens the thriving fishing industry in the Delta lagoons. And, as the rich nutrients of the Nile no longer reach the sea, fish stocks there have been seriously reduced.

Another potentially catastrophic consequence of the dam and lake appears to be the rise in ground water levels. With the water table higher, and salt levels raised, the sandstone blocks of many Egyptian monuments are being eaten away.

You can download a Wadi Rayyan Protected Area atlas, which contains 15 chapters of photos and maps, at www.eiecop.org/ambiente2/projects_2/wadielrayan_atlas.htm.

Survival Guide

Directory A–Z

Accommodation

Rates

» Accommodation in this book is categorised as follows:

- **Budget** ($) Up to E£125
- **Midrange** ($$) E£125–600
- **Top end** ($$$) More than E£600

» Prices listed are for rooms in the winter tourist high season, typically November to February. For budget and most midrange hotels, taxes are included; for high-end hotels, tax is typically separate.

» Breakfast is included in the room price unless indicated otherwise.

» Rates at budget and midrange places can be negotiable in off-peak seasons, generally March to September, except on the Mediterranean coast and during the middle of the week.

» Many hotels will take US dollars or euros in payment, and some higher-end places even request it, though officially this is illegal. Lower-end hotels are usually cash only, though it's not a given that all upmarket hotels accept credit cards.

» Most top-end chains and a few midrange hotels in Egypt offer nonsmoking rooms, though you can't always count on one being available.

Seasons

» Rates often go up by around 10% during the two big feasts (Eid al-Fitr and Eid al-Adha; see boxed text p515) and New Year (20 December to 5 January).

» On the Mediterranean coast, prices may go up by 50% or more in the summer season (approximately 1 July to 15 September).

Types

» Egypt offers visitors the full spectrum of accommodation: hotels, resorts, pensions, B&Bs, youth hostels, cruise boats and even a few camping grounds and ecolodges.

» In Cairo and Upper Egypt, there are options for all budgets, from budget to super-luxury.

» In Middle Egypt (between Cairo and Luxor), options are more limited, with fairly barebones operations that cater to Egyptian travellers only.

» In the oases and much of the Sinai coast (with the exception of Sharm el-Sheikh), budget options range from decent to very good and backpacker-friendly.

» The Red Sea coast and Sharm el-Sheikh are largely dedicated to package tourism. Resorts here typically offer all-inclusive rates that cover most drinks and some activities, though some also offer half- or full-board options (two or three meals). Booking well in advance can yield major discounts, as can booking at the last minute.

Camping

» Officially, camping is allowed at only a few places around Egypt, at a couple of camping grounds and at a few hotels; these facilities are extremely basic.

» To camp in the wilderness, you typically must be with a group. But it's possible to go DIY in a few places in national parks, such as the White Desert; see p296.

» In Sinai the most popular budget choices are beachside camps – all have electricity and 24-hour hot water unless noted in our reviews.

Hostels

» Egypt has eight hostels recognised by **Hostelling International** (HI; www. hihostels.com), where having

---

BOOK YOUR STAY ONLINE

For more accommodation reviews by Lonely Planet authors, check out http://hotels.lonelyplanet.com. You'll find independent reviews, as well as recommendations on the best places to stay. Best of all, you can book online.

a HI card will earn you a discount.

» There are also a number of independent operations offering dorm beds and small private rooms.

» Hostels tend to be noisy and often a bit grimy. In some there are rooms for mixed couples or families but on the whole the sexes are segregated.

» Most of the time you'll be better off staying at a budget hotel instead.

» Reservations are not usually needed.

» Brace yourself for heavy sales pressure for guided tours, especially in Cairo.

Hotels
BUDGET

At the low end, there's little consistency in standards. You can spend as little as E£30 a night for a clean single room with hot water, or E£100 or more for a dirty room without a shower. Generally, rates include a basic breakfast, usually a couple of pieces of bread, a wedge of cheese, a serving of jam, and tea or coffee.

Competition among budget hotels in cities such as Cairo and Luxor is fierce, which keeps standards reasonably high and developing all the time. At this point, most rooms have private bathrooms, but some older hotels still have shared bathrooms only. Air-con is also an option, for an extra E£20. Places that cater to backpackers often have welcoming lounges with satellite TV, internet access and backgammon boards.

Some hotels will tell you they have hot water when they don't. They may not even have warm water. Turn the tap on and check, or look for an electric water heater when inspecting the bathroom. If there's no plug in your bathroom sink, try using the lid of a Baraka mineral-water bottle – it often fits well enough.

PRACTICALITIES

» With the exception of Cairo, tap water in Egypt is not considered safe to drink. In Cairo, a steady diet of tap water can be hard on the stomach, but an occasional glass or ice cube isn't deadly.

» Pack earplugs for noisy Cairo hotel rooms, loud movies on buses and the pre-dawn call to prayer.

» Egypt uses the metric system for weights and measures.

» Egyptian DVDs are region 2 format, the same as Europe.

» Security checkpoints are common on highways outside Cairo. Carry your passport with you.

» Smoking is common in Egypt, including in restaurants and bars. Nonsmoking facilities are rare. Sheesha (hookah or water pipe) is a common social pastime. It delivers substantially more nicotine than you might be used to.

» Alcohol is available, though typically served only at higher-end restaurants. Drinking on the street is taboo, as is public drunkenness.

» International English-language TV news such as CNN and BBC World can be accessed in hotel rooms throughout the country.

» BBC World Service is on the Middle East short-wave schedule, broadcasting from Cyprus. See www.bbc.co.uk/worldservice for details. In Cairo, European-program 95.4FM/557AM runs news in English at 7.30am, 2.30pm and 8pm. Nile Radio 104.2FM (104.2kHz) has English-language pop music.

» The best English newspaper is the *Daily News Egypt*, an insert in the *International Herald-Tribune* (E£14).

» The monthly *Egypt Today* (E£15; also online at www.egypttoday.com) covers social and economic issues.

Many budget establishments economise on sheets and will change linens only on request. Toilet paper is usually supplied, but you'll often need to bring your own soap and shampoo.

MIDRANGE

Midrange options are surprisingly limited, particularly in Cairo and Alexandria, where investment is channelled into top-end accommodation. Moreover, many hotels in this category coast on package-tour bookings. As a result, you could wind up paying more for TV and air-con, in grungy surrounds.

Even if you typically travel in this price bracket, consider budget operations as well – some will be dramatically nicer, for half the price.

TOP END

» Most international luxury and business chains are represented, and amenities are (for the most part) up to international standards.

» Independent luxury hotels can be hit or miss, however, especially at the entry level of this price bracket, so you may want to inspect your room in person before committing any money.

» Most luxury lodging can be booked at a discount in advance, but unlike at cheaper hotels, staff often have little

510

flexibility with set rates in person.

» Beware taxes: quoted rates often don't include them, and they can be as high as 24%.

Activities

See destination chapters for specific options. For wilderness trips you may need military permits, required for the Eastern Desert south of Shams Alam, around Lake Nasser, between Bahariyya and Siwa and off-road in the Western Desert. Safari companies can usually obtain them with two weeks' notice.

Business Hours

The weekend is Friday and Saturday; some businesses close Sunday. During Ramadan, offices, museums and tourist sites keep shorter hours.

Banks 8.30am-2.30pm Sun-Thu

Bars and clubs Early evening until 3am, often later (particularly in Cairo)

Cafes 7am-1am

Government offices 8am-2pm Sun-Thu. Tourist offices are generally open longer.

Post offices 8.30am-2pm Sat-Thu

Private offices 10am-2pm and 4-9pm Sat-Thu

Restaurants Noon-midnight

Shops 9am-1pm and 5-10pm Jun-Sep, 10am-6pm Oct-May

Customs Regulations

» Duty-free allowances on arrival: 1L alcohol, 1L perfume, 200 cigarettes and 25 cigars.

» Up to 48 hours after arrival, you can purchase another 3L alcohol plus up to US$200 in other duty-free articles at dedicated Egypt Free shops at the airport and in Cairo. (Touts in tourist areas may ask you to use

your allotment to buy alcohol for them.)

» Customs Declaration Form D occasionally required for electronics, jewellery and cash.

» Prohibited and restricted articles include tools for espionage as well as books, pamphlets, films and photos 'subversive or constituting a national risk or incompatible with the public interest'.

Discount Cards

The International Student Identity Card (ISIC) gives discounts on museum and site entries. Some travellers have also been able to get the discount with HI cards and Eurail cards. To get an ISIC in Cairo, visit **Egyptian Student Travel Services** (off Map p64; www.estsegypt.com; 23 Sharia al-Manial). You'll need a university ID card, a photocopy of your passport and one photo; the cost is E£90. Beware counterfeit operations in Downtown Cairo.

Electricity

Electricity is generally reliable; Luxor and Upper Egypt occasionally suffer outages.

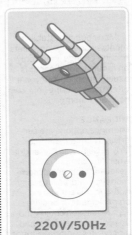

220V/50Hz

Embassies & Consulates

Australia (☏02-2575 0444; www.egypt.embassy.gov.au; 11th fl, World Trade Centre, 1191 Corniche el-Nil, Cairo) Located 1km north of 26th of July Bridge, Cairo.

Canada (off Map p102; ☏02-2791 8700; www.egypt.gc.ca; Sharia Ahmed Raghab, Garden City, Cairo)

Ethiopia (off Map p102; ☏02-3335 3696; 21 Sharia Mohammed al-Ghazali, off Sharia al-Musaddeq, Doqqi, Cairo)

France Alexandria (Map p326; ☏03-484 7950; 2 Midan Orabi, Mansheyya); Cairo (Map p102; www.ambafrance-eg.org; ☏02-3567 3200; www.ambafrance-eg.org; 29 Sharia Charles de Gaulle, Giza)

Germany Alexandria (Map p322; ☏03-486 7503; 9 Sharia el-Fawatem, Bab Sharqi); Cairo (Map p98; ☏02-2728 2000; www.kairo.diplo.de; 2 Sharia Berlin, Zamalek); Hurghada (Map p376; ☏065-344 3605; 365 Sharia al-Gabal al-Shamali)

Iran (Map p102; ☏02-3348 6492; 12 Sharia Refa'a, off Midan al-Misaha, Doqqi, Cairo)

Ireland (Map p98; ☏02-2735 8264; www.embassyofireland.org.eg; 22 Hassan Assem, Zamalek, Cairo)

Israel Alexandria (Map p320; ☏03-544 9501; 15 Sharia Mena, Rushdy); Cairo (Map p102; ☏02-3332 1500; 6 Sharia Ibn Malek, Giza)

Italy Alexandria (Map p326; ☏03-487 9470; 25 Midan Saad Zaghloul); Cairo (Map p102; ☏02-2794 3194; www.ambilcairo.esteri.it; 15 Sharia Abd al-Rahman Fahmy, Garden City)

Jordan (Map p102; ☏02-3749 9912; 6 Sharia Gohainy, Cairo)

Kenya (☏02-3345 3628; www.kenemb-cairo.com; 7 Sharia al-Quds al-Sharif, Mohandiseen, Cairo) Located 800m northwest of Midan Mustafa Mahmoud.

Lebanon Alexandria (Map p322; ☑03-484 6589; 64 Sharia Tariq al-Horreyya); Cairo (Map p98; ☑02-2738 2823; 22 Sharia Mansour Mohammed, Zamalek)

Libya Alexandria (Map p322; ☑03-494 0877; 4 Sharia Batris Lumomba, Bab Sharqi); Cairo (Map p98; ☑02-2735 1269; 7 Sharia al-Saleh Ayoub, Zamalek)

Netherlands (☑02-2739 5500; http://egypt.nlembassy. org; 18 Sharia Hassan Sabry, Zamalek, Cairo) It's 1km north of 26th of July Bridge.

New Zealand (Map p98; ☑02-2461 6000; www.nzem bassy.com; levle 8, North Tower, Nile City Towers, 2005 Corniche el-Nil, Cairo)

Saudi Arabia Alexandria (Map p322; ☑03-497 7951; 12 Sharia Jabarti); Cairo (Map p102; ☑02-3761 4308; 2 Sharia Ahmed Nessim, Giza); Suez (Map p362; ☑062-333 4016; 10 Sharia Abbas al-Akkad, Port Tawfiq)

Spain Alexandria (Map p323; ☑0100 340 7177; 101 Sharia Tariq al-Horreyya); Cairo (Map p98; ☑02-2735 6462; embespeg@mail.mae.es; 41 Sharia Ismail Mohammed, Zamalek)

Sudan Aswan (Map p254; ☑097-230 7231; Bldg 20, Atlas; ☺9am-3pm); Cairo (Map p102; ☑02-2794 9661; 3 Sharia al-Ibrahimi, Garden City)

Syria (Map p102; ☑02-3335 8805; 18 Abdel Rahim Sabry, Doqqi, Cairo)

Turkey Alexandria (Map p322; ☑03-399 0700; 11 Sharia Kamel el-Kilany); Cairo (off Map p64; ☑02-2797 8400; 25 Sharia Falaki, Mounira)

UK Alexandria (Map p320; ☑03-546 7001; Sharia Mena, Rushdy); Cairo (Map p102; ☑02-2791 6000; www. ukinegypt.fco.gov.uk; 7 Sharia Ahmed Ragheb, Garden City)

USA (Map p102; ☑02-2797 3300; www.egypt.usembassy. gov; 5 Sharia Tawfiq Diab, Garden City, Cairo)

Food

In this book, restaurants are assigned a budget rating based on the price of a typical main dish:

Budget ($) Up to E£15

Midrange ($$) E£15–75

Top end ($$$) More than E£75

Many restaurants do not quote taxes (10%) in the menu prices, and will also add 12% for 'service', but this is typically used to cover waitstaff salaries and is not strictly a bonus. So an additional cash tip, paid directly to your server, is nice.

Overall, tipping is appreciated in budget places, advisable in midrange places and essential in all top-end restaurants.

Most budget restaurants do not serve alcohol.

For more information about eating out in Egypt, see p494.

Gay & Lesbian Travellers

Egypt is a conservative society that condemns homosexuality but, at the same time, plenty of same-sex activity goes on. The scene is strictly underground.

Tapping into it can be tricky because signals are ambiguous, as Egyptian men routinely hold hands, link arms and give each other kisses on greeting.

Typically, only the passive partner in a gay relationship is regarded as gay, so foreign male visitors may receive blatant and crudely phrased propositions from Egyptian men. Bar the occasional young crusader, few Egyptian men would openly attest to being gay.

Homosexuality is not strictly criminalised, but statutes against obscenity and public indecency have been used to prosecute gay men, most notably 52 arrested in a raid in Cairo in 2001. Despite a few vocal protesters calling for gay rights during the 2011 revolution, the situation remains tense, and a proposed Pride march in January 2012 was cancelled following aggressive criticism.

The main gay and lesbian Egypt site is www.gayegypt. com, though its basic guide info is not kept up to date.

Health

Before You Go

No vaccines are required for Egypt, but check the status of standard injections (diphtheria, tetanus, pertussis, polio, measles, mumps and rubella), as boosters in adulthood are now recommended for many. In addition, consider the following:

» **Hepatitis A and B** Administered together or separately, at least two weeks before travel

» **Rabies** Only if you'll be in remote areas near animals

» **Typhoid** At least two weeks before travel

» **Yellow fever** Required if you're coming from or travelling to certain countries in southern Africa, including Sudan

Travel insurance is highly recommended, particularly coverage with emergency evacuation services, as road accidents and the like are quite common. Also see your doctor and dentist before travelling. Consider registering with the **International Association for Medical Assistance to Travellers** (IAMAT; www.iamat.org) for a list of reputable doctors.

For longer trips, Lonely Planet's *Africa: Healthy Travel* is packed with advice on pre-trip planning, emergency first aid, immunisation and disease information, as well as what to do if you get sick on the road.

In Egypt

Health care Excellent standards in private and university hospitals, but patchier elsewhere. Dental care is variable. Be prepared to pay upfront for all medical and dental treatment.

Hospitals You may need to provide medicine and sterile dressings from a pharmacy. Nursing care may be rudimentary, as this is something families and friends are expected to provide.

Hygiene Standards are low. Always wash hands thoroughly before and after eating, and choose restaurants with high turnover.

Pharmacies For minor illnesses, consult a pharmacist first. They are well trained, speak English and can dispense all kinds of medication.

Water Generally not safe, but in Cairo tap water is heavily chlorinated and relatively drinkable. We recommend iodine or the Steripen (www.steripen. com) to reduce the use of plastic bottles.

Specific Health Risks

Heat exhaustion is common, given the shadeless settings of most archaeological sites, as well as a lack of sanitary restrooms, which might lead you to drink less water than is required. Symptoms include headache, dizziness and tiredness and can progress to vomiting if untreated. Drink liquids (ideally sports drinks or water with rehydrating salts) before you're thirsty and wear a hat to keep off the sun. Treat yourself to an air-con hotel if necessary.

Heatstroke A much more serious condition, caused by a breakdown in the body's heat-regulating mechanism, that can cause death if untreated. This leads to irrational behaviour, a cessation of sweating and loss of consciousness. Rapid cooling with ice and water, plus intravenous fluid replacement, is required.

Insect bites and stings More annoying than toxic, but look out for sandflies on Mediterranean beaches, and mosquitoes. All bites are at risk of infection, so it's better to avoid them in the first place, with a DEET-based repellent.

Rift Valley fever A rare haemorrhagic fever spread through blood, including from infected animals. It causes a flulike illness with fever, joint pains and occasionally more serious complications. Complete recovery is possible.

Schistosomiasis (bilharzia) An infection of the bowel and bladder caused by a freshwater fluke. It can be contracted through the skin. Avoid all stagnant water, canals and slow-running rivers. Symptoms include a transient fever and rash and, in advanced cases, blood in the stool or in the urine. A blood test can detect antibodies if you have been exposed, and treatment is then possible.

Travellers' diarrhoea This and other mild food poisoning are virtually unavoidable, as food hygiene standards are not high. The best cure is rest, fluids (best with oral rehydration salts, sold as Rehydran in Egypt) and a cool environment. If symptoms persist more than 72 hours or are accompanied by a fever, see a doctor.

Tuberculosis TB is common in Egypt, though nowhere near as rampant as in sub-Saharan Africa. The respiratory infection is spread through close contact and occasionally through milk or milk products. Risk is high only for people in teaching positions or health care.

Typhoid Spread through contaminated food or water and marked by fever or a pink rash on the abdomen.

Yellow fever Mosquito-borne and extremely rare in Egypt. If you need a vaccination for onward travel to

Sudan, you can obtain it at the medical clinic in Terminal 1 of Cairo airport, or at the Giza governorate building (next to the Giza Court by the train station). It costs approximately E£100.

Insurance

» Travel insurance to cover theft, loss and medical problems is a good idea.

» Some policies exclude 'dangerous activities', which can include scuba diving, motorcycling and trekking.

» Insure yourself to the gills if you're driving. Road conditions are hazardous.

» For the same reason, check that the policy covers ambulances and an emergency flight home.

» Worldwide travel insurance is available at www. lonelyplanet.com/travel_ services. You can buy, extend and claim online any time, even if you're already on the road.

Internet Access

» Widely available throughout Egypt, though not always fast.

» Internet cafes are common, if not rampant; rates

are usually between E£5 and E£10 per hour.

» Free wi-fi is surprisingly rare in Cairo and Alexandria, but most hotels offer it (we mark these with 🛜, or @ if only a fixed connection is available).

» In Siwa and Dahab, there are pay-as-you-go services that offer wi-fi all around town for E£10 to E£15 per day.

» A mobile dongle (USB adaptor) for your laptop gives access anywhere with mobile-phone coverage. Vodafone charges E£99 for the USB stick, plus E£50 per 500MB of data.

Language Courses

Studying Arabic in Egypt is popular because the dialect is understood throughout the Arab world, and classes are plentiful and inexpensive. You're entitled to a student visa only if enrolled at an accredited university such as the American University in Cairo (AUC), so bear in mind the need for extending your tourist visa.

Alexandria

Qortoba Institute for Arabic Studies (Map p320; ☑03-556 2959; www.qortoba. net; cnr Muhammad Nabeel Hamdy & Khalid Bin Waleed, Miami; from per hr €5; ☉9am-4pm Sun-Thu) Private tuition options as well as student apartments.

Cairo

Arabic Language Institute (ALI; Map p64; www.aucegypt. edu) For college students or postgrads, this department of the American University in Cairo is the strongest option, but the campus is isolated.

International Language Institute (ILI; off Map p98; ☑02-3346 3087; www.arabic egypt.com; 4 Sharia Mahmoud Azmi, Mohandiseen; 4-week course from €245) The largest school in Cairo, so able to offer the biggest range

of levels. Two-week and four-week sessions. Excellent Egyptian-colloquial textbooks.

Kalimat (Map p98; ☑02-3761 8136; www.kalimategypt.com; 22 Sharia Mohammed Mahmoud Shaaban, Mohandiseen; 4-week course from E£1440) Smaller than ILI, but more convenient Cairo location.

Luxor

Department of Contemporary Arabic Teaching (DEAC; Map p196; ☑0100 639 3466; www.cfcc-eg.com; Gezira al-Bayrat; 2-week course E£2300) This branch of the French Centre for Culture and Cooperation runs a range of Arabic courses at the Hotel Sheherazade.

Sinai

Magana Camp (www.alma gana.de) This beach camp between Taba and Nuweiba runs summer and winter programs, two to six weeks, with three hours of study a day. See the Magana Camp group on Facebook.

Legal Matters

Foreign travellers are subject to Egyptian laws and get no special consideration. If you are arrested you have the right to telephone your embassy immediately (see p510).

Bribes Egypt is notoriously corrupt, but don't assume this means you can pay your way through. You may encounter an official who'd like to further exploit the awkward situation you're in, and of course, your bribe only perpetuates the system.

Drugs Drug use can be penalised by hanging, and you'll get no exemption just because you're a tourist. That said, you will no doubt be offered at least hashish during your travels, especially in the backpacker-friendly zones of Sinai. We can't recommend it.

Political activity Post-revolution, police are particularly suspicious of 'foreign agitators' or anyone who could be perceived as such, including journalists. Both writers and foreign students have been detained on charges of abetting violence. It's best to avoid political affiliation of any kind, and avoid taking photos of government buildings and other sensitive areas.

Maps

Nelles Verlag has one of the most complete general maps of Egypt (scale 1:2,500,000), including a map of the Nile Valley (scale 1:750,000) and a good enlargement of central Cairo. You can find it and a number of other good maps at the AUC bookshop in Cairo; elsewhere in Egypt, selection dwindles.

The top pick for drivers is the Kümmerly & Frey map, which covers all of Egypt on a scale of 1:825,000, though it was last updated in 2000. The Freytag & Berndt map is a lesser scale (1:1,200,000) but includes insets of Cairo and central Alexandria.

Money

Change There is a severe shortage of small change, which is invaluable for tips, taxi fares and more. Withdraw odd amounts from ATMs to avoid a stack of unwieldy E£200 notes, hoard small bills and always try to break big bills at fancier establishments.

Costs For information on costs in Egypt, see p14.

Currency Egyptian pound (E£), *guinay* in Arabic, divided into 100 piastres (pt).

Exchange rate The government sets the exchange rate, and it is fairly stable, changing incrementally only every few years. There is no real black-market exchange. Rates for a range of foreign currencies are given on p15.

TIPPING IN EGYPT

Baksheesh culture is strong – when in doubt, tip.

SERVICE	TIP
Ahwa or cafe	E£1 or E£2
Hotel staff (collective)	E£5-10 per guest per day
Informal mosque or monument guide	E£5-10 (more if you climb a minaret)
Meter taxi	10%
Restaurant	10%
Shoe attendant in mosque	E£1
Toilet attendant	E£1 or E£2

Foreign currency Some tour operators and hotels insist on US dollars or euros, even though this is technically illegal. It's a good idea to travel with a small stash of hard currency, though increasingly you can pay by credit card.

Notes and coins Coins of 5pt, 10pt and 25pt are basically extinct; 50pt notes and coins are on their way. E£1 coins are the most commonly used small change, while E£5, E£10, E£20, E£50, E£100 and E£200 notes are commonly used.

Prices Produce markets and some other venues sometimes write prices in piastres: E£3.50 as 350pt, for example.

ATMs

Cash machines are common, except in Middle Egypt and the oases, where you may find only one. Then you'd be stuck if there's a technical problem, so load up before going somewhere remote. Banque Misr, CIB, Egyptian American Bank and HSBC are the most reliable.

Credit Cards

All major cards are accepted in midrange-and-up establishments. In remote areas they remain useless. You may be charged a percentage of the sale (anywhere between 3% and 10%).

Retain receipts to check later against your statements as there have been cases of shop owners adding extra zeros.

Visa and MasterCard can be used for cash advances at Banque Misr and the National Bank of Egypt, as well as at Thomas Cook offices.

Moneychangers

Money can be officially changed at Amex and Thomas Cook offices, as well as commercial banks, foreign exchange (forex) bureaus and some hotels. Rates don't vary much, but forex bureaus usually don't charge commission.

US dollars, euros and British pounds are the easiest to change (and can be changed back at the end of your stay). Inspect the bills you're given, and don't accept any badly defaced, shabby or torn notes because you'll have difficulty offloading them later.

Travellers Cheques

The only reliable place to cash travellers cheques in Egypt is at the issuing office (Amex or Thomas Cook) in Cairo, Alexandria, Luxor, Aswan, Hurghada and Sharm el-Sheikh. Forex bureaus don't handle them, and even the major banks are unreliable.

Photography

» Egyptians on the whole, and Egyptian women in particular, are relatively camera-shy, so you should always ask before taking pictures.

» Photos are theoretically prohibited inside ancient tombs, though guards often encourage camera use in exchange for tips.

» To combat the glare of sun, a UV filter is recommended.

» A standard daylight filter helps keep dust off your lens. Also pack compressed air and cleaning cloths.

» Avoid taking photos of anything that could be considered of military or other strategic importance. Taking photos out of bus windows especially provokes suspicion.

» Lonely Planet's *Travel Photography*, by Richard l'Anson, provides excellent advice on gear and taking photos on the road.

Post

Parcels Surface mail to the USA, Australia or Europe costs roughly E£150 for the first kilogram, and E£40 for each thereafter. Usually only the main post office in a city will handle parcels; bring them unsealed so the contents can be inspected for customs. Clerks usually have cartons and tape on hand. Many shops provide shipping of goods for a relatively small fee.

Poste restante The service functions well and is generally free. If the clerk can't find your mail, ask him or her to check under Mr, Ms or Mrs in addition to your first and last names.

Service In recent years Egypt Post (☎0800 800 2800; www.egyptpost.org) has improved, and it's reasonably reliable. The express service (EMS) is downright speedy.

Stamps Available at yellow-and-green-signed post offices and some shops and hotels.

Public Holidays

See the 'Major Islamic Holidays' boxed text (right) for additional days on which businesses and government offices close.

New Year's Day (1 Jan) Official national holiday but many businesses stay open.

Coptic Christmas (7 Jan) Most government offices and all Coptic businesses close.

January 25 Revolution Day (25 Jan)

Sham an-Nessim (Mar/Apr) First Monday after Coptic Easter, this tradition with Pharaonic roots is celebrated by all Egyptians, with family picnics. Few businesses close, however.

Sinai Liberation Day (25 Apr) Celebrating Israel's return of the peninsula in 1982.

May Day (1 May) Labour Day.

Revolution Day (23 Jul) Date of the 1952 coup, when the Free Officers seized power from the monarchy.

Armed Forces Day (6 Oct) Celebrating Egyptian successes during the 1973 war with Israel, with some military pomp.

Safe Travel

The incidence of crime, violent or otherwise, in Egypt is negligible compared with most Western countries, and you're generally safe walking around day or night. Following the 2011 revolution, after which police activity was severely curtailed, there has been a spike in petty crime, though it is statistically still quite rare and easily avoided.

Apart from the issues discussed here, you should be aware that the Egyptian authorities take a hard view of illegal drug use (see p513).

Theft

Since 2011, bag and wallet snatchings have been on the rise, usually as drive-bys on mopeds, though very occasionally at knifepoint or gunpoint. Don't let this deter you: you're still more likely to lose your wallet in Barcelona. Simple street-smart precautions should suffice: carry your bag across your body or at least on the side away from the street, and keep it looped around a chair leg in restaurants. Don't walk on empty streets past 1am or 2am. Be aware of your surroundings when you take your wallet out, and don't go to an ATM alone at night.

More common theft, such as items stolen from locked hotel rooms and even from safes, continues, so secure your belongings in a locked suitcase.

Generally, though, unwary visitors are parted from their money through scams, and these are something that you really do have to watch out for; see p517.

Shopping

So great is the quantity of junk souvenirs in Egypt that it can easily hide the good stuff, but if you persist you'll

---

MAJOR ISLAMIC HOLIDAYS

The Islamic calendar is based on the lunar year, approximately 11 days shorter than the Gregorian calendar, so holidays shift through the seasons. These are the principal religious holidays in Egypt, which can cause changes to bus schedules and business openings.

Moulid an-Nabi The birthday of the Prophet Mohammed, and children receive gifts.

Eid al-Fitr (Feast of Fast-Breaking) The end of Ramadan, essentially a three-day feast.

Eid al-Adha (Feast of the Sacrifice) Commemorates Ibrahim's (Abraham's) sacrifice, and families that can afford it buy a sheep to slaughter. The holiday lasts four days, though many businesses reopen by the third day. Many families go out of town, so if you want to travel at this time, book your tickets well in advance.

Ras as-Sana (New Year's Day) A national day off, but only a low-key celebration.

Dates for Ramadan and Eid al-Fitr are approximate, as they rely on the sighting of the new moon.

HOLIDAY	2012	2013	2014	2015
Moulid an-Nabi	4 Feb	24 Jan	13 Jan	2 Jan
Ramadan begins	20 Jul	9 Jul	28 Jun	17 Jun
Eid al-Fitr	19 Aug	8 Aug	28 Jul	17 Jul
Eid al-Adha	26 Oct	15 Oct	4 Oct	23 Sep
New Year begins	15 Nov (1434)	4 Nov (1435)	24 Oct (1436)	14 Oct (1437)

find some treasures. Shop owners have begun commissioning stylish home items from traditional artisans, with some beautiful results. Also look out for traditional Siwan, Bedouin and Nubian handicrafts, such as embroidery.

The undisputed shopping capital is Cairo's medieval souq, Khan al-Khalili, which is just as much a tourist circus as it is one of the Middle East's most storied markets. There are some treasures to be had, assuming you have the time (and the patience). Increasingly, fixed-price shops in Cairo stock familiar Egyptian crafts, often with better quality than you'd fine in the souq. Prices are of course higher than you'd get through bargaining, but rarely outrageous.

The most popular items include the following:

Appliqué & Fabric

Embroidered cloth in intricate patterns and scenes is available as pillow cases, bedspreads and wall hangings. Stitches should be small and barely visible. Printed fabric used for tents is inexpensive when sold by the meter (about E£10) and a bit more if worked into a tablecloth.

Gold & Silver

A gold cartouche with a name in hieroglyphics is a popular gift, as is a silver pendant with a name in Arabic. Gold and silver are sold by weight. Check the international market price before you buy, then add in a bit extra for work.

Inlay

Wood boxes and other items are inlaid with mother-of-pearl and bone in intricate patterns. Surfaces should be smooth and not gummed with glue. An inlaid backgammon set, with pieces, should cost about E£70.

Muski Glass

This bubble-shot glass in blue, green and brown is made from recycled bottles and fashioned into cups and other home items. It's extremely fragile, so pack it well.

Papyrus

Papyrus dealers are as ubiquitous as perfume shops, and this Egyptian invention makes an easy-to-carry souvenir. True papyrus is heavy and difficult to tear; it should not feel delicate, and veins should be visible when it is held up to the light. Good artwork should be hand-painted, not stamped. A small painting on faux papyrus (made from banana leaves) can go for just E£10; a good-quality piece can easily be 10 times as much.

Perfume

You can't escape Egypt without visiting an essential-oils dealer. Most are less than essential, being diluted with vegetable oil. Be sceptical if a salesman drips more than a tiny drop on your arm, then rubs furiously. And watch when your bottles are packed up – make sure they're filled from the stock you sampled. Lotus (sawsan) and jasmine (full) are the most distinctively Egyptian scents.

Spices

Spices are a good buy, particularly kuzbara (coriander), kamoon (cumin), shatta (chilli), filfil iswid (black pepper) and karkadai (hibiscus). Buy whole spices, never ground, for freshness, and skip the 'saffron' – it's really safflower and tastes of little more than dust. The shops that sell these items (attareen) also deal

---

RAMADAN: WHAT TO EXPECT

Travelling in Egypt during the month of Ramadan, when observant Muslims abstain from all food and drink (including waterduring daylight hours, presents some challenges but also affords visitors a unique insight into local culture – provided you can stay up late enough to enjoy it.

Most restaurants that serve Egyptians are closed during the day, and the only reliable place to eat is in hotels – the same goes for finding alcohol of any kind. Don't plan on taking desert tours, as guides will not want to venture far. Shop-owners get cranky as the day wears on, and tend to shut by 2.30pm or so, so do your bargaining early. Avoid taking taxis close to sundown, as everyone wants to get home to their families.

Once night falls and everyone has nibbled on the customary dates, Egyptians regain their energy. Restaurants reopen and lay out a lavish fast-breaking feast called iftar (reserve ahead at high-end places). The streets are decked with glowing lanterns and thronged with families. The goal is to stay up – or at least catnap and get up again – for the sohour, another big meal just before dawn. In Cairo and Alexandria, there's a whole circuit of sohour scenes, from the funkiest fuul vendors trotting out their best spreads to chic waterside pavilions with DJs – think after-party, but with food.

The best way to cope is to keep sightseeing expectations low, don't eat in front of Muslims and take a long nap in the afternoon. Then put on your stretchy pants and accept any invitation to join the feast.

in henna, soaps and herbal treatments. The best are neighbourhood dealers, not in tourist zones.

Telephone

Area codes Listed at the start of each city or town section. Leave off the initial zero when calling from outside Egypt.

Directory assistance ☏140 or ☏141

Egypt country code ☏20

International access code from Egypt ☏00

Mobile Phones

Egypt's GSM network (on the 900MHz/1800MHz band) has thorough coverage, at least in urban areas. SIM cards from any of the three carriers (Vodafone, the largest; Mobinil; Etisalat) cost E£15. You can buy them as well as top-up cards from most kiosks, where you may be asked to show your passport. For pay-as-you-go data service (about E£5 per day or E£50 per month), register at a company phone shop.

Public Phones

Pay phones (from yellow-and-green Menatel and red-and-blue Nile Tel) are card-operated. Cards are sold at shops and kiosks. Once you insert the card into the telephone, press the flag in the top left corner to get instructions in English.

Alternatively, a telephone centrale is an office where you book a call at the desk, pay in advance for three minutes, then take your phone call in a booth. Telephone centrales also offer fax services.

Time

» Egypt is two hours ahead of GMT/UTC.

» In 2011, Egypt did not observe Daylight Saving Time in order to cut the day short for

SCAMS & HUSTLES

Many Egyptians will greet you in the street and offer you tea and other hospitality, all out of genuine kindness. But in tourist hotspots, 'Hello, my friend' can be double-speak for 'This way, sucker'. Next thing you know, you're drinking tea with your new friend...in a perfume shop.

The smoothest operators don't reveal their motives immediately. A kindly professor wants to show you a good restaurant; a mosque 'muezzin' starts by showing off his skills; or a bystander warns you not to get caught up in a (fictitious) demonstration ahead. They adapt tactics rapidly. They've taken up the 'Don't you remember me?' line used in many other African countries, for instance, and use tales of the 2011 revolution as conversational bait.

It's all pretty harmless, and many are genuinely friendly and interesting to talk to. But it can be wearing to be treated like a walking wallet. Everyone works out a strategy to short-circuit a pitch, for when a smile and a quick stride fails. One travelling couple turned the tables: 'We'd love to come to your shop, but yesterday a man scammed us out of all of our money.' Claiming not to speak English, on the other hand, usually backfires, as polyglot touts can perform in nearly any language.

Aside from the hustling, there are touts who lie and misinform to divert travellers to hotels for which they get a commission – see p95 for examples of their ever-ingenious strategies.

If you do get stung, or feel you might crack at the next 'Excuse me, where are you from?', take a deep breath and put it in perspective. According to historical records, Cairene traders bragged about fleecing the king of Mali in the 14th century. Today's touts aren't picking on you because you look like a soft target – they're doing it because it's their job. Your angry tirade won't halt centuries of sales tradition. But it could offend an honest Egyptian who just wants to help.

Ramadan observers. This is expected to continue at least through 2014 as Ramadan continues to fall in the summer months.

Toilets

» Few official public toilets exist, but it's acceptable to use one in a restaurant or hotel even if you're not a customer.

» Toilet paper is seldom in stalls – an attendant may provide it as you enter, for a tip.

» Do not flush paper – deposit it in the bin next to the toilet.

» Many toilets have an integrated bidet tube, which unfortunately can get quite mucky. The knob for the bidet is usually to the right of the toilet tank – open it very slowly to gauge the pressure.

» Some toilets are of the 'squat' variety – use the hose (and bucket, if provided) to 'flush' and to wash your hands.

» In cities it's a good idea to make a mental note of all Western-style fast-food joints and five-star hotels, as these are where you'll find the most sanitary facilities.

» When you're trekking in the desert or camping on a beach, either pack out your toilet paper or burn it. Do not bury it – it will eventually be revealed by the wind.

Tourist Information

The **Egyptian Tourist Authority** (www.egypt.travel) has offices throughout the country. Individual office staff members may be helpful, but often they're just doling out rather dated maps and brochures. The smaller towns and oases tend to have better offices than the big cities. In short, don't rely on these tourist offices, but don't rule them out either.

Travellers with Disabilities

Egypt is not well equipped for travellers with a mobility problem. Ramps are few, public facilities don't necessarily have lifts, curbs are high (except in Alexandria, which has wheelchair-friendly sidewalks), traffic is lethal and gaining entrance to some of the ancient sites – such as the Pyramids of Giza or the tombs on the West Bank near Luxor – is all but impossible due to their narrow entrances and steep stairs.

Despite all this, there is no reason why intrepid travellers with disabilities shouldn't visit Egypt. In general you'll find locals quite willing to assist with any difficulties. Anyone with a wheelchair can take advantage of the large hatchback Peugeot 504s that are often used as taxis (though they're rarer in Cairo now). One of these, together with a driver, can be hired for the day. Chances are the driver will be happy to help you in and out of the vehicle. For getting around the country, most places can be reached via comfortable internal flights.

A few businesses in Egypt making a special effort:
Al-Nakhil Hotel (www.el-nakhil.com; Al-Gezira, Luxor) Rare midrange hotel with special facilities.
Camel Hotel and Dive Club (www.cameldive.com; King of Bahrain St, Sharm El-Sheikh) Specific accommodation and other facilities for divers with disabilities.
Egypt for All (www.egyptforall.com; 334 Sharia Sudan, Mohandiseen, Cairo) Travel arrangements for travellers who are mobility impaired.

Visas & Permits

» Visas required for most foreigners.
» Available for most nationalities at airport on

VISA EXTENSIONS: WHERE TO GO

Wherever you apply, you'll need one photo and two copies each of your passport's data page and the visa page. The fee depends on where you apply, but it's no more than E£15.
Alexandria (Map p326; ☑03-482 7873; 2nd fl, 25 Sharia Talaat Harb; ⊗8.30am-2pm Mon-Thu, 10am-2pm Fri, 9-11am Sat & Sun)
Aswan (off Map p256; ☑097-231 2238; Corniche an-Nil; ⊗8.30am-1pm Sat-Thu)
Cairo (Agouza) (Map p98; ☑02-3338 4226; El Shorta Tower, Sharia Nawal; ⊗8am-1.30pm Sat-Wed) For Giza addresses only: enter at side entrance of police station, go to window 4, 2nd floor.
Cairo (Downtown) (Map p64; Mogamma Bldg, Midan Tahrir; ⊗8am-1.30pm Sat-Wed) Get form from window 12, 1st floor, then stamps from window 43 and file all back at window 12; next-day pickup is at window 38.
Hurghada (Map p374; Sharia an-Nasr, Ad-Dahar; ⊗8am-2pm Sat-Thu)
Ismailia (☑064-391 4559; Midan al-Gomhuriyya; ⊗8am-2pm Sat-Thu)
Luxor (Map p196; ☑095-238 0885; Sharia Khalid ibn al-Walid; ⊗8am-2pm Sat-Thu)
Minya (☑095-236 4193; 2nd fl, above main post office; ⊗8.30am-2pm Sat-Thu) Off Sharia Corniche an-Nil.
Port Said (Governorate Bldg, Sharia 23rd of July; ⊗8am-2pm Sat-Thu) Go to window 7, left wing, 4th floor.
Suez (Sharia al-Horreyya; ⊗8.30am-3pm)

arrival, though check before departure.

» Visa fees:

Australia	A$35
Canada	C$25
Europe	€25
Israel	65NIS
Japan	¥5,500
New Zealand	NZ$45
UK	UK£15
USA	US$15

» When buying visa at airport, payment is accepted in US dollars, UK£ and euros.

» Airport visas typically valid for 30 days in Egypt. If you want more time, apply in advance or get an extension in Egypt.

» Overland from Jordan: visas available at the port in Aqaba.

» Overland from Israel: visas at border only if guaranteed by Egyptian travel agency; otherwise, apply in advance in Tel Aviv or at the consulate in Eilat (65NIS for US or German citizens; 100NIS for others).

» Travel in Sinai between Sharm el-Sheikh and Taba, including St Katherine's Monastery but not Ras Mohammed National Park, requires no visa, only a free entry stamp, good for a 15-day stay.

» Visa extensions used to be routine, but are now subject to scrutiny, especially after repeat extensions. Be polite and say you need more time to appreciate the wonders of Egypt.

» 14-day grace period for extension application, with E£100 late fee. If you leave during this time, you must pay E£135 fine at the airport.

Women Travellers

In public anyway, Egypt is a man's world, and solo women will certainly receive comments in the street – some polite, others less so – and possible groping. As small consolation, street harassment is a major problem for Egyptian women as

THE ART OF BARGAINING

Haggling is part of everyday life in Egypt (though, it should be noted, it's never done between friends). It's essentially a kind of scaled pricing: it can be a discount for people who have more time than money, but if your time is too valuable to discuss a transaction over tea, then you're expected to pay more. Your relative affluence of course factors into the calculations as well.

Shopping this way can seem like a hassle, but it can be fun if you consider it a game, not a fight. The basic procedure:

» Shop around and check fixed-price stores to get an idea of the upper limit.

» Decide how much you would be happy to pay.

» Express a casual interest and ask the vendor the price.

From here, it's up to your own style. The steeliest hagglers start with well below half the starting price, pointing out flaws or quoting a competitor's price. A properly theatrical salesman will respond with indignant shouting or a wounded cry, but it's all bluster. We know one shopper who closed deals in less than five minutes by citing her intense gastrointestinal distress – although unfortunately this was not bluster on her part.

A gentler tactic is to start out just a bit lower than the price you had in mind, or suggest other items in the shop that might be thrown in to sweeten the deal. Resist the vendor's attempts to provoke guilt – he will never sell below cost. If you reach an impasse, relax and drink the tea that's perpetually on offer – or simply walk out, which might close the deal in your favour.

You're never under any obligation to buy – but you should never initiate bargaining on an item you don't actually want, and you shouldn't back out of an agreed-upon price. The 'best' price isn't necessarily the cheapest – it's the one that both you and the seller are happy with. Remember that E£5 or E£10 makes virtually no difference in your budget, and years from now, you won't remember what you paid – but you will have your souvenir of Egypt, and a good story of how you got it.

well. With basic smarts, the constant male attention can be at least relegated to background irritation.

» Wear a sturdy bra and conservative clothing: long sleeves and pants or skirts. Sunglasses also deflect attention.

» Carry a scarf to cover your head inside mosques.

» Outside of Red Sea resorts, swim in shorts and a T-shirt at the least.

» A wedding ring sometimes helps, but it's more effective if your 'husband' (any male travel companion) is present. Most effective: travel with a child.

» Keep your distance. Even innocent, friendly talk can be misconstrued as flirtation, as can any physical contact.

» Ignore obnoxious comments – if you respond to every one, you'll wear yourself out, and public shaming seldom gets satisfying results.

» Text incidents to **Harassmap** (✆0106 987 0900; www.harassmap.org).

» Avoid crowds where testosterone is high: street protests, post–football match celebrations and the like.

» On public transport, sit next to a woman if possible. On the Cairo metro, use the women's cars.

» Avoid city buses at peak times; the crowds make them prime groping zones.

» Bring tampons and contraceptives with you; outside of Cairo, they can be expensive.

» If you need directions or other help, ask a woman first.

» Take any opportunity to befriend an Egyptian woman, for a nonthreatening guide.

» Get older: after your mid-30s, the hassle diminishes.

» Read Rosemary Mahoney's *Down the Nile: Alone in a Fisherman's Skiff* and G Willow Wilson's *The Butterfly Mosque*, two very different tales of solo travel.

» Watch *Cairo 6,7,8*, a great 2011 fiction film about three Egyptian women dealing with sexual harassment.

» For more on the role of women in Egyptian culture, see p485.

MOBILE PHONE NUMBERS IN EGYPT

As of October 2011, all mobile phone numbers are 11 digits, beginning with 01. You may still see old-format numbers in print. Use this table to determine the extra digit:

OLD PREFIX	NEW PREFIX
010	0100
011	0111
012	0122
014	0114
016	0106
017	0127
018	0128
019	0109

Work

Many foreign firms operate in Egypt and hire foreigners, but you must typically be hired before arriving in the country, to have your work visa arranged properly. Consult *Cairo: The Practical Guide* (AUC Press), edited by Claire E Francy and Lesley Lababidi, for possible avenues.

Bars & Hotels

In Sharm el-Sheikh and Dahab, travellers can often find short-term work as bartenders or hotel workers. Masseurs and others with spa skills are also in demand. Most of this work is under the table, however, and often short-term, due to employers' tax concerns.

Diving

If you are a dive master or diving instructor you can find work in Egypt's resorts fairly easily. Owners look also for language and social skills.

Teaching English

The best-paying schools require at least a Certificate in English Language Teaching to Adults (CELTA), but there are other, more informal outlets as well. Cairo's ILI (p513) is one of the better schools, and offers CELTA training as well.

Transport

GETTING THERE & AWAY

Entering the Country

At Cairo International Airport or Burg al-Arab Airport (Alexandria), the main formality is getting a visa, if you haven't arranged one in advance. They are sold at a row of bank booths in every arrivals terminal. Pay cash (see p518) and then present the sticker along with your arrival form and passport at the immigration desks. The procedure is typically speedy, no questions asked, though lines might be long if several flights have arrived at once.

By land or sea, the process is similar.

Passport

Regardless of where you enter, your passport must be valid for at least six months from your date of entry.

Israeli stamps in your passport (and Israeli passports, for that matter) present no problem, unlike in some other Middle Eastern countries.

Air

Airports & Airlines

Cairo, Alexandria and Sharm el-Sheikh receive numerous commercial international flights. Luxor receives many charter flights, but only one commercial one, **easyJet** (www.easyjet.com) from London Gatwick. Aswan, Hurghada and Marsa Alam also handle flights from overseas, but typically only charters.

» Cairo is the most common entry point. Many international flights arrive late at night, but this is in fact preferable, as city traffic is lighter. The airport is served by all the major international carriers. Of note:

- **EgyptAir** (www.egyptair.com) Member of Star Alliance. Tickets are cheap, and its international fleet is in good shape. No alcohol is served.

- **Jetairfly** (www.jetairfly.com) Low-cost carrier from Brussels.

- **Meridiana fly** (www.meridiana.it) Flights from Milan.

- **Air Sinai** (www.egyptair.com) From Tel Aviv. Buy tickets at the unmarked office at Ben Yehuda and Allenby. Run by EgyptAir.

» Alexandria has become a viable alternate airport, especially for low-cost carriers:

- **Air Arabia** (www.airarabia.com) Connects to cities around the Middle East and Milan.

- **flydubai** (www.flydubai.com) Also serves Middle Eastern cities.

» Sharm el-Sheikh is handy if you'll be spending most of your time in Sinai and Jordan. A number of budget

---

CLIMATE CHANGE & TRAVEL

Every form of transport that relies on carbon-based fuel generates CO_2, the main cause of human-induced climate change. Modern travel is dependent on aeroplanes, which might use less fuel per kilometre per person than most cars but travel much greater distances. The altitude at which aircraft emit gases (including CO_2) and particles also contributes to their climate change impact. Many websites offer 'carbon calculators' that allow people to estimate the carbon emissions generated by their journey and, for those who wish to do so, to offset the impact of the greenhouse gases emitted with contributions to portfolios of climate-friendly initiatives throughout the world. Lonely Planet offsets the carbon footprint of all staff and author travel.

Domestic Flights

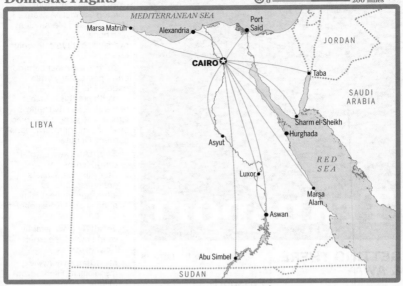

European airlines serve Sharm, but the eight-hour bus ride to Cairo can outweigh any savings.

For EgyptAir offices in Egypt, see the Getting There & Away sections of destination chapters throughout the book. For airport details, see the Getting Around section of destination chapters throughout the book.

Land

Israel & the Palestinian Territories

RAFAH

The border crossing to the Gaza Strip is officially open Saturday to Thursday, but can be closed for days at a time for security reasons. But because Gaza's border with Israel is closed, you likely won't be entering from Gaza, nor can you exit this way and carry on to Israel.

If you do want to visit Gaza, you must also return to Egypt, and you must have special permission from the Palestinian Affairs division of the **Ministry of Foreign Affairs** (☑02-2574 9682; ⊘noon-3pm) in Cairo. Be prepared to wait also for approval (perhaps for weeks) to re-enter Egypt.

TABA

The border at Taba is open 24 hours.

Entering Egypt Advance visa required, unless you're visiting only eastern Sinai or you have prearranged with an Egyptian tour operator. For details see p518. Israeli exit tax is 101NIS, and Egyptian entry tax is E£46, paid at a booth 1km south of the border on the main road. Entry just to eastern Sinai with a travel permit is free.

Exiting Egypt Israeli visa not required for most nationalities. Taxis or city bus 15 (7.5NIS) run 4km to Eilat, for buses onward to Jerusalem or Tel Aviv. Note no buses operate in Israel and the Palestinian Territories from Friday evening to Saturday sundown. Only Israeli-registered cars can cross here.

Bus service A bus operated by **Mazada Tours** (www. mazada.co.il) runs between Cairo and Jerusalem (US$145, 24 hours) via Tel Aviv, though service can be cancelled if there are not enough passengers. In Cairo, bookings are handled by Misr Travel in the Pyramisa Hotel in Doqqi; the office will likely relocate to the Cairo

---

DEPARTURE TAX

Airline tickets include Egypt's exit tax in the price. If you're leaving by ferry to Jordan, expect to pay E£50/US$10 port tax. Crossing overland to Libya, there was no exit tax at the time of research.

Sheraton when renovation is complete in late 2012.

Libya

The border is at Amsaad, officially open 24 hours. The nearest town on the Egyptian side is Sallum, 12km away.

Entering Egypt At the time of research, it was not possible to get an Egyptian visa at the border. You must apply in advance through an embassy or consulate.

Exiting Egypt At the time of research, travellers reported crossing into Libya without a visa or exit tax, though this may be due to the political instability. As a precaution, it's wise to get a visa from the bank in Sallum, or check with the Libyan embassy in Cairo. On the Libyan side, service taxis go to Tobruk.

Bus service A **Super Jet** (☑02-2266 2252; superjet. eg@hotmail.com) bus goes to Benghazi on Sunday and Thursday (E£200, 14 hours) from Al-Mazah depot in Cairo; tickets can be purchased at Cairo Gateway (p119).

Sudan

Despite Egypt and Sudan sharing a 1273km land border, the only way to travel between the two countries is to fly or take the Wadi Halfa ferry (see p523).

Sea

Cyprus

As of 2011, a cruise ship with stops in Port Said and Limassol in Cyprus was suspended due to instability in both Greece and Egypt. It may be restored in the future. Contact operator **Louis Cruises** (www.louiscruises.com) or main agent **Varianos Travel** (www.varianostravel.com) in Cyprus, or check with a Port Said shipping agent such as **Canal Tours** (☑066-332 1874; www.canal-tours.net; 26 Sharia Palestine, Port Said; ⊙8am-3pm & 7pm-midnight).

Europe

At the time of research no passenger boats were operating between Egyptian ports and any ports in Europe, though **Visemar Line** (www. visemarline.com) could restore its Venice–Alexandria (via Tartous, in Syria) service if Syria's political situation stabilises. Tenacious travellers could investigate crossing on a freighter. Try www. cruiseshipportal.com, which books freighter berths.

Israel & the Palestinian Territories

There's been talk about resuming the boat service from Port Said to Haifa. At the time of writing, this service was still nonexistent. Contact **Varianos Travel** (www.varianostravel.com) in Cyprus.

Jordan

A ferry connects Nuweiba in Egypt and Aqaba in Jordan. For more information on this service, see p424. From Cairo, a **Super Jet** (☑02-2266 2252; superjet.eg@hotmail.com) bus service to Amman (US$65/E£220, 15 hours) uses the ferry, but the boat ticket must be purchased separately. The bus runs Tuesday and Saturday at 10pm from Al-Mazah depot; tickets can be purchased at Cairo Gateway (p119).

Saudi Arabia

Ferries run from Hurghada to Duba, though they are not recommended due to erratic schedules, which fluctuate according to work and hajj seasons. Note that tourist visas are not available for Saudi Arabia, though there is an elusive tourist transit visa, which you must apply for well in advance.

Syria

The passenger service between Alexandria and Tartous was cancelled in 2011 due to the political situation. It may be restored. Check with

> ### PORT TAX
>
> All Egyptian international ferries charge US$10/E£50 port tax per person on top of the ticket price.

Visemar Line (www.visemarline.com).

Sudan

The **Nile River Valley Transport Corporation** (Aswan ☑0118 316 0926; in shopping arcade behind tourist police office; ⊙8am-2pm Sat-Thu; Cairo ☑02-2575 9058; Ramses station) runs one passenger ferry per week from Aswan to Wadi Halfa. One-way tickets cost E£500 for 1st class with bed in a cabin, E£322 for an airline seat and E£215 for deck class. The ferry runs on Mondays, though call to confirm. Tickets are typically only sold the Saturday before departure, though you may be able to get one on Monday at the company's **office** (☑097-480 567) in Aswan port. You must show a valid Sudanese visa in your passport.

The trip takes 18 to 24 hours, with tea, soft drinks and snacks available. Departure is sometime in the afternoon, depending on how much there is to load, but it's a good idea to arrive at about 8.30am to clear customs and get a decent seat. Some Sudanese immigration formalities are carried out on the boat, including checking yellow-fever certificates. The return trip departs from Wadi Halfa on Wednesdays.

The Nile River Valley Transport Corporation runs a separate barge for vehicles, which also departs Mondays but takes two or three days. Prices are E£400 for a motorcycle and E£2500 for a car or 4WD. You must have the usual *carnet de passage en douane* and allow plenty of time for customs procedures.

Tours

The majority of visitors see Egypt on an organised tour. The schedules on such trips are usually fairly tight, leaving little room to explore on your own. But a tour often comes with excellent guides, and a group can insulate you from some of the day-to-day hassle and sales pressure that independent travellers receive.

Also see p528 for companies operating solely in Egypt. For specific tour offerings, also check www. lonelyplanet.com/travel_ services.

Abercrombie & Kent (www. abercrombiekent.co.uk) First-class packages, including its own Nile cruisers.

African Trails (www.african trails.co.uk) Overland safari operator, connecting Egypt with the Middle East and sub-Saharan Africa.

Bestway Tours & Safaris (www.bestway.com) Small-group tours, often combining Egypt with neighbouring countries.

Dragoman (www.dragoman. co.uk) Like African Trails, runs sturdy overland trucks around the Middle East, at budget prices.

Imaginative Traveller (www.imaginative-traveller. com) Active tours (trekking etc), some combined with Jordan.

Intrepid Travel (www. intrepidtravel.com) Emphasis on responsible tourism.

Martin Randall (www. martinrandall.com) UK-based experts in cultural tours.

On the Go (www.egypton thego.com) PADI diving-course holidays.

Wind, Sand & Stars (www. windsandstars.co.uk) A Sinai specialist with desert excursions and retreats.

GETTING AROUND

Air

EgyptAir (www.egyptair.com) is the only domestic carrier, and fares can be surprisingly cheap, though they vary considerably depending on season. Domestic one-way fares can be less than US$100.

Bicycle

Cycle tourism is rare, due to long distances plus intense heat. Winter can be manageable, but even in spring and autumn it's necessary to make an early-morning start and finish by early afternoon.

Carry a full kit, as spares are hard to come by, although in a pinch Egyptians are excellent 'bush mechanics'.

The Cairo-based club **Cycle Egypt** (www.cycle -egypt.com), and its very active Facebook group, is a good starting point for making local contacts and getting advice on shops and gear. Also check the Thorn Tree travel forum on www.lonely-planet.com, where there's a dedicated section for cyclists.

Boat

No trip to Egypt is complete without a trip down the Nile River. You can take the trip on a felucca (a traditional sailboat) or opt for a modern steamer or cruise ship. For information on Nile cruises and felucca trips, see p27.

At the time of research, a new boat service from Hurghada to Sharm el-Sheikh was in the works. This bypasses hours of bumpy roads and checkpoints, and it's one of the few chances you have to boat from Africa to Asia! For more information on the ferry, see p378.

Bus

You can get to just about every city, town and village in Egypt on a bus, at a very reasonable price. For many long-distance routes beyond the Nile Valley, it's the best option, and sometimes the only one. Buses aren't necessarily fast, though, and if you're going to or from Cairo, you'll lose at least an hour just in city traffic. Delays are common, especially later in the day as schedules get backed up. When buying tickets, it's a good idea to have a rough idea beforehand of costs, so you don't get sold a standard bus ticket at deluxe-bus prices.

Deluxe Buses

Air-con 'deluxe' buses connect the biggest destinations: Cairo, Alexandria, Ismailia, Port Said, Suez, St Katherine's Monastery, Sharm el-Sheikh, Hurghada and Luxor. Tickets cost a bit more than those for standard buses (which may also make more stops along the way) but they're still cheap.

Most buses have a strict no-smoking rule, and snacks and tea may sometimes be offered for an extra charge. Some buses on long routes have toilets, though they're seldom very clean. Videos are usually shown, often at top volume – ear plugs are a good idea if you want to sleep, as is an extra layer, as overnight buses can often be very cold from the air-con.

Standard Buses

The cheapest buses on long routes, and most on shorter routes, can be markedly more uncomfortable, over-crowded and noisy, and stop frequently. In these cases – trips under two hours or so – minibuses or *servees* are usually preferable.

Companies

Super Jet (☎02-2266 2252; superjet.eg@hotmail.com) serves the longer routes

ROAD DISTANCES (KM)

	Al-Arish	Al-Fayoum	Alexandria	Aswan	Asyut	Beni Suef	Cairo	Giza	Hurghada	Ismailia	Luxor	Marsa Matruh	Minya	Port Said	Sharm el-Sheikh
Al-Fayoum	431														
Alexandria	451	327													
Aswan	1238	822	1133												
Asyut	712	296	607	526											
Beni Suef	453	37	346	785	259										
Cairo	325	106	220	913	387	128									
Giza	333	98	228	903	377	118	8								
Hurghada	668	636	754	496	478	532	530	538							
Ismailia	185	246	266	1053	527	268	140	148	483						
Luxor	955	608	919	209	322	571	699	689	287	770					
Marsa Matruh	741	617	290	1423	897	638	510	518	1040	556	1209				
Minya	579	163	473	659	133	126	254	244	611	394	455	764			
Port Said	200	331	354	1138	612	353	225	233	563	85	850	644	479		
Sharm el-Sheikh	638	610	710	1279	909	632	504	512	783	444	1070	1000	758	529	
Suez	287	273	354	1047	521	262	134	142	395	88	682	644	388	168	388

around the country and internationally, and tends to be most reliable. The other companies are all under the same management, but cover different areas and offer different degrees of service. For Sinai, **East Delta Travel Co** (☎02-3262 3128; www.eastdeltatravel. com) is comparable to Super Jet. But **West & Mid Delta Bus Co** (☎03-427 0916; www.westmidbus-eg.com), to Alexandria and especially to Marsa Matruh and beyond, was showing substantially worse service, with chronic breakdowns, at the time of research. Fairly serviceable **Upper Egypt Bus Co** (☎02-2576 0261; www.uppperegj.com) serves most of the oases and the Nile Valley, though for the latter destinations, the train is preferable.

Within Sinai, the private start-up **Bedouin Bus**

(☎0101 668 4274; www. bedouinbus.com) runs service between Dahab, Nuweiba and St Katherine's Monastery.

Tickets

Buy tickets at bus stations or on the bus. Hang onto your ticket until you get off as inspectors almost always board to check fares. You should also always carry your passport as buses are often stopped at military checkpoints for random identity checks. This is particularly common on the bus between Aswan and Abu Simbel, and on all Sinai buses.

It is advisable to book in advance, especially for the Cairo-to-Sinai service and to the Western Desert, where buses run infrequently. An International Student Identity Card (ISIC) gives discounts on some bus routes. Where you are allowed to buy tickets

on the bus, you generally end up standing if you don't have an assigned seat with a booked ticket. On short runs there are no bookings and it's a case of first on, best seated.

Car & Motorcycle

Proceed with caution. Driving in Cairo is a crazy affair, and only slightly less nerveracking in other parts of the country. Night driving should be completely avoided. But some intrepid readers have reported that self-driving is a wonderful way to leave the tour buses in the dust.

A motorcycle would be a good way to travel around Egypt, but you must bring your own, and the red tape is extensive. Ask your country's automobile association and Egyptian embassy about regulations.

Petrol and diesel are readily available and very cheap. But stations can be scarce outside of Cairo. As a rule, when you see one, fill up.

Bringing Your Own Vehicle

» Stock up on crucial spare parts and tyres. Cars in Egypt are also required to carry a fire extinguisher.

» Registration papers, liability insurance and an International Driving Permit, in addition to your domestic driving licence, are required.

» Get multiple copies of a *carnet de passage en douane*, effectively a passport for the vehicle that waives import duty. The *carnet* should also list any expensive spare parts you're carrying with you.

» At the Egyptian border, you'll be issued with a licence of the same duration as your visa. You can renew the licence, but you'll have to pay a varying fee each time.

» The customs charge is approximately US$200, plus another US$50 for number-plate insurance.

Driving Licence

An International Driving Permit is required to drive in Egypt, and you risk a heavy fine if you're caught without one. Likewise, ensure that you

always have all car registration papers with you while driving.

Hire

Finding a cheap deal with local agencies is virtually impossible – it's advisable to make arrangements via the web before you arrive. Read insurance terms carefully to see whether lower-quality roads are ruled out.

Road Rules

» Driving is on the right-hand side.

» Speed limit outside towns is usually 70km/h to 90km/h, and 100km/h on major highways.

» For traffic violations, the police will confiscate your driving licence and you have to go to the traffic headquarters in the area to get it back.

» Tolls are charged on the Cairo–Alexandria Desert Hwy, the Cairo–Fayoum road and the tunnel under the Suez Canal.

» Checkpoints are frequent. Be ready with identity papers and licence.

» In cities, whoever is in front has the right of way, even if it's only a matter of inches.

» In the countryside, keep an eye out for people and livestock wandering into the road.

» If you have an accident, get to the nearest police station as quickly as possible and report what happened.

Hitching

Hitching is never entirely safe in any country in the world, and it is not recommended. Travellers who decide to hitch should understand that they are taking a small but potentially serious risk. Those who do choose to hitch will be safer if they travel in pairs and let someone know where they are planning to go. Women must never hitch on their own in Egypt, as the general local assumption is that only prostitutes would do such a thing.

Local Transport

Bus

Several of the biggest Egyptian cities have bus systems. Practically speaking, you might use them only in Cairo and Alexandria. They're not particularly visitor-friendly, as numbers are displayed only in Arabic numerals, the routes are unpublished and the buses themselves are often overcrowded to the point of record-breaking.

There's no orderly queue to board – in fact, quite the opposite – and the bus rarely rolls to a complete stop, whether you're getting on or off. If you do make it on, at some point a conductor will manage to squeeze his way through to sell you your ticket.

Metro

Cairo is the only city in Egypt with a metro system (for details, see p123).

Microbus

These 14-seat minivans run informally alongside city bus systems, or sometimes in lieu of them. For the average traveller they can be difficult to use, as they are unmarked. They're easiest to get at their starting point – usually a major *midan* (square) or intersection in a city, where the drivers will be shouting their end destination. You can ask to be let off at any point on the route.

Nabbing a microbus as it's going by is more difficult – sometimes there's a small boy hanging out the doorway yelling the destination, but just as often it's up to you to shout out your destination. If there's room in a van going your way, it will stop.

Typically you pay the driver as you're getting out.

In Cairo, you might have occasion to use a microbus to get to the Pyramids, while in Alexandria they shuttle the length of Tariq al-Horreyya and the Corniche to Montazah. In Sharm el-Sheikh they carry passengers between Old Sharm, Na'ama Bay and Shark's Bay.

Pickup

Toyota and Chevrolet pickup trucks cover some routes between smaller towns and villages off the main roads, especially where passengers might have cargo. A dozen or so people squeeze into the rear of the truck (covered or uncovered), often with goods squeezed in on the floor.

Covered pickup trucks are also sometimes used within towns, similar to microbuses. This is especially so in some of the oases, on Luxor's west bank and in smaller places along the Nile. There are a couple of ways you can indicate to the driver that you want to get out: if you are lucky enough to have a seat, pound on the floor with your foot; alternatively, ask one of the front passengers to hammer on the window behind the driver; or, last, use the buzzer that you'll occasionally find rigged up.

Taxi

Even the smallest cities in Cairo have taxis. They're inexpensive and efficient, even if in some cities the cars themselves have seen better days.

Fares In Cairo metered taxis are taking over, but everywhere else, locals know the accepted price and pay it without (much) negotiation. This book gives guidelines on taxi rates, but check with locals, as fares change as petrol prices rise.

Hailing Just step to the roadside, raise your hand and one will likely come screeching to a halt. Tell the driver where you're headed before getting in – he may decline the fare if there's bad traffic or it's too far.

Negotiating For short fares, setting a price beforehand backfires, as it reveals you don't know the system. But for long distances – from the airport to the city centre,

for instance – you should agree on a price before getting in. And confirm it, as some drivers tend to try to change the deal on arrival.

Paying In unmetered taxis, avoid getting trapped in an argument by getting out first, then handing money through the window. If a driver suspects you don't know the correct fare, you'll get an aghast 'How could you possibly pay me so little?' look, if not a full-on argument. Don't be drawn in if you're sure of your position, but do remember that E£5 makes a far greater difference to your driver than it does to you. And from his perspective, if you can afford to come to Egypt, you can also afford to pay a little above the going rate.

Sharing You may be welcomed into a cab with a passenger, or your cab may stop to pick others up. If you don't mind sharing, sit in the front seat and leave the back free for others (for men only; it's considered a bit forward for women to sit in the front seat).

Tram

Cairo and Alexandria are the only two cities in the country with tram systems. While Alexandria still has a fairly extensive network, Cairo now only has a handful of lines. See p343 and p125 for more details.

Tuk-tuk

These clever scooters-with-seats, ubiquitous in Thailand and India, have arrived in Egypt. Locals call them *tok-tok* (turns out the onomatopoeia of their tiny engines works in Arabic too), and they're especially popular in small towns. They're typically the same price or cheaper than taxis (E£10, say, for a 15-minute ride), with a pounding *shaabi* (music of the working class) soundtrack for free. (Tuk-tuks are popular with young – sometimes too young! – drivers who like to customise their wheels with mega-speakers and other bling.) It's a good idea to negotiate a price before getting in.

THE MAN BEHIND THE WHEEL

Egyptian taxis are a blessing and a curse. They're remarkably convenient and affordable, but outside of Cairo, where meters have yet to be introduced, they can be a frequent source of unpleasantness when it comes to paying the fare. Passengers frequently feel that they've been taken advantage of (which they often have), while drivers may be genuinely (as opposed to just theatrically) aggrieved by what they see as underpayment.

Bear in mind, driving a cab is far from lucrative. Average earnings after fuel has been paid are rarely more than E£10 per hour. Many drivers don't own their car and have to hand over part of their earnings as 'rent'.

Which isn't to say that the next time you flag a taxi for a 10-block hop and the driver declares '10 pounds' that you should smile and say 'OK'. But it might make it easier to see that it was probably worth his while trying. After all, from his point of view, if you can afford to make it all the way to Egypt, you can probably afford to pay a bit more than the going rate.

Microbus

The microbus (pronounced 'meekrobas'), often also called a micro or a minibus, is a Toyota van with seats for 14 passengers. Privately owned and usually unmarked, they run along most of the same routes that buses do, and are a bit cheaper. They also stop anywhere along the route on request, and will pick up riders along the way if there's a free seat.

How to Ride

Microbuses run on no set schedule – they just wait until they're full, then take off. If you're in a hurry or just want more room to yourself, you can buy an extra seat. The two prime seats are next to the driver; savvy solo travellers recommend buying both.

Microbuses can be quite cramped, so you typically don't want to ride one for more than three hours or so. But their flexibility is a huge asset, as you can usually find one headed where you want to go, no matter the time of day.

Where to Find

Microbuses usually congregate outside bus and train stations, or at major highway intersections on the edges of cities. Increasingly, though, they operate from an established depot – ask for the maw'if meekrobas (as opposed to the mahattat bas, or bus station).

Microbus parking areas are usually a mob scene of drivers all shouting their destinations and trying to cajole you into their vehicles. Just shout your destination back, and eventually you'll wind up in the right zone.

Tickets

You pay the microbus driver once you're underway. This usually involves passing your money up hand-to-hand through the rows; your change will be scrupulously returned the same way.

Servees

The servees (service taxi) is the predecessor to the microbus (minivan) and runs on the same principle: buy a seat, wait for the car to fill and you're off. These big Peugeot 504 station wagons, with seats for seven passengers, are now less common than the vans, except in north Sinai and along the Suez Canal and the Red Sea coast. As with microbuses, you'll find them near bus and train stations, and you're welcome to buy extra seats for more space or just to speed along the departure.

Tours

Even if you haven't planned ahead with a full package tour, you can still leave the planning and transport to others for a few days of your trip. The most typical organised tour is a Nile cruise or felucca trip (see p27) or a Western Desert safari (see p280). In addition to specialists recommended there, these local operators can arrange short or long outings.

Backpacker Concierge (📞0106 350 7118; www.back packerconcierge.com) Excellent custom-tour operator, with great connections to Bedouin groups and more; runs the only culinary tour of Egypt.

Experience Egypt (Map p98; 📞02-3302 8364; www. experience-egypt.com; 42 Sharia Abu al-Mahasin al-Shazly, Mohandiseen, Cairo) Egypt-based company with small-group tours.

Wilderness Ventures Egypt (📞0128 282 7182; www.wilderness-ventures-egypt.com) Based in Sinai and rooted in Bedouin culture.

Train

Egypt's British-built rail system comprises more than 5000km of track to almost every major city and town, but not to Sinai. The system is antiquated, and cars are often grubby and battered. Aside from two main routes (Cairo–Alexandria, Cairo–Aswan), you have to be fond of trains to prefer them to a deluxe bus. But for destinations near Cairo, trains win because they don't get stuck in traffic.

For travel times from Cairo, see p121. For specific schedules, see the relevant cities in the book, and consult the Egyptian Railways website, www.egyptrail.gov. eg, where you can also purchase 1st-class tickets.

Classes

1st (darga ula) Preferable if you're going any distance. Air-con (takyeef), padded seats, relatively clean toilet, tea and snack service from a trolley.

2nd (darga tanya) Seats are battered vinyl. Skip air-con if it's an option – it often doesn't work well. Toilets aren't well kept.

3rd (darga talta) Grimy bench seats, glacial pace and crowds, but lots of activity and vendors. Be prepared for attention – you'll probably be the most exciting thing on the train.

Sleepers

Route The private company **Watania Sleeping Trains** (www.wataniasleepingtrains. com) runs daily service from Cairo to Luxor and Aswan. For schedules, see the Getting There & Away sections of those cities.

Tickets Reasonably priced, including two meals. Reservations must be made before 6pm the day of departure, but should really be done at least a few days ahead.

Compartments Spanish- or German-built two-bed sleepers: seats convert to a bed, and an upper bunk folds down. Clean linen, pillows and blankets, plus a small basin with running water. Beds are a bit short. Middle compartments, away from doors, are quieter. Shared toilets are generally clean and have toilet paper. Air-con can get chilly at night.

Meals Serviceable airline-style dinners and breakfasts are served in the compartments. A steward serves drinks (including alcohol), and there's a club car.

Other Upper Egypt Services

Day trains Security rules have been lifted, and tourists can now ride day trains south of Cairo. The best is number 980, the express departing Cairo at 8am, with an enjoyable 10 hours to Luxor and 13 to Aswan, with views of lush plantations and villages along the way.

Night trains (non-sleepers) Also run by Watania, these 1st-class Pullman-car night trains were suspended due to a low volume of tourists, but may be restored. They're cheaper than sleepers, especially if you opt out of meals, but the day trains are far more scenic.

Alexandria

The best trains on the Cairo–Alexandria route are speedy 'Spanish' (esbani) trains. Almost all of them go direct, or with just one stop, in 2½ hours. 'French' (faransawi) trains are less comfortable and make more stops. Both count as 1st class with air-con, though, so specify Spanish when booking. Ordinary trains on this route are very basic and slow.

Nile Delta

The rail system is most extensive in the agricultural region north of Cairo, as it was built to bring cotton to market. If you're headed anywhere in this area, the train is ideal for speed and scenery, though the 1st-class trains run only four or five times a day.

Marsa Matruh

For the summer holiday season, Watania also runs a night train to this Mediterranean resort town, three days a week mid-June to mid-September.

Language

Arabic is the official language of Egypt. Note that there are significant differences between the MSA (Modern Standard Arabic) – the official lingua franca of the Arab world, used in schools, administration and the media – and the colloquial language, ie the everyday spoken variety of a particular region. Of all the Arabic dialects, Egyptian Arabic (provided in this chapter) is probably the most familiar to all Arabic speakers, thanks to the popularity of Egyptian television and cinema.

Read our coloured pronunciation guides as if they were English and you'll be understood. Note that a is pronounced as in 'act', aa as the 'a' in 'father', ai as in 'aisle', aw as in 'law', ay as in 'say', e as in 'bet', ee as in 'see', i as in 'hit', o as in 'pot', oo as in 'zoo', u as in 'put', gh is a guttural sound (like the Parisian French 'r'), r is rolled, kh is pronounced as the 'ch' in the Scottish *loch* and zh as the 's' in 'pleasure'. The apostrophe (') indicates the glottal stop (like the pause in the middle of 'uh-oh'). The stressed syllables are indicated with italics.

BASICS

Hello.	أهلاً.	ah·lan
Goodbye.	مع السلامة.	ma' sa·la·ma
Yes./No.	لأ/أيوة.	ai·wa/la'
Please.	لو سماحت.	law sa·maht (m)
	لو سمحتي.	law sa·mah·tee (f)
Thank you.	شكراً.	shu·kran
Excuse me.	عن إزنك.	'an 'iz·nak (m)
	عن إزنك.	'an 'iz·nik (f)
Sorry.	متأسف.	mu·ta·'as·if (m)
	متأسفة.	mu·ta·'a·si·fa (f)

How are you?
إزيّك؟/إزيّك؟   iz·ay·ak/iz·ay·ik (m/f)

Fine, thanks. And you?
كويّس/كويّسة.   kway·is/kway·is·a (m/f)
الحمدلله؟   il·am·du·li·lah

What's your name?
إسمَك إيه؟   is·mak ay (m)
إسمِك إيه؟   is·mik ay (f)

My name is ...
إسمي ...   is·mee ...

Do you speak English?
بتتكلم/بتتكلمي   bi·tit·ka·lim/bi·tit·ka·lim·ee
إنجليزي؟   in·gi·lee·zee (m/f)

I don't understand.
مش فاهم.   mish fa·him (m)
مش فهمة.   mish fah·ma (f)

Can I take a photo?
ممكن أصوّر؟   mum·kin a·saw·ar

ACCOMMODATION

Where's a ...?	فين ...؟	fayn ...
campsite	المخيّم	il·mu·khay·am
guesthouse	البنسيون	il·ban·see·yon
hotel	الفندق	il·fun·du'
youth hostel	بيت شباب	bayt sha·bab

Question Words		
When?	إمتى؟	im·ta
Where?	فين؟	fayn
Who?	مين؟	meen
Why?	ليه؟	lay

Signs

Entrance	مدخل
Exit	خروج
Open	مفتوح
Closed	مغلق
Information	إستعلامات
Prohibited	ممنوع
Toilets	دورة المّية
Men	رجال
Women	سّيدات

Do you have a ... room?	عندَك/عندِك أوضة ...؟	'an·dak/'an·dik o·da ... (m/f)
single	لواحد	li·wa·hid
double	للإتنين	lil·it·nayn
twin	بسريرين	bi·si·ree·rayn

How much is it per ...?	بكم ...؟	bi kam ...
night	الليلة	il·lay·la
person	الشخس	i·shakhs

Can I get another (blanket)?
عايز/عايزة (بطنية) تنية من فضلَك/فضلِك. 'a·iz/'ai·za (ba·ta·nee·ya) ta·nya min fad·lak/fad·lik (m/f)

The (air conditioning) doesn't work.
(التكييف) مش شغال. (i·tak·yeef) mish sha·ghal

DIRECTIONS

Where's the ...?	فين ...؟	fayn ...
bank	البنك	il·bank
market	السوق	is·soo'
post office	البسطة	il·bus·ta

Can you show me (on the map)?
ممكن تورّيني (على الخريطة)؟ mum·kin ti·wa·ree·nee ('al il·kha·ree·ta)

What's the address?
العنوان أيه؟ il·'un·wan ay

Could you please write it down?
ممكن تكتبه؟ mum·kin tik·ti·booh (m)
ممكن تكتبيه؟ mum·kin tik·ti·beeh (f)

How far is it?
كم كيلو من هنا؟ kam kee·lu min hi·na

How do I get there?
أروح إزّاي؟ a·ruh i·zay

Turn left.
حود شمال. haw·id shi·mal

Turn right.
حود يمين. haw·id yi·meen

It's ...	هو ...	hu·wa ... (m)
	هي ...	hi·ya ... (f)
behind ...	ورا ...	wa·ra ...
in front of ...	قدام ...	'u·dam ...
near to ...	قريب من ...	'u·ray·ib min ...
next to ...	جمب ...	gamb ...
on the corner	على الناصية	'a·lal nas·ya
opposite ...	قصاد ...	'u·saad ...
straight ahead	على طول	'a·la tool

EATING & DRINKING

Can you recommend a ...?	ممكن تقترحلي/ تقترحيلي ...؟	mum·kin tik·ti·rah·lee/ tik·ti·ra·hee·lee ... (m/f)
bar	بار	baar
cafe	قهوة	'ah·wa
restaurant	مطعم	ma·ta'·am

I'd like a table (for four), please.
عايز/عايزة تربيزة (لأربع) من فضلَك/فضلِك. 'a·iz/'ai·za ta·ra·bay·za (li·ar·ba') min fad·lak/fad·lik (m/f)

What would you recommend?
تقترح أيه؟ tik·tar·ah ey

What's the local speciality?
الأطباق المحلية أيه؟ il at·baa' il ma·ha·lee·ya ay

Do you have vegetarian food?
عندَك/عندِك أكل نباتي؟ 'an·dak/'an·dik akl na·ba·tee (m/f)

I'd like (the) ..., please.	عايز/عايزة ... من فضلَك/فضلِك.	'a·iz/'ai·za ... min fad·lak/fad·lik (m/f)
bill	الحساب	il·hi·sab
drink list	لستة مشروبات	lis·tat mash·roo·bat
menu	المنيو	il·men·yu
that dish	التبق ده	il·ta·ba'·da

Could you prepare a meal without ...?	ممكن تعمل أكل من غير ...؟	mum·kin ta'·mil akl min ghayr ...
butter	زبدة	zib·da
eggs	بيض	bayd
meat stock	شربة لحمة	shor·bit lah·ma

I'm allergic to ...	عندي حساسية لـ ...	'an·dee ha·sa·see·ya li ...
dairy produce	الألبان	al·ban
nuts	مكسّرات	mi·ka·sa·raat
seafood	أسماك البحر	as·mak il·bahr

coffee ...	... قهوة	'ah·wa ...
tea ...	... شاي	shay ...
with milk	مع لبن	ma·'a la·ban
without sugar	بدون سكّر	bi·doon su·kar

bottle/glass of beer	إزازة/كباية بيرة	i·za·zit/ku·bay·it bee·ra
(orange) juice	عصير (برتقان)	'as·eer (bur·tu·'aan)
soft drink	حاجة ساقع	ha·ga sa·'a
(mineral) water	ميّة (معدنية)	ma·ya (ma'·da·nee·ya)

... wine	... نبيذ	ni·beet ...
red	أحمر	ah·mar
sparkling	شمبانيا	sham·ban·ya
white	أبيض	ab·yad

EMERGENCIES

| Help! | إلحقني! | il·ha'·nee |
| Go away! | إمشي! | im·shee |

Call ...!	إتصل ب ...!	i·tas·al bi ...
a doctor	دكتور	duk·toor (m)
	دكتورة	duk·too·ra (f)
the police	البوليس	il·bu·lees

I'm lost.

| أنا تايه. | a·na tay·ih (m) |
| أنا تهت. | a·na tuht (f) |

Where are the toilets?

فين التواليت؟ fayn i·tu·wa·leet

I'm sick.

| أنا عيّان. | a·na ay·an (m) |
| أنا عيّانة. | a·na ay·an·a (f) |

It hurts here.

بيوجعني هنا. bi·yiw·ga'·nee hi·na

I'm allergic to (antibiotics).

| عندي حساسية | 'an·dee ha·sa·see·ya |
| من (مضاد حيوي). | min (mu·daad ha·ya·wee) |

SHOPPING & SERVICES

Where's a ...?	فين ...؟	fayn ...
department store	محل	ma·hal
grocery store	بقّال	ba·'al
newsagency	بايع جرايد	bay·aa' ga·ray·id
souvenir shop	محل تذكارات	ma·hal i·tiz·ka·raat
supermarket	سوبرماركت	soo·bir·mar·kit

I'm looking for ...

أنا بدوّر على ... a·na ba·daw·ar 'a·la ...

Can I look at it?

| ممكن أشوفه؟ | mum·kin a·shoo·fuh (m) |
| ممكن أشوفها؟ | mum·kin a·shoof·ha (f) |

Do you have any others?

فيه تاني؟ fee ta·nee

It's faulty.

مش شغّال. mish sha·ghal

How much is it?

بكم؟ bi·kam

Can you write down the price?

| ممكن تكتب/تكتبي | mum·kin tik·tib/tik·ti·bee |
| الثمن؟ | i·ta·man (m/f) |

That's too expensive.

ده غالي قوي. da gha·lee 'aw·ee

What's your lowest price?

الأحسن سعر كم؟ il·ah·san si'r kam

There's a mistake in the bill.

فيه غلطة في الحساب. fee ghal·ta fil his·ab

Where's ...?	فين ...؟	fayn ...
a foreign exchange office	صرّاف	sa·raaf
an ATM	بنك شخصي	bank shakh·see

Numbers

1	١	واحد	wa·hid
2	٢	إثنين	it·nayn
3	٣	ثلاثة	ta·la·ta
4	٤	أربعة	ar·ba'
5	٥	خمسة	kham·sa
6	٦	ستة	si·ta
7	٧	سبعة	sa·ba·'a
8	٨	ثمانية	ta·man·ya
9	٩	تسعة	ti·sa·'a
10	١٠	عشرة	'a·sha·ra
20	٢٠	عشرين	'ish·reen
30	٣٠	ثلاثين	ta·laa·teen
40	٤٠	عربين	ar·ba·'een
50	٥٠	خمسين	kham·seen
60	٦٠	ستين	si·teen
70	٧٠	سبعين	sa·ba·'een
80	٨٠	ثمنين	ta·ma·neen
90	٩٠	تسعين	ti·sa·'een
100	١٠٠	مئة	mee·ya
1000	١٠٠٠	آلف	alf

Note that Arabic numerals, unlike letters, are read from left to right.

SILENT COMMUNICATION

Egyptians have a whole array of nonverbal ways of getting a point across – if you know some of them, you're less likely to get offended, run over or neglected in a restaurant.

For example, 'no' is often expressed with a simple upward nod or a brusque 'tsk' sound. This can seem a bit rude if you're not expecting it or are not familiar with it, but if you use it casually when dealing with touts on the street, they might just leave you alone.

Another signal often misinterpreted by foreigners is a loud hissing sound. No, that guy isn't commenting on your looks – he's trying to get your attention so you don't get trampled by his donkey cart coming down the narrow lane. Interpret a hiss as 'Watch out – coming through!'

The most essential gesture to learn is the one for asking for the bill at a restaurant. Make eye contact with the waiter, hold out your hand (with the palm up), then make a quick chopping motion across it with the side of your other hand, as if to say 'Cut me off'. Works like a charm.

What's the exchange rate?
نسبة التحويل كم؟   nis·bit i·tah·weel kam

Where's the local internet cafe?
فين كفاي إنترنت؟   fayn ka·fay in·ter·net

How much is it per hour?
الساعة بكم؟   i·sa·'a bi·kam

Where's the nearest public phone?
فين الاقرب تليفون؟   fayn il a'·rab ti·li·fon

I'd like to buy a phonecard.
عايز/عايزة أشتري   'a·iz/'ai·za ash·ti·ri
كرت تليفون.   kart ti·li·fon (m/f)

TIME & DATES

What time is it?
الساعة كم؟   is·sa·'a kam

It's (one) o'clock.
الساعة (واحدة).   is·sa·'a (wa·hi·da)

It's (two) o'clock.
الساعة (إثنين).   is·sa·'a (it·nayn)

Half past (two).
الساعة (إثنين) ونص.   is·sa·'a (it·nayn) wi nus

At what time ...?
إمتى ...؟   im·ta ...

yesterday ...	إمبارح ...	im·ba·rih ...
tomorrow ...	بكرة ...	buk·ra ...
morning	الصبح	is·subh
afternoon	الظهر	ba'd·duhr
evening	بالليل	bi·layl
Monday	يوم الإثنين	yom il·it·nayn
Tuesday	يوم الثلاث	yom it·ta·lat
Wednesday	يوم الأربع	yom il·ar·ba'
Thursday	يوم الخميس	yom il·kha·mees
Friday	يوم الجمعة	yom il·gu·ma'
Saturday	يوم السبت	yom is·sabt
Sunday	يوم الحد	yom il·had

TRANSPORT

Is this the ... to (Aswan)?
الى ... (أسوان)؟   ... i·la (as·waan)

boat	دي المركب	dee il·mar·kib
bus	ده الأوتوبيس	da il·o·to·bees
plane	دي الطيّارة	dee i·ta·yaa·ra
train	ده القطر	da il·'atr

What time's the ... bus?
... أتوبيس الساعة كم؟   ... o·to·bees i·sa·'a kam

first	الأوّل	il aw·il
last	الآخر	il a·khir
next	الثاني	i·ta·nee

One ... ticket (to Luxor), please.
تذكرة ... (للقصر)، من فضلك/ فضلِك.   taz·ka·rit ... (li·lu'·sor) min fad·lak/ fad·lik (m/f)

one-way	ذهاب	zi·hab
return	عودة	'aw·da

How long does the trip take?
الرحلة هي كم ساعة؟   i·rih·la hee·ya kam sa·'a

Is it a direct route?
الطريق مباشر؟   it·taa·ree' mu·ba·shir

What station/stop is this?
المحطة دي إسمها/ الموقف ده إسمه إيه؟   il·ma·ha·ta di is·ma·ha/ il·maw·if da is·muh ay

Please tell me when we get to (Minya).
من فضلك/فضلِك ممكن تقولي/ تقوليلي لمّا نوصل (المنيا)؟   min fad·lak/fad·lik mum·kin ti·'ul·ee/ ti·'ul·ee·lee la·ma nuw·sil (il·min·ya) (m/f)

How much is it to ...?
بكم إلى ...؟   bi·kam i·la ...

Please take me to ...
عايز/عايزة أروح ... من فضلك/فضلِك.   'a·iz/'ai·za a·ruh ... min fad·lak/fad·lik (m/f)

ARABIC ALPHABET

Arabic is written from right to left. The form of each letter changes depending on whether it's at the start, in the middle or at the end of a word or whether it stands alone.

Word-Final	Word-Medial	Word-Initial	Alone	Letter
ـا	ـا	ا	ا	alef'
ـب	ـبـ	بـ	ب	'ba
ـت	ـتـ	تـ	ت	'ta
ـث	ـثـ	ثـ	ث	'tha
ـج	ـجـ	جـ	ج	jeem
ـح	ـحـ	حـ	ح	'ha
ـخ	ـخـ	خـ	خ	'kha
ـد	ـد	د ـ	د	daal
ـذ	ـذ	ذـ	ذ	dhaal
ـر	ـر	رـ	ر	'ra
ـز	ـزـ	زـ	ز	'za
ـس	ـسـ	سـ	س	seen
ـش	ـشـ	شـ	ش	sheen
ـص	ـصـ	صـ	ص	saad
ـض	ـضـ	ضـ	ض	daad
ـط	ـطـ	طـ	ط	'ta
ـظ	ـظـ	ظـ	ظ	'dha
ـع	ـعـ	عـ	ع	ain'
ـغ	ـغـ	غـ	غ	ghain
ـف	ـفـ	فـ	ف	'fa
ـق	ـقـ	قـ	ق	kuf
ـك	ـكـ	كـ	ك	kaf
ـل	ـلـ	لـ	ل	lam
ـم	ـمـ	مـ	م	mim
ـن	ـنـ	نـ	ن	nun
ـه	ـهـ	هـ	ه	'ha
ـو	ـوـ	و ـ	و	waw
ـي	ـيـ	يـ	ي	'ya
	ء			hamza
ـَأ	ـَـؤ		أَ	a
ـُأ	ـُـؤ		أُ	u
ـِا	ـِـؤ		اِ	i
ـِا	ـُـؤ		اِ	' (glottal stop)
ـَا	ـَا ـ		اَ	aa
ـُو	ـُو-	أو	أُو	oo
ـِي	ـيـ	إي	إِي	ee
ـَو	ـَو-	أو	أَو	aw
ـَي	ـَيـ	أي	أَي	ay

Please ...	... من فضلَك	min *fad*·lak ... (m)
	... من فضلِك	min *fad*·lik ... (f)
stop here	وقّف هنا	wa·'if *hi*·na
wait here	إستنّى هنا	is·*ta*·na *hi*·na

I'd like to	... عايز	'a·iz a·'*ag*·ar ... (m)
hire a ...	... عايرة	'ai·za a·'*ag*·ar ... (f)
4WD	جيب	zheeb
car	عربية	'a·ra·*bee*·ya

with a driver
مع سوّاق ma' sa·*wa*'

with air conditioning
بتكييف bi·tak·*yeef*

How much for ... hire?	... بكم لإجار ؟	bi·*kam* li·'ig·*aar* ...
daily	يومي	*yom*·ee
weekly	أسبوعي	us·*boo*'·ee

Is this the road to (the Red Sea)?
ده الطريق da i·taa·*ree*'
(للبحر الأحمر)؟ (lil·*bahr* il·*ah*·mar)

ARABIC CHAT ALPHABET

Developed from mobile and internet communication, the so-called 'Arabic chat alphabet' is popping up in advertisements, names of cool clubs, even Arabic textbooks. Though it looks like a jumble of letters and numbers, it's actually a fairly sensible transliteration system. All the sounds peculiar to Arabic are assigned a number, based very loosely on their shape. A '3' for the letter ain' is the most common, as in *Assalaam 3aleikum!* A '7' represents the aspirated 'ha: a popular Cairo DJ goes by the name Amr 7a7a, while *7urya* is Arabic for 'freedom', now commonly seen in graffiti.

I need a mechanic.
محتاج/محتاجة *mih*·tag/*mih*·ta·ga
ميكانيكي mi·ka·*nee*·kee (m/f)

I've run out of petrol.
البنزين خلص il·ben·*zeen* khi·lis

I have a flat tyre.
الكاوتش نائم il·ka·*witsh* nay·im

GLOSSARY

(m) indicates masculine gender, (f) feminine gender and (pl) plural

abd – servant of

abeyya – woman's garment

abu – father, saint

ahwa – coffee, coffeehouse

ain – well, spring

al-jeel – a type of music characterised by a hand-clapping rhythm overlaid with a catchy vocal; literally 'the generation'

ba'al – grocer

bab – gate or door

baksheesh – alms, tip

baladi – local, rural

beit – house

bey – leader; term of respect

bir – spring, well

burg – tower

bustan – walled garden

calèche – horse-drawn carriage

caravanserai – merchants' inn; also called khan

centrale – telephone office

dahabiyya – houseboat

darb – track, street

deir – monastery, convent

domina – dominoes

eid – Islamic feast

emir – Islamic ruler, military commander or governor; literally 'prince'

fellaheen – (singular: fellah) peasant farmers or agricultural workers who make up the majority of Egypt's popu¬lation; 'fellah' literally means ploughman or tiller of the soil

galabiyya – man's full-length robe

gebel – mountain

gezira – island

guinay – pound (currency)

hajj – pilgrimage to Mecca; all Muslims should make the journey at least once in their lifetime

hammam – bathhouse

hantour – horse-drawn carriage

Hejira – Islamic calendar; Mohammed's flight from Mecca to Medina in AD 622

ibn – son of

iconostasis – screen with doors and icons set in tiers, used in Eastern Christian churches

iftar – breaking the fast after sundown during the month of Ramadan

kershef – building material made of large chunks of salt mixed with rock and plastered in local clay

khamsin – a dry, hot wind from the Western Desert

khan – another name for a caravanserai

khanqah – Sufi monastery

khedive – Egyptian viceroy under Ottoman suzerainty

khwaga – foreigner

kuttab – Quranic school

madrassa – school, especially one associated with a mosque

mahattat – station

mammisi – birthhouse

maristan – hospital

mashrabiyya – ornate carved wooden panel or screen; a feature of Islamic architecture

mastaba – mudbrick structure in the shape of a bench above tombs, from which later pyramids developed; Arabic word for 'bench'

matar – airport

midan – town or city square

mihrab – niche in the wall of a mosque that indicates the direction of Mecca

minbar – pulpit in a mosque

Misr – Egypt (also means 'Cairo')

moulid – saints' festival

muezzin – mosque official who calls the faithful to prayer

mugzzabin – Sufi followers who participate in zikrs

muqarnas – stalactite-like decorative device forming tiers and made of stone or wood; used on arches and vaults

oud – a type of lute

piastre – Egyptian currency; one Egyptian pound consists of 100 piastres

qasr – castle or palace

Ramadan – the ninth month of the lunar Islamic calendar during which Muslims fast from sunrise to sunset

ras – headland

sabil – public drinking fountain

sandale – modified felucca

servees – service taxi

shaabi – popular music of the working class

sharia – road or street

sharm – bay

sheesha – water pipe

souq – market

speos – rock-cut tomb or chapel

Sufi – follower of any Islamic mystical order that emphasises dancing, chanting and trances to attain unity with God

tahtib – male dance performed with wooden staves

tarboosh – the hat known elsewhere as a fez

towla – backgammon

umm – mother of

wadi – desert watercourse, dry except in the rainy season

waha – oasis

wikala – another name for a caravanserai

zikr – long sessions of dancing, chanting and trances usually carried out by Sufi mugzzabin to achieve unity with God

behind the scenes

SEND US YOUR FEEDBACK

We love to hear from travellers – your comments keep us on our toes and help make our books better. Our well-travelled team reads every word on what you loved or loathed about this book. Although we cannot reply individually to postal submissions, we always guarantee that your feedback goes straight to the appropriate authors, in time for the next edition. Each person who sends us information is thanked in the next edition – the most useful submissions are rewarded with a selection of digital PDF chapters.

Visit **lonelyplanet.com/contact** to submit your updates and suggestions or to ask for help. Our award-winning website also features inspirational travel stories, news and discussions.

Note: We may edit, reproduce and incorporate your comments in Lonely Planet products such as guidebooks, websites and digital products, so let us know if you don't want your comments reproduced or your name acknowledged. For a copy of our privacy policy visit lonelyplanet.com/privacy.

OUR READERS

Many thanks to the travellers who used the last edition and wrote to us with helpful hints, useful advice and interesting anecdotes:

Phil Abbey, Martin Anzellini, Tressy Arts, Holly Baird, Joseph Banh, Dennis Bowman, Jasmine Browne, Nikki Buran, Jennifer Byrne, Katy Carmichael, Kavita Chaturvedi, Simone Damiano, Paul De Haes, Bec Deacon, Marlon Dekker, Bob Francescone, Pascal Frank, Mirte Fritz-straver, Greta Galeazzi, Stefan Gerke, Joost Golverdingen, Michael Gurman, Jeff Haney, Mark Hanry, Mulle Harbort, Caroline Hughes, Dirk Huyge, Iman, Anders Jeppsson, Gregory Kalkanis, Rasha Khayat, Dido Kooyman, Keith Krause, Nicolas Kucera, Martin Lamarche, Tim Lanzius, Fredy Lauener, Richard Lee, Anne Leroy, Aiden Magee, Margareta Malm, Sharon Mertins, Ian Miller, Vijay Anand Mohan, Christina Neff, Sophie Nuttall & Libby Sutcliffe, Astrid Nyland, Clairie Papazoglou & Panicos Panayides, Laura Pasquero, Ostyn Patrick, Thijs Pepels & Kelly Stewart, Moin Qazi, Torben Retboll, Bert Roebert, Denton Sandlant, Shannon, Joseph Stanik, Tom Stevens, Tim Stonich, Birger Storgaard, Ole Magnus Storset, Stephen Thomson, Nicole Titulaer, Mara Marie Vaughan, Rinske Vellinga, Kelvin Widdows, Penny Yiannakidou, Nicole Zaghlol, Teun Zijlmans.

AUTHOR THANKS

Zora O'Neill

A million thanks to Mandy McClure and Amgad Naguib for great tips and home-cooked meals; to the Roma crew: Cynthia Kling, Philip Weiss and Luc Leclair; to Sudanese tipster Ed Giles; to Heliopolis informant Jenny Kinnear; to Mohamed Shideed for braving the traffic; to Neveen for a delicious lunch, and to Sarah, Esraa and Yousraa for welcoming me in; to Nawal for explaining it all; and to Aatef, Hoda, Hatem, Mohamed and Ghada for a wonderful picnic. Back at the desk, thanks to Michael, Anthony and Jess for dealing with last-minute queries; to Sam (adieu!), Brigitte and Will for wrestling it all into shape; to fellow authors Penny Watson and Alexis Averbuck for giving me such great places to write; and to Peter, for patience.

Michael Benanav

Special thanks go to Eatamad Abdullah, her father Rafallah and their family in Marsa Matruh for their kindness and hospitality. Thanks, too, to Mohammed Khambes in Siwa for many nights of great, informative conversation. Thanks to Reda Esaa in Bawiti for showing me a bit of local life not on the usual tourist itinerary. And thanks most of all to Kelly and Lucas, who make it fun to come home.

Jessica Lee

On the road a big thanks to Claire Craig, Salma Nassar, Eric Monkaba, Muhammad Ali, Gordon Wilkinson, Zoltan Matrahazi, and especially Salama Abd Rabbo and Nori (JJ). Back in Cairo huge cheers to Sameh Tawfik, Mark Walgemoet, Sarah Bruford, Paula Maiorano and Julian 'Whijul' White. While at Lonely Planet, many thanks for awesome advice and putting up with my endless questions to Michael Benanav, Zora O'Neill and Sam Trafford.

Anthony Sattin

Among the many people who helped me on my way up the Nile Valley, many thanks to Elizabeth and Ali Sharawy, Bassem Sobhy, Yehia the brilliant driver, and staff at the Asyut, Minya, Luxor and Aswan tourist offices, welcoming as ever. In Luxor, Mohamed and Marwa Abd er-Rahim, Aladin Elsahaby, Eleonore Kamir, Mamduh Sayed Khalifa, Enrique Cansino, Zeina Aboukheir, Konny Matthews.

At El Kab, Dr Dirk Huyge was immensely informative about his Qurta discovery. In Aswan, Khaled Helmi, Mohamed Arabi, Tim Baily and Mohamed Sobhi provided much assistance.

ACKNOWLEDGMENTS

Climate map data adapted from Peel MC, Finlayson BL & McMahon TA (2007) 'Updated World Map of the Köppen-Geiger Climate Classification', *Hydrology and Earth System Sciences*, 11, 163344.

Illustrations pp128-9, pp212-13 and pp430-1 by Javier Zarracina; pp422-3 by Michael Weldon.

Cover photograph: Rames III's mortuary temple at Medinat Habu on the west bank, Luxor; Julian Love/AWL. Many of the images in this guide are available for licensing from Lonely Planet. Images: www.lonelyplanetimages.com.

THIS BOOK

This 11th edition of Lonely Planet's *Egypt* guidebook was researched and written by Zora O'Neill, Michael Benanav, Jessica Lee and Anthony Sattin. Dr Joann Fletcher wrote the Pharaonic Egypt content. The previous edition was written by Matthew Firestone, Michael Benanav, Thomas Hall and Anthony Sattin. This guidebook was commissioned in Lonely Planet's Melbourne office, and produced by the following:

Commissioning Editors
Sam Trafford, Will Gourlay

Coordinating Editors
Briohny Hooper, Kate James, Shawn Low

Coordinating Cartographer Hunor Csutoros

Coordinating Layout Designer Sandra Helou

Managing Editors Brigitte Ellemor, Angela Tinson

Senior Editor Susan Paterson

Managing Cartographers Corey Hutchison, Adrian Persoglia

Managing Layout Designers Chris Girdler, Jane Hart

Assisting Editors Carolyn Bain

Alice Barker, Carly Hall, Paul Harding, Lauren Hunt, Gabrielle Stefanos

Assisting Cartographer James Leversha

Assisting Layout Designer Kerrianne Southway

Cover Research Naomi Parker

Internal Image Research Rebecca Skinner

Language Content Branislava Vladisavljevic

Thanks to Yvonne Bischofberger, Ryan Evans, Trent Paton, Anthony Phelan, John Taufa, Gerard Walker, Juan Winata

index

how to use this book

These symbols will help you find the listings you want:

- **Sights**
- **Beaches**
- **Activities**
- **Courses**
- **Tours**
- **Festivals & Events**
- **Sleeping**
- **Eating**
- **Drinking**
- **Entertainment**
- **Shopping**
- **Information/ Transport**

Look out for these icons:

- **TOP CHOICE** Our author's recommendation
- **FREE** No payment required
- A green or sustainable option

Our authors have nominated these places as demonstrating a strong commitment to sustainability – for example by supporting local communities and producers, operating in an environmentally friendly way, or supporting conservation projects.

These symbols give you the vital information for each listing:

- Telephone Numbers
- Opening Hours
- Parking
- Nonsmoking
- Air-Conditioning
- Internet Access
- Wi-Fi Access
- Swimming Pool
- Vegetarian Selection
- English-Language Menu
- Family-Friendly
- Pet-Friendly
- Bus
- Ferry
- Metro
- Subway
- London Tube
- Tram
- Train

Reviews are organised by author preference.

Map Legend

Sights
- Beach
- Buddhist
- Castle
- Christian
- Hindu
- Islamic
- Jewish
- Monument
- Museum/Gallery
- Ruin
- Winery/Vineyard
- Zoo
- Other Sight

Activities, Courses & Tours
- Diving/Snorkelling
- Canoeing/Kayaking
- Skiing
- Surfing
- Swimming/Pool
- Walking
- Windsurfing
- Other Activity/ Course/Tour

Sleeping
- Sleeping
- Camping

Eating
- Eating

Drinking
- Drinking
- Cafe

Entertainment
- Entertainment

Shopping
- Shopping

Information
- Bank
- Embassy/ Consulate
- Hospital/Medical
- Internet
- Police
- Post Office
- Telephone
- Toilet
- Tourist Information
- Other Information

Transport
- Airport
- Border Crossing
- Bus
- Cable Car/ Funicular
- Cycling
- Ferry
- Metro
- Monorail
- Parking
- Petrol Station
- Taxi
- Train/Railway
- Tram
- Other Transport

Routes
- Tollway
- Freeway
- Primary
- Secondary
- Tertiary
- Lane
- Unsealed Road
- Plaza/Mall
- Steps
- Tunnel
- Pedestrian Overpass
- Walking Tour
- Walking Tour Detour
- Path

Geographic
- Hut/Shelter
- Lighthouse
- Lookout
- Mountain/Volcano
- Oasis
- Park
- Pass
- Picnic Area
- Waterfall

Population
- Capital (National)
- Capital (State/Province)
- City/Large Town
- Town/Village

Boundaries
- International
- State/Province
- Disputed
- Regional/Suburb
- Marine Park
- Cliff
- Wall

Hydrography
- River, Creek
- Intermittent River
- Swamp/Mangrove
- Reef
- Canal
- Water
- Dry/Salt/ Intermittent Lake
- Glacier

Areas
- Beach/Desert
- Cemetery (Christian)
- Cemetery (Other)
- Park/Forest
- Sportsground
- Sight (Building)
- Top Sight (Building)

Contributing Author

Dr Joann Fletcher wrote the Pharaonic Egypt chapter and several boxed texts. She has a PhD in Egyptology and is a research and teaching fellow at the University of York, where she teaches Egyptian archaeology and undertakes scientific research on everything from mummification to ancient perfumes. Joann regularly appears on TV, has contributed to the BBC History website and has written several books.

OUR STORY

A beat-up old car, a few dollars in the pocket and a sense of adventure. In 1972 that's all Tony and Maureen Wheeler needed for the trip of a lifetime – across Europe and Asia overland to Australia. It took several months, and at the end – broke but inspired – they sat at their kitchen table writing and stapling together their first travel guide, *Across Asia on the Cheap*. Within a week they'd sold 1500 copies. Lonely Planet was born.

Today, Lonely Planet has offices in Melbourne, London and Oakland, with more than 600 staff and writers. We share Tony's belief that 'a great guidebook should do three things: inform, educate and amuse'.

OUR WRITERS

Zora O'Neill

Coordinating Author, Cairo, Egyptian Museum, Cairo Outskirts & the Delta
Zora first visited the Big Mango in 1992. She spent the summer clubbing, and learned a few verb conjugations. Twenty years on, Zora has earned a Master's degree in Arabic literature and has contributed to more than a dozen guidebooks, including an earlier edition of Lonely Planet's *Egypt*. She writes about food and travel for the *New York Times* and *Conde Nast Traveler*, and is working on a book about Arabic language and travel in the Middle East. She lives in Astoria, Queens, and reads the El-Said Badawi *Dictionary of Egyptian Arabic* for fun.

Michael Benanav

Siwa Oasis & the Western Desert, Alexandria & the Mediterranean Coast Michael cut his adventure-travelling teeth in Egypt back in 1998, and his experiences were so bizarre he figured he'd better start writing about them. Since then, he's authored several books, including *Men Of Salt: Crossing the Sahara on the Caravan of White Gold*, about traveling with one of the world's last working camel caravans. He also writes and photographs for the *New York Times* and other publications. Now that he's a father, his Egyptian friends call him Abu Lucas.

Jessica Lee

Suez Canal, Red Sea Coast, Sinai Jessica escaped small-town New Zealand and high-tailed it for the road at the age of 18, spending much of her 20s traipsing extensively through Asia, Africa and Latin America. She washed up in Egypt in 2004 where she fell in love with the Arabic language and the incredible hospitality of the people. Since 2007 she has lived in the Middle East full-time, mostly based in Cairo, and has authored several guidebooks to the region. She tweets about things Middle Eastern @jessofarabia.

Read more about Jessica at:
lonelyplanet.com/members/jessicalee1

Anthony Sattin

Cruising the Nile, Nile Valley chapters, Egypt Today, History, The Egyptians, The Arts, Egyptian Cuisine: Bi-I Hana wa-Shifa!, Environment Anthony has been travelling around and writing about Egypt and Egyptians for more than 20 years. He has contributed to previous editions of Lonely Planet's *Egypt* and *Discover Egypt*, as well as *Morocco* and *Algeria*. He contributes to the *Sunday Times* and *Conde Nast Traveler* and presents documentaries for BBC radio. Anthony's nonfiction includes *A Winter on the Nile* and *Lifting the Veil*. Follow him at anthonysattin.com.

OVER PAGE MORE WRITERS

Published by Lonely Planet Publications Pty Ltd
ABN 36 005 607 983
11th edition – July 2012
ISBN 978 1 74179 959 0
© Lonely Planet 2012   Photographs © as indicated 2012
10 9 8 7 6 5 4 3 2 1
Printed in China

Although the authors and Lonely Planet have taken all reasonable care in preparing this book, we make no warranty about the accuracy or completeness of its content and, to the maximum extent permitted, disclaim all liability arising from its use.